Econometrics of Panel Data

Econometrics of Panel Data

Methods and Applications

Erik Biørn

OXFORD
UNIVERSITY PRESS

OXFORD
UNIVERSITY PRESS

Great Clarendon Street, Oxford, OX2 6DP,
United Kingdom

Oxford University Press is a department of the University of Oxford.
It furthers the University's objective of excellence in research, scholarship,
and education by publishing worldwide. Oxford is a registered trade mark of
Oxford University Press in the UK and in certain other countries

The findings, interpretations, and conclusions expressed in this work are entirely those of the authors and should not be attributed in any manner to the World Bank, its Board of Executive Directors, or the governments they represent.

First Edition published in 2017

Impression: 3

Published in the United States of America by Oxford University Press
198 Madison Avenue, New York, NY 10016, United States of America

British Library Cataloguing in Publication Data
Data available

Library of Congress Control Number: 2016937737

ISBN 978-0-19-875344-5

Printed in Great Britain by
CPI Group (UK) Ltd, Croydon, CR0 4YY

PREFACE

Panel data is a data type used with increasing frequency in empirical research in economics, social sciences, and medicine. Panel data analysis is a core field in modern econometrics and multivariate statistics, and studies based on such data occupy a growing part of the field in all the mentioned disciplines. A substantial literature on methods and applications has accumulated, also synthesized in survey articles and a number of textbooks. Why then write another book on panel data analysis? I hope that some of my motivation and part of the answer will be given in the following paragraphs.

The text collected in this book has originated, and been expanded through several years, partly in parallel with courses I have given at the University of Oslo for master's and doctoral students of economics. I have been interested in the field, both its models and methods and applications to social sciences, for more than forty years. The first drafts were lecture notes, later expanded and synthesized into course compendia, first in Norwegian, later in English. In compiling the text, I have had no ambition of giving an account of the history of panel data analysis and its various subfields, some of which have a longer history than others. Within some 350 pages it is impossible to give a complete coverage, and the choice of topics, and the depth of discussion of each of them, to some extent reflect my preferences. Some readers may miss topics like cross-section-time-series analysis in continuous time, duration analysis, and analysis of non-linear panel data models (outside the limited dependent variables field). Topics I give specific attention to, more than many comparable texts, I think, are coefficient identification of models mixing two-dimensional and individual-specific variables, regression models with two-way random effects, models and methods for handling random coefficients and measurement errors, unbalanced panel data, and panel data in relation to aggregation. Problems at the interface between unbalance and truncation, and between micro-econometrics and panel data analysis, are also discussed.

It goes without saying that in a book dealing with data showing temporal–spatial variation, matrix algebra is unavoidable. Although panel data have a matrix structure, such algebra should not be a core matter. I have experienced that many students starting on the topic feel parts of the matrix algebra, especially when written in a dense, compact style, to be an obstacle. I therefore set out to explain many of the models and methods in some detail to readers coming to panel data analysis for the first time, including students familiar with basic statistics and classical multiple regression analysis, and applied researchers. Some technical material is placed in appendices. Yet some advanced and 'modern' topics are discussed. Since one of my intentions is that students should be given the chance to get an acceptable grasp of basic ideas without having to be involved in extensive matrix-algebraic exercises, most chapters start with a simple example in scalar (or elementary vector) notation, and then attempt to take the reader gradually to more complex cases in fuller matrix notation, even if this necessitates *some* repetition.

The first chapters survey rather elementary materials. I believe that the initial sections of the first eight chapters may be useful for bachelor students, provided their knowledge of multiple regression analysis and basic mathematical statistics is sufficient. Chapters 1–3 and 5 contain mostly basic topics, Chapters 4 and 6–10 contain intermediate level topics, and Chapters 11 and 12 contain somewhat advanced topics. I have, as far as possible, tried to keep each chapter self-contained. Yet some connections exist. It may also be helpful to note that Chapter 6 builds on Chapters 2, 3, and 5, that Chapters 6 and 7 expand topics in Chapters 2–4, that Chapters 7 and 8 are methodologically related, that Chapter 11 builds on Chapters 9 and 10, and that Chapter 12 builds on Chapters 3 and 6. Each chapter has an initial summary, some also have a concluding section.

Some readers may miss exercises with solutions, which would have expanded the size of the book. On the other hand, examples of applications, some from my own research, or experiments, and illustrations utilizing publicly available data are included in several chapters. My view of the panel data field is that the core topics have, to some extent, the character of being building blocks which may be combined, and the number of *potential* combinations is large. Not many combinations are discussed explicitly. Certain potential combinations—for example, dynamic equations with random coefficients for unbalanced panel data and random coefficients interacting with limited dependent variables with measurement errors—have (to my knowledge) hardly been discussed in any existing text.

Although primarily aiming at students and practitioners of econometrics, I believe that my book, or parts of it, may be useful also for students and researchers in social sciences outside economics and for students and research workers in psychology, political science, and medicine, provided they have a sufficient background in statistics. My intention, and hope, is that the book may serve as a main text for lecturing and seminar education at universities. I believe that parts may be useful for students, researchers, and other readers working on their own, *inter alia*, with computer programming of modules for panel data analysis.

During the work, I have received valuable feedback from many colleagues and students, not least PhD students writing their theses, partly under my supervision, on applied panel data topics. Questions frequently posed during such discussions have undoubtedly made their mark on the final text. I want to express my gratitude to the many students who have read, commented on, and in others ways been 'exposed to' my notes, sketches, and chapter drafts. Their efforts have certainly contributed to eliminate errors. I also thank good colleagues for many long and interesting discussions or for having willingly spent their time in reading and commenting on drafts of preliminary versions of the various sections and chapters, sometimes more than once. I regret that I have been unable to take all their advice into account. I specifically want to mention (in alphabetical order) Jørgen Aasness, Anne Line Bretteville-Jensen, John K. Dagsvik, Xuehui Han, Terje Skjerpen, Thor Olav Thoresen, Knut R. Wangen, and Yngve Willassen. Needless to say, none of them are to be held responsible for remaining errors or shortcomings. The text has been prepared by the author in the Latex document preparation software, and I feel obliged to the constructors of this excellent scientific text processor. Last, but not least, I express my sincere gratitude to Oxford University Press, in particular Adam Swallow and Aimee Wright, for their belief in the project and for support, encouragement, and patience.

Erik Biørn

Oslo, March 2016

CONTENTS

LIST OF TABLES

1 Introduction

Panel data, longitudinal data, or combined time-series/cross-section data are terms used in econometrics and statistics to denote data sets which contain repeated observations on a selection of variables from a set of observation units. The observations cover simultaneously the temporal and the spatial dimension. Examples are: (1) time-series for production, factor inputs, and profits in a sample of firms over a succession of years; (2) time-series for consumption, income, wealth, and education in a sample of persons or households over several years; and (3) time-series for manufacturing production, sales of medical drugs, or traffic accidents for all, or a sample of, municipalities or counties, or time-series for variables for countries in the OECD, the EU, etc. Examples (1) and (2) relate to micro-data, (3) exemplifies macro-data.

'Panel data econometrics is one of the most exciting fields of inquiry in econometrics today' (Nerlove, Sevestre, and Balestra (2008, p. 22)), with a history going back to at least 1950. We will not attempt to survey this interesting history. Elements of a survey can be found in Nerlove (2002, Chapter 1); see also Nerlove (2014) as well as Griliches (1986, Sections 5 and 6) and Nerlove, Sevestre and Balestra (2008). A background for the study of panel data, placing it in a wider context, may also be given by a quotation from a text on 'modern philosophy':

> Space and time, or the related concepts of extension and duration, attained special prominence in early modern philosophy because of their importance in the new science... Metaphysical questions surrounding the new science pertained to the nature of space and time and their relation to matter. Epistemological questions pertained to the cognition of space itself or extension in general... and also to the operation of the senses in perceiving the actual spatial order of things. (Hatfield (2006, p. 62))

In this introductory chapter, we first, in Section 1.1, briefly define the main types of panel data. In Section 1.2 we illustrate, by examples, virtues of panel data and explain in which sense they may 'contain more information' than the traditional data types cross-section data and time-series data. Section 1.3 briefly contrasts panel data with experimental data, while some other virtues of panel data, as well as some limitations, are specified in Section 1.4. An overview of the content of the book follows, in Section 1.5.

1.1 Types of panel variables and data

Several types of panel data exist. The one which perhaps first comes to mind is *balanced panel data*, in which *the same individuals* are observed in all periods under consideration.

Using i as subscript for the unit of observation and t as subscript for the time-period, and letting the data set contain N units and T time-periods, the coverage of a balanced panel data set can be denoted as $i=1,\dots,N;\ t=1,\dots,T$.

Balanced panel data have a *matrix structure.* We need, in principle, *three subscripts* to represent the observations: one for the variable number; one for the individual (unit) number; and one for the period (year, quarter, month, etc.). A balanced panel data set can therefore be arranged as *three-dimensional matrices.* Quite often N is much larger than T, but for panels of geographic units, the opposite may well be the case. Regarding asymptotics, the distinction between $N\to\infty$ and $T\to\infty$, often denoted as 'N-asymptotics' (cross-sectional asymptotics) and 'T-asymptotics' (time-serial asymptotics), will often be important. In 'micro' contexts, 'short' panels from 'many' individuals is a frequently occurring constellation.

Quite often, however, some variables do not vary both across observation unit and over time-periods. Examples of variables which do not vary over time, time-invariant variables, are for individuals: birth year; gender; length of the education period (if for all individuals the education has been finished before the sample period starts); and to some extent attitudes, norms, and preferences. For firms they are: year of establishment; sector; location; technical strength; and management ability. Such variables are denoted as *individual-specific* or *firm-specific.* Examples of variables that do not vary across individuals, individual-invariant variables, may be prices, interest rates, tax parameters, and variables representing the macro-economic situation. Such variables are denoted as *time-specific* or *period-specific.* As a common term for individual-specific and time-specific variable we will use *unidimensional variables.* Variables showing variation across both individuals and time-periods are denoted as *two-dimensional variables.* Examples are (usually) income and consumption (for individuals) and production and labour input (for firms).

The second, also very important, category is *unbalanced panel data.* Its characteristic is that *not the same units are observed in all periods,* but some are observed more than once. There are several reasons why a panel data set may become unbalanced. Entry and exit of units in a data base (e.g., establishment and close-down of firms and marriages and dissolution of households) is one reason, another is randomly missing observations in time series. A particular type of unbalance is created by *rotating panel data,* which emerges in *sample surveys* when the sample changes systematically in a way intended by the data collector. Another major reason why unbalanced panel data may occur is *endogenous selection,* meaning, loosely, that the selection of units observed is partly determined by variables our model is intended to explain. This may complicate coefficient estimation and interpretation if the selection mechanism is neglected or improperly accounted for in the modelling and design of inference method. Asserting that selection problems are *potentially* inherent in any micro-data set, panel data as well as cross-section data, is hardly an exaggeration.

1.2 Virtues of panel data: Transformations

Several advantages can be obtained by utilizing panel data instead of time-series data or cross-section data in an empirical investigation. Panel data are in several respects 'richer'. As a general characteristic we may say: *pure time-series data contain no information about individual differences, and pure cross-section data contain no information about period-specific differences.* We therefore are unable from time-series data to explore effects of individual-specific variables and from cross-section data to examine effects of time-specific variables. *Panel data do not have, or have to a far smaller degree, these limitations,* not least because such data admit many useful transformations. Nerlove, Sevestre, and Balestra (2008, pp. 4–5) give the following remarks on the analyst's need to give due attention to the way the actual data type is generated:

> In many applications in the social sciences, especially in economics, the mechanism by which the data are generated is opaque... Understanding the process by which the observations at hand are generated is of equal importance. Were the data for example obtained from a sample of firms selected by stratified random sampling...? In the case of time series, the data are almost always "fabricated" in one way or another, by aggregation, interpolation, or extrapolation, or by all three. The nature of the sampling frame or the way in which the data are fabricated must be part of the model specification on which parametric inference or hypothesis testing is based.

We will, with reference to an *example*, illustrate differences in the 'information' contained in pure time series data and pure cross-section data on the one hand, and in balanced panel data on the other, and the transformations made possible by the latter. Consider an equation explaining the conditional expectation of y linearly by x, z, and q, where y and x are two-dimensional variables, z is individual-specific, and q is period-specific. We assume

$$\mathsf{E}(y_{it}|\boldsymbol{x}, \boldsymbol{z}, \boldsymbol{q}) = k + x_{it}\beta + z_i\alpha + q_t\gamma,$$

where k is an intercept; β, α, and γ are coefficients and $\boldsymbol{x}, \boldsymbol{z}, \boldsymbol{q}$ are (row) vectors containing all values of (x, z, q) in the data set; and i and t are index individuals and time periods, respectively. We assume that $x_{it}, z_i, q_t, \beta, \alpha$, and γ are scalars, but the following argument easily carries over to the case where the variables are row-vectors and the coefficients are column-vectors. *This expression is assumed to describe the relationship between* $\mathsf{E}(y|x, z, q)$ *and* x, z, q *for any values of* i *and* t. Let $u_{it} = y_{it} - \mathsf{E}(y_{it}|\boldsymbol{x}, \boldsymbol{z}, \boldsymbol{q})$, which can be interpreted as a disturbance, giving the equivalent formulation

$$y_{it} = k + x_{it}\beta + z_i\alpha + q_t\gamma + u_{it}, \quad \mathsf{E}(u_{it}|\boldsymbol{x}, \boldsymbol{z}, \boldsymbol{q}) = 0, \text{for all } i, t.$$

First, assume that the data set is balanced panel data from N individuals and T periods, so that we can specify

$$\begin{aligned} &y_{it} = k + x_{it}\beta + z_i\alpha + q_t\gamma + u_{it}, \quad \mathsf{E}(u_{it}|\boldsymbol{x}, \boldsymbol{z}, \boldsymbol{q}) = 0, \\ &i = 1, \ldots, N; \; t = 1, \ldots, T, \end{aligned} \tag{1.1}$$

where now $(\boldsymbol{x}, \boldsymbol{z}, \boldsymbol{q})$ denote vectors containing the values of (x_{it}, z_i, q_t) for $i = 1, \ldots, N;\ t = 1, \ldots, T$. A researcher may sometimes give primary attention to β and wants to estimate it without bias, but α and γ may be of interest as well. Anyway, we include z_i and q_t as explanatory variables because our theory implies that they are relevant in explaining y_{it}, and we do not have experimental data which allow us to 'control for' z_i and q_t by keeping their values constant in repeated samples. If u_{it} has not only zero conditional expectation, but also is homoskedastic and serially uncorrelated, we can from the NT observations on $(y_{it}, x_{it}, z_i, q_t)$ estimate $(k, \beta, \alpha, \gamma)$ by ordinary least squares (OLS), giving Minimum Variance Linear Unbiased Estimators (MVLUE), the 'best possible' linear estimators, or Gauss–Markov estimators of the coefficients.

What would have been the situation if we only had had access to either time-series or cross-section data? Assume first that *pure time-series*, for individual $i=1$ (i.e., $N=1$) in periods $t = 1, \ldots, T$, exist.[1] Then Model (1.1) should be *specialized to this data situation* by (conditioning on z_1 is irrelevant)

$$y_{1t} = (k+z_1\alpha) + x_{1t}\beta + q_t\gamma + u_{1t}, \quad \mathsf{E}(u_{1t}|\boldsymbol{x}_{1\cdot}, \boldsymbol{q}) = 0, \quad t = 1, \ldots, T, \tag{1.2}$$

where $\boldsymbol{x}_{1\cdot} = (x_{11}, \ldots, x_{1T})$. From time-series for y_{1t}, x_{1t}, and q_t, we could estimate β, γ, and the composite intercept $k + z_1\alpha$. This confirms: *(i) pure time-series data contain no information on individual differences or on effects of individual-specific variables*; (ii) the intercept is specific to the individual (unit); *(iii) the coefficient α cannot be identified*, as it belongs to a variable with no variation over the data set (having observed z_1 is of no help); and *(iv) the coefficients β and γ can be identified as long as x_{1t} and q_t are observable and vary over periods*. If u_{1t} is homoskedastic (over t) and shows no serial correlation (over t), then OLS applied on (1.2) will give estimators which are MVLUE for these coefficients *in the pure time-series data case.*

Next, assume that *a cross-section*, for period $t=1$ (i.e., $T=1$), for individuals $i = 1, \ldots, N$, exists. Then (1.1) should be specialized to (conditioning on q_1 is irrelevant):

$$y_{i1} = (k+q_1\gamma) + x_{i1}\beta + z_i\alpha + u_{i1}, \quad \mathsf{E}(u_{i1}|\boldsymbol{x}_{\cdot 1}, \boldsymbol{z}) = 0, \quad i = 1, \ldots, N, \tag{1.3}$$

[1] We here consider the case with time-series from only one individual (unit) to retain symmetry with the pure cross-section case below. Most of our following conclusions, however, carry without essential modifications over to situations with aggregate time-series for a sector or for the entire economy, since the equation is linear. But individual-specific time-series are far from absent. We could, for example, possess annual time-series of sales, stock prices, or employment for a specific company.

where $\boldsymbol{x}_{\cdot 1} = (x_{11}, \dots, x_{N1})$. From cross-section data for y_{i1}, x_{i1}, and z_i, we could estimate β, α, and the composite intercept $k+q_1\gamma$. This confirms: *(i) pure cross-section data contain no information on period-specific differences or on the effects of period-specific variables;* (ii) the intercept is specific to the data period; *(iii) the coefficient γ cannot be identified,* as it belongs to a variable with no variation over the data set (having observed q_1 is of no help); *(iv) the coefficients β and α can be identified as long as x_{i1} and z_i are observable and vary across individuals.* If u_{i1} is homoskedastic (over i) and serially uncorrelated (over i), then OLS applied on (1.3) will give MVLUE for these coefficients *in the pure cross-section data case.*

By panel data we may circumvent the problem of lack of identification of α from times series data, when using the 'time-series equation' (1.2) and of γ from cross-section data, when using the 'cross-section equation' (1.3). Moreover, we may *control for unobserved individual-specific or time-specific heterogeneity.* We illustrate this from (1.1), by first taking the difference between the equations for observations (i, t) and (i, s), giving

$$\begin{aligned} &y_{it}-y_{is}=(x_{it}-x_{is})\beta+(q_t-q_s)\gamma+(u_{it}-u_{is}), \quad \mathsf{E}(u_{it}-u_{is}|\boldsymbol{x},\boldsymbol{q})=0,\\ &i=1,\dots,N;\ t,s=1,\dots,T\ (t\neq s), \end{aligned} \tag{1.4}$$

from which z_i vanishes and, in contrast to (1.1), $\mathsf{E}(u_{it}|\boldsymbol{z})=0$ is not required for consistency of OLS. We consequently 'control for' the effect on y of z and 'retain' only the variation in y, x, and q. Having the opportunity to do so is crucial if z_i is unobservable and reflects unspecified heterogeneity, but still is believed to affect y_{it}. To see this, assume that z_i is unobservable *and correlated with x_{it} (across i)* and consider using OLS on (1.1) with z_i excluded, or on

$$y_{i1} = \text{constant} + x_{i1}\beta + u'_{i1}, \qquad i = 1, \dots, N,$$

where u'_{i1} is a disturbance in which we (tacitly) include the effect of z_i. This gives a biased estimator for β, since u_{i1}, via the correlation and the non-zero value of α, captures the effect of z_i on y_{i1}: we violate $\mathsf{E}(u'_{i1}|\boldsymbol{z}) = 0$. This will not be the case if we instead use OLS on (1.4).

By next in (1.1) taking the difference between the equations for observations (i, t) and (j, t), it likewise follows that

$$\begin{aligned} &y_{it}-y_{jt}=(x_{it}-x_{jt})\beta+(z_i-z_j)\alpha+(u_{it}-u_{jt}), \quad \mathsf{E}(u_{it}-u_{jt}|\boldsymbol{x},\boldsymbol{z})=0,\\ &i,j=1,\dots,N\ (i\neq j);\ t=1,\dots,T, \end{aligned} \tag{1.5}$$

from which q_t vanishes and, in contrast to (1.1), $\mathsf{E}(u_{it}|\boldsymbol{q})=0$ is not required for consistency of OLS. We consequently 'control for' the effect on y of q and 'retain' only the variation in y, x and z. Having the opportunity to do so is crucial if q_t is unobservable and reflects unspecified heterogeneity, but still is believed to affect y_{it}. To see this, assume that q_t is unobservable *and correlated with x_{it} (over t)* and consider using OLS on (1.1) with q_t excluded, or on

$$y_{1t} = \text{constant} + x_{1t}\beta + u''_{1t}, \qquad t = 1, \ldots, T,$$

where u''_{i1} is a disturbance in which we (tacitly) include the effect of q_t. This gives a biased OLS estimator for β, since u''_{1t}, via the correlation and the non-zero value of γ, captures the effect of q_t on y_{1t}: we violate $\mathsf{E}(u''_{1t}|q) = 0$. This not will be the case if we instead use OLS on (1.5).

If only individual time-series ($N = 1$) are available, we may perform the transformation leading to (1.4), but not the one leading to (1.5). Likewise, if one cross-section ($T = 1$) is the only data available, we may perform the transformation leading to (1.5), but not the one leading to (1.4). *Transformations which may give both (1.4) and (1.5) are infeasible unless we have panel data.*

We also have the opportunity to make *other, more complex, transformations* of (1.1). Deducting from (1.4) the corresponding equation when i is replaced by j (or deducting from (1.5) the corresponding equation with t replaced by s) we obtain

$$\begin{aligned}
&(y_{it} - y_{is}) - (y_{jt} - y_{js}) \\
&\qquad = [(x_{it} - x_{is}) - (x_{jt} - x_{js})]\beta + (u_{it} - u_{is}) - (u_{jt} - u_{js}), \\
&\mathsf{E}[(u_{it} - u_{is}) - (u_{jt} - u_{js})|x] = 0, \\
&i, j = 1, \ldots, N\ (i \neq j),\ \ t, s = 1, \ldots, T\ (t \neq s).
\end{aligned} \tag{1.6}$$

By this *double differencing*, z_i and q_t disappear, and neither $\mathsf{E}(u_{it}|z) = 0$ nor $\mathsf{E}(u_{it}|q) = 0$ is needed for consistency of the OLS estimators. We thus control for the effect on y of both z and q and retain only the variation in x. To see this, assume that both z_i and q_t are unobservable and correlated with x_{it} (over i and t, respectively), and consider using OLS on either (1.1) with both z_i and q_t omitted, on

$$y_{1t} = \text{constant} + x_{1t}\beta + u'_{1t}, \qquad t = 1, \ldots, T,$$

or on

$$y_{i1} = \text{constant} + x_{i1}\beta + u''_{i1}, \qquad i = 1, \ldots, N,$$

while (tacitly) including the effect of, respectively, (q_t, z_i), q_t, and z_i in the equation's disturbance, which will give biased (inconsistent) estimators for β. This will not be the case when using OLS on (1.6).

Haavelmo (1944, p. 50), more than 70 years ago, well before panel data became a common term in econometrics, described the relevance of handling unobserved heterogeneity in relation to data variation as follows:

> ... two individuals, or the same individual in two different time periods, may be confronted with exactly the same set of specified influencing factors and still ... may have different quantities y.... We may try to remove such discrepancies by introducing more "explaining" factors, x. But, usually, we shall soon exhaust the number of factors which could be considered as common to all individuals ... and which, at the same time, were not merely of negligible influence upon y. The discrepancies ... may depend upon a great variety of factors, these factors may be different from one individual to another, and they may vary with time for each individual.

Several other linear transformations can be performed on the linear relationship (1.1) when having panel data. We will show five. Summation in (1.1) over, respectively, i, t, and (i,t) and division by N, T, and NT, letting $\bar{z}=\frac{1}{N}\sum_{i=1}^{N} z_i$, $\bar{y}_{\cdot t}=\frac{1}{N}\sum_{i=1}^{N} y_{it}$, $\bar{q}=\frac{1}{T}\sum_{t=1}^{T} q_t$, $\bar{y}_{i\cdot}=\frac{1}{T}\sum_{t=1}^{T} y_{it}$, $\bar{y}=\frac{1}{NT}\sum_{i=1}^{N}\sum_{t=1}^{T} y_{it}$, etc., give

$$\bar{y}_{\cdot t} = (k+\bar{z}\alpha) + \bar{x}_{\cdot t}\beta + q_t\gamma + \bar{u}_{\cdot t}, \tag{1.7}$$

$$\bar{y}_{i\cdot} = (k+\bar{q}\gamma) + \bar{x}_{i\cdot}\beta + z_i\alpha + \bar{u}_{i\cdot}, \tag{1.8}$$

$$\bar{y} = k + \bar{z}\alpha + \bar{q}\gamma + \bar{x}\beta + \bar{u}. \tag{1.9}$$

Here (1.7) and (1.8) are equations in respectively period-specific and individual-specific means, which may have interest in themselves. Deducting these equations from (1.1), we obtain, respectively,

$$y_{it}-\bar{y}_{i\cdot} = (x_{it}-\bar{x}_{i\cdot})\beta + (q_t-\bar{q})\gamma + (u_{it}-\bar{u}_{i\cdot}),\quad \mathsf{E}(u_{it}-\bar{u}_{i\cdot}|\boldsymbol{x},\boldsymbol{q})=0, \tag{1.10}$$

$$y_{it}-\bar{y}_{\cdot t} = (x_{it}-\bar{x}_{\cdot t})\beta + (z_i-\bar{z})\alpha + (u_{it}-\bar{u}_{\cdot t}),\quad \mathsf{E}(u_{it}-\bar{u}_{\cdot t}|\boldsymbol{x},\boldsymbol{z})=0. \tag{1.11}$$

Using (1.10) we can be said to measure the variables from their individual-specific means and therefore, as in (1.4), eliminate z_i, while using (1.11), we measure the variables from their period-specific means and therefore, as in (1.5), eliminate q_t. Consequently, consistency of OLS estimation of β from (1.10) is robust to violation of $\mathsf{E}(u_{it}|\boldsymbol{z})=0$, unlike OLS applied on (1.1), when z_i is unobservable, correlated with x_{it} over i, and omitted from the equation. Likewise, consistency of OLS estimation of β from (1.11) is robust to violation $\mathsf{E}(u_{it}|\boldsymbol{q})=0$, unlike OLS applied on (1.1) when q_t is unobservable, correlated with x_{it}, over t, and omitted from the equation.

We may perform the two last transformations jointly. Subtracting both time-specific means (1.7) and individual-specific means (1.8) from (1.1) and adding the global means (1.9) gives[2]

[2] Equivalently, deduct from (1.10) the period mean of (1.11) or deduct from (1.11) the individual mean of (1.10).

$$\begin{aligned}&y_{it}-\bar{y}_{i\cdot}-\bar{y}_{\cdot t}+\bar{y} = (x_{it}-\bar{x}_{i\cdot}-\bar{x}_{\cdot t}+\bar{x})\beta+(u_{it}-\bar{u}_{i\cdot}-\bar{u}_{\cdot t}+\bar{u}),\\ &\mathsf{E}(u_{it}-\bar{u}_{i\cdot}-\bar{u}_{\cdot t}+\bar{u}|x)=0.\end{aligned} \tag{1.12}$$

Now, we can be said to be measuring the variables from their individual-specific and time-specific means jointly and therefore, as in (1.6), eliminate both the individual-specific variable z_i and the time-specific variable q_t. Consequently, OLS regression on (1.12) is robust to (nuisance) correlation both between x_{it} and z_i and between x_{it} and q_t, which is not the case for OLS regression on (1.1) if z_i and q_t are unobservable and are excluded from the equation.

Example: The following illustration exemplifies the above transformations and shows that running OLS regressions across different 'dimensions' of a panel data set can give rather different results for a model with only one y and one x, while disregarding variables like z and q. Using panel data for $N=229$ firms in the Norwegian chemical manufacturing industry observed over $T=8$ years, the logarithm of input (y) is regressed on the logarithm of the output volume (x). For material input and for labour input the relevant elasticity estimates are, respectively (standard errors in parentheses):

Regression on the full data set (1832 observations):
Materials: 1.0337 (0.0034). Labour: 0.7581 (0.0088)

Regression on the 229 firm means:
Materials: 1.0340 (0.0082). Labour: 0.7774 (0.0227)

Regression on the 8 year means:
Materials: 1.0228 (0.0130). Labour: −0.0348 (0.0752)

The three equations exemplify, respectively, (1.1) with z_i and q_t omitted, (1.8) with z_i omitted, and (1.7) with q_t omitted. The point estimates (of β) are fairly equal for materials, but for labour the estimate exploiting only the time variation is negative and much lower than the two others. There are reasons to believe that the underlying β-coefficient is not the same. Maybe the estimate from the time mean regression reflects that its variation is dominated by an omitted trend, say, a gradual introduction of a labour-saving technology. The question of why cross-sectional and times serial estimates of presumably the same coefficient often differ substantially has occupied econometricians for a long time and was posed almost sixty years ago by Kuh (1959).

1.3 **Panel data versus experimental data**

The linear transformations of (1.1) exemplified in (1.4)–(1.6) and (1.10)–(1.12) show that, when using panel data and linear models, we have the option to exploit; (i) neither the time variation nor the individual variation; (ii) only the time variation; (iii) only the individual variation; or (iv) both types of variation at the same time. It is often said that practitioners of, e.g., econometrics very rarely have access to experimental data. For panel data, however, this is not true without qualification. Such data place the researcher in an intermediate position *closer to an experimental situation* than pure cross-section data and pure time-series data do.

Expressed in technical terms, when using panel data one has the opportunity to separate *intra-individual* differences (differences *within* individuals) from *inter-individual* differences (differences *between* individuals). We have seen that, by performing suitable linear transformations, we can eliminate unobserved individual- or time-specific effects and avoid violating $\mathsf{E}(\text{disturbance}|\text{regressors}) = 0$, the core condition for ensuring unbiased estimation in (classical) regression analysis. *Panel data therefore make it possible to eliminate estimation bias (inconsistency) induced by unobserved nuisance variables which are correlated with the observable explanatory variables in the equation.* Many illustrations of this will be given throughout the book. To quote Lancaster (2006, p. 277): '. . . with panel data we can relax the assumption that the covariates are independent of the errors. They do this by providing what, on certain additional assumptions, amounts to a "controlled experiment".'

1.4 **Other virtues of panel data and some limitations**

The potential of panel data is also illustrated by the possibility they provide for estimating models with *individual-specific or period-specific coefficients.* Allowing for coefficient variability across space or time is another way of representing *individual-specific and/or period-specific heterogeneity* in the model. The coefficients in, for example, the following equations can be estimated by OLS from panel data for $N\ (\geq 2)$ individuals and $T\ (\geq 2)$ periods:

$$y_{it} = k_i + x_{it}\beta_i + u_{it}, \tag{1.13}$$

$$y_{it} = k_{1i} + k_{2t} + x_{1it}\beta_1 + x_{2it}\beta_{2i} + x_{3it}\beta_{3t} + u_{it}, \tag{1.14}$$

where x_{1it}, x_{2it}, and x_{3it} are (row vectors of) two-dimensional explanatory variables; k_i, k_{1i}, and k_{2t} are, respectively, N individual-specific, and T period-specific intercepts; the β_is and β_{2i}s are (column vectors of) individual-specific slope coefficients; the β_{3t}s are period-specific slope coefficients; and β_1 is common to all individuals and periods. Estimating the coefficients in such equations from pure time-series data or pure cross-section data is impossible, as the number of coefficients exceeds the number of observation points.

By panel data we may explore *aggregation problems* for time-series data and time series models. An illustration can be given by (1.13), assuming balanced panel data from N individuals. Summation across i gives

$$\sum_i y_{it} = \sum_i k_i + \sum_i x_{it}\beta_i + \sum_i u_{it}.$$

Let $\bar{k} = \frac{1}{N}\sum_i k_i$ and $\bar{\beta} = \frac{1}{N}\sum_i \beta_i$. The equation in time means, after division by N and a slight rearrangement, can be written as

$$\bar{y}_{\cdot t} = \bar{k} + \bar{x}_{\cdot t}\bar{\beta} + S_{xt,\beta} + \bar{u}_{\cdot t}, \tag{1.15}$$

where $S_{xt,\beta} = \frac{1}{N}\sum_i (x_{it} - \bar{x}_{\cdot t})(\beta_i - \bar{\beta}) \equiv \frac{1}{N}\sum_i x_{it}(\beta_i - \bar{\beta})$, i.e., the empirical covariance between the x_{it}s and the β_is in period t. Letting V_{xt}, V_β, and $R_{xt,\beta}$ denote, respectively, the coefficients of variation[3] of x_{it} (across i) and of β_i and the (empirical) coefficient of correlation between the two, this correctly aggregated equation in period means can be rewritten as

$$\bar{y}_{\cdot t} = \bar{k} + \bar{x}_{\cdot t}\bar{\beta}(1+V_{xt}V_\beta R_{xt,\beta}) + \bar{u}_{\cdot t}. \tag{1.16}$$

Representing the aggregated equation simply as (which is the only thing we could do if we only had linearly aggregated data)

$$\bar{y}_{\cdot t} = \bar{k} + \bar{x}_{\cdot t}\bar{\beta} + \bar{u}_{\cdot t},$$

and interpreting $\bar{\beta}$ as a 'mean slope coefficient' we commit an aggregation error, *unless the micro-coefficients do not show correlation with the variable to which they belong,* $R_{xt,\beta} = 0$. Otherwise, the correct macro-coefficient, $\bar{\beta}(1+V_{xt}V_\beta R_{xt,\beta})$, will either show instability over time or, if V_{xt}, V_β, and $R_{xt,\beta}$ are approximately time-invariant, will differ from $\bar{\beta}$. How it differs is left in the dark. Having panel data, the aggregation bias may be explored and corrected for since $\widehat{\beta_1}, \dots, \widehat{\beta_N}$ and their standard errors can be estimated. For further discussion of individual heterogeneity in aggregation contexts, see, e.g., Stoker (1993) and Blundell and Stoker (2005), as well as Kirman (1992), on the related problems of macro-economic modelling and analysis *as if* a 'representative individual' exists.

Extending from time-series data or cross-section data to panel data usually gives an increased number of observations and hence more degrees of freedom in estimation. Use of panel data frequently contributes to *reducing collinearity* among the explanatory variables and allows more extensive testing of competing model specifications. A common experience is that the correlation between explanatory variables in a regression equation often is stronger over time than across individuals or firms.

[3] Ratios between standard deviations and absolute values of corresponding means.

Another virtue of panel data is that they permit exploration of *dynamics* in behaviour, frequently considered *the primary* virtue of panel relative to cross-section data. We could, for example, estimate relations with lagged response or autoregressive effects, like

$$y_{it} = k + x_{it}\beta_0 + x_{i,t-1}\beta_1 + x_{i,t-2}\beta_2 + u_{it}, \tag{1.17}$$

$$y_{it} = k + x_{it}\beta_0 + y_{i,t-1}\lambda + u_{it}. \tag{1.18}$$

This would have been impossible when using pure cross-section data or data sets from repeated, non-overlapping cross-sections.

Balanced panel data, in particular when obtained from sampling, however, have *disadvantages*. The balanced structure may be felt as a *straitjacket*. Endogenous selection is one problem. Gradually increasing non-response, such that the sample becomes gradually 'less representative' for the underlying population, can be a considerable problem in practice. This is often called *sample attrition*. Following a strategy of always 'curtailing' a panel data set with attrition to obtain a balanced one, we may waste a lot of observations. Choosing an observational design which gives a set of *rotating* panel data—or, at the extreme, time-series of non-overlapping cross-sections—instead of balanced panel data, we can take advantage of observing a larger number of individuals. This means, for a given number of observations, that a larger part of the population will be represented. Hence, although panel data have many advantages, they are not the answer to the researcher's problems in every situation.

Repeated, non-overlapping cross-section data are worth mentioning in this connection. Such data, giving independently drawn cross-sections in two or more time periods, usually are more informative than single cross-sections. By introducing some (often mild) additional assumptions about (latent) homogeneity, attempts have been made to construct artificial panel data, sometimes called *pseudo panel data*, for handling specific problems; see, e.g., Deaton (1985) and Moffitt (1993). Although no individual is repeatedly observed, pseudo panel data may make estimation of equations like (1.17) and (1.18) feasible.

1.5 **Overview**

The contents of the book fall, broadly, into three parts: *basic topics*, rooted in simple and multiple regression analysis, are discussed in Chapters 2 through 5; *extensions*, with focus on various complications arising in panel data regression, and suggested remedies are considered in Chapters 6 through 10; chapters 11 and 12 deal with relatively *advanced topics*, taking selected elements from the discussion in the chapters that have preceded some steps further.

The content of the book is organized as set out below.

In Chapter 2 we first discuss regression models for balanced panel data where individual-specific variation in the intercept, represented by fixed (non-stochastic) parameters, may occur. Their OLS estimators, using, *inter alia*, decomposition of the variation in within- and between-unit variation, are compared with those when all coefficients are common to all individuals and time periods. We further describe ways of testing for different kinds of coefficient heterogeneity. A presentation of algebra for Kronecker-products, a kind of matrix operations which are very useful in handling balanced panel data, is integrated.

Models with fixed shifts in the intercept may require a large number of parameters and a substantial loss of degrees of freedom when the number individuals is large. In Chapter 3, models with a more parsimonious representation of heterogeneity, as realizations of stochastic variables, are considered. They may be viewed as disturbance components models, where the individual-specific intercept shifts can be interpreted as individual-specific components in the equation's disturbance. Suitable inference methods are the Generalized Least Squares (GLS), the Maximum Likelihood (ML), and test procedures rooted in these methods. We also consider extensions with both random individual- and period-specific differences in the intercept, implying that the disturbance has both an individual-specific and a period-specific part.

Regarding heterogeneity, an interesting idea is that the slope coefficients may also vary randomly across individuals and over periods. Chapter 4 brings such extensions of the basic regression models in focus, considering models whose coefficients are individual-specific and generated by a stochastic mechanism with some structure. Problems addressed here are estimation of expected coefficients and their spread, as well as coefficient prediction.

In Chapter 5 problems related to unidimensional regressors are considered. Certain problems, which are, formally, problems of multicollinearity, arise when we combine individual-specific and/or time-specific explanatory variables with fixed effects representations of the heterogeneity, but do not arise if we stick to random effects specifications. The existence of unidimensional explanatory variables and researchers' desire to estimate their effects emerge as strong arguments in favour of either looking for additional restrictions or turning to random effects specifications.

When allowing for stochastic individual- or period-specific effects, it may be questionable to disregard correlation with the explanatory variables. In Chapter 6 we discuss problems then arising, which have the nature partly of identification problems and partly of simultaneity (endogeneity) problems. Such problems, often intractable in unidimensional data, may be handled in panel data, but sometimes they are intractable even then. We demonstrate, *inter alia*, that estimation utilizing instrument variables may be a way of escaping inconsistency following from application of classical methods like OLS and GLS, although not always ensuring efficiency in coefficient estimation.

Chapter 7 is concerned with another important problem in regression analysis, measurement errors in the regressors. The possibility of coming to grips with this problem is often larger and the identification problems less severe when replacing cross-section data with panel data, because we can, by suitable transformations, take advantage of the two-dimensional variation. Procedures discussed in Chapters 2 and 3 are reconsidered in this more general context. Constructing estimators by aggregation of 'micro-estimators' and obtaining consistency by combining inconsistent estimators, are also discussed.

Dynamic mechanisms, in particular autoregressive effects, are our main concern in Chapter 8. Problems then arising are difficulties in distinguishing between persistence arising from unit-specific latent heterogeneity and dependence on the past in the form of autoregressive effects. Relationships between the approaches in this chapter and in Chapter 7, *inter alia*, in the way instrumental variables and the Generalized Method of Moments (GMM) are used, as well as the mixed utilization of equations and variables in levels and in differences, are discussed. The treatment of integrated variables and equations with co-integrated variables, is also briefly discussed.

Chapter 9 is concerned with models for individuals' discrete responses. Since binary regressands will be required, and response probabilities are bound to lie between zero and one, the analysis becomes technically more complicated, *inter alia*, involving non-linear equations and creating problems not arising in linear models. Here logit models for panel data, with focus on situations with only two possible responses for each individual in each period (binomial logit), and estimation by ML will be specifically considered.

Models and procedures for handling unbalanced panel data in the absence of endogenous selection are discussed in Chapter 10. We consider, *inter alia*, ways of modifying models and methods in the preceding chapters (within, between, GLS, and ML) when we are in this more complicated, and often more realistic, data situation. Sometimes a reorganization of the data is recommended.

Chapter 11 extends the discussion in Chapter 10, considering models suited to handling truncated and censored data sets. The common label is systematically unbalanced data sets or models for unbalanced panel data selected endogenously. More elaborate versions of regression procedures, often stepwise, and versions of ML procedures are then required. Some of them are discussed and contrasted with regression procedures.

Finally, Chapter 12 is concerned with multi-equation models for panel data: on the one hand, systems of regression equations; on the other hand, interdependent systems, having endogenous explanatory variables in (some of) the equations. This extends Chapters 3 and 6 in various ways. Procedures considered for single-equation models in the chapters that have preceded, including methods combining GLS and instrumental variable approaches, will here be generalized.

2 Regression analysis: Fixed effects models

CHAPTER SUMMARY

Regression analysis of panel data can handle problems which are unsolvable when having only standard unidimensional data. Linear regression models where the intercepts, and to some extent the coefficients, differ between individuals and/or periods are discussed. These differences, often due to unobserved heterogeneity, are represented by unknown fixed parameters. The chapter gradually extends the models' dimension and the use of matrix algebra, parts of which are explained along the way. The first part considers models with only fixed individual-specific heterogeneity. The second part also includes time-specific heterogeneity, accounting for both spatial and temporal effects. Several applications of Ordinary Least Squares are considered. Integrated in the discussion is an excursion into Kronecker-products, a part of matrix algebra that simplifies the formulation and estimation of panel data models.

Regression models are frequently used in the analysis of panel data, as in general econometrics. Although such models have limitations, to be discussed in later chapters, regression analysis of panel data can handle problems which are unsolvable when only standard unidimensional data are at hand, as indicated by the simple examples in Chapter 1. In this chapter, we consider static, linear regression models where the intercepts, and to some extent the coefficients, differ between individuals and/or between periods. The way the parameters differ will not be modelled. These differences, denoted as *individual-specific and/or time-specific heterogeneity*, will be represented by fixed parameters and, to some extent, by associated binary variables. The models are therefore said to have *fixed effects*.

The chapter is built up step-wise, gradually extending the use of matrix algebra, and consists of two parts, corresponding to the two ways of specifying heterogeneity. The first part (Sections 2.1 and 2.2) gives a fairly elementary exposition. In Section 2.1 a model with fixed unit-specific heterogeneity is considered, and the basic concepts using scalar notation are introduced. The generalization to include any number of regressors is described in Section 2.2. The second part (Sections 2.3 and 2.4) expand by also accounting for time-specific heterogeneity, allowing jointly for cross-sectional (spatial) and time-serial (temporal) heterogeneity. The one-regressor case is considered in Section 2.3 and its generalization to handle any number of regressors in Section 2.4.

2.1 Simple regression model: One-way heterogeneity

We will consider three models. The first allows for full one-way heterogeneity in the parameters, the second for partial one-way heterogeneity, and the third, a benchmark case, assumes a fully homogeneous parameter structure.

2.1.1 INDIVIDUAL-SPECIFIC INTERCEPTS AND COEFFICIENTS

Assume that the scalar variables x and y are observed for N (≥ 2) individuals in T (≥ 2) periods and let (x_{it}, y_{it}) denote the observations from individual i in period t and X denote all observations of x. These variables are related by

$$y_{it} = \alpha_i^* + \beta_i x_{it} + u_{it}, \quad (u_{it}|X) \sim \mathsf{IID}(0, \sigma^2), \quad \begin{matrix} i = 1, \dots, N; \\ t = 1, \dots, T, \end{matrix} \tag{2.1}$$

where α_i^* and β_i are unknown constants, specific to individual i.[1] We want to make inference on these $2N$ constants and see immediately that this requires $T \geq 2$. If $T = 1$, i.e., when the data set is from a cross-section, the number of observations is less than the number of coefficients. Having panel data is essential for estimating and testing hypotheses about individual-specific constants.

The Ordinary Least Squares (OLS) estimators of (α_i^*, β_i) are the solution to

$$\min_{\alpha_1^*,\dots,\alpha_N^*,\beta_1,\dots,\beta_N} \sum_{i=1}^N \sum_{t=1}^T (y_{it} - \alpha_i^* - \beta_i x_{it})^2.$$

This problem, however, can be split into N *simple least squares problems*, one for each individual, because β_i and α_i^* only occur in the T terms of the double sum which relate to individual i. Therefore the solution simplifies to solving the N simple OLS problems[2]

$$\min_{\alpha_i^*, \beta_i} \sum_{t=1}^T (y_{it} - \alpha_i^* - \beta_i x_{it})^2, \qquad i = 1, \dots, N.$$

[1] $\mathsf{IID}(0, \sigma^2)$ denotes *independently, identically distributed* with expectation 0 and variance σ^2. Notice, however, that several of the results do not require an assumption as strong as $(u_{it}|X) \sim \mathsf{IID}(0, \sigma^2)$: zero expectation, constant variances, and no serial correlation will suffice, 'identically' being often superfluous. Sometimes conditioning on parts of X may also be sufficient (without this being explicitly indicated). Extensions allowing for disturbance heteroskedasticity and/or serial correlation will be considered in Sections 3.3.1 and 4.2.1.

[2] Only in estimating σ^2, a gain is obtained when utilizing all NT observations. The estimator $\widehat{\sigma}^2 = \frac{1}{N(T-2)} \sum_{i=1}^N \sum_{t=1}^T \widehat{u}_{it}^2$, where $\widehat{u}_{it} = y_{it} - \widehat{\alpha}_i^* - \widehat{\beta}_i x_{it}$, is unbiased and has a smaller variance than $\widehat{\sigma}_i^2 = \frac{1}{T-2} \sum_{t=1}^T \widehat{u}_{it}^2$, since $\widehat{\sigma}^2 = \frac{1}{N} \sum_{i=1}^N \widehat{\sigma}_i^2$, where $\widehat{\sigma}_1^2, \dots, \widehat{\sigma}_N^2$ are uncorrelated.

Let, for any (z_{it}, q_{it}), $\bar{z}_{i\cdot} = \frac{1}{T}\sum_t z_{it}$, $\bar{q}_{i\cdot} = \frac{1}{T}\sum_t q_{it}$ and

$$W_{ZQii} = \sum_{t=1}^{T}(z_{it} - \bar{z}_{i\cdot})(q_{it} - \bar{q}_{i\cdot}), \qquad i = 1, \dots, N.$$

From the first-order conditions we find the OLS estimators

$$\widehat{\beta}_i = \frac{\sum_{t=1}^{T}(x_{it} - \bar{x}_{i\cdot})(y_{it} - \bar{y}_{i\cdot})}{\sum_{t=1}^{T}(x_{it} - \bar{x}_{i\cdot})^2} = \frac{W_{XYii}}{W_{XXii}}, \tag{2.2}$$

$$\widehat{\alpha}_i^* = \bar{y}_{i\cdot} - \widehat{\beta}_i \bar{x}_{i\cdot}, \qquad i = 1, \dots, N. \tag{2.3}$$

The letter W symbolizes *within-individual* (or simply *within*) and indicates that the variables are measured from their respective individual-specific means; W_{XYii} and W_{XXii} can be said to represent, respectively, the covariation between x and y and the variation of x 'within individual i'. Since inserting (2.1) into (2.2)–(2.3) gives

$$\widehat{\beta}_i - \beta_i = \frac{W_{XUii}}{W_{XXii}}, \qquad \widehat{\alpha}_i^* - \alpha_i^* = \bar{u}_{i\cdot} - (\widehat{\beta}_i - \beta_i)\bar{x}_{i\cdot}, \quad i = 1, \dots, N,$$

where $\mathsf{E}(W_{XUii}|\mathbf{X}) = 0$ and $\text{var}(W_{XUii}|\mathbf{X}) = \sigma^2 W_{XXii}$, $\widehat{\beta}_i$ and $\widehat{\alpha}_i^*$ are unbiased (both conditional on $\mathbf{X}$ and marginally), and

$$\begin{aligned} \text{var}(\widehat{\beta}_i|\mathbf{X}) &= \text{var}\left(\frac{W_{XUii}}{W_{XXii}}|\mathbf{X}\right) \\ &= \frac{\sigma^2}{W_{XXii}} = \frac{\sigma^2}{\sum_{t=1}^{T}(x_{it} - \bar{x}_{i\cdot})^2}, \qquad i = 1, \dots, N. \end{aligned} \tag{2.4}$$

The N sets of individual-specific estimators $(\widehat{\alpha}_i^*, \widehat{\beta}_i)$ are *Minimum Variance Linear Unbiased Estimators (MVLUE), i.e., Gauss–Markov estimators, for any* T (≥ 2). Furthermore, they are consistent if the number of observations in each sub-problem, T, goes to infinity, often denoted as *T-consistency*. On the other hand, if N increases and T is finite, the number of unknown parameters increases. This exemplifies a problem denoted as the *incidental parameter-problem* by Neyman and Scott (1948); see also Lancaster (2000). Each estimator is then inconsistent, according to the definition of consistency.

2.1.2 INDIVIDUAL-SPECIFIC INTERCEPTS, COMMON COEFFICIENT

We next consider a model where the coefficient is the same for all individuals, i.e., we impose on (2.1) $\beta_1 = \cdots = \beta_N = \beta$, giving

$$y_{it} = \alpha_i^* + \beta x_{it} + u_{it}, \quad (u_{it}|X) \sim \mathsf{IID}(0, \sigma^2), \quad \begin{array}{l} i = 1, \dots, N; \\ t = 1, \dots, T. \end{array} \tag{2.5}$$

It has fewer coefficients, but still at least two observations from each individual are needed. The OLS estimators are now determined by

$$\min_{\alpha_1^*,\dots,\alpha_N^*,\beta} \sum_{i=1}^{N} \sum_{t=1}^{T} (y_{it} - \alpha_i^* - \beta x_{it})^2.$$

From the first-order conditions it follows that

$$\widehat{\beta}_W = \frac{\sum_{i=1}^{N} \sum_{t=1}^{T} (x_{it} - \bar{x}_{i\cdot})(y_{it} - \bar{y}_{i\cdot})}{\sum_{i=1}^{N} \sum_{t=1}^{T} (x_{it} - \bar{x}_{i\cdot})^2} \equiv \frac{\sum_{i=1}^{N} W_{XYii}}{\sum_{i=1}^{N} W_{XXii}} \equiv \frac{W_{XY}}{W_{XX}}, \tag{2.6}$$

$$\widehat{\alpha}_{iW}^* = \bar{y}_{i\cdot} - \widehat{\beta}_W \bar{x}_{i\cdot}, \qquad i = 1, \dots, N, \tag{2.7}$$

where, in general,

$$W_{ZQ} = \sum_{i=1}^{N} W_{ZQii} = \sum_{i=1}^{N} \sum_{t=1}^{T} (z_{it} - \bar{z}_{i\cdot})(q_{it} - \bar{q}_{i\cdot}).$$

Now, the OLS problem cannot be reduced to N sub-problems, since β is common to all terms in the minimand.

Technically, the computation can be done by OLS regression with N individual-specific dummy variables (binary variables), one for each individual. The estimator $\widehat{\beta}_W$ is denoted as the *within-individual estimator* of β. An alternative term is the *least squares dummy variables (LSDV) estimator*, since it can be obtained by including N individual dummies, $d_{ij} = 1$ and $= 0$ for $i = j$ and $i \neq j$, respectively, and using OLS after having in (2.5) replaced α_i^* with $\sum_{j=i}^{N} \alpha_j^* d_{ij}$.[3]

Since inserting (2.1) into (2.6)–(2.7) gives

$$\widehat{\beta}_W - \beta = \frac{W_{XU}}{W_{XX}}, \qquad \widehat{\alpha}_{iW}^* - \alpha_i^* = \bar{u}_{i\cdot} - (\widehat{\beta}_W - \beta)\bar{x}_{i\cdot}, \quad i = 1, \dots, N,$$

where $\mathsf{E}(W_{XU}|X) = 0$ and $\text{var}(W_{XU}|X) = \sigma^2 W_{XX}$, $\widehat{\beta}_W$ and $\widehat{\alpha}_{iW}^*$ are unbiased with

$$\text{var}(\widehat{\beta}_W|X) = \text{var}\left(\frac{W_{XU}}{W_{XX}}|X\right) = \frac{\sigma^2}{W_{XX}} \equiv \frac{\sigma^2}{\sum_{i=1}^{N} \sum_{t=1}^{T} (x_{it} - \bar{x}_{i\cdot})^2}. \tag{2.8}$$

[3] We can here refer to the *Frisch–Waugh (1933) theorem*, see Greene (2008, p. 28), which implies that the following two procedures yield the same result. (1) Regress first y_{it} and x_{it} separately on $d_{i1}, \dots, d_{iN}$ and extract the residuals, which in this case become $\tilde{y}_{it} = y_{it} - \bar{y}_{i\cdot}$ and $\tilde{x}_{it} = x_{it} - \bar{x}_{i\cdot}$, respectively. Next, regress $\tilde{y}_{it}$ on $\tilde{x}_{it}$, giving the within estimator. (2) Regress y_{it} on $x_{it}, d_{i1}, \dots, d_{iN}$, giving the LSDV estimator.

The estimator $\widehat{\beta}_W$, like $\widehat{\beta}_1, \dots, \widehat{\beta}_N$, exploits only information about the variation in the observations around their individual mean, the variation *within individuals*. The variation between individuals, the variation in the individual-specific means, is used solely in estimating the intercepts α_i^*, as is seen from (2.7).

The estimators thus obtained are *MVLUE* in Model (2.5). What can be said about their asymptotic properties? When discussing such issues in a panel data context, we must be careful, as both N and T can go to infinity. Since the variance of the estimator of the coefficient, (2.8), normally goes to zero when either N or T, or both, go to infinity, as the denominator goes to infinity, then $N \to \infty$, T finite and $T \to \infty$, N finite are both sufficient for consistency of $\widehat{\beta}_W$. This follows because an unbiased estimator whose variance goes to zero with increasing sample size is consistent. On the other hand, $\widehat{\alpha}_{iW}^*$ *will be consistent only if T goes to infinity*. If N goes to infinity while T is finite, the number of unknown intercepts increase, while the number of observations used in the estimation of each of them remains finite. Then each $\widehat{\alpha}_{iW}^*$ is inconsistent. Briefly, while $\widehat{\beta}_W$ is both N- and T-consistent, $\widehat{\alpha}_{iW}^*$ is only T-consistent.

Now, not only $\widehat{\beta}$, but any of the $\widehat{\beta}_i$s may be considered estimators of β in Model (2.5). They are unbiased, but clearly inefficient as (2.4) exceeds (2.8) by a factor of order N. We find from (2.2), (2.4), and (2.6) that the within-individual estimator can be expressed as

$$\widehat{\beta}_W = \frac{\sum_{i=1}^{N} W_{XXii}\widehat{\beta}_i}{\sum_{i=1}^{N} W_{XXii}} = \frac{\sum_{i=1}^{N}\left(\frac{\widehat{\beta}_i}{\text{var}(\widehat{\beta}_i|X)}\right)}{\sum_{i=1}^{N}\left(\frac{1}{\text{var}(\widehat{\beta}_i|X)}\right)}. \tag{2.9}$$

Hence, *the within-individual estimator of β in Model (2.5) is a weighted average of the individual-specific estimators $\widehat{\beta}_1, \dots, \widehat{\beta}_N$ in Model (2.1), with $\widehat{\beta}_i$ given a weight W_{XXii}, which is inversely proportional to* $\text{var}(\widehat{\beta}_i|X)$. It is easy to derive (2.8) from (2.4) and (2.9), because $\text{cov}(\widehat{\beta}_i, \widehat{\beta}_j|X) = 0$, $i \neq j$. We find

$$\text{var}(\widehat{\beta}_W|X) = \frac{\sum_{i=1}^{N} \text{var}\left(\frac{\widehat{\beta}_i}{\text{var}(\widehat{\beta}_i|X)}|X\right)}{\left[\sum_{i=1}^{N}\left(\frac{1}{\text{var}(\widehat{\beta}_i|X)}\right)\right]^2} \equiv \frac{1}{\sum_{i=1}^{N}\left(\frac{1}{\text{var}(\widehat{\beta}_i|X)}\right)}$$

$$= \frac{1}{\sum_{i=1}^{N}\left(\frac{W_{XXii}}{\sigma^2}\right)} = \frac{\sigma^2}{W_{XX}}.$$

An alternative, and maybe more illuminating, interpretation of this result is: inserting for y_{it} from (2.5) in (2.2) gives

$$\widehat{\beta}_i = \beta + \frac{W_{XUii}}{W_{XXii}}, \qquad i = 1, \dots, N. \tag{2.10}$$

This is, formally, a (degenerate) regression equation with N observations, $\widehat{\beta}_i$ as regressand, β as intercept, no regressor, and W_{XUii}/W_{XXii} as disturbance. The latter is heteroskedastic, with variance σ^2/W_{XXii} (conditional on X). Estimating β from (2.10) by Generalized Least Squares GLS (weighted regression), based on the N $\widehat{\beta}_i$s, gives (2.9). This exemplifies the property of GLS discussed in Appendix 2A, Section 2A.1.

2.1.3 HOMOGENEOUS BENCHMARK MODEL

The third model, a benchmark case, has both intercept and coefficient equal across individuals and periods:

$$y_{it} = \alpha + \beta x_{it} + u_{it}, \quad (u_{it}|X) \sim \mathsf{IID}(0, \sigma^2), \quad \begin{array}{l} i = 1, \dots, N; \\ t = 1, \dots, T. \end{array} \tag{2.11}$$

OLS estimation of α and β solves

$$\min_{\alpha,\beta} \sum_{i=1}^{N} \sum_{t=1}^{T} (y_{it} - \alpha - \beta x_{it})^2$$

and gives

$$\widehat{\beta} = \frac{\sum_{i=1}^{N} \sum_{t=1}^{T} (x_{it} - \bar{x})(y_{it} - \bar{y})}{\sum_{i=1}^{N} \sum_{t=1}^{T} (x_{it} - \bar{x})^2} = \frac{G_{XY}}{G_{XX}}, \tag{2.12}$$

$$\widehat{\alpha} = \bar{y} - \widehat{\beta}\bar{x}, \tag{2.13}$$

where, in general, $\bar{z} = \frac{1}{NT} \sum_i \sum_t z_{it}$ and

$$G_{ZQ} = \sum_{i=1}^{N} \sum_{t=1}^{T} (z_{it} - \bar{z})(q_{it} - \bar{q}),$$

G denoting 'global'. We call (2.12) the *global estimator* of β, since it uses the deviation of each observation from its global mean, therefore exploiting both the variation within and between individuals.

The intuitive reason why (2.12) exploits both kinds of data variation in estimating β, and to the same degree, is that since the intercept is common to all observations, we spend no between-variation in estimating it, making this part 'beneficial' to the estimation of the coefficient. Let

$$B_{ZQ} = T\sum_{i=1}^{N}(\bar{z}_{i\cdot} - \bar{z})(\bar{q}_{i\cdot} - \bar{q}),$$

write the deviation of (z_{it}, q_{it}) from their global means as

$$z_{it} - \bar{z} \equiv (z_{it} - \bar{z}_{i\cdot}) + (\bar{z}_{i\cdot} - \bar{z}), \qquad q_{it} - \bar{q} \equiv (q_{it} - \bar{q}_{i\cdot}) + (\bar{q}_{i\cdot} - \bar{q}),$$

and take their product-sum across (i, t). This gives

$$G_{ZQ} = W_{ZQ} + B_{ZQ}, \tag{2.14}$$

i.e., the global (co)variation can be decomposed into (co)variation within individuals (W) and between individuals (B).

Let us show that the global estimator (2.12), in exploiting both kinds of data variation, has a smaller variance for $\widehat{\beta}$ *in Model (2.11)* than has $\widehat{\beta}_W$. The proof also involves an alternative set of OLS estimators for Model (2.11). Summation across t and division by T gives an *equation in individual-specific means*:

$$\bar{y}_{i\cdot} = \alpha + \beta\bar{x}_{i\cdot} + \bar{u}_{i\cdot}, \quad (\bar{u}_{i\cdot}|X) \sim \mathsf{IID}(0, \sigma^2/T), \quad i = 1, \dots, N, \tag{2.15}$$

for which the OLS problem is

$$\min_{\alpha,\beta} \sum_{i=1}^{N}(\bar{y}_{i\cdot} - \alpha - \beta\bar{x}_{i\cdot})^2.$$

The resulting estimators, called the *between-individual estimators*, become

$$\widehat{\beta}_B = \frac{\sum_{i=1}^{N}(\bar{x}_{i\cdot} - \bar{x})(\bar{y}_{i\cdot} - \bar{y})}{\sum_{i=1}^{N}(\bar{x}_{i\cdot} - \bar{x})^2} = \frac{B_{XY}}{B_{XX}}, \tag{2.16}$$

$$\widehat{\alpha}_B = \bar{y} - \widehat{\beta}_B\bar{x}. \tag{2.17}$$

Since (2.11), (2.12), and (2.16) imply

$$\widehat{\beta} - \beta = \frac{G_{XU}}{G_{XX}}, \qquad \widehat{\beta}_B - \beta = \frac{B_{XU}}{B_{XX}},$$

$\widehat{\beta}$ and $\widehat{\beta}_B$ are both unbiased for β in Model (2.11). It is not difficult to show that $\text{var}(G_{XU}|X) = \sigma^2 G_{XX}$ and $\text{var}(B_{XU}|X) = \sigma^2 B_{XX}$. Hence,

$$\text{var}(\widehat{\beta}|X) = \text{var}\left(\frac{G_{XU}}{G_{XX}}|X\right) = \frac{\sigma^2}{G_{XX}} \equiv \frac{\sigma^2}{\sum_{i=1}^{N}\sum_{t=1}^{T}(x_{it}-\bar{x})^2}, \tag{2.18}$$

$$\text{var}(\widehat{\beta}_B|X) = \text{var}\left(\frac{B_{XU}}{B_{XX}}|X\right) = \frac{\sigma^2}{B_{XX}} \equiv \frac{\sigma^2/T}{\sum_{i=1}^{N}(\bar{x}_{i\cdot}-\bar{x})^2}. \tag{2.19}$$

From (2.8), (2.14), (2.18), and (2.19) we conclude that

$$\text{var}(\widehat{\beta}|X) < \text{var}(\widehat{\beta}_B|X) \text{ if } W_{XX} > 0,$$
$$\text{var}(\widehat{\beta}|X) < \text{var}(\widehat{\beta}_W|X) \text{ if } B_{XX} > 0.$$

2.1.4 HOW ARE THE ESTIMATORS RELATED?

We have defined three estimators for the coefficient β in the homogeneous Model (2.11): the within-individual estimator $\widehat{\beta}_W$; the between-individual estimator $\widehat{\beta}_B$; and the global estimator $\widehat{\beta}$. All are unbiased and consistent, regardless of whether $N\rightarrow\infty$, $T\rightarrow\infty$, or both. Consistency of $\widehat{\beta}_B$ when $T\rightarrow\infty$, N finite, follows from the fact that the disturbance in (2.15), $\bar{u}_{i\cdot}$, has zero plim when $T\rightarrow\infty$. Furthermore, $\widehat{\beta}_W$ and $\widehat{\beta}_B$ are uncorrelated.[4]

On the other hand, we have no guarantee that the between-individual estimator $\widehat{\beta}_B$ and the global estimator $\widehat{\beta}$ are in general unbiased and consistent for β *if the model with individual-specific intercepts, Model (2.5), has generated our data.* As always, it is imperative (i) to be precise about which model is under discussion and (ii) to distinguish sharply between model and method. If (2.5) holds, these estimators can be written as

$$\widehat{\beta}_B = \beta + \frac{\frac{1}{N}\sum_{i=1}^{N}(\bar{x}_{i\cdot}-\bar{x})(\alpha_i^*-\bar{\alpha}^*)}{\frac{1}{N}\sum_{i=1}^{N}(\bar{x}_{i\cdot}-\bar{x})^2} + \frac{\frac{1}{N}\sum_{i=1}^{N}(\bar{x}_{i\cdot}-\bar{x})(\bar{u}_{i\cdot}-\bar{u})}{\frac{1}{N}\sum_{i=1}^{N}(\bar{x}_{i\cdot}-\bar{x})^2}, \tag{2.20}$$

$$\widehat{\beta} = \beta + \frac{\frac{1}{N}\sum_{i=1}^{N}(\bar{x}_{i\cdot}-\bar{x})(\alpha_i^*-\bar{\alpha}^*)}{\frac{1}{NT}\sum_{i=1}^{N}\sum_{t=1}^{T}(x_{it}-\bar{x})^2} + \frac{\frac{1}{NT}\sum_{i=1}^{N}\sum_{t=1}^{T}(x_{it}-\bar{x})(u_{it}-\bar{u})}{\frac{1}{NT}\sum_{i=1}^{N}\sum_{t=1}^{T}(x_{it}-\bar{x})^2}. \tag{2.21}$$

[4] The proof relies on the identity $\sum_i\sum_t(z_{it}-\bar{z}_{i\cdot})(\bar{q}_{i\cdot}-\bar{q})\equiv 0$. See Section 3.2.3 for a more general proof using matrix algebra.

Conditional on $\boldsymbol{X}$, the last term in both expressions has zero expectation. The second term is a ratio between an empirical covariance and an empirical variance. The covariance is zero when the individual-specific effects are *empirically* uncorrelated with the individual-specific means of the xs, and only then are $\widehat{\beta}$ and $\widehat{\beta}_B$ unbiased. Consistency holds if this condition is satisfied asymptotically. But correlation between the α_i^*s and the $\bar{x}_{i\cdot}$s may well occur, so that $\widehat{\beta}$ and $\widehat{\beta}_B$ are biased and do not measure what we want them to measure. Correlation between heterogeneity and regressors is an issue to be explored in Chapter 6.

Conclusions so far are:

(i) The within-individual estimator $\widehat{\beta}_W$ is the MVLUE of β in Model (2.5), and the global estimator $\widehat{\beta}$ is the MVLUE in Model (2.11).

(ii) If x exhibits both within- and between-individual variation ($W_{XX}>0, B_{XX}>0$), neither $\widehat{\beta}_B$ nor $\widehat{\beta}_W$ can be MVLUE in Model (2.11).

From (2.6), (2.8), (2.12), (2.14), (2.16), (2.18), and (2.19) it follows that

$$\widehat{\beta} = \frac{W_{XY}+B_{XY}}{W_{XX}+B_{XX}} = \frac{W_{XX}\widehat{\beta}_W+B_{XX}\widehat{\beta}_B}{W_{XX}+B_{XX}} = \frac{\dfrac{\widehat{\beta}_W}{\mathrm{var}(\widehat{\beta}_W|\boldsymbol{X})}+\dfrac{\widehat{\beta}_B}{\mathrm{var}(\widehat{\beta}_B|\boldsymbol{X})}}{\dfrac{1}{\mathrm{var}(\widehat{\beta}_W|\boldsymbol{X})}+\dfrac{1}{\mathrm{var}(\widehat{\beta}_B|\boldsymbol{X})}}. \tag{2.22}$$

Hence, in Model (2.11), the global estimator of β can be obtained by giving the within-individual and the between-individual *variation* equal weights. Equivalently, it is a weighted mean of the within-individual and the between-individual *estimators*, with weights which are inversely proportional with their respective variances. The *relative efficiency* of the within-individual and the between-individual estimator against the global estimator, i.e., their variance ratios, are

$$f_W = \frac{\mathrm{var}(\widehat{\beta}_W|\boldsymbol{X})}{\mathrm{var}(\widehat{\beta}|\boldsymbol{X})} = \frac{G_{XX}}{W_{XX}} = 1+\frac{B_{XX}}{W_{XX}},$$

$$f_B = \frac{\mathrm{var}(\widehat{\beta}_B|\boldsymbol{X})}{\mathrm{var}(\widehat{\beta}|\boldsymbol{X})} = \frac{G_{XX}}{B_{XX}} = 1+\frac{W_{XX}}{B_{XX}}.$$

If, for example, the between variation of x accounts for 80% of the global variation, $f_W=5, f_B=1.25$.

2.2 Multiple regression model: One-way heterogeneity

We extend to a K-regressor model and change to *matrix notation*, Sections 2.2.1–2.2.4 generalizing Sections 2.1.1–2.1.4. Matrix formulation of regression models for panel data is indispensable except in the very simplest cases. If we had continued using scalar notation, we would need triple subscripted variables (indexing variable, individual, period) to represent the observations, which would often give unwieldy formulae.

2.2.1 INDIVIDUAL-SPECIFIC INTERCEPTS AND COEFFICIENTS

We assume that the equation has K regressors and generalize Model (2.1) to

$$y_{it} = \alpha_i^* + \boldsymbol{x}_{it}\boldsymbol{\beta}_i + u_{it}, \quad (u_{it}|X) \sim \mathsf{IID}(0, \sigma^2), \quad \begin{array}{l} i = 1, \dots, N; \\ t = 1, \dots, T, \end{array} \tag{2.23}$$

where $\boldsymbol{\beta}_i = (\beta_{1i}, \dots, \beta_{Ki})'$ is the coefficient vector for individual i, $\boldsymbol{x}_{it} = (x_{1it}, \dots, x_{Kit})$ is the row vector of observations on the K regressors for individual i in period t. We define

$$\boldsymbol{y}_i = \begin{bmatrix} y_{i1} \\ \vdots \\ y_{iT} \end{bmatrix}, \quad \boldsymbol{X}_i = \begin{bmatrix} \boldsymbol{x}_{i1} \\ \vdots \\ \boldsymbol{x}_{iT} \end{bmatrix} = \begin{bmatrix} x_{1i1} & \dots & x_{Ki1} \\ \vdots & & \vdots \\ x_{1iT} & \dots & x_{KiT} \end{bmatrix}, \quad \boldsymbol{u}_i = \begin{bmatrix} u_{i1} \\ \vdots \\ u_{iT} \end{bmatrix},$$

let $\boldsymbol{e}_T$ be the $(T \times 1)$ vector with all elements equal to 1, $\boldsymbol{I}_T$ the identity matrix of order $(T \times T)$, $\boldsymbol{0}_{T,1}$ the $(T \times 1)$ zero vector, and write (2.23) as

$$\boldsymbol{y}_i = \boldsymbol{e}_T\alpha_i^* + \boldsymbol{X}_i\boldsymbol{\beta}_i + \boldsymbol{u}_i, \quad (\boldsymbol{u}_i|X) \sim \mathsf{IID}(\boldsymbol{0}_{T,1}, \sigma^2\boldsymbol{I}_T), \quad i = 1, \dots, N. \tag{2.24}$$

We introduce two $(T \times T)$ matrices, to be repeatedly used in the following:

$$\boldsymbol{A}_T = \frac{\boldsymbol{e}_T\boldsymbol{e}_T'}{T}, \quad \boldsymbol{B}_T = \boldsymbol{I}_T - \frac{\boldsymbol{e}_T\boldsymbol{e}_T'}{T} = \boldsymbol{I}_T - \boldsymbol{A}_T, \quad T = 1, 2, \dots,$$

$\boldsymbol{A}_T$ having all elements equal to $\frac{1}{T}$ and $\boldsymbol{B}_T$ having all diagonal elements equal to $1 - \frac{1}{T}$ and all off-diagonal elements equal to $-\frac{1}{T}$. They have three crucial properties: (a) symmetry: $\boldsymbol{A}_T' = \boldsymbol{A}_T, \boldsymbol{B}_T' = \boldsymbol{B}_T$; (b) idempotency: $\boldsymbol{A}_T^P = \boldsymbol{A}_T, \boldsymbol{B}_T^P = \boldsymbol{B}_T$ $(P = 2, 3, \dots)$; and (c) orthogonality: $\boldsymbol{A}_T\boldsymbol{B}_T = \boldsymbol{B}_T\boldsymbol{A}_T = \boldsymbol{0}_{T,T}$, and they serve, *inter alia*, the following purpose: *premultiplying the vector* $\boldsymbol{y}_i$ *by* $\boldsymbol{A}_T$ *and by* $\boldsymbol{B}_T$ *replaces all its elements by their means and by the deviation from their means, respectively:* $A_T y_i = \bar{y}_{i\cdot} = e_T \bar{y}_{i\cdot}$, $B_T y_i = y_i - \bar{y}_{i\cdot}$, *while premultiplying the matrix* X_i *by* A_T *and by* B_T *perform similar operations on its columns.*[5]

The OLS estimators for Model (2.24) are the solution to

$$\min_{\alpha_1^*,\ldots,\alpha_N^*,\beta_1,\ldots,\beta_N} \textstyle\sum_{i=1}^N (y_i - e_T\alpha_i^* - X_i\beta_i)'(y_i - e_T\alpha_i^* - X_i\beta_i),$$

which is equivalent to:

$$\min_{\alpha_i^*,\beta_i} (y_i - e_T\alpha_i^* - X_i\beta_i)'(y_i - e_T\alpha_i^* - X_i\beta_i). \quad i = 1,\ldots,N,$$

We solve this problem stepwise. First, minimize the sum of squares with respect to α_i^*, and next set the solution, considered as a function of β_i, into the sum of squares to be minimized with respect to β_i. Since the minimand can be written

$$\begin{aligned}&(y_i - X_i\beta_i)'(y_i - X_i\beta_i) - 2\alpha_i^* e_T'(y_i - X_i\beta_i) + \alpha_i^{*2} e_T' e_T \\ &= (y_i - X_i\beta_i)'(y_i - X_i\beta_i) - 2\alpha_i^*(\bar{y}_{i\cdot} - \bar{x}_{i\cdot}\beta_i) + T\alpha_i^{*2},\end{aligned}$$

we find the following solution to the first sub-problem

$$\widehat{\alpha}_{iW}^* = \widehat{\alpha}_{iW}^*(\beta_i) = \tfrac{1}{T} e_T'(y_i - X_i\beta_i) = \bar{y}_{i\cdot} - \bar{x}_{i\cdot}\beta_i, \quad i = 1,\ldots,N, \tag{2.25}$$

where $\widehat{\alpha}_{iW}^*(\beta_i)$ indicates the solution value as a function of β_i. Next, inserting (2.25) in (2.24) and in the minimand, we get, respectively,

$$\begin{aligned}&B_T y_i = B_T X_i \beta_i + u_i, \\ &[B_T(y_i - X_i\beta_i)]'[B_T(y_i - X_i\beta_i)], \qquad i = 1,\ldots,N.\end{aligned}$$

Regressing $B_T y_i$ on $B_T X_i$ gives

$$\widehat{\beta}_i = [(B_T X_i)'(B_T X_i)]^{-1}[(B_T X_i)'(B_T y_i)],$$

[5] A remark on *notation*: $\bar{y}_{i\cdot}$ (scalar) is the individual-specific mean of y_{it} (scalar); $\bar{y}_{i\cdot}$ is the $(T \times 1)$ vector with all elements equal to this mean; $\bar{x}_{i\cdot} = (e_T'/T)X_i$ is the $(1 \times K)$ vector containing individual i's mean of the K regressors; and $\bar{X}_{i\cdot} = e_T\bar{x}_{i\cdot} = A_T X_i$ is the $(T \times K)$ matrix where this individual-specific row vector is repeated T times and $X_i - \bar{X}_{i\cdot} = B_T X_i$. We conventionally use lowercase letters in standard fonts to represent scalars, lowercase letters in boldface to denote (column or row) vectors, and uppercase letters in boldface to denote matrices.

which, because $\boldsymbol{B}_T$ is symmetric and idempotent, can be simplified to[6]

$$\widehat{\boldsymbol{\beta}}_i = (\boldsymbol{X}_i'\boldsymbol{B}_T\boldsymbol{X}_i)^{-1}(\boldsymbol{X}_i'\boldsymbol{B}_T\boldsymbol{y}_i), \qquad i = 1,\dots,N. \tag{2.26}$$

This is the within-individual estimator. It generalizes (2.2), since in general

$$\boldsymbol{Z}_i'\boldsymbol{B}_T\boldsymbol{Q}_i \equiv (\boldsymbol{Z}_i-\bar{\boldsymbol{Z}}_{i\cdot})'(\boldsymbol{Q}_i-\bar{\boldsymbol{Q}}_{i\cdot}) \equiv \textstyle\sum_{t=1}^{T}(\boldsymbol{z}_{it}-\bar{\boldsymbol{z}}_{i\cdot})'(\boldsymbol{q}_{it}-\bar{\boldsymbol{q}}_{i\cdot}) = \boldsymbol{W}_{ZQii},$$

the last equality defining $\boldsymbol{W}_{ZQii}$ as the generalization of the scalar W_{ZQii}. Therefore (2.26) can be written as

$$\widehat{\boldsymbol{\beta}}_i = \boldsymbol{W}_{XXii}^{-1}\boldsymbol{W}_{XYii}, \qquad i = 1,\dots,N. \tag{2.27}$$

The estimator of α_i^* follows by inserting $\boldsymbol{\beta}_i = \widehat{\boldsymbol{\beta}}_i$ in (2.25). Since inserting for $\boldsymbol{y}_i$ from (2.24) in (2.26), gives

$$\widehat{\boldsymbol{\beta}}_i - \boldsymbol{\beta}_i = (\boldsymbol{X}_i'\boldsymbol{B}_T\boldsymbol{X}_i)^{-1}(\boldsymbol{X}_i'\boldsymbol{B}_T\boldsymbol{u}_i) = \boldsymbol{W}_{XXii}^{-1}\boldsymbol{W}_{XUii},$$

where $\mathsf{E}(\boldsymbol{W}_{XUii}|\boldsymbol{X}) = 0$ and $\mathsf{V}(\boldsymbol{W}_{XUii}|\boldsymbol{X}) \equiv \mathsf{E}(\boldsymbol{W}_{XUii}\boldsymbol{W}_{XUii}'|\boldsymbol{X}) = \sigma^2\boldsymbol{W}_{XXii}$, *using from now on* V *to indicate variance-covariance matrices (covariance matrices, for short)*, the N estimator vectors are unbiased, with

$$\begin{aligned}\mathsf{V}(\widehat{\boldsymbol{\beta}}_i|\boldsymbol{X}) &= \sigma^2(\boldsymbol{X}_i'\boldsymbol{B}_T\boldsymbol{X}_i)^{-1}\\ &= \sigma^2\left[\textstyle\sum_{t=1}^{T}(\boldsymbol{x}_{it}-\bar{\boldsymbol{x}}_{i\cdot})'(\boldsymbol{x}_{it}-\bar{\boldsymbol{x}}_{i\cdot})\right]^{-1} = \sigma^2\boldsymbol{W}_{XXii}^{-1}.\end{aligned} \tag{2.28}$$

This is the matrix generalization of (2.4). Since $\boldsymbol{u}_1,\dots,\boldsymbol{u}_N$ are uncorrelated, $\boldsymbol{W}_{XU11},\dots,\boldsymbol{W}_{XUNN}$ are uncorrelated, and hence $\widehat{\boldsymbol{\beta}}_1,\dots,\widehat{\boldsymbol{\beta}}_N$ are uncorrelated (conditional on $\boldsymbol{X}$). They are also T-consistent. If N increases, while T is finite, the number of OLS problems increases. Each estimator is inconsistent.

2.2.2 INDIVIDUAL-SPECIFIC INTERCEPTS, COMMON COEFFICIENTS

Now let $\boldsymbol{\beta}_1 = \cdots = \boldsymbol{\beta}_N = \boldsymbol{\beta}$ in (2.24), giving

$$\boldsymbol{y}_i = \boldsymbol{e}_T\alpha_i^* + \boldsymbol{X}_i\boldsymbol{\beta} + \boldsymbol{u}_i, \quad (\boldsymbol{u}_i|\boldsymbol{X}) \sim \mathsf{IID}(\boldsymbol{0}_{T,1}, \sigma^2\boldsymbol{I}_T), \quad i=1,\dots,N, \tag{2.29}$$

[6] This again is identical to the estimator obtained by applying OLS on the original equation, (2.24), premultiplied by $\boldsymbol{B}_T$, i.e., $\boldsymbol{B}_T\boldsymbol{y}_i = \boldsymbol{B}_T\boldsymbol{X}_i\boldsymbol{\beta}_i + \boldsymbol{B}_T\boldsymbol{u}_i$, exploiting that $\boldsymbol{B}_T$ and $\boldsymbol{e}_T$ are orthogonal ($\boldsymbol{B}_T\boldsymbol{e}_T = \boldsymbol{0}_{T,1}$). The covariance matrix of $\boldsymbol{B}_T\boldsymbol{u}_i$ is $\sigma^2\boldsymbol{B}_T$, which is singular, while $\boldsymbol{u}_i$ has the scalar covariance matrix $\sigma^2\boldsymbol{I}_T$.

where $\boldsymbol{\beta} = (\beta_1, \dots, \beta_K)'$ is the coefficient column vector of the K regressors. Its OLS problem is

$$\min_{\alpha_1^*,\dots,\alpha_N^*,\boldsymbol{\beta}} \sum_{i=1}^N (\boldsymbol{y}_i - \boldsymbol{e}_T\alpha_i^* - \boldsymbol{X}_i\boldsymbol{\beta})'(\boldsymbol{y}_i - \boldsymbol{e}_T\alpha_i^* - \boldsymbol{X}_i\boldsymbol{\beta}).$$

We first minimize the sum of squares with respect to α_i^* for given $\boldsymbol{\beta}$. The solution follows by replacing $\boldsymbol{\beta}_i$ with $\boldsymbol{\beta}$ in (2.25), giving

$$\widehat{\alpha}_i^* = \widehat{\alpha}_i^*(\boldsymbol{\beta}) = \tfrac{1}{T}\boldsymbol{e}_T'(\boldsymbol{y}_i - \boldsymbol{X}_i\boldsymbol{\beta}) = \bar{y}_{i\cdot} - \bar{\boldsymbol{x}}_{i\cdot}\boldsymbol{\beta}, \quad i = 1, \dots, N, \tag{2.30}$$

which is next inserted in (2.29) and the minimand and gives

$$\begin{aligned} &\boldsymbol{B}_T\boldsymbol{y}_i = \boldsymbol{B}_T\boldsymbol{X}_i\boldsymbol{\beta} + \boldsymbol{u}_i, \qquad i = 1, \dots, N, \\ &\sum_{i=1}^N [\boldsymbol{B}_T(\boldsymbol{y}_i - \boldsymbol{X}_i\boldsymbol{\beta})]'[\boldsymbol{B}_T(\boldsymbol{y}_i - \boldsymbol{X}_i\boldsymbol{\beta})]. \end{aligned}$$

We stack the N equations into

$$\begin{bmatrix} \boldsymbol{B}_T\boldsymbol{y}_1 \\ \vdots \\ \boldsymbol{B}_T\boldsymbol{y}_N \end{bmatrix} = \begin{bmatrix} \boldsymbol{B}_T\boldsymbol{X}_1 \\ \vdots \\ \boldsymbol{B}_T\boldsymbol{X}_N \end{bmatrix}\boldsymbol{\beta} + \begin{bmatrix} \boldsymbol{u}_1 \\ \vdots \\ \boldsymbol{u}_N \end{bmatrix},$$

and use OLS, which gives

$$\begin{aligned} \widehat{\boldsymbol{\beta}}_W &= \left(\begin{bmatrix} \boldsymbol{B}_T\boldsymbol{X}_1 \\ \vdots \\ \boldsymbol{B}_T\boldsymbol{X}_N \end{bmatrix}'\begin{bmatrix} \boldsymbol{B}_T\boldsymbol{X}_1 \\ \vdots \\ \boldsymbol{B}_T\boldsymbol{X}_N \end{bmatrix}\right)^{-1}\left(\begin{bmatrix} \boldsymbol{B}_T\boldsymbol{X}_1 \\ \vdots \\ \boldsymbol{B}_T\boldsymbol{X}_N \end{bmatrix}'\begin{bmatrix} \boldsymbol{B}_T\boldsymbol{y}_1 \\ \vdots \\ \boldsymbol{B}_T\boldsymbol{y}_N \end{bmatrix}\right) \\ &\equiv \left[\sum_{i=1}^N \boldsymbol{X}_i'\boldsymbol{B}_T\boldsymbol{X}_i\right]^{-1}\left[\sum_{i=1}^N \boldsymbol{X}_i'\boldsymbol{B}_T\boldsymbol{y}_i\right]. \end{aligned} \tag{2.31}$$

Since in general

$$\sum_{i=1}^N \boldsymbol{Z}_i'\boldsymbol{B}_T\boldsymbol{Q}_i = \sum_{i=1}^N \sum_{t=1}^T (\boldsymbol{z}_{it} - \bar{\boldsymbol{z}}_{i\cdot})'(\boldsymbol{q}_{it} - \bar{\boldsymbol{q}}_{i\cdot}) = \boldsymbol{W}_{ZQ},$$

where $\boldsymbol{W}_{ZQ}$ is defined by the last equality, (2.31) can be rewritten as the following generalization of (2.6):

$$\widehat{\boldsymbol{\beta}}_W = [\sum_{i=1}^N \boldsymbol{W}_{XXii}]^{-1}[\sum_{i=1}^N \boldsymbol{W}_{XYii}] = \boldsymbol{W}_{XX}^{-1}\boldsymbol{W}_{XY}. \tag{2.32}$$

This is the *within-individual estimator* of $\boldsymbol{\beta}$. The estimators of α_i^* follow by inserting $\boldsymbol{\beta} = \widehat{\boldsymbol{\beta}}_W$ into (2.30). To obtain the covariance matrix we use (2.29) and (2.31), getting

$$\widehat{\boldsymbol{\beta}}_W - \boldsymbol{\beta} = [\sum_{i=1}^N \boldsymbol{X}_i' \boldsymbol{B}_T \boldsymbol{X}_i]^{-1} [\sum_{i=1}^N \boldsymbol{X}_i' \boldsymbol{B}_T \boldsymbol{u}_i] = \boldsymbol{W}_{XX}^{-1} \boldsymbol{W}_{XU},$$

where $\mathsf{V}(\boldsymbol{W}_{XU}|\boldsymbol{X}) = \sigma^2 \boldsymbol{W}_{XX}$, and hence

$$\begin{aligned} \mathsf{V}(\widehat{\boldsymbol{\beta}}_W|\boldsymbol{X}) &= \sigma^2 [\sum_{i=1}^N \boldsymbol{X}_i' \boldsymbol{B}_T \boldsymbol{X}_i]^{-1} \\ &= \sigma^2 [\sum_{i=1}^N \sum_{t=1}^T (\boldsymbol{x}_{it} - \bar{\boldsymbol{x}}_{i\cdot})'(\boldsymbol{x}_{it} - \bar{\boldsymbol{x}}_{i\cdot})]^{-1} = \sigma^2 \boldsymbol{W}_{XX}^{-1}. \end{aligned} \tag{2.33}$$

which generalizes (2.8).

The relationship between $\widehat{\boldsymbol{\beta}}_W$ and $\widehat{\boldsymbol{\beta}}_1, \ldots, \widehat{\boldsymbol{\beta}}_N$, which generalizes (2.9), follows from (2.27), (2.28), and (2.32):

$$\begin{aligned} \widehat{\boldsymbol{\beta}}_W &= [\sum_{i=1}^N \boldsymbol{W}_{XXii}]^{-1} [\sum_{i=1}^N \boldsymbol{W}_{XXii} \widehat{\boldsymbol{\beta}}_i] \\ &= [\sum_{i=1}^N \mathsf{V}(\widehat{\boldsymbol{\beta}}_i|\boldsymbol{X})^{-1}]^{-1} [\sum_{i=1}^N \mathsf{V}(\widehat{\boldsymbol{\beta}}_i|\boldsymbol{X})^{-1} \widehat{\boldsymbol{\beta}}_i]. \end{aligned} \tag{2.34}$$

Hence, $\widehat{\boldsymbol{\beta}}_W$ emerges as a *matrix weighted* mean of the individual-specific estimators with weights proportional to the inverse of the respective covariance matrices.

An alternative interpretation is: from (2.29) and (2.27) we find

$$\widehat{\boldsymbol{\beta}}_i = \boldsymbol{\beta} + \boldsymbol{W}_{XXii}^{-1} \boldsymbol{W}_{XUii}, \qquad i = 1, \ldots, N. \tag{2.35}$$

This equation, which generalizes (2.10), can be considered a system of K (degenerated) regression equations with N observations, with $\widehat{\boldsymbol{\beta}}_i$ as an (observable) $(K \times 1)$ regressand vector, no regressor matrix, $\boldsymbol{\beta}$ as the $(K \times 1)$-vector of intercepts, and $\boldsymbol{W}_{XXii}^{-1} \boldsymbol{W}_{XUii}$ as $(K \times 1)$ disturbance vectors. The latter are serially uncorrelated and heteroskedastic and have covariance matrices $\sigma^2 \boldsymbol{W}_{XXii}^{-1}$. Estimating $\boldsymbol{\beta}$ in (2.35) as a system of regression equations by GLS, which exemplifies Appendix 2A, Section 2A.2, we get (2.34).

2.2.3 HOMOGENEOUS BENCHMARK MODEL

For a fully homogeneous model, generalizing (2.11),

$$y_i = \boldsymbol{e}_T \alpha + \boldsymbol{X}_i \boldsymbol{\beta} + \boldsymbol{u}_i, \ (\boldsymbol{u}_i|\boldsymbol{X}_i) \sim \mathsf{IID}(\boldsymbol{0}_{T,1}, \sigma^2 \boldsymbol{I}_T), \ i = 1, \ldots, N. \tag{2.36}$$

Where α is a scalar and $\boldsymbol{\beta}=(\beta_1,\dots,\beta_K)'$, the OLS problem is

$$\min_{\alpha,\boldsymbol{\beta}} \sum_{i=1}^{N}(y_i - e_T\alpha - X_i\boldsymbol{\beta})'(y_i - e_T\alpha - X_i\boldsymbol{\beta}).$$

We first minimize the sum of squares with respect to α, giving, see (2.30),

$$\widehat{\alpha} = \widehat{\alpha}(\boldsymbol{\beta}) = \bar{y} - \bar{x}\boldsymbol{\beta}, \tag{2.37}$$

where $\bar{y} = \frac{1}{NT}e'_T\sum_{i=1}^{N} y_i$ and $\bar{x} = \frac{1}{NT}e'_T\sum_{i=1}^{N} X_i = \frac{1}{N}\sum_{i=1}^{N}\bar{x}_{i\cdot}$. Inserting (2.37) in (2.36) and in the minimand, we get[7]

$$y_i - \bar{y} = (X_i - \bar{X})\boldsymbol{\beta} + u_i, \qquad i = 1,\dots,N,$$
$$\sum_{i=1}^{N}[y_i - \bar{y} - (X_i - \bar{X})\boldsymbol{\beta})]'[y_i - \bar{y} - (X_i - \bar{X})\boldsymbol{\beta})],$$

where we again stack the N individual-specific equations,

$$\begin{bmatrix} y_1 - \bar{y} \\ \vdots \\ y_N - \bar{y} \end{bmatrix} = \begin{bmatrix} X_1 - \bar{X} \\ \vdots \\ X_N - \bar{X} \end{bmatrix}\boldsymbol{\beta} + \begin{bmatrix} u_1 \\ \vdots \\ u_N \end{bmatrix},$$

and apply OLS, to get

$$\begin{aligned}\widehat{\boldsymbol{\beta}} &= \left(\begin{bmatrix} X_1-\bar{X} \\ \vdots \\ X_N-\bar{X} \end{bmatrix}'\begin{bmatrix} X_1-\bar{X} \\ \vdots \\ X_N-\bar{X} \end{bmatrix}\right)^{-1}\left(\begin{bmatrix} X_1-\bar{X} \\ \vdots \\ X_N-\bar{X} \end{bmatrix}'\begin{bmatrix} y_1-\bar{y} \\ \vdots \\ y_N-\bar{y} \end{bmatrix}\right) \\ &\equiv \left[\sum_{i=1}^{N}(X_i-\bar{X})'(X_i-\bar{X})\right]^{-1}\left[\sum_{i=1}^{N}(X_i-\bar{X})'(y_i-\bar{y})\right].\end{aligned} \tag{2.38}$$

Since, in general,

$$\sum_{i=1}^{N}(Z_i - \bar{Z})'(Q_i - \bar{Q}) \equiv \sum_{i=1}^{N}\sum_{t=1}^{T}(z_{it} - \bar{z})'(q_{it} - \bar{q}) = G_{ZQ},$$

where G_{ZQ} is defined by the last equality, (2.38) can be rewritten as

$$\begin{aligned}\widehat{\boldsymbol{\beta}} &= \left[\sum_{i=1}^{N}\sum_{t=1}^{T}(x_{it}-\bar{x})'(x_{it}-\bar{x})\right]^{-1}\left[\sum_{i=1}^{N}\sum_{t=1}^{T}(x_{it}-\bar{x})'(y_{it}-\bar{y})\right] \\ &= G_{XX}^{-1}G_{XY}.\end{aligned} \tag{2.39}$$

[7] Another remark on notation: $\bar{y} = e_T\bar{y} = \frac{1}{N}A_T\sum_{i=1}^{N} y_i$ is the vector which repeats $\bar{y}$ T times, and $\bar{X} = e_T\bar{x} = A_T\sum_{i=1}^{N} X_i$ is the matrix which repeats the row vector $\bar{x}$ T times.

This is the *global estimator* of $\boldsymbol{\beta}$, which generalizes (2.12). The estimator of α follows by inserting $\boldsymbol{\beta} = \widehat{\boldsymbol{\beta}}$ into (2.37).

We now multiply (2.36) by $\frac{1}{T}\boldsymbol{e}'_T$, giving

$$\bar{y}_{i\cdot} = \alpha + \bar{\boldsymbol{x}}_{i\cdot}\boldsymbol{\beta} + \bar{u}_{i\cdot}, \quad (\bar{u}_{i\cdot}|X) \sim \mathsf{IID}(0, \tfrac{1}{T}\sigma^2), \quad i = 1, \dots, N. \tag{2.40}$$

Inserting the conditional estimator of the intercept, (2.37), we obtain

$$\bar{y}_{i\cdot} - \bar{y} = (\bar{\boldsymbol{x}}_{i\cdot} - \bar{\boldsymbol{x}})\boldsymbol{\beta} + \bar{u}_{i\cdot}, \qquad i = 1, \dots, N,$$

and hence

$$\begin{bmatrix} \bar{y}_{1\cdot} - \bar{y} \\ \vdots \\ \bar{y}_{N\cdot} - \bar{y} \end{bmatrix} = \begin{bmatrix} \bar{\boldsymbol{x}}_{1\cdot} - \bar{\boldsymbol{x}} \\ \vdots \\ \bar{\boldsymbol{x}}_{N\cdot} - \bar{\boldsymbol{x}} \end{bmatrix} \boldsymbol{\beta} + \begin{bmatrix} \bar{u}_{1\cdot} \\ \vdots \\ \bar{u}_{N\cdot} \end{bmatrix},$$

for which the OLS estimator is

$$\begin{aligned} \widehat{\boldsymbol{\beta}}_B &= \left(\begin{bmatrix} \bar{\boldsymbol{x}}_{1\cdot} - \bar{\boldsymbol{x}} \\ \vdots \\ \bar{\boldsymbol{x}}_{N\cdot} - \bar{\boldsymbol{x}} \end{bmatrix}' \begin{bmatrix} \bar{\boldsymbol{x}}_{1\cdot} - \bar{\boldsymbol{x}} \\ \vdots \\ \bar{\boldsymbol{x}}_{N\cdot} - \bar{\boldsymbol{x}} \end{bmatrix} \right)^{-1} \left(\begin{bmatrix} \bar{\boldsymbol{x}}_{1\cdot} - \bar{\boldsymbol{x}} \\ \vdots \\ \bar{\boldsymbol{x}}_{N\cdot} - \bar{\boldsymbol{x}} \end{bmatrix}' \begin{bmatrix} \bar{y}_{1\cdot} - \bar{y} \\ \vdots \\ \bar{y}_{N\cdot} - \bar{y} \end{bmatrix} \right) \\ &\equiv [\textstyle\sum_{i=1}^N (\bar{\boldsymbol{x}}_{i\cdot} - \bar{\boldsymbol{x}})'(\bar{\boldsymbol{x}}_{i\cdot} - \bar{\boldsymbol{x}})]^{-1} [\textstyle\sum_{i=1}^N (\bar{\boldsymbol{x}}_{i\cdot} - \bar{\boldsymbol{x}})'(\bar{y}_{i\cdot} - \bar{y})] \\ &\equiv [\textstyle\sum_{i=1}^N (\boldsymbol{X}_i - \bar{\boldsymbol{X}})'\boldsymbol{A}_T(\boldsymbol{X}_i - \bar{\boldsymbol{X}})]^{-1} [\textstyle\sum_{i=1}^N (\boldsymbol{X}_i - \bar{\boldsymbol{X}})'\boldsymbol{A}_T(\boldsymbol{y}_i - \bar{\boldsymbol{y}})]. \end{aligned} \tag{2.41}$$

This is the matrix version of the *between-individual estimator vector*, which generalizes (2.16). Since in general

$$\textstyle\sum_{i=1}^N (\boldsymbol{Z}_i - \bar{\boldsymbol{Z}})'\boldsymbol{A}_T(\boldsymbol{Q}_i - \bar{\boldsymbol{Q}}) = T \sum_{i=1}^N (\bar{\boldsymbol{z}}_{i\cdot} - \bar{\boldsymbol{z}})'(\bar{\boldsymbol{q}}_{i\cdot} - \bar{\boldsymbol{q}}) = \boldsymbol{B}_{ZQ},$$

where $\boldsymbol{B}_{ZQ}$ is defined by the last equality, a simpler expression is

$$\widehat{\boldsymbol{\beta}}_B = \boldsymbol{B}_{XX}^{-1}\boldsymbol{B}_{XY}. \tag{2.42}$$

Since inserting (2.36) in (2.39) and (2.42) gives

$$\widehat{\boldsymbol{\beta}} - \boldsymbol{\beta} = \boldsymbol{G}_{XX}^{-1}\boldsymbol{G}_{XU}, \qquad \widehat{\boldsymbol{\beta}}_B - \boldsymbol{\beta} = \boldsymbol{B}_{XX}^{-1}\boldsymbol{B}_{XU},$$

$\widehat{\boldsymbol{\beta}}$ and $\widehat{\boldsymbol{\beta}}_B$ are unbiased for $\boldsymbol{\beta}$ in Model (2.36), and since $\mathsf{V}(\boldsymbol{G}_{XU}|X) = \sigma^2\boldsymbol{G}_{XX}$ and $\mathsf{V}(\boldsymbol{B}_{XU}|X) = \sigma^2\boldsymbol{B}_{XX}$, we obtain, as generalizations of (2.18)–(2.19):

$$\begin{aligned}\mathsf{V}(\widehat{\boldsymbol{\beta}}|X) &= \sigma^2\Big[\sum_{i=1}^{N}(X_i-\bar{X})'(X_i-\bar{x})\Big]^{-1}\\ &= \sigma^2\Big[\sum_{i=1}^{N}\sum_{t=1}^{T}(x_{it}-\bar{x})'(x_{it}-\bar{x})\Big]^{-1} = \sigma^2 G_{XX}^{-1}, \qquad (2.43)\\ \mathsf{V}(\widehat{\boldsymbol{\beta}}_B|X) &= \sigma^2\Big[\sum_{i=1}^{N}(X_i-\bar{X})'A_T(X_i-\bar{X})\Big]^{-1}\\ &= \sigma^2\Big[T\sum_{i=1}^{N}(\bar{x}_{i\cdot}-\bar{x})'(\bar{x}_{i\cdot}-\bar{x})\Big]^{-1} = \sigma^2 B_{XX}^{-1}. \qquad (2.44)\end{aligned}$$

2.2.4 HOW ARE THE ESTIMATORS RELATED?

Let us explore the relationships between $\widehat{\boldsymbol{\beta}}_W$, $\widehat{\boldsymbol{\beta}}_B$, and $\widehat{\boldsymbol{\beta}}$, given by (2.31), (2.41), and (2.38), all of which are unbiased, N-consistent, and T-consistent. Furthermore, $\widehat{\boldsymbol{\beta}}_W$ and $\widehat{\boldsymbol{\beta}}_B$ are uncorrelated.[8] Since $\boldsymbol{B}_T+\boldsymbol{A}_T\equiv\boldsymbol{I}_T$, we have

$$\begin{aligned}\sum_{i=1}^{N}(Z_i-\bar{Z})'(Q_i-\bar{Q}) &\equiv \sum_{i=1}^{N}(Z_i-\bar{Z})'(B_T+A_T)(Q_i-\bar{Q})\\ &\equiv \sum_{i=1}^{N}Z_i'B_TQ_i+\sum_{i=1}^{N}(Z_i-\bar{Z})'A_T(Q_i-\bar{Q}),\end{aligned}$$

and hence

$$G_{ZQ} = W_{ZQ}+B_{ZQ}. \qquad (2.45)$$

Using (2.32), (2.33), (2.39), (2.42), (2.43), and (2.44), this gives the following generalization of (2.22)

$$\begin{aligned}\widehat{\boldsymbol{\beta}} &= (W_{XX}+B_{XX})^{-1}(W_{XY}+B_{XY})\\ &= (W_{XX}+B_{XX})^{-1}(W_{XX}\widehat{\boldsymbol{\beta}}_W+B_{XX}\widehat{\boldsymbol{\beta}}_B)\\ &= [\mathsf{V}(\widehat{\boldsymbol{\beta}}_W|X)^{-1}+\mathsf{V}(\widehat{\boldsymbol{\beta}}_B|X)^{-1}]^{-1}\\ &\quad\times[\mathsf{V}(\widehat{\boldsymbol{\beta}}_W|X)^{-1}\widehat{\boldsymbol{\beta}}_W+\mathsf{V}(\widehat{\boldsymbol{\beta}}_B|X)^{-1}\widehat{\boldsymbol{\beta}}_B]. \qquad (2.46)\end{aligned}$$

This means that in Model (2.36), the global estimator $\widehat{\boldsymbol{\beta}}$ emerges as a matrix-weighted mean of the within-individual estimator $\widehat{\boldsymbol{\beta}}_W$ and the between-individual estimator $\widehat{\boldsymbol{\beta}}_B$, with weights proportional to the inverse of their covariance matrices.

On the other hand, $\widehat{\boldsymbol{\beta}}_B$ and $\widehat{\boldsymbol{\beta}}$ are not necessarily unbiased and consistent for $\boldsymbol{\beta}$ if Model (2.29) applies. As in the one-regressor case, only if the individual-specific effects for the

[8] The proof, for a more general model, will be given in Section 3.8.1.

individuals observed are *empirically* uncorrelated with all individual-specific means of the regressors, can $\widehat{\boldsymbol{\beta}}$ and $\widehat{\boldsymbol{\beta}}_B$ be unbiased. Consistency will hold only if this condition is satisfied asymptotically.

Conclusions so far are:

(i) *The within-individual estimator $\widehat{\boldsymbol{\beta}}_W$ is the MVLUE in Model (2.29), and the global estimator $\widehat{\boldsymbol{\beta}}$ is the MVLUE in Model (2.36).*

(ii) *If $\boldsymbol{W}_{XX}$ and $\boldsymbol{B}_{XX}$ are positive definite, neither $\widehat{\boldsymbol{\beta}}_B$ nor $\widehat{\boldsymbol{\beta}}_W$ is MVLUE in Model (2.36).*

Since in general $E^{-1} - (E+F)^{-1} \equiv (E+F)^{-1}FE^{-1}$, we obtain from (2.33) and (2.44)–(2.45)

$$\mathsf{V}(\widehat{\boldsymbol{\beta}}_W|X) - \mathsf{V}(\widehat{\boldsymbol{\beta}}|X) = \sigma^2 \boldsymbol{G}_{XX}^{-1}\boldsymbol{B}_{XX}\boldsymbol{W}_{XX}^{-1},$$
$$\mathsf{V}(\widehat{\boldsymbol{\beta}}_B|X) - \mathsf{V}(\widehat{\boldsymbol{\beta}}|X) = \sigma^2 \boldsymbol{G}_{XX}^{-1}\boldsymbol{W}_{XX}\boldsymbol{B}_{XX}^{-1}.$$

These matrix differences are positive definite whenever $\boldsymbol{W}_{XX}$ and $\boldsymbol{B}_{XX}$ are positive definite.[9] This implies that $\widehat{\boldsymbol{\beta}}$ in Model (2.36) is more efficient than both $\widehat{\boldsymbol{\beta}}_W$ and $\widehat{\boldsymbol{\beta}}_B$, in the following sense: any linear combination of the elements in $\widehat{\boldsymbol{\beta}}$—say $\boldsymbol{a}'\widehat{\boldsymbol{\beta}}$, where $\boldsymbol{a}$ is a $(K\times 1)$-vector of constants, considered as an estimator of $\boldsymbol{a}'\boldsymbol{\beta}$—has a smaller variance than the corresponding linear combination for the two other estimators. The proof is: positive definiteness implies $\boldsymbol{a}'[\mathsf{V}(\widehat{\boldsymbol{\beta}}_Z|X)-\mathsf{V}(\widehat{\boldsymbol{\beta}}|X)]\boldsymbol{a} > 0$ $(Z = W, B)$. Since $\text{var}(\boldsymbol{a}'\widehat{\boldsymbol{\beta}}_Z|X) = \boldsymbol{a}'\mathsf{V}(\widehat{\boldsymbol{\beta}}_Z|X)\boldsymbol{a}$,

$$\text{var}(\boldsymbol{a}'\widehat{\boldsymbol{\beta}}_W|X) > \text{var}(\boldsymbol{a}'\widehat{\boldsymbol{\beta}}|X), \quad Z = W, B.$$

In this sense, $\widehat{\boldsymbol{\beta}}$ is more efficient than both $\widehat{\boldsymbol{\beta}}_W$ and $\widehat{\boldsymbol{\beta}}_B$ as long as (i) the model has both intercept and coefficient vector common to all individuals and (ii) both $\boldsymbol{W}_{XX}$ and $\boldsymbol{B}_{XX}$ are positive definite. The latter assumption will normally hold if all regressors show variation across both individuals and periods.

Example: We consider estimation of *marginal budget shares in consumption*, using a stylized model with total expenditure as the only explanatory variable ($K=1$); see Biørn (1994). The data are from $N=418$ households observed in $T=2$ successive years. Table 2.1 contains within household (WH), between household (BH), and OLS estimates for 28 commodity groups (exhausting total consumption) (although without standard errors, the estimation of which will be discussed in Chapter 3 in relation to a random effects model).

The estimates vary substantially by method used. Notable examples are commodities 01 Flour and bread, 06 Butter and margarine, 10 Tobacco, and 14 Fuel and

[9] We here utilize that the sum of two positive definite matrices is positive definite and that the inverse of a positive definite matrix is itself positive definite.

Table 2.1 Marginal budget share, promille
Within (WH), Between (BH), and OLS estimates

	WH	BH	OLS
01. Flour and bread	2.01	11.05	9.29
02. Meat and eggs	27.79	41.51	39.22
03. Fish	4.29	6.74	6.26
04. Canned meat and fish	0.95	3.48	2.99
05. Dairy products	1.32	10.85	8.99
06. Butter and margarine	−0.20	3.09	2.45
07. Potatoes and vegetables	2.46	21.91	18.12
08. Other food	4.36	16.94	14.49
09. Beverages	10.29	23.76	21.14
10. Tobacco	1.98	11.07	9.29
11. Clothing	61.58	77.36	74.28
12. Footwear	20.96	20.11	20.28
13. Housing	38.17	96.40	85.04
14. Fuel and power	−0.42	7.01	5.56
15. Furniture	37.80	66.41	60.83
16. Household equipment	25.40	37.58	35.21
17. Misc. household goods	11.27	13.61	13.15
18. Medical care	10.94	12.36	12.08
19. Motorcars, bicycles	209.06	91.29	114.28
20. Running costs of vehicles	174.58	135.87	143.42
21. Public transport	48.36	29.24	32.97
22. Post and telecomm. charges	26.09	11.31	14.19
23. Recreation	96.35	90.03	91.26
24. Public entertainment	26.87	22.25	23.15
25. Books and newspapers	19.61	18.96	19.09
26. Personal care	3.27	14.02	11.92
27. Misc. goods and services	107.66	71.22	78.34
28. Restaurants, hotels, etc.	33.35	41.53	39.93

Source: Based on Biørn (1994).

power, of which numbers 06 and 14 appear as 'inferior goods' according to the WH estimates. The OLS estimates, which are always between the BH and the WH estimates, being weighted averages of them, are closest to the BH estimates. This concurs with their weights in the OLS estimates being, respectively, $B_{XX}/G_{XX}=0.8048$ and $W_{XX}/G_{XX}=0.1952$, i.e., the weight of the BH is more than four times the weight of the WH. However, some commodities show small discrepancies, e.g., 12 Footwear, 18 Medical care, and 23 Recreation. A continuation of this example, related to random effects models, follows in Section 3.3.3.

We now extend the models to also account for fixed period-specific intercept heterogeneity. Section 2.3 discusses the one-regressor cases, using scalar notation, and extends via an excursion into a kind of very useful matrix operations when handling panel data, the *Kronecker-products*, to more general models. We refer their basic algebra and give examples to illustrate why they are virtually indispensable in panel data analysis. After this digression, in Section 2.4 we generalize the models to contain an arbitrary number of regressors. Finally, procedures for testing for heterogeneity and for exploring its form are considered in Section 2.5.

2.3 Simple regression model: Two-way heterogeneity

In this section, we consider estimation methods for two one-regressor models, one with two-way intercept heterogeneity and one with full heterogeneity.

2.3.1 INDIVIDUAL- AND PERIOD-SPECIFIC INTERCEPTS

We still let x_{it} and y_{it} be scalars denoting the observation (i, t), now satisfying

$$\begin{aligned} &y_{it} = k+\alpha_i+\gamma_t+\beta x_{it}+u_{it}, \quad (u_{it}|X) \sim \mathsf{IID}(0,\sigma^2), \\ &i = 1,\dots,N;\ t = 1,\dots,T, \end{aligned} \tag{2.47}$$

where α_i and γ_t are effects specific to individual i and period t, respectively, and k is an intercept, satisfying

$$\textstyle\sum_{i=1}^{N} \alpha_i = \sum_{t=1}^{T} \gamma_t = 0. \tag{2.48}$$

The interpretation of these adding-up restrictions is that both the individual-specific and the period-specific effects are on average zero, which means that k measures the intercept for the average individual in the average period. Model (2.1) is the special case where $\gamma_t = 0$ for all t and $\alpha_i^* = k + \alpha_i$.

From (2.47) and (2.48) we can derive the following equations between the individual-specific means, the period-specific means, and the global means:

$$\bar{y}_{i\cdot} = k + \alpha_i + \beta\bar{x}_{i\cdot} + \bar{u}_{i\cdot}, \qquad (\bar{u}_{i\cdot}|X) \sim \mathsf{IID}(0, \tfrac{1}{T}\sigma^2), \qquad i = 1,\dots,N, \tag{2.49}$$

$$\bar{y}_{\cdot t} = k + \gamma_t + \beta\bar{x}_{\cdot t} + \bar{u}_{\cdot t}, \qquad (\bar{u}_{\cdot t}|X) \sim \mathsf{IID}(0, \tfrac{1}{N}\sigma^2), \qquad t = 1,\dots,T, \tag{2.50}$$

$$\bar{y} = k + \beta\bar{x} + \bar{u}, \qquad (\bar{u}|X) \sim (0, \tfrac{1}{NT}\sigma^2), \tag{2.51}$$

where, in general, $\bar{z}_{i\cdot} = \frac{1}{T}\sum_{t=1}^{T} z_{it}$, $\bar{z}_{\cdot t} = \frac{1}{N}\sum_{i=1}^{N} z_{it}$, $\bar{z} = \frac{1}{NT}\sum_{i=1}^{N}\sum_{t=1}^{T} z_{it}$. Combining (2.49)–(2.51) with (2.47), it follows that

$$(y_{it} - \bar{y}_{i\cdot}) = \gamma_t + \beta(x_{it} - \bar{x}_{i\cdot}) + (u_{it} - \bar{u}_{i\cdot}), \tag{2.52}$$

$$(y_{it} - \bar{y}_{\cdot t}) = \alpha_i + \beta(x_{it} - \bar{x}_{\cdot t}) + (u_{it} - \bar{u}_{\cdot t}), \tag{2.53}$$

$$(y_{it} - \bar{y}_{i\cdot} - \bar{y}_{\cdot t} + \bar{y}) = \beta(x_{it} - \bar{x}_{i\cdot} - \bar{x}_{\cdot t} + \bar{x}) + (u_{it} - \bar{u}_{i\cdot} - \bar{u}_{\cdot t} + \bar{u}). \tag{2.54}$$

The transformations (2.52)–(2.54) eliminate (α_i, k), (γ_t, k), and (α_i, γ_t, k), respectively. We can interpret (2.54) as a transformation measuring the variables in (2.52) from their period-specific means, since $(z_{it}-\bar{z}_{i\cdot}) - \frac{1}{N}\sum_{i=1}^{N}(z_{it}-\bar{z}_{i\cdot}) \equiv (z_{it}-\bar{z}_{i\cdot}-\bar{z}_{\cdot t}+\bar{z})$. Symmetrically, we can interpret (2.54) as obtained by measuring the variables in (2.53) from their individual-specific means. Equations (2.52)–(2.54) are basic linear transformations of linear panel data models, to be used extensively in the following.

The OLS estimators of the $1 + (N-1) + (T-1) + 1 = N + T$ unknown constants in (2.47)–(2.48) are those which solve

$$\min_{\alpha_1,\dots,\alpha_N,\gamma_1,\dots,\gamma_T,\beta,k} \sum_{i=1}^{N}\sum_{t=1}^{T}(y_{it} - k - \alpha_i - \gamma_t - \beta x_{it})^2,$$

subject to (2.48). The first-order conditions obtained by setting the first derivatives with respect to k, α_i, γ_t, and β equal to zero, give, respectively,

$$\sum_{i=1}^{N}\sum_{t=1}^{T}(y_{it} - \widehat{k}_R - \widehat{\alpha}_i - \widehat{\gamma}_t - \widehat{\beta}_R x_{it}) = 0, \tag{2.55}$$

$$\sum_{t=1}^{T}(y_{it} - \widehat{k}_R - \widehat{\alpha}_i - \widehat{\gamma}_t - \widehat{\beta}_R x_{it}) = 0, \qquad i = 1,\dots,N, \tag{2.56}$$

$$\sum_{i=1}^{N}(y_{it} - \widehat{k}_R - \widehat{\alpha}_i - \widehat{\gamma}_t - \widehat{\beta}_R x_{it}) = 0, \qquad t = 1,\dots,T, \tag{2.57}$$

$$\sum_{i=1}^{N}\sum_{t=1}^{T}x_{it}(y_{it} - \widehat{k}_R - \widehat{\alpha}_i - \widehat{\gamma}_t - \widehat{\beta}_R x_{it}) = 0, \tag{2.58}$$

denoting the solution by $\widehat{}$, using, for reasons that will become clear later, subscript R on the values for k and β. From (2.55)–(2.57), utilizing (2.48), we find

$$\begin{aligned}
\widehat{k}_R &= \bar{y} - \widehat{\beta}_R\bar{x},\\
\widehat{\alpha}_i + \widehat{k}_R &= \bar{y}_{i\cdot} - \widehat{\beta}_R\bar{x}_{i\cdot},\\
\widehat{\gamma}_t + \widehat{k}_R &= \bar{y}_{\cdot t} - \widehat{\beta}_R\bar{x}_{\cdot t},
\end{aligned}$$

which in combination with (2.58) yields

$$\sum_i\sum_t x_{it}(y_{it}-\bar{y}_{i\cdot}-\bar{y}_{\cdot t}+\bar{y}) - \widehat{\beta}_R\sum_i\sum_t x_{it}(x_{it}-\bar{x}_{i\cdot}-\bar{x}_{\cdot t}+\bar{x}) = 0.$$

Since $\sum_i\sum_t x_{it}(x_{it}-\bar{x}_{i\cdot}-\bar{x}_{\cdot t}+\bar{x}) \equiv \sum_i\sum_t(x_{it}-\bar{x}_{i\cdot}-\bar{x}_{\cdot t}+\bar{x})^2$, we obtain

$$\widehat{\beta}_R = \frac{\sum_{i=1}^{N}\sum_{t=1}^{T}(x_{it}-\bar{x}_{i\cdot}-\bar{x}_{\cdot t}+\bar{x})(y_{it}-\bar{y}_{i\cdot}-\bar{y}_{\cdot t}+\bar{y})}{\sum_{i=1}^{N}\sum_{t=1}^{T}(x_{it}-\bar{x}_{i\cdot}-\bar{x}_{\cdot t}+\bar{x})^2} = \frac{R_{XY}}{R_{XX}}, \tag{2.59}$$

$$\widehat{k}_R = \bar{y} - \widehat{\beta}_R \bar{x}, \tag{2.60}$$
$$\widehat{\alpha}_i = \bar{y}_{i\cdot} - \bar{y} - \widehat{\beta}_R(\bar{x}_{i\cdot} - \bar{x}), \qquad i = 1, \ldots, N, \tag{2.61}$$
$$\widehat{\gamma}_t = \bar{y}_{\cdot t} - \bar{y} - \widehat{\beta}_R(\bar{x}_{\cdot t} - \bar{x}), \qquad t = 1, \ldots, T, \tag{2.62}$$

where, in general,

$$R_{ZQ} = \sum_{i=1}^{N} \sum_{t=1}^{T} (z_{it} - \bar{z}_{i\cdot} - \bar{z}_{\cdot t} + \bar{z})(q_{it} - \bar{q}_{i\cdot} - \bar{q}_{\cdot t} + \bar{q}), \tag{2.63}$$

R symbolizing *residual*, i.e., the variation in the xs and ys remaining when both the individual-specific and the period-specific means have been subtracted from each observation (and the global mean added to compensate for deduction of two means). Obviously, (2.61) and (2.62) always satisfy (2.48). We denote $\widehat{\beta}_R$ as the *residual estimator*, or the *within-individual-and-period estimator* of β.

Since inserting (2.47) in (2.59)–(2.62), using (2.48), gives,

$$\widehat{\beta}_R - \beta = \frac{R_{XU}}{R_{XX}},$$
$$\widehat{k}_R - k = \bar{u} - (\widehat{\beta}_R - \beta)\bar{x},$$
$$\widehat{\alpha}_i - \alpha_i = \bar{u}_{i\cdot} - \bar{u} - (\widehat{\beta}_R - \beta)(\bar{x}_{i\cdot} - \bar{x}),$$
$$\widehat{\gamma}_t - \gamma_t = \bar{u}_{\cdot t} - \bar{u} - (\widehat{\beta}_R - \beta)(\bar{x}_{\cdot t} - \bar{x}),$$

it is then straightforward to show that $\widehat{k}_R$, $\widehat{\alpha}_i$, $\widehat{\gamma}_t$, and $\widehat{\beta}_R$ are unbiased, and since $\mathrm{var}(R_{XU}|\boldsymbol{X}) = \sigma^2 R_{XX}$, we have

$$\mathrm{var}(\widehat{\beta}_R|\boldsymbol{X}) = \mathrm{var}\left[\frac{R_{XU}}{R_{XX}}|\boldsymbol{X}\right] = \frac{\sigma^2}{\sum_{i=1}^{N}\sum_{t=1}^{T}(x_{it} - \bar{x}_{i\cdot} - \bar{x}_{\cdot t} + \bar{x})^2} \equiv \frac{\sigma^2}{R_{XX}}. \tag{2.64}$$

In practice $\widehat{\beta}_R$ can be computed in four ways:

(i) By OLS regression on (2.47), treating the α_is and γ_ts as coefficients of N individual-specific and T period-specific dummy variables.[10]

(ii) By measuring the variables *from their individual-specific means*, as in (2.52), and applying OLS, treating the γ_ts as the coefficients of T *period-specific* dummy variables;

[10] We can incorporate the adding-up restrictions (2.48) by, in (2.47), replacing α_N and γ_T with $-\sum_{i=1}^{N-1} \alpha_i$ and $-\sum_{t=1}^{T-1} \gamma_t$. Then the equation's $N-1+T-1$ dummy arguments in the regression equation will be equal to the dummy-variables for individuals $1, \ldots, N-1$ with the dummy-variable for individual N deducted, and equal to the dummy-variables for periods $1, \ldots, T-1$ with the dummy variable for period T deducted. We have *centred dummies*. The estimators are invariant to which α_i and γ_t we choose to eliminate.

(iii) By measuring the variables *from their period-specific means*, as in (2.53), and applying OLS, treating the α_is as the coefficients of N *individual-specific* dummy variables.

(iv) By transforming the variables into *departures from both their individual-specific and period-specific means*, as in (2.54), and applying OLS.

Using (ii), (iii), or (iv) instead of (i) gives a *reduced dimension* of the regression equation. This can involve a sizeable practical simplification if N and/or T is large, which, for N, often is the case. Therefore (ii) and (iv) are usually preferred to (iii), the number of regressors being $N+T$, T, N, and 1, respectively. Having computed $\widehat{\beta}_R$, the computation of $\widehat{k}_R$, $\widehat{\alpha}_i$, and $\widehat{\gamma}_t$ from (2.60)–(2.62) is straightforward.

As remarked, $\widehat{\beta}_R$ exploits only the part of the variation in the x_{it}s and y_{it}s left when both the individual-specific and the period-specific means have been deducted from each observation. How is the rest of the global variation disposed of? The variation between individuals, as represented by the variation in the individual-specific means, is spent in estimating the individual-specific effects α_i, see (2.61), while the variation between periods, as represented by the variation in the period-specific means, is spent in estimating the period-specific effects γ_t, see (2.62).

The OLS estimators (2.60)–(2.62) and (2.64) are MVLUE in Model (2.47), because its disturbance, u_{it}, satisfies the classical assumptions. What do we know about their asymptotic properties? The estimator $\widehat{\beta}_R$ is consistent regardless of whether N or T goes to infinity. This follows from $\mathsf{E}(u_{it}|X) = 0$, which implies that the plim of $\frac{1}{NT}R_{XU} = \frac{1}{NT}\sum_{i=1}^{N}\sum_{t=1}^{T}(x_{it} - \bar{x}_{i\cdot} - \bar{x}_{\cdot t} + \bar{x})u_{it}$ is zero regardless of whether N or T goes to infinity. However, $\widehat{\alpha}_i$ is only T-consistent. From (2.61), (2.49) and (2.51) it follows that

$$\widehat{\alpha}_i = \alpha_i - (\widehat{\beta}_R - \beta)(\bar{x}_{i\cdot} - \bar{x}) + \bar{u}_{i\cdot} - \bar{u},$$

whose probability limit is α_i, since then $\widehat{\beta}_R \to \beta$, $\bar{u}_{i\cdot} \to 0$, $\bar{u} \to 0$. Symmetrically, $\widehat{\gamma}_t$ is only N-consistent. From (2.62), (2.50), and (2.51) it follows that

$$\widehat{\gamma}_t = \gamma_t - (\widehat{\beta}_R - \beta)(\bar{x}_{\cdot t} - \bar{x}) + \bar{u}_{\cdot t} - \bar{u},$$

whose probability limit is γ_t only if $N \to \infty$, since then $\widehat{\beta}_R \to \beta$, $\bar{u}_{\cdot t} \to 0$, $\bar{u} \to 0$.

2.3.2 HOMOGENEOUS BENCHMARK MODEL

We next consider a model without heterogeneity, i.e., $\alpha_i = \gamma_t = 0$ for all i and t. The model (coinciding with Model (2.11), except that α is renamed as k)

$$y_{it} = k + \beta x_{it} + u_{it}, \quad (u_{it}|X) \sim \mathsf{IID}(0, \sigma^2), \quad \begin{array}{l} i = 1, \ldots, N; \\ t = 1, \ldots, T, \end{array} \tag{2.65}$$

has OLS estimators

$$\widehat{\beta} = \frac{\sum_{i=1}^{N}\sum_{t=1}^{T}(x_{it}-\bar{x})(y_{it}-\bar{y})}{\sum_{i=1}^{N}\sum_{t=1}^{T}(x_{it}-\bar{x})^2} = \frac{G_{XY}}{G_{XX}}, \quad \widehat{k} = \bar{y} - \widehat{\beta}\bar{x}. \tag{2.66}$$

They are the MVLUE in this model. The global estimator $\widehat{\beta}$ exploits the variation *between individuals*, the variation *between periods*, and the *residual variation*.

The intuitive reason why (2.66) exploits all kind of variation is that when assuming an intercept common to all individuals and all periods, no data variation must be spent in estimating the composite intercept $k+\alpha_i+\gamma_t$, as we had to do in Model (2.47). The full data set is exploited in estimating β. Since

$$z_{it} - \bar{z} \equiv (z_{it} - \bar{z}_{i\cdot} - \bar{z}_{\cdot t} + \bar{z}) + (\bar{z}_{i\cdot} - \bar{z}) + (\bar{z}_{\cdot t} - \bar{z}),$$

it follows, taking the product-sum of this expression and a corresponding expression for $q_{it} - \bar{q}$ across all (i, t), that

$$G_{ZQ} = R_{ZQ} + B_{ZQ} + C_{ZQ}, \tag{2.67}$$

where

$$B_{ZQ} = T\sum_{i=1}^{N}(\bar{z}_{i\cdot} - \bar{z})(\bar{q}_{i\cdot} - \bar{q}),$$
$$C_{ZQ} = N\sum_{t=1}^{T}(\bar{z}_{\cdot t} - \bar{z})(\bar{q}_{\cdot t} - \bar{q}),$$

which represent the variation between individuals (B) and the variation between periods (C), respectively.

We can show formally that (2.66) *in Model (2.65)*, by exploiting all three kinds of data variation, in fact has a lower variance than has $\widehat{\beta}_R$. As part of the proof we consider two other estimators of β. We sum (2.65) across t, respectively i, and divide the sum by T, respectively N, giving the following equations in individual-specific and in period-specific means:

$$\bar{y}_{i\cdot} = k + \beta\bar{x}_{i\cdot} + \bar{u}_{i\cdot}, \quad (\bar{u}_{i\cdot}|X) \sim \mathsf{IID}(0, \tfrac{1}{T}\sigma^2), \quad i = 1, \dots, N, \tag{2.68}$$

$$\bar{y}_{\cdot t} = k + \beta\bar{x}_{\cdot t} + \bar{u}_{\cdot t}, \quad (\bar{u}_{\cdot t}|X) \sim \mathsf{IID}(0, \tfrac{1}{N}\sigma^2), \quad t = 1, \dots, T. \tag{2.69}$$

Although it is fairly obvious that estimating β solely from these N or T observations neglects a large part of the data variation, we consider OLS estimation of these two equations, which solve the respective minimization problems:

$$\min_{k,\beta} \sum_{i=1}^{N} (\bar{y}_{i\cdot} - k - \beta \bar{x}_{i\cdot})^2,$$

$$\min_{k,\beta} \sum_{t=1}^{T} (\bar{y}_{\cdot t} - k - \beta \bar{x}_{\cdot t})^2.$$

The estimators become, respectively,

$$\widehat{\beta}_B = \frac{\sum_{i=1}^{N} (\bar{x}_{i\cdot} - \bar{x})(\bar{y}_{i\cdot} - \bar{y})}{\sum_{i=1}^{N} (\bar{x}_{i\cdot} - \bar{x})^2} = \frac{B_{XY}}{B_{XX}}, \qquad \widehat{k}_B = \bar{y} - \widehat{\beta}_B \bar{x}, \tag{2.70}$$

$$\widehat{\beta}_C = \frac{\sum_{t=1}^{T} (\bar{x}_{\cdot t} - \bar{x})(\bar{y}_{\cdot t} - \bar{y})}{\sum_{t=1}^{T} (\bar{x}_{\cdot t} - \bar{x})^2} = \frac{C_{XY}}{C_{XX}}, \qquad \widehat{k}_C = \bar{y} - \widehat{\beta}_C \bar{x}, \tag{2.71}$$

denoted as the *between-individual estimator* and the *between-period estimator.*

Since (2.65), (2.66), (2.70), and (2.71) imply

$$\widehat{\beta} - \beta = \frac{G_{XU}}{G_{XX}}, \qquad \widehat{\beta}_B - \beta = \frac{B_{XU}}{B_{XX}}, \qquad \widehat{\beta}_C - \beta = \frac{C_{XU}}{C_{XX}},$$

$\widehat{\beta}$, $\widehat{\beta}_B$, and $\widehat{\beta}_C$ are unbiased for β in Model (2.65). Since we can show that $\text{var}(B_{XU}|X) = \sigma^2 B_{XX}$ and $\text{var}(C_{XU}|X) = \sigma^2 C_{XX}$, it follows that

$$\text{var}(\widehat{\beta}_B|X) = \text{var}\left(\frac{B_{XU}}{B_{XX}}|X\right) = \frac{\sigma^2}{B_{XX}} \equiv \frac{\sigma^2/T}{\sum_{i=1}^{N} (\bar{x}_{i\cdot} - \bar{x})^2}, \tag{2.72}$$

$$\text{var}(\widehat{\beta}_C|X) = \text{var}\left(\frac{C_{XU}}{C_{XX}}|X\right) = \frac{\sigma^2}{C_{XX}} \equiv \frac{\sigma^2/N}{\sum_{t=1}^{T} (\bar{x}_{\cdot t} - \bar{x})^2}, \tag{2.73}$$

$\text{var}(\widehat{\beta}|X)$ being still given by (2.18).

Since $\widehat{\beta}_R$ also is a possible estimator for β in Model (2.65), we have four suggestions of estimators. From (2.18), (2.64), and (2.72)–(2.73) it follows that

$$\begin{aligned}
\text{var}(\widehat{\beta}|X) &< \text{var}(\widehat{\beta}_B|X) \quad \text{if} \quad R_{XX} > 0,\\
\text{var}(\widehat{\beta}|X) &< \text{var}(\widehat{\beta}_C|X) \quad \text{if} \quad R_{XX} > 0,\\
\text{var}(\widehat{\beta}|X) &< \text{var}(\widehat{\beta}_R|X) \quad \text{if} \quad B_{XX} + C_{XX} > 0.
\end{aligned}$$

In the normal case where x varies along two dimensions, B_{XX}, C_{XX}, and R_{XX} are all positive. We therefore have verified that, generally, $\widehat{\beta}$ *will be more efficient than either of* $\widehat{\beta}_R$, $\widehat{\beta}_B$, *and* $\widehat{\beta}_C$ *in Model (2.65)* because the first, unlike the three last, exploits all kinds of variation in the observed y_{it}s and x_{it}s.

2.3.3 HOW ARE THE ESTIMATORS RELATED?

We have defined four estimators of the coefficient β in Model (2.65): the residual estimator $\widehat{\beta}_R$; the between-individual estimator $\widehat{\beta}_B$; the between-period estimator $\widehat{\beta}_C$; and the global estimator $\widehat{\beta}$. All are unbiased and are consistent regardless of whether $N \to \infty$, $T \to \infty$, or both occur. Notice that T-consistency of $\widehat{\beta}_B$ follows from the fact that the disturbances in (2.68), $\bar{u}_{i\cdot}$, converge to 0 in probability when $T \to \infty$, ensuring $\widehat{\beta}_B$ to exist and be T-consistent as long as $N \geq 2$. Correspondingly, N-consistency of $\widehat{\beta}_C$ follows from the fact that the disturbances in (2.69), $\bar{u}_{\cdot t}$, converge to 0 in probability when $N \to \infty$, ensuring $\widehat{\beta}_C$ to exist and be N-consistent as long as $T \geq 2$. Furthermore, *$\widehat{\beta}_R$, $\widehat{\beta}_B$, and $\widehat{\beta}_C$ are uncorrelated.*[11]

On the other hand, we are not assured that $\widehat{\beta}_B$, $\widehat{\beta}_C$, and $\widehat{\beta}$ are unbiased and consistent for *β if the model with both individual-specific and period-specific effects, (2.47), has generated our data.* If (2.47) and (2.48) hold, these estimators can be written as

$$\widehat{\beta}_B = \beta + \frac{\frac{1}{N}\sum_{i=1}^{N}(\bar{x}_{i\cdot} - \bar{x})\alpha_i}{\frac{1}{N}\sum_{i=1}^{N}(\bar{x}_{i\cdot} - \bar{x})^2} + \frac{\frac{1}{N}\sum_{i=1}^{N}(\bar{x}_{i\cdot} - \bar{x})(\bar{u}_{i\cdot} - \bar{u})}{\frac{1}{N}\sum_{i=1}^{N}(\bar{x}_{i\cdot} - \bar{x})^2}, \tag{2.74}$$

$$\widehat{\beta}_C = \beta + \frac{\frac{1}{T}\sum_{t=1}^{T}(\bar{x}_{\cdot t} - \bar{x})\gamma_t}{\frac{1}{T}\sum_{t=1}^{T}(\bar{x}_{\cdot t} - \bar{x})^2} + \frac{\frac{1}{T}\sum_{t=1}^{T}(\bar{x}_{\cdot t} - \bar{x})(\bar{u}_{\cdot t} - \bar{u})}{\frac{1}{T}\sum_{t=1}^{T}(\bar{x}_{\cdot t} - \bar{x})^2}, \tag{2.75}$$

$$\begin{aligned}\widehat{\beta} = \beta &+ \frac{\frac{1}{N}\sum_{i=1}^{N}(\bar{x}_{i\cdot} - \bar{x})\alpha_i}{\frac{1}{NT}\sum_{i=1}^{N}\sum_{t=1}^{T}(x_{it} - \bar{x})^2} + \frac{\frac{1}{T}\sum_{t=1}^{T}(\bar{x}_{\cdot t} - \bar{x})\gamma_t}{\frac{1}{NT}\sum_{i=1}^{N}\sum_{t=1}^{T}(x_{it} - \bar{x})^2} \\ &+ \frac{\frac{1}{NT}\sum_{i=1}^{N}\sum_{t=1}^{T}(x_{it} - \bar{x})(u_{it} - \bar{u})}{\frac{1}{NT}\sum_{i=1}^{N}\sum_{t=1}^{T}(x_{it} - \bar{x})^2}.\end{aligned} \tag{2.76}$$

Conditional on $\boldsymbol{X}$, the last term in (2.74)–(2.76) has zero expectation. The second term in (2.74) and in (2.75) and the second and third term in (2.76) act as constants in the distribution conditional on $\boldsymbol{X}$. These terms will be zero if (i) the individual-specific effects underlying our data set are empirically uncorrelated with the individual-specific mean of the xs and (ii) the period-specific effects underlying our data set are empirically uncorrelated with the period-specific mean of the xs. Only if both (i) and (ii) are satisfied will $\widehat{\beta}$, $\widehat{\beta}_B$, and $\widehat{\beta}_C$ be unbiased in Model (2.47). Consistency will hold if these conditions are satisfied asymptotically. But correlation may easily occur, which makes $\widehat{\beta}$, $\widehat{\beta}_B$, and

[11] The proof relies on the identities $\sum_i \sum_t (z_{it} - \bar{z}_{i\cdot})(\bar{q}_{i\cdot} - \bar{q}) \equiv \sum_i \sum_t (z_{it} - \bar{z}_{\cdot t})(\bar{q}_{\cdot t} - \bar{q}) \equiv 0$. See Section 3.6.4, for a more general proof using matrix algebra.

$\widehat{\beta}_C$ biased and not measuring what we want them to measure. This indicates a lack of robustness of the global and the between estimators which is of importance, as researchers often meet the challenge of 'navigating' between estimators which are robust and those which are efficient.

Conclusions so far are:

(i) The residual estimator, $\widehat{\beta}_R$, is the MVLUE in Model (2.47), and the global estimator, $\widehat{\beta}$, is the MVLUE in Model (2.65).

(ii) If B_{XX}, C_{XX}, and R_{XX} are all positive, then neither $\widehat{\beta}_B$, $\widehat{\beta}_C$, nor $\widehat{\beta}_R$ can be MVLUE in Model (2.65).

From (2.59), (2.64), (2.66), and (2.70)–(2.73) it follows that

$$\widehat{\beta} = \frac{R_{XY} + B_{XY} + C_{XY}}{R_{XX} + B_{XX} + C_{XX}} = \frac{R_{XX}\widehat{\beta}_R + B_{XX}\widehat{\beta}_B + C_{XX}\widehat{\beta}_C}{R_{XX} + B_{XX} + C_{XX}} = \frac{\dfrac{\widehat{\beta}_R}{\text{var}(\widehat{\beta}_R|X)} + \dfrac{\widehat{\beta}_B}{\text{var}(\widehat{\beta}_B|X)} + \dfrac{\widehat{\beta}_C}{\text{var}(\widehat{\beta}_C|X)}}{\dfrac{1}{\text{var}(\widehat{\beta}_R|X)} + \dfrac{1}{\text{var}(\widehat{\beta}_B|X)} + \dfrac{1}{\text{var}(\widehat{\beta}_C|X)}}. \tag{2.77}$$

In Model (2.65) the global estimator of β can be considered as obtained by giving the residual, the between-individual, and the between-period *variation* the same weight (first equality). Equivalently, the global estimator is a weighted average of the residual, the between-individual, and the between-period *estimators*, with weights which are inversely proportional to their respective variances (second and third equality). The *efficiency* of the three latter estimators relative to the global one can be expressed as

$$f_B = \frac{\text{var}(\widehat{\beta}_B|X)}{\text{var}(\widehat{\beta}|X)} = \frac{G_{XX}}{B_{XX}} = 1 + \frac{R_{XX}}{B_{XX}} + \frac{C_{XX}}{B_{XX}},$$
$$f_C = \frac{\text{var}(\widehat{\beta}_C)|X}{\text{var}(\widehat{\beta}|X)} = \frac{G_{XX}}{C_{XX}} = 1 + \frac{R_{XX}}{C_{XX}} + \frac{B_{XX}}{C_{XX}},$$
$$f_R = \frac{\text{var}(\widehat{\beta}_R|X)}{\text{var}(\widehat{\beta}|X)} = \frac{G_{XX}}{R_{XX}} = 1 + \frac{B_{XX}}{R_{XX}} + \frac{C_{XX}}{R_{XX}}.$$

If, for example, the between-individual, the between-period variation, and the residual variation of x account for, respectively, 80, 15, and 5% of the total variation, $f_B = 1.25$, $f_C = 6.67$, and $f_R = 20$.

2.4 Multiple regression model: Two-way heterogeneity

2.4.1 AN EXCURSION INTO KRONECKER-PRODUCTS: DEFINITION

Before extending the model to an arbitrary dimension, we take a digression by considering an extremely useful kind of matrix operations: Kronecker-products. We will refer, mostly without proofs, important rules for such products and give some applications. Although its definition may seem a bit strange, the algebra of Kronecker-products is in several respects simpler than that of ordinary matrix products. Let

$$A = \begin{bmatrix} a_{11} & a_{12} & \dots & a_{1m} \\ a_{21} & a_{22} & \dots & a_{2m} \\ \vdots & \vdots & & \vdots \\ a_{M1} & a_{M2} & \dots & a_{Mm} \end{bmatrix}, \quad B = \begin{bmatrix} b_{11} & b_{12} & \dots & b_{1n} \\ b_{21} & b_{22} & \dots & b_{2n} \\ \vdots & \vdots & & \vdots \\ b_{N1} & b_{N2} & \dots & b_{Nn} \end{bmatrix},$$

be matrices of dimension $(M \times m)$ and $(N \times n)$, respectively, and let $\boldsymbol{C}$ and $\boldsymbol{D}$ be corresponding matrices of dimension $(P \times p)$ and $(Q \times q)$, respectively. The *Kronecker-product of* $\boldsymbol{A}$ *and* $\boldsymbol{B}$ is defined as the $(MN \times mn)$-matrix

$$A \otimes B = \begin{bmatrix} a_{11}B & a_{12}B & \dots & a_{1m}B \\ a_{21}B & a_{22}B & \dots & a_{2m}B \\ \vdots & \vdots & & \vdots \\ a_{M1}B & a_{M2}B & \dots & a_{Mm}B \end{bmatrix}, \tag{2.78}$$

emerging by 'inflating' each element in $\boldsymbol{A}$ by $\boldsymbol{B}$. Symmetrically, the Kronecker-product of $\boldsymbol{B}$ and $\boldsymbol{A}$,

$$B \otimes A = \begin{bmatrix} b_{11}A & b_{12}A & \dots & b_{1n}A \\ b_{21}A & b_{22}A & \dots & b_{2n}A \\ \vdots & \vdots & & \vdots \\ b_{N1}A & b_{N2}A & \dots & b_{Nn}A \end{bmatrix},$$

emerges by 'inflating' each element in $\boldsymbol{B}$ by $\boldsymbol{A}$. In general, $B \otimes A \neq A \otimes B$: Kronecker-products are—like ordinary matrix products—*non-commutative.*

Important *rules for Kronecker-products*, proofs of which are found in by, e.g., Magnus and Neudecker (1988, chapter 2) and Lütkepohl (1996, Section 2.4), are

$$(A + C) \otimes B = A \otimes B + C \otimes B \quad (P = M, p = m), \tag{2.79}$$

$$(A \otimes B)(C \otimes D) = (A\,C) \otimes (B\,D) \quad (P = m, Q = n), \tag{2.80}$$

$$A \otimes (B \otimes C) = (A \otimes B) \otimes C, \tag{2.81}$$

$$(A \otimes B)' = A' \otimes B', \tag{2.82}$$

$$(A \otimes B)^{-1} = A^{-1} \otimes B^{-1} \qquad (m = M;\ n = N), \tag{2.83}$$

$$|A \otimes B| = |A|^N |B|^M \qquad (m = M; n = N), \tag{2.84}$$

$$\text{rank}(A \otimes B) = \text{rank}(A)\,\text{rank}(B), \tag{2.85}$$

$$\text{tr}(A \otimes B) = \text{tr}(A)\,\text{tr}(B) \qquad (m = M; n = N). \tag{2.86}$$

2.4.2 MATRIX FORMULAE WITH KRONECKER-PRODUCTS: EXAMPLES

Consider specifically the $(T \times T)$-matrices A_T and B_T, introduced in Section 2.2. They satisfy

$$\begin{aligned} \text{rank}(A_T) &= \text{tr}(A_T) = 1, \\ \text{rank}(B_T) &= \text{tr}(B_T) = T - 1, \end{aligned} \tag{2.87}$$

and by using (2.78), we find

$$\begin{aligned} I_N \otimes I_T &= I_{NT}, \\ A_N \otimes A_T &= A_{NT}, \\ B_N \otimes B_T &\neq B_{NT}, \end{aligned}$$

and that

$$I_N \otimes A_T = \begin{bmatrix} A_T & 0_{T,T} & \cdots & 0_{T,T} \\ 0_{T,T} & A_T & \cdots & 0_{T,T} \\ \vdots & \vdots & \ddots & \vdots \\ 0_{T,T} & 0_{T,T} & \cdots & A_T \end{bmatrix}, \quad I_N \otimes B_T = \begin{bmatrix} B_T & 0_{T,T} & \cdots & 0_{T,T} \\ 0_{T,T} & B_T & \cdots & 0_{T,T} \\ \vdots & \vdots & \ddots & \vdots \\ 0_{T,T} & 0_{T,T} & \cdots & B_T \end{bmatrix},$$

$$A_N \otimes I_T = \frac{1}{N} \begin{bmatrix} I_T & I_T & \cdots & I_T \\ I_T & I_T & \cdots & I_T \\ \vdots & \vdots & & \vdots \\ I_T & I_T & \cdots & I_T \end{bmatrix}, \quad B_N \otimes I_T = \begin{bmatrix} I_T - \frac{I_T}{N} & -\frac{I_T}{N} & \cdots & -\frac{I_T}{N} \\ -\frac{I_T}{N} & I_T - \frac{I_T}{N} & \cdots & -\frac{I_T}{N} \\ \vdots & \vdots & \ddots & \vdots \\ -\frac{I_T}{N} & -\frac{I_T}{N} & \cdots & I_T - \frac{I_T}{N} \end{bmatrix}.$$

Hence, $I_N \otimes A_T$ and $I_N \otimes B_T$ are the block-diagonal matrices with diagonal blocks, respectively, A_T and B_T; $A_N \otimes I_T$ has N^2 blocks equal to $\frac{1}{N}I_T$, and $B_N \otimes I_T$ has diagonal blocks equal to $I_T - \frac{1}{N}I_T$ and all off-diagonal blocks equal to $-\frac{1}{N}I_T$.

2.4.3 PANEL DATA 'OPERATORS': BILINEAR AND QUADRATIC FORMS

How are vectors of panel data affected when premultiplied by the above matrices? Let

$$z = [z_{11}, \dots, z_{1T}, \dots, z_{N1}, \dots, z_{NT}]', \quad q = [q_{11}, \dots, q_{1T}, \dots, q_{N1}, \dots, q_{NT}]'.$$

We find

$$(I_N \otimes A_T)z = \begin{bmatrix} \bar{z}_{1\cdot} \\ \vdots \\ \bar{z}_{1\cdot} \\ \vdots \\ \bar{z}_{N\cdot} \\ \vdots \\ \bar{z}_{N\cdot} \end{bmatrix}, \qquad (A_N \otimes I_T)z = \begin{bmatrix} \bar{z}_{\cdot 1} \\ \vdots \\ \bar{z}_{\cdot T} \\ \vdots \\ \bar{z}_{\cdot 1} \\ \vdots \\ \bar{z}_{\cdot T} \end{bmatrix},$$

$$(I_N \otimes B_T)z = \begin{bmatrix} z_{11} - \bar{z}_{1\cdot} \\ \vdots \\ z_{1T} - \bar{z}_{1\cdot} \\ \vdots \\ z_{N1} - \bar{z}_{N\cdot} \\ \vdots \\ z_{NT} - \bar{z}_{N\cdot} \end{bmatrix}, \qquad (B_N \otimes I_T)z = \begin{bmatrix} z_{11} - \bar{z}_{\cdot 1} \\ \vdots \\ z_{1T} - \bar{z}_{\cdot T} \\ \vdots \\ z_{N1} - \bar{z}_{\cdot 1} \\ \vdots \\ z_{NT} - \bar{z}_{\cdot T} \end{bmatrix},$$

expressing that

- $I_N \otimes A_T$ is the *'individual-specific-mean operator'* since premultiplication replaces each element with its individual-specific mean.
- $A_N \otimes I_T$ is the *'period-specific-mean operator'* since premultiplication replaces each element with its period-specific mean.
- $I_N \otimes B_T$ is the *'deviation-from-individual-specific-mean operator'* since premultiplication deducts from each element its individual-specific mean.
- $B_N \otimes I_T$ is the *'deviation-from-period-specific-mean operator'* since premultiplication deducts from each element its period-specific mean.

Recalling that $(\boldsymbol{I}_N \otimes \boldsymbol{A}_T)$, $(\boldsymbol{I}_N \otimes \boldsymbol{B}_T)$, etc., like $\boldsymbol{A}_T$ and $\boldsymbol{B}_T$, are symmetric and idempotent, we find, utilizing (2.80),

$$(\boldsymbol{A}_N \otimes \boldsymbol{A}_T)\boldsymbol{z} = \begin{bmatrix} \bar{z} \\ \vdots \\ \bar{z} \\ \vdots \\ \bar{z} \\ \vdots \\ \bar{z} \end{bmatrix}, \quad (\boldsymbol{B}_N \otimes \boldsymbol{B}_T)\boldsymbol{z} = \begin{bmatrix} z_{11} - \bar{z}_{1\cdot} - \bar{z}_{\cdot 1} + \bar{z} \\ \vdots \\ z_{1T} - \bar{z}_{1\cdot} - \bar{z}_{\cdot T} + \bar{z} \\ \vdots \\ z_{N1} - \bar{z}_{N\cdot} - \bar{z}_{\cdot 1} + \bar{z} \\ \vdots \\ z_{NT} - \bar{z}_{N\cdot} - \bar{z}_{\cdot T} + \bar{z} \end{bmatrix},$$

$$(\boldsymbol{B}_N \otimes \boldsymbol{A}_T)\boldsymbol{z} = \begin{bmatrix} \bar{z}_{1\cdot} - \bar{z} \\ \vdots \\ \bar{z}_{1\cdot} - \bar{z} \\ \vdots \\ \bar{z}_{N\cdot} - \bar{z} \\ \vdots \\ \bar{z}_{N\cdot} - \bar{z} \end{bmatrix}, \quad (\boldsymbol{A}_N \otimes \boldsymbol{B}_T)\boldsymbol{z} = \begin{bmatrix} \bar{z}_{\cdot 1} - \bar{z} \\ \vdots \\ \bar{z}_{\cdot T} - \bar{z} \\ \vdots \\ \bar{z}_{\cdot 1} - \bar{z} \\ \vdots \\ \bar{z}_{\cdot T} - \bar{z} \end{bmatrix},$$

$$(\boldsymbol{I}_N \otimes \boldsymbol{I}_T - \boldsymbol{A}_N \otimes \boldsymbol{A}_T)\boldsymbol{z} = \begin{bmatrix} z_{11} - \bar{z} \\ \vdots \\ z_{1T} - \bar{z} \\ \vdots \\ z_{N1} - \bar{z} \\ \vdots \\ z_{NT} - \bar{z} \end{bmatrix}.$$

Hence:

$$\boldsymbol{q}'(\boldsymbol{I}_N \otimes \boldsymbol{A}_T)\boldsymbol{z} = \tfrac{1}{T}\textstyle\sum_{i=1}^{N}[\sum_{t=1}^{T} z_{it}][\sum_{s=1}^{T} q_{is}], \tag{2.88}$$

$$\boldsymbol{q}'(\boldsymbol{A}_N \otimes \boldsymbol{I}_T)\boldsymbol{z} = \tfrac{1}{N}\textstyle\sum_{t=1}^{T}[\sum_{i=1}^{N} z_{it}][\sum_{j=1}^{N} q_{jt}], \tag{2.89}$$

$$\boldsymbol{q}'(\boldsymbol{I}_N \otimes \boldsymbol{B}_T)\boldsymbol{z} = \textstyle\sum_{i=1}^{N}\sum_{t=1}^{T}(z_{it} - \bar{z}_{i\cdot})(q_{it} - \bar{q}_{i\cdot}), \tag{2.90}$$

$$\boldsymbol{q}'(\boldsymbol{B}_N \otimes \boldsymbol{I}_T)\boldsymbol{z} = \textstyle\sum_{t=1}^{T}\sum_{i=1}^{N}(z_{it} - \bar{z}_{\cdot t})(q_{it} - \bar{q}_{\cdot t}), \tag{2.91}$$

$$\boldsymbol{q}'(\boldsymbol{A}_N \otimes \boldsymbol{A}_T)\boldsymbol{z} = \tfrac{1}{NT}\textstyle[\sum_{i=1}^{N}\sum_{t=1}^{T} z_{it}][\sum_{j=1}^{N}\sum_{s=1}^{T} q_{js}], \tag{2.92}$$

$$\boldsymbol{q}'(\boldsymbol{B}_N \otimes \boldsymbol{A}_T)\boldsymbol{z} = T\textstyle\sum_{i=1}^{N}(\bar{z}_{i\cdot} - \bar{z})(\bar{q}_{i\cdot} - \bar{q}), \tag{2.93}$$

$$\boldsymbol{q}'(\boldsymbol{A}_N \otimes \boldsymbol{B}_T)\boldsymbol{z} = N\textstyle\sum_{t=1}^{T}(\bar{z}_{\cdot t} - \bar{z})(\bar{q}_{\cdot t} - \bar{q}), \tag{2.94}$$

$$q'(B_N \otimes B_T)z = \sum_{i=1}^{N}\sum_{t=1}^{T}(z_{it}-\bar{z}_{i\cdot} - \bar{z}_{\cdot t} + \bar{z})(q_{it}-\bar{q}_{i\cdot} - \bar{q}_{\cdot t} + \bar{q}), \tag{2.95}$$

$$q'(I_{NT}-A_{NT})z = \sum_{i=1}^{N}\sum_{t=1}^{T}(z_{it}-\bar{z})(q_{it}-\bar{q}). \tag{2.96}$$

This enables us to express compactly a variety of *bilinear and quadratic forms.*

As generalizations, we find, by extending z and q to matrices, Z and Q, of dimensions $(NT \times K)$ and $(NT \times L)$, respectively, that $Q'(I_N \otimes A_T)Z$, $Q'(I_N \otimes A_T)Z$, $\dots$, $Q'(I_{NT} - A_{NT})Z$ are the $(L \times K)$ matrix whose element (l, k) is obtained by applying, respectively, (2.88), (2.89), ..., (2.96) on column k of Z and column l of Q.

The following *symmetry* is worth noting: If, in defining z and q, we had *interchanged the ordering of periods and individuals*, i.e., replaced them with

$$z_* = [z_{11},\dots,z_{N1},\dots,z_{1T},\dots,z_{NT}], \quad q_* = [q_{11},\dots,q_{N1},\dots,q_{1T},\dots,q_{NT}],$$

we would obtain the above bilinear and quadratic form by *reversing the order of the factors in the Kronecker-products* in (2.88)–(2.96). For example,

$$q_*'(A_T \otimes I_N)z_* \equiv q'(I_N \otimes A_T)z,$$
$$q_*'(I_T \otimes A_N)z_* \equiv q'(A_N \otimes I_T)z.$$

Two examples illustrate how the primary estimator formulae for the one-way fixed effects model in Section 2.2 can be expressed compactly.

Example 1. The stacked equation for Model (2.29), after having eliminated the individual-specific intercepts, can be written as

$$(I_N \otimes B_T)y = (I_N \otimes B_T)X\beta + u,$$

giving the following alternative expression for $\widehat{\beta}_W$ in (2.32)

$$\widehat{\beta}_W = [X'(I_N \otimes B_T)X]^{-1}[X'(I_N \otimes B_T)y].$$

Example 2. The stacked equation for Model (2.36), after having eliminated the intercept, can be written as

$$(I_N \otimes I_T - A_N \otimes A_T)y = (I_N \otimes I_T - A_N \otimes A_T)X\beta + u,$$

giving the following alternative expression for $\widehat{\beta}$ in (2.38)

$$\widehat{\beta} = [X'(I_N \otimes I_T - A_N \otimes A_T)X]^{-1}[X'(I_N \otimes I_T - A_N \otimes A_T)y].$$

2.4.4 INDIVIDUAL- AND PERIOD-SPECIFIC INTERCEPTS

Having the Kronecker-product algebra in our tool-kit, we can extend Models (2.29) and (2.47) jointly to

$$y_{it} = k+\alpha_i+\gamma_t+\boldsymbol{x}_{it}\boldsymbol{\beta}+u_{it}, \quad (u_{it}|X) \sim \mathsf{IID}(0,\sigma^2), \tag{2.97}$$

where still $\boldsymbol{\beta}=(\beta_1,\ldots,\beta_K)'$ is the column vector of coefficients, and $\boldsymbol{x}_{it}=(x_{1it},\ldots,x_{Kit})$ is the row vector with observations on the K regressors for individual i in period t. Further, we denote the vectors of individual-specific and period-specific effects as, respectively, $\boldsymbol{\alpha} = (\alpha_1,\ldots,\alpha_N)'$ and $\boldsymbol{\gamma} = (\gamma_1,\ldots,\gamma_T)'$. We still impose the *adding-up restrictions* (2.48), now expressed as

$$\boldsymbol{e}_N'\boldsymbol{\alpha} = \boldsymbol{e}_T'\boldsymbol{\gamma} = 0. \tag{2.98}$$

Defining $\boldsymbol{y}_i$, $\boldsymbol{X}_i$, and $\boldsymbol{u}_i$ as in Section 2.2.1, we can write (2.97) as

$$\begin{aligned} &\boldsymbol{y}_i = \boldsymbol{e}_T(k+\alpha_i)+\boldsymbol{\gamma}+\boldsymbol{X}_i\boldsymbol{\beta}+\boldsymbol{u}_i, \\ &(\boldsymbol{u}_i|X) \sim \mathsf{IID}(\boldsymbol{0}_{T,1},\sigma^2\boldsymbol{I}_T), \\ &i = 1,\ldots,N. \end{aligned} \tag{2.99}$$

This generalizes (2.24) ($k+\alpha_i$ corresponding to α_i^* formerly). Letting

$$\boldsymbol{y} = \begin{bmatrix} \boldsymbol{y}_1 \\ \vdots \\ \boldsymbol{y}_N \end{bmatrix}, \quad \boldsymbol{X} = \begin{bmatrix} \boldsymbol{X}_1 \\ \vdots \\ \boldsymbol{X}_N \end{bmatrix}, \quad \boldsymbol{u} = \begin{bmatrix} \boldsymbol{u}_1 \\ \vdots \\ \boldsymbol{u}_N \end{bmatrix},$$

the model is, in compact notation,

$$\begin{aligned} &\boldsymbol{y} = (\boldsymbol{e}_N \otimes \boldsymbol{e}_T)k + \boldsymbol{\alpha}\otimes\boldsymbol{e}_T + \boldsymbol{e}_N\otimes\boldsymbol{\gamma} + \boldsymbol{X}\boldsymbol{\beta} + \boldsymbol{u}, \\ &\mathsf{E}(\boldsymbol{u}|\boldsymbol{X}) = \boldsymbol{0}_{NT,1}, \quad \mathsf{V}(\boldsymbol{u}|\boldsymbol{X}) = \sigma^2\boldsymbol{I}_{NT}, \end{aligned} \tag{2.100}$$

$(\boldsymbol{\alpha}\otimes\boldsymbol{e}_T)$ being the $(NT\times 1)$-vector which repeats α_1 T times, repeats α_2 T times, etc., and $(\boldsymbol{e}_N\otimes\boldsymbol{\gamma})$ being the $(NT\times 1)$-vector which repeats $\boldsymbol{\gamma}$ N times.

It is easy to *reverse the ordering of individuals and periods*. If we define

$$\boldsymbol{y}_{*t} = \begin{bmatrix} y_{1t} \\ \vdots \\ y_{Nt} \end{bmatrix}, \quad \boldsymbol{X}_{*t} = \begin{bmatrix} \boldsymbol{x}_{1t} \\ \vdots \\ \boldsymbol{x}_{Nt} \end{bmatrix}, \quad \boldsymbol{u}_{*t} = \begin{bmatrix} u_{1t} \\ \vdots \\ u_{Nt} \end{bmatrix}, \qquad t = 1,\ldots,T,$$

$$y_* = \begin{bmatrix} y_{*1} \\ \vdots \\ y_{*T} \end{bmatrix}, \quad X_* \begin{bmatrix} X_{*1} \\ \vdots \\ X_{*T} \end{bmatrix}, \quad u_* \begin{bmatrix} u_{*1} \\ \vdots \\ u_{*T} \end{bmatrix},$$

now letting the individual subscript 'run fast' and the period subscript 'run slow', then (2.99) and (2.100) read, respectively,

$$\begin{aligned} &y_{*t} = e_N(k+\gamma_t)+\boldsymbol{\alpha}+X_{*t}\boldsymbol{\beta}+u_{*t}, \\ &(u_{*t}|X_*) \sim \mathsf{IID}(0_{N,1}, \sigma^2 I_N), \quad t=1,\dots,T, \end{aligned}$$

$$\begin{aligned} &y_* = (e_T \otimes e_N)k+e_T \otimes \boldsymbol{\alpha}+\boldsymbol{\gamma} \otimes e_N+X_*\boldsymbol{\beta}+u_*, \\ &\mathsf{E}(u_*|X_*) = 0_{TN,1}, \quad \mathsf{E}(u_*u_*'|X_*) = \sigma^2 I_{TN}, \end{aligned}$$

$(e_T \otimes \boldsymbol{\alpha})$ being the vector which repeats $\boldsymbol{\alpha}$ T times, and $(\boldsymbol{\gamma} \otimes e_N)$ being the vector which repeats γ_1 N times, repeats γ_2 N times, etc. This illustrates that several equivalent ways of expressing a panel data regression model in matrix format exist. Which to choose and how to arrange the observations in a data file to be loaded into a computer programme is a matter of convenience, as several software packages allow both orderings.

The OLS estimators of $(k, \boldsymbol{\alpha}, \boldsymbol{\gamma}, \boldsymbol{\beta})$ in (2.100) are the values which solve

$$\begin{aligned} \min_{k,\boldsymbol{\alpha},\boldsymbol{\gamma},\boldsymbol{\beta}} \; & [y-e_{NT}k-\boldsymbol{\alpha} \otimes e_T-e_N \otimes \boldsymbol{\gamma}-X\boldsymbol{\beta}]' \\ & \times [y-e_{NT}k-\boldsymbol{\alpha} \otimes e_T-e_N \otimes \boldsymbol{\gamma}-X\boldsymbol{\beta}]. \end{aligned}$$

Let us first minimize the sum of squares with respect to k, $\boldsymbol{\alpha}$, and $\boldsymbol{\gamma}$ and next minimize the function obtained with respect to $\boldsymbol{\beta}$. The solution to the first problem has the same form as (2.60)–(2.62), except that the scalars $\bar{x}$, $\bar{x}_{i\cdot}$, and $\bar{x}_{\cdot t}$ are replaced with the $(1 \times K)$-vectors $\bar{\boldsymbol{x}}$, $\bar{\boldsymbol{x}}_{i\cdot}$, and $\bar{\boldsymbol{x}}_{\cdot t}$ and the scalar β is replaced with the $(K \times 1)$-vector $\boldsymbol{\beta}$. In doing this, we notice that

- $\big[(\frac{1}{N}e_N') \otimes (\frac{1}{T}e_T')\big]y$ compresses y into the global mean $\bar{y}$.
- $\big[I_N \otimes (\frac{1}{T}e_T')\big]y$ and $\big[(\frac{1}{N}e_N') \otimes I_T\big]y$ compress y into, respectively, the $(N \times 1)$-vector of repeated $\bar{y}_{i\cdot}$ and the $(T \times 1)$-vector of repeated $\bar{y}_{\cdot t}$.
- $\big[B_N \otimes (\frac{1}{T}e_T')\big]y$ and $\big[(\frac{1}{N}e_N') \otimes B_T\big]y$ take y into, respectively, an $(N \times 1)$-vector of individual-specific means measured from the global mean and a $(T \times 1)$-vector of period-specific means measured from the global mean.

We then find, as matrix analogues to (2.60)–(2.62), that the (conditional) estimators for k, $\boldsymbol{\alpha}$, and $\boldsymbol{\gamma}$ can be written as, respectively,

$$\widehat{k}_R = \widehat{k}_R(\boldsymbol{\beta}) = \tfrac{1}{NT}e_{NT}'(y-X\boldsymbol{\beta}) = \left(\tfrac{1}{N}e_N' \otimes \tfrac{1}{T}e_T'\right)(y-X\boldsymbol{\beta}), \tag{2.101}$$

$$\begin{aligned}\widehat{\alpha} = \widehat{\alpha}(\beta) &= \left[\left(I_N \otimes \tfrac{1}{T}e'_T\right) - e_N\left(\tfrac{1}{N}e'_N \otimes \tfrac{1}{T}e'_T\right)\right](y - X\beta)\\ &\equiv \left(B_N \otimes \tfrac{1}{T}e'_T\right)(y - X\beta),\end{aligned} \tag{2.102}$$

$$\begin{aligned}\widehat{\gamma} = \widehat{\gamma}(\beta) &= \left[\left(\tfrac{1}{N}e'_N \otimes I_T\right) - e_T\left(\tfrac{1}{N}e'_N \otimes \tfrac{1}{T}e'_T\right)\right](y - X\beta)\\ &\equiv \left(\tfrac{1}{N}e'_N \otimes B_T\right)(y - X\beta),\end{aligned} \tag{2.103}$$

by utilizing $e_N \equiv (e_N \otimes 1)$, $e_T \equiv (1 \otimes e_T)$, the definitions of A_T, and B_T and (2.79)–(2.82). These conditional estimators satisfy (2.98):

$$e'_N\widehat{\alpha}(\beta) = (e'_N \otimes 1)\left(B_N \otimes \tfrac{1}{T}e'_T\right)(y - X\beta) = 0,$$
$$e'_T\widehat{\gamma}(\beta) = (1 \otimes e'_T)\left(\tfrac{1}{N}e'_N \otimes B_T\right)(y - X\beta) = 0.$$

Inserting next (2.101)–(2.103) in (2.100) and the minimand, we find

$$\begin{aligned}(e_N \otimes e_T)\widehat{k}_R &= (A_N \otimes A_T)(y - X\beta),\\ \widehat{\alpha} \otimes e_T &\equiv (I_N\widehat{\alpha}) \otimes (e_T\,1) \equiv (I_N \otimes e_T)(\widehat{\alpha} \otimes 1) = (B_N \otimes A_T)(y - X\beta),\\ e_N \otimes \widehat{\gamma} &\equiv (e_N\,1) \otimes (I_T\widehat{\gamma}) \equiv (e_N \otimes I_T)(1 \otimes \widehat{\gamma}) = (A_N \otimes B_T)(y - X\beta),\end{aligned}$$

and hence, since $I_N \otimes I_T \equiv A_N \otimes A_T + A_N \otimes B_T + B_N \otimes A_T + B_N \otimes B_T$,

$$(B_N \otimes B_T)y = (B_N \otimes B_T)X\beta + u. \tag{2.104}$$

Consequently, the simplified minimand becomes

$$(y - X\beta)'(B_N \otimes B_T)(y - X\beta).$$

Its solution defines the residual estimator vector, generalizing (2.59):

$$\widehat{\beta}_R = [X'(B_N \otimes B_T)X]^{-1}[X'(B_N \otimes B_T)y]. \tag{2.105}$$

The corresponding estimators of k, α, and γ follow by inserting $\beta = \widehat{\beta}_R$ in (2.101)–(2.103), respectively,

$$\widehat{k}_R = \widehat{k}_R(\widehat{\beta}_R) = \left(\tfrac{1}{N}e'_N \otimes \tfrac{1}{T}e'_T\right)(y - X\widehat{\beta}_R), \tag{2.106}$$

$$\widehat{\alpha} = \widehat{\alpha}(\widehat{\beta}_R) = \left(B_N \otimes \tfrac{1}{T}e'_T\right)(y - X\widehat{\beta}_R), \tag{2.107}$$

$$\widehat{\gamma} = \widehat{\gamma}(\widehat{\beta}_R) = \left(\tfrac{1}{N}e'_N \otimes B_T\right)(y - X\widehat{\beta}_R). \tag{2.108}$$

Since inserting for y from (2.100) in (2.105) gives

$$\widehat{\boldsymbol{\beta}}_R - \boldsymbol{\beta} = [X'(B_N \otimes B_T)X]^{-1}[X'(B_N \otimes B_T)\boldsymbol{u}],$$

we obtain, as the matrix generalization of (2.64),

$$\mathsf{V}(\widehat{\boldsymbol{\beta}}_R|X) = \sigma^2[X'(B_N \otimes B_T)X]^{-1}. \tag{2.109}$$

The estimators (2.105)–(2.108) are MVLUE in Model (2.100). Regarding asymptotics, we know that $\widehat{\boldsymbol{\beta}}_R$ is both N- and T-consistent, whereas $\widehat{\boldsymbol{\alpha}}$ is only T-consistent and $\widehat{\boldsymbol{\gamma}}$ is only N-consistent, following a reasoning similar to that for the one-regressor model at the end of Section 2.3.1.

2.4.5 HOMOGENEOUS BENCHMARK MODEL

We again consider a model with the same coefficient vector and intercept for all individuals and periods, i.e., $\boldsymbol{\alpha} = \mathbf{0}_{N,1}$ and $\boldsymbol{\gamma} = \mathbf{0}_{T,1}$. Of course, it coincides with (2.36), but now we will, in analogy with (2.100), write it as

$$\begin{aligned} y &= (e_N \otimes e_T)k + X\boldsymbol{\beta} + \boldsymbol{u} = e_{NT}k + X\boldsymbol{\beta} + \boldsymbol{u}, \\ \mathsf{E}(\boldsymbol{u}|X) &= \mathbf{0}_{NT,1}, \ \ \mathsf{V}(\boldsymbol{u}|X) \equiv \mathsf{E}(\boldsymbol{u}\boldsymbol{u}'X) = \sigma^2 I_{NT}. \end{aligned} \tag{2.110}$$

The OLS estimator of the intercept conditional on $\boldsymbol{\beta}$ is still (2.101). Inserting (2.101) into (2.110), we get

$$(I_{NT} - A_{NT})y = (I_{NT} - A_{NT})X\boldsymbol{\beta} + \boldsymbol{u}, \tag{2.111}$$

giving the global estimator

$$\widehat{\boldsymbol{\beta}} = [X'(I_{NT} - A_{NT})X]^{-1}[X'(I_{NT} - A_{NT})y], \tag{2.112}$$

implying

$$\widehat{\boldsymbol{\beta}} - \boldsymbol{\beta} = [X'(I_{NT} - A_{NT})X]^{-1}[X'(I_{NT} - A_{NT})\boldsymbol{u}],$$

from which we obtain

$$\mathsf{V}(\widehat{\boldsymbol{\beta}}|X) = \sigma^2[X'(I_{NT} - A_{NT})X]^{-1}. \tag{2.113}$$

To compare $\widehat{\boldsymbol{\beta}}$ with the estimators exploiting only the between-individual and between-period variation, we proceed as follows: premultiplying (2.110) by $(\boldsymbol{I}_N \otimes \boldsymbol{A}_T)$ and by $(\boldsymbol{A}_N \otimes \boldsymbol{I}_T)$, respectively, we get *equations in individual-specific and period-specific means:*

$$(\boldsymbol{I}_N \otimes \boldsymbol{A}_T)\boldsymbol{y} = (\boldsymbol{e}_N \otimes \boldsymbol{e}_T)k + (\boldsymbol{I}_N \otimes \boldsymbol{A}_T)\boldsymbol{X}\boldsymbol{\beta} + (\boldsymbol{I}_N \otimes \boldsymbol{A}_T)\boldsymbol{u}, \tag{2.114}$$
$$(\boldsymbol{A}_N \otimes \boldsymbol{I}_T)\boldsymbol{y} = (\boldsymbol{e}_N \otimes \boldsymbol{e}_T)k + (\boldsymbol{A}_N \otimes \boldsymbol{I}_T)\boldsymbol{X}\boldsymbol{\beta} + (\boldsymbol{A}_N \otimes \boldsymbol{I}_T)\boldsymbol{u}, \tag{2.115}$$

which after elimination of k, using (2.101), give, respectively,

$$(\boldsymbol{B}_N \otimes \boldsymbol{A}_T)\boldsymbol{y} = (\boldsymbol{B}_N \otimes \boldsymbol{A}_T)\boldsymbol{X}\boldsymbol{\beta} + (\boldsymbol{I}_N \otimes \boldsymbol{A}_T)\boldsymbol{u}, \tag{2.116}$$
$$(\boldsymbol{A}_N \otimes \boldsymbol{B}_T)\boldsymbol{y} = (\boldsymbol{A}_N \otimes \boldsymbol{B}_T)\boldsymbol{X}\boldsymbol{\beta} + (\boldsymbol{A}_N \otimes \boldsymbol{I}_T)\boldsymbol{u}. \tag{2.117}$$

We then have regression equations in, respectively, differences between individual-specific and global means, and differences between period-specific and global means. Applying OLS, we obtain, respectively, the *between-individual estimator* and the *between-period estimator*:

$$\widehat{\boldsymbol{\beta}}_B = [\boldsymbol{X}'(\boldsymbol{B}_N \otimes \boldsymbol{A}_T)\boldsymbol{X}]^{-1}[\boldsymbol{X}'(\boldsymbol{B}_N \otimes \boldsymbol{A}_T)\boldsymbol{y}], \tag{2.118}$$
$$\widehat{\boldsymbol{\beta}}_C = [\boldsymbol{X}'(\boldsymbol{A}_N \otimes \boldsymbol{B}_T)\boldsymbol{X}]^{-1}[\boldsymbol{X}'(\boldsymbol{A}_N \otimes \boldsymbol{B}_T)\boldsymbol{y}], \tag{2.119}$$

and hence

$$\widehat{\boldsymbol{\beta}}_B - \boldsymbol{\beta} = [\boldsymbol{X}'(\boldsymbol{B}_N \otimes \boldsymbol{A}_T)\boldsymbol{X}]^{-1}[\boldsymbol{X}'(\boldsymbol{B}_N \otimes \boldsymbol{A}_T)\boldsymbol{u}],$$
$$\widehat{\boldsymbol{\beta}}_C - \boldsymbol{\beta} = [\boldsymbol{X}'(\boldsymbol{A}_N \otimes \boldsymbol{B}_T)\boldsymbol{X}]^{-1}[\boldsymbol{X}'(\boldsymbol{A}_N \otimes \boldsymbol{B}_T)\boldsymbol{u}],$$

from which we obtain

$$\mathsf{V}(\widehat{\boldsymbol{\beta}}_B|\boldsymbol{X}) = \sigma^2[\boldsymbol{X}'(\boldsymbol{B}_N \otimes \boldsymbol{A}_T)\boldsymbol{X}]^{-1}, \tag{2.120}$$
$$\mathsf{V}(\widehat{\boldsymbol{\beta}}_C|\boldsymbol{X}) = \sigma^2[\boldsymbol{X}'(\boldsymbol{A}_N \otimes \boldsymbol{B}_T)\boldsymbol{X}]^{-1}. \tag{2.121}$$

2.4.6 HOW ARE THE ESTIMATORS RELATED?

We have four estimators of the vector $\boldsymbol{\beta}$ in Model (2.110): the residual estimator $\widehat{\boldsymbol{\beta}}_R$, given by (2.105); the between-individual estimator $\widehat{\boldsymbol{\beta}}_B$, given by (2.118); the between-period estimator $\widehat{\boldsymbol{\beta}}_C$, given by (2.119); and the global estimator $\widehat{\boldsymbol{\beta}}$, given by (2.112). We can express them compactly by means of

$$
\begin{aligned}
G_{ZQ} &= Z'(I_{NT} - A_{NT})Q, \\
B_{ZQ} &= Z'(B_N \otimes A_T)Q, \\
C_{ZQ} &= Z'(A_N \otimes B_T)Q, \\
R_{ZQ} &= Z'(B_N \otimes B_T)Q, \\
B_{Z\boldsymbol{\alpha}} &= Z'(B_N \otimes A_T)(\boldsymbol{\alpha} \otimes e_T), \\
C_{Z\boldsymbol{\gamma}} &= Z'(A_N \otimes B_T)(e_N \otimes \boldsymbol{\gamma}).
\end{aligned}
$$

It follows that, in general, the total variation can be decomposed into residual variation, between-individual variation, and between-period variation:

$$G_{ZQ} = R_{ZQ} + B_{ZQ} + C_{ZQ},$$

and we can express the four estimators and their covariance matrices as follows:

$$\widehat{\boldsymbol{\beta}}_R = R_{XX}^{-1} R_{XY}, \quad \mathsf{V}(\widehat{\boldsymbol{\beta}}_R|X) = \sigma^2 R_{XX}^{-1}, \tag{2.122}$$

$$\widehat{\boldsymbol{\beta}}_B = B_{XX}^{-1} B_{XY}, \quad \mathsf{V}(\widehat{\boldsymbol{\beta}}_B|X) = \sigma^2 B_{XX}^{-1}, \tag{2.123}$$

$$\widehat{\boldsymbol{\beta}}_C = C_{XX}^{-1} C_{XY}, \quad \mathsf{V}(\widehat{\boldsymbol{\beta}}_C|X) = \sigma^2 C_{XX}^{-1}, \tag{2.124}$$

$$\widehat{\boldsymbol{\beta}} = G_{XX}^{-1} G_{XY}, \quad \mathsf{V}(\widehat{\boldsymbol{\beta}}|X) = \sigma^2 G_{XX}^{-1}. \tag{2.125}$$

They are all unbiased *if Model (2.110) has generated our data.* They are also consistent regardless of whether $N \to \infty$ or $T \to \infty$, by an argument similar to that for the simple regression model (confer Section 2.3.3).

The between-individual estimator $\widehat{\boldsymbol{\beta}}_B$, the between-period estimator $\widehat{\boldsymbol{\beta}}_C$, and the global estimator $\widehat{\boldsymbol{\beta}}$ are not necessarily unbiased and consistent for $\boldsymbol{\beta}$ *if Model (2.100), with both individual-specific and period-specific effects, has generated our data.* If (2.100) holds, these three estimators, generalizing (2.74)–(2.76), can be written as, respectively,

$$
\begin{aligned}
\widehat{\boldsymbol{\beta}}_B &= \boldsymbol{\beta} + \left[X'(B_N \otimes A_T)X\right]^{-1} \left[X'(B_N \otimes A_T)[(\boldsymbol{\alpha} \otimes e_T) + \boldsymbol{u}]\right] \\
&= \boldsymbol{\beta} + B_{XX}^{-1} B_{X\boldsymbol{\alpha}} + B_{XX}^{-1} B_{XU},
\end{aligned} \tag{2.126}
$$

$$
\begin{aligned}
\widehat{\boldsymbol{\beta}}_C &= \boldsymbol{\beta} + \left[X'(A_N \otimes B_T)X\right]^{-1} \left[X'(A_N \otimes B_T)[(e_N \otimes \boldsymbol{\gamma}) + \boldsymbol{u}]\right] \\
&= \boldsymbol{\beta} + C_{XX}^{-1} C_{X\boldsymbol{\gamma}} + C_{XX}^{-1} C_{XU},
\end{aligned} \tag{2.127}
$$

$$\begin{aligned}\widehat{\beta} &= \beta + [X'(I_{NT} - A_{NT})X]^{-1} \\ &\quad \times [X'(B_N \otimes A_T)(\alpha \otimes e_T) + X'(A_N \otimes B_T)(e_N \otimes \gamma)] \\ &\quad + [X'(I_{NT} - A_{NT})X]^{-1}[X'(I_{NT} - A_{NT})u] \\ &= \beta + G_{XX}^{-1}(B_{X\alpha} + C_{X\gamma}) + G_{XX}^{-1}G_{XU}. \end{aligned} \tag{2.128}$$

Conditional on X, the last term of each equation has zero expectation. The second term in (2.126), the second term in (2.127), and the second and third terms in (2.123) are vectors of constants, which are zero only if (i) the individual-specific effects generating the data set are empirically uncorrelated with all the individual-specific means of the xs and (ii) the period-specific effects generating the data set are empirically uncorrelated with all the period-specific means of the xs. Only then will $\widehat{\beta}$, $\widehat{\beta}_B$, and $\widehat{\beta}_C$ be unbiased. Consistency will hold if these conditions are satisfied. However, correlation between the α_is and $\bar{x}_{i\cdot}$s and/or between γ_ts and $\bar{x}_{\cdot t}$s may easily make $\widehat{\beta}$, $\widehat{\beta}_B$, and $\widehat{\beta}_C$ biased and not measuring what we want them to measure.

Conclusions are:

(i) *The residual estimator $\widehat{\beta}_R$ is the MVLUE in Model (2.100) and the global estimator $\widehat{\beta}$ is the MVLUE in Model (2.110).*

(ii) *If $C_{XX}+R_{XX}$ is positive definite, the between-individual estimator cannot be an MVLUE in Model (2.110). If $B_{XX}+R_{XX}$ is positive definite, the between-period estimator cannot be an MVLUE in Model (2.110).*

From (2.112) and (2.122)–(2.125) it follows that

$$\begin{aligned}\widehat{\beta} &= [X'(B_N \otimes B_T)X + X'(B_N \otimes A_T)X + X'(A_N \otimes B_T)X]^{-1} \\ &\quad \times [X'(B_N \otimes B_T)X\widehat{\beta}_R + X'(B_N \otimes A_T)X\widehat{\beta}_B + X'(A_N \otimes B_T)X\widehat{\beta}_C] \\ &= [R_{XX}+B_{XX}+C_{XX}]^{-1}[R_{XY}+B_{XY}+C_{XY}] \\ &= [R_{XX}+B_{XX}+C_{XX}]^{-1}[R_{XX}\widehat{\beta}_R+B_{XX}\widehat{\beta}_B+C_{XX}\widehat{\beta}_C] \\ &= [\mathsf{V}(\widehat{\beta}_R|X)^{-1}+\mathsf{V}(\widehat{\beta}_B|X)^{-1}+\mathsf{V}(\widehat{\beta}_C|X)^{-1}]^{-1} \\ &\quad \times [\mathsf{V}(\widehat{\beta}_R|X)^{-1}\widehat{\beta}_R+\mathsf{V}(\widehat{\beta}_B|X)^{-1}\widehat{\beta}_B+\mathsf{V}(\widehat{\beta}_C|X)^{-1}\widehat{\beta}_C]. \end{aligned} \tag{2.129}$$

This matrix generalization of (2.77) implies: in Model (2.110), the global estimator can be interpreted as obtained by giving the residual estimator β_R a (matrix) weight R_{XX}, the between-individual estimator B_{XX} a (matrix) weight B_{XX}, and the between-individual estimator C_{XX} a (matrix) weight C_{XX}. Equivalently, the global estimator is a matrix-weighted average of the residual estimator, the between-individual estimator, and the between-period estimator, the weight matrices being proportional to the inverse of the respective covariance matrices. From the identity $E^{-1} - (E+D)^{-1} \equiv (E+D)^{-1}DE^{-1}$, which implies

$$
\begin{aligned}
R_{XX}^{-1} - G_{XX}^{-1} &\equiv G_{XX}^{-1}(B_{XX}+C_{XX})R_{XX}^{-1},\\
B_{XX}^{-1} - G_{XX}^{-1} &\equiv G_{XX}^{-1}(R_{XX}+C_{XX})B_{XX}^{-1},\\
C_{XX}^{-1} - G_{XX}^{-1} &\equiv G_{XX}^{-1}(R_{XX}+B_{XX})C_{XX}^{-1},
\end{aligned}
$$

and (2.122)–(2.125) we find

$$
\begin{aligned}
\mathsf{V}(\widehat{\beta}_R|X) - \mathsf{V}(\widehat{\beta}|X) &= \sigma^2 G_{XX}^{-1}(B_{XX}+C_{XX})R_{XX}^{-1},\\
\mathsf{V}(\widehat{\beta}_B|X) - \mathsf{V}(\widehat{\beta}|X) &= \sigma^2 G_{XX}^{-1}(R_{XX}+C_{XX})B_{XX}^{-1},\\
\mathsf{V}(\widehat{\beta}_C|X) - \mathsf{V}(\widehat{\beta}|X) &= \sigma^2 G_{XX}^{-1}(R_{XX}+B_{XX})C_{XX}^{-1}.
\end{aligned}
$$

These matrix differences are positive definite whenever R_{XX}, B_{XX}, and C_{XX} have this property. This implies that in Model (2.110), $\widehat{\beta}$ is more efficient than either of $\widehat{\beta}_R$, $\widehat{\beta}_B$, and $\widehat{\beta}_C$, in the following sense. *any linear combination of the elements in* $\widehat{\beta}$*—of the form* $a'\widehat{\beta}$*, where* a *is a* $(K\times 1)$ *vector of constants, considered as an estimator of* $a'\beta$*—has a smaller variance than the corresponding linear combination for the three other estimators.* The proof is: positive definiteness of the difference matrices implies: $a'[\mathsf{V}(\widehat{\beta}_Z|X)-\mathsf{V}(\widehat{\beta}|X)]a > 0$, $(Z = B, C, R)$, for any $a \neq 0_{K,1}$. Therefore, since $\text{var}(a'\widehat{\beta}_Z|X) = a'\mathsf{V}(\widehat{\beta}_Z|X)a$,

$$
\text{var}(a'\widehat{\beta}_Z|X) > \text{var}(a'\widehat{\beta}), \quad \text{for any } a \neq 0_{K,1}, \; Z = B, C, R.
$$

In this sense, $\widehat{\beta}$ is more efficient than either of $\widehat{\beta}_R$, $\widehat{\beta}_B$, and $\widehat{\beta}_C$ as long as (i) both the intercept and the coefficient vector are common to all individuals (and periods) and (ii) R_{XX}, B_{XX}, and C_{XX} are all positive definite. The last assumption is normally satisfied if all regressors show residual variation as well as variation across individuals and periods. Frequently occurring situations where some regressors are individual-specific or period-specific are discussed in Chapter 5.

2.5 Testing for fixed heterogeneity

In this section we consider procedures for testing for the presence of fixed individual-specific intercept and coefficient heterogeneity (Section 2.5.1) and for testing for the presence of fixed individual-specific and time-specific intercept heterogeneity (Section 2.5.2).

A *general statistic* for testing a null hypothesis H_0 against the alternative hypothesis H_1—within a linear multiple regression model, assuming normally distributed disturbances, with one or more linear coefficient restrictions—can be written as, see Greene (2008, Section 5.3.3):

$$F_{01} = \frac{\dfrac{SSR_0 - SSR_1}{\text{Number of restrictions imposed under } H_0}}{\dfrac{SSR_1}{\text{Number of degrees of freedom under } H_1}}, \tag{2.130}$$

where SSR_0 and SSR_1 are the residual sum of squares under, respectively, H_0 and H_1. F_{01} has, under H_0, an F-distribution with numbers of degrees of freedom equal to 'Number of restrictions imposed under H_0' and 'Number of degrees of freedom under H_1'. We reject H_0 when F_{01} exceeds a certain quantile in this F-distribution. Here, 'Number of restrictions imposed under H_0' means the number of (linear) parameter restrictions we impose when going from H_1 to H_0, while 'Number of degrees of freedom under H_1' is the difference between the number of observations and the number of free coefficients (including the intercept) estimated under H_1.

2.5.1 ONE-WAY INTERCEPT AND COEFFICIENT HETEROGENEITY

Hypotheses of interest are:

H_{AI} : Full individual intercept and coefficient heterogeneity: $\alpha_1^*, \dots, \alpha_N^*$ and $\boldsymbol{\beta}_1, \dots, \boldsymbol{\beta}_N$ are unrestricted.

H_{BI} : Individual intercept heterogeneity, homogeneous coefficients: $\alpha_1^*, \dots, \alpha_N^*$ are unrestricted; $\boldsymbol{\beta}_1 = \cdots = \boldsymbol{\beta}_N = \boldsymbol{\beta}$.

H_C : Full homogeneity: $\alpha_1^* = \cdots = \alpha_N^* = \alpha$; $\boldsymbol{\beta}_1 = \cdots = \boldsymbol{\beta}_N = \boldsymbol{\beta}$.

Here H_{AI} corresponds to Model (2.23) (subscript I indicates *individual* heterogeneity). For all models we in addition assume that the disturbances are *normally distributed*, symbolized by $\boldsymbol{u}_i \sim \mathsf{IIN}(\boldsymbol{0}_{T,1}, \sigma^2 \boldsymbol{I}_T)$. The normality assumption ensures the validity of F-tests regardless of the size of N and T. The corresponding sums of squared residuals, $SSR = \sum_{i=1}^{N} \sum_{t=1}^{T} \widehat{u}_{it}^2$ ($\widehat{u}_{it}$ symbolizing OLS residuals), are SSR_{AI}, SSR_{BI}, and SSR_C. The statistic (2.130) leads to F-statistics for comparing H_{BI}, H_{AI}, and H_C. We have

$$\text{Number of (free) coefficients under} \quad \begin{aligned} H_{AI} &= N(K+1), \\ H_{BI} &= K+N, \\ H_C &= K+1. \end{aligned}$$

The relevant statistics for testing H_{BI} against H_{AI}, testing H_C against H_{BI}, and testing H_C against H_{AI} are, respectively,

$$F_{BI,AI} = \frac{SSR_{BI} - SSR_{AI}}{SSR_{AI}} \frac{N(T-K-1)}{K(N-1)}$$
$$\sim F[K(N-1), N(T-K-1)] \text{ under } H_{BI}.$$
$$F_{C,BI} = \frac{SSR_{C} - SSR_{BI}}{SSR_{BI}} \frac{N(T-1)-K}{N-1} \tag{2.131}$$
$$\sim F[N-1, N(T-1)-K] \text{ under } H_C. \tag{2.132}$$
$$F_{C,AI} = \frac{SSR_{C} - SSR_{AI}}{SSR_{AI}} \frac{N(T-K-1)}{(N-1)(K+1)}$$
$$\sim F[(N-1)(K+1), N(T-K-1)] \text{ under } H_C. \tag{2.133}$$

2.5.2 TWO-WAY INTERCEPT HETEROGENEITY

Hypotheses of interest are now (subscripts I and T indicate individual-specific and time-specific intercept heterogeneity, respectively):

H_{BIT} : Full individual-specific and time-specific heterogeneity: $\alpha_1, \dots, \alpha_N$ and $\gamma_1, \dots, \gamma_T$ unrestricted.

H_{BI} : Individual-specific intercept heterogeneity, homogeneity over periods: $\alpha_1, \dots, \alpha_N$ unrestricted; $\gamma_1 = \dots = \gamma_T = 0$.

H_{BT} : Time-specific intercept heterogeneity, homogeneity across individuals: $\alpha_1 = \dots = \alpha_N = 0$; $\gamma_1, \dots, \gamma_T$ unrestricted,

H_C : Full homogeneity: $\alpha_1 = \dots = \alpha_N = 0$; $\gamma_1 = \dots = \gamma_T = 0$.

Model H_{BIT} corresponds to (2.97). The corresponding sums of squared residuals are, respectively, SSR_{BIT}, SSR_{BI}, SSR_{BT}, and SSR_C. The general statistic (2.130) leads to F-statistics for comparing H_{BIT}, H_{BI}, H_{BT}, and H_C. We have

$$\text{Number of (free) coefficients under } \begin{array}{r} H_{BIT} = K + N + T - 1, \\ H_{BI} = K + N, \\ H_{BT} = K + T, \\ H_C = K + 1. \end{array}$$

The relevant statistics for testing, respectively, H_{BI} against H_{BIT} (homogeneity over periods, given heterogeneity across individuals), H_{BT} against H_{BIT} (homogeneity across individuals, given heterogeneity over periods), H_C against H_{BI} (homogeneity across individuals, given homogeneity over periods), H_C against H_{BT} (homogeneity over periods, given homogeneity across individuals), and H_C against H_{BIT} (full homogeneity against full two-way heterogeneity) therefore are, respectively,

$$F_{BI,BIT} = \frac{SSR_{BI}-SSR_{BIT}}{SSR_{BIT}} \frac{NT-K-N-T+1}{T-1}$$
$$\sim F[T-1, NT-K-N-T+1] \text{ under } H_{BI}, \tag{2.134}$$

$$F_{BT,BIT} = \frac{SSR_{BT}-SSR_{BIT}}{SSR_{BIT}} \frac{NT-K-N-T+1}{N-1}$$
$$\sim F[N-1, NT-K-N-T+1] \text{ under } H_{BT}, \tag{2.135}$$

$$F_{C,BI} = \frac{SSR_{C}-SSR_{BI}}{SSR_{BI}} \frac{NT-K-N}{N-1}$$
$$\sim F[N-1, NT-K-N] \text{ under } H_{C}, \tag{2.136}$$

$$F_{C,BT} = \frac{SSR_{C}-SSR_{BT}}{SSR_{BT}} \frac{NT-K-T}{T-1}$$
$$\sim F[T-1, NT-K-T] \text{ under } H_{C}, \tag{2.137}$$

$$F_{C,BIT} = \frac{SSR_{C}-SSR_{BIT}}{SSR_{BIT}} \frac{NT-K-N-T+1}{N+T-2}$$
$$\sim F[N+T-2, NT-K-N-T+1] \text{ under } H_{C}. \tag{2.138}$$

Appendix 2A. **Properties of GLS**

In this appendix, we consider, for models of different generality, properties of the GLS method which are useful for panel data regression models and are referred to in several chapters.

2A.1 The basic scalar case. Assume that N *observable* stochastic variables $\lambda_1, \dots, \lambda_N$ are available, satisfying

$$\lambda_i = \lambda + \theta_i, \qquad i = 1, \dots, N, \tag{2A.1}$$

where λ is an unknown constant, δ_{ij} is the Kronecker-delta, and

$$\mathsf{E}(\theta_i) = 0, \qquad \mathsf{E}(\theta_i\theta_j) = \delta_{ij}\omega_i, \qquad i,j = 1,\dots,N. \tag{2A.2}$$

The MVLUE of λ is

$$\widehat{\lambda} = \frac{\sum_{i=1}^{N}[\lambda_i/\omega_i]}{\sum_{i=1}^{N}[1/\omega_i]}, \tag{2A.3}$$

as it corresponds to estimating a constant by GLS (weighted regression). Its variance,

$$\text{var}(\widehat{\lambda}) = \frac{\sum_{i=1}^{N}\mathsf{E}[\theta_i/\omega_i]^2}{\left[\sum_{i=1}^{N}[1/\omega_i]\right]^2} = \frac{1}{\sum_{i=1}^{N}[1/\omega_i]}, \tag{2A.4}$$

is smaller than the variance of any unbiased estimator of λ constructed as a linear combination of $\lambda_1,\dots,\lambda_N$ with common expectation λ, i.e., an estimator of the form

$$\widetilde{\lambda} = \sum_{i=1}^{N} c_i\lambda_i, \qquad \text{with} \qquad \sum_{i=1}^{N} c_i = 1,$$

where $c_1,\dots,c_N$ are constants. Its variance is

$$\text{var}(\widetilde{\lambda}) = \sum_{i=1}^{N} c_i^2\omega_i.$$

The optimal choice of c_i is therefore

$$c_i = \frac{[1/\omega_i]}{\sum_{i=1}^{N}[1/\omega_i]}, \qquad i = 1,\dots,N.$$

Equations (2.9) and (2.10) exemplify application of (2A.1)–(2A.4) to the one-regressor model with common coefficient in Section 2.1.

2A.2 Generalization. Consider N *observable* $(K \times 1)$-vectors, $\boldsymbol{\lambda}_1,\dots,\boldsymbol{\lambda}_N$, satisfying

$$\boldsymbol{\lambda}_i = \boldsymbol{\lambda} + \boldsymbol{\theta}_i, \qquad i = 1,\dots,N, \tag{2A.5}$$

where $\boldsymbol{\lambda}$ is an *unknown constant vector* and

$$\mathsf{E}(\boldsymbol{\theta}_i) = \mathbf{0}_{K1}, \qquad \mathsf{E}(\boldsymbol{\theta}_i\boldsymbol{\theta}_j') = \delta_{ij}\boldsymbol{\Omega}_i, \qquad i,j = 1,\dots,N. \tag{2A.6}$$

The MVLUE of the K elements of $\boldsymbol{\lambda}$ is

$$\widehat{\boldsymbol{\lambda}} = [\textstyle\sum_{i=1}^{N} \boldsymbol{\Omega}_i^{-1}]^{-1}[\sum_{i=1}^{N} \boldsymbol{\Omega}_i^{-1}\boldsymbol{\lambda}_i]. \tag{2A.7}$$

This estimator is optimal in the following sense: the variance-minimizing linear unbiased estimator of any linear combination of the K elements of $\widehat{\boldsymbol{\lambda}}$s, i.e., of $\boldsymbol{a}'\boldsymbol{\lambda}$ (where $\boldsymbol{a}$ is an arbitrary $(1 \times K)$ vector of constants), is $\boldsymbol{a}'\widehat{\boldsymbol{\lambda}}$. Using this method corresponds to estimating a vector of constants by GLS. The estimator has covariance matrix

$$\mathsf{V}(\widehat{\boldsymbol{\lambda}}) = [\textstyle\sum_{i=1}^{N} \boldsymbol{\Omega}_i^{-1}]^{-1}. \tag{2A.8}$$

Combining (2A.8), (2A.5), and (2A.6), we obtain

$$\mathsf{V}(\widehat{\boldsymbol{\lambda}})^{-1} = \textstyle\sum_{i=1}^{N} \mathsf{V}(\boldsymbol{\lambda}_i)^{-1}. \tag{2A.9}$$

An alternative linear combination of $\boldsymbol{\lambda}_1, \dots, \boldsymbol{\lambda}_N$, with expectation $\boldsymbol{\lambda}$, has the form

$$\widetilde{\boldsymbol{\lambda}} = \textstyle\sum_{i=1}^{N} \boldsymbol{C}_i\boldsymbol{\lambda}_i, \qquad \text{with} \qquad \sum_{i=1}^{N} \boldsymbol{C}_i = \boldsymbol{I}_K,$$

where $\boldsymbol{C}_1, \dots, \boldsymbol{C}_N$ are $(K \times K)$-matrices. Its covariance matrix is

$$\mathsf{V}(\widetilde{\boldsymbol{\lambda}}) = \textstyle\sum_{i=1}^{N} \boldsymbol{C}_i\boldsymbol{\Omega}_i\boldsymbol{C}_i'.$$

It can be shown that the difference matrix $\mathsf{V}(\widetilde{\boldsymbol{\lambda}}) - \mathsf{V}(\widehat{\boldsymbol{\lambda}})$ is positive semi-definite. The optimal choice of $\boldsymbol{C}_i$ is consequently

$$\boldsymbol{C}_i = [\textstyle\sum_{i=1}^{N} \boldsymbol{\Omega}_i^{-1}]^{-1}\boldsymbol{\Omega}_i^{-1}, \qquad i = 1, \dots, N. \tag{2A.10}$$

Equations (2.34) and (2.35) exemplify application of (2A.5)–(2A.8) to the multiple regression model with common coefficient vector in Section 2.2.

2A.3 Regression equation system with unrestricted coefficients. We next consider a system of N regression equations, with T observations and K regressor variables (including intercept),

$$\boldsymbol{q}_i = \boldsymbol{Z}_i\boldsymbol{\mu}_i + \boldsymbol{v}_i, \qquad i = 1, \dots, N, \tag{2A.11}$$

where $\boldsymbol{q}_i$ is a $(T \times 1)$-vector of observations, $\boldsymbol{Z}_i$ is a $(T \times K)$ matrix of observations, $\boldsymbol{\mu}_i$ is the corresponding $(K \times 1)$ coefficient vector, and $\boldsymbol{v}_i$ is a $(T \times 1)$-vector of disturbances, satisfying

$$\mathsf{E}(v_i) = 0_{T1}, \qquad \mathsf{E}(v_i v_j') = \delta_{ij}\Sigma_i, \qquad i,j = 1,\dots,N. \tag{2A.12}$$

If $\mu_1,\dots,\mu_N$ are unrestricted, we know that

$$\widehat{\mu}_i = [Z_i'\Sigma_i^{-1}Z_i]^{-1}[Z_i'\Sigma_i^{-1}q_i], \qquad i = 1,\dots,N, \tag{2A.13}$$

is the MVLUE of μ_i. From (2A.11)–(2A.13) it follows that its covariance matrix is

$$\mathsf{V}(\widehat{\mu}_i|Z) = [Z_i'\Sigma_i^{-1}Z_i]^{-1}, \qquad i = 1,\dots,N. \tag{2A.14}$$

It can be shown that each element in $\widehat{\mu}_i$ has a variance which is smaller than the variance of any other unbiased estimator of the corresponding element in μ_i constructed as a linear combination of the elements in q_i with expectation (conditional on Z_i) equal to $Z_i\mu_i$, i.e., an estimator of the form

$$\widetilde{\mu}_i = G_i q_i \quad \text{with} \quad G_i Z_i = I_K, \qquad i = 1,\dots,N,$$

where G_i is an arbitrary $(K \times T)$ matrix of constants. Equations (2.26) and (2.28) exemplify the application of (2A.13)–(2A.14) to the multiple regression model with individual-specific coefficient vector:

$$(q_i, Z_i, \mu_i, \widehat{\mu}_i, v_i, \Sigma_i) \quad \text{correspond to} \quad (B_T y_i, B_T X_i, \beta_i, \widehat{\beta}_i, u_i, I_T).$$

2A.4 Regression equation system with common coefficients. We still assume (2A.11)–(2A.12), but now impose $\mu_1 = \cdots = \mu_N = \mu$. Utilizing this restriction and combining the N equations (2A.11), we get the following equation system in partitioned form:

$$\begin{bmatrix} q_1 \\ \vdots \\ q_N \end{bmatrix} = \begin{bmatrix} Z_1 \\ \vdots \\ Z_N \end{bmatrix} \mu + \begin{bmatrix} v_1 \\ \vdots \\ v_N \end{bmatrix}, \tag{2A.15}$$

or, in compact notation,

$$q = Z\mu + v. \tag{2A.16}$$

It follows from (2A.12) that v has a block-diagonal $(NT \times NT)$ covariance matrix of the form $\Sigma = \text{diag}\,[\Sigma_1, \cdots, \Sigma_N]$, and its inverse is therefore also block-diagonal, $\Sigma^{-1} = \text{diag}\,[\Sigma_1^{-1}, \cdots, \Sigma_N^{-1}]$.

The GLS estimator of the common coefficient vector $\boldsymbol{\mu}$ can be written as

$$\widehat{\boldsymbol{\mu}} = [\mathbf{Z}'\boldsymbol{\Sigma}^{-1}\mathbf{Z}]^{-1}[\mathbf{Z}'\boldsymbol{\Sigma}^{-1}\boldsymbol{q}] = [\textstyle\sum_{i=1}^{N} \mathbf{Z}_i'\boldsymbol{\Sigma}_i^{-1}\mathbf{Z}_i]^{-1}[\textstyle\sum_{i=1}^{N} \mathbf{Z}_i'\boldsymbol{\Sigma}_i^{-1}\boldsymbol{q}_i]. \tag{2A.17}$$

Since (2A.13) implies that $\mathbf{Z}_i'\boldsymbol{\Sigma}_i^{-1}\boldsymbol{q}_i = \mathbf{Z}_i'\boldsymbol{\Sigma}_i^{-1}\mathbf{Z}_i\widehat{\boldsymbol{\mu}}_i$, which inserted into (2A.17) yields

$$\widehat{\boldsymbol{\mu}} = [\textstyle\sum_{i=1}^{N} \mathbf{Z}_i'\boldsymbol{\Sigma}_i^{-1}\mathbf{Z}_i]^{-1}[\textstyle\sum_{i=1}^{N} \mathbf{Z}_i'\boldsymbol{\Sigma}_i^{-1}\mathbf{Z}_i\widehat{\boldsymbol{\mu}}_i], \tag{2A.18}$$

the common GLS estimator $\widehat{\boldsymbol{\mu}}$ for $\boldsymbol{\mu}$ in (2A.15) emerges as a matrix weighted average of the equation-specific estimators $\widehat{\boldsymbol{\mu}}_1, \dots, \widehat{\boldsymbol{\mu}}_N$ for $\boldsymbol{\mu}_1, \dots, \boldsymbol{\mu}_N$ in (2A.11). Equation (2A.18) has the form

$$\widehat{\boldsymbol{\mu}} = \textstyle\sum_{i=1}^{N} \mathbf{D}_i\widehat{\boldsymbol{\mu}}_i, \tag{2A.19}$$

where

$$\mathbf{D}_i = [\textstyle\sum_{j=1}^{N} \mathbf{Z}_j'\boldsymbol{\Sigma}_i^{-1}\mathbf{Z}_i]^{-1}[\mathbf{Z}_i'\boldsymbol{\Sigma}_i^{-1}\mathbf{Z}_i], \qquad i = 1, \dots, N. \tag{2A.20}$$

In the special case where $\mathbf{Z}_i$ is the identity matrix, (2A.18) can be simplified to expressions of the same form as (2A.7):

$$(\widehat{\boldsymbol{\mu}}, \widehat{\boldsymbol{\mu}}_i, \boldsymbol{\Sigma}_i) \text{ with } \mathbf{Z}_i = \mathbf{I}_K \text{ correspond to } (\widehat{\boldsymbol{\lambda}}, \boldsymbol{\lambda}_i, \boldsymbol{\Omega}_i).$$

From (2A.14) and (2A.18) we find that the covariance matrix of this model is

$$\mathsf{V}(\widehat{\boldsymbol{\mu}}|\mathbf{Z}) = [\mathbf{Z}'\boldsymbol{\Sigma}^{-1}\mathbf{Z}]^{-1} = [\textstyle\sum_{i=1}^{N} \mathbf{Z}_i'\boldsymbol{\Sigma}_i^{-1}\mathbf{Z}_i]^{-1}. \tag{2A.21}$$

Combining (2A.21) with (2A.14), we get a remarkable relationship between the covariance matrices of the 'common' estimator $\widehat{\boldsymbol{\mu}}$ and the equation-specific estimators $\widehat{\boldsymbol{\mu}}_1, \dots, \widehat{\boldsymbol{\mu}}_N$:

$$\mathsf{V}(\widehat{\boldsymbol{\mu}}|\mathbf{Z})^{-1} = \textstyle\sum_{i=1}^{N} \mathsf{V}(\widehat{\boldsymbol{\mu}}_i|\mathbf{Z})^{-1}. \tag{2A.22}$$

This equation generalizes (2A.9).

We can also interpret this model as a subcase of the model in Section 2A.2: inserting for $\boldsymbol{q}_i$ from (2A.15) in (2A.13) we find that the relationship between $\widehat{\boldsymbol{\mu}}_i$ and $\boldsymbol{\mu}$ can be written as

$$\widehat{\mu}_i = \mu + \psi_i, \qquad i = 1, \dots, N, \tag{2A.23}$$

where

$$\psi_i = [\textstyle\sum_{i=1}^{N} Z_i'\Sigma_i^{-1}Z_i]^{-1}[Z_i'\Sigma_i^{-1}v_i], \tag{2A.24}$$

$$\mathsf{V}(\psi_i|X) = Z_i'\Sigma_i^{-1}Z_i, \qquad i = 1, \dots, N. \tag{2A.25}$$

Equation (2A.23), with ψ_i given by (2A.24) has the same form as (2A.5):

$$(\widehat{\mu}_i, \mu, \widehat{\mu}, \psi_i, Z_i'\Sigma_i^{-1}Z_i) \text{ correspond to } (\lambda_i, \lambda, \widehat{\lambda}, \theta_i, \Omega_i).$$

Appendix 2B. **Kronecker-product operations: Examples**

This appendix contains numerical examples illustrating the use of Kronecker-products. Consider the first four examples in Section 2.4.2 for $N = 3$, $T = 2$ and some implications:

$$I_3 \otimes A_2 = \begin{bmatrix} \frac{1}{2} & \frac{1}{2} & 0 & 0 & 0 & 0 \\ \frac{1}{2} & \frac{1}{2} & 0 & 0 & 0 & 0 \\ 0 & 0 & \frac{1}{2} & \frac{1}{2} & 0 & 0 \\ 0 & 0 & \frac{1}{2} & \frac{1}{2} & 0 & 0 \\ 0 & 0 & 0 & 0 & \frac{1}{2} & \frac{1}{2} \\ 0 & 0 & 0 & 0 & \frac{1}{2} & \frac{1}{2} \end{bmatrix}, \tag{2B.1}$$

$$I_3 \otimes B_2 = \begin{bmatrix} \frac{1}{2} & -\frac{1}{2} & 0 & 0 & 0 & 0 \\ -\frac{1}{2} & \frac{1}{2} & 0 & 0 & 0 & 0 \\ 0 & 0 & \frac{1}{2} & -\frac{1}{2} & 0 & 0 \\ 0 & 0 & -\frac{1}{2} & \frac{1}{2} & 0 & 0 \\ 0 & 0 & 0 & 0 & \frac{1}{2} & -\frac{1}{2} \\ 0 & 0 & 0 & 0 & -\frac{1}{2} & \frac{1}{2} \end{bmatrix}, \tag{2B.2}$$

$$\begin{aligned} (I_3 \otimes A_2) + (I_3 \otimes B_2) &= (I_3 \otimes (A_2 + B_2)) = (I_3 \otimes I_2) = I_6, \\ (I_3 \otimes B_2) + (I_3 \otimes A_2) &= (I_3 \otimes (B_2 + A_2)) = (I_3 \otimes I_2) = I_6, \\ (I_3 \otimes A_2)(I_3 \otimes B_2) &= ((I_3I_3) \otimes (A_2B_2)) = (I_3 \otimes 0_{2,2}) = 0_{6,6}, \\ (I_3 \otimes B_2)(I_3 \otimes A_2) &= ((I_3I_3) \otimes (B_2A_2)) = (I_3 \otimes 0_{2,2}) = 0_{6,6}. \end{aligned} \tag{2B.3}$$

$$A_3 \otimes I_2 = \begin{bmatrix} \frac{1}{3} & 0 & \frac{1}{3} & 0 & \frac{1}{3} & 0 \\ 0 & \frac{1}{3} & 0 & \frac{1}{3} & 0 & \frac{1}{3} \\ \frac{1}{3} & 0 & \frac{1}{3} & 0 & \frac{1}{3} & 0 \\ 0 & \frac{1}{3} & 0 & \frac{1}{3} & 0 & \frac{1}{3} \\ \frac{1}{3} & 0 & \frac{1}{3} & 0 & \frac{1}{3} & 0 \\ 0 & \frac{1}{3} & 0 & \frac{1}{3} & 0 & \frac{1}{3} \end{bmatrix}, \tag{2B.4}$$

$$B_3 \otimes I_2 = \begin{bmatrix} \frac{2}{3} & 0 & -\frac{1}{3} & 0 & -\frac{1}{3} & 0 \\ 0 & \frac{2}{3} & 0 & -\frac{1}{3} & 0 & -\frac{1}{3} \\ -\frac{1}{3} & 0 & \frac{2}{3} & 0 & -\frac{1}{3} & 0 \\ 0 & -\frac{1}{3} & 0 & \frac{2}{3} & 0 & -\frac{1}{3} \\ -\frac{1}{3} & 0 & -\frac{1}{3} & 0 & \frac{2}{3} & 0 \\ 0 & -\frac{1}{3} & 0 & -\frac{1}{3} & 0 & \frac{2}{3} \end{bmatrix}, \tag{2B.5}$$

$$(A_3 \otimes I_2) + (B_3 \otimes I_2) = ((A_3 + B_3) \otimes I_2) = (I_3 \otimes I_2) = I_6, \tag{2B.6}$$

$$(B_3 \otimes I_2) + (A_3 \otimes I_2) = ((B_3 + A_3) \otimes I_2) = (I_3 \otimes I_2) = I_6, \tag{2B.7}$$

$$(A_3 \otimes I_2)(B_3 \otimes I_2) = ((A_3B_3) \otimes (I_2I_2)) = (0_{3,3} \otimes I_2) = 0_{6,6}, \tag{2B.8}$$

$$(B_3 \otimes I_2)(A_3 \otimes I_2) = ((B_3A_3) \otimes (I_2I_2)) = (0_{3,3} \otimes I_2) = 0_{6,6}. \tag{2B.9}$$

Kronecker-products *are not commutative.* For example:

$$(A_3 \otimes I_2) = \begin{bmatrix} \frac{1}{3} & \frac{1}{3} & \frac{1}{3} & 0 & 0 & 0 \\ \frac{1}{3} & \frac{1}{3} & \frac{1}{3} & 0 & 0 & 0 \\ \frac{1}{3} & \frac{1}{3} & \frac{1}{3} & 0 & 0 & 0 \\ 0 & 0 & 0 & \frac{1}{3} & \frac{1}{3} & \frac{1}{3} \\ 0 & 0 & 0 & \frac{1}{3} & \frac{1}{3} & \frac{1}{3} \\ 0 & 0 & 0 & \frac{1}{3} & \frac{1}{3} & \frac{1}{3} \end{bmatrix} \neq I_2 \otimes A_3.$$

Kronecker-products of A- and B-matrices are exemplified by

$$A_3 \otimes A_2 = \begin{bmatrix} \frac{1}{6} & \frac{1}{6} & \frac{1}{6} & \frac{1}{6} & \frac{1}{6} & \frac{1}{6} \\ \frac{1}{6} & \frac{1}{6} & \frac{1}{6} & \frac{1}{6} & \frac{1}{6} & \frac{1}{6} \\ \frac{1}{6} & \frac{1}{6} & \frac{1}{6} & \frac{1}{6} & \frac{1}{6} & \frac{1}{6} \\ \frac{1}{6} & \frac{1}{6} & \frac{1}{6} & \frac{1}{6} & \frac{1}{6} & \frac{1}{6} \\ \frac{1}{6} & \frac{1}{6} & \frac{1}{6} & \frac{1}{6} & \frac{1}{6} & \frac{1}{6} \\ \frac{1}{6} & \frac{1}{6} & \frac{1}{6} & \frac{1}{6} & \frac{1}{6} & \frac{1}{6} \end{bmatrix}, \tag{2B.10}$$

$$B_3 \otimes A_2 = \begin{bmatrix} \frac{1}{3} & \frac{1}{3} & -\frac{1}{6} & -\frac{1}{6} & -\frac{1}{6} & -\frac{1}{6} \\ \frac{1}{3} & \frac{1}{3} & -\frac{1}{6} & -\frac{1}{6} & -\frac{1}{6} & -\frac{1}{6} \\ -\frac{1}{6} & -\frac{1}{6} & \frac{1}{3} & \frac{1}{3} & -\frac{1}{6} & -\frac{1}{6} \\ -\frac{1}{6} & -\frac{1}{6} & \frac{1}{3} & \frac{1}{3} & -\frac{1}{6} & -\frac{1}{6} \\ -\frac{1}{6} & -\frac{1}{6} & -\frac{1}{6} & -\frac{1}{6} & \frac{1}{3} & \frac{1}{3} \\ -\frac{1}{6} & -\frac{1}{6} & -\frac{1}{6} & -\frac{1}{6} & \frac{1}{3} & \frac{1}{3} \end{bmatrix}, \tag{2B.11}$$

$$A_3 \otimes B_2 = \begin{bmatrix} \frac{1}{6} & -\frac{1}{6} & \frac{1}{6} & -\frac{1}{6} & \frac{1}{6} & -\frac{1}{6} \\ -\frac{1}{6} & \frac{1}{6} & -\frac{1}{6} & \frac{1}{6} & -\frac{1}{6} & \frac{1}{6} \\ \frac{1}{6} & -\frac{1}{6} & \frac{1}{6} & -\frac{1}{6} & \frac{1}{6} & -\frac{1}{6} \\ -\frac{1}{6} & \frac{1}{6} & -\frac{1}{6} & \frac{1}{6} & -\frac{1}{6} & \frac{1}{6} \\ \frac{1}{6} & -\frac{1}{6} & \frac{1}{6} & -\frac{1}{6} & \frac{1}{6} & -\frac{1}{6} \\ -\frac{1}{6} & \frac{1}{6} & -\frac{1}{6} & \frac{1}{6} & -\frac{1}{6} & \frac{1}{6} \end{bmatrix}, \tag{2B.12}$$

$$B_3 \otimes B_2 = \begin{bmatrix} \frac{1}{3} & -\frac{1}{3} & -\frac{1}{6} & \frac{1}{6} & -\frac{1}{6} & \frac{1}{6} \\ -\frac{1}{3} & \frac{1}{3} & \frac{1}{6} & -\frac{1}{6} & \frac{1}{6} & -\frac{1}{6} \\ -\frac{1}{6} & \frac{1}{6} & \frac{1}{3} & -\frac{1}{3} & -\frac{1}{6} & \frac{1}{6} \\ \frac{1}{6} & -\frac{1}{6} & -\frac{1}{3} & \frac{1}{3} & \frac{1}{6} & -\frac{1}{6} \\ -\frac{1}{6} & \frac{1}{6} & -\frac{1}{6} & \frac{1}{6} & \frac{1}{3} & -\frac{1}{3} \\ \frac{1}{6} & -\frac{1}{6} & \frac{1}{6} & -\frac{1}{6} & -\frac{1}{3} & \frac{1}{3} \end{bmatrix}. \tag{2B.13}$$

Adding (2B.10) and (2B.11) and comparing with (2B.1), adding (2B.12) and (2B.13) and comparing with (2B.2), adding (2B.10) and (2B.12) and comparing with (2B.4), and adding (2B.11) and (2B.13) and comparing with (2B.5), we find, respectively,

$$\begin{aligned} (A_3 \otimes A_2) + (B_3 \otimes A_2) &= I_3 \otimes A_2, \\ (A_3 \otimes B_2) + (B_3 \otimes B_2) &= I_3 \otimes B_2, \\ (A_3 \otimes A_2) + (A_3 \otimes B_2) &= A_3 \otimes I_2, \\ (B_3 \otimes A_2) + (B_3 \otimes B_2) &= B_3 \otimes I_2. \end{aligned}$$

Adding (2B.10)–(2B.13), we find

$$\begin{aligned} &(A_3 \otimes A_2) + (B_3 \otimes A_2) + (A_3 \otimes B_2) + (B_3 \otimes B_2) \\ &\quad = ((A_3 + B_3) \otimes A_2) + ((A_3 + B_3) \otimes B_2) \\ &\quad = (I_3 \otimes (A_2 + B_2)) = (I_3 \otimes I_2) = I_6. \end{aligned}$$

The addition and multiplication rules (2.79)–(2.80) are exemplified by: multiplying (2B.1) and (2B.4) and comparing with (2B.10); multiplying (2B.2) and (2B.4) and comparing with (2B.12); multiplying (2B.1) and (2B.5) and comparing with (2B.11); and multiplying (2B.2) and (2B.5) and comparing with (2B.13). We find, respectively,

$$(I_3 \otimes A_2)(A_3 \otimes I_2) = (A_3 \otimes A_2),$$
$$(I_3 \otimes B_2)(A_3 \otimes I_2) = (A_3 \otimes B_2),$$
$$(I_3 \otimes A_2)(B_3 \otimes I_2) = (B_3 \otimes A_2),$$
$$(I_3 \otimes B_2)(B_3 \otimes I_2) = (B_3 \otimes B_2).$$

3 Regression analysis: Random effects models

CHAPTER SUMMARY

Regression equations with random intercept heterogeneity are considered. Compared with Chapter 2, assumptions are strengthened. First, we consider one-way disturbance component models, representing only unspecified individual differences not captured by the specified regressors, next, two-way disturbance component models, also representing period-specific differences not captured by the specified regressors. This gives a disturbance structure with variance components, which invites estimation by GLS or ML. Estimation of the variance components from residuals is explained, as is also testing for random heterogeneity. Extensions allowing for heteroskedastic or autocorrelated disturbances, including test procedures, are presented. Empirical examples, *inter alia*, contrasting fixed and random effects specifications, are given.

Also this chapter will deal with single-equation regression models with heterogeneous intercepts. Heterogeneity will be represented by *random variables* with specific properties. This imposes stronger restrictions than the fixed effects models in Chapter 2, where virtually no assumption was made about the heterogeneity pattern. This has both its pros and cons. Heterogeneity in the form of varying disturbance spread, heteroskedasticity, and disturbance serial correlation are also worth considering.

This chapter has two parts. The first part (Sections 3.1–3.4) deals with models allowing for unobserved spatial heterogeneity. The models then become *one-way disturbance component models*, the disturbance term being the sum of an individual-specific component and a 'classical' disturbance. The resulting *gross disturbances* get properties different from the classical ones: the variance is the sum of the variances of its components, and several covariances are positive (Section 3.1). The *GLS* method ensures MVLUE. We first consider GLS when the variance components are known, and compare it with OLS and within and between estimation (Section 3.2). Next, we consider estimation of the variance components, leading to the Feasible GLS (FGLS) estimators of the slope coefficients (Section 3.3), before we, finally, take a step into *Maximum Likelihood (ML)*, estimating simultaneously the coefficients and the variance components (Section 3.4). Ways of testing for the occurrence of random individual-specific effects are also discussed.

The second part of the chapter (Sections 3.5–3.8) deals with models also allowing for unobserved temporal heterogeneity. The models then become *two-way disturbance component models*, the disturbance term being the sum of an individual-specific component, a period-specific component, and a 'classical' disturbance. An implication is that correlation prevails between all gross disturbances from the same individual and between all gross disturbances from the same period (Section 3.5). There are stronger deviations from the assumptions in classical regression analysis. Again, GLS, in a more complex version, assuming that the variance components are known, gives MVLUE. The coefficient estimator is compared with alternatives (Section 3.6). We next discuss estimation of the variance components, which takes us to the FGLS estimators (Section 3.7). Again, we finally outline joint estimation, by ML, of the regression coefficient vector and the variance components (Section 3.8). Testing for the occurrence of unobserved random two-way intercept heterogeneity is also discussed.

However, *mixing random and fixed heterogeneity* is sometimes worth considering, for example, to treat individual effects as random and time effects as fixed. Interpreting the former as draws from a 'population of individual effects' may seem more sensible than interpreting the latter as draws from a 'population of time effects'. That time periods, unlike persons, firms, and geographical units, have a natural ordering is an argument drawing in the same direction.[1]

3.1 One-way variance component model

The fixed effects model in Chapter 2 imposed no restrictions on the intercepts, $\alpha_1^*, \dots, \alpha_N^*$. We might consider them as representing specific properties of the *sample* of units observed, often a random sample, and a purpose of the analysis may be to estimate them. If we have a moderate number of identifiable units, say countries or regions in a country, we may well attach specific interest to these N intercepts, and then the fixed effects approach may be considered appropriate. On the other hand, if N is large, say representing 10000 persons, we would get 10000 intercept estimates and could test whether there is significant heterogeneity, as discussed in Appendix 2A. What else might these $N = 10000$ individual (unit) specific estimates tell us? We may be invited to perform a *data reduction*, for example, to compute the empirical mean and variance, or the quantiles, of the $\widehat{\alpha}_i^*$s. Making no other assumptions, we might get no further.

3.1.1 BASIC MODEL

Here random heterogeneity comes into play. We consider $\alpha_1^*, \dots, \alpha_N^*$ as realizations of N independent draws from a probability distribution which characterizes the *population*

[1] If, however, the 'second dimension' is not calendar time, modelling heterogeneity symmetrically along the two dimensions of the panel may raise few objections.

from which the N individuals, say households or firms, are selected. The regression equation is

$$y_{it} = \alpha_i^* + \boldsymbol{x}_{it}\boldsymbol{\beta} + u_{it}, \qquad i = 1,\dots,N;\ t = 1,\dots,T,$$

where $\boldsymbol{x}_{it} = (x_{1it},\dots,x_{Kit})$ contains the observations on the K regressors from individual i in period t, and $\boldsymbol{\beta} = (\beta_1,\dots,\beta_K)'$ is its coefficient vector, common to all individuals. The individual-specific intercepts, α_i^*, satisfy

$$\mathsf{E}(\alpha_i^*|X)=k,\ \text{var}(\alpha_i^*|X)=\sigma_\alpha^2,\ \text{cov}(\alpha_i^*,\alpha_j^*|X)=0\ (i\neq j);\ \ i,j=1,\dots,N,$$

where k and σ_α^2 are unknown constants and X symbolizes all values of $\boldsymbol{x}_{it}$ in the data set. Choosing this formulation instead of that in Section 2.2.2, we reduce the number of unknown parameters describing the individual-specific intercepts from N to two: the expectation k and the variance σ_α^2. We economize on the number of unknown parameters as compared with using fixed individual-specific effects, and the reduction is substantial since N will often be large.

Letting $\alpha_i=\alpha_i^*-\mathsf{E}(\alpha_i^*)=\alpha_i^*-k$, the *model with K regressors, stochastic individual-specific effects*, and disturbance homoskedasticity reads:[2]

$$\begin{aligned}&y_{it}=k+\boldsymbol{x}_{it}\boldsymbol{\beta}+\alpha_i+u_{it}=k+\boldsymbol{x}_{it}\boldsymbol{\beta}+\epsilon_{it},\ \epsilon_{it}=\alpha_i+u_{it},\\&(u_{it}|X)\sim\mathsf{IID}(0,\sigma^2),\ \ (\alpha_i|X)\sim\mathsf{IID}(0,\sigma_\alpha^2),\ \ u_{it}\perp\alpha_i,\\&i=1,\dots,N;t=1,\dots,T,\end{aligned}\tag{3.1}$$

where $\perp$ denotes 'orthogonal to' and ϵ_{it} can be interpreted as a composite, *gross disturbance*, generated by one simple random draw for individual i and one random draw made repeatedly for individual i in each period.

3.1.2 SOME IMPLICATIONS

This kind of regression model is denoted as a *disturbance component, or error component, model*. It implies that two ϵ_{it}s from the same individual have the same covariance and correlation regardless of the time distance between them: $\text{cov}(\epsilon_{it},\epsilon_{is}|X) = \text{var}(\alpha_i|X) = \sigma_\alpha^2$, $t\neq s$, sometimes denoted as *equi-correlation*: $\text{corr}(\epsilon_{it},\epsilon_{is}|X) = \rho = \sigma_\alpha^2/(\sigma_\alpha^2+\sigma^2)$, $t\neq s$. The components α_i and u_{it} have variances σ_α^2 and σ^2, respectively, of which the first may also be interpreted as a covariance.

[2] The notation '$u_{it}\perp\alpha_i$' is strictly a bit imprecise, but will be used for convenience in the following to denote that *any* u_{it} and α_j $(i,j = 1,\dots,N;\ t = 1,\dots,T)$ are uncorrelated.

Since the α_is are uncorrelated, *we cannot impose an adding-up restriction,* $\sum_{i=1}^{N} \alpha_i = 0$, as in the fixed effects model. In the latter, we could set the average intercept equal to $k = \frac{1}{N}\sum_{i=1}^{N} \alpha_i^* = \bar{\alpha}^*$ and define the individual-specific effects as $\alpha_i = \alpha_i^* - k$. Zero *expectation* $\mathsf{E}(\alpha_i|X)$ in the *random* effects model has its counterpart in zero *average* $\bar{\alpha} = \frac{1}{N}\sum_{i=1}^{N} \alpha_i$ in the *fixed* effects model. For both, the regression equation has a composite intercept $k+\alpha_i = \alpha_i^*$, where

$$\begin{array}{lll} \textit{in the random effects case:} & \alpha_i = \alpha_i^* - \mathsf{E}(\alpha_i^*|X), & k = \mathsf{E}(\alpha_i^*|X), \\ \textit{in the fixed effects case:} & \alpha_i = \alpha_i^* - \bar{\alpha}^*, & k = \bar{\alpha}^*. \end{array}$$

The stacked equation for individual i, $\boldsymbol{e}_T$ being the $(T\times 1)$-vector of ones, is

$$\boldsymbol{y}_i = \boldsymbol{e}_T k + \boldsymbol{X}_i \boldsymbol{\beta} + \boldsymbol{\epsilon}_i, \quad \boldsymbol{\epsilon}_i = \boldsymbol{e}_T \alpha_i + \boldsymbol{u}_i, \qquad i = 1, \dots, N.$$

It follows from (3.1) that $\boldsymbol{\epsilon}_1, \dots, \boldsymbol{\epsilon}_N$ are uncorrelated, with

$$\mathsf{V}(\boldsymbol{\epsilon}_i|X) \equiv \mathsf{E}(\boldsymbol{\epsilon}_i \boldsymbol{\epsilon}_i'|X) = \sigma_\alpha^2(\boldsymbol{e}_T \boldsymbol{e}_T') + \sigma^2 \boldsymbol{I}_T.$$

Compactly, Model (3.1) can therefore be written as

$$\boldsymbol{y}_i = \boldsymbol{e}_T k + \boldsymbol{X}_i \boldsymbol{\beta} + \boldsymbol{\epsilon}_i, \;\; (\boldsymbol{\epsilon}_i|X) \sim \mathsf{IID}(\boldsymbol{0}_{T,1}, \boldsymbol{\Omega}_T), \;\; i = 1, \dots, N, \tag{3.2}$$

where

$$\boldsymbol{\Omega}_T = \sigma_\alpha^2(\boldsymbol{e}_T \boldsymbol{e}_T') + \sigma^2 \boldsymbol{I}_T = \begin{bmatrix} \sigma_\alpha^2 + \sigma^2 & \sigma_\alpha^2 & \dots & \sigma_\alpha^2 \\ \sigma_\alpha^2 & \sigma_\alpha^2 + \sigma^2 & \dots & \sigma_\alpha^2 \\ \vdots & \vdots & \ddots & \vdots \\ \sigma_\alpha^2 & \sigma_\alpha^2 & \dots & \sigma_\alpha^2 + \sigma^2 \end{bmatrix}. \tag{3.3}$$

This kind of model is often denoted as a *variance component model*. All elements outside the main diagonal of $\boldsymbol{\Omega}_T$ being equal to σ_α^2.

3.2 **GLS with known variance components**

3.2.1 THE GLS PROBLEM AND ITS REFORMULATION

We first assume that σ_α^2 and σ^2 are *known*. This is a rigid assumption which will later (Section 3.3) be relaxed. Since the disturbance covariance matrix is not diagonal, it is GLS which gives MVLUE. To explain the derivation of the estimators we proceed stepwise, first state the minimization problem, next describe a reformulation of the GLS problem to eliminate the intercept, and finally explain how the GLS problem can be solved as an OLS problem in transformed variables. The GLS problem is

$$\min_{k,\boldsymbol{\beta}} \sum_{i=1}^{N} (y_i - e_T k - X_i\boldsymbol{\beta})' \boldsymbol{\Omega}_T^{-1} (y_i - e_T k - X_i\boldsymbol{\beta}) = \min_{k,\boldsymbol{\beta}} \sum_{i=1}^{N} \epsilon_i' \boldsymbol{\Omega}_T^{-1} \epsilon_i.$$

Let $\epsilon = (\epsilon_1', \dots, \epsilon_N')'$, $y = (y_1', \dots, y_N')'$, $X = (X_1', \dots, X_N')'$, where, from (3.2), $\mathsf{V}(\epsilon|X) = \boldsymbol{\Omega} = I_N \otimes \boldsymbol{\Omega}_T$.[3] The GLS problem can then be reformulated as

$$\min_{k,\boldsymbol{\beta}} [y - (e_N \otimes e_T)k - X\boldsymbol{\beta}]' [I_N \otimes \boldsymbol{\Omega}_T^{-1}] [y - (e_N \otimes e_T)k - X\boldsymbol{\beta}]. \tag{3.4}$$

Its solution involves two theorems, proved in Appendix 3A. They relate to the inversion of a specific class of matrices, which $\boldsymbol{\Omega}_T^{-1}$ exemplifies, and to the estimation of the intercept in a class of regression equations.

We use the theorem Appendix 3A, Section 3A.1, rewrite (3.3) as[4]

$$\boldsymbol{\Omega}_T = \boldsymbol{\Omega}_T(\sigma^2, \sigma_\alpha^2) = \sigma^2 \boldsymbol{B}_T + (\sigma^2 + T\sigma_\alpha^2)\boldsymbol{A}_T, \tag{3.5}$$

and obtain, since $\boldsymbol{A}_T$ and $\boldsymbol{B}_T$ are symmetric, idempotent, and orthogonal,

$$\boldsymbol{\Omega}_T^{-1} = \frac{\boldsymbol{B}_T}{\sigma^2} + \frac{\boldsymbol{A}_T}{\sigma^2 + T\sigma_\alpha^2} \equiv \sigma^{-2}[\boldsymbol{B}_T + \theta_B \boldsymbol{A}_T], \tag{3.6}$$

where

$$\theta_B = \frac{\sigma^2}{\sigma^2 + T\sigma_\alpha^2} \equiv \frac{1-\rho}{1+(T-1)\rho}. \tag{3.7}$$

Since $e_T'\boldsymbol{B}_T = \boldsymbol{0}$, $e_T'\boldsymbol{A}_T = e_T'$ and hence $e_T'\boldsymbol{\Omega}_T^{-1} = \sigma^{-2}\theta_B e_T' \Longrightarrow e_{NT}'\boldsymbol{\Omega}^{-1} = (e_N' \otimes e_T')(I_N \otimes \boldsymbol{\Omega}_T^{-1}) = \sigma^{-2}\theta_B e_{NT}'$, all column sums of $\boldsymbol{\Omega}^{-1}$ equal $\sigma^{-2}\theta_B$. Therefore, we find, using the theorem in Appendix 3A, Section 3A.2, that the value of k which solves the GLS problem for given $\boldsymbol{\beta}$ is

$$\widehat{k} = \widehat{k}(\boldsymbol{\beta}) = \left[\tfrac{1}{N}e_N' \otimes \tfrac{1}{T}e_T'\right](y - X\boldsymbol{\beta}) = \tfrac{1}{NT}e_{NT}'(y - X\boldsymbol{\beta}) = \bar{y} - \bar{x}\boldsymbol{\beta}. \tag{3.8}$$

[3] Here and in the following we repeatedly utilize algebra for Kronecker-products. The most useful rules for models with balanced panel data are collected in Section 2.4.1 and Appendix 2B.

[4] This corresponds to the *spectral-decomposition* of $\boldsymbol{\Omega}_T$, which implies that σ^2 and $\sigma^2 + T\sigma_\alpha^2$ are its eigenvalues, with multiplicity $T-1$ and 1, respectively; see Lütkepohl (1996, p. 70).

Utilizing (3.6)–(3.8), the minimand in (3.4) is simplified to

$$(y-X\boldsymbol{\beta})'(I_{NT}-A_{NT})(I_N\otimes\boldsymbol{\Omega}_T^{-1})(I_{NT}-A_{NT})(y-X\boldsymbol{\beta}) \equiv$$
$$\sigma^{-2}(y-X\boldsymbol{\beta})'[(I_N\otimes B_T)+\theta_B(B_N\otimes A_T)](y-X\boldsymbol{\beta}),$$

since $A_T\boldsymbol{\Omega}_T^{-1}A_T = A_T\boldsymbol{\Omega}_T^{-1} = \sigma^{-2}\theta_B A_T$, and hence

$$(I_{NT}-A_{NT})(I_N\otimes\boldsymbol{\Omega}_T^{-1})(I_{NT}-A_{NT})$$
$$\equiv I_N\otimes\boldsymbol{\Omega}_T^{-1} - \sigma^{-2}\theta_B A_N\otimes A_T \equiv \sigma^{-2}[I_N\otimes B_T + \theta_B B_N\otimes A_T].$$

This implies that the GLS estimators of $\boldsymbol{\beta}$ and k in Model (3.2) become

$$\widehat{\boldsymbol{\beta}}_{GLS} = [X'(I_N\otimes B_T)X+\theta_B X'(B_N\otimes A_T)X]^{-1}$$
$$\times [X'(I_N\otimes B_T)y+\theta_B X'(B_N\otimes A_T)y], \tag{3.9}$$
$$\widehat{k}_{GLS} = \widehat{k}(\widehat{\boldsymbol{\beta}}_{GLS}) = \bar{y} - \bar{\boldsymbol{x}}\widehat{\boldsymbol{\beta}}_{GLS}. \tag{3.10}$$

3.2.2 GLS AS OLS ON TRANSFORMED DATA

From classical regression analysis it is known that any GLS problem can be transformed into an OLS problem through a suitable factorization of the inverse disturbance covariance matrix. A closer look at the transformation in the present case illuminates the interpretation of $\widehat{\boldsymbol{\beta}}_{GLS}$. Utilizing (3.6), (3.7), and

$$\boldsymbol{\Omega}_T^{-1} = S_T^2,\ \ S_T = \sigma^{-1}\Big[B_T + \sqrt{\theta_B}A_T\Big] = \sigma^{-1}\Big[I_T - (1-\sqrt{\theta_B})A_T\Big], \tag{3.11}$$

we can, letting $k^* = \sqrt{\theta_B}k$, write the minimand as

$$\sigma^{-2}\textstyle\sum_{i=1}^{N}(y_i-e_Tk - X_i\boldsymbol{\beta})'(\sigma S_T)'(\sigma S_T)(y_i-e_Tk-X_i\boldsymbol{\beta})=\sigma^{-2}\sum_{i=1}^{N}\boldsymbol{\epsilon}_i^{*\prime}\boldsymbol{\epsilon}_i^*,$$

where

$$\boldsymbol{\epsilon}_i^* = \sigma S_T\boldsymbol{\epsilon}_i = y_i^* - e_Tk^* - X_i^*\boldsymbol{\beta},$$
$$y_i^* = y_i - (1-\sqrt{\theta_B})A_Ty_i, \tag{3.12}$$
$$X_i^* = X_i - (1-\sqrt{\theta_B})A_TX_i.$$

To solve the GLS problem we can therefore: *(i) deduct from y_i and X_i a share $(1-\sqrt{\theta_B})$ of their individual means, giving $y_i^* = e_Tk^*+X_i^*\boldsymbol{\beta}+\boldsymbol{\epsilon}_i^*$; and (ii) apply OLS on this equation.*

Table 3.1 Transforming the GLS problem into an OLS problem
Example: $(1-\sqrt{\theta_B})$ *as function of* T *and* $\rho=\sigma_\alpha^2/(\sigma^2+\sigma_\alpha^2)$

T	$\rho=0$	$\rho=0.01$	$\rho=0.1$	$\rho=0.2$	$\rho=0.5$	$\rho=0.8$	$\rho=0.9$	$\rho=0.99$
5	0	0.0243	0.1982	0.3333	0.5918	0.7818	0.8526	0.9859
10	0	0.0470	0.3118	0.4655	0.6985	0.8438	0.8952	0.9900
20	0	0.0879	0.4429	0.5918	0.7818	0.8889	0.9257	0.9929
100	0	0.2947	0.7127	0.8039	0.9005	0.9501	0.9667	0.9968
1000	0	0.6999	0.9056	0.9369	0.9684	0.9842	0.9895	0.9990
∞	0	1	1	1	1	1	1	1

This shows that *the GLS estimator emerges as a compromise between the OLS and the within-individual estimators*, as the former corresponds to $\theta_B=1$ and the latter corresponds to $\theta_B=0$. From (3.9) we then get

$$\begin{aligned}\widehat{\boldsymbol{\beta}}_{\mathrm{OLS}} &= [\boldsymbol{X}'(\boldsymbol{I}_N\otimes\boldsymbol{B}_T)\boldsymbol{X}+\boldsymbol{X}'(\boldsymbol{B}_N\otimes\boldsymbol{A}_T)\boldsymbol{X}]^{-1}\\ &\quad\times[\boldsymbol{X}'(\boldsymbol{I}_N\otimes\boldsymbol{B}_T)\boldsymbol{y}+\boldsymbol{X}'(\boldsymbol{B}_N\otimes\boldsymbol{A}_T)\boldsymbol{y}],\\ \widehat{\boldsymbol{\beta}}_W &= [\boldsymbol{X}'(\boldsymbol{I}_N\otimes\boldsymbol{B}_T)\boldsymbol{X}]^{-1}[\boldsymbol{X}'(\boldsymbol{I}_N\otimes\boldsymbol{B}_T)\boldsymbol{y}].\end{aligned}$$

Treating individual heterogeneity as random makes much stronger assumptions than in the fixed effects case. The message from (3.9) is to choose an estimator between the two above extremes: (i) for given T, it should be closer to the OLS estimator the smaller σ_α^2/σ^2 is (the larger θ_B is) and closer to the within estimator the larger σ_α^2/σ^2 is (the smaller θ_B is); (ii) for given σ^2 and σ_α^2, it should be closer to the within estimator the larger T is. Table 3.1 illustrates this, for selected T and $\rho=\sigma_\alpha^2/(\sigma^2+\sigma_\alpha^2)$, showing that $(1-\sqrt{\theta_B})$ is monotonically increasing in both. If, for example, $\rho=0.5$ and $T=20$, 78.2% of the respective individual means should be deducted before applying OLS; shortening the time series length to $T=5$, we should deduct 59.2%, etc.

3.2.3 FOUR ESTIMATORS AND A SYNTHESIS

Let us compare $\widehat{\boldsymbol{\beta}}_{GLS}$ with the within-individual estimator $\widehat{\boldsymbol{\beta}}_W$, the between-individual estimator $\widehat{\boldsymbol{\beta}}_B$, and the global (OLS) estimator $\widehat{\boldsymbol{\beta}}_{OLS}$, the three last also considered in Sections 2.2.2 and 2.2.3. Using the (general) notation

$$\begin{aligned}\boldsymbol{G}_{ZQ} &= \boldsymbol{Z}'(\boldsymbol{I}_{NT}-\boldsymbol{A}_{NT})\boldsymbol{Q} = \textstyle\sum_{i=1}^N\sum_{t=1}^T(\boldsymbol{z}_{it}-\bar{\boldsymbol{z}})'(\boldsymbol{q}_{it}-\bar{\boldsymbol{q}}),\\ \boldsymbol{W}_{ZQ} &= \boldsymbol{Z}'(\boldsymbol{I}_N\otimes\boldsymbol{B}_T)\boldsymbol{Q} = \textstyle\sum_{i=1}^N\sum_{t=1}^T(\boldsymbol{z}_{it}-\bar{\boldsymbol{z}}_{i\cdot})'(\boldsymbol{q}_{it}-\bar{\boldsymbol{q}}_{i\cdot}),\\ \boldsymbol{B}_{ZQ} &= \boldsymbol{Z}'(\boldsymbol{B}_N\otimes\boldsymbol{A}_T)\boldsymbol{Q} = T\textstyle\sum_{i=1}^N(\bar{\boldsymbol{z}}_{i\cdot}-\bar{\boldsymbol{z}})'(\bar{\boldsymbol{q}}_{i\cdot}-\bar{\boldsymbol{q}}),\end{aligned}$$

they can be written as

$$\widehat{\boldsymbol{\beta}}_{GLS} = (\boldsymbol{W}_{XX}+\theta_B \boldsymbol{B}_{XX})^{-1}(\boldsymbol{W}_{XY}+\theta_B \boldsymbol{B}_{XY}), \tag{3.13}$$

$$\widehat{\boldsymbol{\beta}}_{W} = \boldsymbol{W}_{XX}^{-1}\boldsymbol{W}_{XY}, \tag{3.14}$$

$$\widehat{\boldsymbol{\beta}}_{B} = \boldsymbol{B}_{XX}^{-1}\boldsymbol{B}_{XY}, \tag{3.15}$$

$$\widehat{\boldsymbol{\beta}}_{OLS} = \boldsymbol{G}_{XX}^{-1}\boldsymbol{G}_{XY} = (\boldsymbol{W}_{XX}+\boldsymbol{B}_{XX})^{-1}(\boldsymbol{W}_{XY}+\boldsymbol{B}_{XY}), \tag{3.16}$$

where $\widehat{\boldsymbol{\beta}}_W$ is the MVLUE of $\boldsymbol{\beta}$ in Model (2.29) (fixed individual-specific effects), $\widehat{\boldsymbol{\beta}}_{GLS}$ is the MVLUE in the present model (stochastic individual-specific effects), and $\widehat{\boldsymbol{\beta}}_{OLS}$ is the MVLUE in Model (2.11) (no heterogeneity). Since $\widehat{\boldsymbol{\beta}}_{OLS}$ can be interpreted as a compromise between $\widehat{\boldsymbol{\beta}}_W$ and $\widehat{\boldsymbol{\beta}}_B$ (Section 2.2.4) and $\widehat{\boldsymbol{\beta}}_{GLS}$ also can be interpreted as a compromise between $\widehat{\boldsymbol{\beta}}_W$ and $\widehat{\boldsymbol{\beta}}_{OLS}$ (Section 3.2.2), $\widehat{\boldsymbol{\beta}}_{GLS}$ is also a compromise between $\widehat{\boldsymbol{\beta}}_W$ and $\widehat{\boldsymbol{\beta}}_B$. We have from (3.13)–(3.15)

$$\widehat{\boldsymbol{\beta}}_{GLS} = \left[\boldsymbol{W}_{XX} + \theta_B \boldsymbol{B}_{XX}\right]^{-1} [\boldsymbol{W}_{XX}\widehat{\boldsymbol{\beta}}_W + \theta_B \boldsymbol{B}_{XX}\widehat{\boldsymbol{\beta}}_B]. \tag{3.17}$$

Consider a general unbiased estimator of $\boldsymbol{\beta}$ obtained by giving the within and the between (co)variation weights λ_W *and* λ_B:

$$\widehat{\boldsymbol{\beta}} = \left[\lambda_W \boldsymbol{W}_{XX}+\lambda_B \boldsymbol{B}_{XX}\right]^{-1}\left[\lambda_W \boldsymbol{W}_{XY}+\lambda_B \boldsymbol{B}_{XY}\right]. \tag{3.18}$$

Since $\boldsymbol{W}_{XY} = \boldsymbol{W}_{XX}\boldsymbol{\beta}+\boldsymbol{W}_{X\epsilon}$ and $\boldsymbol{B}_{XY} = \boldsymbol{B}_{XX}\boldsymbol{\beta}+\boldsymbol{B}_{X\epsilon}$, we have

$$\widehat{\boldsymbol{\beta}} - \boldsymbol{\beta} = \left[\lambda_W \boldsymbol{W}_{XX} + \lambda_B \boldsymbol{B}_{XX}\right]^{-1}\left[\lambda_W \boldsymbol{W}_{X\epsilon} + \lambda_B \boldsymbol{B}_{X\epsilon}\right].$$

Now, $\mathsf{V}(\boldsymbol{\epsilon}|\boldsymbol{X}) = \boldsymbol{I}_N \otimes \boldsymbol{\Omega}_T$, $\boldsymbol{B}_T\boldsymbol{\Omega}_T\boldsymbol{B}_T = \sigma^2\boldsymbol{B}_T$, $\boldsymbol{A}_T\boldsymbol{\Omega}_T\boldsymbol{A}_T = (\sigma^2+T\sigma_\alpha^2)\boldsymbol{A}_T$, and hence

$$\begin{aligned}\mathsf{V}(\boldsymbol{W}_{X\epsilon}|\boldsymbol{X}) &= \boldsymbol{X}'(\boldsymbol{I}_N\otimes\boldsymbol{B}_T)(\boldsymbol{I}_N\otimes\boldsymbol{\Omega}_T)(\boldsymbol{I}_N\otimes\boldsymbol{B}_T)\boldsymbol{X}\\ &= \sigma^2\boldsymbol{X}'(\boldsymbol{I}_N\otimes\boldsymbol{B}_T)\boldsymbol{X} = \sigma^2\boldsymbol{W}_{XX},\end{aligned} \tag{3.19}$$

$$\begin{aligned}\mathsf{V}(\boldsymbol{B}_{X\epsilon}|\boldsymbol{X}) &= \boldsymbol{X}'(\boldsymbol{B}_N\otimes\boldsymbol{A}_T)(\boldsymbol{I}_N\otimes\boldsymbol{\Omega}_T)(\boldsymbol{B}_N\otimes\boldsymbol{A}_T)\boldsymbol{X},\\ &= (\sigma^2+T\sigma_\alpha^2)(\boldsymbol{B}_N\otimes\boldsymbol{A}_T)\boldsymbol{X} = (\sigma^2+T\sigma_\alpha^2)\boldsymbol{B}_{XX},\end{aligned} \tag{3.20}$$

while $\boldsymbol{A}_T\boldsymbol{B}_T = \boldsymbol{0}_{T,T} \Longrightarrow \mathsf{E}(\boldsymbol{W}_{X\epsilon}\boldsymbol{B}_{X\epsilon}'|\boldsymbol{X}) = \boldsymbol{0}_{K,K}$, and hence $\widehat{\boldsymbol{\beta}}_W$ and $\widehat{\boldsymbol{\beta}}_B$ are uncorrelated (conditional on $\boldsymbol{X}$). Therefore,

$$\begin{aligned}\mathsf{V}(\widehat{\boldsymbol{\beta}}|\boldsymbol{X}) = {}& [\lambda_W \boldsymbol{W}_{XX}+\lambda_B \boldsymbol{B}_{XX}]^{-1} \times [\lambda_W^2\sigma^2\boldsymbol{W}_{XX}+\lambda_B^2(\sigma^2+T\sigma_\alpha^2)\boldsymbol{B}_{XX}]\\ &\times[\lambda_W \boldsymbol{W}_{XX}+\lambda_B \boldsymbol{B}_{XX}]^{-1}.\end{aligned} \tag{3.21}$$

Since the four estimators are obtained for $(\lambda_W, \lambda_B) = (1, \theta_B), (1, 0), (0, 1), (1, 1)$, respectively, the covariance matrices of (3.13)–(3.16) are given by

$$\mathsf{V}(\widehat{\boldsymbol{\beta}}_{GLS}|\boldsymbol{X}) = \sigma^2(\boldsymbol{W}_{XX} + \theta_B \boldsymbol{B}_{XX})^{-1}, \tag{3.22}$$

$$\mathsf{V}(\widehat{\boldsymbol{\beta}}_{W}|\boldsymbol{X}) = \sigma^2 \boldsymbol{W}_{XX}^{-1}, \tag{3.23}$$

$$\mathsf{V}(\widehat{\boldsymbol{\beta}}_{B}|\boldsymbol{X}) = (\sigma^2 + T\sigma_\alpha^2)\boldsymbol{B}_{XX}^{-1} = (\sigma^2/\theta_B)\boldsymbol{B}_{XX}^{-1}, \tag{3.24}$$

$$\mathsf{V}(\widehat{\boldsymbol{\beta}}_{OLS}|\boldsymbol{X}) = \boldsymbol{G}_{XX}^{-1}(\sigma^2 + T\sigma_\alpha^2 \boldsymbol{B}_{XX}\boldsymbol{G}_{XX}^{-1}). \tag{3.25}$$

In the *one-regressor case*, b denoting the share of the regressor's variation which is between-individual variation, the more transparent scalar counterparts read, see Appendix 3B, (3B.6)–(3B.9):

$$\text{var}(\widehat{\beta}_{GLS}|X) = \frac{\sigma^2}{G_{XX}} \frac{1}{1 - b(1 - \theta_B)},$$

$$\text{var}(\widehat{\beta}_{W}|X) = \frac{\sigma^2}{G_{XX}} \frac{1}{1 - b},$$

$$\text{var}(\widehat{\beta}_{B}|X) = \frac{\sigma^2}{G_{XX}} \frac{1}{b\theta_B},$$

$$\text{var}(\widehat{\beta}_{OLS}|X) = \frac{\sigma^2}{G_{XX}} \left[1 + b\left(\frac{1}{\theta_B} - 1\right)\right].$$

The relative OLS/GLS-efficiency is, see Appendix B3, (3B.12)–(3B.13):

$$\frac{\text{var}(\widehat{\beta}_{OLS}|X)}{\text{var}(\widehat{\beta}_{GLS}|X)} = \left[1+b\left(\frac{1}{\theta_B}-1\right)\right]\left[1-b(1-\theta_B)\right],$$

which exceeds one when $0 < b < 1$ and $0 < \theta_B < 1$ $(\sigma_\alpha^2 > 0)$.[5]

Using the identity $\boldsymbol{E}^{-1} - (\boldsymbol{E}+\boldsymbol{D})^{-1} \equiv (\boldsymbol{E}+\boldsymbol{D})^{-1}\boldsymbol{D}\boldsymbol{E}^{-1}$, we have

$$\mathsf{V}(\widehat{\boldsymbol{\beta}}_{W}|\boldsymbol{X}) - \mathsf{V}(\widehat{\boldsymbol{\beta}}_{GLS}|\boldsymbol{X}) = \sigma^2\theta_B(\boldsymbol{W}_{XX} + \theta_B\boldsymbol{B}_{XX})^{-1}\boldsymbol{B}_{XX}\boldsymbol{W}_{XX}^{-1}, \tag{3.26}$$

$$\mathsf{V}(\widehat{\boldsymbol{\beta}}_{B}|\boldsymbol{X}) - \mathsf{V}(\widehat{\boldsymbol{\beta}}_{GLS}|\boldsymbol{X}) = (\sigma^2/\theta_B)(\boldsymbol{W}_{XX} + \theta_B\boldsymbol{B}_{XX})^{-1}\boldsymbol{W}_{XX}\boldsymbol{B}_{XX}^{-1}, \tag{3.27}$$

[5] This result extends Malinvaud (1978, p. 330); see also Biørn (2001).

which are positive definite when $\theta_B > 0$. Inserting in (3.22) and (3.25), respectively, $W_{XX} = G_{XX} - B_{XX}$ and $T\sigma_\alpha^2 = \sigma^2(\theta_B^{-1} - 1)$, we obtain[6]

$$\begin{aligned} &\mathsf{V}(\widehat{\boldsymbol{\beta}}_{OLS}|X) - \mathsf{V}(\widehat{\boldsymbol{\beta}}_{GLS}|X) \\ &= \sigma^2(1-\theta_B)(\theta_B^{-1}-1)[\boldsymbol{W}_{XX}+\theta_B \boldsymbol{B}_{XX}]^{-1}\boldsymbol{W}_{XX}\boldsymbol{G}_{XX}^{-1}\boldsymbol{B}_{XX}\boldsymbol{G}_{XX}^{-1}. \end{aligned} \tag{3.28}$$

This difference is positive definite when $0 < \theta_B < 1$ and $\boldsymbol{B}_{XX}$ and $\boldsymbol{W}_{XX}$ are positive definite.

This confirms that $\widehat{\boldsymbol{\beta}}_{GLS}$ is more efficient than the other three estimators. *Any linear combination of the elements in $\widehat{\boldsymbol{\beta}}_{GLS}$, $\boldsymbol{a}'\widehat{\boldsymbol{\beta}}_{GLS}$, where $\boldsymbol{a}$ is a $(K \times 1)$-vector, as an estimator of $\boldsymbol{a}'\boldsymbol{\beta}$, has a smaller variance than the corresponding linear combination for the other estimators* because, since $\text{var}(\boldsymbol{a}'\widehat{\boldsymbol{\beta}}_Z|X) \equiv \boldsymbol{a}'\mathsf{V}(\widehat{\boldsymbol{\beta}}_Z|X)\boldsymbol{a}$ $(Z = W, B, OLS)$, positive definiteness of the matrix differences means that[7]

$$\begin{aligned} &\boldsymbol{a}'[\mathsf{V}(\widehat{\boldsymbol{\beta}}_Z|X) - \mathsf{V}(\widehat{\boldsymbol{\beta}}_{GLS}|X)]\boldsymbol{a} > 0 \implies \\ &\text{var}(\boldsymbol{a}'\widehat{\boldsymbol{\beta}}_Z|X) > \text{var}(\boldsymbol{a}'\widehat{\boldsymbol{\beta}}_{GLS}|X), \quad Z = W, B, OLS. \end{aligned}$$

3.3 **GLS with unknown variance components**

3.3.1 THE PROBLEM

Assuming σ^2 and σ_α^2 known is rarely realistic. To explain how they can be estimated, we first construct from (3.1) the within-individual and the between-individual transformation

$$y_{it} - \bar{y}_{i\cdot} = (\boldsymbol{x}_{it} - \bar{\boldsymbol{x}}_{i\cdot})\boldsymbol{\beta} + (\epsilon_{it} - \bar{\epsilon}_{i\cdot}), \tag{3.29}$$

$$\bar{y}_{i\cdot} - \bar{y} = (\bar{\boldsymbol{x}}_{i\cdot} - \bar{\boldsymbol{x}})\boldsymbol{\beta} + (\bar{\epsilon}_{i\cdot} - \bar{\epsilon}), \tag{3.30}$$

[6] The detailed algebra is:

$$\begin{aligned} &\sigma^{-2}[\mathsf{V}(\widehat{\boldsymbol{\beta}}_{OLS}|X) - \mathsf{V}(\widehat{\boldsymbol{\beta}}_{GLS}|X)] \\ &= \boldsymbol{G}_{XX}^{-1} + (\theta_B^{-1} - 1)\,\boldsymbol{G}_{XX}^{-1}\boldsymbol{B}_{XX}\boldsymbol{G}_{XX}^{-1} - [\boldsymbol{G}_{XX} - (1-\theta_B)\boldsymbol{B}_{XX}]^{-1} \\ &= (\theta_B^{-1}-1)\boldsymbol{G}_{XX}^{-1}\,\boldsymbol{B}_{XX}\,\boldsymbol{G}_{XX}^{-1} - [\boldsymbol{G}_{XX} - (1-\theta_B)\boldsymbol{B}_{XX}]^{-1}(1-\theta_B)\boldsymbol{B}_{XX}\,\boldsymbol{G}_{XX}^{-1} \\ &= (1-\theta_B)\left\{(\theta_B\boldsymbol{G}_{XX})^{-1} - [(\theta_B\boldsymbol{G}_{XX}) + (1-\theta_B)\boldsymbol{W}_{XX}]^{-1}\right\}\boldsymbol{B}_{XX}\boldsymbol{G}_{XX}^{-1} \\ &= (1-\theta_B)^2[\theta_B\boldsymbol{G}_{XX} + (1-\theta_B)\boldsymbol{W}_{XX}]^{-1}\boldsymbol{W}_{XX}(\theta_B\boldsymbol{G}_{XX})^{-1}\boldsymbol{B}_{XX}\,\boldsymbol{G}_{XX}^{-1}, \end{aligned}$$

in the second equality using $E^{-1} - (E+D)^{-1} = (E+D)^{-1}DE^{-1}$ with $E = \boldsymbol{G}_{XX}$ and $D = -(1-\theta_B)\,\boldsymbol{B}_{XX}$, and in the fourth equality transforming the expression in the square bracket by letting $E = \theta_B\,\boldsymbol{G}_{XX}$ and $D = (1-\theta_B)(\boldsymbol{G}_{XX} - \boldsymbol{B}_{XX})$.

[7] Equation (3.25) also implies that the 'standard' expression for the covariance matrix of the OLS estimator, $\mathsf{V}^*(\widehat{\boldsymbol{\beta}}_{OLS}|X) = \sigma^2\boldsymbol{G}_{XX}^{-1} = \sigma^2(\boldsymbol{W}_{XX}+\boldsymbol{B}_{XX})^{-1}$, leads to *underestimation*: $\mathsf{V}(\widehat{\boldsymbol{\beta}}_{OLS}|X) - \mathsf{V}^*(\widehat{\boldsymbol{\beta}}_{OLS}|X) = T\sigma_\alpha^2\boldsymbol{G}_{XX}^{-1}\boldsymbol{B}_{XX}\boldsymbol{G}_{XX}^{-1}$, which is a positive definite matrix when $\sigma_\alpha^2 > 0$ and $\boldsymbol{B}_{XX}$ are positive definite.

in matrix notation,

$$(I_N \otimes B_T)y = (I_N \otimes B_T)X\boldsymbol{\beta} + (I_N \otimes B_T)\boldsymbol{\epsilon}, \tag{3.31}$$
$$\big[B_N \otimes \tfrac{1}{T}e'_T\big]y = [B_N \otimes \tfrac{1}{T}e'_T]X\boldsymbol{\beta} + [B_N \otimes \tfrac{1}{T}e'_T]\boldsymbol{\epsilon}. \tag{3.32}$$

Since (3.5) implies

$$\mathsf{V}(\boldsymbol{\epsilon}|X) = I_N \otimes \boldsymbol{\Omega}_T = \sigma^2(I_N \otimes B_T) + (\sigma^2 + T\sigma_\alpha^2)(I_N \otimes A_T), \tag{3.33}$$

the disturbance vectors in (3.31) and (3.32) satisfy

$$\mathsf{V}[(I_N \otimes B_T)\boldsymbol{\epsilon}|X] = \sigma^2(I_N \otimes B_T), \tag{3.34}$$
$$\mathsf{V}[(B_N \otimes \tfrac{1}{T}e'_T)\boldsymbol{\epsilon}|X] = (\sigma_\alpha^2 + \tfrac{1}{T}\sigma^2)B_N. \tag{3.35}$$

Their diagonal elements are $\sigma^2(1-\frac{1}{T})$ and $(\sigma_\alpha^2+\frac{1}{T}\sigma^2)(1-\frac{1}{N})$. In general,

$$\mathsf{E}[(\epsilon_{it}-\bar{\epsilon}_{i\cdot})(\epsilon_{js}-\bar{\epsilon}_{j\cdot})|X] = \sigma^2\delta_{ij}(\delta_{ts}-\tfrac{1}{T}), \tag{3.36}$$
$$\mathsf{E}[(\bar{\epsilon}_{i\cdot}-\bar{\epsilon})(\bar{\epsilon}_{j\cdot}-\bar{\epsilon})|X] = (\sigma_\alpha^2+\tfrac{1}{T}\sigma^2)(\delta_{ij}-\tfrac{1}{N}). \tag{3.37}$$

3.3.2 'ESTIMATION' OF VARIANCE COMPONENTS FROM DISTURBANCES

We first pretend that ϵ_{it} is observable, so that we can estimate the above variances by their empirical counterparts, giving:[8]

$$\widehat{\sigma}^2 = \frac{1}{N(T-1)}\sum_{i=1}^N\sum_{t=1}^T(\epsilon_{it}-\bar{\epsilon}_{i\cdot})^2 = \frac{1}{N(T-1)}W_{\epsilon\epsilon}, \tag{3.38}$$
$$\widehat{\sigma_\alpha^2+\tfrac{\sigma^2}{T}} = \frac{1}{N-1}\sum_{i=1}^N(\bar{\epsilon}_{i\cdot}-\bar{\epsilon})^2 = \frac{1}{(N-1)T}B_{\epsilon\epsilon}, \tag{3.39}$$

and hence

$$\widehat{\sigma}_\alpha^2 = \frac{1}{T}\left[\frac{B_{\epsilon\epsilon}}{N-1} - \frac{W_{\epsilon\epsilon}}{N(T-1)}\right], \tag{3.40}$$
$$\widehat{\theta}_B = \frac{\widehat{\sigma}^2}{\widehat{\sigma}^2 + T\widehat{\sigma}_\alpha^2} = \frac{N-1}{N(T-1)}\frac{W_{\epsilon\epsilon}}{B_{\epsilon\epsilon}}. \tag{3.41}$$

[8] When T and N are small it may happen that $\widehat{\sigma}_\alpha^2$ becomes negative, giving $\widehat{\theta}_B > 1$. This may reflect a mis-specified model. What to do in such cases is not obvious. A remedy may be to use the boundary value, $\sigma_\alpha^2 = 0$, i.e., $\theta_B = 1$, and proceed by using OLS.

The 'estimators' of σ^2 and σ_α^2 are unbiased. The proof, involving rules for trace operations, is that since (3.33) implies

$$\begin{aligned}
\mathsf{E}(W_{\epsilon\epsilon}|X) &= \mathsf{E}[\boldsymbol{\epsilon}'(\boldsymbol{I}_N\otimes \boldsymbol{B}_T)\boldsymbol{\epsilon}|X] \\
&= \mathsf{E}[\mathrm{tr}(\boldsymbol{\epsilon}'(\boldsymbol{I}_N\otimes \boldsymbol{B}_T)\boldsymbol{\epsilon})|X] = \mathsf{E}[\mathrm{tr}(\boldsymbol{\epsilon}\boldsymbol{\epsilon}'(\boldsymbol{I}_N\otimes \boldsymbol{B}_T))|X] \\
&= \mathrm{tr}[\mathsf{E}(\boldsymbol{\epsilon}\boldsymbol{\epsilon}')(\boldsymbol{I}_N\otimes \boldsymbol{B}_T)|X] = \sigma^2\mathrm{tr}(\boldsymbol{I}_N\otimes \boldsymbol{B}_T), \\
\mathsf{E}(B_{\epsilon\epsilon}|X) &= \mathsf{E}[\boldsymbol{\epsilon}'(\boldsymbol{B}_N\otimes \boldsymbol{A}_T)\,\boldsymbol{\epsilon}] \\
&= \mathsf{E}[\mathrm{tr}(\boldsymbol{\epsilon}'(\boldsymbol{B}_N\otimes \boldsymbol{A}_T)\boldsymbol{\epsilon})|X] = \mathsf{E}[\mathrm{tr}(\boldsymbol{\epsilon}\boldsymbol{\epsilon}'(\boldsymbol{B}_N\otimes \boldsymbol{A}_T))|X] \\
&= \mathrm{tr}[(\boldsymbol{I}_N\otimes \boldsymbol{\Omega}_T)(\boldsymbol{B}_N\otimes \boldsymbol{A}_T)|X] = (T\sigma_\alpha^2+\sigma^2)\mathrm{tr}(\boldsymbol{B}_N\otimes \boldsymbol{A}_T),
\end{aligned}$$

and (2.86)–(2.87) give $\mathrm{tr}(\boldsymbol{I}_N\otimes \boldsymbol{B}_T) = N(T-1)$, $\mathrm{tr}(\boldsymbol{B}_N\otimes \boldsymbol{A}_T) = N-1$, we get

$$\mathsf{E}(W_{\epsilon\epsilon}|X) = \sigma^2 N(T-1), \tag{3.42}$$

$$\mathsf{E}(B_{\epsilon\epsilon}|X) = (T\sigma_\alpha^2+\sigma^2)(N-1). \tag{3.43}$$

These equations combined with (3.38) and (3.40) give $\mathsf{E}(\widehat{\sigma}^2|X)=\sigma^2$ and $\mathsf{E}(\widehat{\sigma}_\alpha^2|X)=\sigma_\alpha^2$, which completes the proof.

3.3.3 SYNTHESIS: STEPWISE ESTIMATION

When ϵ_{it} is unobservable we use (consistent) residuals in estimating the variance components. This motivates a stepwise procedure for *FGLS estimation*:

1. Estimate $\boldsymbol{\beta}$ and k by OLS and extract the residuals, $\widehat{\epsilon}_{it}$.
2. Compute $\widehat{\theta}_B$ from (3.41), replacing ϵ_{it} by $\widehat{\epsilon}_{it}$.
3. Compute $\widehat{\boldsymbol{\beta}}_{GLS}$ and $\mathsf{V}(\widehat{\boldsymbol{\beta}}_{GLS})$ from (3.13) and (3.22), with $\theta_B = \widehat{\theta}_B$.
4. Estimate k, using (3.10), by $\widehat{k}_{GLS} = \widehat{k}(\widehat{\boldsymbol{\beta}}_{GLS}) = \bar{y} - \bar{\boldsymbol{x}}\widehat{\boldsymbol{\beta}}_{GLS}$.

We may continue by recomputing residuals $\widehat{\epsilon}_{it}$ and repeating steps 2–4 iteratively until convergence, according to some criterion.

Is it obvious that OLS should be used in step 1 to obtain ϵ-residuals? Different answers have been given: Wallace and Hussain (1969, p. 65) propose replacing ϵ_{it} by OLS residuals. Amemiya (1971, p. 6) proposes computing the ϵ-residuals from within-individual coefficient estimates and shows that they give more asymptotically efficient estimators than those obtained from OLS residuals (the latter having an asymptotic distribution which depends on the relative increase in N and T). Nerlove (1971 a) proposes estimating σ^2 by the residuals from the within-individual regression and estimating σ_α^2 by the empirical variance of the N individual-specific $\widehat{\alpha}_i^*$s. Swamy and Arora (1972, p. 274) conclude that if N, T, and σ_α^2 are small, FGLS tends to be inferior to OLS because the σ^2 and σ_α^2 estimates may be unreliable, and that if N and T are small and σ_α^2 large, FGLS tends to be inferior to the within-individual estimator and a fixed effects approach should be preferred. Taylor (1980, p. 222) concludes that if N is not 'too small', FGLS is more efficient than the within-individual estimator. Baltagi (1981a, p. 47) concludes from Monte Carlo evidence that improved σ^2 and σ_α^2 estimators do not necessarily improve the FGLS estimates.

Example: This example, from Biørn (1994), which is a continuation of the example in Section 2.2.4, relates to the estimation of *marginal budget shares in consumption*, using a stylized (and obviously simplistic) model with total expenditure as the only explanatory variable ($K=1$). The data are from $N=418$ households observed in $T=2$ successive years. Table 3.2, contains within household (WH), between household (BH), residual (R), OLS, and FGLS estimates for five aggregated commodity groups, exhausting total consumption, and five selected (among 28) disaggregated groups, with standard errors obtained from the (one-way) random effects model, as described above.

For three aggregated and four disaggregated groups the estimates differ substantially. One disaggregated group, Butter and margarine, even has a negative WH estimate (although with a large standard error). The results confirm that OLS and FGLS are in

Table 3.2 Marginal budget share, promille.
Within (WH), Between (BH), OLS, and FGLS estimates

	WH	BH	OLS	FGLS
Aggregated				
Food, beverages, tobacco	58.1	151.4	133.2	115.9
	(10.0)	(7.9)	(6.6)	(6.2)
Clothing, footwear	82.7	97.7	94.7	93.5
	(9.6)	(5.9)	(5.1)	(5.0)
Housing, fuel, furniture	110.3	217.9	196.9	194.3
	(18.8)	(10.0)	(8.8)	(8.8)
Travel, recreation	603.6	398.5	438.5	462.1
	(21.9)	(14.7)	(12.6)	(12.2)
Other	155.5	139.1	142.3	142.3
	(17.6)	(8.7)	(7.8)	(7.8)
Selected disaggregated				
Flour and bread	2.01	11.05	9.29	7.57
	(1.18)	(0.93)	(0.79)	(0.73)
Butter and margarine	-0.20	3.09	2.45	1.98
	(0.72)	(0.51)	(0.44)	(0.42)
Tobacco	1.98	11.07	9.29	4.83
	(1.10)	(1.63)	(1.33)	(0.92)
Medical care	10.94	12.36	12.08	12.11
	(5.04)	(2.30)	(2.10)	(2.09)
Public transport	48.36	29.24	32.97	33.21
	(8.95)	(4.59)	(4.08)	(4.08)

Source: Based on Biørn (1994), Tables 5 and 7.
Standard errors, based on (3.75), in parentheses.

Table 3.3 Relative efficiency of estimators: OLS = 1

	WH	BH	R	FGLS
Aggregated				
Food, beverages, tobacco	2.30	1.41	2.35	0.873
Clothing, footwear	3.51	1.34	3.58	0.968
Housing, fuel, furniture	4.55	1.28	4.65	0.997
Travel and recreation	3.05	1.37	3.10	0.942
Other	5.13	1.24	5.24	1.000
Selected disaggregated				
Flour and bread	2.25	1.41	2.01	0.868
Butter and margarine	2.71	1.38	2.77	0.916
Tobacco	0.69	1.50	0.70	0.472
Medical care	5.81	1.20	5.93	0.996
Public transport	4.81	1.26	4.92	0.997

Source: Based on Biørn (1994), Table 8.

the interval spanned by the BH and the WH estimates. As shown in Appendix 3B, the weights of the BH and the WH estimators in OLS are the share of the overall variation in the regressor, total expenditure, which is BH and WH variation, respectively, in the present example $B_{XX}/G_{XX} = 0.8048$ and $W_{XX}/G_{XX} = 0.1952$. This means that the weight of the former is more than four times the weight of the latter. In GLS, the BH variation is given a relatively smaller and the WH variation a relatively larger weight when $\rho = \sigma_\alpha^2/(\sigma^2+\sigma_\alpha^2) > 0$. Since (3.7) with $T=2$ implies $\theta_B = \sigma^2/(\sigma^2+2\sigma_\alpha^2) = (1-\rho)/(1+\rho)$, the weights are, respectively, $(1-\rho)/(1+\rho)\,0.8048$ and 0.1952. This implies that the BH estimate is given a larger weight than the WH estimate in the GLS estimate as long as $(1-\rho)/(1+\rho)\,0.8048 > 0.1952 \implies \rho < 0.6096$.

Table 3.3, containing estimated variance ratios, shows that the OLS estimator is more efficient than the WH and the R estimators for all aggregate commodities and all disaggregate ones, with tobacco as a notable exception. The variance ratios of the WH and the R estimators for the latter are 69% and 70%, respectively. The BH estimator is more efficient than the WH estimator for all the five aggregate commodities and all the selected disaggregate ones except tobacco (variance ratios 1.50 and 0.69). In terms of efficiency, OLS estimation is always superior to BH estimation, as confirmed by these examples.

3.3.4 TESTING FOR RANDOM ONE-WAY HETEROGENEITY

Breusch and Pagan (1979) have constructed a chi-square procedure for testing for latent random heterogeneity by using residuals in the case with normally distributed disturbances, based on the Lagrange Multiplier test principle. Briefly, it can be explained as follows. Let $\widehat{\ }$ denote OLS (or ML) residuals from Model (3.1) under $H_0: \sigma_\alpha^2 = 0$, and let

$E_T = e_T e_T'$ and $\widehat{\epsilon} = [\widehat{\epsilon}_{11}, \dots, \widehat{\epsilon}_{1T}, \dots, \widehat{\epsilon}_{N1}, \dots, \widehat{\epsilon}_{NT}]'$. For the case with one-way heterogeneity, its test statistic is, see, e.g., Baltagi (2008, Section 4.2.1):

$$\begin{aligned} \text{BP}_\alpha &= \frac{NT}{2(T-1)} \left[\frac{\sum_{i=1}^N [\sum_{t=1}^T \widehat{\epsilon}_{it}]^2}{\sum_{i=1}^N \sum_{t=1}^T \widehat{\epsilon}_{it}^2} - 1 \right]^2 \equiv \frac{NT}{2(T-1)} \left[\frac{\widehat{\epsilon}'[I_N \otimes E_T]\widehat{\epsilon}}{\widehat{\epsilon}'\widehat{\epsilon}} - 1 \right]^2 \\ &\equiv \frac{NT}{2(T-1)} \left[\frac{\sum_{i=1}^N \sum_{t=1}^T \sum_{s \neq t} \widehat{\epsilon}_{it} \widehat{\epsilon}_{is}}{\sum_{i=1}^N \sum_{t=1}^T \widehat{\epsilon}_{it}^2} \right]^2 . \end{aligned} \tag{3.44}$$

The test criterion is to *reject* H_0*, at an approximate level* θ*, when* $\text{BP}_\alpha > \chi^2_{1-\theta}(1)$*, the* $(1-\theta)$*-quantile in the* $\chi^2(1)$*-distribution.*[9] Intuitively, $\widehat{\epsilon}_{it}\widehat{\epsilon}_{is}$ $(t \neq s)$ tends to be 'small', and hence BP_α tends to be 'small', when $\alpha_i = 0$, which makes ϵ_{it} and ϵ_{is} uncorrelated.

3.3.5 DISTURBANCE SERIAL CORRELATION AND HETEROSKEDASTICITY

Model (3.1) assumes homoskedastic disturbances, i.e., equal variances both across periods and individuals and no serial correlation of the genuine disturbance. These assumptions, in particular the implied equi-correlation ($\text{corr}(\epsilon_{it}, \epsilon_{is})$ i-invariant and (t,s)-invariant) may be too restrictive for panels where the units have varying size and hence may exhibit different variability of the 'unexplained' part of the equation. Among the advantages of relaxing them are the gains by being able to include a larger data set and to 'explain' a larger part of the variation. However, since we rarely know the 'correct' form of the disturbance second-order moments, there is a risk that an inappropriate generalization is chosen.

We now outline extensions which relax, in various ways, $(u_{it}|X) \sim \mathsf{IID}(0, \sigma^2)$ and $(\alpha_i|X) \sim \mathsf{IID}(0, \sigma_\alpha^2)$, which we know imply

$$\text{cov}(\epsilon_{it}, \epsilon_{js}|X) \equiv \sigma_{\epsilon,ij,ts} = \delta_{ij}\sigma_\alpha^2 + \delta_{ij}\delta_{ts}\sigma^2,$$

where δ_{ij} and δ_{ts} are Kronecker deltas. Cases allowing for heteroskedasticity and for serial correlation are labelled by H and S, respectively.

Five ways of modelling *heteroskedasticity* are:[10]

H1: α_i *has i-specific variance:* $(\alpha_i|\boldsymbol{x}_{it}) \sim (0, \sigma_{\alpha i}^2)$, $\alpha_i \perp \alpha_j$, $i \neq j$.
H2: u_{it} *has i-specific variance:* $(u_{it}|\boldsymbol{x}_{it}) \sim (0, \sigma_i^2)$, $u_{it} \perp u_{js}$, $i \neq j$ or $t \neq s$.

[9] A problem with this test is that it assumes that the alternative hypothesis is two-sided, while $\sigma_\alpha^2 \geq 0$ always holds. Honda (1985) proposes a variant more suited to the *one-sided alternative* $\sigma_\alpha^2 > 0$, based on the positive square root of BP_α, which under H_0 is shown to be approximately distributed as $\mathsf{N}(0,1)$.

[10] We let $v \sim (\mu, \sigma^2)$ denote 'v has a distribution with $\mathsf{E}(v) = \mu$, $\text{var}(v) = \sigma^2$' and let $v \perp w$ symbolize that v and w (or their elements) are uncorrelated (orthogonal).

H3: u_{it} has t-specific variance: $(u_{it}|x_{it}) \sim (0, \sigma_t^2)$, $u_{it} \perp u_{js}$, $i \neq j$ or $t \neq s$.
H4: α_i and u_{it} have i-specific variances: combines H1 and H2.
H5: α_i has i-specific, and u_{it} has t-specific variance: combines H1 and H3.

The variances and covariances are then given by, respectively:

H1:	$\sigma_{\epsilon,ij,ts} = \delta_{ij}(\sigma_{\alpha i}^2 + \delta_{ts}\sigma^2)$	($N+1$ parameters),
H2:	$\sigma_{\epsilon,ij,ts} = \delta_{ij}(\sigma_{\alpha}^2 + \delta_{ts}\sigma_i^2)$	($N+1$ parameters),
H3:	$\sigma_{\epsilon,ij,ts} = \delta_{ij}(\sigma_{\alpha}^2 + \delta_{ts}\sigma_t^2)$	($T+1$ parameters),
H4:	$\sigma_{\epsilon,ij,ts} = \delta_{ij}(\sigma_{\alpha i}^2 + \delta_{ts}\sigma_i^2)$,	($2N$ parameters),
H5:	$\sigma_{\epsilon,ij,ts} = \delta_{ij}(\sigma_{\alpha i}^2 + \delta_{ts}\sigma_t^2)$	($N+T$ parameters).

Parameter saving variants, *inter alia*, to escape incidental parameter problems (e.g., for large N in H2, H4, and H5), can be obtained by letting $\sigma_{\alpha i}^2 = g(\bar{x}_{i\cdot})\sigma_\alpha^2$ (g known); $\sigma_i^2 = f(x_{it})\sigma^2$ or $= f(\bar{x}_{i\cdot})\sigma^2$; or $\sigma_t^2 = f(x_{it})\sigma^2$ or $= f(\bar{x}_{\cdot t})\sigma^2$ (f known), or by letting *groups* of units or time periods (defined in some way) have the same σ_i^2 or σ_t^2. Heteroskedasticity in 'gross' disturbances is also implied when letting slope coefficients have random individual- or period-specific slacks, see Section 4.3. This gives another way of ensuring parsimony and coming to grips with incidental parameter problems.

Three ways of modelling *serial correlation*, extending u_{it} to an AR(1) process, are:

S1: common AR parameter: $u_{it} = \rho u_{i,t-1} + \eta_{it}$, $|\rho| < 1$, $\eta_{it} \sim \mathsf{IID}(0, \sigma_\eta^2)$.
S2: i-dependent variance: as S1 with σ_η^2 replaced by $\sigma_{\eta i}^2$.
S3: i-dependent AR parameter and variance: as S2 with ρ replaced by ρ_i.

Since S1 and S2 imply $u_{it} = \sum_{s=0}^{\infty} \rho^s \eta_{i,t-s}$ and S3 implies $u_{it} = \sum_{s=0}^{\infty} \rho_i^s \eta_{i,t-s}$, with $\text{var}(u_{it}) = \sigma_\eta^2/(1-\rho^2)$ and $= \sigma_{\eta i}^2/(1-\rho_i^2)$, respectively, it follows that:

S1:	$\sigma_{\epsilon,ij,ts} = \delta_{ij}\left(\sigma_\alpha^2 + \dfrac{\rho^{\lvert t-s\rvert}\sigma_\eta^2}{1-\rho^2}\right)$	(3 parameters),
S2:	$\sigma_{\epsilon,ij,ts} = \delta_{ij}\left(\sigma_\alpha^2 + \dfrac{\rho^{\lvert t-s\rvert}\sigma_{\eta i}^2}{1-\rho^2}\right)$	($N+2$ parameters),
S3:	$\sigma_{\epsilon,ij,ts} = \delta_{ij}\left(\sigma_\alpha^2 + \dfrac{\rho_i^{\lvert t-s\rvert}\sigma_{\eta i}^2}{1-\rho_i^2}\right)$	($2N+1$ parameters).

Combinations of $H1, \ldots, H5$ and $S1$, $S2$, and $S3$ are also possible.[11]

[11] The Stata routines `xtgls` and `xtregar` are useful for handling some of these models.

Allowing for *cross-sectional dependence*, by weakening at least one of the rather strong assumptions $u_{it} \perp u_{js}$ $(i \neq j)$ or $\alpha_i \perp \alpha_j$ $(i \neq j)$—hence weakening $\text{cov}(\epsilon_{it}, \epsilon_{js}) = 0$ for all $i \neq j$—would give extensions in other directions, some of which are discussed in the recent panel data literature. For an overview of the field, see Sarafidis and Wansbeek (2012).

A substantial literature exists on estimation *and testing* in models allowing for heteroskedastic or serially correlated disturbances. Versions of (F)GLS or ML, using models of the kind outlined above, may then be the answer to coefficient estimation. Transformations useful for handling heteroskedastic disturbance components in estimating slope coefficients are discussed in Randolph (1987), Baltagi and Griffin (1988), Li and Stengos (1994), and Baltagi, Bresson, and Pirotte (2005). Transformations useful for handling serially correlated disturbance components are discussed in Baltagi and Li (1991). Testing for heteroskedasticity is considered in Holly and Gardiol (2000) and Baltagi, Bresson, and Pirotte (2006), testing for serial correlation in, *inter alia*, Drukker (2003) and Baltagi, Jung, and Song (2010), the former presenting a Stata procedure (`xtserial`) for testing for serial correlation in the genuine disturbance, the latter considering tests for heteroskedasticity and serial correlation jointly. Bhargava, Franzini, and Narendranathan (1982) extend the *Durbin–Watson* (1950, 1951) statistics for testing for AR(1) disturbances in pure time-series models to test OLS residuals from a fixed effect panel data model for AR(1) serial correlation. Burke, Godfrey, and Tremayne (1990) and Baltagi and Li (1995) consider tests to contrast AR(1) and MA(1) serial correlation, utilizing, *inter alia*, correlograms of individual-specific residuals.

3.4 **Maximum Likelihood estimation**

3.4.1 THE PROBLEM

We return to Model (3.1) and proceed to the problem of joint estimation of $(k, \boldsymbol{\beta}, \sigma^2, \sigma_\alpha^2)$. From (3.2), assuming that α_i and $\boldsymbol{u}_i$, and hence ϵ_{it}, are *normally distributed*, we have

$$y_i = \boldsymbol{e}_T k + \boldsymbol{X}_i \boldsymbol{\beta} + \boldsymbol{\epsilon}_i, \quad (\boldsymbol{\epsilon}_i | \boldsymbol{X}) \sim \mathsf{IIN}(\boldsymbol{0}_{T,1}, \boldsymbol{\Omega}_T), \quad i = 1, \dots, N, \tag{3.45}$$

where $\boldsymbol{\Omega}_T$ is given by (3.3). The density of $\boldsymbol{\epsilon}_i$ is

$$\mathcal{L}_i = (2\pi)^{-\frac{T}{2}} |\boldsymbol{\Omega}_T|^{-\frac{1}{2}} \exp[-\tfrac{1}{2} \boldsymbol{\epsilon}_i' \boldsymbol{\Omega}_T^{-1} \boldsymbol{\epsilon}_i].$$

Since (3.45) implies that $\boldsymbol{\epsilon}_1', \dots, \boldsymbol{\epsilon}_N'$ are stochastically independent, the density function of $\boldsymbol{\epsilon} = (\boldsymbol{\epsilon}_1', \dots, \boldsymbol{\epsilon}_N')'$ is $\prod_{i=1}^N \mathcal{L}_i$, and hence the log-density is

$$\textstyle\sum_{i=1}^N \ln(\mathcal{L}_i) = -\frac{NT}{2} \ln(2\pi) - \frac{N}{2} \ln(|\boldsymbol{\Omega}_T|) - \frac{1}{2} \sum_{i=1}^N \boldsymbol{\epsilon}_i' \boldsymbol{\Omega}_T^{-1} \boldsymbol{\epsilon}_i.$$

Inserting $\boldsymbol{\epsilon}_i = \boldsymbol{y}_i - \boldsymbol{e}_T k - \boldsymbol{X}_i \boldsymbol{\beta}$ and $\sum_{i=1}^{N} \boldsymbol{\epsilon}_i' \boldsymbol{\Omega}_T^{-1} \boldsymbol{\epsilon}_i \equiv \boldsymbol{\epsilon}'(\boldsymbol{I}_N \otimes \boldsymbol{\Omega}_T^{-1})\boldsymbol{\epsilon}$ gives the *log-likelihood function of* $\boldsymbol{y}_1, \ldots, \boldsymbol{y}_N$, *conditional on* $\boldsymbol{X}_1, \ldots, \boldsymbol{X}_N$:

$$\begin{aligned}\ln(\mathcal{L}) = & -\tfrac{N}{2}[T \ln(2\pi) + \ln(|\boldsymbol{\Omega}_T|] \\ & - \tfrac{1}{2}[\boldsymbol{y} - \boldsymbol{e}_{NT} k - \boldsymbol{X}\boldsymbol{\beta}]'(\boldsymbol{I}_N \otimes \boldsymbol{\Omega}_T^{-1})[\boldsymbol{y} - \boldsymbol{e}_{NT} k - \boldsymbol{X}\boldsymbol{\beta}]. \end{aligned} \tag{3.46}$$

The ML estimators of $(\boldsymbol{\beta}, k, \sigma^2, \sigma_\alpha^2)$ are the values that maximize (3.46). How to solve this problem will be explained stepwise in Sections 3.4.2 and 3.4.3.

3.4.2 SIMPLIFYING THE LOG-LIKELIHOOD

To formulate the conditions for maximization of (3.46) we use

$$|\boldsymbol{\Omega}_T| = \sigma^{2(T-1)} (\sigma^2 + T\sigma_\alpha^2), \tag{3.47}$$

which can be shown in two ways. First, the determinant of a matrix is the product of its eigenvalues, and $\boldsymbol{\Omega}_T$ has eigenvalues σ^2 with multiplicity $T-1$ and $\sigma^2 + T\sigma_\alpha^2$ with multiplicity 1.[12] Second, the determinant of a matrix is unchanged if a multiple of a row/column is added to the other rows/columns. Deducting row T in $\boldsymbol{\Omega}_T$ from rows $1, \ldots, T-1$, and next adding columns $1, \ldots, T-1$ to column T, we obtain

$$|\boldsymbol{\Omega}_T| = \begin{vmatrix} \sigma^2 \boldsymbol{I}_{T-1} & -\sigma^2 \boldsymbol{e}_{T-1} \\ \sigma_\alpha^2 \boldsymbol{e}_{T-1}' & \sigma_\alpha^2 + \sigma^2 \end{vmatrix} = \begin{vmatrix} \sigma^2 \boldsymbol{I}_{T-1} & \boldsymbol{0}_{T-1,1} \\ \sigma_\alpha^2 \boldsymbol{e}_{T-1}' & \sigma^2 + T\sigma_\alpha^2 \end{vmatrix}.$$

Since the matrix in the last expression is triangular, the determinant value is the product of the diagonal elements.

Inserting (3.6) and (3.47) in (3.46) gives

$$\ln(\mathcal{L}) = -\tfrac{N}{2}[T \ln(2\pi) + (T-1)\ln(\sigma^2) + \ln(\sigma^2 + T\sigma_\alpha^2)] + Q(\boldsymbol{\beta}, k, \sigma^2, \sigma_\alpha^2)], \tag{3.48}$$

where

$$\begin{aligned} & Q(\boldsymbol{\beta}, k, \sigma^2, \sigma_\alpha^2) \\ & = \sigma^{-2}[\boldsymbol{y} - (\boldsymbol{e}_N \otimes \boldsymbol{e}_T)k - \boldsymbol{X}\boldsymbol{\beta}]'(\boldsymbol{I}_N \otimes \boldsymbol{B}_T)[\boldsymbol{y} - (\boldsymbol{e}_N \otimes \boldsymbol{e}_T)k - \boldsymbol{X}\boldsymbol{\beta}] \\ & \quad + (\sigma^2 + T\sigma_\alpha^2)^{-2}[\boldsymbol{y} - (\boldsymbol{e}_N \otimes \boldsymbol{e}_T)k - \boldsymbol{X}\boldsymbol{\beta}]'(\boldsymbol{I}_N \otimes \boldsymbol{A}_T)[\boldsymbol{y} - (\boldsymbol{e}_N \otimes \boldsymbol{e}_T)k - \boldsymbol{X}\boldsymbol{\beta}]. \end{aligned}$$

[12] See Nerlove (1971b), whose proof is for the model with both individual-specific and period-specific variance components; see Section 3.8.2.

3.4.3 STEPWISE SOLUTION

The first-order conditions $\partial \ln(\mathcal{L})/\partial \boldsymbol{\beta} = \mathbf{0}_{K,1}$ and $\partial \ln(\mathcal{L})/\partial k = \partial \ln(\mathcal{L})/\partial \sigma^2 = \partial \ln(\mathcal{L})/\partial \sigma_\alpha^2 = 0$ do not admit a solution in closed form. However, the structure of (3.48) can be utilized to simplify the conditions. For given σ^2 and σ_α^2,

$$\max_{k,\boldsymbol{\beta}} \ln(\mathcal{L}) \iff \min_{k,\boldsymbol{\beta}}(Q).$$

Since the latter is the GLS problem, the ML-estimators of $(\boldsymbol{\beta}, k)$, conditional on $(\sigma^2, \sigma_\alpha^2)$, equal the GLS estimators.

Eliminating k from $\ln(\mathcal{L})$ by inserting $\widehat{k}(\boldsymbol{\beta})$ from (3.8) in (3.48), gives

$$\ln(\mathcal{L}) = -\tfrac{N}{2}[T\ln(2\pi)+(T-1)\ln(\sigma^2)+\ln(\kappa_B^2)] - \tfrac{1}{2}Q^*(\boldsymbol{\beta}, \sigma^2, \kappa_B^2), \tag{3.49}$$

where

$$\kappa_B^2 = \sigma^2 + T\sigma_\alpha^2,$$
$$Q^*(\boldsymbol{\beta}, \sigma^2, \kappa_B^2) = (y - X\boldsymbol{\beta})'[\sigma^{-2}(I_N \otimes B_T) + \kappa_B^{-2}(B_N \otimes A_T)](y - X\boldsymbol{\beta}).$$

Maximizing $\ln(\mathcal{L})$ with respect to $(\boldsymbol{\beta}, k, \sigma^2, \sigma_\alpha^2)$ is then reduced to maximizing it with respect to $(\boldsymbol{\beta}, \sigma^2, \sigma_\alpha^2)$. This is equivalent to maximizing it with respect to $(\boldsymbol{\beta}, \sigma^2, \kappa_B^2)$, since the transformation from $(\boldsymbol{\beta}, \sigma^2, \sigma_\alpha^2)$ to $(\boldsymbol{\beta}, \sigma^2, \kappa_B^2)$ is one-to-one. Now (3.49) has an additive form where σ^2 and κ_B^2 enter the expression in the square bracket, while they occur together with $\boldsymbol{\beta}$ in Q^*. We can therefore split the simplified ML problem into:

Sub-problem A: Maximization of $\ln(\mathcal{L})$ *with respect to* $\boldsymbol{\beta}$ *for given* σ^2, κ_B^2.
Sub-problem B: Maximization of $\ln(\mathcal{L})$ *with respect to* σ^2, κ_B^2 *for given* $\boldsymbol{\beta}$.

Sub-problem A is identical to the GLS problem. We therefore obtain the (conditional) estimator directly from (3.13).

Sub-problem B has first-order conditions $\partial \ln(\mathcal{L})/\partial \sigma^2 = \partial \ln(\mathcal{L})/\partial \kappa_B^2 = 0$, which lead to the conditional estimators

$$\widetilde{\sigma}^2 = \widetilde{\sigma}^2(\boldsymbol{\beta}) = \tfrac{1}{N(T-1)}(y - X\boldsymbol{\beta})'(I_N \otimes B_T)(y - X\boldsymbol{\beta}),$$
$$\widetilde{\kappa}_B^2 = \widetilde{\kappa}_B^2(\boldsymbol{\beta}) = \tfrac{1}{N}(y - X\boldsymbol{\beta})'(B_N \otimes A_T)(y - X\boldsymbol{\beta}).$$

Since $W_{\epsilon\epsilon}(\boldsymbol{\beta}) = \boldsymbol{\epsilon}'(I_N \otimes B_T)\boldsymbol{\epsilon}$, $B_{\epsilon\epsilon}(\boldsymbol{\beta}) = \boldsymbol{\epsilon}'(B_N \otimes A_T)\boldsymbol{\epsilon}$, we have

$$\widetilde{\sigma}^2 = \tfrac{1}{N(T-1)} W_{\epsilon\epsilon}(\boldsymbol{\beta}), \tag{3.50}$$
$$\widetilde{\kappa}_B^2 = \tfrac{1}{N} B_{\epsilon\epsilon}(\boldsymbol{\beta}), \tag{3.51}$$

and hence[13]

$$\widetilde{\sigma}_{\alpha}^{2} = \widetilde{\sigma}_{\alpha}^{2}(\boldsymbol{\beta}) = \tfrac{1}{T}\widetilde{\kappa}_{B}^{2}(\boldsymbol{\beta}) - \widetilde{\sigma}^{2}(\boldsymbol{\beta}) = \tfrac{1}{NT}\Big[B_{\epsilon\epsilon}(\boldsymbol{\beta}) - \tfrac{1}{T-1}W_{\epsilon\epsilon}(\boldsymbol{\beta})\Big], \tag{3.52}$$

$$\widetilde{\theta}_{B} = \widetilde{\theta}_{B}(\boldsymbol{\beta}) = \frac{\widetilde{\sigma}^{2}(\boldsymbol{\beta})}{\widetilde{\kappa}_{B}^{2}(\boldsymbol{\beta})} = \frac{W_{\epsilon\epsilon}(\boldsymbol{\beta})}{(T-1)B_{\epsilon\epsilon}(\boldsymbol{\beta})}. \tag{3.53}$$

Comparing these estimators with the method of moments estimators derived in Section 3.3.2, we see that the conditional ML estimator of σ^2, (3.50), coincides with (3.38), while the conditional ML estimator of σ_{α}^2, (3.52), equals (3.40), except that $B_{\epsilon\epsilon}/(N-1)$ is replaced by $B_{\epsilon\epsilon}/N$, so that if N is large, the two sets of estimators are in practice indistinguishable.

An iterative procedure, switching between solving sub-problems A and B is:[14]

1. Estimate $\boldsymbol{\beta}$ and k by OLS and extract the residuals $\widehat{\epsilon}_{it}$.
2. Compute $\widetilde{\theta}_B(\widetilde{\boldsymbol{\beta}})$ and $\widetilde{\kappa}_B^2(\widetilde{\boldsymbol{\beta}})$ from (3.53) and (3.51), replacing ϵ_{it} by $\widehat{\epsilon}_{it}$.
3. Compute $\widehat{\boldsymbol{\beta}}_{GLS}$ from (3.13) with θ_B replaced by $\widetilde{\theta}_B$.
4. Compute $\ln(\mathcal{L})$ and check for convergence. If convergence is confirmed, go to step 5. Otherwise, return to step 2 and repeat steps 2–4.
5. Finally, estimate $\sigma_{\alpha}^2(\widetilde{\boldsymbol{\beta}})$ and k by $\widetilde{k}=\widehat{k}(\widetilde{\boldsymbol{\beta}})$ from (3.52) and (3.8).

3.5 Two-way variance component model

We turn to models with *both individual and time specific heterogeneity*, treated as random. They can be labelled regression models with random individual-specific and period-specific effects. Then we make stronger assumptions than when including corresponding fixed effects. This approach has both its pros and cons.

3.5.1 BASIC ASSUMPTIONS

We consider $\alpha_1,\dots,\alpha_N$ and $\gamma_1,\dots,\gamma_T$ as (realizations of) *stochastic variables*, N independent draws from one distribution and T independent draws from another, characterizing the population from which the sample defining the panel data set originates. The regression equation is

[13] The estimate of σ_{α}^2 may be negative. This problem is discussed in Berzeg (1979).

[14] Oberhofer and Kmenta (1974) and Breusch (1987) show that this kind of algorithm, under mild conditions, gives a result which converges towards the ML solution.

$$y_{it} = k + \alpha_i + \gamma_t + \boldsymbol{x}_{it}\boldsymbol{\beta} + u_{it}, \qquad i = 1,\dots,N;\ t = 1,\dots,T,$$

where $\boldsymbol{x}_{it} = (x_{1it},\dots,x_{Kit})$ and $\boldsymbol{\beta} = (\beta_1,\dots,\beta_K)'$. The individual-specific and period-specific intercept elements satisfy, respectively,

$$\begin{aligned}
&\mathsf{E}(\alpha_i|X) = 0, &&\text{var}(\alpha_i|X) = \sigma_\alpha^2, &&\text{cov}(\alpha_i,\alpha_j|X) = 0, &&i \neq j;\ i,j = 1,\dots,N,\\
&\mathsf{E}(\gamma_t|X) = 0, &&\text{var}(\gamma_t|X) = \sigma_\gamma^2, &&\text{cov}(\gamma_t,\gamma_s|X) = 0, &&t \neq s;\ t,s = 1,\dots,T,
\end{aligned}$$

where σ_α^2 and σ_γ^2 are unknown constants. Further, all values of α_i, γ_t, and u_{it} are uncorrelated. This formulation may seem 'aesthetically attractive', and it ensures a reduction in the number of parameters describing individual heterogeneity from $N-1$ to one, σ_α^2, and in the number of unknown parameters describing period heterogeneity from $T-1$ to one, σ_γ^2. However, as remarked in the introduction to the chapter, the objections against a symmetric modelling of individual- and period-specific heterogeneity should not be forgotten. Time-heterogeneity may sometimes be more adequately modelled by (deterministic or stochastic) trends or other kinds of time-series processes.

3.5.2 SOME IMPLICATIONS

The model can be rewritten as

$$\begin{aligned}
&y_{it} = k+\boldsymbol{x}_{it}\boldsymbol{\beta}+\alpha_i+\gamma_t+u_{it} = k+\boldsymbol{x}_{it}\boldsymbol{\beta}+\epsilon_{it},\ \ \epsilon_{it} = \alpha_i+\gamma_t+u_{it},\\
&(\alpha_i|X) \sim \mathsf{IID}(0,\sigma_\alpha^2),\ \ (\gamma_t|X) \sim \mathsf{IID}(0,\sigma_\gamma^2),\ \ (u_{it}|X) \sim \mathsf{IID}(0,\sigma^2),\\
&\alpha_i \perp \gamma_t \perp u_{it},\ \ i = 1,\dots,N;\ t = 1,\dots,T,
\end{aligned} \tag{3.54}$$

where ϵ_{it} can be interpreted as a *composite disturbance* obtained by adding *one random draw for individual i to one draw for period t and one draw for each individual in each period*. It is a *disturbance (error) component model* with three components. Two ϵ_{it}s from the same individual have equally strong correlation regardless of from which period they come: $\text{cov}(\epsilon_{it},\epsilon_{is}|X) = \sigma_\alpha^2$, $t \neq s$, and two ϵ_{it}s from the same period have equally strong correlation regardless of from which individual they come: $\text{cov}(\epsilon_{it},\epsilon_{jt}|X) = \sigma_\gamma^2$, $i \neq j$—again a kind of *equi-correlation*: $\text{corr}(\epsilon_{it},\epsilon_{jt}|X) = \rho_\alpha = \sigma_\alpha^2/(\sigma_\alpha^2+\sigma_\gamma^2+\sigma^2)$, $i \neq j$, and $\text{corr}(\epsilon_{it},\epsilon_{is}|X) = \rho_\gamma = \sigma_\gamma^2/(\sigma_\alpha^2+\sigma_\gamma^2+\sigma^2)$, $t \neq s$. The disturbance components are α_i, γ_t, and u_{it}, with variances σ_α^2, and σ_γ^2, and σ^2, of which the first and second also have interpretations as covariances.

Since the α_is and the γ_ts are independent, we cannot impose adding-up restrictions, $\sum \alpha_i = \sum \gamma_t = 0$, as in the fixed effects model. $\mathsf{E}(\alpha_i) = 0$ and $\mathsf{E}(\gamma_t) = 0$ in the *random* effects model are the counterparts to $\bar{\alpha} = \frac{1}{N}\sum \alpha_i = 0$ and $\bar{\gamma} = \frac{1}{T}\sum \gamma_t = 0$ in the *fixed* effects model. Imagine that we had specified individual-specific and time-specific components, α_i^* and γ_t^*, without restricting their expectations or means to be zero. We could then interpret (3.54) as having a composite intercept equal to $k+\alpha_i+\gamma_t = k^*+\alpha_i^*+\gamma_t^*$, where:

In the random effects case:

$$\alpha_i = \alpha_i^* - \mathsf{E}(\alpha_i^*|X),\;\; \gamma_t = \gamma_t^* - \mathsf{E}(\gamma_t^*|X),\;\; k = k^* + \mathsf{E}(\alpha_i^*|X) + \mathsf{E}(\gamma_t^*|X).$$

In the fixed effects case:

$$\alpha_i = \alpha_i^* - \bar{\alpha}^*,\;\; \gamma_t = \gamma_t^* - \bar{\gamma}^*,\;\; k = k^* + \bar{\alpha}^* + \bar{\gamma}^*.$$

Letting $\boldsymbol{\alpha} = (\alpha_1,\dots,\alpha_N)'$, $\boldsymbol{\gamma} = (\gamma_1,\dots,\gamma_T)'$, (3.54) can be written compactly as

$$\begin{aligned} &\boldsymbol{y} = \boldsymbol{e}_{NT}k + \boldsymbol{X\beta} + \boldsymbol{\epsilon},\;\; \boldsymbol{\epsilon} = (\boldsymbol{\alpha}\otimes\boldsymbol{e}_T) + (\boldsymbol{e}_N\otimes\boldsymbol{\gamma}) + \boldsymbol{u}, \\ &\mathsf{E}(\boldsymbol{\epsilon}|\boldsymbol{X}) = \boldsymbol{0}_{NT,1},\;\; \mathsf{V}(\boldsymbol{\epsilon}|\boldsymbol{X}) = \boldsymbol{\Omega},\;\; \boldsymbol{\alpha}\perp\boldsymbol{\gamma}\perp\boldsymbol{u}. \end{aligned} \tag{3.55}$$

Its disturbance covariance matrix, $\boldsymbol{\Omega}$, has $(N\times N)$ blocks of dimension $(T\times T)$:

$$\begin{aligned} \boldsymbol{\Omega} &= \sigma_\alpha^2 \boldsymbol{I}_N\otimes(\boldsymbol{e}_T\boldsymbol{e}_T') + \sigma_\gamma^2(\boldsymbol{e}_N\boldsymbol{e}_N')\otimes\boldsymbol{I}_T + \sigma^2(\boldsymbol{I}_N\otimes\boldsymbol{I}_T) \\ &= \begin{bmatrix} \boldsymbol{\Omega}_{T1}+\boldsymbol{\Omega}_{T2} & \cdots & \boldsymbol{\Omega}_{T2} \\ \vdots & \ddots & \vdots \\ \boldsymbol{\Omega}_{T2} & \cdots & \boldsymbol{\Omega}_{T1}+\boldsymbol{\Omega}_{T2} \end{bmatrix}, \end{aligned} \tag{3.56}$$

where

$$\boldsymbol{\Omega}_{T1} = \sigma_\alpha^2(\boldsymbol{e}_T\boldsymbol{e}_T') + \sigma^2\boldsymbol{I}_T = \begin{bmatrix} \sigma_\alpha^2+\sigma^2 & \cdots & \sigma_\alpha^2 \\ \vdots & \ddots & \vdots \\ \sigma_\alpha^2 & \cdots & \sigma_\alpha^2+\sigma^2 \end{bmatrix},$$

$$\boldsymbol{\Omega}_{T2} = \sigma_\gamma^2\boldsymbol{I}_T = \begin{bmatrix} \sigma_\gamma^2 & \cdots & 0 \\ \vdots & \ddots & \vdots \\ 0 & \cdots & \sigma_\gamma^2 \end{bmatrix}.$$

Since the mechanism generating $\boldsymbol{\epsilon}$ is described by $(\sigma_\alpha^2, \sigma_\gamma^2, \sigma^2)$, the label *variance component model with three components* is appropriate.[15]

[15] The three-component model specializes to a two-component model with only period-specific effects when $\alpha_i = \sigma_\alpha^2 = 0$, symmetric to the two-component model with $\gamma_t = \sigma_\gamma^2 = 0$.

3.6 GLS with known variance components

3.6.1 THE PROBLEM AND ITS REFORMULATION

We first assume that σ_α^2, σ_γ^2, and σ^2 are known. Again, we proceed stepwise: first state the minimization problem, next transform the minimand to eliminate the intercept, and finally explain how the GLS problem can be solved as an OLS problem in transformed variables. The GLS problem is

$$\min_{k,\boldsymbol{\beta}}\{[y - e_{NT}k - X\boldsymbol{\beta}]'\boldsymbol{\Omega}^{-1}[y - e_{NT}k - X\boldsymbol{\beta}]\} = \min_{k,\boldsymbol{\beta}} \boldsymbol{\epsilon}'\boldsymbol{\Omega}^{-1}\boldsymbol{\epsilon}. \tag{3.57}$$

To obtain an expression for $\boldsymbol{\Omega}^{-1}$ we rearrange $\boldsymbol{\Omega}$ as[16]

$$\begin{aligned}\boldsymbol{\Omega} &= \sigma^2(\boldsymbol{B}_N\otimes\boldsymbol{B}_T)+(\sigma^2+T\sigma_\alpha^2)(\boldsymbol{B}_N\otimes\boldsymbol{A}_T)\\ &\quad + (\sigma^2+N\sigma_\gamma^2)(\boldsymbol{A}_N\otimes\boldsymbol{B}_T)+(\sigma^2+T\sigma_\alpha^2+N\sigma_\gamma^2)(\boldsymbol{A}_N\otimes\boldsymbol{A}_T)\end{aligned} \tag{3.58}$$

and obtain from *Theorem 1* in Appendix 3A, Section 3A.1:

$$\begin{aligned}\boldsymbol{\Omega}^{-1} &= \frac{\boldsymbol{B}_N\otimes\boldsymbol{B}_T}{\sigma^2}+\frac{\boldsymbol{B}_N\otimes\boldsymbol{A}_T}{\sigma^2+T\sigma_\alpha^2}+\frac{\boldsymbol{A}_N\otimes\boldsymbol{B}_T}{\sigma^2+N\sigma_\gamma^2}+\frac{\boldsymbol{A}_N\otimes\boldsymbol{A}_T}{\sigma^2+T\sigma_\alpha^2+N\sigma_\gamma^2}\\ &= \sigma^{-2}[\boldsymbol{B}_N\otimes\boldsymbol{B}_T+\theta_B\boldsymbol{B}_N\otimes\boldsymbol{A}_T+\theta_C\boldsymbol{A}_N\otimes\boldsymbol{B}_T+\theta_D\boldsymbol{A}_N\otimes\boldsymbol{A}_T],\end{aligned} \tag{3.59}$$

where, recalling $\rho_\alpha = \sigma_\alpha^2/(\sigma^2+\sigma_\alpha^2+\sigma_\gamma^2)$ and $\rho_\gamma = \sigma_\gamma^2/(\sigma^2+\sigma_\alpha^2+\sigma_\gamma^2)$,

$$\begin{aligned}\theta_B &= \frac{\sigma^2}{\sigma^2+T\sigma_\alpha^2} \equiv \frac{1-\rho_\alpha-\rho_\gamma}{1+(T-1)\rho_\alpha-\rho_\gamma},\\ \theta_C &= \frac{\sigma^2}{\sigma^2+N\sigma_\gamma^2} \equiv \frac{1-\rho_\alpha-\rho_\gamma}{1+(N-1)\rho_\gamma-\rho_\alpha},\\ \theta_D &= \frac{\sigma^2}{\sigma^2+T\sigma_\alpha^2+N\sigma_\gamma^2} \equiv \frac{1-\rho_\alpha-\rho_\gamma}{1+(T-1)\rho_\alpha+(N-1)\rho_\gamma}.\end{aligned} \tag{3.60}$$

See Wansbeek and Kapteyn (1982, 1983) for an extended treatment of covariance matrix decomposition.

Since $\boldsymbol{e}_N'\boldsymbol{B}_N=\boldsymbol{0}$, $\boldsymbol{e}_N'\boldsymbol{A}_N=\boldsymbol{e}_N' \Longrightarrow \boldsymbol{e}_{NT}'\boldsymbol{\Omega}^{-1}=\sigma^{-2}\theta_D\boldsymbol{e}_{NT}'$, all column sums of $\boldsymbol{\Omega}^{-1}$ equal $\sigma^{-2}\theta_D$. Theorem 2 in Appendix 3A, Section 3A.2, therefore implies

$$\widehat{k} = \widehat{k}(\boldsymbol{\beta}) = \tfrac{1}{NT}\boldsymbol{e}_{NT}'(y - X\boldsymbol{\beta}) = \bar{y} - \bar{x}\boldsymbol{\beta}. \tag{3.61}$$

[16] This corresponds to the spectral decomposition of $\boldsymbol{\Omega}$; see Lütkepohl (1996, p. 70).

Utilizing (3.57), (3.59), and (3.61), the minimand can be simplified to

$$(y-X\boldsymbol{\beta})'(I_{NT}-A_{NT})\boldsymbol{\Omega}^{-1}(I_{NT}-A_{NT})(y-X\boldsymbol{\beta}) \equiv$$
$$\sigma^{-2}(y-X\boldsymbol{\beta})'[(B_N\otimes B_T)+\theta_B(B_N\otimes A_T)+\theta_C(A_N\otimes B_T)](y-X\boldsymbol{\beta}),$$

since $A_{NT}\boldsymbol{\Omega}^{-1}=A_{NT}\boldsymbol{\Omega}^{-1}A_{NT}=\sigma^{-2}\theta_D A_{NT}$, and hence

$$\begin{aligned}(I_{NT}-A_{NT})\,\boldsymbol{\Omega}^{-1}\,(I_{NT}-A_{NT})\\ &\equiv \boldsymbol{\Omega}^{-1}-\sigma^{-2}\theta_D A_N\otimes A_{NT}\\ &\equiv \sigma^{-2}[(B_N\otimes B_T)+\theta_B(B_N\otimes A_T)+\theta_C(A_N\otimes B_T)].\end{aligned}$$

This implies that the GLS estimator of $\boldsymbol{\beta}$ in Model (3.55) becomes

$$\begin{aligned}\widehat{\boldsymbol{\beta}}_{GLS} &= [X'(B_N\otimes B_T)X+\theta_B X'(B_N\otimes A_T)X+\theta_C X'(A_N\otimes B_T)X]^{-1}\\ &\quad\times [X'(B_N\otimes B_T)y+\theta_B X'(B_N\otimes A_T)y+\theta_C X'(A_N\otimes B_T)y],\end{aligned} \tag{3.62}$$

while (3.61) gives

$$\widehat{k}_{GLS}=\widehat{k}(\widehat{\boldsymbol{\beta}}_{GLS})=\bar{y}-\bar{\boldsymbol{x}}\widehat{\boldsymbol{\beta}}_{GLS}. \tag{3.63}$$

Equation (3.62) generalizes (3.9) (obtained for $\sigma_\gamma^2=0 \Longrightarrow \theta_C=1$).

3.6.2 GLS AS OLS ON TRANSFORMED DATA

Once again, the transformation of the GLS problem into an OLS problem illuminates the interpretation of the GLS estimators. From (3.59) we obtain the factorization

$$\begin{aligned}&\boldsymbol{\Omega}^{-1}=S^2,\\ &S=\sigma^{-1}[B_N\otimes B_T+\sqrt{\theta_B}B_N\otimes A_T+\sqrt{\theta_C}A_N\otimes B_T+\sqrt{\theta_D}A_N\otimes A_T],\end{aligned} \tag{3.64}$$

so that the minimand in (3.57), letting $k^*=\sqrt{\theta_D}k$, can be written as

$$\sigma^{-2}[y-e_{NT}k-X\boldsymbol{\beta}]'(\sigma S)'(\sigma S)\left[y-e_{NT}k-X\boldsymbol{\beta}\right]=\sigma^{-2}\boldsymbol{\epsilon}^{*\prime}\boldsymbol{\epsilon}^*,$$

where

$$\sigma S = I_N\otimes I_T-\eta_B I_N\otimes A_T-\eta_C A_N\otimes I_T+\eta_D A_N\otimes A_T,$$

$$\eta_B=1-\sqrt{\theta_B},\;\; \eta_C=1-\sqrt{\theta_C},\;\; \eta_D=1-\sqrt{\theta_B}-\sqrt{\theta_C}+\sqrt{\theta_D},$$

$$\begin{aligned}
\boldsymbol{\epsilon}^* &= \sigma S\boldsymbol{\epsilon} = \boldsymbol{y}^* - (\boldsymbol{e}_N \otimes \boldsymbol{e}_T)k^* - \boldsymbol{X}^*\boldsymbol{\beta},\\
\boldsymbol{y}^* &= \boldsymbol{y} - \eta_B(\boldsymbol{I}_N \otimes \boldsymbol{A}_T)\boldsymbol{y} - \eta_C(\boldsymbol{A}_N \otimes \boldsymbol{I}_T)\boldsymbol{y} + \eta_D(\boldsymbol{A}_N \otimes \boldsymbol{A}_T)\boldsymbol{y},\\
\boldsymbol{X}^* &= \boldsymbol{X} - \eta_B(\boldsymbol{I}_N \otimes \boldsymbol{A}_T)\boldsymbol{X} - \eta_C(\boldsymbol{A}_N \otimes \boldsymbol{I}_T)\boldsymbol{X} + \eta_D(\boldsymbol{A}_N \otimes \boldsymbol{A}_T)\boldsymbol{X}.
\end{aligned}$$

Therefore, to solve the GLS problem (3.57) we can:[17] *(i) deduct from* $\boldsymbol{y}$ *and* $\boldsymbol{X}$ *a share* η_B *of their individual-specific means and a share* η_C *of their period-specific means and add a share* η_D *of their global means, giving the regression equation* $\boldsymbol{y}^* = (\boldsymbol{e}_N \otimes \boldsymbol{e}_T)k^* + \boldsymbol{X}^*\boldsymbol{\beta} + \boldsymbol{\epsilon}^*$; *and (ii) apply OLS on this equation.* This shows that the *GLS estimator emerges as a compromise between OLS, the within-individual, the within-period, and the residual estimators,* corresponding to, respectively, $\theta_B = \theta_C = \theta_D = 1$; $\theta_B = \theta_D = 0, \theta_C = 1$; $\theta_C = \theta_D = 0, \theta_B = 1$; and $\theta_B = \theta_C = \theta_D = 0$.

We know from Section 2.4 that the OLS estimator of $\boldsymbol{\beta}$ is the MVLUE in the absence of heterogeneity and that the residual estimator is the MVLUE if fixed heterogeneity occurs along both dimensions. The within-individual estimator is the MVLUE if there is fixed *individual-specific*, but no period-specific heterogeneity, and the within-period estimator is the MVLUE in the opposite case. The above results for the two-way random effects model supports our intuition that an optimal solution to the GLS problem lies between these four extremes, and (3.60) and (3.62) give the optimal weights.

3.6.3 FIVE ESTIMATORS AND A SYNTHESIS

Let us compare $\widehat{\boldsymbol{\beta}}_{GLS}$ with the residual estimator $\widehat{\boldsymbol{\beta}}_R$, the between-individual estimator $\widehat{\boldsymbol{\beta}}_B$, the between-period estimator $\widehat{\boldsymbol{\beta}}_C$, and the global estimator $\widehat{\boldsymbol{\beta}}_{OLS}$. Using the (general) notation,

$$\begin{aligned}
G_{ZQ} &= \boldsymbol{Z}'(\boldsymbol{I}_{NT} - \boldsymbol{A}_{NT})\boldsymbol{Q} = \textstyle\sum_{i=1}^N \sum_{t=1}^T (z_{it} - \bar{z})'(q_{it} - \bar{q}),\\
R_{ZQ} &= \boldsymbol{Z}'(\boldsymbol{B}_N \otimes \boldsymbol{B}_T)\boldsymbol{Q} = \textstyle\sum_{i=1}^N \sum_{t=1}^T (z_{it} - \bar{z}_{i\cdot} - \bar{z}_{\cdot t} + \bar{z})'(q_{it} - \bar{q}_{i\cdot} - \bar{q}_{\cdot t} + \bar{q}),\\
B_{ZQ} &= \boldsymbol{Z}'(\boldsymbol{B}_N \otimes \boldsymbol{A}_T)\boldsymbol{Q} = T\textstyle\sum_{i=1}^N (\bar{z}_{i\cdot} - \bar{z})'(\bar{q}_{i\cdot} - \bar{q}),\\
C_{ZQ} &= \boldsymbol{Z}'(\boldsymbol{A}_N \otimes \boldsymbol{B}_T)\boldsymbol{Q} = N\textstyle\sum_{t=1}^T (\bar{z}_{\cdot t} - \bar{z})'(\bar{q}_{\cdot t} - \bar{q}),
\end{aligned}$$

they can be rewritten as

$$\widehat{\boldsymbol{\beta}}_{GLS} = (\boldsymbol{R}_{XX} + \theta_B \boldsymbol{B}_{XX} + \theta_C \boldsymbol{C}_{XX})^{-1}(\boldsymbol{R}_{XY} + \theta_B \boldsymbol{B}_{XY} + \theta_C \boldsymbol{C}_{XY}), \tag{3.65}$$

$$\widehat{\boldsymbol{\beta}}_R = \boldsymbol{R}_{XX}^{-1}\boldsymbol{R}_{XY}, \tag{3.66}$$

[17] This is the procedure proposed by Fuller and Battese (1973; 1974, p. 77).

$$\widehat{\boldsymbol{\beta}}_B = \boldsymbol{B}_{XX}^{-1}\boldsymbol{B}_{XY}, \tag{3.67}$$

$$\widehat{\boldsymbol{\beta}}_C = \boldsymbol{C}_{XX}^{-1}\boldsymbol{C}_{XY}, \tag{3.68}$$

$$\widehat{\boldsymbol{\beta}}_{OLS} = (\boldsymbol{R}_{XX}+\boldsymbol{B}_{XX}+\boldsymbol{C}_{XX})^{-1}(\boldsymbol{R}_{XY}+\boldsymbol{B}_{XY}+\boldsymbol{C}_{XY}), \tag{3.69}$$

where $\widehat{\boldsymbol{\beta}}_R$ is the MVLUE of $\boldsymbol{\beta}$ in Model (2.100), $\widehat{\boldsymbol{\beta}}_{GLS}$ is the MVLUE in Model (3.55), and $\widehat{\boldsymbol{\beta}}_{OLS}$ is the MVLUE in the homogeneous model. Both $\widehat{\boldsymbol{\beta}}_{GLS}$ and $\widehat{\boldsymbol{\beta}}_{OLS}$ are linear combinations of $\widehat{\boldsymbol{\beta}}_R$, $\widehat{\boldsymbol{\beta}}_B$, and $\widehat{\boldsymbol{\beta}}_C$. The relationship between $\widehat{\boldsymbol{\beta}}_{GLS}$, $\widehat{\boldsymbol{\beta}}_R$, $\widehat{\boldsymbol{\beta}}_B$, and $\widehat{\boldsymbol{\beta}}_C$, which generalizes (3.17), is

$$\begin{aligned}\widehat{\boldsymbol{\beta}}_{GLS} &= [\boldsymbol{R}_{XX}+\theta_B\boldsymbol{B}_{XX}+\theta_C\boldsymbol{C}_{XX}]^{-1}\\ &\quad\times[\boldsymbol{R}_{XX}\widehat{\boldsymbol{\beta}}_R+\theta_B\boldsymbol{B}_{XX}\widehat{\boldsymbol{\beta}}_B+\theta_C\boldsymbol{C}_{XX}\widehat{\boldsymbol{\beta}}_C].\end{aligned} \tag{3.70}$$

Consider a general unbiased estimator obtained by giving the residual-, the between-individual, and the between-period (co)variation weights λ_R, λ_B, and λ_C:

$$\begin{aligned}\widehat{\boldsymbol{\beta}} &= [\lambda_R\boldsymbol{R}_{XX}+\lambda_B\boldsymbol{B}_{XX}+\lambda_C\boldsymbol{C}_{XX}]^{-1}\\ &\quad\times[\lambda_R\boldsymbol{R}_{XY}+\lambda_B\boldsymbol{B}_{XY}+\lambda_C\boldsymbol{C}_{XY}].\end{aligned} \tag{3.71}$$

Since $\boldsymbol{R}_{XY}=\boldsymbol{R}_{XX}\boldsymbol{\beta}+\boldsymbol{R}_{X\epsilon}$, $\boldsymbol{B}_{XY}=\boldsymbol{B}_{XX}\boldsymbol{\beta}+\boldsymbol{B}_{X\epsilon}$, $\boldsymbol{C}_{XY}=\boldsymbol{C}_{XX}\boldsymbol{\beta}+\boldsymbol{C}_{X\epsilon}$,

$$\begin{aligned}\widehat{\boldsymbol{\beta}}-\boldsymbol{\beta} &= [\lambda_R\boldsymbol{R}_{XX}+\lambda_B\boldsymbol{B}_{XX}+\lambda_C\boldsymbol{C}_{XX}]^{-1}\\ &\quad\times[\lambda_R\boldsymbol{R}_{X\epsilon}+\lambda_B\boldsymbol{B}_{X\epsilon}+\lambda_C\boldsymbol{C}_{X\epsilon}].\end{aligned}$$

From (3.58) it follows that

$$\begin{aligned}\mathsf{V}(\boldsymbol{R}_{X\epsilon}|\boldsymbol{X}) &= \boldsymbol{X}'(\boldsymbol{B}_N\otimes\boldsymbol{B}_T)\boldsymbol{\Omega}(\boldsymbol{B}_N\otimes\boldsymbol{B}_T)\boldsymbol{X}\\ &= \sigma^2\boldsymbol{X}'(\boldsymbol{B}_N\otimes\boldsymbol{B}_T)\boldsymbol{X} = \sigma^2\boldsymbol{R}_{XX},\end{aligned} \tag{3.72}$$

$$\begin{aligned}\mathsf{V}(\boldsymbol{B}_{X\epsilon}|\boldsymbol{X}) &= \boldsymbol{X}'(\boldsymbol{B}_N\otimes\boldsymbol{A}_T)\boldsymbol{\Omega}(\boldsymbol{B}_N\otimes\boldsymbol{A}_T)\boldsymbol{X}\\ &= (\sigma^2+T\sigma_\alpha^2)\boldsymbol{X}'(\boldsymbol{B}_N\otimes\boldsymbol{A}_T)\boldsymbol{X} = (\sigma^2+T\sigma_\alpha^2)\boldsymbol{B}_{XX},\end{aligned} \tag{3.73}$$

$$\begin{aligned}\mathsf{V}(\boldsymbol{C}_{X\epsilon}|\boldsymbol{X}) &= \boldsymbol{X}'(\boldsymbol{A}_N\otimes\boldsymbol{B}_T)\boldsymbol{\Omega}(\boldsymbol{A}_N\otimes\boldsymbol{B}_T)\boldsymbol{X}\\ &= (\sigma^2+N\sigma_\gamma^2)\boldsymbol{X}'(\boldsymbol{A}_N\otimes\boldsymbol{B}_T)\boldsymbol{X} = (\sigma^2+N\sigma_\gamma^2)\boldsymbol{C}_{XX},\end{aligned} \tag{3.74}$$

while $\boldsymbol{A}_T\boldsymbol{B}_T=\boldsymbol{0}_{T,T} \Longrightarrow \mathsf{E}(\boldsymbol{R}_{X\epsilon}\boldsymbol{B}'_{X\epsilon}|\boldsymbol{X})=\mathsf{E}(\boldsymbol{R}_{X\epsilon}\boldsymbol{C}'_{X\epsilon}|\boldsymbol{X})=\mathsf{E}(\boldsymbol{B}_{X\epsilon}\boldsymbol{C}'_{X\epsilon}|\boldsymbol{X})=\boldsymbol{0}_{KK}$, and hence *$\widehat{\boldsymbol{\beta}}_R$, $\widehat{\boldsymbol{\beta}}_B$, and $\widehat{\boldsymbol{\beta}}_C$ are uncorrelated (conditional on $\boldsymbol{X}$)*. Therefore,

$$\begin{aligned}\mathsf{V}(\widehat{\boldsymbol{\beta}}|\boldsymbol{X}) = {} & [\lambda_R \boldsymbol{R}_{XX} + \lambda_B \boldsymbol{B}_{XX} + \lambda_C \boldsymbol{C}_{XX}]^{-1} \\ & \times [\lambda_R^2 \sigma^2 \boldsymbol{R}_{XX} + \lambda_B^2 (\sigma^2 + T\sigma_\alpha^2) \boldsymbol{B}_{XX} + \lambda_C^2 (\sigma^2 + N\sigma_\gamma^2) \boldsymbol{C}_{XX}] \\ & \times [\lambda_R \boldsymbol{R}_{XX} + \lambda_B \boldsymbol{B}_{XX} + \lambda_C \boldsymbol{C}_{XX}]^{-1}. \end{aligned} \tag{3.75}$$

This equation generalizes (3.21). Since the five estimators are obtained for $(\lambda_R, \lambda_B, \lambda_C) = (1, \theta_B, \theta_C), (1, 0, 0), (0, 1, 0), (0, 0, 1), (1, 1, 1)$, respectively, the covariance matrices of (3.65)–(3.69) are given by

$$\mathsf{V}(\widehat{\boldsymbol{\beta}}_{GLS}|\boldsymbol{X}) = \sigma^2 (\boldsymbol{R}_{XX} + \theta_B \boldsymbol{B}_{XX} + \theta_C \boldsymbol{C}_{XX})^{-1}, \tag{3.76}$$

$$\mathsf{V}(\widehat{\boldsymbol{\beta}}_R|\boldsymbol{X}) = \sigma^2 \boldsymbol{R}_{XX}^{-1}, \tag{3.77}$$

$$\mathsf{V}(\widehat{\boldsymbol{\beta}}_B|\boldsymbol{X}) = (\sigma^2 + T\sigma_\alpha^2) \boldsymbol{B}_{XX}^{-1} = (\sigma^2/\theta_B) \boldsymbol{B}_{XX}^{-1}, \tag{3.78}$$

$$\mathsf{V}(\widehat{\boldsymbol{\beta}}_C|\boldsymbol{X}) = (\sigma^2 + N\sigma_\gamma^2) \boldsymbol{C}_{XX}^{-1} = (\sigma^2/\theta_C) \boldsymbol{C}_{XX}^{-1}, \tag{3.79}$$

$$\mathsf{V}(\widehat{\boldsymbol{\beta}}_{OLS}|\boldsymbol{X}) = \boldsymbol{G}_{XX}^{-1} (\sigma^2 + T\sigma_\alpha^2 \boldsymbol{B}_{XX} \boldsymbol{G}_{XX}^{-1} + N\sigma_\gamma^2 \boldsymbol{C}_{XX} \boldsymbol{G}_{XX}^{-1}). \tag{3.80}$$

In the *one-regressor case*, b and c denoting the between-individual and the between-period share of the regressor's total variation, the more transparent scalar counterparts read, see Appendix 3B, (3B.19)–(3B.23),

$$\begin{aligned} \text{var}(\widehat{\beta}_{GLS}|\boldsymbol{X}) &= \frac{\sigma^2}{G_{XX}} \frac{1}{1 - b(1-\theta_B) - c(1-\theta_C)}, \\ \text{var}(\widehat{\beta}_R|\boldsymbol{X}) &= \frac{\sigma^2}{G_{XX}} \frac{1}{1 - b - c}, \\ \text{var}(\widehat{\beta}_B|\boldsymbol{X}) &= \frac{\sigma^2}{G_{XX}} \frac{1}{b\theta_B}, \\ \text{var}(\widehat{\beta}_C|\boldsymbol{X}) &= \frac{\sigma^2}{G_{XX}} \frac{1}{c\theta_C}, \\ \text{var}(\widehat{\beta}_{OLS}|\boldsymbol{X}) &= \frac{\sigma^2}{G_{XX}} \left[1 + b\left(\frac{1}{\theta_B} - 1\right) + c\left(\frac{1}{\theta_C} - 1\right)\right]. \end{aligned}$$

The relative OLS/GLS-efficiency, see Appendix B3, (3B.27), is:

$$\frac{\text{var}(\widehat{\beta}_{OLS}|\boldsymbol{X})}{\text{var}(\widehat{\beta}_{GLS}|\boldsymbol{X})} = \left[1 + b\left(\frac{1}{\theta_B} - 1\right) + c\left(\frac{1}{\theta_C} - 1\right)\right] \left[1 - b(1-\theta_B) - c(1-\theta_C)\right],$$

which exceeds one in the normal case where $0 < b+c < 1, 0 < \theta_B < 1, 0 < \theta_C < 1$.

Using again the identity $E^{-1}-(E+D)^{-1} \equiv (E+D)^{-1}DE^{-1}$, we have

$$\begin{aligned}
&\mathsf{V}(\widehat{\boldsymbol{\beta}}_R|X)-\mathsf{V}(\widehat{\boldsymbol{\beta}}_{GLS}|X)\\
&=\sigma^2(\boldsymbol{R}_{XX}+\theta_B\boldsymbol{B}_{XX}+\theta_C\boldsymbol{C}_{XX})^{-1}(\theta_B\boldsymbol{B}_{XX}+\theta_C\boldsymbol{C}_{XX})\boldsymbol{R}_{XX}^{-1}, \qquad (3.81)\\
&\mathsf{V}(\widehat{\boldsymbol{\beta}}_B|X)-\mathsf{V}(\widehat{\boldsymbol{\beta}}_{GLS}|X)\\
&=(\sigma^2/\theta_B)(\boldsymbol{R}_{XX}+\theta_B\boldsymbol{B}_{XX}+\theta_C\boldsymbol{C}_{XX})^{-1}(\boldsymbol{R}_{XX}+\theta_C\boldsymbol{C}_{XX})\boldsymbol{B}_{XX}^{-1}, \qquad (3.82)\\
&\mathsf{V}(\widehat{\boldsymbol{\beta}}_C|X)-\mathsf{V}(\widehat{\boldsymbol{\beta}}_{GLS}|X)\\
&=(\sigma^2/\theta_C)(\boldsymbol{R}_{XX}+\theta_B\boldsymbol{B}_{XX}+\theta_C\boldsymbol{C}_{XX})^{-1}(\boldsymbol{R}_{XX}+\theta_B\boldsymbol{B}_{XX})\boldsymbol{C}_{XX}^{-1}. \qquad (3.83)
\end{aligned}$$

They are positive definite when $\boldsymbol{R}_{XX}$, $\boldsymbol{B}_{XX}$, and $\boldsymbol{C}_{XX}$ are positive definite and $\theta_B>0, \theta_C>0$.

This confirms that $\widehat{\boldsymbol{\beta}}_{GLS}$ is more efficient than $\widehat{\boldsymbol{\beta}}_R$, $\widehat{\boldsymbol{\beta}}_B$, and $\widehat{\boldsymbol{\beta}}_C$ (the same can be shown to hold when comparing it with $\widehat{\boldsymbol{\beta}}_{OLS}$): *any linear combination of the elements in* $\widehat{\boldsymbol{\beta}}_{GLS}$, $\boldsymbol{a}'\widehat{\boldsymbol{\beta}}_{GLS}$, *where* $\boldsymbol{a}$ *is a* $(K \times 1)$*-vector, as an estimator of* $\boldsymbol{a}'\boldsymbol{\beta}$*, has smaller variance than the corresponding linear combination for the other estimators:* since $\text{var}(\boldsymbol{a}'\widehat{\boldsymbol{\beta}}_Z|X)= \boldsymbol{a}'\mathsf{V}(\widehat{\boldsymbol{\beta}}_Z|X)\boldsymbol{a}$ $(Z = R, B, C, OLS)$, positive definiteness of the matrix differences means that[18]

$$\begin{aligned}
&\boldsymbol{a}'[\mathsf{V}(\widehat{\boldsymbol{\beta}}_Z|X)-\mathsf{V}(\widehat{\boldsymbol{\beta}}_{GLS}|X)]\boldsymbol{a}>0 \implies\\
&\text{var}(\boldsymbol{a}'\widehat{\boldsymbol{\beta}}_Z|X)>\text{var}(\boldsymbol{a}'\widehat{\boldsymbol{\beta}}_{GLS}|X),\; Z=R,B,C,OLS.
\end{aligned}$$

3.7 **GLS with unknown variance components**

3.7.1 THE PROBLEM

Assuming $(\sigma^2, \sigma_\alpha^2, \sigma_\gamma^2)$ known is rarely realistic. To explain how can they be estimated we start by transforming (3.54) as follows:

$$\begin{aligned}
y_{it}-\bar{y}_{i\cdot}-\bar{y}_{\cdot t}+\bar{y} &= (\boldsymbol{x}_{it}-\bar{\boldsymbol{x}}_{i\cdot}-\bar{\boldsymbol{x}}_{\cdot t}+\bar{\boldsymbol{x}})\boldsymbol{\beta} + (\epsilon_{it}-\bar{\epsilon}_{i\cdot}-\bar{\epsilon}_{\cdot t}+\bar{\epsilon})\\
&= (\boldsymbol{x}_{it}-\bar{\boldsymbol{x}}_{i\cdot}-\bar{\boldsymbol{x}}_{\cdot t}+\bar{\boldsymbol{x}})\boldsymbol{\beta} + (u_{it}-\bar{u}_{i\cdot}-\bar{u}_{\cdot t}+\bar{u}), \qquad (3.84)
\end{aligned}$$

[18] Equation (3.80) also implies that the 'standard' expression for the covariance matrix of the OLS estimator when the disturbances are uncorrelated and homoskedastic, which is $\mathsf{V}^*(\widehat{\boldsymbol{\beta}}_{OLS}|X) = \sigma^2\boldsymbol{G}_{XX}^{-1}$, *underestimates* the true covariance matrix:

$$\mathsf{V}(\widehat{\boldsymbol{\beta}}_{OLS}|X) - \mathsf{V}^*(\widehat{\boldsymbol{\beta}}_{OLS}|X) = \boldsymbol{G}_{XX}^{-1}[T\sigma_\alpha^2\boldsymbol{B}_{XX} + N\sigma_\gamma^2\boldsymbol{C}_{XX}]\boldsymbol{G}_{XX}^{-1}$$

is positive definite for (i) $\boldsymbol{B}_{XX}$ positive definite, $\sigma_\alpha^2>0$ or (ii) $\boldsymbol{C}_{XX}$ positive definite, $\sigma_\gamma^2>0$.

$$\bar{y}_{i\cdot} - \bar{y} = (\bar{x}_{i\cdot} - \bar{x})\boldsymbol{\beta} + (\bar{\epsilon}_{i\cdot} - \bar{\epsilon})$$
$$= (\bar{x}_{i\cdot} - \bar{x})\boldsymbol{\beta} + (\alpha_i - \bar{\alpha}) + (\bar{u}_{i\cdot} - \bar{u}), \tag{3.85}$$
$$\bar{y}_{\cdot t} - \bar{y} = (\bar{x}_{\cdot t} - \bar{x})\boldsymbol{\beta} + (\bar{\epsilon}_{\cdot t} - \bar{\epsilon})$$
$$= (\bar{x}_{\cdot t} - \bar{x})\,\boldsymbol{\beta} + (\gamma_t - \bar{\gamma}) + (\bar{u}_{\cdot t} - \bar{u}), \tag{3.86}$$

in matrix notation, using (3.55),

$$(B_N \otimes B_T)y = (B_N \otimes B_T)X\boldsymbol{\beta} + (B_N \otimes B_T)\boldsymbol{\epsilon}$$
$$= (B_N \otimes B_T)X\boldsymbol{\beta} + (B_N \otimes B_T)u, \tag{3.87}$$
$$(B_N \otimes \tfrac{1}{T}e_T')y = (B_N \otimes \tfrac{1}{T}e_T')X\boldsymbol{\beta} + (B_N \otimes \tfrac{1}{T}e_T')\boldsymbol{\epsilon}$$
$$= (B_N \otimes \tfrac{1}{T}e_T')X\boldsymbol{\beta} + B_N\boldsymbol{\alpha} + (B_N \otimes \tfrac{1}{T}e_T')u, \tag{3.88}$$
$$(\tfrac{1}{N}e_N' \otimes B_T)y = (\tfrac{1}{N}e_N' \otimes B_T)X\boldsymbol{\beta} + (\tfrac{1}{N}e_N' \otimes B_T)\boldsymbol{\epsilon}$$
$$= (\tfrac{1}{N}e_N' \otimes B_T)X\boldsymbol{\beta} + B_T\boldsymbol{\gamma} + (\tfrac{1}{N}e_N' \otimes B_T)u. \tag{3.89}$$

Using (3.58), it follows that

$$\mathsf{V}[(B_N \otimes B_T)\boldsymbol{\epsilon}|X] = \sigma^2(B_N \otimes B_T), \tag{3.90}$$
$$\mathsf{V}[(B_N \otimes \tfrac{1}{T}e_T')\boldsymbol{\epsilon}|X] = (\sigma_\alpha^2 + \tfrac{1}{T}\sigma^2)B_N, \tag{3.91}$$
$$\mathsf{V}[(\tfrac{1}{N}e_N' \otimes B_T)\boldsymbol{\epsilon}|X] = (\sigma_\gamma^2 + \tfrac{1}{N}\sigma^2)B_T. \tag{3.92}$$

Their diagonal elements are, respectively,

$$\sigma^2\left(1-\tfrac{1}{T}\right)\left(1-\tfrac{1}{N}\right), \qquad (\sigma_\alpha^2+\tfrac{1}{T}\sigma^2)\left(1-\tfrac{1}{N}\right), \qquad \left(\sigma_\gamma^2+\tfrac{1}{N}\sigma^2\right)\left(1-\tfrac{1}{T}\right).$$

3.7.2 'ESTIMATION' OF VARIANCE COMPONENTS FROM DISTURBANCES

Assume first (hypothetically) that the ϵ_{it}s are observable. We could then estimate the above variances by their empirical counterparts, giving

$$\widehat{\sigma}^2 = \frac{1}{(N-1)(T-1)} \sum_{i=1}^{N} \sum_{t=1}^{T} (\epsilon_{it} - \bar{\epsilon}_{i\cdot} - \bar{\epsilon}_{\cdot t} + \bar{\epsilon})^2 = \frac{1}{(N-1)(T-1)} R_{\epsilon\epsilon}, \tag{3.93}$$
$$\widehat{(\sigma_\alpha^2+\tfrac{1}{T}\sigma^2)} = \frac{1}{N-1} \sum_{i=1}^{N} (\bar{\epsilon}_{i\cdot} - \bar{\epsilon})^2 = \frac{1}{(N-1)T} B_{\epsilon\epsilon}, \tag{3.94}$$

$$(\widehat{\sigma_\gamma^2+\tfrac{1}{N}\sigma^2}) = \tfrac{1}{T-1}\sum_{t=1}^{T}(\bar{\epsilon}_{\cdot t}-\bar{\epsilon})^2 = \tfrac{1}{N(T-1)}C_{\epsilon\epsilon}, \tag{3.95}$$

and hence

$$\widehat{\sigma}_\alpha^2 = \tfrac{1}{T(N-1)}[B_{\epsilon\epsilon}-\tfrac{1}{T-1}R_{\epsilon\epsilon}], \tag{3.96}$$

$$\widehat{\sigma}_\gamma^2 = \tfrac{1}{N(T-1)}[C_{\epsilon\epsilon}-\tfrac{1}{N-1}R_{\epsilon\epsilon}], \tag{3.97}$$

$$\widehat{\theta}_B = \frac{\widehat{\sigma}^2}{\widehat{\sigma}^2+T\widehat{\sigma}_\alpha^2} = \frac{R_{\epsilon\epsilon}}{(T-1)B_{\epsilon\epsilon}}, \tag{3.98}$$

$$\widehat{\theta}_C = \frac{\widehat{\sigma}^2}{\widehat{\sigma}^2+N\widehat{\sigma}_\gamma^2} = \frac{R_{\epsilon\epsilon}}{(N-1)C_{\epsilon\epsilon}}. \tag{3.99}$$

The 'estimators' of σ^2, σ_α^2, and σ_γ^2 are unbiased. The proof, again utilizing rules for trace operations, is that since (3.58) implies

$$\begin{aligned}
\mathsf{E}(R_{\epsilon\epsilon}|X) &= \mathsf{E}[\boldsymbol{\epsilon}'(\boldsymbol{B}_N\otimes\boldsymbol{B}_T)\boldsymbol{\epsilon}|X]\\
&= \mathsf{E}[\mathrm{tr}(\boldsymbol{\epsilon}'(\boldsymbol{B}_N\otimes\boldsymbol{B}_T)\boldsymbol{\epsilon})|X] = \mathsf{E}[\mathrm{tr}(\boldsymbol{\epsilon}\boldsymbol{\epsilon}'(\boldsymbol{B}_N\otimes\boldsymbol{B}_T))|X]\\
&= \mathrm{tr}[\mathsf{E}(\boldsymbol{\epsilon}\boldsymbol{\epsilon}')(\boldsymbol{B}_N\otimes\boldsymbol{B}_T)|X] = \sigma^2\mathrm{tr}(\boldsymbol{B}_N\otimes\boldsymbol{B}_T),\\
\mathsf{E}(B_{\epsilon\epsilon}|X) &= \mathsf{E}[\boldsymbol{\epsilon}'(\boldsymbol{B}_N\otimes\boldsymbol{A}_T)\,\boldsymbol{\epsilon}|X]\\
&= \mathsf{E}[\mathrm{tr}(\boldsymbol{\epsilon}'(\boldsymbol{B}_N\otimes\boldsymbol{A}_T)\boldsymbol{\epsilon})|X] = \mathsf{E}[\mathrm{tr}(\boldsymbol{\epsilon}\boldsymbol{\epsilon}'(\boldsymbol{B}_N\otimes\boldsymbol{A}_T))|X]\\
&= \mathrm{tr}[\mathsf{E}(\boldsymbol{\epsilon}\boldsymbol{\epsilon}'|X)(\boldsymbol{B}_N\otimes\boldsymbol{A}_T)] = (T\sigma_\alpha^2+\sigma^2)\mathrm{tr}(\boldsymbol{B}_N\otimes\boldsymbol{A}_T),\\
\mathsf{E}(C_{\epsilon\epsilon}|X) &= \mathsf{E}[\boldsymbol{\epsilon}'(\boldsymbol{A}_N\otimes\boldsymbol{B}_T)\,\boldsymbol{\epsilon}|X]\\
&= \mathsf{E}[\mathrm{tr}(\boldsymbol{\epsilon}'(\boldsymbol{A}_N\otimes\boldsymbol{B}_T)\boldsymbol{\epsilon})|X] = \mathsf{E}[\mathrm{tr}(\boldsymbol{\epsilon}\boldsymbol{\epsilon}'(\boldsymbol{A}_N\otimes\boldsymbol{B}_T))|X]\\
&= \mathrm{tr}[\mathsf{E}(\boldsymbol{\epsilon}\boldsymbol{\epsilon}')(\boldsymbol{A}_N\otimes\boldsymbol{B}_T)|X] = (N\sigma_\gamma^2+\sigma^2)\mathrm{tr}(\boldsymbol{A}_N\otimes\boldsymbol{B}_T),
\end{aligned}$$

and (2.86)–(2.87) give $\mathrm{tr}(\boldsymbol{B}_N\otimes\boldsymbol{B}_T)=(N-1)(T-1)$, $\mathrm{tr}(\boldsymbol{B}_N\otimes\boldsymbol{A}_T)=N-1$, $\mathrm{tr}(\boldsymbol{A}_N\otimes\boldsymbol{B}_T)=T-1$, we get

$$\mathsf{E}(R_{\epsilon\epsilon}|X) = \sigma^2(N-1)(T-1), \tag{3.100}$$

$$\mathsf{E}(B_{\epsilon\epsilon}|X) = (T\sigma_\alpha^2+\sigma^2)(N-1), \tag{3.101}$$

$$\mathsf{E}(C_{\epsilon\epsilon}|X) = (N\sigma_\gamma^2+\sigma^2)(T-1). \tag{3.102}$$

These equations combined with (3.93), (3.96), and (3.97), give $\mathsf{E}(\widehat{\sigma}^2|X)=\sigma^2$, $\mathsf{E}(\widehat{\sigma}_\alpha^2|X)=\sigma_\alpha^2$, and $\mathsf{E}(\widehat{\sigma}_\gamma^2|X)=\sigma_\gamma^2$, which completes the proof.

3.7.3 SYNTHESIS: STEPWISE ESTIMATION

When ϵ_{it} in unobservable, we use residuals in estimating the variance components. This motivates the following stepwise procedure for FGLS estimation:

1. Estimate $\boldsymbol{\beta}$ and k by OLS and extract the residuals $\widehat{\epsilon}_{it}$.
2. Compute $\widehat{\theta}_B$ and $\widehat{\theta}_C$ from (3.98) and (3.99), replacing ϵ_{it} by $\widehat{\epsilon}_{it}$.
3. Compute $\widehat{\boldsymbol{\beta}}_{GLS}$ and $\mathsf{V}(\widehat{\boldsymbol{\beta}}_{GLS}|X)$ from (3.65) and (3.76) with (θ_B, θ_C) replaced by $(\widehat{\theta}_B, \widehat{\theta}_C)$.
4. Estimate k by $\widehat{k}_{GLS} = \widehat{k}(\widehat{\boldsymbol{\beta}}_{GLS}) = \bar{y} - \bar{\boldsymbol{x}}\widehat{\boldsymbol{\beta}}_{GLS}$.

We may continue by recomputing residuals $\widehat{\epsilon}_{it}$ and repeating steps 2 and 3 iteratively until convergence, according to some criterion.

3.7.4 TESTING FOR RANDOM TWO-WAY HETEROGENEITY

We finally describe an extension of the test for latent random heterogeneity in the one-way model, considered in Section 3.3.4, to also account for two-dimensional heterogeneity, also due to Breusch and Pagan (1979). Let $\widehat{}$ denote OLS (or ML) residuals obtained from Model (3.54) under $H_0 : \sigma_\alpha^2 = \sigma_\gamma^2 = 0$. The test consists in supplementing BP_α, given by (3.44), with the symmetric statistic,

$$\begin{aligned} \text{BP}_\gamma &= \frac{NT}{2(N-1)}\left[\frac{\sum_{t=1}^{T}[\sum_{i=1}^{N}\widehat{\epsilon}_{it}]^2}{\sum_{t=1}^{T}\sum_{i=1}^{N}\widehat{\epsilon}_{it}^2} - 1\right]^2 \equiv \frac{NT}{2(N-1)}\left[\frac{\widehat{\boldsymbol{\epsilon}}'[E_N \otimes I_T]\widehat{\boldsymbol{\epsilon}}}{\widehat{\boldsymbol{\epsilon}}'\widehat{\boldsymbol{\epsilon}}} - 1\right]^2 \\ &\equiv \frac{NT}{2(N-1)}\left[\frac{\sum_{t=1}^{T}\sum_{i=1}^{N}\sum_{j\neq i}\widehat{\epsilon}_{it}\widehat{\epsilon}_{jt}}{\sum_{t=1}^{T}\sum_{i=1}^{N}\widehat{\epsilon}_{it}^2}\right]^2, \end{aligned} \tag{3.103}$$

and define the composite test statistic for the above null hypothesis as their sum

$$\begin{aligned} \text{BP}_{\alpha\gamma} \equiv \text{BP}_\alpha + \text{BP}_\gamma &= \frac{NT}{2(T-1)}\left[\frac{\sum_{i=1}^{N}\sum_{t=1}^{T}\sum_{s\neq t}\widehat{\epsilon}_{it}\widehat{\epsilon}_{is}}{\sum_{i=1}^{N}\sum_{t=1}^{T}\widehat{\epsilon}_{it}^2}\right]^2 \\ &+ \frac{NT}{2(N-1)}\left[\frac{\sum_{t=1}^{T}\sum_{i=1}^{N}\sum_{j\neq i}\widehat{\epsilon}_{it}\widehat{\epsilon}_{jt}}{\sum_{t=1}^{T}\sum_{i=1}^{N}\widehat{\epsilon}_{it}^2}\right]^2. \end{aligned} \tag{3.104}$$

The test criterion is to *reject* H_0*, at an approximate level* θ*, when* $\text{BP}_{\alpha\gamma} > \chi^2_{1-\theta}(2)$*, the* $(1-\theta)$*-quantile in the* $\chi^2(2)$*-distribution.* The number of degrees of freedom is raised from 1 to 2 since one additional parameter is under test. Intuitively, $\widehat{\epsilon}_{it}\widehat{\epsilon}_{is}$ $(t \neq s)$ tends to be 'small', and hence BP_α tends to be 'small', when $\alpha_i = 0$, making ϵ_{it} and ϵ_{is} uncorrelated; and $\widehat{\epsilon}_{it}\widehat{\epsilon}_{jt}$ $(i \neq j)$ tends to be 'small', and hence BP_γ tends to be 'small', when $\gamma_t = 0$, which makes ϵ_{it} and ϵ_{jt} uncorrelated.

3.8 Maximum Likelihood estimation

3.8.1 THE PROBLEM

We proceed to the problem of joint estimation of $(k, \boldsymbol{\beta}, \sigma^2, \sigma_\alpha^2, \sigma_\gamma^2)$. From (3.55), assuming that $\boldsymbol{\alpha}$, $\boldsymbol{\gamma}$, and $\boldsymbol{u}$ are *normally distributed*, we have

$$y = (e_N \otimes e_T)k + X\boldsymbol{\beta} + \boldsymbol{\epsilon}, \quad (\boldsymbol{\epsilon}|X) \sim \mathsf{N}(\mathbf{0}_{NT,1}, \boldsymbol{\Omega}), \tag{3.105}$$

where $\boldsymbol{\Omega}$ is given by (3.58). The density of $\boldsymbol{\epsilon}$ is

$$\mathcal{L} = (2\pi)^{-\frac{NT}{2}} |\boldsymbol{\Omega}|^{-\frac{1}{2}} \exp[-\tfrac{1}{2}\boldsymbol{\epsilon}'\boldsymbol{\Omega}^{-1}\boldsymbol{\epsilon}].$$

Inserting $\boldsymbol{\epsilon} = y - (e_N \otimes e_T)k - X\boldsymbol{\beta}$ we get the *log-likelihood function of* $y|X$:

$$\begin{aligned} \ln(\mathcal{L}) &= -\tfrac{NT}{2}\ln(2\pi) - \tfrac{1}{2}\ln(|\boldsymbol{\Omega}|) \\ &\quad - \tfrac{1}{2}\left[y - (e_N \otimes e_T)k - X\boldsymbol{\beta}\right]' \boldsymbol{\Omega}^{-1}[y - (e_N \otimes e_T)k - X\boldsymbol{\beta}]. \end{aligned} \tag{3.106}$$

The ML estimators of $(\boldsymbol{\beta}, k, \sigma^2, \sigma_\alpha^2, \sigma_\gamma^2)$ are the values that maximize (3.106).

3.8.2 SIMPLIFYING THE LOG-LIKELIHOOD

The determinant value of $\boldsymbol{\Omega}$ is

$$|\boldsymbol{\Omega}| = \sigma^{2(N-1)(T-1)}\,(\sigma^2 + T\sigma_\alpha^2)^{N-1}(\sigma^2 + N\sigma_\gamma^2)^{T-1}(\sigma^2 + T\sigma_\alpha^2 + N\sigma_\gamma^2), \tag{3.107}$$

which can be verified from $\boldsymbol{\Omega}$'s eigenvalues, see Nerlove (1971b), and the fact that the determinant value of a matrix is the product of its eigenvalues:

$$\begin{array}{lll} \sigma^2 & \text{with multiplicity} & (N-1)(T-1), \\ \kappa_B^2 = \sigma^2 + T\sigma_\alpha^2 & \text{with multiplicity} & N-1, \\ \kappa_C^2 = \sigma^2 + N\sigma_\gamma^2 & \text{with multiplicity} & T-1, \\ \kappa_D^2 = \sigma^2 + T\sigma_\alpha^2 + N\sigma_\gamma^2 & \text{with multiplicity} & 1 \end{array}$$

Inserting (3.59) and (3.107) in (3.106), the log-likelihood function becomes

$$\begin{aligned}\ln(\mathcal{L}) = -\tfrac{1}{2}\{&NT\ln(2\pi) + (N-1)(T-1)\ln(\sigma^2)\\ &+ (N-1)\ln(\sigma^2+T\sigma_\alpha^2) + (T-1)\ln(\sigma^2+N\sigma_\gamma^2)\\ &+ \ln(\sigma^2+T\sigma_\alpha^2+N\sigma_\gamma^2) + Q(\boldsymbol{\beta},k,\sigma^2,\sigma_\alpha^2,\sigma_\gamma^2)\},\end{aligned} \tag{3.108}$$

where

$$\begin{aligned}&Q(\boldsymbol{\beta},k,\sigma^2,\sigma_\alpha^2,\sigma_\gamma^2)\\ &= \sigma^{-2}[y-(e_N\otimes e_T)k-\boldsymbol{X\beta}]'(\boldsymbol{B}_N\otimes\boldsymbol{B}_T)[y-(e_N\otimes e_T)k-\boldsymbol{X\beta}]\\ &+(\sigma^2+T\sigma_\alpha^2)^{-2}[y-(e_N\otimes e_T)k-\boldsymbol{X\beta}]'(\boldsymbol{B}_N\otimes\boldsymbol{A}_T)[y-(e_N\otimes e_T)k-\boldsymbol{X\beta}]\\ &+(\sigma^2+N\sigma_\gamma^2)^{-2}[y-(e_N\otimes e_T)k-\boldsymbol{X\beta}]'(\boldsymbol{A}_N\otimes\boldsymbol{B}_T)[y-(e_N\otimes e_T)k-\boldsymbol{X\beta}]\\ &+(\sigma^2+T\sigma_\alpha^2+N\sigma_\gamma^2)^{-2}[y-(e_N\otimes e_T)k-\boldsymbol{X\beta}]'(\boldsymbol{A}_N\otimes\boldsymbol{A}_T)[y-(e_N\otimes e_T)k-\boldsymbol{X\beta}].\end{aligned}$$

The first-order conditions for maximizing $\ln(\mathcal{L})$ are: $\partial\ln(\mathcal{L})/\partial\boldsymbol{\beta} = \mathbf{0}_{K,1}$ and $\partial\ln(\mathcal{L})/\partial k = \partial\ln(\mathcal{L})/\partial\sigma^2 = \partial\ln(\mathcal{L})/\partial\sigma_\alpha^2 = \partial\ln(\mathcal{L})/\partial\sigma_\gamma^2 = 0$.

3.8.3 STEPWISE SOLUTION

Solving these conditions is complicated and does not admit a closed form solution. As in the one-way case, the maximand has a particular structure, which can be utilized to simplify the solution conditions. For given σ^2, σ_α^2, and σ_γ^2 we have

$$\max_{k,\boldsymbol{\beta}}\ln(\mathcal{L}) \iff \min_{k,\boldsymbol{\beta}}(Q).$$

The latter is the GLS problem. Hence, conditional on $(\sigma^2,\sigma_\alpha^2,\sigma_\gamma^2)$, the ML estimators for $\boldsymbol{\beta}$ and k equal the GLS estimators.

Eliminating k from $\ln(\mathcal{L})$ by inserting $\widehat{k}(\boldsymbol{\beta})$ from (3.61) in (3.108) gives

$$\begin{aligned}\ln(\mathcal{L}) = -\tfrac{1}{2}[&NT\ln(2\pi)+(N-1)(T-1)\ln(\sigma^2)\\ &+ (N-1)\ln(\kappa_B^2) + (T-1)\ln(\kappa_C^2) + \ln(\kappa_D^2)]\\ &- \tfrac{1}{2}Q^*(\boldsymbol{\beta},\sigma^2,\kappa_B^2,\kappa_C^2),\end{aligned} \tag{3.109}$$

where

$$\kappa_B^2 = \sigma^2 + T\sigma_\alpha^2,$$

$$\kappa_C^2 = \sigma^2 + N\sigma_\gamma^2,$$
$$\kappa_D^2 = \sigma^2 + T\sigma_\alpha^2 + N\sigma_\gamma^2,$$
$$Q^*(\boldsymbol{\beta},\sigma^2,\kappa_B^2,\kappa_C^2),$$
$$= (y-X\boldsymbol{\beta})'[\sigma^{-2}(B_N\otimes B_T)+\kappa_B^{-2}(B_N\otimes A_T)+\kappa_C^{-2}(A_N\otimes B_T)](y-X\boldsymbol{\beta}).$$

Now (3.109) has an additive form where in the expression in the square bracket, $(\sigma^2,\kappa_B^2,\kappa_C^2)$ occur alone, while in Q^* they occur together with $\boldsymbol{\beta}$. Since the transformation from $(\boldsymbol{\beta},\sigma^2,\sigma_\alpha^2,\sigma_\gamma^2)$ to $(\boldsymbol{\beta},\sigma^2,\kappa_B^2,\kappa_C^2)$ is one-to-one, we can split the ML problem into:

Sub-problem A: maximization of $\ln(\mathcal{L})$ *with respect to* $\boldsymbol{\beta}$ *for given* $\sigma^2,\kappa_B^2,\kappa_C^2$.
Sub-problem B: maximization of $\ln(\mathcal{L})$ *with respect to* $\sigma^2,\kappa_B^2,\kappa_C^2$ *for given* $\boldsymbol{\beta}$.

Sub-problem A is identical to the GLS-problem. We therefore obtain the (conditional) estimator directly from (3.65).

Sub-problem B has first-order conditions $\partial\ln(\mathcal{L})/\partial\sigma^2 = \partial\ln(\mathcal{L})/\partial\kappa_B^2 = \partial\ln(\mathcal{L})/\partial\kappa_C^2 = 0$. Exploiting (3.109), letting

$$R_{\epsilon\epsilon}(\boldsymbol{\beta}) = \boldsymbol{\epsilon}'(B_N\otimes B_T)\boldsymbol{\epsilon} = (y-X\boldsymbol{\beta})'(B_N\otimes B_T)(y-X\boldsymbol{\beta}),$$
$$B_{\epsilon\epsilon}(\boldsymbol{\beta}) = \boldsymbol{\epsilon}'(B_N\otimes A_T)\boldsymbol{\epsilon} = (y-X\boldsymbol{\beta})'(B_N\otimes A_T)(y-X\boldsymbol{\beta}),$$
$$C_{\epsilon\epsilon}(\boldsymbol{\beta}) = \boldsymbol{\epsilon}'(A_N\otimes B_T)\boldsymbol{\epsilon} = (y-X\boldsymbol{\beta})'(A_N\otimes B_T)(y-X\boldsymbol{\beta}),$$

we find that the (conditional) estimators of $(\sigma^2,\kappa_B^2,\kappa_C^2)$ satisfy

$$\widetilde{\sigma}^2(\boldsymbol{\beta}) = \frac{1}{(N-1)(T-1)}\left[R_{\epsilon\epsilon}(\boldsymbol{\beta}) + \frac{\widetilde{\sigma}^4(\boldsymbol{\beta})}{\widetilde{\kappa}_B^2(\boldsymbol{\beta})+\widetilde{\kappa}_C^2(\boldsymbol{\beta})-\widetilde{\sigma}^2(\boldsymbol{\beta})}\right], \tag{3.110}$$

$$\widetilde{\kappa}_B^2(\boldsymbol{\beta}) = \frac{1}{N-1}\left[B_{\epsilon\epsilon}(\boldsymbol{\beta}) - \frac{\widetilde{\kappa}_B^4(\boldsymbol{\beta})}{\widetilde{\kappa}_B^2(\boldsymbol{\beta})+\widetilde{\kappa}_C^2(\boldsymbol{\beta})-\widetilde{\sigma}^2(\boldsymbol{\beta})}\right], \tag{3.111}$$

$$\widetilde{\kappa}_C^2(\boldsymbol{\beta}) = \frac{1}{T-1}\left[C_{\epsilon\epsilon}(\boldsymbol{\beta}) - \frac{\widetilde{\kappa}_C^4(\boldsymbol{\beta})}{\widetilde{\kappa}_B^2(\boldsymbol{\beta})+\widetilde{\kappa}_C^2(\boldsymbol{\beta})-\widetilde{\sigma}^2(\boldsymbol{\beta})}\right], \tag{3.112}$$

These expressions do not admit closed form solution. However, since $\widetilde{\sigma}^2(\boldsymbol{\beta})$, $\widetilde{\kappa}_B^2(\boldsymbol{\beta})$, and $\widetilde{\kappa}_C^2(\boldsymbol{\beta})$ are all less than $\widetilde{\kappa}_B^2(\boldsymbol{\beta})+\widetilde{\kappa}_C^2(\boldsymbol{\beta})-\widetilde{\sigma}^2(\boldsymbol{\beta})$, it is not difficult to show that the conditional estimators which solve (3.110)–(3.112) satisfy:

$$\frac{1}{(N-1)(T-1)}R_{\epsilon\epsilon}(\boldsymbol{\beta}) < \widetilde{\sigma}^2(\boldsymbol{\beta}) < \frac{1}{(N-1)(T-1)-1}R_{\epsilon\epsilon}(\boldsymbol{\beta}), \tag{3.113}$$

$$\frac{1}{N}B_{\epsilon\epsilon}(\boldsymbol{\beta}) < \widetilde{\kappa}_B^2(\boldsymbol{\beta}) < \frac{1}{N-1}B_{\epsilon\epsilon}(\boldsymbol{\beta}), \tag{3.114}$$

$$\frac{1}{T}C_{\epsilon\epsilon}(\boldsymbol{\beta}) < \widetilde{\kappa}_C^2(\boldsymbol{\beta}) < \frac{1}{T-1}C_{\epsilon\epsilon}(\boldsymbol{\beta}). \tag{3.115}$$

The conditional ML estimators of σ^2, $\frac{1}{T}\kappa_B^2 = \sigma_\alpha^2 + \frac{1}{T}\sigma^2$ and $\frac{1}{N}\kappa_C^2 = \sigma_\gamma^2 + \frac{1}{N}\sigma^2$ are approximately equal to the unbiased 'estimators' (3.93)–(3.95). The method of moment estimator of σ^2, (3.93), coincides with the *lower* bound in (3.113), while (3.94) and (3.95) give estimators for κ_B^2 and κ_C^2 coinciding with the *upper* bound in, respectively, (3.114) and (3.115). For large N and T the two sets of estimators are for practical purposes equal. Anyway, knowing that the solution values are inside the intervals (3.113)–(3.115) is useful when solving iteratively (3.110)–(3.112) with respect to $\widetilde{\sigma}^2(\boldsymbol{\beta})$, $\widetilde{\kappa}_B^2(\boldsymbol{\beta})$, and $\widetilde{\kappa}_C^2(\boldsymbol{\beta})$.

An iterative procedure, solving alternatively sub-problems A and B is:[19]

1. Compute $\widetilde{\boldsymbol{\beta}} = \boldsymbol{G}_{XX}^{-1}\boldsymbol{G}_{XY} = \widehat{\boldsymbol{\beta}}_{OLS}$, $\widetilde{k} = \bar{y} - \bar{\boldsymbol{x}}\widetilde{\boldsymbol{\beta}}$ and extract the residuals $\widehat{\epsilon}_{it}$.
2. Compute $\widetilde{\sigma}^2 = \widetilde{\sigma}^2(\widetilde{\boldsymbol{\beta}})$, $\widetilde{\kappa}_B^2 = \widetilde{\kappa}_B^2(\widetilde{\boldsymbol{\beta}})$ and $\widetilde{\kappa}_C^2 = \widetilde{\kappa}_C^2(\widetilde{\boldsymbol{\beta}})$ by (3.113)–(3.115).
3. Compute $\widehat{\boldsymbol{\beta}}_{GLS}$ from (3.65).
4. Compute $\ln(\mathcal{L})$ and check for convergence. If convergence is confirmed, go to step 5. Otherwise, return to step 2, and repeat steps 2–4.
5. Finally, compute $\widetilde{\sigma}_\alpha^2 = \widetilde{\sigma}_\alpha^2(\widetilde{\boldsymbol{\beta}})$, $\widetilde{\sigma}_\gamma^2 = \widetilde{\sigma}_\gamma^2(\widetilde{\boldsymbol{\beta}})$, $\widetilde{\theta}_B = \widetilde{\theta}_B(\widetilde{\boldsymbol{\beta}})$, and $\widetilde{\theta}_C = \widetilde{\theta}_C(\widetilde{\boldsymbol{\beta}})$ from the estimates obtained for $\widetilde{\sigma}^2 = \widetilde{\sigma}^2(\widetilde{\boldsymbol{\beta}})$, $\widetilde{\kappa}_B^2 = \widetilde{\kappa}_B^2(\widetilde{\boldsymbol{\beta}})$ and $\widetilde{\kappa}_C^2 = \widetilde{\kappa}_C^2(\widetilde{\boldsymbol{\beta}})$ and $\widehat{k}(\widetilde{\boldsymbol{\beta}})$ from (3.61).

Appendix 3A. **Two theorems related to GLS estimation**

In this appendix we prove two theorems useful in solving several types of GLS problems.

3A.1. Theorem 1, on matrix inversion. *Let $\boldsymbol{M}$ be a quadratic, non-singular matrix of the form*

$$\boldsymbol{M} = \sum_{j=1}^{J} a_j \boldsymbol{M}_j, \quad \sum_{j=1}^{J} \boldsymbol{M}_j = \boldsymbol{I}, \tag{3A.1}$$

where $\boldsymbol{M}_1, \dots, \boldsymbol{M}_J$ are symmetric, idempotent, and orthogonal, add to the identity matrix all $a_j \neq 0$, and $\boldsymbol{M}$ has full rank, but the $\boldsymbol{M}_j$'s may well be singular. Then

$$\boldsymbol{M}^{-1} = \sum_{j=1}^{J} a_j^{-1} \boldsymbol{M}_j = \boldsymbol{S}'\boldsymbol{S}, \text{ where } \boldsymbol{S} = \sum_{j=1}^{J} a_j^{-1/2} \boldsymbol{M}_j. \tag{3A.2}$$

Proof: inserting $\boldsymbol{M}$ and $\boldsymbol{M}^{-1}$ from (3A.1) and (3A.2), we get

$$\begin{aligned} \boldsymbol{M}\boldsymbol{M}^{-1} &= [\textstyle\sum_{j=1}^{J} a_j \boldsymbol{M}_j][\sum_{j=1}^{J} a_j^{-1} \boldsymbol{M}_j] = \sum_{j=1}^{J} \boldsymbol{M}_j = \boldsymbol{I}, \\ \boldsymbol{S}'\boldsymbol{S} &= [\textstyle\sum_{j=1}^{J} a_j^{-\frac{1}{2}} \boldsymbol{M}_j]^2 = \sum_{j=1}^{J} a_j^{-1} \boldsymbol{M}_j = \boldsymbol{M}^{-1}, \end{aligned}$$

[19] See again Oberhofer and Kmenta (1974) and Breusch (1987).

whose second equality follows from $M_1, \dots, M_J$ being idempotent and orthogonal. The essence of the theorem is simple: to invert M, invert the a_js. To factorize M^{-1}, invert the square roots of the a_js.

3A.2. Theorem 2, on intercept estimation. *Consider a regression equation with n observations,*

$$y = e_n k + X\boldsymbol{\beta} + \boldsymbol{\epsilon}, \quad \mathsf{E}(\boldsymbol{\epsilon}|X) = 0_{n,1}, \quad \mathsf{V}(\boldsymbol{\epsilon}|X) = \mathsf{E}(\boldsymbol{\epsilon}\boldsymbol{\epsilon}'|X) = \boldsymbol{\Omega}, \tag{3A.3}$$

where y, X, $\boldsymbol{\beta}$, and $\boldsymbol{\epsilon}$ are vectors/matrices and k is a scalar. Assume that the disturbance covariance matrix has an inverse, $\boldsymbol{\Omega}^{-1}$, whose column sums are c:

$$e_n'\boldsymbol{\Omega}^{-1} = c\,e_n'. \tag{3A.4}$$

Then, letting $\bar{y} = \frac{1}{n}e_n'y$, $\bar{x} = \frac{1}{n}e_n'X$, the GLS estimator of k, conditional on $\boldsymbol{\beta}$, is for any $(\boldsymbol{\Omega}, c)$

$$\widehat{k} = \widehat{k}(\boldsymbol{\beta}) = \tfrac{1}{n}e_n'(y - X\boldsymbol{\beta}) = \bar{y} - \bar{x}\boldsymbol{\beta}, \tag{3A.5}$$

Proof: GLS estimation of k for given $(\boldsymbol{\beta}, \boldsymbol{\Omega})$ means minimizing

$$\begin{aligned}
&(y - X\boldsymbol{\beta} - e_n k)'\boldsymbol{\Omega}^{-1}(y - X\boldsymbol{\beta} - e_n k) \\
&\quad \equiv (y - X\boldsymbol{\beta})'\boldsymbol{\Omega}^{-1}(y - X\boldsymbol{\beta}) - 2ke_n'\boldsymbol{\Omega}^{-1}(y - X\boldsymbol{\beta}) + k^2 e_n'\boldsymbol{\Omega}^{-1}e_n \\
&\quad \equiv (y - X\boldsymbol{\beta})'\boldsymbol{\Omega}^{-1}(y - X\boldsymbol{\beta}) - c[k^2 n - 2k(y - X\boldsymbol{\beta})],
\end{aligned}$$

in the last equality using $e_n'e_n = n$ and assumption (3A.4). The minimizing value of k is the value that maximizes the expression in the square brackets, which is $\widehat{k} = \frac{1}{n}e_n'(y - X\boldsymbol{\beta})$ for any c and $\boldsymbol{\Omega}$.

Appendix 3B. **Efficiency in the one-regressor case**

In this appendix we examine more closely the efficiency of the estimators considered in Sections 3.2 and 3.6 in the one-regressor case ($K = 1$), $\boldsymbol{x}_{it}$ and $\boldsymbol{\beta}$ being scalars, symbolized by x_{it} and β.

3B.1. One-way model. Expressions (3.18) and (3.21) for $K = 1$ read

$$\widehat{\beta} = \frac{\lambda_W W_{XY} + \lambda_B B_{XY}}{\lambda_W W_{XX} + \lambda_B B_{XX}}, \tag{3B.1}$$

$$\mathrm{var}(\widehat{\beta}|\mathbf{X}) = \frac{\lambda_W^2\sigma^2 W_{XX} + \lambda_B^2(\sigma^2 + T\sigma_\alpha^2)B_{XX}}{(\lambda_W W_{XX} + \lambda_B B_{XX})^2}. \tag{3B.2}$$

Since $\widehat{\beta}_W = W_{XY}/W_{XX}$ and $\widehat{\beta}_B = B_{XY}/B_{XX}$, we have, letting $b = B_{XX}/G_{XX}$,

$$\widehat{\beta} = \frac{\lambda_W(1-b)\,\widehat{\beta}_W + \lambda_B b\widehat{\beta}_B}{\lambda_W(1-b) + \lambda_B b}, \tag{3B.3}$$

$$\mathrm{var}(\widehat{\beta}|\mathbf{X}) = \frac{\sigma^2}{G_{XX}} \frac{\lambda_W^2(1-b) + \lambda_B^2 b/\theta_B}{[\lambda_W(1-b) + \lambda_B b]^2}. \tag{3B.4}$$

Hence, $\widehat{\beta}$ emerges as a weighted average of $\widehat{\beta}_W$ and $\widehat{\beta}_B$, with weights $\lambda_W(1-b)$ and $\lambda_B b$. The variance expression emerges by multiplying the 'standard' expression in the case with no (random) heterogeneity ($\lambda_B = \lambda_W = 1$), which is σ^2/G_{XX}, by the inflation factor

$$f = f(\lambda_W, \lambda_B, b, \theta_B) = \frac{\lambda_W^2(1-b) + \lambda_B^2 b/\theta_B}{[\lambda_W(1-b) + \lambda_B b]^2}. \tag{3B.5}$$

It satisfies:

(i) f has its minimum, $f_{\min} = (1 - b + \theta_B b)^{-1}$, obtained for $\lambda_B/\lambda_W = \theta_B$.
(ii) f is decreasing in θ_B for $b > 0$, $\lambda_B/\lambda_W > 0$.

From (3.22)–(3.25) follow

$$\mathrm{var}(\widehat{\beta}_{GLS}|\mathbf{X}) = \frac{\sigma^2}{G_{XX}} \frac{1}{1 - b(1-\theta_B)}, \tag{3B.6}$$

$$\mathrm{var}(\widehat{\beta}_W|\mathbf{X}) = \frac{\sigma^2}{G_{XX}} \frac{1}{1-b}, \tag{3B.7}$$

$$\mathrm{var}(\widehat{\beta}_B|\mathbf{X}) = \frac{\sigma^2}{G_{XX}} \frac{1}{b\theta_B}, \tag{3B.8}$$

$$\mathrm{var}(\widehat{\beta}_{OLS}|\mathbf{X}) = \frac{\sigma^2}{G_{XX}} \left[1 + b\left(\frac{1}{\theta_B} - 1\right)\right], \tag{3B.9}$$

$$\mathrm{var}(\widehat{\beta}_W|\mathbf{X}) > \mathrm{var}(\widehat{\beta}_{GLS}|\mathbf{X}) \text{ for } b\theta_B > 0, \tag{3B.10}$$

$$\mathrm{var}(\widehat{\beta}_B|\mathbf{X}) > \mathrm{var}(\widehat{\beta}_{GLS}|\mathbf{X}) \text{ for } b < 1, \tag{3B.11}$$

$$\mathrm{var}(\widehat{\beta}_{OLS}|\mathbf{X}) > \mathrm{var}(\widehat{\beta}_{GLS}|\mathbf{X}) \text{ for } 0 < b < 1,\ 0 < \theta_B < 1. \tag{3B.12}$$

Let

$$e_{OLS} \equiv \frac{\mathrm{var}(\widehat{\beta}_{OLS}|\mathbf{X})}{\mathrm{var}(\widehat{\beta}_{GLS}|\mathbf{X})} = \left[1+b\left(\frac{1}{\theta_B}-1\right)\right]\left[1-b(1-\theta_B)\right], \tag{3B.13}$$

which satisfies

$$\begin{aligned} e_{OLS} > 1 &\iff (1-\theta_B)\left(\frac{1}{\theta_B}-1\right)b(1-b) > 0, \\ \frac{\partial e_{OLS}}{\partial \theta_B} &= -b(1-b)\left(\frac{1}{\theta_B^2}-1\right), \\ \frac{\partial e_{OLS}}{\partial b} &= (1-\theta_B)\left(\frac{1}{\theta_B}-1\right)(1-2b). \end{aligned}$$

Hence:

(i) If $0<b<1$ and $0<\theta_B<1$, e_{OLS} decreases with increasing θ_B, implying that $\widehat{\beta}_{OLS}$ is relatively more inefficient the larger are T and σ_α^2.

(ii) If $\theta_B<1$, e_{OLS} increases in b when $b<\frac{1}{2}$ and decreases thereafter, i.e., $\widehat{\beta}_{OLS}$ is maximally inefficient relative to $\widehat{\beta}_{GLS}$ when x has an equal share as between- and within-variation.

For the relative efficiency of $\widehat{\beta}_W$, $\widehat{\beta}_B$, and $\widehat{\beta}_{OLS}$ we find

$$\begin{aligned} \frac{\mathrm{var}(\widehat{\beta}_B|\mathbf{X})}{\mathrm{var}(\widehat{\beta}_{OLS}|\mathbf{X})} &= \frac{1}{\theta_B b[1-b+b/\theta_B]} = \frac{1}{b[\theta_B(1-b)+b]} > 1, \text{ for } 0<b<1,\ 0<\theta_B<1, \\ \frac{\mathrm{var}(\widehat{\beta}_W|\mathbf{X})}{\mathrm{var}(\widehat{\beta}_{OLS}|\mathbf{X})} &= \frac{1}{(1-b)[1-b+b/\theta_B]} = \frac{\theta_B}{(1-b)[\theta_B(1-b)+b]}. \end{aligned}$$

Two critical constellations, $1-b=\theta_B/(1+\theta_B)$ and $=\theta_B/(1-\theta_B)$ equivalent to $\theta_B=(1-b)/b$ and $=(1-b)/(2-b)$, are relevant for the ranking of $\widehat{\beta}_W$ and $\widehat{\beta}_{OLS}$:

$$\begin{aligned} &\mathrm{var}(\widehat{\beta}_B|\mathbf{X}) > \mathrm{var}(\widehat{\beta}_{OLS}|\mathbf{X}) > \mathrm{var}(\widehat{\beta}_W|\mathbf{X}) \text{ for } 1-b > \frac{\theta_B}{1-\theta_B} \iff \theta_B < \frac{1-b}{2-b}, \\ &\mathrm{var}(\widehat{\beta}_B|\mathbf{X}) > \mathrm{var}(\widehat{\beta}_W|\mathbf{X}) > \mathrm{var}(\widehat{\beta}_{OLS}|\mathbf{X}) \text{ for } 1-b \in \left(\frac{\theta_B}{1+\theta_B}, \frac{\theta_B}{1-\theta_B}\right) \iff \theta_B \in \left(\frac{1-b}{2-b}, \frac{1-b}{b}\right), \\ &\mathrm{var}(\widehat{\beta}_W|\mathbf{X}) > \mathrm{var}(\widehat{\beta}_B|\mathbf{X}) > \mathrm{var}(\widehat{\beta}_{OLS}|\mathbf{X}) \text{ for } 1-b < \frac{\theta_B}{1+\theta_B} \iff \theta_B > \frac{1-b}{b}. \end{aligned}$$

3B.2. Two-way model. Expressions (3.71) and (3.75) for $K=1$ read

$$\widehat{\beta} = \frac{\lambda_R R_{XY} + \lambda_B B_{XY} + \lambda_C C_{XY}}{\lambda_R R_{XX} + \lambda_B B_{XX} + \lambda_C C_{XX}}, \tag{3B.14}$$

$$\text{var}(\widehat{\beta}|\boldsymbol{X}) = \frac{\lambda_R^2 \sigma^2 R_{XX} + \lambda_B^2(\sigma^2 + T\sigma_\alpha^2)B_{XX} + \lambda_C^2(\sigma^2 + N\sigma_\gamma^2)C_{XX}}{(\lambda_R R_{XX} + \lambda_B B_{XX} + \lambda_C C_{XX})^2}. \tag{3B.15}$$

Since $\widehat{\beta}_R = R_{XY}/R_{XX}$, $\widehat{\beta}_B = B_{XY}/B_{XX}$, and $\widehat{\beta}_C = C_{XY}/C_{XX}$, we have, letting $b = B_{XX}/G_{XX}$ and $c = C_{XX}/G_{XX}$,

$$\widehat{\beta} = \frac{\lambda_R(1-b-c)\,\widehat{\beta}_R + \lambda_B b\,\widehat{\beta}_B + \lambda_C c\,\widehat{\beta}_C}{\lambda_R(1-b-c) + \lambda_B b + \lambda_C c}, \tag{3B.16}$$

$$\text{var}(\widehat{\beta}|\boldsymbol{X}) = \frac{\sigma^2}{G_{XX}} \frac{\lambda_R^2(1-b-c) + \lambda_B^2 \dfrac{b}{\theta_B} + \lambda_C^2 \dfrac{c}{\theta_C}}{[\lambda_R(1-b-c) + \lambda_B b + \lambda_C c]^2}. \tag{3B.17}$$

The variance expression emerges by multiplying the 'standard' expression in the case with no (random) heterogeneity ($\lambda_B = \lambda_C = \lambda_R = 1$), which is σ^2/G_{XX}, by the inflation factor

$$f = f(\lambda_R, \lambda_B, \lambda_C, b, c, \theta_B, \theta_C) = \frac{\lambda_R^2(1-b-c) + \lambda_B^2 \dfrac{b}{\theta_B} + \lambda_C^2 \dfrac{c}{\theta_C}}{[\lambda_R(1-b-c) + \lambda_B b + \lambda_C c]^2}. \tag{3B.18}$$

It satisfies:

(i) f has its minimum, $f_{min} = [1 - b(1-\theta_B) - c(1-\theta_C)]^{-1}$, for $\lambda_B/\lambda_R = \theta_B$, $\lambda_C/\lambda_R = \theta_C$.
(ii) f is decreasing in θ_B for $b > 0, \lambda_B/\lambda_R > 0$, and decreasing in θ_C for $c > 0$, $\lambda_C/\lambda_R > 0$.

From (3.76)–(3.80) follow

$$\text{var}(\widehat{\beta}_{GLS}|\boldsymbol{X}) = \frac{\sigma^2}{G_{XX}} \frac{1}{1 - b(1-\theta_B) - c(1-\theta_C)}, \tag{3B.19}$$

$$\text{var}(\widehat{\beta}_R|\boldsymbol{X}) = \frac{\sigma^2}{G_{XX}} \frac{1}{1-b-c}, \tag{3B.20}$$

$$\text{var}(\widehat{\beta}_B|\boldsymbol{X}) = \frac{\sigma^2}{G_{XX}} \frac{1}{b\theta_B}, \tag{3B.21}$$

$$\text{var}(\widehat{\beta}_C|\boldsymbol{X}) = \frac{\sigma^2}{G_{XX}} \frac{1}{c\theta_C}, \tag{3B.22}$$

$$\text{var}(\widehat{\beta}_{OLS}|X) = \frac{\sigma^2}{G_{XX}}\left[1+b\left(\frac{1}{\theta_B}-1\right)+c\left(\frac{1}{\theta_C}-1\right)\right], \tag{3B.23}$$

$$\text{var}(\widehat{\beta}_R|X) > \text{var}(\widehat{\beta}_{GLS}|X) \text{ for } b\theta_B + c\theta_C > 0, \tag{3B.24}$$

$$\text{var}(\widehat{\beta}_B|X) > \text{var}(\widehat{\beta}_{GLS}|X) \text{ for } b + c(1-\theta_C) < 1, \tag{3B.25}$$

$$\text{var}(\widehat{\beta}_C|X) > \text{var}(\widehat{\beta}_{GLS}|X) \text{ for } c + b(1-\theta_B) < 1. \tag{3B.26}$$

Hence, $\widehat{\beta}_R$ is less efficient than $\widehat{\beta}_{GLS}$ when x has *between-individual or between-period variation* ($b>0$ or $c>0$) and $\theta_B>0$ and $\theta_C>0$, while $\widehat{\beta}_B$ and $\widehat{\beta}_C$ are less efficient than $\widehat{\beta}_{GLS}$ as long as x has some *residual-variation* ($b+c<1$). Further,

$$e_{OLS} \equiv \frac{\text{var}(\widehat{\beta}_{OLS}|X)}{\text{var}(\widehat{\beta}_{GLS}|X)} = \left[1+b\left(\frac{1}{\theta_B}-1\right)+c\left(\frac{1}{\theta_C}-1\right)\right]\left[1-b(1-\theta_B)-c(1-\theta_C)\right], \tag{3B.27}$$

which satisfies

$$e_{OLS} > 1 \iff \left[\frac{b}{\theta_B}(1-\theta_B)^2 + \frac{c}{\theta_C}(1-\theta_C)^2\right](1-b-c) + \frac{b}{\theta_B}\frac{c}{\theta_C}(\theta_B-\theta_C)^2 > 0,$$

$$\frac{\partial e_{OLS}}{\partial \theta_B} = -b(1-b-c)\left(\frac{1}{\theta_B^2}-1\right) - \frac{bc}{\theta_C}\left(\frac{\theta_C^2}{\theta_B^2}-1\right),$$

$$\frac{\partial e_{OLS}}{\partial \theta_C} = -c(1-b-c)\left(\frac{1}{\theta_C^2}-1\right) - \frac{bc}{\theta_B}\left(\frac{\theta_B^2}{\theta_C^2}-1\right),$$

$$\frac{\partial e_{OLS}}{\partial b} = (1-\theta_B)\left[(1-2b)\left(\frac{1}{\theta_B}-1\right) - c(1-\theta_C)\left(\frac{1}{\theta_B}+\frac{1}{\theta_C}\right)\right],$$

$$\frac{\partial e_{OLS}}{\partial c} = (1-\theta_C)\left[(1-2c)\left(\frac{1}{\theta_C}-1\right) - b(1-\theta_B)\left(\frac{1}{\theta_B}+\frac{1}{\theta_C}\right)\right],$$

and therefore

$$\theta_C = 1, \theta_B < 1,\ 0 < b < 1 \Longrightarrow \frac{\partial e_{OLS}}{\partial \theta_B} < 0,$$

$$\theta_B = 1, \theta_C < 1,\ 0 < c < 1 \Longrightarrow \frac{\partial e_{OLS}}{\partial \theta_C} < 0,$$

$$\theta_B < 1,\ c(1-\theta_C) = 0 \quad \Longrightarrow \frac{\partial e_{OLS}}{\partial b} \geq 0 \text{ for } b \leq \tfrac{1}{2},\ \frac{\partial e_{OLS}}{\partial b} \leq 0 \text{ for } b \geq \tfrac{1}{2},$$

$$\theta_C < 1,\ b(1-\theta_B) = 0 \quad \Longrightarrow \frac{\partial e_{OLS}}{\partial c} \geq 0 \text{ for } c \leq \tfrac{1}{2},\ \frac{\partial e_{OLS}}{\partial c} \leq 0 \text{ for } c \geq \tfrac{1}{2}.$$

Hence:

(i) In the absence of a period-specific disturbance component ($\sigma_\gamma^2=0$) while $0<b<1$ and $\sigma_\alpha^2>0$, e_{OLS} is decreasing in θ_B. This implies that if x has both within- and between-individual variation, $\widehat{\beta}_{OLS}$ is less efficient relative to $\widehat{\beta}_{GLS}$ the larger T and σ_α^2 are.

(ii) In the absence of an individual-specific disturbance component ($\sigma_\alpha^2=0$) while $0<c<1$ and $\sigma_\gamma^2>0$, e_{OLS} is decreasing in θ_C. This implies that if x has both within- and between-period variation, $\widehat{\beta}_{OLS}$ is less efficient relative to $\widehat{\beta}_{GLS}$ the larger are N and σ_γ^2.

(iii) If $c(1-\theta_C)=0$, e_{OLS} is increasing in b when $b<\frac{1}{2}$, $\widehat{\beta}_{OLS}$ is maximally inefficient relative to $\widehat{\beta}_{GLS}$ when half of the variation in x is between-individual.

(iv) If $b(1-\theta_B)=0$, e_{OLS} is increasing in c when $c<\frac{1}{2}$, $\widehat{\beta}_{OLS}$ is maximally inefficient relative to $\widehat{\beta}_{GLS}$ when half of the variation in x is between-period.

For the relative efficiency of $\widehat{\beta}_R$, $\widehat{\beta}_B$, $\widehat{\beta}_C$, and $\widehat{\beta}_{OLS}$ (3B.20)–(3B.23) imply:

$$\mathrm{var}(\widehat{\beta}_B|\mathbf{X}) \gtreqless \mathrm{var}(\widehat{\beta}_R|\mathbf{X}) \iff b \lesseqgtr \frac{1-c}{1+\theta_B},$$

$$\mathrm{var}(\widehat{\beta}_C|\mathbf{X}) \gtreqless \mathrm{var}(\widehat{\beta}_R|\mathbf{X}) \iff c \lesseqgtr \frac{1-b}{1+\theta_C},$$

$$\mathrm{var}(\widehat{\beta}_C|\mathbf{X}) \gtreqless \mathrm{var}(\widehat{\beta}_B|\mathbf{X}) \iff b\theta_B \gtreqless c\theta_C,$$

$$\begin{aligned}\mathrm{var}(\widehat{\beta}_{OLS}|\mathbf{X}) \gtreqless \mathrm{var}(\widehat{\beta}_R|\mathbf{X}) &\iff (1-b-c)\left[1+b\left(\frac{1}{\theta_B}-1\right)+c\left(\frac{1}{\theta_C}-1\right)\right] \gtreqless 1\\ &\iff 1-b-c \gtreqless \frac{\sigma^2}{\sigma^2+bT\sigma_\alpha^2+cN\sigma_\gamma^2},\end{aligned}$$

$$\begin{aligned}\mathrm{var}(\widehat{\beta}_B|\mathbf{X}) > \mathrm{var}(\widehat{\beta}_{OLS}|\mathbf{X}) &\iff b\theta_B\left[1+b\left(\frac{1}{\theta_B}-1\right)+c\left(\frac{1}{\theta_C}-1\right)\right] < 1,\\ &\iff b\left[\theta_B(1-b-c)+b+c\frac{\theta_B}{\theta_C}\right] < 1,\end{aligned}$$

$$\begin{aligned}\mathrm{var}(\widehat{\beta}_C|\mathbf{X}) > \mathrm{var}(\widehat{\beta}_{OLS}|\mathbf{X}) &\iff c\theta_C\left[1+b\left(\frac{1}{\theta_B}-1\right)+c\left(\frac{1}{\theta_C}-1\right)\right] < 1,\\ &\iff c\left[\theta_C(1-b-c)+c+b\frac{\theta_C}{\theta_B}\right] < 1.\end{aligned}$$

Hence:

Sufficient for $\text{var}(\widehat{\beta}_B|X) > \text{var}(\widehat{\beta}_{OLS}|X)$ is that $b < 1, \theta_B \leq \theta_C$.
Sufficient for $\text{var}(\widehat{\beta}_C|X) > \text{var}(\widehat{\beta}_{OLS}|X)$ is that $c < 1, \theta_C \leq \theta_B$.

This means that under two-way heterogeneity, it is possible that a between estimator may be superior to OLS. Such a case may occur for $c > 0$ when θ_B/θ_C is sufficiently large and for $b > 0$ when θ_C/θ_B is sufficiently large. The relative efficiency of $\widehat{\beta}_R$ against $\widehat{\beta}_{OLS}$ is also in general indeterminate.

4 Regression analysis with heterogeneous coefficients

CHAPTER SUMMARY

Models and methods for panel data having (slope) coefficients that vary between individuals are considered. Fixed and random heterogeneity are discussed; OLS and GLS are relevant estimation methods. In certain cases GLS degenerates to applying OLS on each equation. Modifications allowing for heteroskedastic or serially correlated disturbances are considered. Coefficient prediction in the random heterogeneity case is discussed, *inter alia*, by contrasting coefficient estimation in the fixed coefficient case and coefficient prediction in the random coefficient case. An empirical example is given.

4.1 Introduction

In panel data regression analysis we may need to extend the modelling of heterogeneity in order to allow not only the intercepts, but also the coefficients to vary across individuals or periods. Heterogeneity may be represented as fixed coefficients or as realizations of stochastic variables. Random coefficients are usually assumed to have a common expectation, representing *average* responses, which then become parameters in the model. *Estimating* random coefficients is not a meaningful problem (at least within the 'frequentist' approach), while coefficient *prediction* is. This modelling approach is considerably more flexible than that in Chapters 2 and 3, by not only allowing shifts in the intercept. In a linear model of Engel functions, we may, for example, allow for marginal propensities to consume varying across households, being interested in both the average income response and its spread. In a Cobb–Douglas or Translog production function, we may allow for varying input and scale elasticities across firms, being interested in both the average elasticity and its spread. And motivated by economic or statistical theory, we may want to impose some structure on this variation.

In this chapter, we consider selected models and methods for panel data where the *coefficients vary between observation units*. Models with coefficients varying both over units and periods, obtained by, for example, replacing β or β_i by a set of unstructured β_{it}s, will in general be overparameterized, having NT coefficients, N intercepts, and disturbance second order moments. This by far exceeds the number of parameters estimable from one panel data set. We would need multiple observations for each (i, t), i.e., a higher-order panel data set, to be able to identify coefficients like β_{it}. Replacing β with, e.g., $\beta_{1i}+\beta_{2t}$ is a feasible, more parsimonious alternative.[1]

The rest of the chapter is organized as follows. In Section 4.2 models with *fixed coefficients* are discussed. Cases with no intercept are considered as intermediate specifications. Section 4.3 gives examples of models with *random coefficients*, and their relationship to fixed coefficient models, also with respect to estimation methods, is considered. Suitable estimation methods are GLS, which in certain cases degenerate to OLS applied separately on the individual-specific equations. An interesting application of the methods for models with random slope coefficients models is *coefficient prediction*, which is also discussed, partly by an example. We also explain the contrast between coefficient estimation in the fixed coefficient case and coefficient prediction in the random coefficient case.[2]

4.2 Fixed coefficient models

4.2.1 SINGLE-REGRESSOR MODELS WITHOUT INTERCEPT

We specify three models, labelled F1, F2, and F3, with one regressor and fixed individual-specific coefficient, of increasing complexity.

Model F1. Consider a regression model having both its single coefficient and disturbance variance individual-dependent. In scalar notation it reads:

$$\begin{aligned} &y_{it} = x_{it}\beta_i+u_{it}, \quad \mathsf{E}(u_{it}|X)=0, \quad \mathsf{E}(u_{it}u_{js}|X)=\delta_{ij}\delta_{ts}\sigma_{ii}, \\ &i,j = 1,\dots,N; \; t,s = 1,\dots,T, \end{aligned}$$

where δ_{ij} and δ_{ts} are Kronecker deltas (see Section 3.3.5). An equivalent formulation, letting $\boldsymbol{x}_i=(x_{i1},\dots,x_{iT})'$, $\boldsymbol{y}_i=(y_{i1},\dots,y_{iT})'$, and $\boldsymbol{u}_i=(u_{i1},\dots,u_{iT})'$, is

$$\begin{aligned} &\boldsymbol{y}_i = \boldsymbol{x}_i\beta_i+\boldsymbol{u}_i, \quad \mathsf{E}(\boldsymbol{u}_i|X) = \boldsymbol{0}_{T,1}, \quad \mathsf{E}(\boldsymbol{u}_i\boldsymbol{u}_j'|X) = \delta_{ij}\sigma_{ii}\boldsymbol{I}_T, \\ &i,j = 1,\dots,N. \end{aligned} \tag{4.1}$$

Since no connection exists between the β_is and between the σ_{ii}s, an MVLUE of β_i is obtained by simply applying OLS for each individual separately, giving

[1] When extending model descriptions in this way, a look at the terminology of classical econometrics is relevant. Following this terminology, a clear distinction should be drawn between exogenous variables and (structural) parameters; the former have varied 'in the past', the latter have not; see Marschak (1953, p.7) and Section 5.5.1. 'Varying parameters' may seem alien to this terminology, and *pseudo*-parameters or similar terms might be more appropriate.

[2] Extensions of the models and methods considered in this chapter, *inter alia*, with extended use of linear algebra and further references to Bayesian interpretations, can be found in Swamy (1970, 1971, 1974), Hsiao (1974, 1975, 1996b), Wansbeek and Kapteyn (1981, 1982), and Hsiao and Pesaran (2008).

$$\widehat{\beta}_i = \frac{\sum_{t=1}^{T} x_{it} y_{it}}{\sum_{t=1}^{T} x_{it}^2} = \frac{\boldsymbol{x}_i' \boldsymbol{y}_i}{\boldsymbol{x}_i' \boldsymbol{x}_i}, \tag{4.2}$$

$$\text{var}(\widehat{\beta}_i|\boldsymbol{X}) = \frac{\sigma_{ii}}{\sum_{t=1}^{T} x_{it}^2} = \frac{\sigma_{ii}}{\boldsymbol{x}_i' \boldsymbol{x}_i}. \qquad i = 1, \dots, N. \tag{4.3}$$

Letting $\widehat{\boldsymbol{u}}_i = \boldsymbol{y}_i - \boldsymbol{x}_i \widehat{\beta}_i$, the corresponding estimator of σ_{ii} is

$$\widehat{\sigma}_{ii} = \frac{1}{T-1} \sum_{t=1}^{T} \widehat{u}_{it}^2 = \frac{1}{T-1} \widehat{\boldsymbol{u}}_i' \widehat{\boldsymbol{u}}_i. \tag{4.4}$$

We may consider $\widehat{\beta}_{it} = y_{it}/x_{it}$ as a very simple estimator of β_i, with $\text{var}(\widehat{\beta}_{it}|\boldsymbol{X}) = \sigma_{ii}/x_{it}^2$, based solely on observation (i, t), and write $\widehat{\beta}_i$ as a weighted mean of $\widehat{\beta}_{i1}, \dots, \widehat{\beta}_{iT}$, with the squared value of the regressor, $x_{i1}^2, \dots, x_{iT}^2$, as weight:

$$\widehat{\beta}_i = \frac{\sum_{t=1}^{T} x_{it}^2 \widehat{\beta}_{it}}{\sum_{t=1}^{T} x_{it}^2} = \frac{\sum_{t=1}^{T} \text{var}(\widehat{\beta}_{it}|\boldsymbol{X})^{-1} \widehat{\beta}_{it}}{\sum_{t=1}^{T} \text{var}(\widehat{\beta}_{it}|\boldsymbol{X})^{-1}}, \qquad i = 1, \dots, N, \tag{4.5}$$

the weights being inversely proportional to the respective variances.

Model F2. We generalize (4.1) by letting the disturbance show not only *heteroskedasticity across individuals*, but also *heteroskedasticity and serial correlation over periods*. This is a sensible extension, since heteroskedasticity typically arises in cross-section data, while serial correlation typically arises in time series data. For panel data, having ingredients from both, it is sensible to allow the disturbances to have both properties. We then specify

$$y_{it} = x_{it}\beta_i + u_{it}, \quad \mathsf{E}(u_{it}|\boldsymbol{X}) = 0, \quad \mathsf{E}(u_{it}u_{js}|\boldsymbol{X}) = \delta_{ij}\sigma_{ii}\omega_{ts},$$

where the ω_{ts}s, collected in

$$\boldsymbol{\Omega}_T = \begin{bmatrix} \omega_{11} & \cdots & \omega_{1T} \\ \vdots & & \vdots \\ \omega_{T1} & \cdots & \omega_{TT} \end{bmatrix}, \quad \text{tr}(\boldsymbol{\Omega}_T) \equiv \sum_{t=1}^{T} \omega_{tt} = T, \tag{4.6}$$

represent the common serial correlation. In matrix notation, the model reads

$$\begin{aligned} &\boldsymbol{y}_i = \boldsymbol{x}_i \beta_i + \boldsymbol{u}_i, \\ &\mathsf{E}(\boldsymbol{u}_i|\boldsymbol{X}) = \boldsymbol{0}, \quad \mathsf{E}(\boldsymbol{u}_i \boldsymbol{u}_j'|\boldsymbol{X}) = \delta_{ij}\sigma_{ii}\boldsymbol{\Omega}_T, \\ &i, j = 1, \dots, N. \end{aligned} \tag{4.7}$$

The adding-up restriction $\sum_{t=1}^{T} \omega_{tt} = T$ is motivated by the fact that the σ_{ii}s and ω_{ts}s are not identified unless at least one of the sets is normalized.

Because $u_{i1},\dots,u_{iT}$, via $\boldsymbol{\Omega}_T$, have period-specific variances and are serially correlated, OLS is not optimal. If $\boldsymbol{\Omega}_T$ is known, we can estimate the β_is separately for each individual by GLS, to obtain the MVLUE

$$\widetilde{\beta}_i = \frac{\boldsymbol{x}_i'\boldsymbol{\Omega}_T^{-1}\boldsymbol{y}_i}{\boldsymbol{x}_i'\boldsymbol{\Omega}_T^{-1}\boldsymbol{x}_i}, \qquad i=1,\dots,N. \tag{4.8}$$

Since (4.7) and (4.8) imply $\widetilde{\beta}_i-\beta_i=(\boldsymbol{x}_i'\boldsymbol{\Omega}_T^{-1}\boldsymbol{u}_i)/(\boldsymbol{x}_i'\boldsymbol{\Omega}_T^{-1}\boldsymbol{x}_i)$, we get

$$\begin{aligned} \text{var}(\widetilde{\beta}_i|X) &= \frac{\sigma_{ii}}{\boldsymbol{x}_i'\boldsymbol{\Omega}_T^{-1}\boldsymbol{x}_i}, \\ \text{cov}(\widetilde{\beta}_i,\widetilde{\beta}_j|X) &= 0,\ i\neq j, \end{aligned} \qquad i,j=1,\dots,N. \tag{4.9}$$

If the disturbances are serially uncorrelated, i.e., $\omega_{ts}=\delta_{ts}\omega_{tt}$, we have

$$\widetilde{\beta}_i = \frac{\sum_{t=1}^{T}\left(\frac{x_{it}y_{it}}{\omega_{tt}}\right)}{\sum_{t=1}^{T}\left(\frac{x_{it}^2}{\omega_{tt}}\right)} \equiv \frac{\sum_{t=1}^{T}\left(\frac{x_{it}^2}{\omega_{tt}}\right)\widehat{\beta}_{it}}{\sum_{t=1}^{T}\left(\frac{x_{it}^2}{\omega_{tt}}\right)}. \tag{4.10}$$

This estimator is formally a weighted mean of the T estimators for individual i, $\widehat{\beta}_{it}=y_{it}/x_{it}$, with weights x_{it}^2/ω_{tt}, being inversely proportional (across t) to $\text{var}(\widehat{\beta}_{it}|X)=\sigma_{ii}\omega_{tt}/x_{it}^2$. This exemplifies the properties of GLS considered in Appendix 2A, Section 2A.1.

Estimation of σ_{ii} and ω_{ts} from residuals, $\widehat{u}_{it}$, subject to the normalization restriction, is straightforward. Since (4.6)–(4.7) imply

$$\begin{aligned} \mathsf{E}(\textstyle\sum_{i=1}^{N}\boldsymbol{u}_i\boldsymbol{u}_i'|X) &= (\textstyle\sum_{i=1}^{N}\sigma_{ii})\boldsymbol{\Omega}_T, \\ \mathsf{E}(\textstyle\sum_{t=1}^{T}u_{it}^2|X) &= \sigma_{ii}\textstyle\sum_{t=1}^{T}\omega_{tt} = \sigma_{ii}T, \end{aligned}$$

and hence

$$\frac{\mathsf{E}(\sum_{i=1}^{N}u_{it}u_{is}|X)}{\sum_{i=1}^{N}\sigma_{ii}} = \omega_{ts},$$

we are motivated to use

$$\widehat{\sigma}_{ii} = \frac{\sum_{t=1}^{T}\widehat{u}_{it}^2}{T}, \qquad i=1,\dots,N, \tag{4.11}$$

$$\widehat{\omega}_{ts} = \frac{T\sum_{i=1}^{N}\widehat{u}_{it}\widehat{u}_{is}}{\sum_{i=1}^{N}\sum_{t=1}^{T}\widehat{u}_{it}^{2}}, \qquad t,s=1,\dots,T. \tag{4.12}$$

Model F3. In Models F1 and F2 nothing connected the disturbances of different individuals. A model allowing for *correlation between disturbances from different individuals* (cross-sectional dependence) is:

$$\begin{aligned} &y_i = x_i\beta_i + u_i, \\ &\mathsf{E}(u_i|X) = 0, \quad \mathsf{E}(u_i u_j'|X) = \sigma_{ij} I_T, \\ &i,j = 1,\dots,N. \end{aligned} \tag{4.13}$$

It generalizes Model F1 by allowing for *heteroskedasticity and contemporaneous cross-individual correlation.* Since period-dependent disturbance variances are ruled out and the serial correlation only goes across individuals, Model F3 is not a generalization of Model F2. The equations, stacked into

$$\begin{bmatrix} y_1 \\ \vdots \\ y_N \end{bmatrix} = \begin{bmatrix} x_1 & \dots & 0 \\ \vdots & \ddots & \vdots \\ 0 & \dots & x_N \end{bmatrix} \begin{bmatrix} \beta_1 \\ \vdots \\ \beta_N \end{bmatrix} + \begin{bmatrix} u_1 \\ \vdots \\ u_N \end{bmatrix},$$

have the 'seemingly unrelated regression' (SUR) format (Zellner (1961)) with *one equation per individual* and contemporaneous cross-equation correlation. Letting y, X, $\boldsymbol{\beta}$, and u denote the stacked vectors/matrices of dimensions $(NT\times 1)$, $(NT\times N)$, $(N\times 1)$, and $(NT\times 1)$, respectively (4.13) can be written as

$$y = X\boldsymbol{\beta} + u, \;\; \mathsf{E}(u|X) = 0_{NT,1}, \;\; \mathsf{E}(uu'|X) = \boldsymbol{\Sigma}_N \otimes I_T, \tag{4.14}$$

where

$$\boldsymbol{\Sigma}_N = \begin{bmatrix} \sigma_{11} & \dots & \sigma_{1N} \\ \vdots & & \vdots \\ \sigma_{N1} & \dots & \sigma_{NN} \end{bmatrix}. \tag{4.15}$$

If $\boldsymbol{\Sigma}_N$ is known, $\boldsymbol{\beta}$ can be estimated by *GLS*, which gives

$$\boldsymbol{\beta}^* = [X'(\boldsymbol{\Sigma}_N^{-1} \otimes I_T)X]^{-1}[X'(\boldsymbol{\Sigma}_N^{-1} \otimes I_T)y], \tag{4.16}$$

and by using (4.14), $\boldsymbol{\beta}^* - \boldsymbol{\beta} = [X'(\boldsymbol{\Sigma}_N^{-1}\otimes I_T)X]^{-1}[X'(\boldsymbol{\Sigma}_N^{-1}\otimes I_T)u]$. Hence,

$$\mathsf{V}(\boldsymbol{\beta}^*|X) = [X'(\boldsymbol{\Sigma}_N^{-1}\otimes I_T)X]^{-1}. \tag{4.17}$$

Model F3, unlike F1 and F2, has the property that a gain, as a reduced estimator variance, is in general obtained by estimating the N individual-specific coefficients jointly by GLS. However, in two cases the gain vanishes; the procedure degenerates to OLS applied equation by equation if the disturbances are uncorrelated across individuals or the regressor vector is individual-invariant. The proofs are as follows.

Uncorrelated disturbances. If $\sigma_{ij}=0$ for all $i \neq j$, $\boldsymbol{\Sigma}_N$ and $\boldsymbol{\Sigma}_N^{-1}$ are diagonal matrices, and we get, since $\boldsymbol{X}$ is block-diagonal,

$$\boldsymbol{X}'(\boldsymbol{\Sigma}_N^{-1} \otimes \boldsymbol{I}_T)\boldsymbol{X} = \begin{bmatrix} \frac{\boldsymbol{x}_1'\boldsymbol{x}_1}{\sigma_{11}} & \cdots & 0 \\ \vdots & \ddots & \vdots \\ 0 & \cdots & \frac{\boldsymbol{x}_N'\boldsymbol{x}_N}{\sigma_{NN}} \end{bmatrix},$$

$$\boldsymbol{X}'(\boldsymbol{\Sigma}_N^{-1} \otimes \boldsymbol{I}_T)\boldsymbol{y} = \begin{bmatrix} \frac{\boldsymbol{x}_1'\boldsymbol{y}_1}{\sigma_{11}} \\ \vdots \\ \frac{\boldsymbol{x}_N'\boldsymbol{y}_N}{\sigma_{NN}} \end{bmatrix}.$$

Inserting these expressions in (4.16), $\sigma_{11}, \dots, \sigma_{NN}$ vanish, and the estimator vector simplifies to a vector of individual-specific OLS estimators:

$$\boldsymbol{\beta}^* = \begin{bmatrix} (\boldsymbol{x}_1'\boldsymbol{x}_1)^{-1}(\boldsymbol{x}_1'\boldsymbol{y}_1) \\ \vdots \\ (\boldsymbol{x}_N'\boldsymbol{x}_N)^{-1}(\boldsymbol{x}_N'\boldsymbol{y}_N) \end{bmatrix} = \begin{bmatrix} \widehat{\boldsymbol{\beta}}_1 \\ \vdots \\ \widehat{\boldsymbol{\beta}}_N \end{bmatrix}.$$

Identical regressors. Inserting $\boldsymbol{x}_i = \widetilde{\boldsymbol{x}}$ $(i = 1, \dots, N) \implies \boldsymbol{X} = \boldsymbol{I}_N \otimes \widetilde{\boldsymbol{x}}$ in (4.16), we get, using rules for Kronecker-products,

$$\begin{aligned}
\boldsymbol{\beta}^* &= [(\boldsymbol{I}_N \otimes \widetilde{\boldsymbol{x}}')(\boldsymbol{\Sigma}_N^{-1} \otimes \boldsymbol{I}_T)(\boldsymbol{I}_N \otimes \widetilde{\boldsymbol{x}})]^{-1}[(\boldsymbol{I}_N \otimes \widetilde{\boldsymbol{x}}')(\boldsymbol{\Sigma}_N^{-1} \otimes \boldsymbol{I}_T)\boldsymbol{y}] \\
&\equiv [\boldsymbol{\Sigma}_N^{-1} \otimes (\widetilde{\boldsymbol{x}}'\widetilde{\boldsymbol{x}})]^{-1}[\boldsymbol{\Sigma}_N^{-1} \otimes \widetilde{\boldsymbol{x}}']\boldsymbol{y} = [\boldsymbol{I}_N \otimes ((\widetilde{\boldsymbol{x}}'\widetilde{\boldsymbol{x}})^{-1}\widetilde{\boldsymbol{x}}')]\boldsymbol{y} \\
&\equiv \begin{bmatrix} (\widetilde{\boldsymbol{x}}'\widetilde{\boldsymbol{x}})^{-1}\widetilde{\boldsymbol{x}}' & \cdots & 0 \\ \vdots & \ddots & \vdots \\ 0 & \cdots & (\widetilde{\boldsymbol{x}}'\widetilde{\boldsymbol{x}})^{-1}\widetilde{\boldsymbol{x}}' \end{bmatrix} \begin{bmatrix} \boldsymbol{y}_1 \\ \vdots \\ \boldsymbol{y}_N \end{bmatrix} \\
&\equiv \begin{bmatrix} (\widetilde{\boldsymbol{x}}'\widetilde{\boldsymbol{x}})^{-1}\widetilde{\boldsymbol{x}}'\boldsymbol{y}_1 \\ \vdots \\ (\widetilde{\boldsymbol{x}}'\widetilde{\boldsymbol{x}})^{-1}\widetilde{\boldsymbol{x}}'\boldsymbol{y}_N \end{bmatrix} \equiv \begin{bmatrix} \widehat{\boldsymbol{\beta}}_1 \\ \vdots \\ \widehat{\boldsymbol{\beta}}_N \end{bmatrix},
\end{aligned}$$

which also is a vector of individual-specific OLS estimators.

4.2.2 SYNTHESIS

We can combine Models F1–F3 into:

$$y_{it} = x_{it}\beta_i + u_{it}, \quad \mathsf{E}(u_{it}|X) = 0, \quad \mathsf{E}(u_{it}u_{js}|X) = \sigma_{ij}\omega_{ts},$$
$$i, j = 1, \dots, N; \; t, s = 1, \dots, T,$$

where the σ_{ij}s and the ω_{ts}s are assumed unrestricted, except that, as in Model F2, $\sum_{t=1}^{T} \omega_{tt} = T$ is imposed to ensure identification. The model can be expressed as individual-specific matrix equations:

$$y_i = x_i\beta_i + u_i, \quad \mathsf{E}(u_i|X) = \mathbf{0}, \quad \mathsf{E}(u_i u_j'|X) = \sigma_{ij}\mathbf{\Omega}_T, \quad i, j = 1, \dots, N, \tag{4.18}$$

which after stacking, with $\mathbf{\Omega}_T$ and $\mathbf{\Sigma}_N$ defined in (4.6) and (4.15), reads

$$y = X\boldsymbol{\beta} + u, \quad \mathsf{E}(u|X) = \mathbf{0}_{NT,1}, \quad \mathsf{E}(uu'|X) = \mathbf{\Sigma}_N \otimes \mathbf{\Omega}_T. \tag{4.19}$$

It generalizes both (4.7) and (4.13): Model F3 lets $\omega_{ts} = \delta_{ts}$, Model F2 lets $\sigma_{ij} = 0 \; (i \neq j)$, while Model F1 imposes both.

Since $\mathsf{E}(u_{it}u_{js}|X) = \sigma_{ij}\omega_{ts}$ implies

$$\mathsf{E}(\textstyle\sum_{i=1}^{N} u_{it}u_{is}) = \omega_{ts} \sum_{i=1}^{N} \sigma_{ii},$$
$$\mathsf{E}(\textstyle\sum_{t=1}^{N} u_{it}u_{jt}) = \sigma_{ij} \sum_{t=1}^{T} \omega_{tt} = T\sigma_{ij},$$

σ_{ij} and ω_{ts} can be estimated from consistent (say OLS) residuals, $\widehat{u}_{it}$, giving the following generalizations of (4.11)–(4.12):

$$\widehat{\sigma}_{ij} = \frac{\sum_{t=1}^{T} \widehat{u}_{it}\widehat{u}_{jt}}{T}, \qquad i, j = 1, \dots, N \tag{4.20}$$

$$\widehat{\omega}_{ts} = \frac{T\sum_{i=1}^{N} \widehat{u}_{it}\widehat{u}_{is}}{\sum_{i=1}^{N}\sum_{t=1}^{T} \widehat{u}_{it}^2}, \qquad t, s = 1, \dots, T. \tag{4.21}$$

The GLS estimator of $\boldsymbol{\beta}$ is the following generalization of (4.8) and (4.16):

$$\boldsymbol{\beta}^* = [X'(\mathbf{\Sigma}_N^{-1} \otimes \mathbf{\Omega}_T^{-1})X]^{-1}[X'(\mathbf{\Sigma}_N^{-1} \otimes \mathbf{\Omega}_T^{-1})y]. \tag{4.22}$$

Since it follows that $\boldsymbol{\beta}^* - \boldsymbol{\beta} = [X'(\mathbf{\Sigma}_N^{-1} \otimes \mathbf{\Omega}_T^{-1})X]^{-1}[X'(\mathbf{\Sigma}_N^{-1} \otimes \mathbf{\Omega}_T^{-1})u]$, we obtain

$$\mathsf{V}(\boldsymbol{\beta}^*|X) = [X'(\boldsymbol{\Sigma}_N^{-1} \otimes \boldsymbol{\Omega}_T^{-1})X]^{-1}. \tag{4.23}$$

The FGLS estimator of $\boldsymbol{\beta}$ and the estimator of $\mathsf{V}(\boldsymbol{\beta}^*|X)$ are obtained by replacing $\boldsymbol{\Sigma}_N$ and $\boldsymbol{\Omega}_T$ by $\widehat{\boldsymbol{\Sigma}}_N$ and $\widehat{\boldsymbol{\Omega}}_T$, as defined by (4.20) and (4.21).

Since the covariance structure is characterized by $\frac{1}{2}[N(N+1) + T(T+1)] - 1$ parameters if $\boldsymbol{\Sigma}_N$ or $\boldsymbol{\Omega}_T$ are unrestricted, it may be easily overparameterized when N is large. Hence, the primary function of this synthesis model may be in completing the 'model hierarchy'.

4.2.3 INCLUDING INTERCEPTS

The results for Models F1–F3 hold, with minor modifications, also when an individual-specific intercept α_i^* is added to the equation. We briefly reconsider F1 and F2.

Model F1 with intercept. Replacing $y_{it} = x_{it}\beta_i + u_{it}$ with $y_{it} = \alpha_i^* + x_{it}\beta_i + u_{it}$, OLS gives the following generalization of (4.2)–(4.3):

$$\widehat{\beta}_i = \frac{\sum_{t=1}^{T}(x_{it} - \bar{x}_{i\cdot})(y_{it} - \bar{y}_{i\cdot})}{\sum_{t=1}^{T}(x_{it} - \bar{x}_{i\cdot})^2}, \qquad \widehat{\alpha}_i^* = \bar{y}_{i\cdot} - \bar{x}_{i\cdot}\widehat{\beta}_i, \tag{4.24}$$

$$\mathrm{var}(\widehat{\beta}_i|X) = \frac{\sigma_{ii}}{\sum_{t=1}^{T}(x_{it} - \bar{x}_{i\cdot})^2}, \qquad i = 1, \dots, N. \tag{4.25}$$

The conclusion is that $\widehat{\beta}_i$ in the zero-intercept version of Model F1 is a weighted mean of $\widehat{\beta}_{it} = y_{it}/x_{it}$ $(t = 1, \dots, T)$ carries over to the case with intercept, except that all weights are no longer positive. This is seen by rewriting (4.24) as

$$\widehat{\beta}_i = \frac{\sum_{t=1}^{T}(x_{it} - \bar{x}_{i\cdot})y_{it}}{\sum_{t=1}^{T}(x_{it} - \bar{x}_{i\cdot})x_{it}} \equiv \frac{\sum_{t=1}^{T}(x_{it} - \bar{x}_{i\cdot})x_{it}\widehat{\beta}_{it}}{\sum_{t=1}^{T}(x_{it} - \bar{x}_{i\cdot})x_{it}}, \qquad i = 1, \dots, N, \tag{4.26}$$

where the weight $(x_{it} - \bar{x}_{i\cdot})x_{it}$ may have either sign.

Model F2 with intercept. Let $\boldsymbol{X}_i = [\boldsymbol{e}_T, \boldsymbol{x}_i]$ and $\boldsymbol{\beta}_i = [\alpha_i^*, \beta_i]'$, and write the equation as $\boldsymbol{y}_i = \alpha_i^* + \boldsymbol{x}_i\boldsymbol{\beta}_i + \boldsymbol{u}_i = \boldsymbol{X}_i\boldsymbol{\beta}_i + \boldsymbol{u}_i$. The modified GLS estimator and its covariance matrix, replacing (4.8)–(4.9), then become

$$\widetilde{\boldsymbol{\beta}}_i = \begin{bmatrix} \widetilde{\alpha}_i^* \\ \widetilde{\beta}_i \end{bmatrix} = [\boldsymbol{X}_i'\boldsymbol{\Omega}_T^{-1}\boldsymbol{X}_i]^{-1}[\boldsymbol{X}_i'\boldsymbol{\Omega}_T^{-1}\boldsymbol{y}_i], \tag{4.27}$$

$$\mathsf{V}(\widetilde{\boldsymbol{\beta}}_i|X) = \sigma_{ii}[\boldsymbol{X}_i'\boldsymbol{\Omega}_T^{-1}\boldsymbol{X}_i]^{-1}. \tag{4.28}$$

With serially uncorrelated disturbances, $\boldsymbol{\Omega}_T = \mathrm{diag}(\omega_{11}, \dots, \omega_{TT})$, $\widetilde{\boldsymbol{\beta}}_i$ simplifies to

$$\widetilde{\boldsymbol{\beta}}_i = \begin{bmatrix} \sum_t (1/\omega_{tt}) & \sum_t (x_{it}/\omega_{tt}) \\ \sum_t (x_{it}/\omega_{tt}) & \sum_t (x_{it}^2/\omega_{tt}) \end{bmatrix}^{-1} \begin{bmatrix} \sum_t (y_{it}/\omega_{tt}) \\ \sum_t (x_{it} y_{it}/\omega_{tt}) \end{bmatrix}$$

$$= \frac{1}{|\mathbf{X}_i' \boldsymbol{\Omega}_T^{-1} \mathbf{X}_i|} \begin{bmatrix} \sum_t (x_{it}^2/\omega_{tt}) & -\sum_t (x_{it}/\omega_{tt}) \\ -\sum_t (x_{it}/\omega_{tt}) & \sum_t (1/\omega_{tt}) \end{bmatrix} \begin{bmatrix} \sum_t (y_{it}/\omega_{tt}) \\ \sum_t (x_{it} y_{it}/\omega_{tt}) \end{bmatrix},$$

where

$$|\mathbf{X}_i' \boldsymbol{\Omega}_T^{-1} \mathbf{X}_i| = \left[\sum_t (1/\omega_{tt})\right]\left[\sum_t (x_{it}^2/\omega_{tt})\right] - \left[\sum_t (x_{it}/\omega_{tt})\right]^2.$$

The counterpart to (4.10) then becomes:

$$\widetilde{\beta}_i = \frac{\sum_{t=1}^{T}\left[\frac{x_{it}y_{it}}{\omega_{tt}}\right]\sum_{t=1}^{T}\left[\frac{1}{\omega_{tt}}\right] - \sum_{t=1}^{T}\left[\frac{y_{it}}{\omega_{tt}}\right]\sum_{t=1}^{T}\left[\frac{x_{it}}{\omega_{tt}}\right]}{\sum_{t=1}^{T}\left[\frac{1}{\omega_{tt}}\right]\sum_{t=1}^{T}\left[\frac{x_{it}^2}{\omega_{tt}}\right] - \left[\sum_{t=1}^{T}\left[\frac{x_{it}}{\omega_{tt}}\right]\right]^2}$$

$$= \frac{\sum_{t=1}^{T} (x_{it} - \bar{\bar{x}}_{i\cdot})(x_{it}/\omega_{tt})\widehat{\beta}_{it}}{\sum_{t=1}^{T} (x_{it} - \bar{\bar{x}}_{i\cdot})(x_{it}/\omega_{tt})}, \tag{4.29}$$

where $\bar{\bar{x}}_{i\cdot}$ is a weighted individual mean, the weight of each x_{it} being the inverse of the corresponding disturbance variance,

$$\bar{\bar{x}}_{i\cdot} = \frac{\sum_{t=1}^{T} (x_{it}/\omega_{tt})}{\sum_{t=1}^{T} (1/\omega_{tt})}.$$

Still, $\widetilde{\beta}_i$ is a mean of $\widehat{\beta}_{i1}, \dots, \widehat{\beta}_{iT}$, now with weights $(x_{it} - \bar{\bar{x}}_{i\cdot})(x_{it}/\omega_{tt})$, and (4.29) modifies both (4.10) and (4.26).

4.2.4 MULTI-REGRESSOR MODELS

The step from the one-regressor to the K-regressor model is rather short and is considered briefly.

For *Models F1 and F2* the equation is extended to

$$y_i = X_i \boldsymbol{\beta}_i + \boldsymbol{u}_i,$$

where

$$\begin{aligned} X_i &= [\boldsymbol{e}_T, \boldsymbol{x}_{1i}, \dots, \boldsymbol{x}_{Ki}], \\ \boldsymbol{x}_{ki} &= [x_{ki1}, \dots, x_{kiT}]', \\ \boldsymbol{\beta}_i &= (\alpha_i^*, \beta_{1i}, \dots, \beta_{Ki})'. \end{aligned}$$

The MVLUE of $\boldsymbol{\beta}_i$ and its covariances matrix, generalizing (4.2)–(4.3) and (4.8)–(4.9), are, respectively,

$$\widehat{\boldsymbol{\beta}}_i = (X_i'X_i)^{-1}(X_i'y_i), \tag{4.30}$$

$$\mathsf{V}(\widehat{\boldsymbol{\beta}}_i|X) = \sigma_{ii}(X_i'X_i)^{-1}, \qquad i = 1, \dots, N, \tag{4.31}$$

and

$$\widetilde{\boldsymbol{\beta}}_i = [X_i'\boldsymbol{\Omega}_T^{-1}X_i]^{-1}[X_i'\boldsymbol{\Omega}_T^{-1}y_i], \tag{4.32}$$

$$\mathsf{V}(\widetilde{\boldsymbol{\beta}}_i|X) = \sigma_{ii}[X_i'\boldsymbol{\Omega}_T^{-1}X_i]^{-1}, \qquad i = 1, \dots, N. \tag{4.33}$$

For *Model F3* and the synthesis of F1–F3, the matrix formulations in, respectively, (4.14), (4.16), (4.17), (4.19), (4.22), and (4.23) are unchanged.

An example of estimation of unit-specific coefficients, where the units are $N=47$ Norwegian hospitals observed over $T=10$ years, and the coefficients represent impact on efficiency measures, is given in Table 4.1, columns 1 and 5. See Section 4.3.3 for details and discussion.

4.3 Random coefficient models

An essentially different description of heterogeneity is now introduced: random coefficients imagined drawn from a probability distribution. We again proceed stepwise, from a single-regressor zero-intercept model to versions of increasing complexity.

As a start, it is worth noticing that regression analysis of panel data with random coefficients has some resemblance to approaches in *Bayesian econometrics*, and more so than models with random intercepts only. The Bayesian viewpoint, for example, provides an interesting interpretation of the distinction between 'fixed' and 'random' coefficient versions of the model, also invoking *hyperparameters*:[3]

In the Bayesian framework both 'fixed' and 'random' effects are treated as random parameters defined within a three-stage hierarchical model: the dependent variable is distributed around a mean value that depends, together with regressors, on certain parameters; these parameters are, in turn, distributed around a mean value determined by other parameters called 'hyperparameters', which are also random. While a fixed effects estimation updates the distribution of the parameters, a random effects estimation updates the distribution of the hyperparameters. (Rendon (2013, p. 461))

4.3.1 SINGLE-REGRESSOR MODELS AND THEIR ESTIMATORS

We specify two models, labelled R1 and R2, with one regressor, R2 generalizing R1 by including a random intercept.

Model R1. In the simplest random coefficient model we assume

$$y_{it} = x_{it}\beta_i + u_{it}, \qquad i = 1,\dots,N;\ t = 1,\dots,T, \tag{4.34}$$

and imagine that the individual-specific coefficients are draws from a probability distribution with homoskedastic coefficients and heteroskedastic disturbances,

$$\beta_i = \beta+\delta_i,\ (u_{i1},\dots,u_{iT}|X) \sim \mathsf{IID}(0,\sigma_{ii}),\ \ (\delta_i|X) \sim \mathsf{IID}(0,\sigma_\delta^2).$$

Here β can be interpreted as the *common expectation* of the N individual coefficients, δ_i as the 'coefficient slack' of individual i, and σ_δ^2 as the common variance of the slacks. The coefficients vary randomly around a common value β, which represents the average response to a change in x_{it}. This way of specifying heterogeneity requires a much lower number of parameters than the fixed coefficient counterparts (when N by far exceeds 2), since the distribution of $\beta_1,\dots,\beta_N$ is characterized by only two parameters. The assumption $\mathsf{E}(\delta_i|X) = 0$ implies that *the coefficients do not vary systematically with the variable to which they belong.*[4] It follows that

[3] Demidenko (2004, p. 8) sets out to 'convince the reader' of his book on 'mixed models' that this model class, to which models with random intercepts and coefficients belong, see Demidenko (2004, Section 1.3), 'may serve as a compromise between the frequentist (classical) and Bayesian approaches'.

[4] Confer the example with aggregation in Section 1.4.

$$y_{it} = x_{it}\beta + v_{it}, \quad v_{it} = x_{it}\delta_i + u_{it} \qquad i = 1, \dots, N; \; t = 1, \dots, T, \tag{4.35}$$

where v_{it} can be interpreted as a composite disturbance, with

$$\mathsf{E}(v_{it}|X) = 0, \quad \mathsf{E}(v_{it}v_{js}|X) = \delta_{ij}[x_{it}x_{is}\sigma_\delta^2 + \delta_{ts}\sigma_{ii}], \tag{4.36}$$

δ_{ij} and δ_{ts} still being Kronecker-deltas. The implied composite disturbance v_{it} is heteroskedastic both across individuals and over periods, and this heteroskedasticity has a double origin, provided that x_{it} has a time variation. Further, this disturbance is autocorrelated over periods, but cross-individual correlation is absent.[5] The form of the heteroskedasticity and of the autocorrelation are determined by the covariates. The gross disturbance v_{it} therefore has important properties in common with u_{it} in the fixed coefficient model (4.7); the random coefficient approach may be seen as a way of *modelling* (disturbance) heteroskedasticity. Its distribution, however, is described by fewer parameters.

The v_{it} disturbance has two other notable properties. First,

$$\begin{aligned} \text{cov}(v_{it}, x_{it}^s) &= \mathsf{E}(v_{it}x_{it}^s) = \mathsf{E}_x[\mathsf{E}_v(v_{it}x_{it}^s|x_{it})] \\ &= \mathsf{E}_x[x_{it}^s\mathsf{E}_v(v_{it}|x_{it})] = 0, \quad s = 0, 1, 2, \dots, \end{aligned}$$

so that although x_{it} enters the expression for v_{it}, the two variables are uncorrelated. Yet, they are stochastically dependent, as stochastic independence requires coinciding conditional and marginal distributions, and we know that $\text{var}(v_{it}|x_{it})$ depends on x_{it}. Second, it follows from (4.36) that $\mathsf{E}(v_{it}^2 x_{it}^s) = \mathsf{E}_x[\mathsf{E}_v(v_{it}^2 x_{it}^s|x_{it})] = \mathsf{E}(x_{it}^{s+2})\sigma_\delta^2 + \mathsf{E}(x_{it}^s)\sigma_{ii}$, and hence

$$\begin{aligned} \text{cov}(v_{it}^2, x_{it}^s) &= \mathsf{E}(v_{it}^2 x_{it}^s) - \mathsf{E}(v_{it}^2)\mathsf{E}(x_{it}^s) \\ &= \left[\mathsf{E}(x_{it}^{s+2}) - \mathsf{E}(x_{it}^2)\mathsf{E}(x_{it}^s)\right]\sigma_\delta^2 = \text{cov}(x_{it}^2, x_{it}^s)\sigma_\delta^2. \end{aligned}$$

Thus, when $\sigma_\delta^2 > 0$, v_{it}^2 is correlated with x_{it}, x_{it}^2, etc.

Formally, we have an N-equation system with common slope coefficient β:[6]

$$\begin{aligned} &\boldsymbol{y}_i = \boldsymbol{x}_i\beta + \boldsymbol{v}_i, \quad \boldsymbol{v}_i = \boldsymbol{x}_i\delta_i + \boldsymbol{u}_i, \\ &\mathsf{E}(\boldsymbol{v}_i|X) = 0, \;\; \mathsf{E}(\boldsymbol{v}_i\boldsymbol{v}_j'|X) = \delta_{ij}\boldsymbol{\Sigma}_{ii}, \\ &\boldsymbol{\Sigma}_{ii} = \boldsymbol{x}_i\boldsymbol{x}_i'\sigma_\delta^2 + \sigma_{ii}\boldsymbol{I}_T, \\ &i, j = 1, \dots, N, \end{aligned} \tag{4.37}$$

[5] Cases where $x_{it}x_{is} = 0$ for all $s \neq t$ have minor practical interest.

[6] Confers again the distinction between parameters and exogenous variables.

which in stacked form, with

$$y = \begin{bmatrix} y_1 \\ \vdots \\ y_N \end{bmatrix}, \quad x = \begin{bmatrix} x_1 \\ \vdots \\ x_N \end{bmatrix}, \quad v = \begin{bmatrix} v_1 \\ \vdots \\ v_N \end{bmatrix}, \quad \boldsymbol{\Sigma} = \begin{bmatrix} \boldsymbol{\Sigma}_{11} & \dots & 0 \\ \vdots & \ddots & \vdots \\ 0 & \dots & \boldsymbol{\Sigma}_{NN} \end{bmatrix},$$

can be written as

$$y = x\beta + v, \quad \mathsf{E}(v|X) = 0, \quad \mathsf{E}(vv'|X) = \boldsymbol{\Sigma}. \tag{4.38}$$

The GLS estimator of the expected coefficient, β, and its variance are, respectively,

$$\beta^* = \frac{x'\boldsymbol{\Sigma}^{-1}y}{x'\boldsymbol{\Sigma}^{-1}x} \equiv \frac{\sum_{i=1}^{N} \boldsymbol{x}_i'\boldsymbol{\Sigma}_{ii}^{-1}\boldsymbol{y}_i}{\sum_{i=1}^{N} \boldsymbol{x}_i'\boldsymbol{\Sigma}_{ii}^{-1}\boldsymbol{x}_i}, \tag{4.39}$$

$$\mathsf{V}(\beta^*|x) = \mathsf{V}\left(\frac{x'\boldsymbol{\Sigma}^{-1}v}{x'\boldsymbol{\Sigma}^{-1}x}|X\right) = \frac{1}{x'\boldsymbol{\Sigma}^{-1}x} = \frac{1}{\sum_{i=1}^{N} \boldsymbol{x}_i'\boldsymbol{\Sigma}_{ii}^{-1}\boldsymbol{x}_i}. \tag{4.40}$$

The corresponding expressions involving only observations from individual i are

$$\beta_i^* = \frac{\boldsymbol{x}_i'\boldsymbol{\Sigma}_{ii}^{-1}\boldsymbol{y}_i}{\boldsymbol{x}_i'\boldsymbol{\Sigma}_{ii}^{-1}\boldsymbol{x}_i}, \tag{4.41}$$

$$\mathsf{V}(\beta_i^*|X) = \mathsf{V}\left(\frac{\boldsymbol{x}_i'\boldsymbol{\Sigma}_{ii}^{-1}\boldsymbol{v}_i}{\boldsymbol{x}_1'\boldsymbol{\Sigma}_{ii}^{-1}\boldsymbol{x}_i}|X\right) = \frac{1}{\boldsymbol{x}_i'\boldsymbol{\Sigma}_{ii}^{-1}\boldsymbol{x}_i}, \qquad i = 1, \dots, N. \tag{4.42}$$

Clearly, β^* is a weighted mean of these i-specific GLS estimators, satisfying

$$\beta^* = \frac{\sum_{i=1}^{N} \mathsf{V}(\beta_i^*|X)^{-1}\beta_i^*}{\sum_{i=1}^{N} \mathsf{V}(\beta_i^*|X)^{-1}}, \tag{4.43}$$

$$\mathsf{V}(\beta^*|X) = [\textstyle\sum_{i=1}^{N} \mathsf{V}(\beta_i^*|X)^{-1}]^{-1}. \tag{4.44}$$

This again exemplifies the property of GLS discussed in Appendix 2A.

More instructive interpretations exist. Using the theorem in Appendix 4A, Section 4A.1, it follows that

$$\begin{aligned}
\boldsymbol{\Sigma}_{ii}^{-1} &= \left(\boldsymbol{x}_i\boldsymbol{x}_i'\sigma_\delta^2 + \sigma_{ii}\boldsymbol{I}_T\right)^{-1} \\
&\equiv \frac{1}{\sigma_{ii}}\left[\boldsymbol{I}_T - \boldsymbol{x}_i\left(\boldsymbol{x}_i'\boldsymbol{x}_i + \frac{\sigma_{ii}}{\sigma_\delta^2}\right)^{-1}\boldsymbol{x}_i'\right] \\
&\equiv \frac{1}{\sigma_{ii}}\left[\boldsymbol{I}_T - \frac{\sigma_\delta^2}{\sigma_\delta^2\boldsymbol{x}_i'\boldsymbol{x}_i + \sigma_{ii}}\boldsymbol{x}_i\boldsymbol{x}_i'\right],
\end{aligned} \tag{4.45}$$

and hence,

$$x_i'\boldsymbol{\Sigma}_{ii}^{-1}x_i = \frac{1}{\sigma_{ii}}\left[x_i'x_i - \frac{\sigma_\delta^2(x_i'x_i)^2}{\sigma_\delta^2 x_i'x_i + \sigma_{ii}}\right] \equiv \frac{1}{\sigma_\delta^2 + \sigma_{ii}(x_i'x_i)^{-1}}, \tag{4.46}$$

$$x_i'\boldsymbol{\Sigma}_{ii}^{-1}y_i = \frac{1}{\sigma_{ii}}\left[x_i'y_i - \frac{\sigma_\delta^2(x_i'x_i)(x_i'y_i)}{\sigma_\delta^2 x_i'x_i + \sigma_{ii}}\right] \equiv \frac{(x_i'x_i)^{-1}(x_i'y_i)}{\sigma_\delta^2 + \sigma_{ii}(x_i'x_i)^{-1}}. \tag{4.47}$$

Inserting these expressions in (4.41) and (4.42), the common factor

$$\Psi_i = \sigma_\delta^2 + \sigma_{ii}(x_i'x_i)^{-1}, \qquad i = 1,\dots,N, \tag{4.48}$$

cancels, and we can conclude: *the GLS estimator of β based on the observations from individual i in the random coefficients model equals the OLS estimator of β_i in the corresponding fixed coefficients model:*

$$\beta_i^* = \frac{x_i'\boldsymbol{\Sigma}_{ii}^{-1}y_i}{x_i'\boldsymbol{\Sigma}_{ii}^{-1}x_i} = \frac{x_i'y_i}{x_i'x_i} = \widehat{\beta}_i, \tag{4.49}$$

$$\mathsf{V}(\beta_i^*|X) = \frac{1}{x_i'\boldsymbol{\Sigma}_{ii}^{-1}x_i} = \sigma_\delta^2 + \sigma_{ii}(x_i'x_i)^{-1} = \Psi_i, \quad i = 1,\dots,N. \tag{4.50}$$

It follows from (4.39) and (4.43) that β^* can be written as a weighted mean:

$$\beta^* = \frac{\sum_{i=1}^N[\sigma_\delta^2 + \sigma_{ii}(x_i'x_i)^{-1}]^{-1}\beta_i^*}{\sum_{i=1}^N[\sigma_\delta^2 + \sigma_{ii}(x_i'x_i)^{-1}]^{-1}} \equiv \frac{\sum_{i=1}^N \Psi_i^{-1}\beta_i^*}{\sum_{i=1}^N \Psi_i^{-1}}. \tag{4.51}$$

Since (4.37) and (4.49) imply

$$\beta_i^* - \beta_i = \frac{x_i'u_i}{x_i'x_i}, \quad \beta_i^* - \beta = \frac{x_i'v_i}{x_i'x_i} \equiv \delta_i + \frac{x_i'u_i}{x_i'x_i},$$

the variances of β_i^*, conditional on β_i and marginally, are, respectively,

$$\mathsf{V}(\beta_i^*|X,\beta_i) = \frac{x_i'\mathsf{V}(u_i|X)x_i}{(x_i'x_i)^2} = \frac{\sigma_{ii}}{x_i'x_i}, \tag{4.52}$$

$$\mathsf{V}(\beta_i^*|X) = \frac{x_i'\mathsf{V}(v_i|X)x_i}{(x_i'x_i)^2} = \sigma_\delta^2 + \frac{\sigma_{ii}}{x_i'x_i}. \tag{4.53}$$

This concurs with the law of iterated expectations, which implies[7]

$$\mathsf{V}(\beta_i^*|X) = \mathsf{V}[\mathsf{E}(\beta_i^*|X,\beta_i)] + \mathsf{E}[\mathsf{V}(\beta_i^*|X,\beta_i)].$$

Since $\mathsf{E}(\beta_i^*|X,\beta_i)=\beta_i$ and $\mathsf{V}(\beta_i^*|X,\beta_i)=\sigma_{ii}(\boldsymbol{x}_i'\boldsymbol{x}_i)^{-1}$, we can give the following interpretation of (4.48) and (4.53):

$$\Psi_i = \mathsf{V}(\beta_i^*|X)=\mathsf{V}(\beta_i|X)+\mathsf{V}(\beta_i^*|X,\beta_i) = \sigma_\delta^2+\sigma_{ii}(\boldsymbol{x}_i'\boldsymbol{x}_i)^{-1}. \tag{4.54}$$

We can therefore conclude: *the GLS estimator of the expected coefficient β, as given by (4.51), is a weighted mean of the i-specific OLS estimators with weights depending on the variance of the coefficient slack in the random coefficient model and the variances of the i-specific OLS estimator in the fixed coefficient model.*

Computation of β^* requires that $\Psi_1,\dots,\Psi_N$ are known, which in practice means $\sigma_{11},\dots,\sigma_{NN}$ and σ_δ^2 are known. To obtain its FGLS counterpart, we can estimate the former from the OLS residual vectors, $\widehat{\boldsymbol{u}}_i = \boldsymbol{y}_i - \boldsymbol{x}_i\widehat{\beta}_i$, where $\widehat{\beta}_i\ (=\beta_i^*)$ is given by (4.49), confer (4.2),

$$\widehat{\sigma}_{ii} = \tfrac{1}{T-1}\widehat{\boldsymbol{u}}_i'\widehat{\boldsymbol{u}}_i, \qquad\qquad i=1,\dots,N, \tag{4.55}$$

and the latter from

$$\widehat{\sigma}_\delta^2 = \tfrac{1}{N-1}\textstyle\sum_{i=1}^N \widehat{\delta}_i^2, \qquad \widehat{\delta}_i = \widehat{\beta}_i - \tfrac{1}{N}\textstyle\sum_{j=1}^N \widehat{\beta}_j,\quad i=1,\dots,N. \tag{4.56}$$

Finally, we estimate Ψ_i by, in (4.48), replacing $(\sigma_{ii},\sigma_\delta^2)$ by $(\widehat{\sigma}_{ii},\widehat{\sigma}_\delta^2)$, and next replacing Ψ_i in (4.51) by $\widehat{\Psi}_i=\widehat{\sigma}_\delta^2+\widehat{\sigma}_{ii}(\boldsymbol{x}_i'\boldsymbol{x}_i)^{-1}$.

Consider two boundary cases to support intuition.

No coefficient slack. If $\sigma_\delta^2=0 \Longrightarrow \boldsymbol{\Sigma}_{ii}=\sigma_{ii}\boldsymbol{I}_T$, $\Psi_i^{-1}=\sigma_{ii}^{-1}(\boldsymbol{x}_i'\boldsymbol{x}_i)$, (4.51) gives

$$\beta^* = \frac{\sum_{i=1}^N \sigma_{ii}^{-1}\boldsymbol{x}_i'\boldsymbol{y}_i}{\sum_{i=1}^N \sigma_{ii}^{-1}\boldsymbol{x}_i'\boldsymbol{x}_i} = \frac{\sum_{i=1}^N \sigma_{ii}^{-1}\boldsymbol{x}_i'\boldsymbol{x}_i\boldsymbol{\beta}_i^*}{\sum_{i=1}^N \sigma_{ii}^{-1}\boldsymbol{x}_i'\boldsymbol{x}_i} = \frac{\sum_{i=1}^N\sum_{t=1}^T\left(\frac{x_{it}^2}{\sigma_{ii}}\right)\widehat{\beta}_{it}}{\sum_{i=1}^N\sum_{t=1}^T\left(\frac{x_{it}^2}{\sigma_{ii}}\right)},$$

so that this estimator is a weighted mean of the N individual-specific OLS estimators in the fixed coefficient model with $\boldsymbol{x}_i'\boldsymbol{x}_i/\sigma_{ii}$ as weights, or, equivalently, an x_{it}^2/σ_{ii}-weighted mean of the NT observation-specific 'estimators' $\widehat{\beta}_{it}=y_{it}/x_{it}$.

[7] For any (Q,Z) this 'law' implies $\mathsf{V}(Q) = \mathsf{V}_Q[\mathsf{E}_Z(Z|Q)]+\mathsf{E}_Q[\mathsf{V}_Z(Z|Q)]$. See, e.g., Greene (2008, Appendix B8).

No disturbance. If $y_i = \beta_i x_i$, $\sigma_{ii} = 0 \Longrightarrow \boldsymbol{\Sigma}_{ii} = \boldsymbol{x}_i\boldsymbol{x}_i'\sigma_\delta^2$, $\Psi_i = \sigma_\delta^2$, then $\boldsymbol{\Sigma}_{ii}$ becomes singular with rank 1,[8] and (4.51) is simplified to

$$\beta^* = \tfrac{1}{N}\sum_{i=1}^N \widehat{\beta}_i.$$

This means that the GLS estimator of β degenerates to an unweighted mean of the individual-specific OLS estimators. Since (4.49) with $y_i = \beta_i x_i$ implies $\beta_i^* = \widehat{\beta}_i = \beta_i$; we have $\beta^* = \frac{1}{N}\sum_{i=1}^N \beta_i$, which can be given an interesting interpretation. The MVLUE of β can be obtained by applying OLS on

$$\beta_i = \frac{y_{it}}{x_{it}} = \beta + \delta_i,$$

which has regressand $\beta_i = \beta_{it} = y_{it}/x_{it}$, no regressor, intercept β, and disturbance $\delta_i \sim \mathsf{IID}(0, \sigma_\delta^2)$, giving

$$\beta^* = \tfrac{1}{NT}\sum_{i=1}^N \sum_{t=1}^T \left(\tfrac{y_{it}}{x_{it}}\right),$$

i.e., an unweighted mean of the NT values of $\widehat{\beta}_{it} = y_{it}/x_{it}$.

Model R2. We include a *random intercept*, $\alpha_i^* = k + \alpha_i$, in (4.34) and let

$$\boldsymbol{X}_i = [\boldsymbol{e}_T, \boldsymbol{x}_i],\ \ \boldsymbol{\beta} = \begin{bmatrix} k \\ \beta \end{bmatrix},\ \ \boldsymbol{\delta}_i = \begin{bmatrix} \alpha_i \\ \beta_i \end{bmatrix} \sim \mathsf{IID}(\boldsymbol{0}, \boldsymbol{\Sigma}_\delta),\ \ \boldsymbol{\Sigma}_\delta = \begin{bmatrix} \sigma_\alpha^2 & \sigma_{\alpha\delta} \\ \sigma_{\alpha\delta} & \sigma_\delta^2 \end{bmatrix},$$

where $\boldsymbol{\delta}_i$ is the (2×1) vector containing the slacks in the intercept and the coefficient. It then follows that (4.37) is generalized to

$$\begin{aligned}
&\boldsymbol{y}_i = \boldsymbol{X}_i\boldsymbol{\beta} + \boldsymbol{v}_i, \qquad \boldsymbol{v}_i = \boldsymbol{X}_i\boldsymbol{\delta}_i + \boldsymbol{u}_i, \\
&\mathsf{E}(\boldsymbol{v}_i|\boldsymbol{X}) = \boldsymbol{0}, \qquad \mathsf{E}(\boldsymbol{v}_i\boldsymbol{v}_j'|\boldsymbol{X}) = \delta_{ij}\boldsymbol{\Sigma}_{ii}, \\
&\boldsymbol{\Sigma}_{ii} = \boldsymbol{X}_i\boldsymbol{\Sigma}_\delta\boldsymbol{X}_i' + \sigma_{ii}\boldsymbol{I}_T \\
&\qquad = \boldsymbol{e}_T\boldsymbol{e}_T'\sigma_\alpha^2 + (\boldsymbol{e}_T\boldsymbol{x}_i' + \boldsymbol{x}_i\boldsymbol{e}_T')\sigma_{\alpha\delta} + \boldsymbol{x}_i\boldsymbol{x}_i'\sigma_\delta^2 + \sigma_{ii}\boldsymbol{I}_T, \\
&i, j = 1, \dots, N.
\end{aligned} \tag{4.57}$$

The GLS estimator of $\boldsymbol{\beta}$ then becomes

$$\boldsymbol{\beta}^* = [\textstyle\sum_{i=1}^N \boldsymbol{X}_i'\boldsymbol{\Sigma}_{ii}^{-1}\boldsymbol{X}_i]^{-1}[\sum_{i=1}^N \boldsymbol{X}_i'\boldsymbol{\Sigma}_{ii}^{-1}\boldsymbol{y}_i]. \tag{4.58}$$

[8] We see from (4.45) that its inverse does not exist in this case, $\boldsymbol{x}_i\boldsymbol{x}_i'$ has rank 1.

Since the corresponding estimator based on observations from individual i is

$$\boldsymbol{\beta}_i^* = [X_i'\boldsymbol{\Sigma}_{ii}^{-1}X_i]^{-1}[X_i'\boldsymbol{\Sigma}_{ii}^{-1}y_i], \tag{4.59}$$

we can rewrite (4.58) as the matrix-weighted mean:

$$\boldsymbol{\beta}^* = [\textstyle\sum_{i=1}^N X_i'\boldsymbol{\Sigma}_{ii}^{-1}X_i]^{-1}[\sum_{i=1}^N X_i'\boldsymbol{\Sigma}_{ii}^{-1}X_i\boldsymbol{\beta}_i^*] \tag{4.60}$$

with

$$\mathsf{V}(\boldsymbol{\beta}^*|X) = [\textstyle\sum_{i=1}^N X_i'\boldsymbol{\Sigma}_{ii}^{-1}X_i]^{-1}. \tag{4.61}$$

Equations (4.58)–(4.61) generalize (4.39), (4.41), (4.43), and (4.44).

FGLS estimation of the single-regressor model (4.57), with both random coefficient and intercept can be synthesized in the prescription:

1. Form the OLS residual vectors $\widehat{\boldsymbol{u}}_i = \boldsymbol{y}_i - \boldsymbol{e}_T\widehat{\alpha}_i^* - \boldsymbol{x}_i\widehat{\beta}_i$, where $\widehat{\alpha}_i^*$ and $\widehat{\beta}_i$ are the OLS estimators of α_i^* and β_i, when they are considered as fixed.
2. Estimate σ_{ii} by $\widehat{\sigma}_{ii} = \widehat{\boldsymbol{u}}_i'\widehat{\boldsymbol{u}}_i/(T-2)$, $i = 1,\dots,N$.
3. Estimate $\sigma_\alpha^2, \sigma_{\alpha\delta}$, and σ_δ^2 from their analogues: $\widehat{\sigma}_\alpha^2 = \frac{1}{N-1}\sum_{i=1}^N \widehat{\alpha}_i^2$, $\widehat{\sigma}_{\alpha\delta} = \frac{1}{N-1}\sum_{i=1}^N \widehat{\alpha}_i\widehat{\delta}_i$, and $\widehat{\sigma}_\delta^2 = \frac{1}{N-1}\sum_{i=1}^N \widehat{\delta}_i^2$, where $\widehat{\alpha}_i = \widehat{\alpha}_i^* - \frac{1}{N}\sum_{j=1}^N \widehat{\alpha}_j^*$ and $\widehat{\delta}_i = \widehat{\beta}_i - \frac{1}{N}\sum_{j=1}^N \widehat{\beta}_j$.
4. Compute $\widehat{\boldsymbol{\Sigma}}_{ii} = \boldsymbol{e}_T\boldsymbol{e}_T'\widehat{\sigma}_\alpha^2 + (\boldsymbol{e}_T\boldsymbol{x}_i' + \boldsymbol{x}_i\boldsymbol{e}_T')\widehat{\sigma}_{\alpha\delta} + \boldsymbol{x}_i\boldsymbol{x}_i'\widehat{\sigma}_\delta^2 + \widehat{\sigma}_{ii}\boldsymbol{I}_T$ and replace in (4.60) and (4.61) $\boldsymbol{\Sigma}_{ii}$ by $\widehat{\boldsymbol{\Sigma}}_{ii}$.

4.3.2 MULTI-REGRESSOR MODEL AND ITS GLS ESTIMATOR

The generalization of Model R2 to include K regressors is straightforward. The equation is

$$y_{it} = \boldsymbol{x}_{it}\,\boldsymbol{\beta}_i + u_{it} \qquad i = 1,\dots,N;\ t = 1,\dots,T, \tag{4.62}$$

where now $\boldsymbol{\beta}_i = (\alpha_i^*, \beta_{1i},\dots,\beta_{Ki})'$ and $\boldsymbol{x}_{it} = (1, x_{1it},\dots,x_{Kit})$. We consider $\boldsymbol{\beta}_i$ as random and generalize (4.35)–(4.36) to

$$\begin{aligned}
&\boldsymbol{y}_i = \boldsymbol{X}_i\boldsymbol{\beta}_i + \boldsymbol{u}_i,\ \ \boldsymbol{\beta}_i = \boldsymbol{\beta} + \boldsymbol{\delta}_i,\ \ \boldsymbol{u}_i \perp \boldsymbol{\delta}_i,\\
&\mathsf{E}(\boldsymbol{u}_i|X) = \boldsymbol{0}_{T,1},\ \ \mathsf{E}(\boldsymbol{u}_i\boldsymbol{u}_j'|X) = \delta_{ij}\sigma_{ii}\boldsymbol{I}_T,\\
&(\boldsymbol{\delta}_i|X) \sim \mathsf{IID}(\boldsymbol{0}_{T,1}, \boldsymbol{\Sigma}_\delta),\\
&i,j = 1,\dots,N,
\end{aligned} \tag{4.63}$$

equivalent to the following generalization of (4.37):

$$\begin{aligned}
&y_i = X_i\boldsymbol{\beta} + v_i, \quad v_i = X_i\boldsymbol{\delta}_i + u_i,\\
&\mathsf{E}(v_i|X) = 0_{T,1}, \quad \mathsf{E}(v_iv_j'|X) = \delta_{ij}\boldsymbol{\Sigma}_{ii},\\
&\boldsymbol{\Sigma}_{ii} = \delta_{ij}[X_i\boldsymbol{\Sigma}_\delta X_i' + \sigma_{ii}I_T],\\
&i,j = 1,\dots,N,
\end{aligned} \tag{4.64}$$

where $X_i = (x_{i1}',\dots,x_{iT}')'$, $\boldsymbol{\beta} = \mathsf{E}(\boldsymbol{\beta}_i) = (k, \beta_1',\dots,\beta_K')'$ contains the common expectation of the $\boldsymbol{\beta}_i$s, and $\boldsymbol{\delta}_i = (\alpha_i, \delta_{1i},\dots,\delta_{Ki})'$ is the random slack vector of individual i. Letting

$$y = \begin{bmatrix} y_1 \\ \vdots \\ y_N \end{bmatrix}, \; X = \begin{bmatrix} X_1 \\ \vdots \\ X_N \end{bmatrix}, \; v = \begin{bmatrix} v_1 \\ \vdots \\ v_N \end{bmatrix}, \; \boldsymbol{\Sigma} = \begin{bmatrix} \boldsymbol{\Sigma}_{11} & \dots & 0 \\ \vdots & \ddots & \vdots \\ 0 & \dots & \boldsymbol{\Sigma}_{NN} \end{bmatrix},$$

the model can be written compactly as

$$y = X\boldsymbol{\beta} + v, \quad \mathsf{E}(v|X) = 0, \quad \mathsf{E}(vv'|X) = \boldsymbol{\Sigma}. \tag{4.65}$$

This model belongs to a *wider model class*, denoted by Jones (1993, Chapter 2) as the 'general linear *mixed model*', by Rao (1997, Section 6.2) as the 'general mixed model', and by Demidenko (2004, p. 6) as the 'linear mixed effects (LME) model'. It can be written in the form

$$y = X\boldsymbol{\beta} + v, \; v = \textstyle\sum_p Z_p\boldsymbol{\xi}_p, \; \mathsf{E}(\boldsymbol{\xi}_p) = 0, \; \mathsf{E}(\boldsymbol{\xi}_p\boldsymbol{\xi}_p') = \sigma_p I_p,$$

where X and $Z_1, Z_2, \dots$ are known matrices and $\boldsymbol{\xi}_1, \boldsymbol{\xi}_2, \dots$ are random vectors.

Estimation of (4.65) by GLS gives

$$\begin{aligned}
\boldsymbol{\beta}^* &= [X'\boldsymbol{\Sigma}^{-1}X]^{-1}[X'\boldsymbol{\Sigma}^{-1}y]\\
&\equiv [\textstyle\sum_{i=1}^N X_i'\boldsymbol{\Sigma}_{ii}^{-1}X_i]^{-1}[\sum_{i=1}^N X_i'\boldsymbol{\Sigma}_{ii}^{-1}y_i],
\end{aligned} \tag{4.66}$$

$$\mathsf{V}(\boldsymbol{\beta}^*|X) = [X'\boldsymbol{\Sigma}^{-1}X]^{-1} \equiv [\textstyle\sum_{i=1}^N X_i'\boldsymbol{\Sigma}_{ii}^{-1}X_i]^{-1}. \tag{4.67}$$

The corresponding expressions when using observations from individual i are

$$\boldsymbol{\beta}_i^* = \left[X_i'\boldsymbol{\Sigma}_{ii}^{-1}X_i\right]^{-1}\left[X_i'\boldsymbol{\Sigma}_{ii}^{-1}y_i\right], \tag{4.68}$$

$$\mathsf{V}(\boldsymbol{\beta}_i^*|X) = \left[X_i'\boldsymbol{\Sigma}_{ii}^{-1}X_i\right]^{-1}, \qquad i = 1,\dots,N. \tag{4.69}$$

Hence, $\boldsymbol{\beta}^*$ emerges as a matrix-weighted mean of these individual-specific estimator vectors with the inverse covariance matrices as weights:

$$\begin{aligned}\boldsymbol{\beta}^* &= [\textstyle\sum_{i=1}^N (X_i'\boldsymbol{\Sigma}_{ii}^{-1}X_i)]^{-1}[\sum_{i=1}^N (X_i'\boldsymbol{\Sigma}_{ii}^{-1}X_i)\boldsymbol{\beta}_i^*] \\ &= [\textstyle\sum_{i=1}^N \mathsf{V}(\boldsymbol{\beta}_i^*|X)^{-1}]^{-1}[\sum_{i=1}^N \mathsf{V}(\boldsymbol{\beta}_i^*|X)^{-1}\boldsymbol{\beta}_i^*],\end{aligned} \tag{4.70}$$

$$\mathsf{V}(\boldsymbol{\beta}^*|X) = [\textstyle\sum_{i=1}^N \mathsf{V}(\boldsymbol{\beta}_i^*|X)^{-1}]^{-1}. \tag{4.71}$$

Equations (4.66)–(4.71), which give another example of the general property of GLS in Appendix 2A, generalize (4.39)–(4.44).

As in the case with scalar β^* and β_i^*, more instructive interpretations that show the anatomy of the GLS estimator exist. From the theorem in Appendix 4A, Section 4A.1, we have the following generalization of (4.45):

$$\begin{aligned}\boldsymbol{\Sigma}_{ii}^{-1} &= \left(X_i\boldsymbol{\Sigma}_\delta X_i' + \sigma_{ii}I_T\right)^{-1} \\ &= \sigma_{ii}^{-1}[I_T - X_i(X_i'X_i + \sigma_{ii}\boldsymbol{\Sigma}_\delta)^{-1}X_i'],\end{aligned} \tag{4.72}$$

and hence the theorem in Appendix 4A, Section 4A.2 gives

$$X_i'\boldsymbol{\Sigma}_{ii}^{-1}X_i = [\boldsymbol{\Sigma}_\delta + \sigma_{ii}(X_i'X_i)^{-1}]^{-1}, \tag{4.73}$$

$$X_i'\boldsymbol{\Sigma}_{ii}^{-1}y_i = [\boldsymbol{\Sigma}_\delta + \sigma_{ii}(X_i'X_i)^{-1}]^{-1}(X_i'X_i)^{-1}(X_i'y_i). \tag{4.74}$$

Inserting these expressions in (4.68) and (4.69), the common factor

$$\boldsymbol{\Psi}_i = \boldsymbol{\Sigma}_\delta + \sigma_{ii}(X_i'X_i)^{-1}, \qquad i = 1, \dots, N, \tag{4.75}$$

which generalizes (4.48), cancels. Hence, *the GLS estimator of $\boldsymbol{\beta}$ based on the observations from individual i equals the OLS estimator in the corresponding fixed coefficient model*, as in the single-regressor model without intercept:

$$\begin{aligned}\boldsymbol{\beta}_i^* &= [X_i'\boldsymbol{\Sigma}_{ii}^{-1}X_i]^{-1}[X_i'\boldsymbol{\Sigma}_{ii}^{-1}y_i] \\ &= (X_i'X_i)^{-1}(X_i'y_i) = \widehat{\boldsymbol{\beta}}_i,\end{aligned} \tag{4.76}$$

$$\mathsf{V}(\boldsymbol{\beta}_i^*|X) = [X_i'\boldsymbol{\Sigma}_{ii}^{-1}X_i]^{-1}. \tag{4.77}$$

It therefore follows from (4.69) and (4.70) that

$$\begin{aligned}\boldsymbol{\beta}^* &= [\textstyle\sum_{i=1}^N [\boldsymbol{\Sigma}_\delta + \sigma_{ii}(X_i'X_i)^{-1}]^{-1}]^{-1} \\ &\quad \times [\textstyle\sum_{i=1}^N [\boldsymbol{\Sigma}_\delta + \sigma_{ii}(X_i'X_i)^{-1}]^{-1}\boldsymbol{\beta}_i^*] \\ &= [\textstyle\sum_{i=1}^N \boldsymbol{\Psi}_i^{-1}]^{-1}[\sum_{i=1}^N \boldsymbol{\Psi}_i^{-1}\boldsymbol{\beta}_i^*],\end{aligned} \tag{4.78}$$

$$\mathsf{V}(\boldsymbol{\beta}^*|X) = [\textstyle\sum_{i=1}^N [\boldsymbol{\Sigma}_\delta + \sigma_{ii}(X_i'X_i)^{-1}]^{-1}]^{-1}$$
$$= [\textstyle\sum_{i=1}^N \boldsymbol{\Psi}_i^{-1}]^{-1}. \tag{4.79}$$

In Appendix 4B, a more illuminating and direct way of obtaining $\boldsymbol{\beta}^*$ is shown.

Since (4.63), (4.64), and (4.76) imply

$$\boldsymbol{\beta}_i^* - \boldsymbol{\beta}_i = [X_i'X_i]^{-1}[X_i'\boldsymbol{u}_i],$$
$$\boldsymbol{\beta}_i^* - \boldsymbol{\beta} = [X_i'X_i]^{-1}[X_i'\boldsymbol{v}_i] = \boldsymbol{\delta}_i + [X_i'X_i]^{-1}[X_i'\boldsymbol{u}_i],$$

we have the following generalizations of (4.52) and (4.53):

$$\mathsf{V}(\boldsymbol{\beta}_i^*|X,\boldsymbol{\beta}_i) = [X_i'X_i]^{-1}[X_i'\mathsf{V}(\boldsymbol{u}_i|X)X_i][X_i'X_i]^{-1} \tag{4.80}$$
$$= \sigma_{ii}[X_i'X_i]^{-1},$$
$$\mathsf{V}(\boldsymbol{\beta}_i^*|X) = [X_i'X_i]^{-1}[X_i'\mathsf{V}(\boldsymbol{v}_i|X)X_i][X_i'X_i]^{-1} \tag{4.81}$$
$$= \boldsymbol{\Sigma}_\delta + \sigma_{ii}[X_i'X_i]^{-1}.$$

Equations (4.72)–(4.81) are the matrix generalizations of (4.45)–(4.53). This concurs with the (vector version of the) law of iterated expectations, which implies

$$\mathsf{V}(\boldsymbol{\beta}_i^*|X) = \mathsf{V}[\mathsf{E}(\boldsymbol{\beta}_i^*|X,\boldsymbol{\beta}_i)] + \mathsf{E}[\mathsf{V}(\boldsymbol{\beta}_i^*|X,\boldsymbol{\beta}_i)].$$

Since $\mathsf{E}(\boldsymbol{\beta}_i^*|X,\boldsymbol{\beta}_i) = \boldsymbol{\beta}_i$ and $\mathsf{V}(\boldsymbol{\beta}_i^*|X,\boldsymbol{\beta}_i) = \sigma_{ii}(X_i'X_i)^{-1}$, we can reinterpret (4.75) and (4.81) as:

$$\boldsymbol{\Psi}_i = \mathsf{V}(\boldsymbol{\beta}_i^*|X)$$
$$= \mathsf{V}(\boldsymbol{\beta}_i|X) + \mathsf{V}(\boldsymbol{\beta}_i^*|X,\boldsymbol{\beta}_i)$$
$$= \boldsymbol{\Sigma}_\delta + \sigma_{ii}(X_i'X_i)^{-1}. \tag{4.82}$$

We therefore conclude: *the GLS estimator of the expected coefficient vector* $\boldsymbol{\beta}$, *given by (4.78), can be interpreted as a matrix weighted mean of the i-specific OLS estimator vectors, where the weights depend on the covariance matrices of the coefficient slack vector in the random coefficient model and the i-specific OLS estimator vector in the fixed coefficient model.*

Again, two boundary cases may support intuition.

No coefficient slack. If $\boldsymbol{\Sigma}_\delta = \boldsymbol{0} \Longrightarrow \boldsymbol{\Sigma}_{ii} = \sigma_{ii}\boldsymbol{I}_T, \boldsymbol{\Psi}_i = \sigma_{ii}(X_i'X_i)^{-1}$, then $\boldsymbol{\beta}^*$ can be interpreted as a matrix weighted mean of the individual-specific OLS estimators with $\mathsf{V}(\boldsymbol{\beta}_i^*|X,\boldsymbol{\beta}_i)^{-1} = (X_i'X_i)/\sigma_{ii}$ as weights:

$$\boldsymbol{\beta}^* = \left[\sum_{i=1}^{N}\left(\frac{\boldsymbol{X}_i'\boldsymbol{X}_i}{\sigma_{ii}}\right)\right]^{-1}\left[\sum_{i=1}^{N}\left(\frac{\boldsymbol{X}_i'\boldsymbol{Y}_i}{\sigma_{ii}}\right)\right]$$

$$= \left[\sum_{i=1}^{N}\left(\frac{\boldsymbol{X}_i'\boldsymbol{X}_i}{\sigma_{ii}}\right)\right]^{-1}\left[\sum_{i=1}^{N}\left(\frac{\boldsymbol{X}_i'\boldsymbol{X}_i}{\sigma_{ii}}\right)\widehat{\boldsymbol{\beta}}_i\right].$$

No disturbance. If $y_i = X_i\boldsymbol{\beta}_i$, $\sigma_{ii} = 0 \Longrightarrow \boldsymbol{\Sigma}_{ii} = X_i\boldsymbol{\Sigma}_\delta X_i'$, $\boldsymbol{\Psi}_i = \boldsymbol{\Sigma}_\delta$, then $\boldsymbol{\beta}^*$ is simply the mean of the individual-specific OLS estimators:

$$\boldsymbol{\beta}^* = \tfrac{1}{N}\textstyle\sum_{i=1}^{N}(X_i'X_i)^{-1}(X_i'y_i) = \tfrac{1}{N}\sum_{i=1}^{N}\widehat{\boldsymbol{\beta}}_i.$$

The above results can be briefly summarized. To compute $\boldsymbol{\beta}^*$ in Model (4.63) with unknown $\boldsymbol{\Sigma}_{ii}$, we can proceed stepwise as follows:[9]

1. Form the OLS residual vectors $\widehat{\boldsymbol{u}}_i = \boldsymbol{y}_i - \boldsymbol{X}_i\widehat{\boldsymbol{\beta}}_i$, where $\widehat{\boldsymbol{\beta}}_i$ is given by (4.76).
2. Estimate σ_{ii} by $\widehat{\sigma}_{ii} = \widehat{\boldsymbol{u}}_i'\widehat{\boldsymbol{u}}_i/(T-K-1)$, $i = 1,\dots,N$.
3. Let $\widehat{\boldsymbol{\delta}}_i = \widehat{\boldsymbol{\beta}}_i - \frac{1}{N}\sum_{j=1}^{N}\widehat{\boldsymbol{\beta}}_j$ and estimate $\boldsymbol{\Sigma}_\delta$ by $\widehat{\boldsymbol{\Sigma}}_\delta = \frac{1}{N-1}\sum_{i=1}^{N}\widehat{\boldsymbol{\delta}}_i\widehat{\boldsymbol{\delta}}_i'$.
4. Let $\widehat{\boldsymbol{\Psi}}_i = \widehat{\boldsymbol{\Sigma}}_\delta + \widehat{\sigma}_{ii}(X_i'X_i)^{-1}$ and replace in (4.78) and (4.79) $\boldsymbol{\Psi}_i$ by $\widehat{\boldsymbol{\Psi}}_i$ to obtain the FGLS estimators of $\boldsymbol{\beta}$ and its covariance matrix.

4.3.3 COEFFICIENT PREDICTION

Requesting coefficient estimation in a regression model with random coefficients is usually not meaningful (according to the 'frequentist paradigm'), while estimation of the *expectation or spread* of random coefficients is quite sensible. Predicting values of stochastic coefficients, like predicting (unrealized) values of regressands in classical regression equations, is also a quite sensible problem, which is indeed interesting for several purposes. Having panel data, substantial insight can be obtained by contrasting OLS *estimates* of individual-specific coefficients in a fixed coefficient model (Sections 4.2.1 and 4.2.4) with *predicted* counterparts in a random coefficient model (Sections 4.3.1 and 4.3.2). We will briefly discuss this, supplementing discussion with an illustration.

In the simple *scalar, no intercept case*, the *Minimum Variance Linear Unbiased Predictor (MVLUP)* of β_i is:

$$\beta_i^P = \beta^* + \sigma_\delta^2 \boldsymbol{x}_i'\boldsymbol{\Sigma}_{ii}^{-1}(y_i - \boldsymbol{x}_i\beta^*) \equiv \beta^* + \sigma_\delta^2 \boldsymbol{x}_i'\boldsymbol{\Sigma}_{ii}^{-1}\widehat{\boldsymbol{v}}_i, \qquad (4.83)$$

[9] A further discussion of this model and estimation procedures based on a generalization of the approach to *unbalanced* panel data (confer Chapter 10) and to systems of regression equations (SUR) (confer Chapter 12) is given in Biørn (2014), which also contains an application to cost and input data for Norwegian manufacturing.

see Goldberger (1962), Jones (1993, Section 2.7), Rao (1997, Section 11.3), and Demidenko (2004, Section 3.7), where β^* is given by (4.39), or equivalently by (4.51), and $\widehat{v}_i = y_i - x_i\beta^*$, i.e., the residual vector corresponding to the gross disturbance vector $v_i = x_i\delta_i + u_i$. Using (4.41), this predictor can be expressed as a weighted mean of β^* and β_i^* as follows:

$$\begin{aligned}\beta_i^P &= (1 - \sigma_\delta^2 x_i'\boldsymbol{\Sigma}_{ii}^{-1}x_i)\beta^* + \sigma_\delta^2 x_i'\boldsymbol{\Sigma}_{ii}^{-1}y_i \\ &\equiv (1 - \sigma_\delta^2 x_i'\boldsymbol{\Sigma}_{ii}^{-1}x_i)\beta^* + \sigma_\delta^2 x_i'\boldsymbol{\Sigma}_{ii}^{-1}x_i\beta_i^*.\end{aligned} \tag{4.84}$$

Utilizing (4.46), the latter expression can be rewritten as

$$\begin{aligned}\beta_i^P &= \left(1 - \frac{\sigma_\delta^2}{\sigma_\delta^2 + \sigma_{ii}(x_i'x_i)^{-1}}\right)\beta^* + \frac{\sigma_\delta^2}{\sigma_\delta^2 + \sigma_{ii}(x_i'x_i)^{-1}}\beta_i^* \\ &\equiv \frac{\sigma_{ii}(x_i'x_i)^{-1}\beta^* + \sigma_\delta^2\beta_i^*}{\sigma_\delta^2 + \sigma_{ii}(x_i'x_i)^{-1}},\end{aligned}$$

and again as an inverse-variance-weighted mean:

$$\begin{aligned}\beta_i^P &= \frac{\mathsf{V}(\beta_i^*|X, \beta_i)\beta^* + \mathsf{V}(\beta_i|X)\beta_i^*}{\mathsf{V}(\beta_i^*|X, \boldsymbol{\beta}_i) + \mathsf{V}(\beta_i|X)} \\ &\equiv \frac{\mathsf{V}(\beta_i|X)^{-1}\beta^* + \mathsf{V}(\beta_i^*|X, \beta_i)^{-1}\beta_i^*}{\mathsf{V}(\beta_i|X)^{-1} + \mathsf{V}(\beta_i^*|X, \beta_i)^{-1}}.\end{aligned} \tag{4.85}$$

From this we conclude: *(1) β_i^P is closer to β^* the larger is the conditional (with respect to β_i) variance of the i-specific (conditional) estimator, $\mathsf{V}(\beta_i^*|X, \beta_i)$, and the smaller is the unconditional (with respect to β_i) variance of the i-specific coefficient, $\mathsf{V}(\beta_i|X)$; and (2) β_i^P is closer to β_i^* the larger is the unconditional (with respect to β_i) variance of the i-specific coefficient, $\mathsf{V}(\beta_i|X)$, and the smaller is the conditional (with respect to β_i) variance of the i-specific (conditional) estimator, $\mathsf{V}(\beta_i^*|X, \beta_i)$.*

In the *general multi-regressor case*, the MVLUP of the vector $\boldsymbol{\beta}_i$ is

$$\boldsymbol{\beta}_i^P = \boldsymbol{\beta}^* + \boldsymbol{\Sigma}_\delta X_i'\boldsymbol{\Sigma}_{ii}^{-1}(y_i - X_i\boldsymbol{\beta}^*) \equiv \boldsymbol{\beta}^* + \boldsymbol{\Sigma}_\delta X_i'\boldsymbol{\Sigma}_{ii}^{-1}\widehat{v}_i, \tag{4.86}$$

where $\widehat{v}_i = y_i - X_i\boldsymbol{\beta}^*$. It generalizes (4.83). Using (4.66), $\boldsymbol{\beta}_i^P$ can be written as a matrix-weighted mean of $\boldsymbol{\beta}^*$ and $\boldsymbol{\beta}_i^*$, generalizing (4.84):

$$\begin{aligned}\boldsymbol{\beta}_i^P &= (I - \boldsymbol{\Sigma}_\delta X_i'\boldsymbol{\Sigma}_{ii}^{-1}X_i)\boldsymbol{\beta}^* + \boldsymbol{\Sigma}_\delta X_i'\boldsymbol{\Sigma}_{ii}^{-1}y_i \\ &\equiv (I - \boldsymbol{\Sigma}_\delta X_i'\boldsymbol{\Sigma}_{ii}^{-1}X_i)\boldsymbol{\beta}^* + \boldsymbol{\Sigma}_\delta X_i'\boldsymbol{\Sigma}_{ii}^{-1}X_i\boldsymbol{\beta}_i^*.\end{aligned} \tag{4.87}$$

Utilizing (4.73), the latter expression can be rewritten as

$$\begin{aligned}\boldsymbol{\beta}_i^P &= (I - \boldsymbol{\Sigma}_\delta[\boldsymbol{\Sigma}_\delta + \sigma_{ii}(X_i'X_i)^{-1}]^{-1})\boldsymbol{\beta}^* + \boldsymbol{\Sigma}_\delta[\boldsymbol{\Sigma}_\delta + \sigma_{ii}(X_i'X_i)^{-1}]^{-1}\boldsymbol{\beta}_i^*,\\ &\equiv \sigma_{ii}(X_i'X_i)^{-1}[\boldsymbol{\Sigma}_\delta + \sigma_{ii}(X_i'X_i)^{-1}]^{-1}\boldsymbol{\beta}^* + \boldsymbol{\Sigma}_\delta[\boldsymbol{\Sigma}_\delta + \sigma_{ii}(X_i'X_i)^{-1}]^{-1}\boldsymbol{\beta}_i^*,\end{aligned}$$

and again as an inverse-covariance-matrix-weighted mean:[10]

$$\begin{aligned}\boldsymbol{\beta}_i^P &= \mathsf{V}(\boldsymbol{\beta}_i^*|X,\boldsymbol{\beta}_i)[\mathsf{V}(\boldsymbol{\beta}_i|X) + \mathsf{V}(\boldsymbol{\beta}_i^*|X,\boldsymbol{\beta}_i)]^{-1}\boldsymbol{\beta}^*\\ &\quad + \mathsf{V}(\boldsymbol{\beta}_i|X)[\mathsf{V}(\boldsymbol{\beta}_i|X) + \mathsf{V}(\boldsymbol{\beta}_i^*|X,\boldsymbol{\beta}_i)]^{-1}\boldsymbol{\beta}_i^*\\ &\equiv [\mathsf{V}(\boldsymbol{\beta}_i^*|X,\boldsymbol{\beta}_i)^{-1} + \mathsf{V}(\boldsymbol{\beta}_i|X)^{-1}]^{-1}\mathsf{V}(\boldsymbol{\beta}_i|X)^{-1}\boldsymbol{\beta}^*\\ &\quad + [\mathsf{V}(\boldsymbol{\beta}_i^*|X,\boldsymbol{\beta}_i)^{-1} + \mathsf{V}(\boldsymbol{\beta}_i|X)^{-1}]^{-1}\mathsf{V}(\boldsymbol{\beta}_i^*|X,\boldsymbol{\beta}_i)^{-1}\boldsymbol{\beta}_i^*. \end{aligned} \tag{4.88}$$

Conclusion: $\boldsymbol{\beta}_i^P$ *is (1) closer to* $\boldsymbol{\beta}^*$ *the more* $\mathsf{V}(\boldsymbol{\beta}_i^*|X,\boldsymbol{\beta}_i)$ *dominates over* $\mathsf{V}(\boldsymbol{\beta}_i|X)$, *and (2) closer to* $\boldsymbol{\beta}_i^*$ *the more* $\mathsf{V}(\boldsymbol{\beta}_i|X)$ *dominates over* $\mathsf{V}(\boldsymbol{\beta}_i^*|X,\boldsymbol{\beta}_i)$.

Example: In Biørn *et al.* (2010) an attempt is made to explain the variation in efficiency if Norwegian hospitals, defined and measured alternatively as Cost Efficiency (CE) and as Technical Efficiency (TE), by four regressors: a dummy for being exposed to 'activity-based financing' (ABF) as an efficiency improving measure; the number of hospital beds; the hospital revenue per bed; and the share of within-hospital days of patients representing irregularly long stays (all two-dimensional). Panel data for $N=47$ Norwegian hospital observed in $T=10$ years (1992–2001) are used.

Table 4.1 shows for each hospital and each efficiency indicator the OLS estimate of the ABF dummy (columns 1 and 5), the corresponding predicted coefficient (columns 3 and 7), and their *ranking numbers* (in descending order, columns 2, 4, 6, 8). Overall, the rankings of the estimates and the corresponding predictions agree well. Most estimates and predictions are positive, although with varying significance: among the 47 hospitals, 27 have positive coefficient estimates and 29 have positive coefficient predictions for the CE indicator. The corresponding numbers for the TE indicator are 25 and 28.

Table 4.2, columns 1 and 2, contain the OLS estimate of the ABF coefficient based on all observations when disregarding heterogeneity, while columns 3 and 4 give FGLS estimates of the expected coefficient vector in the corresponding random coefficient model. Columns 5 and 6 contain GLS estimates when the two coefficient vectors are estimated jointly with corresponding vectors in equations for cost efficiency and

[10] We here utilize (twice) that any positive definite matrices, A and B, satisfy $A(A+B)^{-1} \equiv [(A+B)A^{-1}]^{-1} \equiv [B(B^{-1}+A^{-1})]^{-1} \equiv [B^{-1}+A^{-1}]^{-1}B^{-1}$.

Table 4.1 Hospital-specific coefficient of ABF dummy

Hosp.	Efficiency indicator: CE				Efficiency indicator: TE			
no.	Est. coef.	Rank no.	Pred. coef.	Rank no.	Est. coef.	Rank no.	Pred. coef.	Rank no.
1	2.789	22	2.831	21	1.951	19	2.787	18
2	−14.062	46	−11.607	46	−2.952	37	−2.290	36
3	−7.488	44	−5.859	45	4.425	15	4.435	14
4	8.198	9	5.588	9	4.864	14	3.150	16
5	5.707	14	5.022	10	10.323	8	9.248	9
6	1.744	24	1.457	23	1.853	20	0.638	27
7	8.389	8	3.712	15	26.828	2	15.426	5
8	−4.616	42	−3.476	41	−5.681	41	−4.474	42
9	4.252	18	3.186	18	6.476	13	4.615	12
10	6.450	12	4.641	12	18.963	6	14.901	6
11	14.889	2	8.417	5	24.470	4	18.580	3
12	11.308	4	10.124	4	8.289	11	7.195	10
13	−1.009	32	−0.941	33	1.023	22	1.603	22
14	14.668	3	12.387	2	20.628	5	18.644	2
15	−3.711	40	−3.157	40	−1.006	32	−0.436	32
16	−1.083	33	−2.179	38	−10.288	45	−2.917	37
17	7.918	11	6.221	8	6.930	12	6.036	11
18	5.856	13	2.946	19	42.803	1	21.634	1
19	−2.106	37	1.358	24	−2.177	35	−0.021	29
20	−8.446	45	−4.344	43	−12.028	46	−6.694	44
21	8.847	6	6.553	7	−2.106	34	−1.863	34
22	−0.933	31	−0.342	32	−0.955	31	1.842	21
23	−3.880	41	−2.462	39	0.223	25	0.706	26
24	4.570	17	4.791	11	−2.825	36	−1.143	33
25	−1.948	36	−2.016	36	0.721	24	0.294	28
26	−18.281	47	−12.722	47	−13.190	47	−7.540	46
27	8.641	7	10.663	3	10.308	9	10.625	8
28	15.189	1	13.371	1	−6.316	43	−5.543	43
29	−3.604	39	−2.079	37	−4.738	40	−3.361	39
30	5.103	15	3.348	17	−8.944	44	−7.297	45
31	2.502	23	1.940	22	−0.314	27	−3.269	38
32	1.329	25	1.064	26	−3.785	38	−3.545	40
33	3.044	21	2.946	20	−0.908	30	−0.389	31
34	0.449	27	0.667	28	2.249	18	2.243	20
35	−0.118	29	−0.122	31	−0.714	29	−2.044	35
36	8.178	10	3.470	16	4.265	16	4.443	13
37	4.222	19	3.926	14	1.798	21	2.703	19
38	3.638	20	1.185	25	8.289	10	4.030	15
39	0.547	26	0.513	29	−0.176	26	0.941	25
40	−4.773	43	−5.817	44	−5.863	42	−12.785	47
41	−1.665	35	−1.261	34	−4.609	39	−4.040	41
42	−2.832	38	−3.492	42	−0.460	28	−0.068	30
43	−1.257	34	−1.330	35	−1.569	33	1.036	24
44	9.868	5	7.885	6	15.405	7	12.420	7
45	4.912	16	4.441	13	2.788	17	3.086	17
46	−0.007	28	−0.097	30	0.819	23	1.511	23
47	−0.237	30	0.706	27	25.721	3	17.093	4

Note: Additional regressors: no. of hospital beds, hospital revenue per bed, share of within-hospital days representing irregularly long stays.

Table 4.2 Estimated coefficient mean of ABF dummy

Homogeneous, OLS		Heterogenous, Single-eq., GLS		Heterogenous, Multi-eq., GLS	
CE	TE	CE	TE	CE	TE
0.277 (0.828)	3.894 (1.013)	1.241 (1.053)	1.760 (1.479)	2.839 (0.962)	2.349 (1.406)

Notes: Standard errors in parentheses

The OLS standard error estimates are obtained from 'standard' formulae (neglecting coefficient heterogeneity).

Additional regressors: no. of hospital beds, hospital revenue per bed, share of within-hospital days representing irregularly long stays.

Table 4.3 ABF coefficient: distribution of estimates. Descriptive statistics

	CE	TE
Mean	1.491	2.438
St.dev.	6.392	9.458
Skew	−0.340	1.780
Kurt	4.262	6.183

technical efficiency. (This is a two-equation model, whose setup is not explained in the text; see Biørn *et al.* (2010, Appendix A) and Chapter 12.) The single equation GLS estimates have larger standard errors than the system GLS estimates, which agree with the former being a less efficient estimator. The coefficient estimate of the ABF dummy is positive in all cases. While the OLS estimates suggest that introduction of ABF has a stronger effect on technical efficiency (TE) than on cost-efficiency (CE), the system FGLS estimates do not show marked differences; the single equation FGLS takes an intermediate position.

Summary statistics describing the distribution of the coefficient estimates of the ABF dummy are given in Table 4.3. The large standard deviations give *prima facie* evidence of strong heterogeneity. The mean and standard deviation are 1.49 and 6.39 for CE and 2.44 and 9.46 for TE. The skewness and kurtosis of the coefficient estimates, which would equal 0 and 3, respectively, if the coefficients were generated by a normal (Gaussian) distribution, are informative: a positive skewness and a non-negligible excess kurtosis, 3.18, for the ABF-coefficient in the equation of TE; and a negative skewness and a minor excess kurtosis, 1.26, for the ABF-coefficient in the equation of CE.

Appendix 4A. **Matrix inversion and matrix products: Useful results**

In this appendix, we prove a result on inversion of a certain class of matrices which frequently occur in GLS estimation in regression models with stochastic coefficients. We will next consider a certain kind matrix products involving such inverses.

4A.1 Theorem on the inversion of a class of matrices

Consider a non-singular and symmetric $(T \times T)$-matrix $\boldsymbol{M}$ of the form

$$\boldsymbol{M} = a\boldsymbol{I}_T + c\boldsymbol{BDB}', \tag{4A.1}$$

where (i) $\boldsymbol{B}$ has dimension $(T \times S)$ and rank$(\boldsymbol{B}) = S$, (ii) $\boldsymbol{D}$ is symmetric, has dimension $(S \times S)$ and rank$(\boldsymbol{D}) = S$, and (iii) a and c are arbitrary (scalar) non-zero constants. Then

$$\boldsymbol{M}^{-1} = \frac{1}{a}\boldsymbol{I}_T - \frac{1}{a}\boldsymbol{B}\left(\boldsymbol{B}'\boldsymbol{B} + \frac{a}{c}\boldsymbol{D}^{-1}\right)^{-1}\boldsymbol{B}'. \tag{4A.2}$$

Note that when $T > S$, the $(T \times T)$ matrix $\boldsymbol{BDB}'$ does not have full rank, while the $(S \times S)$ matrix $\boldsymbol{B}'\boldsymbol{B}$ has full rank S. This implies that when $T > S$, $\boldsymbol{M}$ is singular for $a=0$.

The *proof* proceeds by showing that the product of the expressions on the right-hand side in (4A.1) and (4A.2), denoted by $\boldsymbol{E}$, equals the identity matrix $\boldsymbol{I}_T$. We have

$$\begin{aligned}\boldsymbol{E} &= (a\boldsymbol{I}_T + c\boldsymbol{BDB}')\left[\tfrac{1}{a}\boldsymbol{I}_T - \tfrac{1}{a}\boldsymbol{B}\left(\boldsymbol{B}'\boldsymbol{B} + \tfrac{a}{c}\boldsymbol{D}^{-1}\right)^{-1}\boldsymbol{B}'\right]\\ &= (\boldsymbol{I}_T + k\boldsymbol{BDB}')[\boldsymbol{I}_T - \boldsymbol{B}(\boldsymbol{B}'\boldsymbol{B} + \tfrac{1}{k}\boldsymbol{D}^{-1})^{-1}\boldsymbol{B}'],\end{aligned} \tag{4A.3}$$

where $k = c/a$. Now, since

$$\boldsymbol{B}(\boldsymbol{B}'\boldsymbol{B} + \tfrac{1}{k}\boldsymbol{D}^{-1})^{-1}\boldsymbol{B}' = \boldsymbol{B}(\boldsymbol{B}'\boldsymbol{BD} + \tfrac{1}{k}\boldsymbol{I}_T)^{-1}\boldsymbol{DB}',$$

we find

$$\begin{aligned}\boldsymbol{E} &= (\boldsymbol{I}_T + k\boldsymbol{BDB}')[\boldsymbol{I}_T - \boldsymbol{B}(\boldsymbol{B}'\boldsymbol{BD} + \tfrac{1}{k}\boldsymbol{I}_T)^{-1}\boldsymbol{DB}']\\ &= \boldsymbol{I}_T + k\boldsymbol{BDB}' - \boldsymbol{B}(\boldsymbol{B}'\boldsymbol{BD} + \tfrac{1}{k}\boldsymbol{I}_T)^{-1}\boldsymbol{DB}' - k\boldsymbol{BDB}'\boldsymbol{B}(\boldsymbol{B}'\boldsymbol{BD} + \tfrac{1}{k}\boldsymbol{I}_T)^{-1}\boldsymbol{DB}'\\ &= \boldsymbol{I}_T + k\boldsymbol{BDB}' - \boldsymbol{B}(\boldsymbol{I}_T + k\boldsymbol{DB}'\boldsymbol{B})(\boldsymbol{B}'\boldsymbol{BD} + \tfrac{1}{k}\boldsymbol{I}_T)^{-1}\boldsymbol{DB}'.\end{aligned}$$

Since $\boldsymbol{D}$ is symmetric, $\boldsymbol{B}'\boldsymbol{BD} = \boldsymbol{DB}'\boldsymbol{B}$, which implies

$$(I_T + kDB'B)(B'BD + \tfrac{1}{k}I_T)^{-1} = k(I_T + k\,DB'B)(kDB'B + I_T)^{-1} = kI_T,$$

and therefore

$$E = I_T + k\,BDB' - kBDB' = I_T,$$

which completes the proof.

4A.2 Theorem relating to a class of matrix products

Let **F** *be a matrix of dimension* $(T \times P)$, *where* P *is arbitrary, and let* a, c, **B**, *and* **D** *have the same properties as in 4A.1 and let again*

$$M = aI_T + cBDB'. \tag{4A.4}$$

Then

$$\begin{aligned} Q &\equiv B'M^{-1}F \equiv B'[aI_T + cBDB']^{-1}F \\ &= [cD + a(B'B)^{-1}]^{-1}(B'B)^{-1}(B'F). \end{aligned} \tag{4A.5}$$

Proof. First, because

$$\begin{aligned} &B'B + \tfrac{a}{c}\,D^{-1} \equiv (B'B)\left[D + \tfrac{a}{c}(B'B)^{-1}\right]D^{-1} \implies \\ &\left[B'B + \tfrac{a}{c}\,D^{-1}\right]^{-1} \equiv D\left[D + \tfrac{a}{c}(B'B)^{-1}\right]^{-1}(B'B)^{-1}, \end{aligned}$$

it follows from (4A.2) that

$$\begin{aligned} Q &= B'\left[\tfrac{1}{a}I_T - \tfrac{1}{a}BD\left(D + \tfrac{a}{c}(B'B)^{-1}\right)^{-1}(B'B)^{-1}B'\right]F \\ &\equiv \tfrac{1}{a}B'F - \tfrac{1}{a}B'BD\left(D + \tfrac{a}{c}(B'B)^{-1}\right)^{-1}(B'B)^{-1}B'F \\ &\equiv \tfrac{1}{a}\left[I_S - B'BD\left(D + \tfrac{a}{c}(B'B)^{-1}\right)^{-1}(B'B)^{-1}\right]B'F. \end{aligned}$$

Second, we have

$$\begin{aligned} Q &= \tfrac{1}{a}\left[(B'B)\left(D + \tfrac{a}{c}(B'B)^{-1}\right) - B'BD\right]\left[D + \tfrac{a}{c}(B'B)^{-1}\right]^{-1}(B'B)^{-1}(B'F) \\ &\equiv \tfrac{1}{a}\left[B'BD + \tfrac{a}{c} - B'BD\right]\left[D + \tfrac{a}{c}(B'B)^{-1}\right]^{-1}(B'B)^{-1}(B'F) \qquad \implies \end{aligned}$$

$$Q = \tfrac{1}{a}\tfrac{a}{c}\left[D + \tfrac{a}{c}(B'B)^{-1}\right]^{-1}(B'B)^{-1}(B'F) \qquad \Longrightarrow$$

$$Q = [cD + a(B'B)^{-1}]^{-1}(B'B)^{-1}(B'F).$$

This completes the proof.

Consider two special cases:

Case 1: $F = B$ (and therefore $P = S$). Then (4A.5) specializes to

$$Q \equiv B'M^{-1}B \equiv B'[aI_T + cBDB']^{-1}B = [cD + a(B'B)^{-1}]^{-1}. \tag{4A.6}$$

Case 2: $P = S = 1$. This makes B and F $(T \times 1)$ vectors, denoted as b and f, and D, Q, R *scalars*, denoted as d, q, r. The scalar expressions corresponding to (4A.5) and (4A.6) then become, respectively,

$$q = \frac{1}{cd + a/(b'b)}\,\frac{b'f}{b'b} \equiv \frac{b'f}{cd(b'b) + a},$$

$$q = \frac{1}{cd + a/(b'b)} \equiv \frac{b'b}{cd(b'b) + a}.$$

Appendix 4B. **A reinterpretation of the GLS estimator**

In this appendix is shown an alternative and more illuminating way of deriving the estimator (4.78), which does not rely on the results in Appendix 4A. Its essence is that before applying GLS we premultiply the equation in (4.64) by

$$P_i = (X_i'X_i)^{-1}X_i'.$$

Since $P_iX_i = I$ and $P_iP_i' = (X_i'X_i)^{-1}$, this gives

$$P_iy_i = I\beta + w_i, \qquad w_i = P_iu_i, \tag{4B.1}$$

$$\mathsf{E}(w_iw_i'|X) = P_i\Sigma_{ii}P_i' = \Sigma_\delta + \sigma_{ii}(X_i'X_i)^{-1} = \Psi_i. \tag{4B.2}$$

The implied GLS estimator of β based on observations from individual i, which also equals the estimator obtained by using *OLS* on (4B.1): $(II)^{-1}(IP_iy_i) = P_iy_i \equiv \widehat{\beta}_i$, is

$$\widetilde{\beta}_i = (I\Psi_i^{-1}I)^{-1}(I\Psi_i^{-1}P_iy_i) \equiv P_iy_i. \tag{4B.3}$$

Stacking (4B.1) across i and using (4B.3) gives

$$\begin{bmatrix} P_1 y_1 \\ \vdots \\ P_N y_N \end{bmatrix} = \begin{bmatrix} \widetilde{\boldsymbol{\beta}}_1 \\ \vdots \\ \widetilde{\boldsymbol{\beta}}_N \end{bmatrix} = \begin{bmatrix} I \\ \vdots \\ I \end{bmatrix} \boldsymbol{\beta} + \begin{bmatrix} w_1 \\ \vdots \\ w_N \end{bmatrix},$$

and hence

$$\widetilde{\boldsymbol{\beta}} = (e_N \otimes I)\boldsymbol{\beta} + w, \tag{4B.4}$$

where

$$\mathsf{E}(ww'|X) = \begin{bmatrix} \boldsymbol{\Psi}_1 & \dots & 0 \\ \vdots & \ddots & \vdots \\ 0 & \dots & \boldsymbol{\Psi}_N \end{bmatrix} = \boldsymbol{\Psi}. \tag{4B.5}$$

Applying GLS on (4B.4) gives the estimator

$$\begin{aligned} \boldsymbol{\beta}^{**} &= [(e_N' \otimes I)\boldsymbol{\Psi}^{-1}(e_N \otimes I)]^{-1}[(e_N' \otimes I)\boldsymbol{\Psi}^{-1}\widetilde{\boldsymbol{\beta}}] \\ &= [\textstyle\sum_{i=1}^N \boldsymbol{\Psi}_i^{-1}]^{-1}[\sum_{i=1}^N \boldsymbol{\Psi}_i^{-1}\widehat{\boldsymbol{\beta}}_i] = \boldsymbol{\beta}^*. \end{aligned} \tag{4B.6}$$

This is identical to (4.78).

5 Regression analysis with unidimensional variables

CHAPTER SUMMARY

Basic properties of second-order moments and moment matrices involving unidimensional variables are described. Next, one-way regression models containing unobserved fixed or random effects along with unidimensional regressors are considered. Extensions to two-way models with individual-specific and period-specific regressors are discussed. For the fixed effects versions, collinearity and identification problems relating to the effect of the unidimensional variables arise, unless additional, parameter-reducing restrictions are imposed. This partial estimability of fixed-effects models may, in many situations, reduce their attraction in treating heterogeneity.

5.1 Introduction

Regression analysis of panel data very often requires variables which do not vary over both periods and individuals. In certain cases, the regressand itself is time-invariant or individual-invariant. Examples of frequently occurring time-invariant regressors are cohort and gender of a person, and year of establishment and industry of a firm. Examples of frequently occurring individual-invariant regressors are calendar-related variables and (often) consumer prices, tax rates, and temperature. We denote the first as *individual-specific* and the second as *period-specific variables* and use *unidimensional variables* as a common term. Their counterparts are the variables which vary both over individuals and time periods, which are *two-dimensional*. Examples of the latter are (usually) a person's age, income, and savings, and a firm's labour force and production. Certain variables which are two-dimensional in principle may show unidimensional variation in the available data set. For example, the number of persons in a household and its location, which in principle vary along both dimensions, may in a panel data set, collected over a short time span, be observed as household-specific because each household has the same number of members or lives in the same region through the entire observation period. Another example is an interest rate facing borrowing firms or households, which is in principle two-dimensional (because the lenders differentiate the interest rates claimed according to borrower characteristics), but is observed as time specific means from aggregate statistics.

When unidimensional variables occur, the data set may be said to be 'degenerate', as it does not fully represent within- and between-variation. The examples in Chapter 1 provide some motivation. For a researcher choosing between specifications with fixed and stochastic effects, the situation when some regressors are unidimensional therefore deviates from the situation when all regressors are two-dimensional. The purpose of this chapter is to explain and illustrate some of these differences.

The chapter is organized as follows. In Section 5.2, we first call attention to some properties of second-order moments involving unidimensional variables. Models with one-way heterogeneity and fixed effects are then discussed in Section 5.3. In Section 5.4, we consider corresponding models with random effects: first, a regression model with two regressors, one two-dimensional and one unidimensional (individual specific); and next generalizations with an arbitrary number of regressors. Finally, in Section 5.5, we consider generalizations to two-way models, which allow for both kinds of heterogeneity, and individual-specific and period-specific explanatory variables along with two-dimensional ones. We here contrast the fixed effects and the random effects specifications.

5.2 **Properties of moment matrices in unidimensional variables**

5.2.1 BASICS

Regression equations with unidimensional regressors have certain properties that restrict coefficient estimability relative to the equations with all variables two-dimensional, as discussed in Chapters 2, 3, and 4. In this section, we clarify some formal properties. For an *individual-specific* variable $\{z_i\}_{i=1}^{i=N}$, all variation goes across individuals, and for a *period-specific* variable $\{q_t\}_{t=1}^{t=T}$, all variation goes over periods, implying $z_{it} = \bar{z}_{i\cdot} = z_i$, $\bar{z}_{\cdot t} = \bar{z}$, $q_{it} = \bar{q}_{\cdot t} = q_t$, $\bar{q}_{i\cdot} = \bar{q}$. We therefore have

$$
\begin{aligned}
G_{ZZ} &= B_{ZZ} = T\sum_{i=1}^{N}(z_i - \bar{z})^2, \\
G_{QQ} &= C_{QQ} = N\sum_{t=1}^{T}(q_t - \bar{q})^2, \\
B_{QQ} &= R_{QQ} = C_{ZZ} = R_{ZZ} = 0,
\end{aligned}
$$

still letting G, B, C, and R symbolize, respectively, global, between-individual, between-period, and residual (within-individual-and-period jointly). Furthermore, z_i and q_t are orthogonal, so that

$$
G_{ZQ} = B_{ZQ} = C_{ZQ} = R_{ZQ} = 0 \quad (z \text{ individual-specific, } q \text{ period-specific}). \tag{5.1}
$$

If x_{it} is two-dimensional, s_i individual-specific, and p_t period-specific—a particular case of orthogonal variation—we have, since $\sum_{t=1}^{T}(x_{it}-\bar{x}) \equiv T(\bar{x}_{i\cdot}-\bar{x})$ and $\sum_{i=1}^{N}(x_{it}-\bar{x}) \equiv N(\bar{x}_{\cdot t}-\bar{x})$:

$$\begin{aligned} &G_{ZS} = B_{ZS} = T\sum_{i=1}^{N}(z_i-\bar{z})(s_i-\bar{s}),\\ &C_{ZS} = R_{ZS} = 0,\\ &G_{XZ} = B_{XZ} = T\sum_{i=1}^{N}(\bar{x}_{i\cdot}-\bar{x})(z_i-\bar{z}),\\ &C_{XZ} = R_{XZ} = 0 \end{aligned} \qquad \begin{array}{c}(z, s \text{ individual-specific}\\ x \text{ two-dimensional}),\end{array} \tag{5.2}$$

$$\begin{aligned} &G_{QP} = C_{QP} = N\sum_{t=1}^{T}(q_t-\bar{q})(p_t-\bar{p}),\\ &B_{QP} = R_{QP} = 0,\\ &G_{XQ} = C_{XQ} = N\sum_{t=1}^{T}(\bar{x}_{\cdot t}-\bar{x})(q_t-\bar{q}),\\ &B_{XQ} = R_{XQ} = 0 \end{aligned} \qquad \begin{array}{c}(q, p \text{ period-specific}\\ x \text{ two-dimensional}),\end{array} \tag{5.3}$$

i.e., the global covariation between x_{it} and z_i collapses to the between-individual covariation, and the global covariation between x_{it} and q_t collapses to the between-period covariation. Therefore: *all between-period and residual covariation involving at least one individual-specific variable vanishes; all between individual and residual covariation involving at least one period-specific variable vanishes.*

5.2.2 IMPLICATIONS FOR REGRESSION ANALYSIS

This has important consequences. Let y be a *two-dimensional* regressand vector, X its regressor matrix X, and $\boldsymbol{\beta}$ its coefficient vector. Consider three cases:

1. X has *at least one individual-specific, but no period-specific variables.* Then (5.2) implies G_{XX} and B_{XX} are positive definite, C_{XX} and R_{XX} are singular (at least one row and one column having only zeros). *The global and the between-individual estimators of* $\boldsymbol{\beta}$ *exist, but not its between-period and residual estimators.* If all regressors are individual-specific, then $G_{XX}=B_{XX}$ (positive definite) and $G_{XY}=B_{XY}$, while $C_{XX}=R_{XX}$ is a zero matrix and $C_{XY}=R_{XY}$ is a zero vector. Then *the global estimator equals the between-individual estimator.*
2. X has *at least one period-specific, but no individual-specific variables.* Then (5.3) implies G_{XX} and C_{XX} are positive definite and B_{XX} and R_{XX} are singular (at least one row and one column having only zeros). *The global and the between-period estimators of* $\boldsymbol{\beta}$ *exist, but not its between-period and residual estimators.* If all regressors are period-specific, then $G_{XX}=C_{XX}$ (positive definite) and $G_{XY}=C_{XY}$, while $B_{XX}=R_{XX}$ is a zero matrix and $B_{XY}=R_{XY}$ is a zero vector. Then *the global estimator equals the between-period estimator.*
3. X has *at least one individual-specific and at least one period-specific variable.* Then (5.2)–(5.3) imply G_{XX} is positive definite and *the global estimator of* $\boldsymbol{\beta}$ *exists*; B_{XX}, C_{XX},

and $\boldsymbol{R}_{XX}$ are singular (all having at least one zero row and zero column). *Neither the between-individual, the between-period, nor the residual estimators of* $\boldsymbol{\beta}$ *exist.*

When considering estimability of coefficients of unidimensional regressors, it is even more important than before to distinguish between fixed and random effects specifications. We will discuss this in Sections 5.3 and 5.4, concentrating on models with individual-specific heterogeneity and individual-specific regressors. Models with period-specific heterogeneity and period-specific regressors can be treated symmetrically.

5.3 **One-way fixed effects models**

We first discuss fixed effects models in the simplest case with one two-dimensional and one unidimensional regressor (Section 5.3.1) and next their generalization to models with regressor vectors of arbitrary dimensions (Section 5.3.2).

5.3.1 SIMPLE MODEL WITH TWO REGRESSORS

Consider the model

$$\begin{aligned} & y_{it} = k + \beta x_{it} + \delta z_i + \alpha_i + u_{it}, \\ & (u_{it}|X, Z) \sim \mathsf{IID}(0, \sigma^2), \\ & i = 1, \dots, N;\ t = 1, \dots, T, \end{aligned} \tag{5.4}$$

where x_{it} and z_i (scalars) are, respectively, the two-dimensional and the unidimensional variables, and β, δ, k, and $\alpha_1, \dots, \alpha_N$ are unknown constants. We can give two interpretations of the latter assumptions: (A) the individual-specific effects, $\alpha_1, \dots, \alpha_N$, are unknown constants; (B) the mechanism generating $\alpha_1, \dots, \alpha_N$ has some structure, which we could have represented by a (probably complex) stochastic model, but want *our inference to be conditional on the* α_i*-values realized in the sample of individuals (units) actually drawn.* The information we might have about the α_is will then be neglected when making inference on β and δ. The units may, for example, be known geographic regions (municipalities, counties, etc.), the α_i-values of which we may want to know.

If we had known *a priori* that δ was zero, we know that the within-individual estimator had been the MVLUE of β. This corresponds to using OLS on (5.4) with the α_is considered as unknown constants and $\delta = 0$. Is this method also feasible when δ is free? The answer, from Section 5.1, is that problems are likely to arise: the within-individual estimator for $(\beta, \delta)'$ does not exist, since $W_{ZZ} = W_{XZ} = W_{ZY} = 0$, while $W_{XX} > 0$ (and usually $W_{XY} \neq 0$). To compute these estimators we would have to solve

$$\begin{bmatrix} W_{XX} & W_{XZ} \\ W_{ZX} & W_{ZZ} \end{bmatrix} \begin{bmatrix} \widehat{\beta}_W \\ \widehat{\delta}_W \end{bmatrix} = \begin{bmatrix} W_{XY} \\ W_{ZY} \end{bmatrix},$$

which implies solving

$$\begin{bmatrix} W_{XX} & 0 \\ 0 & 0 \end{bmatrix} \begin{bmatrix} \widehat{\beta}_W \\ \widehat{\delta}_W \end{bmatrix} = \begin{bmatrix} W_{XY} \\ 0 \end{bmatrix}. \tag{5.5}$$

As solution value for $\widehat{\beta}_W$ we would obtain

$$\widehat{\beta}_W = \frac{W_{XY}}{W_{XX}},$$

which is a well-defined estimator since $W_{XX} > 0$, while $\widehat{\delta}_W$ is indeterminate—a '$\frac{0}{0}$-expression'. The formal reason is that the regressors have a moment matrix with *reduced rank* 1, implying that we only obtain a *partial solution* to the estimation problem: an estimator for the coefficient of the two-dimensional variable, but no estimator for the coefficient of the unidimensional variable.

On the other hand, if no unknown individual-specific effect had occurred, i.e., if we could impose *a priori* $\alpha_i = 0$, we could have used OLS or the between-individual estimator, which would, by (5.2), have given, respectively,

$$\begin{bmatrix} G_{XX} & B_{XZ} \\ B_{ZX} & B_{ZZ} \end{bmatrix} \begin{bmatrix} \widehat{\beta}_{OLS} \\ \widehat{\delta}_{OLS} \end{bmatrix} = \begin{bmatrix} G_{XY} \\ B_{ZY} \end{bmatrix}, \tag{5.6}$$

which defines $\widehat{\beta}_{OLS}$ and $\widehat{\delta}_{OLS}$, and

$$\begin{bmatrix} B_{XX} & B_{XZ} \\ B_{ZX} & B_{ZZ} \end{bmatrix} \begin{bmatrix} \widehat{\beta}_B \\ \widehat{\delta}_B \end{bmatrix} = \begin{bmatrix} B_{XY} \\ B_{ZY} \end{bmatrix}, \tag{5.7}$$

which defines $\widehat{\beta}_B$ and $\widehat{\delta}_B$. Both would have given well-defined estimators since the regressor moment matrix has rank 2, and both would have been consistent, OLS giving the MVLUE. *The only problem with Model (5.4) is the joint occurrence of the individual-specific variables and the fixed individual-specific effects.*

The anatomy of the OLS problem for Model (5.4), minimization of

$$\textstyle\sum_i \sum_t (y_{it} - k - \beta x_{it} - \delta z_i - \alpha_i)^2,$$

can be explained as follows. Setting the first derivatives with respect to, respectively, k, β, δ, and α_i equal to zero gives $N+3$ (normal) equations defining the estimators $(\widehat{k}_W, \widehat{\beta}_W, \widehat{\delta}_W, \widehat{\alpha}_{iW})$:

$$\sum_i \sum_t (y_{it} - \widehat{k}_W - \widehat{\beta}_W x_{it} - \widehat{\delta}_W z_i - \widehat{\alpha}_{iW}) = 0,$$
$$\sum_i \sum_t (y_{it} - \widehat{k}_W - \widehat{\beta}_W x_{it} - \widehat{\delta}_W z_i - \widehat{\alpha}_{iW}) x_{it} = 0,$$
$$\sum_i \sum_t (y_{it} - \widehat{k}_W - \widehat{\beta}_W x_{it} - \widehat{\delta}_W z_i - \widehat{\alpha}_{iW}) z_i = 0,$$
$$\sum_t (y_{it} - \widehat{k}_W - \widehat{\beta}_W x_{it} - \widehat{\delta}_W z_i - \widehat{\alpha}_{iW}) = 0, \quad i = 1, \dots, N.$$

These equations are not independent, since from the N last equations we can derive both the first and the third, which means that the system has only $N+1$ *independent* equations. It follows from its N last equations that

$$\widehat{k}_W + \widehat{\delta}_W z_i + \widehat{\alpha}_{iW} = \bar{y}_{i\cdot} - \widehat{\beta}_W \bar{x}_{i\cdot}, \qquad i = 1, \dots, N,$$

which in combination with its second equation gives

$$\widehat{\beta}_W = \frac{\sum_{i=1}^{N} \sum_{t=1}^{T} (x_{it} - \bar{x}_{i\cdot})(y_{it} - \bar{y}_{i\cdot})}{\sum_{i=1}^{N} \sum_{t=1}^{T} (x_{it} - \bar{x}_{i\cdot})^2} = \frac{W_{XY}}{W_{XX}}. \tag{5.8}$$

Hence, we can estimate β and the composite 'parameters'

$$k+\delta z_i+\alpha_i, \qquad i = 1, \dots, N,$$

in total $N+1$ 'parameters',[1] by, respectively, $\widehat{\beta}_W$ and $\bar{y}_{i\cdot} - \widehat{\beta}_W \bar{x}_{i\cdot}$, $i = 1, \dots, N$. Therefore we have: (i) the estimator of the coefficient of the two-dimensional variable x_{it} equals the one obtained if the individual-specific variable z_i had been excluded from the equation; and (ii) we are unable to separate the fixed individual-specific effect α_i from the effect of the individual-specific variable. Model (5.4) has a *collinearity problem*: the individual-specific variable depends linearly on the individual-specific binary variables. Individual-specific effects have to represent all (observable and unobservable) individual-specific variables that have an effect on y_{it}.

A frequently occurring *example* is: a theory implies that birth year is a relevant explanatory variable for some other variable, as people born in different years have different experiences and 'norms' (often termed *cohort-effects*). Then it would have been impossible also to include individual fixed effects (individual dummies), i.e., we would be unable to uncover the partial effect of the birth year. It can well be argued that this a major drawback of the approach and a strong argument against including a full set of fixed individual effects. *We often are genuinely interested in identifying effects of observable*

[1] Calling $k+\delta z_i+\alpha_i$ a parameter is not without problems in relation to classical econometric terminology; see Marschak (1953, Sections 3 and 5) and Section 5.5.1.

individual-specific variables and do not want the effects of all such variables to be lumped together in composite 'individual effects', $\alpha_1,\dots,\alpha_N$, with a rather diffuse interpretation.[2]

What we could do is to impose an additional normalization constraint making the individual-specific effects add to zero: $\sum_{i=1}^{N}\alpha_i = \sum_{i=1}^{N}\widehat{\alpha}_{iW} = 0$. The system of normal equations would then give $N+2$ equations between $N+3$ unknowns, from which we obtain

$$\widehat{k}_W = \bar{y} - \widehat{\beta}_W\bar{x} - \widehat{\delta}_W\bar{z},$$
$$\widehat{\alpha}_{iW} = (\bar{y}_{i\cdot} - \bar{y}) - \widehat{\beta}_W(\bar{x}_{i\cdot} - \bar{x}) - \widehat{\delta}_W(z_i - \bar{z}), \qquad i = 1,\dots,N.$$

For known $\widehat{\beta}_W$, this gives $N+1$ equations between $\widehat{k}_W$, $\widehat{\delta}_W$, and $\widehat{\alpha}_1,\dots,\widehat{\alpha}_N$. One additional restriction, say knowledge of δ or α_1, would suffice to uncover the remaining unknowns. Another (and frequently used) way of 'solving' the collinearity problem is to let *groups of* individuals have the same α_i.

Having no additional information, could we still make interesting statements about δ, for example, instead of the within-individual estimator, use OLS on (5.4) with all $\alpha_i=0$? Its solution for δ, obtained from (5.6), is

$$\widehat{\delta}_{OLS} = \frac{B_{ZY}G_{XX} - G_{XY}B_{XZ}}{G_{XX}B_{ZZ} - B_{XZ}^2}. \tag{5.9}$$

Is this a well-behaved estimator when some $\alpha_i \neq 0$? Equation (5.4) implies

$$G_{XY} = \beta G_{XX} + \delta B_{XZ} + B_{X\alpha} + G_{XU},$$
$$B_{ZY} = \beta B_{ZX} + \delta B_{ZZ} + B_{Z\alpha} + B_{ZU},$$

which when inserted in (5.9) yields

$$\widehat{\delta}_{OLS} - \delta = \frac{(B_{Z\alpha}+B_{ZU})G_{XX} - (B_{X\alpha}+G_{XU})B_{XZ}}{G_{XX}B_{ZZ} - B_{XZ}^2}. \tag{5.10}$$

Conditional on the xs and the zs, G_{XU} and B_{ZU} have zero expectation when $\mathsf{E}(u_{it}|X,Z)=0$. Therefore their marginal expectations are also zero. However, $B_{X\alpha}$ and $B_{Z\alpha}$ do not necessarily have zero expectations neither conditionally nor unconditionally. The fractional expressions after the equality signs could be non-zero if the individual-specific effects *in the sample of individuals observed show (empirical) correlation with*

[2] A symmetric example that creates a collinearity (reduced rank) problem is a model for annual data that includes prices (period-specific) along with a full set of year dummies with unrestricted coefficients: the time-specific variable depends linearly on the year dummy. A full set of year-specific effects will have to represent all (observable and unobservable) variables that are year-specific. Price effects cannot be isolated.

at least one regressor. (Recall that $\frac{1}{NT}B_{X\alpha}$ and $\frac{1}{NT}B_{Z\alpha}$ are empirical between-individual covariances.) More precisely, we have

$$\mathsf{E}(\widehat{\delta}_{OLS}-\delta|X,Z) \neq 0 \text{ if either}$$
$$\mathsf{E}(B_{Z\alpha}|X,Z) \neq 0 \text{ or } \mathsf{E}(B_{X\alpha}|X,Z) \times B_{XZ} \neq 0.$$

A corresponding result holds for probability limits (when $N \to \infty$)

$$\text{plim}(\widehat{\delta}_{OLS}-\delta) \neq 0 \text{ if either}$$
$$\text{plim}[\tfrac{1}{NT}B_{Z\alpha}] \neq 0 \text{ or plim}[\tfrac{1}{NT}B_{X\alpha}] \times \text{plim}[\tfrac{1}{NT}B_{XZ}] \neq 0.$$

Correlation between α_i and $(\bar{x}_{i\cdot}, z_i)$ may well occur. This implies that the global estimators are biased and do not measure what we want them to measure (see Section 2.1.4). What arises here is essentially an *omitted variables problem*. Therefore, it may be little reason to replace $\widehat{\beta}_W$, whose consistency is not vulnerable to such correlation, with $\widehat{\beta}_{OLS}$, which is. Could we then accept to estimate δ by $\widehat{\delta}_{OLS}$ and accordingly use

$$\widehat{\alpha}_{iW/OLS} = (\bar{y}_{i\cdot} - \bar{y}) - \widehat{\beta}_W(\bar{x}_{i\cdot} - \bar{x}) - \widehat{\delta}_{OLS}(z_i - \bar{z}), \qquad i = 1, \ldots, N,$$

rather than having no estimators of $\delta, \alpha_1, \ldots, \alpha_N$ at all? A more satisfactory suggestion would be to formalize the dependence and reformulate the model and the estimations procedure accordingly. We leave this idea here and return to it in Chapter 6, when addressing, in a more general setting, the important problem correlation between latent individual-specific effects and structural variables, considering the α_is as stochastic.

5.3.2 THE GENERAL CASE

We extend Model (5.4) to include an arbitrary number of two-dimensional and unidimensional variables, K_2 and K_1, respectively, specifying

$$\begin{aligned} &y_{it} = k + \boldsymbol{x}_{it}\boldsymbol{\beta} + \boldsymbol{z}_i\boldsymbol{\delta} + \alpha_i + u_{it}, \\ &(u_{it}|X,Z) \sim \mathsf{IID}(0,\sigma^2), \\ &i = 1, \ldots, N;\ t = 1, \ldots, T, \end{aligned} \tag{5.11}$$

where $\boldsymbol{x}_{it}$ is the $(1 \times K_2)$-vector of two-dimensional regressors and $\boldsymbol{z}_i$ is the $(1 \times K_1)$-vector of unidimensional regressors; $\boldsymbol{\beta}$ and $\boldsymbol{\delta}$ are the corresponding coefficient vectors.

We need some additional notation for $\boldsymbol{G}$-, $\boldsymbol{W}$-, and $\boldsymbol{B}$-matrices, and let them occur in two versions. Symbols in non-tilded boldface letters denote full matrices, symbols in tilded boldface letters denote *submatrices* of the non-tilded matrices when expressed in *partitioned* form. For example, what we denoted as $\boldsymbol{W}_{XX}$ and $\boldsymbol{W}_{XY}$ earlier, will now be expressed as, respectively,

$$\begin{bmatrix} \widetilde{\boldsymbol{W}}_{XX} & \widetilde{\boldsymbol{W}}_{XZ} \\ \widetilde{\boldsymbol{W}}_{ZX} & \widetilde{\boldsymbol{W}}_{ZZ} \end{bmatrix} \text{ and } \begin{bmatrix} \widetilde{\boldsymbol{W}}_{XY} \\ \widetilde{\boldsymbol{W}}_{ZY} \end{bmatrix}.$$

If we had known that $\boldsymbol{\delta}$ was a zero-vector, the within-individual estimator would have been the MVLUE of $\boldsymbol{\beta}$. Is this method feasible also when $\boldsymbol{\delta}$ is unknown? The answer is that to compute the within-individual estimators for $(\boldsymbol{\beta}', \boldsymbol{\delta}')$, we would have to solve

$$\begin{bmatrix} \widetilde{\boldsymbol{W}}_{XX} & \widetilde{\boldsymbol{W}}_{XZ} \\ \widetilde{\boldsymbol{W}}_{ZX} & \widetilde{\boldsymbol{W}}_{ZZ} \end{bmatrix} \begin{bmatrix} \widehat{\boldsymbol{\beta}}_W \\ \widehat{\boldsymbol{\delta}}_W \end{bmatrix} = \begin{bmatrix} \widetilde{\boldsymbol{W}}_{XY} \\ \widetilde{\boldsymbol{W}}_{ZY} \end{bmatrix},$$

which simplifies to the following generalization of (5.5)

$$\begin{bmatrix} \widetilde{\boldsymbol{W}}_{XX} & \boldsymbol{0} \\ \boldsymbol{0} & \boldsymbol{0} \end{bmatrix} \begin{bmatrix} \widehat{\boldsymbol{\beta}}_W \\ \widehat{\boldsymbol{\delta}}_W \end{bmatrix} = \begin{bmatrix} \widetilde{\boldsymbol{W}}_{XY} \\ \boldsymbol{0}_{K_1,1} \end{bmatrix}. \tag{5.12}$$

The solution for $\widehat{\boldsymbol{\beta}}_W$ is

$$\widehat{\boldsymbol{\beta}}_W = \widetilde{\boldsymbol{W}}_{XX}^{-1} \widetilde{\boldsymbol{W}}_{XY},$$

while $\widehat{\boldsymbol{\delta}}_W$ is undefined, as the moment matrix of the regressors has reduced rank, K_2. Full solution would require rank $K_2 + K_1$. We therefore only obtain a *partial solution* to the estimation problem.

On the other hand, if all $\alpha_i = 0$, the estimation problem would have been straightforward for both $\boldsymbol{\beta}$ and $\boldsymbol{\delta}$, using either OLS or the between-individual estimator. This would, in view of (5.2), have given the following generalization of (5.6) and (5.7):

$$\begin{bmatrix} \widetilde{\boldsymbol{G}}_{XX} & \widetilde{\boldsymbol{B}}_{XZ} \\ \widetilde{\boldsymbol{B}}_{ZX} & \widetilde{\boldsymbol{B}}_{ZZ} \end{bmatrix} \begin{bmatrix} \widehat{\boldsymbol{\beta}}_{OLS} \\ \widehat{\boldsymbol{\delta}}_{OLS} \end{bmatrix} = \begin{bmatrix} \widetilde{\boldsymbol{G}}_{XY} \\ \widetilde{\boldsymbol{B}}_{ZY} \end{bmatrix}, \tag{5.13}$$

$$\begin{bmatrix} \widetilde{\boldsymbol{B}}_{XX} & \widetilde{\boldsymbol{B}}_{XZ} \\ \widetilde{\boldsymbol{B}}_{ZX} & \widetilde{\boldsymbol{B}}_{ZZ} \end{bmatrix} \begin{bmatrix} \widehat{\boldsymbol{\beta}}_{B} \\ \widehat{\boldsymbol{\delta}}_{B} \end{bmatrix} = \begin{bmatrix} \widetilde{\boldsymbol{B}}_{XY} \\ \widetilde{\boldsymbol{B}}_{ZY} \end{bmatrix}, \tag{5.14}$$

since in both cases the moment matrix of the regressors has full rank, K_2+K_1. Both estimators would be consistent, OLS giving the MVLUE. Thus, the problem with Model

(5.11) seems to be that the K_1 individual-specific regressors and the fixed individual-specific effects occur simultaneously.

What could be done if both $\boldsymbol{\delta}$ and $\alpha_1, \dots, \alpha_N$ are unknown is to estimate $\boldsymbol{\beta}$ by the within estimator. After imposing $\sum_{i=1}^{N} \alpha_i = \sum_{i=1}^{N} \widehat{\alpha}_{iW} = 0$, we find

$$\widehat{k}_W = \bar{y} - \bar{\boldsymbol{x}}\widehat{\boldsymbol{\beta}}_W - \bar{\boldsymbol{z}}\widehat{\boldsymbol{\delta}}_W,$$
$$\widehat{\alpha}_{iW} = (\bar{y}_{i\cdot} - \bar{y}) - (\bar{\boldsymbol{x}}_{i\cdot} - \bar{\boldsymbol{x}})\widehat{\boldsymbol{\beta}}_W - (\boldsymbol{z}_i - \bar{\boldsymbol{z}})\widehat{\boldsymbol{\delta}}_W, \quad i = 1, \dots, N.$$

In the absence of further restrictions we might estimate $\boldsymbol{\delta}$ by either $\widehat{\boldsymbol{\delta}}_{OLS}$, from (5.13), or $\widehat{\boldsymbol{\delta}}_B$, from (5.14). This would create essentially the same type of problems as described in Section 5.3.1 when $K_2 = K_1 = 1$.

5.4 **One-way random effects models**

We next consider models with two-dimensional and unidimensional regressors similar to those in Section 5.3, except that $\alpha_1, \dots, \alpha_N$ are random variables, obtained from N independent draws from a probability distribution, which characterizes the *population* from which we imagine the individual-specific being drawn.

5.4.1 SIMPLE MODEL WITH TWO REGRESSORS

The regression model with one two-dimensional and one unidimensional regressor and with stochastic individual-specific effects is:

$$\begin{aligned} &y_{it} = k + \beta x_{it} + \delta z_i + \alpha_i + u_{it} = k + \beta x_{it} + \delta z_i + \epsilon_{it}, \quad u_{it} \perp \alpha_i, \\ &(\alpha_i | X, Z) \sim \mathsf{IID}(0, \sigma_\alpha^2), \quad (u_{it} | X, Z) \sim \mathsf{IID}(0, \sigma^2), \\ &i = 1, \dots, N; \; t = 1, \dots, T. \end{aligned} \tag{5.15}$$

Stacking the observations from individual i into vectors and matrices, $\boldsymbol{y}_i = (y_{i1}, \dots, y_{iT})'$, $\boldsymbol{u}_i = (u_{i1}, \dots, u_{iT})'$, $\boldsymbol{x}_i = (x_{i1}, \dots, x_{iT})'$, $\boldsymbol{\epsilon}_i = (\epsilon_{i1}, \dots, \epsilon_{iT})'$, (5.15) can be written as

$$\begin{aligned} &\boldsymbol{y}_i = \boldsymbol{e}_T k + \boldsymbol{x}_i \beta + \boldsymbol{e}_T z_i \delta + \boldsymbol{\epsilon}_i, \\ &(\boldsymbol{\epsilon}_i | X, Z) \sim \mathsf{IID}(\boldsymbol{0}_{T1}, \boldsymbol{\Omega}_T), \quad \boldsymbol{\Omega}_T = \sigma_\alpha^2 \boldsymbol{e}_T \boldsymbol{e}_T' + \sigma^2 \boldsymbol{I}_T, \\ &i = 1, \dots, N. \end{aligned} \tag{5.16}$$

This is a special case of the model considered in Section 3.1 for $K = 2$, with the second x-variable individual-specific. Therefore, we can to a large extent draw on procedures for GLS estimation developed in Section 3.2. Letting

$$y = \begin{bmatrix} y_1 \\ \vdots \\ y_N \end{bmatrix}, \quad x = \begin{bmatrix} x_1 \\ \vdots \\ x_N \end{bmatrix}, \quad z = \begin{bmatrix} z_1 \\ \vdots \\ z_N \end{bmatrix},$$

so that the matrix X in Section 3.2.1 corresponds to $[x, (z \otimes e_T)]$, we find

$$W_{XX} = \begin{bmatrix} x' \\ (z \otimes e_T)' \end{bmatrix} (I_N \otimes B_T)\,[x, (z \otimes e_T)] = \begin{bmatrix} W_{XX} & 0 \\ 0 & 0 \end{bmatrix},$$

$$B_{XX} = \begin{bmatrix} x' \\ (z \otimes e_T)' \end{bmatrix} (B_N \otimes A_T)\,[x, (z \otimes e_T)] = \begin{bmatrix} B_{XX} & B_{XZ} \\ B_{ZX} & B_{ZZ} \end{bmatrix},$$

$$W_{XY} = \begin{bmatrix} x' \\ (z \otimes e_T)' \end{bmatrix} (I_N \otimes B_T) y = \begin{bmatrix} W_{XY} \\ 0 \end{bmatrix},$$

$$B_{XY} = \begin{bmatrix} x' \\ (z \otimes e_T)' \end{bmatrix} (B_N \otimes A_T) y = \begin{bmatrix} B_{XY} \\ B_{ZY} \end{bmatrix},$$

W_{XX}, W_{XY}, B_{XX}, B_{XY}, B_{ZZ}, B_{XZ}, B_{ZY} being scalars. Inserting these expressions in $\widehat{\boldsymbol{\beta}}_{GLS} = (\boldsymbol{W}_{XX} + \theta_B \boldsymbol{B}_{XX})^{-1}(\boldsymbol{W}_{XY} + \theta_B \boldsymbol{B}_{XY})$, where $\theta_B = \sigma^2/(\sigma^2 + T\sigma_\alpha^2)$, we find that the GLS estimators of $(\beta, \delta)'$ can be expressed as

$$\begin{bmatrix} \widehat{\beta}_{GLS} \\ \widehat{\delta}_{GLS} \end{bmatrix} = \begin{bmatrix} W_{XX} + \theta_B B_{XX} & \theta_B B_{XZ} \\ \theta_B B_{ZX} & \theta_B B_{ZZ} \end{bmatrix}^{-1} \begin{bmatrix} W_{XY} + \theta_B B_{XY} \\ \theta_B B_{ZY} \end{bmatrix}. \tag{5.17}$$

This shows that *the GLS estimators of the coefficients of all the variables always exist when* $\theta_B > 0 \iff \sigma^2 > 0$. Consequently, the situation with respect to identification of δ is more favourable if the individual-specific effect is random and uncorrelated with both regressors than if we desist from making this assumption and rely on the individual-specific effects being fixed and unstructured. It follows from Theorem 2 in Appendix 3A, Section 3A.2, that

$$\begin{aligned} \widehat{k}_{GLS} &= [\tfrac{1}{N} e_N' \otimes \tfrac{1}{T} e_T'][y - x\widehat{\beta}_{GLS} - (z \otimes e_T)\widehat{\delta}_{GLS}] \\ &= \bar{y} - \bar{x}\widehat{\beta}_{GLS} - \bar{z}\widehat{\delta}_{GLS}. \end{aligned} \tag{5.18}$$

As explained in Section 3.2, any GLS estimator can be obtained by an OLS estimation on suitably transformed variables. In the present case, the transformed disturbances are: $\epsilon_i^* = y_i^* - e_T k^* - x_i^* \beta - (e_T z_i^*)\delta$, where

$$y_i^* = y_i - (1 - \sqrt{\theta_B}) A_T y_i = (B_T + \sqrt{\theta_B} A_T) y_i,$$

$$\begin{aligned}
\boldsymbol{x}_i^* &= \boldsymbol{x}_i - (1-\sqrt{\theta_B})\boldsymbol{A}_T\boldsymbol{x}_i = (\boldsymbol{B}_T+\sqrt{\theta_B}\boldsymbol{A}_T)\boldsymbol{x}_i,\\
\boldsymbol{e}_T z_i^* &= \boldsymbol{e}_T z_i - (1-\sqrt{\theta_B})\boldsymbol{A}_T\boldsymbol{e}_T z_i = \boldsymbol{e}_T\sqrt{\theta_B} \Longleftrightarrow z_i^* = \sqrt{\theta_B}z_i,\\
\boldsymbol{e}_T k^* &= \boldsymbol{e}_T k - (1-\sqrt{\theta_B})\boldsymbol{A}_T\boldsymbol{e}_T k = \boldsymbol{e}_T\sqrt{\theta_B}k \Longleftrightarrow k^* = \sqrt{\theta_B}k.
\end{aligned}$$

Hence, the prescription is: *deduct from the two-dimensional variables $\boldsymbol{y}_i$ and $\boldsymbol{x}_i$ a share $(1-\sqrt{\theta_B})$ of the individual-specific means, multiply the unidimensional variable z_i by $\sqrt{\theta_B}$, and apply OLS on the resulting equation, $\boldsymbol{y}_i^* = \boldsymbol{e}_T k^* + \boldsymbol{x}_i^*\beta + (\boldsymbol{e}_T z_i^*)\delta + \boldsymbol{\epsilon}_i^*$.*

5.4.2 THE GENERAL CASE

Extending the model to include K_2 two-dimensional and K_1 unidimensional variables is straightforward. We extend the scalars x_{it}, z_i, β, and δ to vectors $\boldsymbol{x}_{it}, \boldsymbol{z}_i, \boldsymbol{\beta}$, and $\boldsymbol{\delta}$, of dimensions $(1\times K_2)$, $(1\times K_1)$, $(K_2\times 1)$, and $(K_1\times 1)$, respectively, obtaining

$$\begin{aligned}
&y_{it} = k+\boldsymbol{x}_{it}\boldsymbol{\beta}+\boldsymbol{z}_i\boldsymbol{\delta}+\alpha_i+u_{it} = k+\boldsymbol{x}_{it}\boldsymbol{\beta}+\boldsymbol{z}_i\boldsymbol{\delta}+\epsilon_{it},\\
&(\alpha_i|X,Z) \sim \mathsf{IID}(0,\sigma_\alpha^2),\quad (u_{it}|X,Z) \sim \mathsf{IID}(0,\sigma^2),\\
&i = 1,\dots,N;\ t = 1,\dots,T.
\end{aligned} \tag{5.19}$$

Stacking the observations as $\boldsymbol{y}_i=(y_{i1},\dots,y_{iT})'$, $\boldsymbol{u}_i=(u_{i1},\dots,u_{iT})'$, $\boldsymbol{X}_i=(\boldsymbol{x}_{i1}',\dots,\boldsymbol{x}_{iT}')'$, $\boldsymbol{\epsilon}_i=(\epsilon_{i1},\dots,\epsilon_{iT})'$, we have[3]

$$\begin{aligned}
&\boldsymbol{y}_i = \boldsymbol{e}_T k + \boldsymbol{X}_i\boldsymbol{\beta} + (\boldsymbol{z}_i \otimes \boldsymbol{e}_T)\boldsymbol{\delta} + \boldsymbol{\epsilon}_i,\\
&(\boldsymbol{\epsilon}_i|X,Z) \sim \mathsf{IID}(\boldsymbol{0}_{T1},\boldsymbol{\Omega}_T),\quad \boldsymbol{\Omega}_T = \sigma_\alpha^2\boldsymbol{e}_T\boldsymbol{e}_T' + \sigma^2\boldsymbol{I}_T,\\
&i = 1,\dots,N.
\end{aligned} \tag{5.20}$$

This is a special version of the K-regressor model considered in Section 3.1, with $K = K_2 + K_1$ and the K_1 last x-variables individual-specific. We introduce

$$\boldsymbol{y} = \begin{bmatrix} \boldsymbol{y}_1 \\ \vdots \\ \boldsymbol{y}_N \end{bmatrix},\quad \boldsymbol{X} = \begin{bmatrix} \boldsymbol{X}_1 \\ \vdots \\ \boldsymbol{X}_N \end{bmatrix},\quad \boldsymbol{Z} = \begin{bmatrix} \boldsymbol{z}_1 \\ \vdots \\ \boldsymbol{z}_N \end{bmatrix},$$

[3] Note that $\boldsymbol{X}_i$ is the $(T \times K_2)$-matrix of observations from the K_2 two-dimensional variables in the T periods, while $(\boldsymbol{z}_i \otimes \boldsymbol{e}_T)$ is the $(T \times K_1)$-matrix which repeats the $(1 \times K_1)$-vector of the K_1 unidimensional variables T times.

so that the matrix X in Section 3.2.1 corresponds to $[X, (Z \otimes e_T)]$, and

$$W_{XX} = \begin{bmatrix} X' \\ (Z \otimes e_T)' \end{bmatrix} (I_N \otimes B_T)[X, (Z \otimes e_T)] = \begin{bmatrix} \tilde{W}_{XX} & 0 \\ 0 & 0 \end{bmatrix},$$

$$B_{XX} = \begin{bmatrix} X' \\ (Z \otimes e_T)' \end{bmatrix} (B_N \otimes A_T)\,[X, (Z \otimes e_T)] = \begin{bmatrix} \tilde{B}_{XX} & \tilde{B}_{XZ} \\ \tilde{B}_{ZX} & \tilde{B}_{ZZ} \end{bmatrix},$$

$$W_{XY} = \begin{bmatrix} X' \\ (Z \otimes e_T)' \end{bmatrix} (I_N \otimes B_T)\, y = \begin{bmatrix} \tilde{W}_{XY} \\ 0 \end{bmatrix},$$

$$B_{XY} = \begin{bmatrix} X' \\ (Z \otimes e_T)' \end{bmatrix} (B_N \otimes A_T)\, y = \begin{bmatrix} \tilde{B}_{XY} \\ \tilde{B}_{ZY} \end{bmatrix}.$$

Inserting these expressions in $\widehat{\boldsymbol{\beta}}_{GLS} = (W_{XX} + \theta_B B_{XX})^{-1}(W_{XY} + \theta_B B_{XY})$, we find that the estimators of β and δ can be expressed as

$$\begin{bmatrix} \widehat{\boldsymbol{\beta}}_{GLS} \\ \widehat{\boldsymbol{\delta}}_{GLS} \end{bmatrix} = \begin{bmatrix} \tilde{W}_{XX} + \theta_B \tilde{B}_{XX} & \theta_B \tilde{B}_{XZ} \\ \theta_B \tilde{B}_{ZX} & \theta_B \tilde{B}_{ZZ} \end{bmatrix}^{-1} \begin{bmatrix} \tilde{W}_{XY} + \theta_B \tilde{B}_{XY} \\ \theta_B \tilde{B}_{ZY} \end{bmatrix}. \tag{5.21}$$

These GLS estimators always exist when $\theta_B > 0 \iff \sigma^2 > 0$.

We consequently are in a more favourable situation with respect to identification of $\boldsymbol{\delta}$ when the individual-specific effect is random and uncorrelated with both regressors than if we rely on the individual effects being fixed and unstructured. It follows from Appendix 3A, Section 3A.2, that the GLS estimator of k is

$$\begin{aligned} \widehat{k}_{GLS} &= [\tfrac{1}{N} e_N' \otimes \tfrac{1}{T} e_T'][y - X\widehat{\boldsymbol{\beta}}_{GLS} - (Z \otimes e_T)\widehat{\boldsymbol{\delta}}_{GLS}] \\ &= \bar{y} - \bar{x}\widehat{\boldsymbol{\beta}}_{GLS} - \bar{z}\widehat{\boldsymbol{\delta}}_{GLS}. \end{aligned} \tag{5.22}$$

From Section 3.2 we know the GLS estimator can be obtained by solving a transformed OLS problem, minimizing a sum of squares in $\boldsymbol{\epsilon}_i^* = y_i^* - e_T k^* - X_i^* \boldsymbol{\beta} - (z_i^* \otimes e_T)\boldsymbol{\delta}$, where

$$\begin{aligned} y_i^* &= y_i - (1 - \sqrt{\theta_B}) A_T y_i = (B_T + \sqrt{\theta_B} A_T) y_i, \\ X_i^* &= X_i - (1 - \sqrt{\theta_B}) A_T X_i = (B_T + \sqrt{\theta_B} A_T) X_i, \\ z_i^* \otimes e_T &= z_i \otimes e_T - (1 - \sqrt{\theta_B}) A_T (z_i \otimes e_T) = \sqrt{\theta_B} z_i \otimes e_T \\ &\iff z_i^* = \sqrt{\theta_B} z_i, \\ e_T k^* &= e_T k - (1 - \sqrt{\theta_B}) A_T e_T k = e_T \sqrt{\theta_B}\, k \\ &\iff k^* = \sqrt{\theta_B} k. \end{aligned}$$

Hence, the prescription is: *deduct from the two-dimensional variables in y_i and X_i the share $(1-\sqrt{\theta_B})$ of the individual-specific means, multiply the unidimensional vector z_i by $\sqrt{\theta_B}$, and apply OLS on the resulting equation, $y_i^* = e_T k^* + X_i^* \beta + (z_i^* \otimes e_T)\delta + \epsilon_i^*$.*

Example: From a US data set for wage rates and its determinants, used in Cornwell and Rupert (1988) (downloaded from http://www.stata-press.com/data/r8, variables renamed; last accessed March 2016), are estimated random effects, GLS regressions, and fixed effects, OLS regressions for a simple wage equation (columns 1 and 2) with both two-dimensional and individual-specific regressors. The results, supplemented with comparable OLS estimates for a corresponding homogeneous model (column 3), are given in Table 5.1. The regressand is the logarithm of the wage rate, the regressor set contains six two-dimensional variables—`occ`, `metr`, `ind`, `exper`, `work`, `union`, all except `exper` and `work` being binary variables (see table footnote for definitions)—and two individual-specific variables—dummy for female (`fem`) and number of years of education (`educ`). The balanced panel contains $N = 595$ individuals observed in $T = 7$ years. As expected, we obtain no within (fixed effects) estimates for the impact of `fem` and `educ`. This appears as a substantial 'loss', considering the large interest often paid to 'returns to schooling' in policy recommendations and academic discussions. The GLS and OLS estimates of their coefficients

Table 5.1 Equation with individual specific regressors: Wage equation with random versus fixed effects

	GLS,RE	Within,FE	OLS
`occ`	−0.0567	−0.0249	−0.1547
	(0.0169)	(0.0138)	(0.0151)
`metr`	−0.0319	−0.0459	0.1369
	(0.0204)	(0.0194)	(0.0123)
`ind`	0.0078	0.0204	0.0634
	(0.0176)	(0.0156)	(0.0121)
`exper`	0.0493	0.0966	0.0106
	(0.0011)	(0.0012)	(0.0005)
`work`	0.0840	0.0590	0.2654
	(0.0406)	(0.0314)	(0.0581)
`union`	0.0666	0.0341	0.1123
	(0.0174)	(0.0150)	(0.0130)
`fem`	−0.3023	–	−0.4384
	(0.0485)		(0.0185)
`educ`	0.1057	–	0.0607
	(0.0059)		(0.0027)
`intercept`	4.3205	4.7269	5.4200
	(0.0952)	(0.0405)	(0.0699)

Notes: Standard errors in parentheses. The two-dimensional regressors include four dummies: `occ`, `metr`, `ind`, `union`, for, respectively, working in blue-collar occupation, living in a metropolitan area, working in manufacturing industry, and having wage set by a union contract, and: `exper`=years of full-time work experience, and `work`= share of the year being in work.

are quite different. The F-statistic for testing for absence of individual fixed effects is $F(594, 3562) = 47.37$, with $p = 0.0000$. The correlation (across i) between $\widehat{\alpha}_i^*$ and $\bar{x}_{i\cdot}\widehat{\boldsymbol{\beta}}_W$ is -0.91, indicating that unobserved heterogeneity varies systematically with the (two-dimensional) regressor vector. It therefore comes as no surprise that the GLS and the within estimates of working in blue-collar occupation (`occ`), working in manufacturing industry (`ind`), years of full-time work experience (`exper`), and share of the year being in work (`work`) differ substantially. A continuation of the example, using more elaborate methods, follows in Section 6.5.

5.5 **Two-way models**

In this section we outline extensions of the models in Sections 5.3.1 and 5.4.1 by including a *period-specific regressor*. Correspondingly, we let the intercept be shifted by including both individual-specific and period-specific effects. The fixed effects case will be considered in Section 5.5.1 and the random effects case in Section 5.5.2. The corresponding matrix extension with arbitrary numbers of (two-dimensional, individual-specific, and period-specific) regressors is straightforward in principle, but bringing few results beyond those from the scalar version, it will not be explained in detail.

5.5.1 FIXED EFFECTS TWO-REGRESSOR MODEL

Consider a model with fixed effects in both dimensions:

$$\begin{aligned} &y_{it} = k + \beta x_{it} + \delta z_i + \phi q_t + \alpha_i + \gamma_t + u_{it}, \\ &(u_{it}|\mathbf{X}, \mathbf{Z}, \mathbf{Q}) \sim \mathsf{IID}(0, \sigma^2), \\ &i = 1, \dots, N;\ t = 1, \dots, T, \end{aligned} \tag{5.23}$$

where x_{it}, z_i, and q_t are, respectively, the two-dimensional, the individual-specific, and the period-specific variable, and $\beta, \delta, \phi, \alpha_1, \dots, \alpha_N, \gamma_1, \dots, \gamma_T$, and k are $N+T+4$ unknown constants satisfying $\sum_{i=1}^N \alpha_i = \sum_{t=1}^T \gamma_t = 0$.

If we had known *a priori* that δ and ϕ were zero, the residual estimator (the combined within-individual-within-period estimator) would have been the MVLUE of β and could be obtained by OLS on (5.23) with z_i and q_t omitted. Is this method feasible also when δ and ϕ are unknown? Again, problems are likely to arise.

The residual estimators of $(\beta, \delta, \phi)'$ do not exist, since $R_{ZZ} = R_{XZ} = R_{ZY} = R_{QQ} = R_{XQ} = R_{QY} = R_{ZQ} = 0$, while $R_{XX} > 0$ and R_{XY} usually is non-zero. To compute them we would have to solve for $\widehat{\beta}_R$, $\widehat{\delta}_R$, and $\widehat{\phi}_R$ from

$$\begin{bmatrix} R_{XX} & R_{XZ} & R_{XQ} \\ R_{ZX} & R_{ZZ} & R_{ZQ} \\ R_{QX} & R_{QZ} & R_{QQ} \end{bmatrix} \begin{bmatrix} \widehat{\beta}_R \\ \widehat{\delta}_R \\ \widehat{\phi}_R \end{bmatrix} = \begin{bmatrix} R_{XY} \\ R_{ZY} \\ R_{QY} \end{bmatrix},$$

which degenerates to

$$\begin{bmatrix} R_{XX} & 0 & 0 \\ 0 & 0 & 0 \\ 0 & 0 & 0 \end{bmatrix} \begin{bmatrix} \widehat{\beta}_R \\ \widehat{\delta}_R \\ \widehat{\phi}_R \end{bmatrix} = \begin{bmatrix} R_{XY} \\ 0 \\ 0 \end{bmatrix}. \tag{5.24}$$

As solution value for $\widehat{\beta}_R$ we would obtain

$$\widehat{\beta}_R = \frac{R_{XY}}{R_{XX}},$$

which is a well-defined estimator since $R_{XX} > 0$, while $\widehat{\delta}_R$ and $\widehat{\phi}_R$ are undefined—being '$\frac{0}{0}$ expressions'. The regressor moment matrix has a reduced rank, 1, while full solution requires rank 3. This implies that we only obtain a *partial solution* to the estimation problem: an estimator for the coefficient of the two-dimensional variable, but none for the coefficients of the unidimensional variables.

On the other hand, if no unknown individual-specific and period-specific effects had occurred, i.e., if we had known that $\alpha_i = \gamma_t = 0$ for all i and t, we could have used OLS. This would, in view of (5.2)–(5.3), have given

$$\begin{bmatrix} G_{XX} & B_{XZ} & C_{XQ} \\ B_{ZX} & B_{ZZ} & 0 \\ C_{QX} & 0 & C_{QQ} \end{bmatrix} \begin{bmatrix} \widehat{\beta}_{OLS} \\ \widehat{\delta}_{OLS} \\ \widehat{\phi}_{OLS} \end{bmatrix} = \begin{bmatrix} G_{XY} \\ B_{ZY} \\ C_{QY} \end{bmatrix}, \tag{5.25}$$

which would yield $\widehat{\beta}_{OLS}$, $\widehat{\delta}_{OLS}$, and $\widehat{\phi}_{OLS}$. Alternatively, we could have used the *between-individual estimators*, defined by

$$\begin{bmatrix} B_{XX} & B_{XZ} & 0 \\ B_{ZX} & B_{ZZ} & 0 \\ 0 & 0 & 0 \end{bmatrix} \begin{bmatrix} \widehat{\beta}_B \\ \widehat{\delta}_B \\ \widehat{\phi}_B \end{bmatrix} = \begin{bmatrix} B_{XY} \\ B_{ZY} \\ 0 \end{bmatrix},$$

which implies

$$\begin{bmatrix} B_{XX} & B_{XZ} \\ B_{ZX} & B_{ZZ} \end{bmatrix} \begin{bmatrix} \widehat{\beta}_B \\ \widehat{\delta}_B \end{bmatrix} = \begin{bmatrix} B_{XY} \\ B_{ZY} \end{bmatrix}, \tag{5.26}$$

giving $\widehat{\beta}_B$ and $\widehat{\delta}_B$, but no solution for $\widehat{\phi}_B$. Or we could have used

$$\begin{bmatrix} C_{XX} & 0 & C_{XQ} \\ 0 & 0 & 0 \\ C_{QX} & 0 & C_{QQ} \end{bmatrix} \begin{bmatrix} \widehat{\beta}_C \\ \widehat{\delta}_C \\ \widehat{\phi}_C \end{bmatrix} = \begin{bmatrix} C_{XY} \\ 0 \\ C_{QY} \end{bmatrix},$$

which implies

$$\begin{bmatrix} C_{XX} & C_{XQ} \\ C_{QX} & C_{QQ} \end{bmatrix} \begin{bmatrix} \widehat{\beta}_C \\ \widehat{\phi}_C \end{bmatrix} = \begin{bmatrix} C_{XY} \\ C_{QY} \end{bmatrix}, \tag{5.27}$$

giving $\widehat{\beta}_C$ and $\widehat{\phi}_C$, but no solution for $\widehat{\delta}_C$.

The system (5.25) would have given well-defined solutions to the estimation problem for all three coefficients, because its matrix would (normally) have had rank 3. The systems (5.26) and (5.27) would give solutions to only two of the three estimators, as their matrices have (at most) rank 2. *The problem with model (5.23) (with unknown δ, ϕ, $\alpha_1, \ldots, \alpha_N$, and $\gamma_1, \ldots, \gamma_T$) is thus the joint occurrence of (a) the individual-specific regressor and the fixed individual-specific effects and (b) the period-specific regressor and the fixed period-specific effects.*

Let us examine the nature of the OLS problem for (5.23), i.e., to minimize

$$\textstyle\sum_i \sum_t (y_{it} - k - \beta x_{it} - \delta z_i - \phi q_t - \alpha_i - \gamma_t)^2.$$

Setting its first derivatives with respect to k, β, δ, ϕ, α_i, and γ_t equal to zero, gives the following $N+T+4$ linear (normal) equations in the residual estimators:

$$\begin{aligned}
&\textstyle\sum_i \sum_t (y_{it} - \widehat{k}_R - \widehat{\beta}_R x_{it} - \widehat{\delta}_R z_i - \widehat{\phi}_R q_t - \widehat{\alpha}_{iR} - \widehat{\gamma}_{tR}) = 0, \\
&\textstyle\sum_i \sum_t (y_{it} - \widehat{k}_R - \widehat{\beta}_R x_{it} - \widehat{\delta}_R z_i - \widehat{\phi}_R q_t - \widehat{\alpha}_{iR} - \widehat{\gamma}_{tR}) x_{it} = 0, \\
&\textstyle\sum_i \sum_t (y_{it} - \widehat{k}_R - \widehat{\beta}_R x_{it} - \widehat{\delta}_R z_i - \widehat{\phi}_R q_t - \widehat{\alpha}_{iR} - \widehat{\gamma}_{tR}) z_i = 0, \\
&\textstyle\sum_i \sum_t (y_{it} - \widehat{k}_R - \widehat{\beta}_R x_{it} - \widehat{\delta}_R z_i - \widehat{\phi}_R q_t - \widehat{\alpha}_{iR} - \widehat{\gamma}_{tR}) q_t = 0, \\
&\textstyle\sum_t (y_{it} - \widehat{k}_R - \widehat{\beta}_R x_{it} - \widehat{\delta}_R z_i - \widehat{\phi}_R q_t - \widehat{\alpha}_{iR} - \widehat{\gamma}_{tR}) = 0, \quad i = 1, \ldots, N, \\
&\textstyle\sum_i (y_{it} - \widehat{k}_R - \widehat{\beta}_R x_{it} - \widehat{\delta}_R z_i - \widehat{\phi}_R q_t - \widehat{\alpha}_{iR} - \widehat{\gamma}_{tR}) = 0, \quad t = 1, \ldots, T.
\end{aligned}$$

These equations are not independent: the N next last equations imply that the first and the third also hold, and the T last equations imply that the first and the fourth also hold. We therefore have only $N+T+1$ *independent* linear equations. From the $N+T$ last equations and the adding-up restrictions it follows that

$$\begin{aligned}
&\widehat{k}_R + \widehat{\delta}_R z_i + \widehat{\phi}_R \bar{q} + \widehat{\alpha}_{iR} = \bar{y}_{i\cdot} - \widehat{\beta}_R \bar{x}_{i\cdot}, && i = 1, \ldots, N, \\
&\widehat{k}_R + \widehat{\delta}_R \bar{z} + \widehat{\phi}_R q_t + \widehat{\gamma}_{tR} = \bar{y}_{\cdot t} - \widehat{\beta}_R \bar{x}_{\cdot t}, && t = 1, \ldots, T.
\end{aligned}$$

Using the adding-up restrictions, we further have

$$\widehat{k}_R + \widehat{\delta}_R\bar{z} + \widehat{\phi}_R\bar{q} = \bar{y} - \widehat{\beta}_R\bar{x}.$$

Combining the three last equations with the second normal equation, we obtain

$$\widehat{\beta}_R = \frac{\sum_{i=1}^{N}\sum_{t=1}^{T}(x_{it} - \bar{x}_{i\cdot} - \bar{x}_{\cdot t} + \bar{x})(y_{it} - \bar{y}_{i\cdot} - \bar{y}_{\cdot t} + \bar{y})}{\sum_{i=1}^{N}\sum_{t=1}^{T}(x_{it} - \bar{x}_{i\cdot} - \bar{x}_{\cdot t} + \bar{x})^2} = \frac{R_{XY}}{R_{XX}}. \tag{5.28}$$

Hence, we can estimate β and the $N+T+1$ composite 'parameters'

$$\begin{aligned} &k+\delta z_i+\phi\bar{q}+\alpha_i, \quad i = 1,\dots,N,\\ &k+\delta\bar{z}+\phi q_t+\gamma_t, \quad t = 1,\dots,T,\\ &k+\delta\bar{z}+\phi\bar{q}, \end{aligned}$$

by, respectively, $\widehat{\beta}_R$ and

$$\begin{aligned} &\bar{y}_{i\cdot} - \widehat{\beta}_R\bar{x}_{i\cdot}, \quad i = 1,\dots,N,\\ &\bar{y}_{\cdot t} - \widehat{\beta}_R\bar{x}_{\cdot t}, \quad t = 1,\dots,T,\\ &\bar{y} - \widehat{\beta}_R\bar{x}. \end{aligned}$$

Therefore: (i) the estimator of the coefficient of the two-dimensional regressor x_{it} is the same as the one obtained if the individual-specific and period-specific regressors z_i and q_t had been excluded from the model; and (ii) we are unable to separate the individual-specific effect α_i from the effect of the individual-specific regressor z_i and to separate the period-specific effect γ_t from the effect of the period-specific regressor q_t. Now the *collinearity problem* is: (i) the individual-specific variable depends linearly on the set of the individual-specific binary variables we could use to represent the individual-specific effects; and (ii) the period-specific variable depends linearly on the set of the period-specific binary variables we could use to represent the period-specific effects. For individual-specific effects α_i and period-specific effects γ_t to be estimable they would have to capture the effect of *any* individual-specific, respectively *any* period-specific variable, in explaining the variation in y_{it}.

Conclusion (ii) can be a strong argument against utilizing models with *full sets of* fixed individual-specific and period-specific effects in practice. We often are genuinely interested in effects of observable individual-specific and period-specific explanatory variables and do not want them to be mixed with composite individual-specific effects, $\alpha_1,\dots,\alpha_N$, and period-specific effects, $\gamma_1,\dots,\gamma_T$, with diffuse interpretations.

From the above normal equations and the adding-up restrictions, we derive

$$\begin{aligned}
\widehat{\alpha}_{iR} &= (\bar{y}_{i\cdot} - \bar{y}) - \widehat{\beta}_R(\bar{x}_{i\cdot} - \bar{x}) - \widehat{\delta}_R(z_i - \bar{z}), && i = 1,\dots,N,\\
\widehat{\gamma}_{tR} &= (\bar{y}_{\cdot t} - \bar{y}) - \widehat{\beta}_R(\bar{x}_{\cdot t} - \bar{x}) - \widehat{\phi}_R(q_t - \bar{q}), && t = 1,\dots,T,\\
\widehat{k}_R &= \bar{y} - \widehat{\beta}_R\bar{x} - \widehat{\delta}_R\bar{z} - \widehat{\phi}_R\bar{q},
\end{aligned}$$

which satisfy $\sum_{i=1}^{N}\widehat{\alpha}_{iR} = \sum_{t=1}^{T}\widehat{\gamma}_{tR} = 0$. Unless we have more restrictions, identification of $k, \delta, \alpha_1,\dots,\alpha_N, \phi$, and $\gamma_1,\dots,\gamma_T$ cannot get any further. Were additional information at hand for (at least) two coefficients, for example δ and ϕ, the remaining coefficients could have been uncovered. Another (and frequently used) way of 'solving' the collinearity problem is to let *groups of* units (individuals, firms) or of periods have the same α_i and γ_t, respectively.

In classical econometrics, a sharp distinction is usually drawn between 'parameters' and 'exogenous variables'. Marschak, for example, obviously referring to the temporal context, states

If the decision variable has varied in the past, it is called an exogenous variable: if it has not, it is usually called a structural parameter . . . Some may find it more convenient to give the set of exogenous variables and structural parameters a more general name: 'conditions' . . . Conditions that undergo changes during the period of observation correspond to 'exogenous variables'. Conditions that remain constant throughout the observation period but may or may not change in the future constitute the 'structure'. (1953, pp. 7, 10)

How his points should be transmitted to a panel data context is an interesting question with no obvious answer. Clearly, if the equation considered is a structural equation, k, δ, and ϕ are *structural parameters* in the classical sense, while $k+\delta z_i + \phi\bar{q} + \alpha_i$ and $k + \delta\bar{z} + \phi q_t + \gamma_t$ are in general not. Strictly, they are *unobserved exogenous variables* involving observable elements. However, in a pure time-series context, the former, but not the latter, may be regarded as a (pseudo-)parameter, although non-identifiable from one set of time-series. Likewise, in a pure cross-sectional context the latter, but not the former, may be regarded as a (pseudo-)parameter, although non-identifiable from one set of cross-section data.

5.5.2 RANDOM EFFECTS TWO-REGRESSOR MODEL

The final model has individual-specific and period-specific effects, α_i and γ_t, that are random and satisfy strong distributional assumptions. We consider the following generalization of Model (5.15):

$$
\begin{aligned}
&y_{it} = k+\beta x_{it}+\delta z_i+\phi q_t+\alpha_i+\gamma_t+u_{it},\\
&(\alpha_i|X,Z,Q) \sim \mathsf{IID}(0,\sigma_\alpha^2),\\
&(\gamma_t|X,Z,Q) \sim \mathsf{IID}(0,\sigma_\gamma^2),\\
&(u_{it}|X,Z,Q) \sim \mathsf{IID}(0,\sigma^2),\\
&i = 1,\dots,N;\ t = 1,\dots,T,
\end{aligned}
\tag{5.29}
$$

and again let $\epsilon_{it}=\alpha_i+\gamma_t+u_{it}$. Stacking the observations as in Section 5.4.2, we have the equivalent formulation

$$
\begin{aligned}
&y = (e_N \otimes e_T)k + x\beta + (z \otimes e_T)\delta + (e_N \otimes q)\phi + \epsilon,\\
&\epsilon = \alpha \otimes e_T + e_N \otimes \gamma + u,\\
&\mathsf{E}(\epsilon|X,Z,Q) = 0,\quad \mathsf{V}(\epsilon|X,Z,Q) = \Omega,\\
&\Omega = \sigma_\alpha^2 I_N \otimes (e_T e_T') + \sigma_\gamma^2 (e_N e_N') \otimes I_T + \sigma^2 I_N \otimes I_T.
\end{aligned}
\tag{5.30}
$$

This is a special version of a multiple regression model with K regressors and stochastic individual- and period-specific effects, as discussed in Section 3.5 for $K=3$, the second x-variable is individual-specific, and the third x-variable is period-specific. We can therefore, for GLS estimation, to a large extent, draw on the results in Section 3.6.

Letting $z = (z_1,\dots,z_N)'$, $q = (q_1,\dots,q_T)'$, etc., the general $(NT \times K)$-matrix X corresponds to the $(NT \times 3)$-matrix $[x, (z \otimes e_T), (e_N \otimes q)]$, and we have

$$
R_{XX} = \begin{bmatrix} x' \\ (z \otimes e_T)' \\ (e_N \otimes q)' \end{bmatrix} (B_N \otimes B_T)\big[x, (z \otimes e_T), (e_N \otimes q)\big] = \begin{bmatrix} R_{XX} & 0 & 0 \\ 0 & 0 & 0 \\ 0 & 0 & 0 \end{bmatrix},
$$

$$
B_{XX} = \begin{bmatrix} x' \\ (z \otimes e_T)' \\ (e_N \otimes q)' \end{bmatrix} (B_N \otimes A_T)\big[x, (z \otimes e_T), (e_N \otimes q)\big] = \begin{bmatrix} B_{XX} & B_{XZ} & 0 \\ B_{ZX} & B_{ZZ} & 0 \\ 0 & 0 & 0 \end{bmatrix},
$$

$$
C_{XX} = \begin{bmatrix} x' \\ (z \otimes e_T)' \\ (e_N \otimes q)' \end{bmatrix} (A_N \otimes B_T)\big[x, (z \otimes e_T), (e_N \otimes q)\big] = \begin{bmatrix} C_{XX} & 0 & C_{XQ} \\ 0 & 0 & 0 \\ C_{QX} & 0 & C_{QQ} \end{bmatrix},
$$

$$
R_{XY} = \begin{bmatrix} x' \\ (z \otimes e_T)' \\ (e_N \otimes q)' \end{bmatrix} (B_N \otimes B_T) y = \begin{bmatrix} R_{XY} \\ 0 \\ 0 \end{bmatrix},
$$

$$B_{XY} = \begin{bmatrix} x' \\ (z \otimes e_T)' \\ (e_N \otimes q)' \end{bmatrix} (B_N \otimes A_T) y = \begin{bmatrix} B_{XY} \\ B_{ZY} \\ 0 \end{bmatrix},$$

$$C_{XY} = \begin{bmatrix} x' \\ (z \otimes e_T)' \\ (e_N \otimes q)' \end{bmatrix} (A_N \otimes B_T) y = \begin{bmatrix} C_{XY} \\ 0 \\ C_{QY} \end{bmatrix},$$

which when inserted into

$$\widehat{\beta}_{GLS} = (R_{XX} + \theta_B B_{XX} + \theta_C C_{XX})^{-1}(R_{XY} + \theta_B B_{XY} + \theta_C C_{XY}),$$

where $\theta_B = \sigma^2/(\sigma^2 + T\sigma_\alpha^2)$, $\theta_C = \sigma^2/(\sigma^2 + N\sigma_\gamma^2)$, see (3.60), gives

$$\begin{bmatrix} \widehat{\beta}_{GLS} \\ \widehat{\delta}_{GLS} \\ \widehat{\phi}_{GLS} \end{bmatrix} = \begin{bmatrix} R_{XX} + \theta_B B_{XX} + \theta_C C_{XX} & \theta_B B_{XZ} & \theta_C C_{XQ} \\ \theta_B B_{ZX} & \theta_B B_{ZZ} & 0 \\ \theta_C C_{QX} & 0 & \theta_C C_{QQ} \end{bmatrix}^{-1} \times \begin{bmatrix} R_{XY} + \theta_B B_{XY} + \theta_C C_{XY} \\ \theta_B B_{ZY} \\ \theta_C C_{QY} \end{bmatrix}. \tag{5.31}$$

It follows from Theorem 2 in Appendix 3A, Section 3A.2, that

$$\begin{aligned} \widehat{k}_{GLS} &= [\tfrac{1}{N} e_N' \otimes \tfrac{1}{T} e_T'][y - x\widehat{\beta}_{GLS} - (z \otimes e_T)\widehat{\delta}_{GLS} - (e_N \otimes q)\widehat{\phi}_{GLS}] \\ &= \bar{y} - \bar{x}\widehat{\beta}_{GLS} - \bar{z}\widehat{\delta}_{GLS} - \bar{q}\widehat{\phi}_{GLS}. \end{aligned} \tag{5.32}$$

Consequently, we are in a more favourable situation with respect to identification of δ and ϕ is when the individual-specific and period-specific effects are random and uncorrelated with both regressors than if we rely on these effects being fixed and unstructured.

6 Latent heterogeneity correlated with regressors

CHAPTER SUMMARY

This chapter discusses problems for the use of regression models raised by correlation between latent individual-specific heterogeneity and the specified regressors, and ways of resolving them. This is an important extension which exploits the potential of panel data to address nuisance variables problems, in particular related to time-invariant regressors. instrumental variables and GLS elements are important in the procedures. The Hausman–Taylor type of specifications, with extensions, an order condition for identification, as well as applications of Hausman specification tests are discussed. Empirical examples are given.

6.1 Introduction

Latent heterogeneity, when treated as stochastic shifts in the intercept of an equation, has so far been assumed random and uncorrelated with the specified regressors. Quite often this occurs as an unduly strong restriction. We have touched upon ways of relaxing it for models with fixed effects, e.g., in Section 5.3, without giving it a thorough discussion. In this chapter we discuss problems raised by such correlation in the case with individual-specific heterogeneity and ways of resolving them. This is an important extension, which more than many of the previous models exploits the potential of panel data to address the nuisance variables problem specifically related to time-invariant covariates.

We proceed step-wise, starting from a model with one two-dimensional regressor, augment it by including one individual-specific variable, and then generalize to models of arbitrary dimension. A further extension will be to split the regression vector into two parts, one correlated with the latent heterogeneity and one with correlation absent. Instrumental variables (IVs) will be used extensively. Giving instruments a *theoretical* underpinning is crucial because the general requirements for instrument validity rely on *theoretical (population)* correlation as well as absence of correlation rather than on empirical (sample) correlation. We will show that the occurrence of unidimensional regressors may create identification problems for their coefficients, but the orthogonality of the within and the between variation may help us so that we do not need (to postulate the existence of) external instruments. We can, by appropriate transformations, obtain variables that fulfil the conditions for valid IVs 'inside' the model.

The chapter proceeds as follows. First, in Section 6.2, we consider the simplest model in this category, with only two-dimensional regressors, all correlated with the individual-specific latent effect. In Section 6.3, we extend this by including time-invariant (individual-specific) regressors. Section 6.4 is concerned with mixed situations where the latent individual effect is correlated with only a subset of the *time-invariant* regressors, but is uncorrelated with all other variables. At this stage IVs enter the scene. For expositional reasons, in Sections 6.2, 6.3, and 6.4, we start by considering simple cases with scalar regressors, keeping the matrix notation to a minimum, before extending to more general formulations. Section 6.5 considers generalizations. First, we generalize to situations where instruments are needed for an arbitrary subset of individual-specific regressors, and next to situations where an arbitrary number of two-dimensional and individual-specific variables occur as regressors and where some of the variables in each category are correlated with the individual effect.

Throughout the chapter the regressors are assumed to be uncorrelated with the genuine disturbance. Multi-equation models which take the modelling of 'endogeneity' and 'simultaneity' further—in also addressing the 'classical' problem of correlation between explanatory variables and genuine disturbances, sometimes denoted as '*double endogeneity*', see, e.g., Biørn and Krishnakumar (2008, p. 323)—will be discussed in the second part of Chapter 12.

6.2 **Models with only two-dimensional regressors**

6.2.1 A SIMPLE CASE

We start by considering the following equation with regressand y_{it}, one scalar regressor x_{it}, a stochastic individual effect, α_i, and a disturbance, u_{it}:

$$y_{it} = k^* + x_{it}\beta + \alpha_i + u_{it}, \qquad i = 1, \dots, N;\ t = 1, \dots, T, \tag{6.1}$$

k^* and β being constants. In Chapter 3 orthogonality between x_{it}, α_i, and u_{it} was not questioned. We now relax these strong assumptions, by allowing for correlation between x_{it} and α_i, but retain orthogonality between u_{it} and (x_{it}, α_i). One motivating example may be that latent tastes or preferences in household i, included in α_i, is correlated with its income, x_{it}, both explaining expenditure on the commodity, y_{it}, in an Engel function. Another example is that the latent quality of the labour force or the management of firm i, α_i, may be correlated with capital input, x_{it}, both explaining firm performance. *We are interested in quantifying the partial effect of x_{it} on y_{it}*—for example the effect of income on consumption or the effect of capital on output—represented by β, and do *not* want our estimates to be biased by x_{it} being correlated with α_i.

It is convenient (though not necessary) to *formalize the correlation* between x_{it} and α_i by a linear equation. Rather than pretending that a two-dimensional variable x_{it} determines the individual-specific α_i in a structural equation, we formalize the relationship as a linear equation, with λ an unknown constant:

$$\alpha_i = [\bar{x}_{i\cdot} - \mathsf{E}(\bar{x}_{i\cdot})]\lambda + w_i, \qquad i = 1, \dots, N. \tag{6.2}$$

We let $\boldsymbol{x}_i = (x_{i1}, \dots, x_{iT})$ and assume

$$(u_{it}|\boldsymbol{x}_i) \sim \mathsf{IID}(0, \sigma^2), \quad (w_i|\boldsymbol{x}_i) \sim \mathsf{IID}(0, \sigma_w^2), \quad u_{it} \perp w_i. \tag{6.3}$$

Conditional on $\boldsymbol{x}_i$, the expectation of α_i is not constant since

$$\mathsf{E}(\alpha_i|\boldsymbol{x}_i) = [\bar{x}_{i\cdot} - \mathsf{E}(\bar{x}_{i\cdot})]\lambda,$$

while (6.2)–(6.3) imply $\mathsf{E}(\alpha_i) = 0$. On the other hand, while the variance of α_i is constant conditional on $\boldsymbol{x}_i$, it is marginally i-dependent when $\text{var}(\bar{x}_{i\cdot})$ has this property:

$$\begin{aligned} \text{var}(\alpha_i|\boldsymbol{x}_i) &= \text{var}(w_i|\boldsymbol{x}_i) = \sigma_w^2, \\ \text{var}(\alpha_i) &= \text{var}[\mathsf{E}(\alpha_i|\boldsymbol{x}_i)] + \mathsf{E}[\text{var}(\alpha_i|\boldsymbol{x}_i)] = \text{var}(\bar{x}_{i\cdot})\lambda^2 + \sigma_w^2. \end{aligned}$$

Assume $\mathsf{E}(\bar{x}_{i\cdot}) = \mu_x$ $(i = 1, \dots, N)$, let $k = k^* - \mu_x\lambda$, and write the model as

$$\begin{aligned} &y_{it} = k + x_{it}\beta + \bar{x}_{i\cdot}\lambda + w_i + u_{it}, \\ &(u_{it}|X) \sim \mathsf{IID}(0, \sigma^2), \quad (w_i|X) \sim \mathsf{IID}(0, \sigma_w^2), \quad u_{it} \perp w_i, \\ &i = 1, \dots, N; \; t = 1, \dots, T, \end{aligned} \tag{6.4}$$

conditioning (slightly stronger) on $\boldsymbol{X}$ (all values on $\boldsymbol{x}_i$) rather than $\boldsymbol{x}_i$ only.

Now, since (6.4) represents the data-generating process, estimating β from (6.1) by OLS or GLS, neglecting (6.2), can be interpreted as estimation from a model where *the individual mean of the regressor is an erroneously omitted regressor*. The OLS estimator of β based on (6.1) will then be affected by omitted variables bias since x_{it} and $\bar{x}_{i\cdot}$ are undoubtedly correlated. A crucial general property of (balanced) panel data, useful at this stage, is the *orthogonality of the within and between variation*, implied by $\boldsymbol{A}_T\boldsymbol{B}_T = \boldsymbol{0}$. It therefore is convenient to perform the following one-to-one transformation of (6.4):

$$\begin{aligned} &(y_{it} - \bar{y}_{i\cdot}) + \bar{y}_{i\cdot} = k + (x_{it} - \bar{x}_{i\cdot})\beta + \bar{x}_{i\cdot}(\beta + \lambda) + \varepsilon_{it}, \quad \varepsilon_{it} = w_i + u_{it}, \\ &(u_{it}|X) \sim \mathsf{IID}(0, \sigma^2), \quad (w_i|X) \sim \mathsf{IID}(0, \sigma_w^2), \quad u_{it} \perp w_{it}, \end{aligned} \tag{6.5}$$

in which $(y_{it} - \bar{y}_{i\cdot})$ and $(x_{it} - \bar{x}_{i\cdot})$ are (empirically) uncorrelated with $\bar{y}_{i\cdot}$ and $\bar{x}_{i\cdot}$.

This invites estimating β and $(\beta+\lambda)$ by OLS or GLS regression on (6.5), rather than on (6.4). OLS estimation is reduced to simply estimating β by regressing $y_{it}-\bar{y}_{i\cdot}$ on $x_{it}-\bar{x}_{i\cdot}$, and estimating $(\beta+\lambda)$ by regressing $\bar{y}_{i\cdot}$ on $\bar{x}_{i\cdot}$. This leads to the following estimators of β, $\beta+\lambda$, and λ:[1]

$$\widehat{\beta}_{OLS} = \widehat{\beta}_{W} = \frac{\sum_{i=1}^{N}\sum_{t=1}^{T}(x_{it}-\bar{x}_{i\cdot})(y_{it}-\bar{y}_{i\cdot})}{\sum_{i=1}^{N}\sum_{t=1}^{T}(x_{it}-\bar{x}_{i\cdot})^2} = \frac{W_{XY}}{W_{XX}},$$

$$(\widehat{\beta+\lambda})_{OLS} = (\widehat{\beta+\lambda})_{B} = \frac{T\sum_{i=1}^{N}(\bar{x}_{i\cdot}-\bar{x})(\bar{y}_{i\cdot}-\bar{y})}{T\sum_{i=1}^{N}(\bar{x}_{i\cdot}-\bar{x})^2} = \frac{B_{XY}}{B_{XX}},$$

$$\widehat{\lambda}_{OLS} = (\widehat{\beta+\lambda})_{OLS} - \widehat{\beta}_{OLS} = (\widehat{\beta+\lambda})_{B} - \widehat{\beta}_{W} = \frac{B_{XY}}{B_{XX}} - \frac{W_{XY}}{W_{XX}}.$$

A pertinent question is why estimate (6.5) by OLS when its disturbance, ε_{it}, shows serial correlation, equi-correlation, owing to its individual-specific component, w_i? It is GLS that gives MVLUE. However, surprisingly, in this case OLS and GLS give the same result. The proof is simple. As shown in Section 3.2.3, GLS can be implemented as OLS after deducting from all observations a share of the individual means:

$$\mu_B = 1-\sqrt{\theta_B} = 1-\left(\frac{\sigma^2}{\sigma^2+T\sigma_w^2}\right)^{\frac{1}{2}}. \tag{6.6}$$

This leaves $(y_{it}-\bar{y}_{i\cdot})$ and $(x_{it}-\bar{x}_{i\cdot})$ unchanged, while $\bar{y}_{i\cdot}$ and $\bar{x}_{i\cdot}$ are multiplied by $(1-\mu_B) = \sqrt{\theta_B}$. Therefore, *the GLS estimators equal the OLS estimators*, as regressing $\sqrt{\theta_B}\bar{y}_{i\cdot}$ on $\sqrt{\theta_B}\bar{x}_{i\cdot}$ implies regressing $\bar{y}_{i\cdot}$ on $\bar{x}_{i\cdot}$.[2]

Users of panel data often experience that between and within estimates of *presumably* the same parameter differ markedly (see the example below); the differences, judged from t-tests, seem 'significant'. We now are in a position to interpret such a discrepancy: an estimator of λ in an equation of the form (6.2). A researcher using the between estimator may believe themselves to be estimating β, while actually estimating $\beta+\lambda$. When $\lambda \neq 0$, $\widehat{\beta}_B = B_{XY}/B_{XX}$ is inconsistent for β and *consistent* for $\beta+\lambda$. We therefore conclude:[3]

$$\widehat{\beta}_{GLS} = \widehat{\beta}_{W} = \frac{W_{XY}}{W_{XX}}, \tag{6.7}$$

$$(\widehat{\beta+\lambda})_{GLS} = (\widehat{\beta+\lambda})_{B} = \frac{B_{XY}}{B_{XX}}, \tag{6.8}$$

[1] Note that the OLS subscript refers to OLS applied on the transformed model (6.5).
[2] See Maddala (1987, pp. 309–11) for a related exposition of the argument.
[3] Note that the GLS subscript refers to GLS applied on the reformulated model (6.5).

Table 6.1 Wage equation: impact of work experience on wage rate

	OLS	RE, FGLS	FE, Within	Between
`exper`	0.00881	0.06121	0.09693	0.00578
	(0.00064)	(0.00116)	(0.00119)	(0.00148)

Notes: RE = Random effects.
FE = Fixed effects.
Standard errors in parentheses

$$\widehat{\lambda}_{GLS} = (\widehat{\beta+\lambda})_{GLS} - \widehat{\beta}_{GLS} = \frac{B_{XY}}{B_{XX}} - \frac{W_{XY}}{W_{XX}}. \tag{6.9}$$

Example: We want to explore the impact of longer work experience (`exper`) on (the logarithm of) an individual's wage rate (`lwage`) by using an equation like (6.1). Stata modules for OLS (appropriate for no heterogeneity), FGLS (appropriate for random effects), within estimation (appropriate for fixed effects), and between estimation are combined with US data (National Longitudinal Survey) for young women 14–28 years of age in 1968, $N = 595$, $T = 7$ (*source*: http://www.stata-press.com/data/r9; last accessed March 2016). The results, given in Table 6.1, show that the OLS and FGLS estimates, both lying in the interval spanned by the between and the within estimate, differ substantially. The OLS result is closest to the between estimate and the FGLS result is closest to the within estimate. It is very likely that latent heterogeneity explaining earnings varies non-randomly and is correlated with work experience, so that differences in education may account for parts of the unspecified heterogeneity that is correlated with work experience. An equation of the form (6.2) may well be in effect. Interpreting in (6.1) $\widehat{\beta}_{OLS}$, $\widehat{\beta}_{GLS}$, $\widehat{\beta}_{W}$, and $\widehat{\beta}_{B}$ as measuring the partial effect on the wage rate of a one year additional work experience, we have to conclude that only $\widehat{\beta}_{W}$ accounts for fixed heterogeneity. Interpreting the results relative to Model (6.4), we find the quite large discrepancy $\widehat{\lambda} = \widehat{\beta}_B - \widehat{\beta}_W = 0.00578 - 0.09693 = -0.09115$. What does this estimate measure? A tentative answer, as a continuation of the example, will be given in Section 6.3.1.

6.2.2 GENERALIZATION

We extend to a model with K regressors, represented by the $(1 \times K)$-vector $\boldsymbol{x}_{it}$, and replace (6.1)–(6.3) with

$$\begin{aligned}
&y_{it} = k^* + \boldsymbol{x}_{it}\boldsymbol{\beta} + \alpha_i + u_{it},\\
&\alpha_i = [\bar{\boldsymbol{x}}_{i\cdot} - \mathsf{E}(\bar{\boldsymbol{x}}_{i\cdot})]\boldsymbol{\lambda} + w_i,\\
&(u_{it}|X) \sim \mathsf{IID}(0,\sigma^2), \quad (w_i|X) \sim \mathsf{IID}(0,\sigma_w^2), \quad u_{it} \perp w_i,\\
&i = 1,\dots,N;\ t = 1,\dots,T,
\end{aligned} \tag{6.10}$$

where $\boldsymbol{\beta}$ and $\boldsymbol{\lambda}$ are unknown vectors. It follows that α_i is homoskedastic conditional on $\bar{\boldsymbol{x}}_{i\cdot}$, but marginally, it has this property only when $\bar{\boldsymbol{x}}_{1\cdot},\dots,\bar{\boldsymbol{x}}_{N\cdot}$ have identical covariance matrices:

$$\begin{aligned}
\mathsf{E}(\alpha_i|\boldsymbol{x}_{i1},\dots,\boldsymbol{x}_{iT}) &= [\bar{\boldsymbol{x}}_{i\cdot} - \mathsf{E}(\bar{\boldsymbol{x}}_{i\cdot})]\boldsymbol{\lambda},\\
\mathsf{E}(\alpha_i) &= 0,\\
\mathrm{var}(\alpha_i|\boldsymbol{x}_{i1},\dots,\boldsymbol{x}_{iT}) &= \sigma_w^2,\\
\mathrm{var}(\alpha_i) &= \boldsymbol{\lambda}'\mathsf{V}(\bar{\boldsymbol{x}}_{i\cdot})\boldsymbol{\lambda} + \sigma_w^2.
\end{aligned}$$

Assuming $\mathsf{E}(\bar{\boldsymbol{x}}_{i\cdot}) = \boldsymbol{\mu}_x$ $(i = 1,\dots,N)$, the model can be written as the following extension of (6.4):

$$\begin{aligned}
&y_{it} = k + \boldsymbol{x}_{it}\boldsymbol{\beta} + \bar{\boldsymbol{x}}_{i\cdot}\boldsymbol{\lambda} + w_i + u_{it}, \quad k = k^* - \boldsymbol{\mu}_x\boldsymbol{\lambda},\\
&(u_{it}|X) \sim \mathsf{IID}(0,\sigma^2), \quad (w_i|X) \sim \mathsf{IID}(0,\sigma_w^2), \quad u_{it} \perp w_i,\\
&i = 1,\dots,N;\ t = 1,\dots,T,
\end{aligned} \tag{6.11}$$

This shows that if, when estimating β from (6.10) by OLS or GLS, we proceed as if α_i is uncorrelated with $\boldsymbol{x}_{it}$, we erroneously omit $\bar{\boldsymbol{x}}_{i\cdot}$. The corresponding generalization of (6.5) is

$$\begin{aligned}
(y_{it} - \bar{y}_{i\cdot}) + \bar{y}_{i\cdot} = k + (\boldsymbol{x}_{it} - \bar{\boldsymbol{x}}_{i\cdot})\boldsymbol{\beta} + \bar{\boldsymbol{x}}_{i\cdot}(\boldsymbol{\beta} + \boldsymbol{\lambda}) + \varepsilon_{it}, \quad \varepsilon_{it} = w_i + u_{it},\\
(u_{it}|X) \sim \mathsf{IID}(0,\sigma^2), \quad (w_i|X) \sim \mathsf{IID}(0,\sigma_w^2), \quad u_{it} \perp w_i.
\end{aligned} \tag{6.12}$$

The within–between orthogonality ensures that any element in $(y_{it} - \bar{y}_{i\cdot}, \boldsymbol{x}_{it} - \bar{\boldsymbol{x}}_{i\cdot})$ is orthogonal to any element in $(\bar{y}_{i\cdot}, \bar{\boldsymbol{x}}_{i\cdot})$. Therefore, OLS estimation of (6.12) simplifies to estimate $\boldsymbol{\beta}$ by regressing $y_{it} - \bar{y}_{i\cdot}$ on $\boldsymbol{x}_{it} - \bar{\boldsymbol{x}}_{i\cdot}$ and estimate $(\boldsymbol{\beta} + \boldsymbol{\lambda})$ by regressing $\bar{y}_{i\cdot}$ on $\bar{\boldsymbol{x}}_{i\cdot}$. This gives the following unbiased and consistent estimators for, respectively, $\boldsymbol{\beta}$, $\boldsymbol{\beta} + \boldsymbol{\lambda}$, and $\boldsymbol{\lambda}$:

$$\begin{aligned}
\widehat{\boldsymbol{\beta}}_{OLS} &= [\textstyle\sum_{i=1}^N \sum_{t=1}^T (\boldsymbol{x}_{it} - \bar{\boldsymbol{x}}_{i\cdot})'(\boldsymbol{x}_{it} - \bar{\boldsymbol{x}}_{i\cdot})]^{-1}\\
&\quad \times [\textstyle\sum_{i=1}^N \sum_{t=1}^T (\boldsymbol{x}_{it} - \bar{\boldsymbol{x}}_{i\cdot})'(y_{it} - \bar{y}_{i\cdot})]\\
&= \widehat{\boldsymbol{\beta}}_W = \boldsymbol{W}_{XX}^{-1}\boldsymbol{W}_{XY},
\end{aligned}$$

$$\begin{aligned}
\widehat{(\boldsymbol{\beta}+\boldsymbol{\lambda})}_{OLS} &= [\textstyle\sum_{i=1}^{N}\sum_{t=1}^{T}(\bar{\boldsymbol{x}}_{i\cdot}-\bar{\boldsymbol{x}})'(\bar{\boldsymbol{x}}_{i\cdot}-\bar{\boldsymbol{x}})]^{-1} \\
&\quad \times [\textstyle\sum_{i=1}^{N}\sum_{t=1}^{T}(\bar{\boldsymbol{x}}_{i\cdot}-\bar{\boldsymbol{x}})'(\bar{y}_{i\cdot}-\bar{y})] \\
&= \widehat{(\boldsymbol{\beta}+\boldsymbol{\lambda})}_{B} = \boldsymbol{B}_{XX}^{-1}\boldsymbol{B}_{XY}, \\
\widehat{\boldsymbol{\lambda}}_{OLS} &= \widehat{(\boldsymbol{\beta}+\boldsymbol{\lambda})}_{OLS} - \widehat{\boldsymbol{\beta}}_{OLS} = \boldsymbol{B}_{XX}^{-1}\boldsymbol{B}_{XY} - \boldsymbol{W}_{XX}^{-1}\boldsymbol{W}_{XY}.
\end{aligned}$$

Again, OLS and GLS give identical estimators: GLS on (6.12) can be implemented as OLS after deducting from all observations a share μ_B of the individual mean. This leaves $(y_{it}-\bar{y}_{i\cdot})$ and $(\boldsymbol{x}_{it}-\bar{\boldsymbol{x}}_{i\cdot})$ unchanged, while $\bar{y}_{i\cdot}$ and $\bar{\boldsymbol{x}}_{i\cdot}$ are multiplied by $(1-\mu_B)=\sqrt{\theta_B}$. Since regressing $\sqrt{\theta_B}\bar{y}_{i\cdot}$ on $\sqrt{\theta_B}\bar{\boldsymbol{x}}_{i\cdot}$ is equivalent to regressing $\bar{y}_{i\cdot}$ on $\bar{\boldsymbol{x}}_{i\cdot}$, the generalizations of (6.7)–(6.9) become

$$\widehat{\boldsymbol{\beta}}_{GLS} = \widehat{\boldsymbol{\beta}}_{W} = \boldsymbol{W}_{XX}^{-1}\boldsymbol{W}_{XY}, \tag{6.13}$$

$$\widehat{(\boldsymbol{\beta}+\boldsymbol{\lambda})}_{GLS} = \widehat{(\boldsymbol{\beta}+\boldsymbol{\lambda})}_{B} = \boldsymbol{B}_{XX}^{-1}\boldsymbol{B}_{XY}, \tag{6.14}$$

$$\widehat{\boldsymbol{\lambda}}_{GLS} = \widehat{(\boldsymbol{\beta}+\boldsymbol{\lambda})}_{GLS} - \widehat{\boldsymbol{\beta}}_{GLS} = \boldsymbol{B}_{XX}^{-1}\boldsymbol{B}_{XY} - \boldsymbol{W}_{XX}^{-1}\boldsymbol{W}_{XY}. \tag{6.15}$$

We therefore conclude:

(i) *The GLS estimator of $\boldsymbol{\beta}$ in (6.11) equals the OLS estimator, which again equals the within estimator obtained from (6.10). Hence, the GLS estimator of $\boldsymbol{\beta}$ when treating α_i as stochastic, with $\mathsf{E}(\alpha_i|\bar{\boldsymbol{x}}_{i\cdot})$ linear in $\bar{\boldsymbol{x}}_{i\cdot}$ is the same as when treating α_i as an unstructured fixed effect.*

(ii) *When $\boldsymbol{\lambda}\neq 0$, GLS on the first equation of (6.10) is inconsistent for $\boldsymbol{\beta}$, because $\bar{\boldsymbol{x}}_{i\cdot}$ is erroneously omitted. GLS estimation of $\boldsymbol{\lambda}$ from (6.11) coincides with OLS, and follows by deducting the within estimator of $\boldsymbol{\beta}$ based on (6.10) from the between estimator.*

It has been forcefully asserted by, e.g., Mundlak (1978), that since GLS estimation of β when $\mathsf{E}(\alpha_i|\boldsymbol{x}_{i1},\dots\boldsymbol{x}_{iT})$ is linear in $\bar{\boldsymbol{x}}_{i\cdot}$ (and otherwise unstructured) corresponds to using the within estimator, no essential difference exists between considering α_i as fixed and considering it as random, since the individual effects are always potentially correlated with the specified regressor(s) ($\boldsymbol{\lambda}\neq 0$ and unstructured). The random effects models in Chapter 3 are from this viewpoint unrealistic. In the following sections, we will examine this rather radical and, to some extent, premature conclusion more closely and modify it.

So far all regressors have been assumed two-dimensional. The identification problems created by the interplay between fixed effects and unidimensional regressors, discussed in Chapter 5, may create identification problems which carry over to models with random effects correlated with the regressors. This will be shown in Section 6.3. Sections 6.4 and 6.5 discuss ways of handling these problems.

6.3 Models with time-invariant regressors

6.3.1 A SIMPLE CASE

We include in (6.1) a time-invariant variable z_i, giving

$$y_{it} = k^* + x_{it}\beta + z_i\delta + \alpha_i + u_{it}, \qquad i = 1,\dots,N;\ t = 1,\dots,T, \tag{6.16}$$

where k^*, β, and δ are constants. We assume that $\mathsf{E}(u_{it}|x_{it}, z_i, \alpha_i) = 0$, but allow x_{it}, z_i, α_i to be correlated. One example is that α_i reflects preferences of household i, correlated with both a two-dimensional x_{it}, income or age, and an individual-specific z_i, cohort or a gender dummy, in an *expenditure function* of a commodity. Another example is an equation describing firm performance in which α_i reflects unobserved quality of the labour stock of firm i, correlated with a two-dimensional capital stock, x_{it}, and a firm-specific year of establishment or a dummy for localization, z_i. A third example is to let (6.16) represent a *wage equation* with y_{it} an individual wage rate, explained by a measure of work experience, x_{it}, and a measure of the length, intensity, or quality of education, z_i, while α_i represents ability, intelligence, etc. Work experience (observable) as well as education (observable) and ability and intelligence (unobservable) are likely to affect the wage rate, and the length of education and ability are most likely correlated. Clever persons, on average, choose longer and more challenging education than less clever ones; confer the comments to Table 6.1. In such a model, δ can be taken to represent the (marginal) returns to education when controlling for ability.[4]

In all these examples our aim is to assess the partial effect of x_{it} and z_i on y_{it}—provided it is possible. We do not want our estimates of β and δ in (6.16) to be 'polluted' by the correlation between (x_{it}, z_i) and α_i. To formalize this we extend (6.2)–(6.3) to

$$\begin{aligned} &\alpha_i = [\bar{x}_{i\cdot} - \mathsf{E}(\bar{x}_{i\cdot})]\lambda + [z_i - \mathsf{E}(z_i)]\pi + w_i, \\ &(u_{it}|X, Z) \sim \mathsf{IID}(0, \sigma^2), \quad (w_i|X, Z) \sim \mathsf{IID}(0, \sigma_w^2), \quad u_{it} \perp w_i, \end{aligned} \tag{6.17}$$

where λ and π are constants and w_i is a disturbance. Conditional on $\boldsymbol{x}_i$ and z_i, the expectation of α_i cannot be i-invariant, since

$$\begin{aligned} \mathsf{E}(\alpha_i|\boldsymbol{x}_i, z_i) &= [\bar{x}_{i\cdot} - \mathsf{E}(\bar{x}_{i\cdot})]\lambda + [z_i - \mathsf{E}(z_i)]\pi, \\ \mathsf{E}(\alpha_i) &= 0, \\ \operatorname{var}(\alpha_i|\boldsymbol{x}_i, z_i) &= \sigma_w^2, \\ \operatorname{var}(\alpha_i) &= \operatorname{var}(\bar{x}_{i\cdot})\lambda^2 + \operatorname{var}(z_i)\pi^2 + 2\operatorname{cov}(\bar{x}_{i\cdot}, z_i)\lambda\pi + \sigma_w^2. \end{aligned}$$

[4] Early examples following this line of attack, explaining wage rates by, *inter alia*, education and ability, are discussed in Griliches (1977).

Assuming $\mathsf{E}(\bar{x}_{i\cdot}) = \mu_x$ and $\mathsf{E}(z_i) = \mu_z$ $(i = 1, \dots, N)$, the model can be condensed into the following generalization of (6.4):

$$\begin{aligned} &y_{it} = k + x_{it}\beta + \bar{x}_{i\cdot}\lambda + z_i(\delta+\pi) + w_i + u_{it}, \; k = k^* - \mu_x\lambda - \mu_z\pi, \\ &(u_{it}|X, Z) \sim \mathsf{IID}(0, \sigma^2), \;\; (w_i|X, Z) \sim \mathsf{IID}(0, \sigma_w^2), \;\;\; u_{it} \perp w_i, \\ &i = 1, \dots, N; \; t = 1, \dots, T. \end{aligned} \tag{6.18}$$

Hence, using (6.16) in estimating β and proceeding as if α_i is uncorrelated with x_{it} and z_i when (6.17) holds, can be interpreted as erroneously omitting $\bar{x}_{i\cdot}$ and neglecting the changed interpretation of the coefficient of z_i. The resulting generalization of (6.5) is

$$\begin{aligned} (y_{it} - \bar{y}_{i\cdot}) + \bar{y}_{i\cdot} &= k + (x_{it} - \bar{x}_{i\cdot})\beta + \bar{x}_{i\cdot}(\beta+\lambda) + z_i(\delta+\pi) + \varepsilon_{it}, \\ \varepsilon_{it} = w_i + u_{it}, \;\;\; &(u_{it}|X, Z) \sim \mathsf{IID}(0, \sigma^2), \;\;\; (w_i|X, Z) \sim \mathsf{IID}(0, \sigma_w^2), \end{aligned} \tag{6.19}$$

where $(\bar{y}_{i\cdot}, \bar{x}_{i\cdot}, z_i)$ are uncorrelated with $(y_{it} - \bar{y}_{i\cdot}, x_{it} - \bar{x}_{i\cdot})$. Feasible estimation methods for β, $(\beta+\lambda)$, and $(\delta+\pi)$ are OLS or GLS.

We are then led, by an argument similar to that in Section 6.2.1, to estimate β by regressing $y_{it} - \bar{y}_{i\cdot}$ on $x_{it} - \bar{x}_{i\cdot}$ and to estimate $(\beta+\lambda)$ and $(\delta+\pi)$ by regressing $\bar{y}_{i\cdot}$ on $\bar{x}_{i\cdot}$ and z_i, which gives

$$\widehat{\beta}_{OLS} = \widehat{\beta}_W = \frac{W_{XY}}{W_{XX}},$$

$$\begin{bmatrix} \widehat{(\beta+\lambda)}_{OLS} \\ \widehat{(\delta+\pi)}_{OLS} \end{bmatrix} = \begin{bmatrix} \widehat{(\beta+\lambda)}_B \\ \widehat{(\delta+\pi)}_B \end{bmatrix} = \begin{bmatrix} B_{XX} & B_{XZ} \\ B_{ZX} & B_{ZZ} \end{bmatrix}^{-1} \begin{bmatrix} B_{XY} \\ B_{ZY} \end{bmatrix},$$

$$\widehat{\lambda}_{OLS} = \widehat{(\beta+\lambda)}_{OLS} - \widehat{\beta}_{OLS} = \widehat{(\beta+\lambda)}_B - \widehat{\beta}_W.$$

These estimates are unbiased and consistent for, respectively, β, $\beta+\lambda$, $\delta+\pi$, and λ. If δ and π are *a priori* unknown, only their sum can be identified.

Still GLS and OLS give identical estimators: GLS can be implemented as OLS after deducting from all observations a share μ_B of the individual means, which leaves $(y_{it} - \bar{y}_{i\cdot})$ and $(x_{it} - \bar{x}_{i\cdot})$ unaffected, while $\bar{y}_{i\cdot}$, $\bar{x}_{i\cdot}$ and z_i are multiplied by $(1 - \mu_B) = \sqrt{\theta_B}$. Since regressing $\sqrt{\theta_B}\bar{y}_{i\cdot}$ on $(\sqrt{\theta_B}\bar{x}_{i\cdot}, \sqrt{\theta_B}z_i)$ implies regressing $\bar{y}_{i\cdot}$ on $(\bar{x}_{i\cdot}, z_i)$, we have the following generalization of (6.7)–(6.9):

$$\widehat{\beta}_{GLS} = \widehat{\beta}_W = \frac{W_{XY}}{W_{XX}}, \tag{6.20}$$

$$\begin{bmatrix} \widehat{(\beta+\lambda)}_{GLS} \\ \widehat{(\delta+\pi)}_{GLS} \end{bmatrix} = \begin{bmatrix} \widehat{(\beta+\lambda)}_B \\ \widehat{(\delta+\pi)}_B \end{bmatrix} = \begin{bmatrix} B_{XX} & B_{XZ} \\ B_{ZX} & B_{ZZ} \end{bmatrix}^{-1} \begin{bmatrix} B_{XY} \\ B_{ZY} \end{bmatrix}, \tag{6.21}$$

Table 6.2 Wage equation example: including education

	OLS	RE, FGLS	FE, Within	Between
exper	0.01305	0.05742	0.09693	0.01001
	(0.00058)	(0.00111)	(0.00119)	(0.00130)
educ	0.07640	0.11449	–	0.07380
	(0.00228)	(0.00625)		(0.00504)

Notes: RE = Random effects.
FE = Fixed effects.
Standard errors in parentheses

$$\widehat{\lambda}_{GLS} = (\widehat{\beta+\lambda})_{GLS} - \widehat{\beta}_{GLS} = (\widehat{\beta+\lambda})_B - \widehat{\beta}_W. \tag{6.22}$$

Example *(continued)*: We continue the wage equation example in Table 6.1, by including in the equation an obviously omitted variable, the length of education, (educ). It is time invariant and comes out with a clear effect when accounted for in OLS, FGLS, and between estimation. The results are given in Table 6.2. The correlation coefficients of the three variables involved (taken across all observations),

(lwage, exper): 0.2093, (lwage, educ): 0.3939, (exper, educ): -0.2182,

show that both educ and exper are positively correlated with lwage, while being negatively correlated. This extended model therefore implies $\widehat{\lambda} = 0.01001 - 0.09693 = -0.08692$ (for exper), while π (for educ) is unidentified. The estimate of the coefficient of educ, $\delta+\pi$, represents the joint impact of an additional year of education (δ) and the fact that able persons usually take longer education (π). Concluding that the implied annual education premium is as large as 8% (OLS) or 11% (GLS) would then be unjustified.

6.3.2 GENERALIZATION

We include in Model (6.10) K_1 time-invariant and K_2 two-dimensional regressors, the $(1\times K_1)$-vector z_i, and the $(1\times K_2)$-vector $\boldsymbol{x}_{it}$, giving

$$\begin{aligned}
&y_{it} = k^* + \boldsymbol{x}_{it}\boldsymbol{\beta} + z_i\boldsymbol{\delta} + \alpha_i + u_{it},\\
&\alpha_i = [\bar{\boldsymbol{x}}_{i\cdot} - \mathsf{E}(\bar{\boldsymbol{x}}_{i\cdot})]\boldsymbol{\lambda} + [z_i - \mathsf{E}(z_i)]\boldsymbol{\pi} + w_i,\\
&(u_{it}|X,Z) \sim \mathsf{IID}(0,\sigma^2),\;\; (w_i|X,Z) \sim \mathsf{IID}(0,\sigma_w^2),\;\; u_{it} \perp w_i,\\
&i = 1,\dots,N;\; t = 1,\dots,T,
\end{aligned} \tag{6.23}$$

where k^* is a constant, $\boldsymbol{\beta}$ and $\boldsymbol{\delta}$ are $(K_2 \times 1)$ and $(K_1 \times 1)$ vectors, and $\boldsymbol{\lambda}$ and $\boldsymbol{\pi}$ have the same dimension as $\boldsymbol{\beta}$ and $\boldsymbol{\delta}$. It follows that

$$\begin{aligned} \mathsf{E}(\alpha_i|X,Z) &= [\bar{\boldsymbol{x}}_{i\cdot} - \mathsf{E}(\bar{\boldsymbol{x}}_{i\cdot})]\boldsymbol{\lambda} + [\boldsymbol{z}_i - \mathsf{E}(\boldsymbol{z}_i)]\boldsymbol{\pi}, \\ \mathsf{E}(\alpha_i) &= 0, \\ \mathrm{var}(\alpha_i|X,Z) &= \sigma_w^2, \\ \mathrm{var}(\alpha_i) &= \boldsymbol{\lambda}'\mathsf{V}(\bar{\boldsymbol{x}}_{i\cdot})\boldsymbol{\lambda} + \boldsymbol{\pi}'\mathsf{V}(\boldsymbol{z}_i)\boldsymbol{\pi} + 2\boldsymbol{\lambda}'\mathsf{C}(\bar{\boldsymbol{x}}_{i\cdot},\boldsymbol{z}_i)\boldsymbol{\pi} + \sigma_w^2. \end{aligned}$$

Assuming $\mathsf{E}(\bar{\boldsymbol{x}}_{i\cdot}) = \boldsymbol{\mu}_x$ and $\mathsf{E}(\boldsymbol{z}_i) = \boldsymbol{\mu}_z$ $(i = 1, \dots, N)$, we obtain

$$\begin{aligned} & y_{it} = k + \boldsymbol{x}_{it}\boldsymbol{\beta} + \bar{\boldsymbol{x}}_{i\cdot}\boldsymbol{\lambda} + \boldsymbol{z}_i(\boldsymbol{\delta}+\boldsymbol{\pi}) + w_i + u_{it}, \; k = k^* - \boldsymbol{\mu}_x\boldsymbol{\lambda} - \boldsymbol{\mu}_z\boldsymbol{\delta}, \\ & (u_i|X,Z) \sim \mathsf{IID}(0,\sigma^2), \quad (w_i|X,Z) \sim \mathsf{IID}(0,\sigma_w^2), \quad u_{it} \perp w_i, \\ & i = 1,\dots,N; \; t = 1,\dots,T. \end{aligned} \tag{6.24}$$

If, when estimating $\boldsymbol{\beta}$ and $\boldsymbol{\delta}$ by OLS or GLS, we proceed as if α_i is uncorrelated with $\boldsymbol{x}_{it}$ and $\boldsymbol{z}_i$, we erroneously omit $\bar{\boldsymbol{x}}_{i\cdot}$ and neglect that the coefficient vector of $\boldsymbol{z}_i$ has changed from $\boldsymbol{\delta}$ to $\boldsymbol{\delta}+\boldsymbol{\pi}$.

This leads to the following generalization of (6.19):

$$\begin{aligned} (y_{it} - \bar{y}_{i\cdot}) + \bar{y}_{i\cdot} &= k + (\boldsymbol{x}_{it} - \bar{\boldsymbol{x}}_{i\cdot})\boldsymbol{\beta} + \bar{\boldsymbol{x}}_{i\cdot}(\boldsymbol{\beta}+\boldsymbol{\lambda}) + \boldsymbol{z}_i(\boldsymbol{\delta}+\boldsymbol{\pi}) + \varepsilon_{it}, \\ \varepsilon_{it} = w_i + u_{it}, & \quad (u_i|X,Z) \sim \mathsf{IID}(0,\sigma^2), \quad (w_i|X,Z) \sim \mathsf{IID}(0,\sigma_w^2). \end{aligned} \tag{6.25}$$

Since all elements in $(y_{it} - \bar{y}_{i\cdot}, \boldsymbol{x}_{it} - \bar{\boldsymbol{x}}_{i\cdot})$ are orthogonal to all elements in $(\bar{y}_{i\cdot}, \bar{\boldsymbol{x}}_{i\cdot}, \boldsymbol{z}_i)$, OLS and GLS ensure unbiased and consistent estimation of $\boldsymbol{\beta}$, $(\boldsymbol{\beta}+\boldsymbol{\lambda})$, and $(\boldsymbol{\delta}+\boldsymbol{\pi})$. This simplifies to estimating $\boldsymbol{\beta}$ by regressing $y_{it} - \bar{y}_{i\cdot}$ on $\boldsymbol{x}_{it} - \bar{\boldsymbol{x}}_{i\cdot}$, and $(\boldsymbol{\beta}+\boldsymbol{\lambda})$ and $(\boldsymbol{\delta}+\boldsymbol{\pi})$ by regressing $\bar{y}_{i\cdot}$ on $\bar{\boldsymbol{x}}_{i\cdot}$ and $\boldsymbol{z}_i$.

To elaborate, we need some notation for blocks of partitioned matrices, and symbolize them with bars: $\bar{\boldsymbol{W}}_{XX}$ and $\bar{\boldsymbol{B}}_{XX}$ contain the within (co)variation and the between (co)variation of $\boldsymbol{x}_{it}$, $\bar{\boldsymbol{B}}_{ZZ}$ contains the (co)variation of $\boldsymbol{z}_i$, $\bar{\boldsymbol{B}}_{XZ}$ contains the between covariation of the two-dimensional versus the individual-specific regressors, $\bar{\boldsymbol{W}}_{XY}$ and $\bar{\boldsymbol{B}}_{XY}$ contain the within covariation and the between covariation of $\boldsymbol{x}_{it}$ versus y_{it}, and $\bar{\boldsymbol{B}}_{ZY}$ contains the between covariation of $\boldsymbol{z}_i$ versus y_{it}. We have

$$\widehat{\boldsymbol{\beta}}_{OLS} = \widehat{\boldsymbol{\beta}}_W = \bar{\boldsymbol{W}}_{XX}^{-1}\bar{\boldsymbol{W}}_{XY},$$

$$\begin{bmatrix} \widehat{(\boldsymbol{\beta}+\boldsymbol{\lambda})}_{OLS} \\ \widehat{(\boldsymbol{\delta}+\boldsymbol{\pi})}_{OLS} \end{bmatrix} = \begin{bmatrix} \widehat{(\boldsymbol{\beta}+\boldsymbol{\lambda})}_{B} \\ \widehat{(\boldsymbol{\delta}+\boldsymbol{\pi})}_{B} \end{bmatrix} = \begin{bmatrix} \bar{\boldsymbol{B}}_{XX} & \bar{\boldsymbol{B}}_{XZ} \\ \bar{\boldsymbol{B}}_{ZX} & \bar{\boldsymbol{B}}_{ZZ} \end{bmatrix}^{-1} \begin{bmatrix} \bar{\boldsymbol{B}}_{XY} \\ \bar{\boldsymbol{B}}_{ZY} \end{bmatrix},$$

$$\widehat{\boldsymbol{\lambda}}_{OLS} = \widehat{(\boldsymbol{\beta}+\boldsymbol{\lambda})}_{OLS} - \widehat{\boldsymbol{\beta}}_{OLS} = \widehat{(\boldsymbol{\beta}+\boldsymbol{\lambda})}_{B} - \widehat{\boldsymbol{\beta}}_{W}.$$

GLS estimation implemented as OLS after deducting a share μ_B of the individual means from all observations leaves $(y_{it}-\bar{y}_{i\cdot})$, $(\boldsymbol{x}_{it}-\bar{\boldsymbol{x}}_{i\cdot})$ unaffected, while $\bar{y}_{i\cdot}, \bar{\boldsymbol{x}}_{i\cdot}, \boldsymbol{z}_i$ are multiplied by $(1-\mu_B)=\sqrt{\theta_B}$. Altogether, this gives the following generalization of (6.20)–(6.22):

$$\widehat{\boldsymbol{\beta}}_{GLS} = \widehat{\boldsymbol{\beta}}_W = \bar{W}_{XX}^{-1}\bar{W}_{XY}, \tag{6.26}$$

$$\begin{bmatrix} (\widehat{\boldsymbol{\beta}+\boldsymbol{\lambda}})_{GLS} \\ (\widehat{\boldsymbol{\delta}+\boldsymbol{\pi}})_{GLS} \end{bmatrix} = \begin{bmatrix} (\widehat{\boldsymbol{\beta}+\boldsymbol{\lambda}})_B \\ (\widehat{\boldsymbol{\delta}+\boldsymbol{\pi}})_B \end{bmatrix} = \begin{bmatrix} \bar{B}_{XX} & \bar{B}_{XZ} \\ \bar{B}_{ZX} & \bar{B}_{ZZ} \end{bmatrix}^{-1} \begin{bmatrix} \bar{B}_{XY} \\ \bar{B}_{ZY} \end{bmatrix} \tag{6.27}$$

$$\widehat{\boldsymbol{\lambda}}_{GLS} = (\widehat{\boldsymbol{\beta}+\boldsymbol{\lambda}})_{GLS} - \widehat{\boldsymbol{\beta}}_{GLS} = (\widehat{\boldsymbol{\beta}+\boldsymbol{\lambda}})_B - \widehat{\boldsymbol{\beta}}_W. \tag{6.28}$$

We therefore conclude:

(i) *The GLS estimator of $\boldsymbol{\beta}$ in (6.24) equals the OLS estimator, which also is the within estimator from (6.23). This again emerges by applying OLS on (6.23), while representing $\boldsymbol{z}_i\boldsymbol{\delta}+\alpha_i$ by individual dummies. If $\boldsymbol{\pi}$ is unknown, estimation of $\boldsymbol{\delta}$ is impossible. Only $\boldsymbol{\delta}+\boldsymbol{\pi}$ is identifiable.*

(ii) *The GLS estimators of $\boldsymbol{\beta}+\boldsymbol{\lambda}$ and $\boldsymbol{\delta}+\boldsymbol{\pi}$ in (6.25) equal the OLS estimators, which coincide with the between estimators for $\boldsymbol{\beta}$ and $\boldsymbol{\delta}$ from (6.23). GLS and OLS estimation of $\boldsymbol{\lambda}$ coincide, giving as estimator the difference between the between and the within estimator of $\boldsymbol{\beta}$ obtained from (6.23).*

6.3.3 THE WU–HAUSMAN TEST

Sometimes one may be in doubt whether to choose the parsimonious random effects specification or the far less restrictive and parameter-rich fixed effect alternative for a specific problem. We now consider a test procedure for contrasting the two models formally. As a start, reconsider Model (6.23), with K_1 individual-specific and K_2 two-dimensional explanatory variables, the $(1 \times K_1)$- and $(1 \times K_2)$-vectors $\boldsymbol{z}_i$ and $\boldsymbol{x}_{it}$, and write it as (6.24). The relevant test can be conducted by formulating

$$H_0 : \boldsymbol{\lambda} = \boldsymbol{0}\ (\Longrightarrow \textit{RE acceptable}).$$
$$H_1 : \boldsymbol{\lambda} \neq \boldsymbol{0}\ (\Longrightarrow \textit{RE invalid, FE acceptable}).$$

Under H_0, GLS estimation of (6.24) is MVLUE; the relevant equation reads

$$y_{it} = k + \boldsymbol{x}_{it}\boldsymbol{\beta} + \boldsymbol{z}_i(\boldsymbol{\delta}+\boldsymbol{\pi}) + w_i + u_{it}. \tag{6.29}$$

Under H_1, within estimation of (6.24) is consistent and is, see Section 6.3.2, equivalent to within estimation of (6.29) and GLS estimation of (6.24).

Consider first the following *general test problem*. Two estimators of a $(K \times 1)$ parameter vector $\boldsymbol{\beta}$ based on n observations, $\widehat{\boldsymbol{\beta}}_0$ and $\widehat{\boldsymbol{\beta}}_1$, are available. We formulate H_0 : the regressor vector is uncorrelated with the disturbance, against H_1 : the regressor vector is correlated with the disturbance. The latter may be due to, e.g., the existence of explanatory variables jointly endogenous with y_{it}, or random measurement errors. The estimators have the following properties:

$\widehat{\boldsymbol{\beta}}_0$ is *consistent and efficient* for $\boldsymbol{\beta}$ under H_0, but *inconsistent* under H_1.
$\widehat{\boldsymbol{\beta}}_1$ is *consistent* for $\boldsymbol{\beta}$ under both H_0 and H_1, but *inefficient* under H_0.

Loosely expressed, $\widehat{\boldsymbol{\beta}}_1$ is *more robust to inconsistency* than $\widehat{\boldsymbol{\beta}}_0$. The price to be paid when applying $\widehat{\boldsymbol{\beta}}_1$ is, however, its *loss of efficiency* when H_0 is true and the latter estimator should be preferred. Intuition says that the 'distance' between the vectors $\widehat{\boldsymbol{\beta}}_0$ and $\widehat{\boldsymbol{\beta}}_1$ should 'on average' be 'smaller' when H_0 is true than when H_1 is true. This suggests that we might proceed by estimating $\boldsymbol{\beta}$ by both methods and investigate whether the discrepancy between the estimate vectors seems 'large' or 'small': $\widehat{\boldsymbol{\beta}}_1-\widehat{\boldsymbol{\beta}}_0$ 'large' suggests rejection, and $\widehat{\boldsymbol{\beta}}_1-\widehat{\boldsymbol{\beta}}_0$ 'small' suggests non-rejection of H_0. Such a 'strategy' can be nothing more than an informal approach since it does not prescribe which distances should be judged as 'large' and 'small'. A formal method determining a critical region in a test criterion is needed. At this point the Wu–Hausman test is called upon.

The test essentially examines whether the discrepancy between $\widehat{\boldsymbol{\beta}}_1$ and $\widehat{\boldsymbol{\beta}}_0$, $\widehat{\boldsymbol{\Delta}}=\widehat{\boldsymbol{\beta}}_1-\widehat{\boldsymbol{\beta}}_0$ is statistically large enough to call H_0 into doubt. Hausman (1978), building on Wu (1973), showed that: (i) *asymptotically*, the discrepancy vector and the preferred estimator under H_0, $\widehat{\boldsymbol{\beta}}_0$, are uncorrelated: $C(\widehat{\boldsymbol{\beta}}_0, \widehat{\boldsymbol{\Delta}})=\mathbf{0} \Longrightarrow \mathsf{V}(\widehat{\boldsymbol{\beta}}_1-\widehat{\boldsymbol{\beta}}_0)=\mathsf{V}(\widehat{\boldsymbol{\beta}}_1)-\mathsf{V}(\widehat{\boldsymbol{\beta}}_0)$; and (ii) *under* H_0 we have:

$$\sqrt{n}(\widehat{\boldsymbol{\beta}}_0-\boldsymbol{\beta}) \stackrel{d}{\rightarrow} \mathcal{N}(\mathbf{0}, V_0),\ \sqrt{n}(\widehat{\boldsymbol{\beta}}_1-\boldsymbol{\beta}) \stackrel{d}{\rightarrow} \mathcal{N}(\mathbf{0}, V_1),$$

$$V_1 - V_0 \text{ is positive definite,}$$

$$S = \mathsf{V}(\widehat{\boldsymbol{\beta}}_1 - \widehat{\boldsymbol{\beta}}_0) = \mathsf{V}(\widehat{\boldsymbol{\beta}}_1)-\mathsf{V}(\widehat{\boldsymbol{\beta}}_0) \text{ is positive definite,}$$

$$Q = n(\widehat{\boldsymbol{\beta}}_1-\widehat{\boldsymbol{\beta}}_0)'\widehat{S}^{-1}(\widehat{\boldsymbol{\beta}}_1-\widehat{\boldsymbol{\beta}}_0) \stackrel{d}{\rightarrow} \chi^2(K),$$

where $\widehat{S}$ is a consistent estimator of $S=\mathsf{V}(\widehat{\boldsymbol{\Delta}})=\mathsf{V}(\widehat{\boldsymbol{\beta}}_1-\widehat{\boldsymbol{\beta}}_0)$. The quadratic form Q is a scalar measure of the distance between the vectors. Then, under H_0, Q is approximately distributed as χ^2 with K degrees of freedom, and tends to be larger under H_1 than under H_0. The test criterion therefore becomes: reject H_0, at a level of significance ε, when $Q > \chi^2_{1-\varepsilon}(K)$.

Leaving the general test problem, we return to the panel data model and let $\widehat{\boldsymbol{\beta}}_{GLS}$ and $\widehat{(\boldsymbol{\delta}+\boldsymbol{\pi})}_{GLS}$ be the GLS estimators of $\boldsymbol{\beta}$ and $\boldsymbol{\delta}+\boldsymbol{\pi}$ under H_0 ($\boldsymbol{\lambda}=\mathbf{0}$, random effects specification valid), i.e., obtained from (6.29). Let $\widehat{\boldsymbol{\beta}}_W$ be the within estimator of $\boldsymbol{\beta}$

under H_1 ($\boldsymbol{\lambda}$ unrestricted, fixed effects specification valid), i.e., obtained from (6.24). This estimator is then consistent and efficient. The estimators symbolized by $(\widehat{\boldsymbol{\beta}}_0, \widehat{\boldsymbol{\beta}}_1)$ in the general case correspond to $(\widehat{\boldsymbol{\beta}}_{GLS}, \widehat{\boldsymbol{\beta}}_W)$ in the panel data case. This is because when $\boldsymbol{\lambda}$ is unknown, the GLS estimator coincides with the within estimator, and the within estimator of $\boldsymbol{\delta}+\boldsymbol{\pi}$ does not exist, and hence cannot be subject to test: $H_0 : \boldsymbol{\lambda} = \mathbf{0}$ seems 'unlikely' when $|\widehat{\boldsymbol{\beta}}_W - \widehat{\boldsymbol{\beta}}_{GLS}|$ is 'large', and the test statistic becomes

$$Q = NT(\widehat{\boldsymbol{\beta}}_W - \widehat{\boldsymbol{\beta}}_{GLS})'\widehat{\mathbf{S}}^{-1}(\widehat{\boldsymbol{\beta}}_W - \widehat{\boldsymbol{\beta}}_{GLS}) \xrightarrow{d} \chi^2(K_2) \text{ under } H_0,$$

where $\widehat{\mathbf{S}}$ is a consistent estimator of $\mathsf{V}(\widehat{\boldsymbol{\beta}}_W - \widehat{\boldsymbol{\beta}}_{GLS})$ under H_0.

Example: We want to explore the possible relationship between petrol consumption per car (`gaspercar`) and income per capita (`incpercap`), relative petrol price (`realgaspr`) (all in logs), and the number of cars per capita (`carpercap`), using panel data for 18 OECD countries, years 1960–78: $N=18$, $T=19$ (*data source: Baltagi (2005), Table F9.2; see Baltagi and Griffin (1983)*). A likely hypothesis is that the three regressors are correlated with the country-specific effect, violating the random effects specification (no time-invariant variables occur). Estimation results are given in Table 6.3, columns 1 and 2, while column 3 gives the difference between the within and the FGLS estimates, with their standard errors. For the two first regressors, the difference is substantial. First, according to both models, absence of heterogeneity is strongly rejected: the F-statistic (with 17 and 321 degrees of freedom) for the fixed effects model is 84, while the χ^2-distributed Wald-test-statistic (with 3 degrees of freedom) for the random effects model is 1642, both having $p = 0.0000$. Second, the χ^2-statistic for the Hausman test (with 3 degrees of freedom) is 303, corresponding to $p = 0.0000$, so that zero correlation between the latent country-specific heterogeneity in petrol consumption and the regressor vector is clearly rejected.

Table 6.3 Fixed vs. Random effects: petrol consumption. Input in Wu–Hausman-test (regressand=gaspercar)

	FE, Within	RE, FGLS	Difference
`incpercap`	0.6622 (0.0734)	0.5550 (0.0591)	0.1072 (0.0435)
`realgaspr`	–0.3217 (0.0441)	–0.4204 (0.0400)	0.0987 (0.0186)
`carpercap`	–0.6405 (0.0297)	–0.6068 (0.0255)	–0.0336 (0.0152)

Notes: RE = Random effects.
FE = Fixed effects.
Standard errors in parentheses

6.4 Exploiting instruments: Initial attempts

We have considered GLS and within estimation of suitably transformed equations as remedies to handle latent heterogeneity correlated with observed regressors. Such correlation, frequently labelled 'endogeneity'—regressors correlated with *only* the α_i component of the gross disturbance α_i+u_{it}, sometimes labelled '*single endogeneity*'—may well motivate the use of IVs. This, however, is a rather shallow motivation for calling upon IVs unless we invoke some theory supplementing the equation under consideration.

We now pursue this IV-approach, proceeding stepwise. The first models rely on rigid assumptions, but serve to put the more attractive models, and the more complex methods they require, in perspective. We first explore the case with one two-dimensional and one time-invariant explanatory variable (Section 6.4.1), the latter correlated with the individual effects; next, we extend from scalars to vectors *of equal dimension* (Section 6.4.2); and finally, we give a reinterpretation (Section 6.4.3). Further generalizations to models of arbitrary dimension, and with arbitrary subsets of two-dimensional and time-invariant explanatory variables subject to such 'endogeneity', are considered in Section 6.5, giving more elaborate applications of IVs and combining them with other methods.

6.4.1 A SIMPLE EXAMPLE

Returning to the model in Section 6.3.1, we consider

$$\begin{aligned}
&y_{it} = k^* + x_{it}\beta + z_i\delta + \alpha_i + u_{it},\\
&\mathsf{E}(u_{it}|X,Z,\alpha_i) = 0, \quad \mathsf{E}(\alpha_i|X) = 0,\\
&i = 1,\dots,N;\ t = 1,\dots,T.
\end{aligned} \tag{6.30}$$

While in Model (6.16)–(6.17) correlation between x_{it}, z_i, α_i was allowed, our assumptions now imply that α_i *is uncorrelated with* x_{it}, while α_i and z_i are allowed to be correlated, which corresponds to, respectively, $\lambda=0$ and π unrestricted in (6.17). For the wage equation example these assumptions would imply that work experience and ability are uncorrelated,[5] while both are correlated with the length of the education period.

We proceed in two steps: first, estimate β by the within estimator; next estimate δ by using an IV. Since the within transformation eliminates z_i and α_i, the first step gives, see (6.20),

[5] This, admittedly, is a strong assumption, especially if the panel contains some young persons, who, because of having a long education period, may not yet have had time for a long working career. It could have been controlled for by, e.g., including age and job characteristics as regressors, if such variables were in the data set.

$$\widehat{\beta} = \widehat{\beta}_W = \frac{\sum_{i=1}^{N}\sum_{t=1}^{T}(x_{it}-\bar{x}_{i\cdot})(y_{it}-\bar{y}_{i\cdot})}{\sum_{i=1}^{N}\sum_{t=1}^{T}(x_{it}-\bar{x}_{i\cdot})^2} = \frac{W_{XY}}{W_{XX}}. \tag{6.31}$$

An alternative interpretation of this step is that $x_{it}-\bar{x}_{i\cdot}$ is an IV for x_{it}, since an equivalent expression is

$$\widehat{\beta} = \frac{\sum_{i=1}^{N}\sum_{t=1}^{T}(x_{it}-\bar{x}_{i\cdot})y_{it}}{\sum_{i=1}^{N}\sum_{t=1}^{T}(x_{it}-\bar{x}_{i\cdot})x_{it}}.$$

For the second step we construct

$$\bar{d}_{i\cdot} = \bar{y}_{i\cdot} - \bar{x}_{i\cdot}\widehat{\beta} = k^* + z_i\delta + \alpha_i + \bar{u}_{i\cdot} - \bar{x}_{i\cdot}(\widehat{\beta}-\beta),$$

and from this equation estimate δ by using $\bar{x}_{i\cdot}$ as IV for z_i. We then utilize that the two variables are theoretically correlated, while $\bar{x}_{i\cdot}$ is asymptotically uncorrelated with $\alpha_i + \bar{u}_{i\cdot} - \bar{x}_{i\cdot}(\widehat{\beta}-\beta)$ because $\widehat{\beta}$ is N-consistent. This gives

$$\widehat{\delta} = \frac{\sum_{i=1}^{N}\sum_{t=1}^{T}(\bar{x}_{i\cdot}-\bar{x})(d_{it}-\bar{d})}{\sum_{i=1}^{N}\sum_{t=1}^{T}(\bar{x}_{i\cdot}-\bar{x})(z_i-\bar{z})} \equiv \frac{B_{XD}}{B_{XZ}}. \tag{6.32}$$

Since $B_{XD}=B_{XY}-B_{XX}\widehat{\beta}$, the estimator can be written as

$$\widehat{\delta} = \frac{B_{XY}-B_{XX}\widehat{\beta}}{B_{XZ}} = \frac{\dfrac{B_{XY}}{B_{XX}} - \dfrac{W_{XY}}{W_{XX}}}{\dfrac{B_{XZ}}{B_{XX}}}. \tag{6.33}$$

6.4.2 GENERALIZATION

We extend the scalar regressors in (6.30) to $(1 \times K)$-vectors, $\boldsymbol{x}_{it}$ and $\boldsymbol{z}_i$, giving

$$\begin{aligned} &y_{it} = k^* + \boldsymbol{x}_{it}\boldsymbol{\beta} + \boldsymbol{z}_i\boldsymbol{\delta} + \alpha_i + u_{it},\\ &\mathsf{E}(u_{it}|X,Z,\alpha_i) = 0, \quad \mathsf{E}(\alpha_i|X) = 0,\\ &i = 1,\dots,N;\ t = 1,\dots,T, \end{aligned} \tag{6.34}$$

where k^* is a constant and $\boldsymbol{\beta}$ and $\boldsymbol{\delta}$ are $(K \times 1)$ vectors. Rather than letting $(\boldsymbol{x}_{it}, \boldsymbol{z}_i, \alpha_i)$ be correlated, we assume that α_i is uncorrelated with $\boldsymbol{x}_{it}$ and allow it to be correlated with $\boldsymbol{z}_i$, corresponding to imposing on (6.23) $\boldsymbol{\lambda} = \boldsymbol{0}$ and having $\boldsymbol{\pi}$ unrestricted.

In the first step we *estimate* $\boldsymbol{\beta}$ *by the within estimator*

$$\widehat{\boldsymbol{\beta}} = \boldsymbol{W}_{XX}^{-1}\boldsymbol{W}_{XY}, \tag{6.35}$$

and construct

$$\bar{d}_{i\cdot} = \bar{y}_{i\cdot} - \bar{\boldsymbol{x}}_{i\cdot}\widehat{\boldsymbol{\beta}} = k^* + \boldsymbol{z}_i\boldsymbol{\delta} + \alpha_i + \bar{u}_{i\cdot} - \bar{\boldsymbol{x}}_{i\cdot}(\widehat{\boldsymbol{\beta}} - \boldsymbol{\beta}).$$

In the second step, we estimate $\boldsymbol{\delta}$, using in this equation $\bar{\boldsymbol{x}}_{i\cdot}$ as IV vector for $\boldsymbol{z}_i$, giving

$$\begin{aligned}\widehat{\boldsymbol{\delta}} &= [\textstyle\sum_i\sum_t(\bar{\boldsymbol{x}}_{i\cdot}-\bar{\boldsymbol{x}})'(\boldsymbol{z}_i-\bar{\boldsymbol{z}})]^{-1}[\sum_i\sum_t(\bar{\boldsymbol{x}}_{i\cdot}-\bar{\boldsymbol{x}})'(\bar{d}_{i\cdot}-\bar{d})]\\ &= \boldsymbol{B}_{XZ}^{-1}\boldsymbol{B}_{XD}.\end{aligned} \tag{6.36}$$

Since $\boldsymbol{B}_{XD} = \boldsymbol{B}_{XY} - \boldsymbol{B}_{XX}\widehat{\boldsymbol{\beta}}$, it follows that

$$\begin{aligned}\widehat{\boldsymbol{\delta}} &= \boldsymbol{B}_{XZ}^{-1}[\boldsymbol{B}_{XY} - \boldsymbol{B}_{XX}\widehat{\boldsymbol{\beta}}]\\ &= \boldsymbol{B}_{XZ}^{-1}\boldsymbol{B}_{XX}[\boldsymbol{B}_{XX}^{-1}\boldsymbol{B}_{XY} - \boldsymbol{W}_{XX}^{-1}\boldsymbol{W}_{XY}].\end{aligned} \tag{6.37}$$

Equations (6.35)–(6.37) generalize (6.31)–(6.33).

Consistency of $\widehat{\boldsymbol{\delta}}$ is easily shown. From (6.37), inserting $\boldsymbol{B}_{XY} = \boldsymbol{B}_{XX}\boldsymbol{\beta} + \boldsymbol{B}_{XZ}\boldsymbol{\delta} + \boldsymbol{B}_{X\alpha} + \boldsymbol{B}_{XU}$, we get

$$\widehat{\boldsymbol{\delta}} = \boldsymbol{\delta} + \boldsymbol{B}_{XZ}^{-1}[\boldsymbol{B}_{X\alpha} + \boldsymbol{B}_{XU} - \boldsymbol{B}_{XX}(\widehat{\boldsymbol{\beta}} - \boldsymbol{\beta})].$$

Since, for $N \to \infty$, $\text{plim}(\frac{1}{NT}\boldsymbol{B}_{X\alpha})$ and $\text{plim}(\frac{1}{NT}\boldsymbol{B}_{XU})$ are zero vectors and $\text{plim}(\frac{1}{NT}\boldsymbol{B}_{XZ})$ is non-singular, then $\text{plim}(\widehat{\boldsymbol{\delta}}) = \boldsymbol{\delta}$. Essential for this conclusion is the assumption $\text{plim}(\frac{1}{NT}\boldsymbol{B}_{X\alpha}) = \boldsymbol{0}_{K1}$.

This estimation procedure for $\boldsymbol{\beta}$ and $\boldsymbol{\delta}$ relies on $\boldsymbol{x}_{it}$ and $\boldsymbol{z}_i$ having the same dimension, making $\boldsymbol{B}_{XZ}$ quadratic. A reinterpretation, using an auxiliary equation to represent the correlation of $(\boldsymbol{z}_i, \bar{\boldsymbol{x}}_{i\cdot}, \alpha_i)$, is given below.

6.4.3 REINTERPRETATION USING A RECURSIVE SYSTEM

We reformulate the model as a two-equation, recursive system, whose second equation, in one individual-specific variable and one individual-specific mean, in some cases may be given a structural interpretation.

Reconsidering the simple scalar case in Section 6.4.1, we formulate the model's second equation as

$$z_i = \mu_0 + \bar{x}_{i\cdot}\mu + \alpha_i\eta + \kappa_i, \quad \mathsf{E}(\kappa_{it}|\bar{x}_{i\cdot}, \alpha_i) = 0, \quad \kappa_i \perp u_{it}, \tag{6.38}$$

where (μ_0, μ, η) are constants, and the recursivity follows from $\kappa_i \perp u_{it}$. Inserting (6.38) in (6.30) gives the reduced form equation

$$\begin{aligned} y_{it} &= k + x_{it}\beta + \bar{x}_{i\cdot}\mu\delta + \alpha_i^* + u_{it} \implies \\ (y_{it} - \bar{y}_{i\cdot}) + \bar{y}_{i\cdot} &= k + (x_{it} - \bar{x}_{i\cdot})\beta + \bar{x}_{i\cdot}(\beta + \mu\delta) + \varepsilon_{it}, \end{aligned}$$

where

$$\begin{aligned} k &= k^* + \mu_0\delta, \\ \alpha_i^* &= \alpha_i(1+\eta\delta) + \kappa_i\delta, \\ \varepsilon_{it} &= \alpha_i^* + u_{it}. \end{aligned}$$

Applying OLS (=GLS), confer (6.7)–(6.8), we get

$$\begin{aligned} \widehat{\beta} &= \frac{W_{XY}}{W_{XX}}, \\ \widehat{(\beta + \mu\delta)} &= \frac{B_{XY}}{B_{XX}}. \end{aligned} \tag{6.39}$$

To estimate μ we use OLS on (6.38) and obtain

$$\widehat{\mu} = \frac{B_{XZ}}{B_{XX}}, \tag{6.40}$$

which in combination with (6.39) gives the following estimator of δ:

$$\widetilde{\delta} = \frac{\widehat{(\beta + \mu\delta)} - \widehat{\beta}}{\widehat{\mu}}, \tag{6.41}$$

This expression is identical to (6.33).

Reconsidering the generalization in Section 6.4.2, we formulate the following second block of the block-recursive system in individual-specific variables (or means)

$$z_i = \boldsymbol{\mu}_0 + \bar{\boldsymbol{x}}_{i\cdot}\boldsymbol{\mu} + \alpha_i\boldsymbol{\eta} + \boldsymbol{\kappa}_i, \quad \mathsf{E}(\kappa_{it}|\bar{x}_{i\cdot}, \alpha_i) = 0, \quad \boldsymbol{\kappa}_i \perp u_{it}, \tag{6.42}$$

where $\boldsymbol{\mu}_0$, $\boldsymbol{\mu}$, $\boldsymbol{\eta}$ are matrices of constants, $\boldsymbol{\kappa}_i$ is an error vector, and the block-recursivity follows from $\boldsymbol{\kappa}_i \perp u_{it}$. Inserting (6.42) in (6.34) gives the reduced form equation

$$\begin{aligned} y_{it} &= k + \boldsymbol{x}_{it}\boldsymbol{\beta} + \bar{\boldsymbol{x}}_{i\cdot}\boldsymbol{\mu}\boldsymbol{\delta} + \alpha_i^* + u_{it} \implies \\ (y_{it} - \bar{y}_{i\cdot}) + \bar{y}_{i\cdot} &= k + (\boldsymbol{x}_{it} - \bar{\boldsymbol{x}}_{i\cdot})\boldsymbol{\beta} + \bar{\boldsymbol{x}}_{i\cdot}(\boldsymbol{\beta} + \boldsymbol{\mu}\boldsymbol{\delta}) + \varepsilon_{it}, \end{aligned}$$

where

$$k = k^* + \mu_0 \delta,$$
$$\alpha_i^* = \alpha_i(1 + \eta\delta) + \kappa_i \delta$$
$$\varepsilon_{it} = \alpha_i^* + u_{it}.$$

Applying OLS (=GLS), confer (6.13)–(6.14), we get

$$\begin{aligned} \widehat{\beta} &= W_{XX}^{-1} W_{XY}, \\ (\widehat{\beta + \mu\delta}) &= B_{XX}^{-1} B_{XY}. \end{aligned} \tag{6.43}$$

We estimate μ consistently by OLS on (6.42) and get

$$\widehat{\mu} = B_{XX}^{-1} B_{XZ}, \tag{6.44}$$

which in combination with (6.43) gives the following estimator of the 'structural' coefficient vector

$$\widetilde{\delta} = \widehat{\mu}^{-1}[(\widehat{\beta + \mu\delta}) - \widehat{\beta}]. \tag{6.45}$$

This expression is identical to (6.37).

6.5 Exploiting instruments: Further steps

In this final section we consider a framework which contains all models in Sections 6.2–6.4 as special cases. It is practically more appealing than the framework in Section 6.4, which restricted $\boldsymbol{x}_{it}$ and z_i to have the same dimension and $\boldsymbol{x}_{it}$ and α_i to be uncorrelated. Now we let *the explanatory variables which are correlated with α_i include both two-dimensional and time-invariant variables* and do not restrict $\boldsymbol{x}_{it}$ and z_i (as well as $\boldsymbol{\beta}$ and $\boldsymbol{\delta}$) to have the same dimension. This extension requires a slight modification of the notation.

The size of the vectors of variables and coefficients will be indicated as follows. C_d and U_d are the number of variables of dimension $d\,(d=1,2)$ which are, respectively, *correlated (C)* and *uncorrelated (U)* with α_i. The $(1\times U_2)$-vector $\boldsymbol{x}_{Uit}$ and the $(1\times U_1)$-vector z_{Ui} contain, respectively, the two-dimensional and the time-invariant variables which are *uncorrelated* with α_i, and the $(1\times C_2)$-vector $\boldsymbol{x}_{Cit}$ and the $(1\times C_1)$-vector z_{Ci} contain, respectively, the two-dimensional and the time-invariant variables which are *correlated* with α_i.

In this framework, the fixed effects and the random effects specifications *emerge as two extremes*: the former by allowing for correlation between latent heterogeneity and *all* regressors, the latter by imposing zero correlation throughout. In other words, with respect to the correlation allowed for, they are 'all or nothing' cases. The model's applicability is then substantially extended. On the other hand, it gives the user the challenge to motivate theoretically in which 'basket' to put the two sets of variables.

The extended model is

$$\begin{aligned} & y_{it} = k^* + \boldsymbol{x}_{Uit}\boldsymbol{\beta}_U + \boldsymbol{x}_{Cit}\boldsymbol{\beta}_C + \boldsymbol{z}_{Ui}\boldsymbol{\delta}_U + \boldsymbol{z}_{Ci}\boldsymbol{\delta}_C + \epsilon_{it}, \\ & \epsilon_{it} = \alpha_i + u_{it}, \ \alpha_i \perp u_{it} \\ & (u_{it}|X,Z) \sim \mathsf{IID}(0,\sigma^2), \quad (\alpha_i|X_U,Z_U) \sim \mathsf{IID}(0,\sigma_\alpha^2), \\ & i = 1,\dots,N; \ t = 1,\dots,T, \end{aligned} \tag{6.46}$$

where X_U and Z_U are matrices containing all values of $\boldsymbol{x}_{Uit}$ and $\boldsymbol{z}_{Ui}$, respectively, X and Z are the matrix containing X_U, Z_U, X_C and Z_C, while $\boldsymbol{\beta}_U$ $(U_2 \times 1)$, $\boldsymbol{\beta}_C$ $(C_2 \times 1)$, $\boldsymbol{\delta}_U$ $(U_1 \times 1)$, and $\boldsymbol{\delta}_C$ $(C_1 \times 1)$ are associated coefficient vectors, and k^* is an intercept. We assume that the disturbance u_{it} is uncorrelated with all regressors as well as with the latent effect α_i: $\boldsymbol{x}_{Uit}$ and $\boldsymbol{z}_{Ui}$ are *doubly exogenous*, while for $\boldsymbol{x}_{Cit}$ and $\boldsymbol{z}_{Ci}$ *single endogeneity* and *single exogeneity* are assumed, as $\mathsf{E}(u_{it}|X_C, Z_C) = 0$ is implied.

The models in Sections 6.3 and 6.4 are special cases. In *Section 6.3* we had no variables uncorrelated with α_i, imposing $U_1 = U_2 = 0$. We then concluded that estimation of the coefficients of the time-invariant variables is infeasible, whilst the coefficients of the two-dimensional variables could be identified. In *Section 6.4* neither time-invariant variables uncorrelated with α_i nor two-dimensional variables correlated with α_i occurred, and in addition there was an equal number of individual-specific variables (correlated with α_i) and of two-dimensional variables (uncorrelated with α_i), i.e., $U_1 = C_2 = 0$, $U_2 = C_1$ $(= K)$. We then concluded that consistent estimation of the coefficients of both the U_2 $(=K)$ two-dimensional and the C_1 $(=K)$ individual-specific variables was within reach.

The core question for the present model becomes: is identification possible, and in particular, when are all of $\boldsymbol{\beta}_U$, $\boldsymbol{\beta}_C$, $\boldsymbol{\delta}_U$, and $\boldsymbol{\delta}_C$ identifiable?

6.5.1 CHOOSING INSTRUMENTS: GENERAL REMARKS

Application of IVs is still attractive. The doubly exogenous variables $\boldsymbol{x}_{Uit}$ and $\boldsymbol{z}_{Ui}$ raise no problems, so a first suggestion is to let $\boldsymbol{x}_{Uit}$ and $\boldsymbol{z}_{Ui}$ be IVs for themselves and seek IVs for $\boldsymbol{x}_{Cit}$ and $\boldsymbol{z}_{Ci}$ elsewhere, invoking theoretical arguments. It may, however, be questioned whether $C_2 + C_1$ 'extraneous' IVs are needed. Could we exploit our *a priori* knowledge, including the orthogonality $(\boldsymbol{x}_{Uit}, \boldsymbol{x}_{Cit}, \boldsymbol{z}_{Ui}, \boldsymbol{z}_{Ci}) \perp u_{it}$ implied by $\mathsf{E}(u_{it}|X,Z) = 0$, in a more parsimonious way by calling upon fewer IVs, or by not seeking for IVs 'outside the model' at all? The answer is yes if we make one additional assumption, utilizing:

(a) *Usually,* $\boldsymbol{x}_{Uit}$ *and* $\boldsymbol{x}_{Cit}$ *are correlated with* $\boldsymbol{x}_{Uit}-\bar{\boldsymbol{x}}_{Ui\cdot}$ *and* $\boldsymbol{x}_{Cit}-\bar{\boldsymbol{x}}_{Ci\cdot}$. *When* $\boldsymbol{x}_{Uit}$ *is uncorrelated with* α_i, *the same is true for* $\boldsymbol{x}_{Uit}-\bar{\boldsymbol{x}}_{Ui\cdot}$ *and* $\bar{\boldsymbol{x}}_{Ui\cdot}$. *However, although* $\boldsymbol{x}_{Cit}$ *is correlated with* α_i, *the within–between orthogonality ensures that* $\boldsymbol{x}_{Cit}-\bar{\boldsymbol{x}}_{Ci\cdot}$ *is uncorrelated with* α_i.

(b) *The individual means of the two-dimensional variables which are uncorrelated with* α_i, *i.e.,* $\bar{\boldsymbol{x}}_{Ui\cdot}$, *are assumed to be (theoretically) correlated with the time-invariant variables which are correlated with* α_i, *i.e.,* $\boldsymbol{z}_{Ci}$.

Here (a) exemplifies how access to panel data can give a considerable gain over cross-section data. Whether (b) is untrue or true depends on the interpretation of $\boldsymbol{x}_{Uit}, \boldsymbol{x}_{Cit}, \boldsymbol{z}_{Ui}, \boldsymbol{z}_{Ci}$ and theoretical arguments.

Motivated by (a) and (b), we suggest the IVs for (6.46) to be chosen as follows:

$$\begin{array}{lll} \boldsymbol{x}_{Uit}-\bar{\boldsymbol{x}}_{Ui\cdot} & \text{is IV vector for } \boldsymbol{x}_{Uit} & (U_2 \text{ IVs for } U_2 \text{ variables}), \\ \boldsymbol{x}_{Cit}-\bar{\boldsymbol{x}}_{Ci\cdot} & \text{is IV vector for } \boldsymbol{x}_{Cit} & (C_2 \text{ IVs for } C_2 \text{ variables}), \\ \boldsymbol{z}_{Ui} & \text{is IV vector for } \boldsymbol{z}_{Ui} & (U_1 \text{ IVs for } U_1 \text{ variables}), \\ \bar{\boldsymbol{x}}_{Ui\cdot} & \text{is IV vector for } \boldsymbol{z}_{Ci} & (U_2 \text{ IVs for } C_1 \text{ variables}). \end{array} \tag{6.47}$$

The salient points are: (i) using $\boldsymbol{x}_{Uit}$ as IV for itself is wasteful, it may be interpreted as containing $2U_2$ potential IVs: $\boldsymbol{x}_{Uit}-\bar{\boldsymbol{x}}_{Ui\cdot}$ and $\bar{\boldsymbol{x}}_{Ui\cdot}$, which serve for $\boldsymbol{x}_{Uit}$, and for $\boldsymbol{z}_{Ci}$, respectively; (ii) $\boldsymbol{x}_{Cit}-\bar{\boldsymbol{x}}_{Ci\cdot}$ (unlike $\boldsymbol{x}_{Cit}$) is a valid IV for $\boldsymbol{x}_{Cit}$. Will (6.47) give a sufficiently large IV-set? Since we have $U_2+C_2+U_1+U_2$ potential IVs for $U_2+C_2+U_1+C_1$ variables, we can formulate the *order condition*:

The number of IVs is sufficient if $U_2 \geq C_1$, *i.e., if there are at least as many two-dimensional variables uncorrelated with* α_i, *as time-invariant variables correlated with* α_i. (6.48)

We now examine estimation procedures implied by this prescription, distinguishing between the cases where the order condition holds with equality ('exact identification', Section 6.5.2) and the practically more interesting case where it holds with strict inequality ('overidentification', Section 6.5.3). Full identification cannot be achieved when $U_2 < C_1$, yet *some* coefficients are estimable.

6.5.2 ESTIMATION IN CASE OF EXACT IDENTIFICATION

We describe two equivalent procedures for the case where the number of two-dimensional variables uncorrelated with α_i equals the number of time-invariant variables correlated with α_i ($U_2 = C_1$). Let

$$X_U = \begin{bmatrix} x_{U11} \\ \vdots \\ x_{U1T} \\ \vdots \\ x_{UN1} \\ \vdots \\ x_{UNT} \end{bmatrix}, \quad X_C = \begin{bmatrix} x_{C11} \\ \vdots \\ x_{C1T} \\ \vdots \\ x_{CN1} \\ \vdots \\ x_{CNT} \end{bmatrix}, \quad y = \begin{bmatrix} y_{11} \\ \vdots \\ y_{1T} \\ \vdots \\ y_{N1} \\ \vdots \\ y_{NT} \end{bmatrix}, \quad u = \begin{bmatrix} u_{11} \\ \vdots \\ u_{1T} \\ \vdots \\ u_{N1} \\ \vdots \\ u_{NT} \end{bmatrix},$$

$$Z_U = \begin{bmatrix} z_{U1} \\ \vdots \\ z_{UN} \end{bmatrix}, \quad Z_C = \begin{bmatrix} z_{C1} \\ \vdots \\ z_{CN} \end{bmatrix}, \quad \boldsymbol{\alpha} = \begin{bmatrix} \alpha_1 \\ \vdots \\ \alpha_N \end{bmatrix}.$$

A two-step procedure which extends that in Section 6.4, is: first, estimate $\boldsymbol{\beta}_U$ and $\boldsymbol{\beta}_C$ by the within estimators, equivalent to using $x_{Uit} - \bar{x}_{Ui\cdot}$ and $x_{Cit} - \bar{x}_{Ci\cdot}$ as IVs for, respectively, x_{Uit} and x_{Cit}. Second, estimate $\boldsymbol{\delta}_U$ and $\boldsymbol{\delta}_C$ by another IV approach.

The *first-step* estimators are

$$\begin{bmatrix} \widehat{\boldsymbol{\beta}}_U \\ \widehat{\boldsymbol{\beta}}_C \end{bmatrix} = \begin{bmatrix} W_{XUXU} & W_{XUXC} \\ W_{XCXU} & W_{XCXC} \end{bmatrix}^{-1} \begin{bmatrix} W_{XUY} \\ W_{XCY} \end{bmatrix}, \tag{6.49}$$

where

$$W_{XPXQ} = X'_P(I_N \otimes B_T)X_Q,$$
$$W_{XPY} = X'_P(I_N \otimes B_T)y, \qquad P, Q = U, C.$$

Define

$$d_{it} = y_{it} - x_{Uit}\widehat{\boldsymbol{\beta}}_U - x_{Cit}\widehat{\boldsymbol{\beta}}_C, \tag{6.50}$$

which implies

$$\begin{bmatrix} B_{ZUD} \\ B_{XUD} \end{bmatrix} = \begin{bmatrix} B_{ZUY} \\ B_{XUY} \end{bmatrix} - \begin{bmatrix} B_{ZUXU} & B_{ZUXC} \\ B_{XUXU} & B_{XUXC} \end{bmatrix} \begin{bmatrix} \widehat{\boldsymbol{\beta}}_U \\ \widehat{\boldsymbol{\beta}}_C \end{bmatrix},$$

where

$$B_{XUXQ} = X'_U(B_N \otimes A_T)X_Q,$$
$$B_{XUZQ} = X'_U(B_N \otimes A_T)(Z_Q \otimes e_T),$$

$$
\begin{aligned}
B_{ZUZQ} &= (Z_U' \otimes e_T')(B_N \otimes A_T)(Z_Q \otimes e_T),\\
B_{XUY} &= X_U'(B_N \otimes B_T)y,\\
B_{ZUY} &= (Z_U' \otimes e_T')(B_N \otimes A_T)y, \;\; Q = U, C,
\end{aligned}
$$

etc. In the *second step* we use $(z_{Ui}, \bar{x}_{Ui\cdot})$ as IVs for (z_{Ui}, z_{Ci}), giving

$$
\begin{bmatrix} \widehat{\delta}_U \\ \widehat{\delta}_C \end{bmatrix} = \begin{bmatrix} B_{ZUZU} & B_{ZUZC} \\ B_{XUZU} & B_{XUZC} \end{bmatrix}^{-1} \begin{bmatrix} B_{ZUD} \\ B_{XUD} \end{bmatrix}, \tag{6.51}
$$

or

$$
\begin{aligned}
\begin{bmatrix} \widehat{\delta}_U \\ \widehat{\delta}_C \end{bmatrix} = &\begin{bmatrix} B_{ZUZU} & B_{ZUZC} \\ B_{XUZU} & B_{XUZC} \end{bmatrix}^{-1} \\
&\times \left\{ \begin{bmatrix} B_{ZUY} \\ B_{XUY} \end{bmatrix} - \begin{bmatrix} B_{ZUXU} & B_{ZUXC} \\ B_{XUXU} & B_{XUXC} \end{bmatrix} \begin{bmatrix} \widehat{\beta}_U \\ \widehat{\beta}_C \end{bmatrix} \right\}.
\end{aligned} \tag{6.52}
$$

Equations (6.51)–(6.52) generalize (6.36)–(6.37). Consistency of the four estimator vectors is demonstrated in Appendix 6B.

A one-step procedure. We exploit the IV set (6.47) to jointly estimate the four coefficient vectors in one step, first writing the equation in (6.46) as

$$
\begin{aligned}
y &= e_{NT}k^* + X_U\beta_U + X_C\beta_C \\
&\quad + (Z_U \otimes e_T)\delta_U + (Z_C \otimes e_T)\delta_C + (\alpha \otimes e_T) + u \\
&= e_{NT}k^* + X\gamma + (\alpha \otimes e_T) + u,
\end{aligned} \tag{6.53}
$$

where, after the necessary reordering,

$$
\begin{aligned}
X &= [X_U, X_C, (Z_U \otimes e_T), (Z_C \otimes e_T)],\\
\gamma' &= [\beta_U', \beta_C', \delta_U', \delta_C'].
\end{aligned}
$$

The IV matrix for X prescribed by (6.47) is[6]

$$
Q = [(I_N \otimes B_T)[X_U \; X_C], (B_N \otimes A_T)[(Z_U \otimes e_T) \; X_U]]. \tag{6.54}
$$

[6] Recall (see Section 2.4.3) that premultiplication by $(I_N \otimes B_T)$ and $(B_N \otimes A_T)$ form from $(NT \times 1)$-vectors, respectively, deviations from individual means and individual means minus global means.

Since X and Q have equal dimension, this leads to[7]

$$\widehat{\gamma} = \begin{bmatrix} \widehat{\beta} \\ \widehat{\delta} \end{bmatrix} = \begin{bmatrix} \widehat{\beta}_U \\ \widehat{\beta}_C \\ \widehat{\delta}_U \\ \widehat{\delta}_C \end{bmatrix} = [Q'X]^{-1}[Q'y], \tag{6.55}$$

where

$$Q'X = \begin{bmatrix} W_{XX} & 0 \\ B_{XZ1} & B_{XZ2} \end{bmatrix}, \qquad Q'y = \begin{bmatrix} W_{XY} \\ B_{XZY} \end{bmatrix},$$

whose blocks are

$$W_{XX} = \begin{bmatrix} W_{XUXU} & W_{XUXC} \\ W_{XCXU} & W_{XCXC} \end{bmatrix},$$

$$B_{XZ1} = \begin{bmatrix} B_{ZUXU} & B_{ZUXC} \\ B_{XUXU} & B_{XUXC} \end{bmatrix}, \qquad B_{XZ2} = \begin{bmatrix} B_{ZUZU} & B_{ZUZC} \\ B_{XUZU} & B_{XUZC} \end{bmatrix},$$

$$W_{XY} = \begin{bmatrix} W_{XUY} \\ W_{XCY} \end{bmatrix}, \qquad B_{XZY} = \begin{bmatrix} B_{ZUY} \\ B_{XUY} \end{bmatrix}.$$

Now, (6.55) can be rewritten as[8]

$$\widehat{\gamma} = \begin{bmatrix} W_{XX} & 0 \\ B_{XZ1} & B_{XZ2} \end{bmatrix}^{-1} \begin{bmatrix} W_{XY} \\ B_{XZY} \end{bmatrix},$$

which implies

$$\widehat{\beta} = W_{XX}^{-1} W_{XY}, \tag{6.56}$$

$$\widehat{\delta} = B_{XZ2}^{-1} B_{XZY} - B_{XZ2}^{-1} B_{XZ1} \widehat{\beta}. \tag{6.57}$$

These estimators, with the interpretation of the elements given above, are identical to (6.49) and (6.52). Mathematically, this is due to the block-triangularity of $Q'X$ that follows

[7] When using the IV-matrix Q, k^* is eliminated. Its estimation is explained in Section 6.5.3.

[8] Any non-singular, quadratic block-triangular matrix satisfies

$$\begin{bmatrix} C & 0 \\ D & E \end{bmatrix}^{-1} = \begin{bmatrix} C^{-1} & 0 \\ -E^{-1}DC^{-1} & E^{-1} \end{bmatrix}.$$

from the within–between orthogonality and implies that estimation of $\boldsymbol{\beta}$ can be done before estimation of $\boldsymbol{\delta}$.

Our conclusion then is: if the number of two-dimensional variables which are uncorrelated with the individual-specific effects equals the number of individual-specific variables which are correlated with the individual-specific effects ($U_2 = C_1$), equivalent ways of estimating (6.46) are:

- First estimate $(\boldsymbol{\beta}_U, \boldsymbol{\beta}_C)$ by (6.49), next estimate $(\boldsymbol{\delta}_U, \boldsymbol{\delta}_C)$ by (6.52).
- Use $\boldsymbol{Q}$, given by (6.54), as IV for $\boldsymbol{X}$.

A third interpretation is given in Appendix 6A.

6.5.3 ESTIMATION IN CASE OF OVERIDENTIFICATION

The assumption that the order condition for identification, (6.48), is satisfied with equality, is particular. In this section, we consider the case $U_2 > C_1$. Elements from 2SLS and GLS will then be involved. We first consider simple application of 2SLS and next a more efficient application, which also includes elements from GLS, to account for the disturbance components structure, and proposed by Hausman and Taylor (1981). In addition we consider briefly two modifications later proposed by other authors. They differ from the Hausman–Taylor approach with respect to the exact definition of the IV set and orthogonality conditions.

An IV application resembling two-stage least squares (2SLS). When $U_2 > C_1$, we might still have used (6.49) for estimation of $(\boldsymbol{\beta}_U, \boldsymbol{\beta}_C)$, but (6.52) would no longer define estimators for $(\boldsymbol{\delta}_U, \boldsymbol{\delta}_C)$, *as* $\boldsymbol{B}_{XUZC}$ *is not quadratic.* We could either use $(\boldsymbol{z}_{Ui}, \bar{\boldsymbol{x}}_{Ui\cdot})$ as IVs for $(\boldsymbol{z}_{Ui}, \boldsymbol{z}_{Ci})$ and modify (6.51) to take into account that $(\boldsymbol{z}_{Ui}, \bar{\boldsymbol{x}}_{Ui\cdot})$ has more columns than $(\boldsymbol{z}_{Ui}, \boldsymbol{z}_{Ci})$, or stick to (6.54) and modify (6.55) to account for $\boldsymbol{Q}$ having more columns than $\boldsymbol{X}$, $G = U_2+C_2+U_1+U_2$ and $H = U_2+C_2+U_1+C_1$, respectively. The latter motivates using *2SLS*, which, in case of overidentification, can be considered an optimal IV procedure.

We formalize the procedure by introducing H *auxiliary regression equations*, one for each column of $\boldsymbol{X}$ in (6.53),

$$\boldsymbol{X} = \boldsymbol{Q}\boldsymbol{\Pi} + \boldsymbol{E},$$

where $\boldsymbol{X}$ and $\boldsymbol{Q}$ are $(NT\times H)$ and $(NT\times G)$ matrices, $\boldsymbol{\Pi}$ is a $(G\times H)$ coefficient matrix, and $\boldsymbol{E}$ is a $(NT\times H)$ matrix of disturbances.[9] First, estimate $\boldsymbol{\Pi}$ by OLS, obtaining

[9] This equation can be interpreted as a *reduced-form equation system* of a multi-equation model and is a generalization of the auxiliary regression equations (6A.1), formalized for the case with exact identification in Appendix 6A.

$\widehat{\Pi} = (Q'Q)^{-1}(Q'X)$, which gives the matrix of 'X-hat'-values, $\widehat{X} = Q\widehat{\Pi} = P_Q X$, where $P_Q = Q(Q'Q)^{-1}Q'$, satisfying $P_Q X \equiv P_Q \widehat{X}$, since P_Q is idempotent. Next, estimate $\boldsymbol{\gamma}$ by OLS, after having replaced X by $\widehat{X}$. This is equivalent to using $\widehat{X}$ as IV matrix for X, and gives[10]

$$\begin{aligned}\widehat{\gamma} &= (\widehat{X}'\widehat{X})^{-1}(\widehat{X}'y) \equiv (\widehat{X}'X)^{-1}(\widehat{X}'y)\\ &\equiv [X'P_Q X]^{-1}[X'P_Q y].\end{aligned} \tag{6.58}$$

From Section 3.2.2 the following estimator for the common intercept k^* in (6.46) (conditional on the coefficient vector) is motivated:

$$\widehat{k}^*(\boldsymbol{\gamma}) = \left(\tfrac{1}{N}e_N' \otimes \tfrac{1}{T}e_T'\right)(y - X\boldsymbol{\gamma}),$$

which after substituting $\boldsymbol{\gamma} = \widehat{\boldsymbol{\gamma}}$ gives

$$\widehat{k}^* = \widehat{k}^*(\widehat{\boldsymbol{\gamma}}) = \left(\tfrac{1}{N}e_N' \otimes \tfrac{1}{T}e_T'\right)(y - X\widehat{\boldsymbol{\gamma}}). \tag{6.59}$$

An extension exploiting GLS: the Hausman–Taylor procedure. The 2SLS method just described is modified by Hausman and Taylor (1981, Section 3.2), who propose an extension that *combines GLS and 2SLS.* From (6.53) we have

$$y = (e_N \otimes e_T)k^* + X\boldsymbol{\gamma} + \boldsymbol{\epsilon}, \qquad \boldsymbol{\epsilon} = (\boldsymbol{\alpha} \otimes e_T) + \boldsymbol{u},$$

for which we know, confer Sections 3.2.1–3.2.3, that

$$\mathsf{E}(\boldsymbol{\epsilon}\boldsymbol{\epsilon}'|X_U, Z_U) = \boldsymbol{\Omega} = I_N \otimes \boldsymbol{\Omega}_T, \qquad \boldsymbol{\Omega}_T = \sigma^2 B_T + (\sigma^2 + T\sigma_\alpha^2)A_T,$$

where

$$\begin{aligned}\boldsymbol{\Omega}_T^{-1} &= S_T^2, &\qquad S_T &= B_T/\sqrt{\sigma^2} + A_T/\sqrt{\sigma^2 + T\sigma_\alpha^2},\\ \boldsymbol{\Omega}^{-1} &= S^2, & S &= I_N \otimes S_T,\end{aligned}$$

and hence $S_T\boldsymbol{\Omega}_T S_T = I_T$ and $S\boldsymbol{\Omega}S = I_{NT}$.

[10] When $G = H$, $Q'X$ is quadratic and (6.58) can be simplified to (6.55).

Essentially, the procedure has three steps, which may be used iteratively:[11]

1. Form, using (6.58)–(6.59), the residual vector $\widehat{\boldsymbol{\epsilon}} = \boldsymbol{y} - (\boldsymbol{e}_N \otimes \boldsymbol{e}_T)\widehat{k}^* - \boldsymbol{X}\widehat{\boldsymbol{\gamma}}$,
2. Estimate from $\widehat{\epsilon}_{it}$, σ^2, σ_α^2, $\boldsymbol{S}_T$, and $\boldsymbol{S}$ by using, see (3.38) and (3.40):

$$\widehat{\sigma}^2 = \frac{\sum_i \sum_t (\widehat{\varepsilon}_{it} - \bar{\widehat{\varepsilon}}_{i\cdot})^2}{N(T-1)} = \frac{W_{\widehat{\varepsilon}\widehat{\varepsilon}}}{N(T-1)},$$

$$\widehat{\sigma}_\alpha^2 = \frac{\sum_i (\bar{\widehat{\varepsilon}}_{i\cdot} - \bar{\widehat{\varepsilon}})^2}{N-1} - \frac{\sum_i \sum_t (\widehat{\varepsilon}_{it} - \bar{\widehat{\varepsilon}}_{i\cdot})^2}{NT(T-1)} = \frac{1}{T}\left[\frac{B_{\widehat{\varepsilon}\widehat{\varepsilon}}}{N-1} - \frac{W_{\widehat{\varepsilon}\widehat{\varepsilon}}}{N(T-1)}\right],$$

$$\widehat{\boldsymbol{S}}_T = (\widehat{\sigma}^2)^{-\frac{1}{2}}\boldsymbol{B}_T + (\widehat{\sigma}^2 + T\widehat{\sigma}_\alpha^2)^{-\frac{1}{2}}\boldsymbol{A}_T, \quad \widehat{\boldsymbol{S}} = \boldsymbol{I}_N \otimes \widehat{\boldsymbol{S}}_T.$$

3. Premultiply (6.53) by $\widehat{\boldsymbol{S}}$, let $\boldsymbol{y}^\Delta = \widehat{\boldsymbol{S}}\boldsymbol{y}$, $\boldsymbol{X}^\Delta = \widehat{\boldsymbol{S}}\boldsymbol{X}$, $\boldsymbol{\epsilon}^\Delta = \widehat{\boldsymbol{S}}\boldsymbol{\epsilon}$, and $k^\Delta = k^*(\widehat{\sigma}^2 + T\widehat{\sigma}_\alpha^2)^{-1/2}$, giving

$$\boldsymbol{y}^\Delta = (\boldsymbol{e}_N \otimes \boldsymbol{e}_T)k^\Delta + \boldsymbol{X}^\Delta\boldsymbol{\gamma} + \boldsymbol{\epsilon}^\Delta, \tag{6.60}$$

where $\mathsf{E}(\boldsymbol{\epsilon}^\Delta\boldsymbol{\epsilon}^{\Delta\prime}) = \boldsymbol{I}_{NT}$. How should this equation be instrumented in estimating $\boldsymbol{\gamma}$ and k^Δ? One answer is to *use* $\boldsymbol{Q}$ *as IV matrix for* $\boldsymbol{X}^\Delta$, giving

$$\begin{aligned}\widetilde{\boldsymbol{\gamma}} &= [(\boldsymbol{X}^\Delta)'\boldsymbol{Q}(\boldsymbol{Q}'\boldsymbol{Q})^{-1}\boldsymbol{Q}'(\boldsymbol{X}^\Delta)]^{-1}[(\boldsymbol{X}^\Delta)'\boldsymbol{Q}(\boldsymbol{Q}'\boldsymbol{Q})^{-1}\boldsymbol{Q}'(\boldsymbol{y}^\Delta)] \\ &= [(\boldsymbol{X}^\Delta)'\boldsymbol{P}_Q(\boldsymbol{X}^\Delta)]^{-1}[(\boldsymbol{X}^\Delta)'\boldsymbol{P}_Q(\boldsymbol{y}^\Delta)], \end{aligned} \tag{6.61}$$

$$\widetilde{k}^\Delta = \left(\tfrac{1}{N}\boldsymbol{e}_N' \otimes \tfrac{1}{T}\boldsymbol{e}_T'\right)(\boldsymbol{y}^\Delta - \boldsymbol{X}^\Delta\widetilde{\boldsymbol{\gamma}}). \tag{6.62}$$

This modification of (6.58)–(6.59) is a mixture of FGLS and 2SLS. The former serves to handle the (non-scalar) covariance matrix of the original disturbance vector in (6.53), the latter accounts for the single endogeneity of some of the regressors.

Modifications of the Hausman–Taylor procedure. Two modifications have been proposed in the way orthogonality conditions and IVs are selected. First, Amemiya and MaCurdy (1986) (AM) propose utilizing somewhat stronger exogeneity assumptions than Hausman and Taylor (1981) (HT) and are able to improve efficiency. They assume that α_i is uncorrelated with the realization of $\boldsymbol{x}_{Uit}$ *for each* t, rather than with the mean taken over t only. This modification, of course, only concerns the two-dimensional variables. Second, Breusch, Mizon, and Schmidt (1989) (BMS) suggest including an even

[11] This interpretation departs somewhat from the description in Hausman and Taylor (1981).

stronger set of orthogonality conditions, in addition to the HT prescription by assuming that the correlation between α_i and $\boldsymbol{x}_{Cit}$ is due to the time-invariant part of the latter. This implies, briefly, that the applicability of the $\boldsymbol{x}_{Cit}-\bar{\boldsymbol{x}}_{Ci\cdot}$ instrument set relative to GLS in step 3 is extended. For elaboration, see Cornwell and Rupert (1988), Wyhowski (1994), and Boumahdi and Thomas (2008). Cornwell and Rupert, in an empirical comparison of the three procedures, conclude that

> noticeable efficiency gains to the methods put forward by AM and BMS are limited to the estimated coefficients of the time-invariant variables ... The impact of ... estimators falls primarily on the time-invariant endogenous variables ... because the extra instruments employed by these methods are time invariant. (1988, p. 155)

while BMS remark:

> As we progress from the HT to the AM and then to the BMS estimator, we require successively stronger exogeneity assumptions, and we achieve successively more efficient estimators ... Nevertheless, it is somewhat disconcerting to have the choice of estimators depend on the properties of reduced form equations that are more or less devoid of behavioral content. (1989, p. 700)

Example: We continue discussing the example in Chapter 5 (Table 5.1). A data set for wage rates and its determinants from USA (from Cornwell and Rupert (1988), source: http://www.stata-press.com/data/r8, variables renamed; last accessed March 2016) is used to estimate versions of a simple wage equation by using the HT procedure and the AM modification, see Table 6.4, columns 1–6 (see notes to Table 5.1 for variable definitions). The individual-specific length of education, `educ`, is treated as (singly) endogenous (i.e., correlated with the latent individual effect) throughout. Three selections of endogenous explanatory variables are considered: IV1: four variables (the first three of which two-dimensional) `exper, work, union, educ` (columns 1–2); IV2: only `exper, educ` (columns 3–4); and IV3: only `educ` (columns 5–6). Comparable results based on the standard random effects (RE) approach (all explanatory variables assumed exogenous) are given in column 7. 'Endogenization' of `exper, educ`, as in HT and AM, increases their coefficient estimates, while the negative impacts of the `fem` and `occ` dummies are weakened. While the gender effect is insignificant in the HT and AM results, it emerges as clearly significant in the RE results. The effect of replacing HT with AM is on the whole modest. However, changing the status of `exper` from endogenous to exogenous increases the coefficient estimate of the (still) endogenous `educ` from about 0.14 to 0.23–0.24 (compare columns 1–4 with 5–6), which is an inexplicably large 'education premium'. Its counterpart in the RE result is 'only' 0.11, still a substantial estimated 'returns to schooling'.

Table 6.4 Wage equation example: estimates from Hausman–Taylor procedure

	HT,IV1	AM,IV1	HT,IV2	AM,IV2	HT,IV3	AM,IV3	RE
`occ`	−0.0245	−0.0247	−0.0252	−0.0252	−0.0195	−0.0209	−0.0567
	(0.0138)	(0.0138)	(0.0138)	(0.0138)	(0.0137)	(0.0137)	(0.0169)
`metr`	−0.0460	−0.0460	−0.0459	−0.0463	−0.0561	−0.0555	−0.0319
	(0.0190)	(0.0190)	(0.0190)	(0.0190)	(0.0189)	(0.0189)	(0.0204)
`ind`	0.0152	0.0151	0.0149	0.0150	0.0210	0.0204	0.0078
	(0.0154)	(0.0154)	(0.0154)	(0.0154)	(0.0153)	(0.0153)	(0.0176)
`exper`	0.0965	0.0964	0.0964	0.0961	0.0900	0.0899	0.0493
	(0.0012)	(0.0012)	(0.0012)	(0.0012)	(0.0011)	(0.0011)	(0.0011)
`work`	0.0590	0.0590	0.0626	0.0626	0.0608	0.0609	0.0840
	(0.0314)	(0.0314)	(0.0313)	(0.0313)	(0.0311)	(0.0311)	(0.0406)
`union`	0.0344	0.0342	0.0363	0.0365	0.0415	0.0410	0.0666
	(0.0150)	(0.0150)	(0.0149)	(0.0149)	(0.0148)	(0.0148)	(0.0174)
`fem`	−0.1485	−0.1491	−0.1486	−0.1495	−0.1633	−0.1642	−0.3023
	(0.1258)	(0.1258)	(0.1258)	(0.1258)	(0.1318)	(0.1316)	(0.0485)
`educ`	0.1438	0.1414	0.1393	0.1417	0.2413	0.2266	0.1057
	(0.0216)	(0.0210)	(0.0216)	(0.0206)	(0.0220)	(0.0211)	(0.0059)
`intercept`	2.8998	2.9341	2.9563	2.9319	1.7766	1.9684	4.3205
	(0.2852)	(0.2774)	(0.2846)	(0.2732)	(0.2912)	(0.2807)	(0.0952)
ρ	0.9755	0.9755	0.9755	0.9755	0.9779	0.9779	0.7631

Notes: For variable definitions, see notes to Table 5.1. Standard errors in parentheses.
HT: Hausman–Taylor procedure. AM: Amemiya–MaCurdy modification of HT.
RE = Standard Random Effects model.
Exogenous variables throughout: `occ, metr, ind, fem`
IV1: Endogenous = `exper, work, union` (2-dim), `educ` (1-dim).
IV2: Endogenous = `exper` (2-dim), `educ` (1-dim).
IV3: Endogenous = `educ` (1-dim)

Appendix 6A. **Reinterpretation: Block-recursive system**

This appendix gives a reinterpretation of the IV procedure in Section 6.5.2, with reference to the block-recursive reformulation of the model. Specifically, we consider $(\bar{x}_{Ci\cdot}, z_{Ci})$ as determined by $(\bar{x}_{Ui\cdot}, z_{Ui}, \alpha_i)$, via C_2+C_1 equations supplementing (6.46). The block of equation added is:

$$\begin{aligned}
&\bar{x}_{Ci\cdot} = \mu_{X0} + \bar{x}_{Ui\cdot}\mu_{XX} + z_{Ui\cdot}\mu_{XZ} + \alpha_i\eta_X + \kappa_{Xi},\\
&z_{Ci} = \mu_{Z0} + \bar{x}_{Ui\cdot}\mu_{ZX} + z_{Ui\cdot}\mu_{ZZ} + \alpha_i\eta_Z + \kappa_{Zi},\\
&(\bar{x}_{Ui\cdot}, z_{Ui\cdot}) \perp \alpha_i \perp \kappa_{Xi} \perp u_{it},\\
&(\bar{x}_{Ui\cdot}, z_{Ui\cdot}) \perp \alpha_i \perp \kappa_{Zi} \perp u_{it},
\end{aligned} \tag{6A.1}$$

where $\boldsymbol{\mu}_{X0}, \boldsymbol{\mu}_{Z0}, \boldsymbol{\mu}_{XX}, \boldsymbol{\mu}_{XZ}, \boldsymbol{\mu}_{ZX}, \boldsymbol{\mu}_{ZZ}, \boldsymbol{\eta}_X, \boldsymbol{\eta}_Z$ are coefficient matrices and $\boldsymbol{\kappa}_{Xi}$ and $\boldsymbol{\kappa}_{Zi}$ are disturbance vectors. We insert (6A.1) in (6.46), letting

$$\begin{aligned}
\begin{bmatrix}\boldsymbol{\phi}_X\\ \boldsymbol{\phi}_Z\end{bmatrix} &= \begin{bmatrix} I & \boldsymbol{\mu}_{XX}\\ 0 & \boldsymbol{\mu}_{XZ}\end{bmatrix}\begin{bmatrix}\boldsymbol{\beta}_U\\ \boldsymbol{\beta}_C\end{bmatrix} + \begin{bmatrix} 0 & \boldsymbol{\mu}_{ZX}\\ I & \boldsymbol{\mu}_{ZZ}\end{bmatrix}\begin{bmatrix}\boldsymbol{\delta}_U\\ \boldsymbol{\delta}_C\end{bmatrix}, \\
k &= k^* + \boldsymbol{\mu}_{X0}\boldsymbol{\beta}_C + \boldsymbol{\mu}_{Z0}\boldsymbol{\delta}_C, \\
\varepsilon_{it} &= \alpha_i(1+\boldsymbol{\eta}_X\boldsymbol{\beta}_C+\boldsymbol{\eta}_Z\boldsymbol{\delta}_C) + u_{it},
\end{aligned} \tag{6A.2}$$

and obtain

$$(y_{it}-\bar{y}_{i\cdot})+\bar{y}_{i\cdot} = k+(\boldsymbol{x}_{Uit}-\bar{\boldsymbol{x}}_{Ui\cdot})\boldsymbol{\beta}_U+(\boldsymbol{x}_{Cit}-\bar{\boldsymbol{x}}_{Ci\cdot})\boldsymbol{\beta}_C+\bar{\boldsymbol{x}}_{Ui\cdot}\boldsymbol{\phi}_X+\boldsymbol{z}_{Ui}\boldsymbol{\phi}_Z+\varepsilon_{it}, \tag{6A.3}$$

which can be considered as a reduced form equation suitable for OLS (or equivalently GLS) estimation since ε_{it} is uncorrelated with all regressors. The within–between orthogonality implies that the estimator of $(\boldsymbol{\beta}'_U, \boldsymbol{\beta}'_C)'$ obtained equals the within estimator $(\widehat{\boldsymbol{\beta}}'_U, \widehat{\boldsymbol{\beta}}'_C)'$, confer (6.49). Similarly, $\boldsymbol{\phi}_X$ and $\boldsymbol{\phi}_Z$ can be estimated from the between variation, which gives

$$\begin{bmatrix}\widehat{\boldsymbol{\phi}}_X\\ \widehat{\boldsymbol{\phi}}_Z\end{bmatrix} = \begin{bmatrix} \boldsymbol{B}_{XUXU} & \boldsymbol{B}_{XUZU}\\ \boldsymbol{B}_{ZUXU} & \boldsymbol{B}_{ZUZU}\end{bmatrix}^{-1}\begin{bmatrix}\boldsymbol{B}_{XUY}\\ \boldsymbol{B}_{ZUY}\end{bmatrix}. \tag{6A.4}$$

Now, $\boldsymbol{\mu}_{XX}, \boldsymbol{\mu}_{XZ}\ \boldsymbol{\mu}_{ZX}, \boldsymbol{\mu}_{ZZ}$ can be estimated by using OLS on (6A.1), which gives

$$\begin{aligned}
\begin{bmatrix}\widehat{\boldsymbol{\mu}}_{XX}\\ \widehat{\boldsymbol{\mu}}_{XZ}\end{bmatrix} &= \begin{bmatrix} \boldsymbol{B}_{XUXU} & \boldsymbol{B}_{XUZU}\\ \boldsymbol{B}_{ZUXU} & \boldsymbol{B}_{ZUZU}\end{bmatrix}^{-1}\begin{bmatrix}\boldsymbol{B}_{XUXC}\\ \boldsymbol{B}_{ZUXC}\end{bmatrix}, \\
\begin{bmatrix}\widehat{\boldsymbol{\mu}}_{ZX}\\ \widehat{\boldsymbol{\mu}}_{ZZ}\end{bmatrix} &= \begin{bmatrix} \boldsymbol{B}_{XUXU} & \boldsymbol{B}_{XUZU}\\ \boldsymbol{B}_{ZUXU} & \boldsymbol{B}_{ZUZU}\end{bmatrix}^{-1}\begin{bmatrix}\boldsymbol{B}_{XUZC}\\ \boldsymbol{B}_{ZUZC}\end{bmatrix}.
\end{aligned} \tag{6A.5}$$

We then obtain estimators for $\boldsymbol{\delta}_U$ and $\boldsymbol{\delta}_C$ from (6A.2) by inserting the estimators for $\boldsymbol{\beta}_U$, $\boldsymbol{\beta}_C, \boldsymbol{\phi}_X, \boldsymbol{\phi}_Z, \boldsymbol{\mu}_{XX}, \boldsymbol{\mu}_{XZ}, \boldsymbol{\mu}_{ZX}$, and $\boldsymbol{\mu}_{ZZ}$ from (6.49), (6A.4), and (6A.5). This gives

$$\begin{bmatrix}\widehat{\boldsymbol{\phi}}_X\\ \widehat{\boldsymbol{\phi}}_Z\end{bmatrix} = \begin{bmatrix} I & \widehat{\boldsymbol{\mu}}_{XX}\\ 0 & \widehat{\boldsymbol{\mu}}_{XZ}\end{bmatrix}\begin{bmatrix}\widehat{\boldsymbol{\beta}}_U\\ \widehat{\boldsymbol{\beta}}_C\end{bmatrix} + \begin{bmatrix} 0 & \widehat{\boldsymbol{\mu}}_{ZX}\\ I & \widehat{\boldsymbol{\mu}}_{ZZ}\end{bmatrix}\begin{bmatrix}\widehat{\boldsymbol{\delta}}_U\\ \widehat{\boldsymbol{\delta}}_C\end{bmatrix}.$$

Since a slight reformulation of (6A.4) and (6A.5) yields

$$\begin{bmatrix} \boldsymbol{B}_{XUXU} & \boldsymbol{B}_{XUZU}\\ \boldsymbol{B}_{ZUXU} & \boldsymbol{B}_{ZUZU}\end{bmatrix}\begin{bmatrix}\widehat{\boldsymbol{\phi}}_X\\ \widehat{\boldsymbol{\phi}}_Z\end{bmatrix} = \begin{bmatrix}\boldsymbol{B}_{XUY}\\ \boldsymbol{B}_{ZUY}\end{bmatrix},$$

$$\begin{bmatrix} B_{XUXU} & B_{XUZU} \\ B_{ZUXU} & B_{ZUZU} \end{bmatrix} \begin{bmatrix} I & \widehat{\mu}_{XX} \\ 0 & \widehat{\mu}_{XZ} \end{bmatrix} = \begin{bmatrix} B_{XUXU} & B_{XUXC} \\ B_{ZUXU} & B_{ZUXC} \end{bmatrix},$$

$$\begin{bmatrix} B_{XUXU} & B_{XUZU} \\ B_{ZUXU} & B_{ZUZU} \end{bmatrix} \begin{bmatrix} 0 & \widehat{\mu}_{ZX} \\ I & \widehat{\mu}_{ZZ} \end{bmatrix} = \begin{bmatrix} B_{XUZU} & B_{XUZC} \\ B_{ZUZU} & B_{ZUZC} \end{bmatrix},$$

it follows that

$$\begin{bmatrix} B_{ZUY} \\ B_{XUY} \end{bmatrix} = \begin{bmatrix} B_{ZUXU} & B_{ZUXC} \\ B_{XUXU} & B_{XUXC} \end{bmatrix} \begin{bmatrix} \widehat{\boldsymbol{\beta}}_U \\ \widehat{\boldsymbol{\beta}}_C \end{bmatrix} + \begin{bmatrix} B_{ZUZU} & B_{ZUZC} \\ B_{XUZU} & B_{XUZC} \end{bmatrix} \begin{bmatrix} \widehat{\boldsymbol{\delta}}_U \\ \widehat{\boldsymbol{\delta}}_C \end{bmatrix}.$$

This equation is equivalent to (6.52). It can be written compactly as

$$B_{XZY} = B_{XZ1}\widehat{\boldsymbol{\beta}} + B_{XZ2}\widehat{\boldsymbol{\delta}},$$

which is equivalent to (6.57).

Appendix 6B. **Proof of consistency in case of exact identification**

In this appendix we prove consistency of the two-step estimators. We first insert for y_{it} from (6.46) in (6.49), which gives

$$\begin{bmatrix} \widehat{\boldsymbol{\beta}}_U - \boldsymbol{\beta}_U \\ \widehat{\boldsymbol{\beta}}_C - \boldsymbol{\beta}_C \end{bmatrix} = \begin{bmatrix} \frac{1}{NT} W_{XUXU} & \frac{1}{NT} W_{XUXC} \\ \frac{1}{NT} W_{XCXU} & \frac{1}{NT} W_{XCXC} \end{bmatrix}^{-1} \begin{bmatrix} \frac{1}{NT} W_{XUU} \\ \frac{1}{NT} W_{XCU} \end{bmatrix}. \quad (6B.1)$$

Since $\text{plim}(\frac{1}{NT} W_{XUU})$ and $\text{plim}(\frac{1}{NT} W_{XCU})$ are zero vectors, consistency of $\widehat{\boldsymbol{\beta}}_U$ and $\widehat{\boldsymbol{\beta}}_C$ follows. Next, inserting in (6.52)

$$\begin{bmatrix} B_{ZUY} \\ B_{XUY} \end{bmatrix} = \begin{bmatrix} B_{ZUZU} & B_{ZUZC} \\ B_{XUZU} & B_{XUZC} \end{bmatrix} \begin{bmatrix} \boldsymbol{\beta}_U \\ \boldsymbol{\beta}_C \end{bmatrix} + \begin{bmatrix} B_{ZUXU} & B_{ZUXC} \\ B_{XUXU} & B_{XUXC} \end{bmatrix} \begin{bmatrix} \boldsymbol{\delta}_U \\ \boldsymbol{\delta}_C \end{bmatrix} + \begin{bmatrix} B_{ZU\epsilon} \\ B_{XU\epsilon} \end{bmatrix},$$

it follows that

$$\begin{bmatrix} \widehat{\boldsymbol{\delta}}_U - \boldsymbol{\delta}_U \\ \widehat{\boldsymbol{\delta}}_C - \boldsymbol{\delta}_C \end{bmatrix} = - \begin{bmatrix} \frac{1}{NT}\boldsymbol{B}_{ZUZU} & \frac{1}{NT}\boldsymbol{B}_{ZUZC} \\ \frac{1}{NT}\boldsymbol{B}_{XUZU} & \frac{1}{NT}\boldsymbol{B}_{XUZC} \end{bmatrix}^{-1}$$
$$\times \left\{ \begin{bmatrix} \frac{1}{NT}\boldsymbol{B}_{ZUXU} & \frac{1}{NT}\boldsymbol{B}_{ZUXC} \\ \frac{1}{NT}\boldsymbol{B}_{XUXU} & \frac{1}{NT}\boldsymbol{B}_{XUXC} \end{bmatrix} \begin{bmatrix} \widehat{\boldsymbol{\beta}}_U - \boldsymbol{\beta}_U \\ \widehat{\boldsymbol{\beta}}_C - \boldsymbol{\beta}_C \end{bmatrix} + \begin{bmatrix} \frac{1}{NT}\boldsymbol{B}_{ZU\epsilon} \\ \frac{1}{NT}\boldsymbol{B}_{XU\epsilon} \end{bmatrix} \right\}. \tag{6B.2}$$

Since our assumptions imply that $\text{plim}(\frac{1}{NT}\boldsymbol{B}_{ZU\epsilon})$ and $\text{plim}(\frac{1}{NT}\boldsymbol{B}_{XU\epsilon})$ are zero vectors and $\text{plim}(\widehat{\boldsymbol{\beta}}_U) = \boldsymbol{\beta}_U$ and $\text{plim}(\widehat{\boldsymbol{\beta}}_C) = \boldsymbol{\beta}_C$, it follows that $\widehat{\boldsymbol{\delta}}_U$ and $\widehat{\boldsymbol{\delta}}_C$ are consistent. This, which relies on $\boldsymbol{B}_{XUZC}$ being quadratic and $\text{plim}(\frac{1}{NT}\boldsymbol{B}_{XUZC})$ non-singular, completes the proof.

7 Measurement errors

CHAPTER SUMMARY

The chapter demonstrates how measurement error problems which are untractable in cross-section data can be handled when using panel data. Measuring variables from individual means or taking differences, recommended, in error-free regression models, to eliminate fixed effects, can magnify the relative variation of the measurement error and the 'true' value, i.e., the noise–signal ratio increases. Questions arising are: is the consistency of the within, OLS, GLS, and various difference estimators retained when random measurement errors occur? If consistency fails, can we, by combining inconsistent estimators, construct consistent estimators? The anatomy of the problems is illustrated by contrasting 'disaggregate' and 'aggregate' estimators, the former utilizing only part of the data set. The contrast between N- and T-consistency is important. We first consider models with one regressor, using simple IV procedures. Next generalizations to multi-regressor models and the use of the Generalized Method of Moments are discussed. Different kinds of measurement error processes are discussed. Empirical examples illustrate some of the points.

7.1 Introduction

An essential assumption so far has been that the variables are correctly measured, as prescribed by a theory. Since this assumption is often unlikely to be met, it is highly interesting to reconsider estimation procedures when the *explanatory variables* observed are affected by *measurement errors*, often called errors-in-variables (EIVs). Why is the intersection of measurement errors and panel data of specific interest?

Part of the answer lies in the two-dimensional nature of panel data. When using unidimensional data where the measurement errors in the regressors (noise) are uncorrelated with the true value (signal), the following is known. First, OLS regression with the observed error-ridden variables substituted for the true, latent variables gives inconsistent estimates. Second, the coefficients are not identified unless additional information (from some specified theory) exists, e.g., instrument variables (IV) for the error-ridden regressors; see, e.g., Greene (2008, Section 12.5.2), and, for extended discussion, Fuller (1987) and Wansbeek and Meijer (2000). An early contribution on measurement errors in panel data is Griliches and Hausman (1986), extended in Wansbeek and Koning (1991), Biørn (1992, 1996, 2000), and Wansbeek (2001). A primary purpose of this chapter, to some extent relying on these contributions, is to demonstrate how to come to grips with measurement error problems which are untractable for unidimensional data.

A recurring theme in the first six chapters has been exploiting the possibility that panel data offer for controlling for unobserved time-invariant heterogeneity. In Chapter 6 we specifically examined the treatment of heterogeneity correlated with observable regressors. To eliminate heterogeneity we were led to measure all variables from their individual means or to take differences. When measurement errors occur, such transformations can, however, magnify the variation in the measurement error relative to the variation in the 'true' value: the noise-signal ratio may increase.

Questions then arising are: (a) is the consistency of the within, between, OLS and GLS estimators, and difference estimators retained when there are measurement errors? (b) If they are inconsistent, can we, by combining inconsistent estimators, construct consistent estimators? Often, the answer to (a) is negative, while the answer to (b) is that several consistent estimators exist, *and we do not have to call upon additional information involving extraneous variables.* This raises the question of whether consistent estimators can be combined to increase efficiency.

The chapter proceeds as follows. Section 7.2 presents the simplest model with an error-ridden regressor, without any heterogeneity. Selected estimators, some of which have been considered earlier for error-free models, and some 'disaggregate' estimators, which only exploit fractions of the observation set, are discussed, *inter alia*, with respect to bias. The chapter's sections extend along three lines. Section 7.3 introduces individual heterogeneity, allowed to be correlated with the latent regressor. We show, *inter alia*, how, by combining two inconsistent estimators, consistency can be achieved. In Section 7.4 heterogeneity in the measurement error process is modelled, and its impact on estimator bias discussed. An extension allowing for memory in the error process is considered in Section 7.5. In Section 7.6 several applications of the Generalized Method of Moments (GMM) are considered. Focus here is on transforming the equation to differences to eliminate heterogeneity and using as IVs level values of the regressor not involved in constructing the difference. Another application, with the roles of the levels and differences reversed, is briefly commented on. In Section 7.7 we conclude and outline some extensions.

7.2 A homogeneous model

In this section we are concerned with a baseline model for error-ridden panel data without any heterogeneity. After presenting some notation, three kinds of estimators, denoted as basic (disaggregate) estimators, aggregate estimators, and difference estimators, will be considered. The section is intended to serve as a *preamble*, containing points of reference for the following discussion, considering more complex approaches for cases with various forms of heterogeneity.

7.2.1 MODEL SETUP: BASIC PROBABILITY LIMITS

Assume that N (≥ 2) individuals are observed in T (≥ 2) periods, and consider:

$$\begin{aligned} &y_{it} = k + x^*_{it}\beta + u_{it}, \quad (u_{it}|X^*) \sim \mathsf{IID}(0, \sigma^2), \\ &i = 1, \dots, N;\ t = 1, \dots, T, \end{aligned} \tag{7.1}$$

where y_{it} (observable) and x^*_{it} (latent) are the values of y and x^* for individual i in period t, β and k are unknown constants, u_{it} is a disturbance, and X^* symbolizes all values of the latent exogenous variable x^*_{it} which correspond to the data set. We observe x_{it}, a counterpart to x^*_{it} with measurement error η_{it} and assume

$$\begin{aligned} &x_{it} = x^*_{it} + \eta_{it}, \quad (\eta_{it}|X^*) \sim \mathsf{IID}(0, \sigma^2_\eta), \\ &u_{it} \perp \eta_{it}, \quad i = 1, \dots, N;\ t = 1, \dots, T. \end{aligned} \tag{7.2}$$

After elimination of x^*_{it}, the model can be rewritten as

$$\begin{aligned} &y_{it} = k + x_{it}\,\beta + u_{it} - \eta_{it}\beta, \quad u_{it} \perp \eta_{it}, \\ &(u_{it}|X^*) \sim \mathsf{IID}(0, \sigma^2), \quad (\eta_{it}|X^*) \sim \mathsf{IID}(0, \sigma^2_\eta), \\ &i = 1, \dots, N;\ t = 1, \dots, T. \end{aligned} \tag{7.3}$$

Hence, $\text{cov}(x_{it}, \eta_{it}) = \sigma^2_\eta$ and $\text{cov}(x_{it}, u_{it} - \eta_{it}\beta) = -\beta\sigma^2_\eta$, so that the composite error $u_{it} - \eta_{it}\beta$ is negatively (positively) correlated with x_{it} if β is positive (negative). An implication is that the OLS estimator of β in a regression of y_{it} on x_{it}, using all NT observations, is biased towards zero, an effect often denoted as *attenuation*.

As in earlier chapters, W, V, B, C (or w, v, b, c) indicate within-individual, within-period, between-individual, and between-period (co)variation, respectively. Further, D, E (or d, e) indicate product-sums in between-individual and between-period differences, respectively. Some compact general notation is required for probability limits of certain normalized product-sums:

$$\begin{aligned} w_{ij}(z, q) &= \operatorname*{plim}_{T\to\infty}\left[\tfrac{1}{T}\textstyle\sum_{t=1}^{T}(z_{it} - \bar{z}_{i\cdot})(q_{jt} - \bar{q}_{j\cdot})\right], \quad i, j = 1, \dots, N, \\ v_{ts}(z, q) &= \operatorname*{plim}_{N\to\infty}\left[\tfrac{1}{N}\textstyle\sum_{i=1}^{N}(z_{it} - \bar{z}_{\cdot t})(q_{is} - \bar{q}_{\cdot s})\right], \quad t, s = 1, \dots, T, \end{aligned} \tag{7.4}$$

$$\begin{aligned} d_{ij}(z, q) &= \operatorname*{plim}_{T\to\infty}\left[\tfrac{1}{T}\textstyle\sum_{t=1}^{T}(z_{it} - z_{jt})(q_{it} - q_{jt})\right], \quad i, j = 1, \dots, N, \\ e_{ts}(z, q) &= \operatorname*{plim}_{N\to\infty}\left[\tfrac{1}{N}\textstyle\sum_{i=1}^{N}(z_{it} - z_{is})(q_{it} - q_{is})\right], \quad t, s = 1, \dots, T. \end{aligned} \tag{7.5}$$

From (7.1)–(7.2) and the law of large numbers it follows that $\text{plim}_{T\to\infty}(\bar{\eta}_{i\cdot}) = \text{plim}_{N\to\infty}(\bar{\eta}_{\cdot t}) = 0$, that $w_{ij}(\eta, \eta) = \delta_{ij}\sigma^2_\eta$, $v_{ts}(\eta, \eta) = \delta_{ts}\sigma^2_\eta$, and that

$$\begin{aligned} w_{ij}(x,y) &= w_{ij}(x^*,x^*)\beta, \\ w_{ij}(x,x) &= w_{ij}(x^*,x^*) + \delta_{ij}\sigma_\eta^2, \end{aligned} \quad i,j=1,\dots,N, \tag{7.6}$$

$$\begin{aligned} v_{ts}(x,y) &= v_{ts}(x^*,x^*)\beta, \\ v_{ts}(x,x) &= v_{ts}(x^*,x^*) + \delta_{ts}\sigma_\eta^2, \end{aligned} \quad t,s=1,\dots,T, \tag{7.7}$$

where δ_{ij} and δ_{ts} are Kronecker-deltas. Further, $d_{ij}(\eta,\eta)=e_{ts}(\eta,\eta)=2\sigma_\eta^2$ for all (i,j) and (t,s), and

$$\begin{aligned} d_{ij}(x,y) &= d_{ij}(x^*,x^*)\beta, \\ d_{ij}(x,x) &= d_{ij}(x^*,x^*) + 2\sigma_\eta^2, \end{aligned} \quad i,j=1,\dots,N;\ i\neq j, \tag{7.8}$$

$$\begin{aligned} e_{ts}(x,y) &= e_{ts}(x^*,x^*)\beta, \\ e_{ts}(x,x) &= e_{ts}(x^*,x^*) + 2\sigma_\eta^2, \end{aligned} \quad t,s=1,\dots,T;\ t\neq s. \tag{7.9}$$

Regarding identification and estimation, the *time-serial properties* of x_{it}^* and η_{it} are crucial. Implications of (7.1) and (7.2) are that the measurement errors and disturbances are stationary, while x_{it}^* may be *non-stationary*. Under non-stationarity of x_{it}^*, certain plims of empirical second-order moments of x_{it}^*s when $T\to\infty$, N finite, for example $w_{ij}(x^*,x^*)$, $d_{ij}(x^*,x^*)$ or functions of them, may not exist. On the other hand, when $N\to\infty$, T finite, plims of moments of the type $v_{ts}(x^*,x^*)$ and $e_{ts}(x^*,x^*)$ and functions of them may well exist. This should be kept in mind when interpreting plims of estimators of β below.

Three kinds of estimators for β will be considered, denoted as *basic estimators* or *disaggregate estimators* (Section 7.2.2), *aggregate estimators* (Section 7.2.3), and *difference estimators* (Section 7.2.4). Aggregate estimators include within, between, residual estimators, etc., in Chapters 2, 3, 5, and 6 discussed for models without measurement errors. Examining how they can be constructed from disaggregate estimators will give insight. Although the disaggregate estimators will in most cases be (far) less efficient than the aggregate ones, we give them attention because they illustrate possibilities for estimating slope coefficients consistently which are not available when only pure cross-section or pure time-series data are at hand, and they may act as building blocks in the construction of aggregate estimators and may illustrate their anatomy.

7.2.2 BASIC (DISAGGREGATE) ESTIMATORS

Let, in general,

$$\begin{aligned} W_{ZQij} &= \textstyle\sum_{t=1}^{T}(z_{it}-\bar{z}_{i\cdot})(q_{jt}-\bar{q}_{j\cdot}), \quad i,j=1,\dots,N, \\ V_{ZQts} &= \textstyle\sum_{i=1}^{N}(z_{it}-\bar{z}_{\cdot t})(q_{is}-\bar{q}_{\cdot s}), \quad t,s=1,\dots,T, \end{aligned}$$

which represent, respectively, the *within-individual-covariation* between z for individual i and q for individual j, and the *within-period covariation* between z in period t and q in period s. Consider two sets of estimators of β:

$$\widehat{\beta}_{Wij} = \frac{W_{XYij}}{W_{XXij}} = \frac{\sum_{t=1}^{T}(x_{it} - \bar{x}_{i\cdot})(y_{jt} - \bar{y}_{j\cdot})}{\sum_{t=1}^{T}(x_{it} - \bar{x}_{i\cdot})(x_{jt} - \bar{x}_{j\cdot})}, \quad i,j = 1,\dots,N, \tag{7.10}$$

$$\widehat{\beta}_{Vts} = \frac{V_{XYts}}{V_{XXts}} = \frac{\sum_{i=1}^{N}(x_{it} - \bar{x}_{\cdot t})(y_{is} - \bar{y}_{\cdot s})}{\sum_{i=1}^{N}(x_{it} - \bar{x}_{\cdot t})(x_{is} - \bar{x}_{\cdot s})}, \quad t,s = 1,\dots,T. \tag{7.11}$$

They have the following interpretation: *(i)* $\widehat{\beta}_{Wij}$ $(i \neq j)$ *is an IV estimator for individual j using individual i's within-variation in the observed regressor as IV for individual j's within-variation.* There are $N(N-1)$ such estimators. *(ii)* $\widehat{\beta}_{Wii}$ *is the OLS estimator based on data from individual i only. (iii)* $\widehat{\beta}_{Vts}$ $(t \neq s)$ *is an IV estimator for period s, when using the period t within-variation in the observed regressor as IV for the period s within-variation.* There are $T(T-1)$ such estimators. (iv) $\widehat{\beta}_{Vtt}$ is the OLS estimator based on data from period t. We denote these estimators as *basic, disaggregate estimators.*

Are the requirements for $\widehat{\beta}_{Wij}$ $(i \neq j)$ and $\widehat{\beta}_{Vts}$ $(t \neq s)$ being IV estimators for β relative to (7.3) satisfied? We know that: $x_{it} - \bar{x}_{i\cdot}$ *is uncorrelated with both* $u_{jt} - \bar{u}_{j\cdot}$ *and* $\eta_{jt} - \bar{\eta}_{j\cdot}$ *for* $i \neq j$, *and if in addition* $x_{it} - \bar{x}_{i\cdot}$ *is correlated with* $x_{jt} - \bar{x}_{j\cdot}$ *(asymptotically when* $T \to \infty$*),* $x_{it} - \bar{x}_{i\cdot}$ *will be a valid IV for* $x_{jt} - \bar{x}_{j\cdot}$. Correlation between $x_{it} - \bar{x}_{i\cdot}$ and $x_{jt} - \bar{x}_{j\cdot}$ is ensured if x^*_{it} and x^*_{jt} have a common *period-specific* component, which an IID property for x^*_{it} violates. Likewise, $x_{it} - \bar{x}_{\cdot t}$ *is uncorrelated with both* $u_{is} - \bar{u}_{\cdot s}$ *and* $\eta_{is} - \bar{\eta}_{\cdot s}$ *for* $t \neq s$, *and if in addition* $x_{it} - \bar{x}_{\cdot t}$ *is correlated with* $x_{is} - \bar{x}_{\cdot s}$ *(asymptotically when* $N \to \infty$*),* $x_{it} - \bar{x}_{\cdot t}$ *will be a valid IV for* $x_{is} - \bar{x}_{\cdot s}$. Correlation between $x_{it} - \bar{x}_{\cdot t}$ and $x_{is} - \bar{x}_{\cdot s}$ is ensured if x^*_{it} and x^*_{is} have a common *individual-specific* component, by way of symmetry, which again an IID property for x^*_{it} violates.

It follows from (7.6) and (7.10) that the plims of the *individual-specific* basic estimators when T goes to infinity and $w_{ij}(x^*, x^*) \neq 0$, are

$$\underset{T\to\infty}{\text{plim}}\,(\widehat{\beta}_{Wij}) = \frac{w_{ij}(x,y)}{w_{ij}(x,x)} = \beta - \frac{\delta_{ij}\sigma_\eta^2\beta}{w_{ij}(x^*,x^*) + \delta_{ij}\sigma_\eta^2}, \quad i,j = 1,\dots,N. \tag{7.12}$$

All IV estimators $\widehat{\beta}_{Wij}$ $(i \neq j)$ *exist and are T-consistent,* while all OLS estimators $\widehat{\beta}_{Wii}$ are negatively (positively) biased when β is positive (negative). Symmetrically, it follows from (7.7) and (7.11) that the plims of the *period-specific* basic estimators when N goes to infinity and $v_{ts}(x^*, x^*) \neq 0$, are

$$\underset{N\to\infty}{\text{plim}}\,(\widehat{\beta}_{Vts}) = \frac{v_{ts}(x,y)}{v_{ts}(x,x)} = \beta - \frac{\delta_{ts}\sigma_\eta^2\beta}{v_{ts}(x^*,x^*) + \delta_{ts}\sigma_\eta^2}, \quad t,s = 1,\dots,T. \tag{7.13}$$

All IV estimators $\widehat{\beta}_{Vts}$ $(t \neq s)$ *exist and are* N*-consistent*, while all OLS estimators $\widehat{\beta}_{Vtt}$ are negatively (positively) biased when β is positive (negative).

Needless to say, these $N(N-1)+T(T-1)$ IV estimators are far from efficient, as each utilizes only a minor part of the data set. Any weighted mean of them will be consistent. If $w_{ij}(x^*,x^*)=0\ (i\neq j)$, $\text{plim}_{T\to\infty}(\widehat{\beta}_{Wij})$ does not exist, and if $v_{ts}(x^*,x^*)=0\ (t\neq s)$, $\text{plim}_{N\to\infty}(\widehat{\beta}_{Vts})$ does not exist. Sufficient for such non-existence is that all x^*_{it} are IID. An IID-structure for the latent exogenous variable is therefore unattractive and gives rise to identification problems similar to those in standard measurement error models. Biørn (2000) expands this argument.

7.2.3 AGGREGATE ESTIMATORS

We next reconsider, in the measurement error context, five estimators previously (Sections 2.1.2 and 2.3.2) considered for fixed effects models with no measurement errors. It is convenient now to reinterpret them as obtained by *aggregating the* N^2+T^2 *basic estimators (7.10)–(7.11)* in suitable ways.

Again, prototype aggregate *within-individual* and *within-period* (co)variation are defined as

$$W_{ZQ} = \textstyle\sum_{i=1}^{N} W_{ZQii}, \quad V_{ZQ} = \sum_{t=1}^{T} V_{ZQtt}, \tag{7.14}$$

Since $\bar{z}_{i\cdot}-\bar{z} \equiv \frac{1}{T}\sum_t(z_{it}-\bar{z}_{\cdot t})$, $\bar{z}_{\cdot t}-\bar{z} \equiv \frac{1}{N}\sum_i(z_{it}-\bar{z}_{i\cdot})$, etc., *the between-individual* (co)variation can be expressed by means the *period-specific within* (co)variation, and the *between-period* (co)variation can be expressed by means of the *individual-specific within* (co)variation:

$$B_{ZQ} = T\textstyle\sum_{i=1}^{N}(\bar{z}_{i\cdot}-\bar{z})(\bar{q}_{i\cdot}-\bar{q}) = \frac{1}{T}\sum_{t=1}^{T}\sum_{s=1}^{T} V_{ZQts}, \tag{7.15}$$

$$C_{ZQ} = N\textstyle\sum_{t=1}^{T}(\bar{z}_{\cdot t}-\bar{z})(\bar{q}_{\cdot t}-\bar{q}) = \frac{1}{N}\sum_{i=1}^{N}\sum_{j=1}^{N} W_{ZQij}. \tag{7.16}$$

Since the global covariation can be decomposed as

$$\begin{aligned} G_{ZQ} &\equiv W_{ZQ}+B_{ZQ} \equiv V_{ZQ}+C_{ZQ} \\ &\equiv B_{ZQ}+C_{ZQ}+R_{ZQ}, \end{aligned}$$

we have

$$\begin{aligned} R_{ZQ} &= \textstyle\sum_{i=1}^{N}\sum_{t=1}^{T}(z_{it}-\bar{z}_{i\cdot}-\bar{z}_{\cdot t}+\bar{z})(q_{it}-\bar{q}_{i\cdot}-\bar{q}_{\cdot t}+\bar{q}) \\ &\equiv W_{ZQ}-C_{ZQ} = V_{ZQ}-B_{ZQ}, \end{aligned}$$

and therefore,

$$R_{ZQ} = \sum_{i=1}^{N}[W_{ZQii} - \tfrac{1}{N}\sum_{j=1}^{N} W_{ZQij}]$$
$$= \sum_{t=1}^{T}[V_{ZQtt} - \tfrac{1}{T}\sum_{s=1}^{T} V_{ZQts}]. \quad (7.17)$$

The within, between, and residual estimators of β considered in matrix notation in Sections 3.2.3 and 3.6.3—now being labelled aggregate estimators—can therefore be expressed by means of the basic estimators (7.10) and (7.11) as, respectively:

$$\widehat{\beta}_W = \frac{W_{XY}}{W_{XX}} = \frac{\sum_{i=1}^{N} W_{XXii}\,\widehat{\beta}_{Wii}}{\sum_{i=1}^{N} W_{XXii}}, \quad (7.18)$$

$$\widehat{\beta}_B = \frac{B_{XY}}{B_{XX}} = \frac{\sum_{t=1}^{T}\sum_{s=1}^{T} V_{XXts}\,\widehat{\beta}_{Vts}}{\sum_{t=1}^{T}\sum_{s=1}^{T} V_{XXts}}, \quad (7.19)$$

$$\widehat{\beta}_V = \frac{V_{XY}}{V_{XX}} = \frac{\sum_{t=1}^{T} V_{XXtt}\,\widehat{\beta}_{Vtt}}{\sum_{t=1}^{T} V_{XXtt}}, \quad (7.20)$$

$$\widehat{\beta}_C = \frac{C_{XY}}{C_{XX}} = \frac{\sum_{i=1}^{N}\sum_{j=1}^{N} W_{XXij}\,\widehat{\beta}_{Wij}}{\sum_{i=1}^{N}\sum_{j=1}^{N} W_{XXij}}, \quad (7.21)$$

$$\widehat{\beta}_R = \frac{R_{XY}}{R_{XX}} = \frac{\sum_{i=1}^{N}[W_{XXii}\,\widehat{\beta}_{Wii} - \frac{1}{N}\sum_{j=1}^{N} W_{XXij}\,\widehat{\beta}_{Wij}]}{\sum_{i=1}^{N}[W_{XXii} - \frac{1}{N}\sum_{j=1}^{N} W_{XXij}]}$$
$$= \frac{\sum_{t=1}^{T}[V_{XXtt}\,\widehat{\beta}_{Vtt} - \frac{1}{T}\sum_{t=1}^{T} V_{XXts}\,\widehat{\beta}_{Vts}]}{\sum_{t=1}^{T}[V_{XXtt} - \frac{1}{T}\sum_{s=1}^{T} V_{XXts}]}. \quad (7.22)$$

The anatomy of the estimators can be described as follows:[1]

1. $\widehat{\beta}_W$ and $\widehat{\beta}_C$ are weighted means of the disaggregate within-*individual* estimators $\widehat{\beta}_{Wij}$. The former utilizes only the N individual-specific OLS estimators ($i\!=\!j$), the latter also the $N(N-1)$ IV estimators ($i \neq j$).
2. $\widehat{\beta}_V$ and $\widehat{\beta}_B$ are weighted means of the disaggregate within-*period* estimators $\widehat{\beta}_{Vts}$. The former utilizes only the T period-specific OLS estimators ($t\!=\!s$), the latter also the $T(T-1)$ IV estimators ($t \neq s$).
3. $\widehat{\beta}_R$ is a weighted mean of either the N^2 within-individual estimators or the T^2 within-period estimators.

[1] See Biørn (2005) for an extension of the argument.

When considering asymptotics, the following general notation is convenient:

$$w_N(z,q) = \operatorname*{plim}_{N\to\infty}[\tfrac{1}{NT}W_{ZQ}],$$
$$w_T(z,q) = \operatorname*{plim}_{T\to\infty}[\tfrac{1}{NT}W_{ZQ}],$$
$$w_{NT}(z,q) = \operatorname*{plim}_{N,T\to\infty}[\tfrac{1}{NT}W_{ZQ}].$$

In Appendix 7A, (7A.17)–(7A.31), it is shown that (7.18)–(7.22) converge in probability, when, respectively $N\to\infty$, $T\to\infty$, and both N and $T\to\infty$, to the respective expressions collected in Table 7.1. Here w_N^*, w_T^*, v_N^*, v_T^*, etc., are shorthand notation for $w_N(x^*,x^*)$, $w_T(x^*,x^*)$, $v_N(x^*,x^*)$, $v_T(x^*,x^*)$, etc. We see that:

(a) *The between-period estimator $\widehat{\beta}_C$ is N-consistent, but not T-consistent.*
(b) *The between-individual estimator $\widehat{\beta}_B$ is T-consistent, but not N-consistent.*
(c) *The biases in $\widehat{\beta}_W, \widehat{\beta}_V, \widehat{\beta}_R$ depend on the ratios between the measurement error variance σ_η^2 and the within-individual, the within-period, and the residual variation in the 'signal' x_{it}^*, respectively.*

The N-consistency of $\widehat{\beta}_C$ follows because it depends only on period-specific means, while $\text{plim}_{N\to\infty}(\bar{x}_{\cdot t} - \bar{x}_{\cdot t}^*) = \text{plim}_{N\to\infty}(\bar{\eta}_{\cdot t}) = \text{plim}_{N\to\infty}(\bar{u}_{\cdot t}) = 0$. Symmetrically, the T-consistency of $\widehat{\beta}_B$ follows because it depends only on individual-specific means, while $\text{plim}_{T\to\infty}(\bar{x}_{i\cdot} - \bar{x}_{i\cdot}^*) = \text{plim}_{T\to\infty}(\bar{\eta}_{i\cdot}) = \text{plim}_{T\to\infty}(\bar{u}_{i\cdot}) = 0$. Regressing $\bar{y}_{\cdot t}$ on $\bar{x}_{\cdot t}$ coin-

Table 7.1 Probability limits of aggregate estimators in Model (7.1)–(7.2)

Estimator	$\operatorname*{plim}_{N\to\infty}$	$\operatorname*{plim}_{T\to\infty}$	$\operatorname*{plim}_{N,T\to\infty}$
$\widehat{\beta}_W$	$\beta - \frac{\sigma_\eta^2(1-\frac{1}{T})\beta}{w_N^*+\sigma_\eta^2(1-\frac{1}{T})}$	$\beta - \frac{\sigma_\eta^2\beta}{w_T^*+\sigma_\eta^2}$	$\beta - \frac{\sigma_\eta^2\beta}{w_{NT}^*+\sigma_\eta^2}$
$\widehat{\beta}_B$	$\beta - \frac{\sigma_\eta^2\frac{1}{T}\beta}{b_N^*+\sigma_\eta^2\frac{1}{T}}$	β	β
$\widehat{\beta}_V$	$\beta - \frac{\sigma_\eta^2\beta}{v_N^*+\sigma_\eta^2}$	$\beta - \frac{\sigma_\eta^2(1-\frac{1}{N})\beta}{v_T^*+\sigma_\eta^2(1-\frac{1}{N})}$	$\beta - \frac{\sigma_\eta^2\beta}{v_{NT}^*+\sigma_\eta^2}$
$\widehat{\beta}_C$	β	$\beta - \frac{\sigma_\eta^2\frac{1}{N}\beta}{c_T^*+\sigma_\eta^2\frac{1}{N}}$	β
$\widehat{\beta}_R$	$\beta - \frac{\sigma_\eta^2(1-\frac{1}{T})\beta}{r_N^*+\sigma_\eta^2(1-\frac{1}{T})}$	$\beta - \frac{\sigma_\eta^2(1-\frac{1}{N})\beta}{r_T^*+\sigma_\eta^2(1-\frac{1}{N})}$	$\beta - \frac{\sigma_\eta^2\beta}{r_{NT}^*+\sigma_\eta^2}$

cides asymptotically with regressing $\bar{y}_{\cdot t}$ on $\bar{x}^*_{\cdot t}$ (since N-asymptotically $\bar{x}_{\cdot t}$ measures $\bar{x}^*_{\cdot t}$). Regressing $\bar{y}_{i\cdot}$ on $\bar{x}_{i\cdot}$ coincides asymptotically with regressing $\bar{y}_{i\cdot}$ on $\bar{x}^*_{i\cdot}$ (since T-asymptotically $\bar{x}_{i\cdot}$ measures $\bar{x}^*_{i\cdot}$). In short,

$$\underset{N\to\infty}{\text{plim}}\,(\bar{y}_{\cdot t}) = k + \underset{N\to\infty}{\text{plim}}\,(\bar{x}_{\cdot t})\beta,$$

$$\underset{T\to\infty}{\text{plim}}\,(\bar{y}_{i\cdot}) = k + \underset{T\to\infty}{\text{plim}}\,(\bar{x}_{i\cdot})\beta.$$

Assumptions required for this approach to work, underlying the above conclusions, are that, respectively, $\text{plim}_{N\to\infty}(\bar{x}_{\cdot t})$ is t-dependent and $\text{plim}_{T\to\infty}(\bar{x}_{i\cdot})$ is i-dependent.

We know from Section 2.3.2, that $\widehat{\beta}_W$ and $\widehat{\beta}_V$ can be interpreted as weighted means of $\widehat{\beta}_C$ and $\widehat{\beta}_R$ and of $\widehat{\beta}_B$ and $\widehat{\beta}_R$, respectively. Their plims have the same properties. Using $\bar{\beta}_{WN}, \bar{\beta}_{BN}, \dots$ as shorthand notation for $\text{plim}_{N\to\infty}(\widehat{\beta}_W)$, $\text{plim}_{N\to\infty}(\widehat{\beta}_B), \dots$, we find from Table 7.1, when $\beta > 0$, that:

$$\begin{aligned}
&\bar{\beta}_{RN} < \bar{\beta}_{WN} < \bar{\beta}_{CN} = \beta,\\
&\bar{\beta}_{RN} < \bar{\beta}_{VN} < \bar{\beta}_{BN} < \beta \iff r^*_N < (T-1)b^*_N,\\
&\bar{\beta}_{BN} < \bar{\beta}_{VN} < \bar{\beta}_{RN} < \beta \iff r^*_N > (T-1)b^*_N,
\end{aligned}$$

$$\begin{aligned}
&\bar{\beta}_{RT} < \bar{\beta}_{VT} < \bar{\beta}_{BT} = \beta,\\
&\bar{\beta}_{RT} < \bar{\beta}_{WT} < \bar{\beta}_{CT} < \beta \iff r^*_T < (N-1)c^*_T,\\
&\bar{\beta}_{CT} < \bar{\beta}_{WT} < \bar{\beta}_{RT} < \beta \iff r^*_T > (N-1)c^*_T.
\end{aligned}$$

For these results to hold, *the latent regressor, x^*_{it}, must satisfy some mild requirements*, in particular *it should not be* IID: why should $x^*_{it} \sim \text{IID}(\chi, \sigma^2_\kappa)$ be ruled out? It follows that in such a case,

$$\begin{aligned}
w^*_N &= r^*_N = (1-\tfrac{1}{T})\sigma^2_\kappa,\\
b^*_N &= \tfrac{1}{T}\sigma^2_\kappa,\\
v^*_N &= \sigma^2_\kappa,\\
c^*_N &= 0,
\end{aligned}$$

while, symmetrically,

$$\begin{aligned}
v^*_T &= r^*_T = (1-\tfrac{1}{N})\sigma^2_\kappa,\\
c^*_T &= \tfrac{1}{N}\sigma^2_\kappa,\\
w^*_T &= \sigma^2_\kappa,\\
b^*_T &= 0,
\end{aligned}$$

which when combined with the expressions in Table 7.1 imply

$$\begin{aligned}
&\bar{\beta}_{WN} = \bar{\beta}_{BN} = \bar{\beta}_{VN} = \bar{\beta}_{RN} = \beta\sigma_\kappa^2/(\sigma_\kappa^2+\sigma_\eta^2), && \text{for any } T,\\
&\bar{\beta}_{WT} = \bar{\beta}_{VT} = \bar{\beta}_{CT} = \bar{\beta}_{RT} = \beta\sigma_\kappa^2/(\sigma_\kappa^2+\sigma_\eta^2), && \text{for any } N,\\
&\bar{\beta}_{CN} \text{ does not exist,}\\
&\bar{\beta}_{BT} \text{ does not exist.}
\end{aligned}$$

To conclude: if x_{it}^* and η_{it} are IID, with variances σ_κ^2 and σ_η^2, respectively, then:

1. The two within estimators, the between individual estimator, and the residual estimator for β converge in probability to $\beta\sigma_\kappa^2/(\sigma_\kappa^2+\sigma_\eta^2)$ when $N \to \infty$ for any $T \geq 2$, while the plim of the between-period estimator does not exist.
2. The two within estimators, the between period estimator, and the residual estimator for β converge in probability to $\beta\sigma_\kappa^2/(\sigma_\kappa^2+\sigma_\eta^2)$ when $T \to \infty$, for any $N \geq 2$, while the plim of the between-individual estimator does not exist.

7.2.4 COMBINING INCONSISTENT ESTIMATORS

We have so far considered several inconsistent estimators of β. Such estimators have obvious methodical interest, although their practical appeal may seem limited. However, it is possible—if $x_{it}^* \sim$ IID is ruled out—to *estimate coefficients consistently by combining inconsistent estimators*. We will illustrate this when $N \to \infty$. From (7A.9) and (7A.11) in Appendix 7A, after elimination of $b_N(x^*, x^*)$ and $r_N(x^*, x^*)$, respectively, it follows that

$$\begin{aligned}
b_N(x,x) &= b_N(x,y)/\beta + \sigma_\eta^2/T,\\
r_N(x,x) &= r_N(x,y)/\beta + \sigma_\eta^2(1-1/T).
\end{aligned}$$

Eliminating σ_η^2 we get

$$\beta = \frac{(T-1)b_N(x,y) - r_N(x,y)}{(T-1)b_N(x,x) - r_N(x,x)}, \tag{7.23}$$

provided that $r_N(x,x) \neq (T-1)b_N(x,x)$. Estimating $b_N(x,x)$ and $b_N(x,y)$ by the finite-sample counterparts $B_{XX}/(NT)$ and $B_{XY}/(NT)$, and estimating $r_N(x,x)$ and $r_N(x,y)$ by $R_{XX}/(NT)$ and $R_{XY}/(NT)$, the following N-consistent estimator of β emerges:

$$\widehat{\beta}_{BR} = \frac{(T-1)B_{XY} - R_{XY}}{(T-1)B_{XX} - R_{XX}} = \frac{(T-1)B_{XX}\widehat{\beta}_B - R_{XX}\widehat{\beta}_R}{(T-1)B_{XX} - R_{XX}}. \tag{7.24}$$

This estimator combines the inconsistent between-individual and residual-estimators.

We can explain the N-consistency of $\widehat{\beta}_{BR}$ by giving an alternative interpretation of (7.24), exploiting (7.11). From (7.7) it follows that $v_{t,s}(x,y) = \beta[v_{t,s}(x,x) - \delta_{ts}\sigma_\eta^2]$ and hence

$$\beta = \frac{\sum_{t=1}^T \sum_{s=1,t\neq s}^T v_{ts}(x,y)}{\sum_{t=1}^T \sum_{s=1,t\neq s}^T v_{ts}(x,x)}, \tag{7.25}$$

Combining (7.15), (7.17), and (7.24), we obtain

$$\widehat{\beta}_{BR} = \frac{\sum_{t=1}^T \sum_{s=1,t\neq s}^T V_{XYts}}{\sum_{t=1}^T \sum_{s=1,t\neq s}^T V_{XXts}}. \tag{7.26}$$

This is simply the estimator we obtain from (7.25) when for all $t \neq s$ we replace $v_{ts}(x,x)$ and $v_{ts}(x,y)$ by V_{XXts}/N and V_{XYts}/N. The latter expression can be written as a weighted mean of the $T(T-1)$ N-consistent within-period IV estimators $\widehat{\beta}_{Vts}$:

$$\widehat{\beta}_{BR} = \frac{\sum_{t=1}^T \sum_{s=1,t\neq s}^T V_{XXts}\widehat{\beta}_{Vts}}{\sum_{t=1}^T \sum_{s=1,t\neq s}^T V_{XXts}}. \tag{7.27}$$

The N-consistency therefore follows because the inconsistent period-specific estimators $\widehat{\beta}_{Vtt}$ $(t = 1,\dots,T)$ have been removed from $\widehat{\beta}_B$, as given in (7.19), when constructing $\widehat{\beta}_{BR}$. Hence, $\widehat{\beta}_{BR}$ is N-consistent *for any* T, while $\widehat{\beta}_B$, although T-consistent, is not N-consistent.

7.2.5 DIFFERENCE ESTIMATORS

The third set of estimators for β we consider is constructed from *differences* between y_{it}s and between x_{it}s taken across individuals or over periods. Although differences over periods are usually of most interest, we look at both.

Let, in general,

$$D_{ZQij} = \sum_{t=1}^T (z_{it} - z_{jt})(q_{it} - q_{jt}), \qquad i,j = 1,\dots,N; i \neq j,$$
$$E_{ZQts} = \sum_{i=1}^N (z_{it} - z_{is})(q_{it} - q_{is}), \qquad t,s = 1,\dots,T; t \neq s,$$

and construct the *individual-specific difference-estimator* for individuals (i,j) and the *period-specific difference estimator* for periods (t,s) as, respectively,

$$\widehat{\beta}_{Dij} = \frac{D_{XYij}}{D_{XXij}} = \frac{\sum_{t=1}^{T}(x_{it}-x_{jt})(y_{it}-y_{jt})}{\sum_{t=1}^{T}(x_{it}-x_{jt})^2}, \qquad i,j = 1,\dots,N;\; i \neq j, \tag{7.28}$$

$$\widehat{\beta}_{Ets} = \frac{E_{XYts}}{E_{XXts}} = \frac{\sum_{i=1}^{N}(x_{it}-x_{is})(y_{it}-y_{is})}{\sum_{i=1}^{N}(x_{it}-x_{is})^2}, \qquad t,s = 1,\dots,T;\; t \neq s. \tag{7.29}$$

Utilizing (7.5), (7.8), and (7.9) it follows that:[2]

$$\operatorname*{plim}_{T\to\infty}(\widehat{\beta}_{Dij}) = \frac{d_{ij}(x,y)}{d_{ij}(x,x)} = \beta - \frac{2\sigma_\eta^2\,\beta}{d_{ij}(x^*,x^*)+2\sigma_\eta^2}, \qquad i \neq j, \tag{7.30}$$

$$\operatorname*{plim}_{N\to\infty}(\widehat{\beta}_{Ets}) = \frac{e_{ts}(x,y)}{e_{ts}(x,x)} = \beta - \frac{2\sigma_\eta^2\,\beta}{e_{ts}(x^*,x^*)+2\sigma_\eta^2}, \qquad t \neq s. \tag{7.31}$$

Again, we can *combine inconsistent estimators* to achieve consistency. Eliminating $d_{ij}(x^*,x^*)$ from (7.8) and $e_{ts}(x^*,x^*)$ from (7.9) we obtain

$$d_{ij}(x,x) = d_{ij}(x,y)/\beta + 2\sigma_\eta^2, \quad i \neq j,$$
$$e_{ts}(x,x) = e_{ts}(x,y)/\beta + 2\sigma_\eta^2, \quad t \neq s.$$

Letting a_{ij} $(i,j = 1,\dots,N)$ and b_{ts} $(t,s = 1,\dots,T)$ be constants, we derive

$$\textstyle\sum_i\sum_j a_{ij}d_{ij}(x,x) = (1/\beta)\sum_i\sum_j a_{ij}d_{ij}(x,y) + 2\sigma_\eta^2\sum_i\sum_j a_{ij},$$
$$\textstyle\sum_t\sum_s b_{ts}e_{ts}(x,x) = (1/\beta)\sum_t\sum_s b_{ts}e_{ts}(x,y) + 2\sigma_\eta^2\sum_t\sum_s b_{ts}.$$

Choosing the a_{ij}s and b_{ts}s so that $\sum_i\sum_j a_{ij} = \sum_t\sum_s b_{ts} = 0$, we obtain

$$\beta = \frac{\sum_i\sum_j a_{ij}d_{ij}(x,y)}{\sum_i\sum_j a_{ij}d_{ij}(x,x)} = \frac{\sum_t\sum_s b_{ts}e_{ts}(x,y)}{\sum_t\sum_s b_{ts}e_{ts}(x,x)}. \tag{7.32}$$

By replacing $d_{ij}(x,y)$ and $d_{ij}(x,x)$ by D_{XYij}/T and D_{XXij}/T, and replacing $e_{ts}(x,y)$ and $e_{ts}(x,x)$ by E_{XYts}/N and E_{XXts}/N, this can serve as an *estimator-generating equation*. If, for example,

$$b_{ts} = b_{t,s}^{\theta} - b_{t,s}^{\tau}, \quad t,s = 1,\dots,T;\; \theta = 2,\dots,T-1;\; \tau = 1,\dots,\theta-1,$$

[2] If $x_{it}^* \sim \mathsf{IID}(\chi,\sigma_\kappa^2) \Longrightarrow d_{ij}(x^*,x^*) = e_{ts}(x^*,x^*) = 2\sigma_\kappa^2,\ i \neq j;\ t \neq s$, it follows that

$$\operatorname*{plim}_{T\to\infty}(\widehat{\beta}_{Dij}) = \operatorname*{plim}_{N\to\infty}(\widehat{\beta}_{Ets}) = \frac{\sigma_\kappa^2}{\sigma_\kappa^2+\sigma_\eta^2}\beta.$$

where

$$b^{\theta}_{t,s} = \begin{cases} \frac{1}{T-\theta}, s < t-\theta, \\ 0, \quad s \geq t-\theta, \end{cases}$$

$$b^{\tau}_{t,s} = \begin{cases} \frac{1}{T-\tau}, s < t-\tau, \\ 0, \quad s \geq t-\tau, \end{cases}$$

we get

$$\beta = \frac{\frac{1}{T-\theta}\sum_{t=\theta+1}^{T} e_{t,t-\theta}(x,y) - \frac{1}{T-\tau}\sum_{t=\tau+1}^{T} e_{t,t-\tau}(x,y)}{\frac{1}{T-\theta}\sum_{t=\theta+1}^{T} e_{t,t-\theta}(x,x) - \frac{1}{T-\tau}\sum_{t=\tau+1}^{T} e_{t,t-\tau}(x,x)}, \tag{7.33}$$

provided that the denominator is non-zero. This motivates, for alternative (θ, τ)-combinations, the following estimators of β, all of which are N-consistent:

$$\widehat{\beta}_{\Delta\theta\tau} = \frac{\frac{1}{T-\theta}\sum_{t=\theta+1}^{T} E_{XYt,t-\theta} - \frac{1}{T-\tau}\sum_{t=\tau+1}^{T} E_{XYt,t-\tau}}{\frac{1}{T-\theta}\sum_{t=\theta+1}^{T} E_{XXt,t-\theta} - \frac{1}{T-\tau}\sum_{t=\tau+1}^{T} E_{XXt,t-\tau}}, \tag{7.34}$$

Consistent difference estimators can also be constructed by *utilizing as IVs for Δxs either x-differences or x-levels relating to other periods* than those occurring in the actual differences. Two examples, using as IVs for $x_{it}-x_{is}$, respectively, $x_{ip}-x_{ir}$ $(p, r \neq t, s)$, and x_{ip} $(p \neq t, s)$, illustrate this:

$$\widehat{\beta}_{\Delta(ts),\Delta(pr)} = \frac{\sum_i (x_{ip}-x_{ir})(y_{it}-y_{is})}{\sum_i (x_{ip}-x_{ir})(x_{it}-x_{is})}, \qquad t, s, p, r = 1, \dots, T; \; t \neq s \neq p \neq r, \tag{7.35}$$

$$\widehat{\beta}_{\Delta(ts),p} = \frac{\sum_i x_{ip}(y_{it}-y_{is})}{\sum_i x_{ip}(x_{it}-x_{is})}, \qquad t, s, p = 1, \dots, T; \; t \neq s \neq p. \tag{7.36}$$

They exist and are consistent if, respectively,

$$\operatorname*{plim}_{N\to\infty} [\tfrac{1}{N}\sum_i (x^*_{ip}-x^*_{ir})(x^*_{it}-x^*_{is})] \neq 0,$$

$$\operatorname*{plim}_{N\to\infty} [\tfrac{1}{N}\sum_i x^*_{ip}(x^*_{it}-x^*_{is})] \neq 0.$$

These conditions may be satisfied if x^*_{it} is autocorrelated or non-stationary, while an IID structure would still create an unsolvable estimation problem.

Model (7.1)–(7.2) is very simple and since it neglects any heterogeneity, its practical appeal may seem limited. However, several estimators involve within- and difference-transformations, which are usually motivated as a way of eliminating heterogeneity. Considering such estimators for homogeneous models is therefore primarily intended as a preamble to the construction of more complex procedures. Three extended models will be examined: heterogeneity in the equation (Section 7.3); heterogeneity in the error process (Section 7.4); and memory in the error process (Section 7.5).

7.3 **Extension I: Heterogeneity in the equation**

7.3.1 MODEL

We generalize the homogeneous model by including individual intercept heterogeneity, retaining (7.2) and extending (7.1) to

$$\begin{aligned} &y_{it} = k^* + x^*_{it}\beta + \alpha_i + u_{it}, \quad (u_{it}|X^*) \sim \mathsf{IID}(0,\sigma^2),\\ &i = 1,\dots,N;\ t = 1,\dots,T, \end{aligned} \tag{7.37}$$

where k^* is an intercept and α_i an individual effect. We proceed by letting, as in Section 6.1, α_i represent omitted individual-specific variables which are (potentially) correlated with the unobserved regressor, formalized as

$$\alpha_i = [\bar{x}^*_{i\cdot} - \mathsf{E}(\bar{x}^*_{i\cdot})]\lambda + w_i, \quad (w_i|X^*) \sim \mathsf{IID}(0,\sigma^2_w), \quad i = 1,\dots,N, \tag{7.38}$$

where λ is an unknown constant and w_i is an error term. From (7.1), (7.2), and (7.38) it follows that

$$\begin{aligned} &y_{it} = k + x^*_{it}\beta + \bar{x}^*_{i\cdot}\lambda + w_i + u_{it},\\ &x_{it} = x^*_{it} + \eta_{it}, \quad u_{it} \perp \eta_{it} \perp w_i,\\ &(u_{it}|X^*) \sim \mathsf{IID}(0,\sigma^2),\ (\eta_{it}|X^*) \sim \mathsf{IID}(0,\sigma^2_\eta),\ (w_i|X^*) \sim \mathsf{IID}(0,\sigma^2_w),\\ &i = 1,\dots,N;\ t = 1,\dots,T, \end{aligned} \tag{7.39}$$

where $k = k^* - \mathsf{E}(\bar{x}^*_{i\cdot})\lambda$. In Appendix 7A, see (7A.7) and (7A.9), it is shown that the following plims are implied when $N \to \infty$:

$$\begin{aligned} w_N(x,y) &= w_N(x^*,x^*)\beta,\\ w_N(x,x) &= w_N(x^*,x^*) + \sigma^2_\eta(1 - \tfrac{1}{T}), \end{aligned} \tag{7.40}$$

$$\begin{aligned} b_N(x,y) &= b_N(x^*,x^*)(\beta + \lambda),\\ b_N(x,x) &= b_N(x^*,x^*) + \sigma^2_\eta \tfrac{1}{T}. \end{aligned} \tag{7.41}$$

7.3.2 BETWEEN AND WITHIN ESTIMATION

From (7.39), after elimination of x^*_{it} and $\bar{x}^*_{i\cdot}$, we obtain

$$y_{it} = k + x_{it}\beta + \bar{x}_{i\cdot}\lambda + (u_{it} - \eta_{it}\beta) + (w_i - \bar{\eta}_{i\cdot}\lambda), \tag{7.42}$$

and hence,

$$\bar{y}_{i\cdot} = k + \bar{x}_{i\cdot}(\beta + \lambda) + \bar{u}_{i\cdot} + w_i - \bar{\eta}_{i\cdot}(\beta + \lambda), \tag{7.43}$$

$$(y_{it} - \bar{y}_{i\cdot}) = (x_{it} - \bar{x}_{i\cdot})\beta + (u_{it} - \bar{u}_{i\cdot}) - (\eta_{it} - \bar{\eta}_{i\cdot})\beta, \tag{7.44}$$

$$(y_{it} - \bar{y}_{i\cdot}) + \bar{y}_{i\cdot} = k + (x_{it} - \bar{x}_{i\cdot})\beta + \bar{x}_{i\cdot}(\beta + \lambda) + (u_{it} - \eta_{it}\beta) + (w_i - \bar{\eta}_{i\cdot}\lambda). \tag{7.45}$$

Applying OLS on (7.43) and (7.44), or on their sum (7.45), gives respectively, the *between-individual-estimator* and the *within-individual estimator*, formerly expressed as (7.19) and (7.18). Taking plim when $N \to \infty$ (after dividing the numerator and the denominator by NT) and utilizing (7.40) and (7.41), we get, respectively,

$$\operatorname*{plim}_{N\to\infty}(\widehat{\beta}_W) = \frac{w_N(x,y)}{w_N(x,x)} = \beta\left[1 - \frac{\sigma^2_\eta(1-\frac{1}{T})}{w^*_N + \sigma^2_\eta(1-\frac{1}{T})}\right], \tag{7.46}$$

$$\operatorname*{plim}_{N\to\infty}(\widehat{\beta}_B) = \frac{b_N(x,y)}{b_N(x,x)} = (\beta+\lambda)\left[1 - \frac{\sigma^2_\eta\frac{1}{T}}{b^*_N + \sigma^2_\eta\frac{1}{T}}\right]. \tag{7.47}$$

Therefore,

$$0 < \operatorname*{plim}_{N\to\infty}(\widehat{\beta}_W) < \beta \qquad (\beta > 0),$$

$$0 < \operatorname*{plim}_{N\to\infty}(\widehat{\beta}_B) < \beta+\lambda \qquad (\beta+\lambda > 0).$$

The plim of $\widehat{\beta}_B$ depends on $\beta+\lambda, \sigma^2_\eta$, and T. This estimator can alternatively be interpreted as the between-individual estimator of β in (7.37) when the correlation between α_i and $\bar{x}^*_{i\cdot}$ is neglected, or as the OLS estimator for $(\beta+\lambda)$ in (7.43) when correlation between α_i and $\bar{x}^*_{i\cdot}$ is allowed for—as explained in Section 6.2. If $\lambda \neq 0$ and $\sigma^2_\eta > 0$, $\widehat{\beta}_B$ is inconsistent for both β and $(\beta+\lambda)$ (when $N \to \infty$ and T is finite). If, however, both N and $T \to \infty$, $\widehat{\beta}_B$ is consistent for $(\beta+\lambda)$. Equivalently, as also explained in Section 6.2, $\widehat{\beta}_W$ and $\widehat{\beta}_B$ can be reinterpreted as OLS and GLS estimators for, respectively, β and $(\beta+\lambda)$ in (7.45).

It follows from (7.46) and (7.47) that the implied estimator for λ,

$$\widehat{\lambda} = \frac{B_{XY}}{B_{XX}} - \frac{W_{XY}}{W_{XX}} = \widehat{\beta}_B - \widehat{\beta}_W, \tag{7.48}$$

is inconsistent when $N \to \infty$. The bias in $\widehat{\beta}_B$ (as estimator of $\beta+\lambda$) and in $\widehat{\beta}_W$ (as estimator of β) are transmitted into $\widehat{\lambda}$. The bias can go in either direction, since

$$\operatorname*{plim}_{N\to\infty}(\widehat{\lambda}) - \lambda = -\frac{\sigma_\eta^2(\beta+\lambda)}{Tb_N^* + \sigma_\eta^2} + \frac{\sigma_\eta^2\beta}{\frac{T}{T-1}w_N^* + \sigma_\eta^2}. \tag{7.49}$$

If both β and λ are positive,

$$\operatorname*{plim}_{N,T\to\infty}(\widehat{\lambda}) > \lambda,$$

while

$$w_N^* \geq (T-1)b_N^* \Longrightarrow \operatorname*{plim}_{N\to\infty}(\widehat{\lambda}) < \lambda.$$

The overestimation of λ when $N, T \to \infty$ follows because then $\widehat{\beta}_W$ underestimates β, while $\widehat{\beta}_B$ is consistent for $(\beta+\lambda)$; see Table 7.1.

The main conclusions so far are:

1. $\widehat{\beta}_W$, considered as an estimator of β, has a bias which draws it towards zero (attenuation). $\widehat{\beta}_B$, considered as an estimator for $(\beta+\lambda)$, has a bias which draws it towards zero (it is attenuated for $\beta+\lambda$), while if considered as an estimator of β, its bias can have either sign.
2. The bias of the implied estimator of λ can have either sign. If $\beta > 0$, $\lambda > 0$, then $\operatorname{plim}_{N,T\to\infty}(\widehat{\lambda}) > \lambda$. If $w_N^* \geq (T-1)b_N^*$ (T finite), $\operatorname{plim}_{N\to\infty}(\widehat{\lambda}) < \lambda$.

In Section 7.2.4 we discussed, for Model (7.1)–(7.2), estimators constructed from variables differenced across individuals, $\widehat{\beta}_{Dij}$, and over periods, $\widehat{\beta}_{Ets}$. When the heterogeneity has the form (7.38), $\widehat{\beta}_{Ets}$ is usually the most interesting difference estimator, as the differencing eliminates the heterogeneity.

7.3.3 COMBINING INCONSISTENT ESTIMATORS

Consider, for this heterogeneous model, again the idea of combining inconsistent estimators to construct N-consistent estimators. Let

$$e_{N,\Delta\theta}(z,q) = \tfrac{1}{T-\theta}\textstyle\sum_{t=\theta+1}^{T} e_{t,t-\theta}(z,q),$$
$$E_{ZQ,\Delta\theta} = \textstyle\sum_{t=\theta+1}^{T} E_{ZQ,t,t-\theta} = \sum_{i=1}^{N}\sum_{t=\theta+1}^{T}(z_{it}-z_{i,t-\theta})(q_{it}-q_{i,t-\theta}).$$

It follows from (7.9) that since

$$\begin{aligned} e_{N,\Delta\theta}(x,y) &= e_{N,\Delta\theta}(x^*,x^*)\beta, \\ e_{N,\Delta\theta}(x,x) &= e_{N,\Delta\theta}(x^*,x^*) + 2\sigma_\eta^2, \end{aligned} \tag{7.50}$$

the θ-period difference estimator,

$$\widehat{\beta}_{\Delta\theta} = \frac{E_{XY,\Delta\theta}}{E_{XX,\Delta\theta}} = \frac{\sum_{t=\theta+1}^{T}\widehat{\beta}_{Et,t-\theta}E_{XX,t,t-\theta}}{\sum_{t=\theta+1}^{T}E_{XX,t,t-\theta}},\quad \theta=1,\dots,T-1, \tag{7.51}$$

satisfies

$$\operatorname*{plim}_{N\to\infty}(\widehat{\beta}_{\Delta\theta}) = \frac{e_{N,\Delta\theta}(x,y)}{e_{N,\Delta\theta}(x,x)} = \beta - \frac{2\sigma_\eta^2\beta}{e_{N,\Delta\theta}(x^*,x^*)+2\sigma_\eta^2}. \tag{7.52}$$

From (7.40) and (7.50) we find, respectively,

$$w_N(x,x) = w_N(x,y)/\beta + (1-\tfrac{1}{T})\sigma_\eta^2,$$
$$e_{N,\Delta\theta}(x,x) = e_{N,\Delta\theta}(x,y)/\beta + 2\sigma_\eta^2,$$

which after elimination of σ_η^2 gives, provided that $w_N(x,x) \neq \frac{1}{2}(1-\frac{1}{T})e_{N,\Delta\theta}(x,x)$,

$$\beta = \frac{2Tw_N(x,y) - (T-1)\,e_{N,\Delta\theta}(x,y)}{2Tw_N(x,x) - (T-1)\,e_{N,\Delta\theta}(x,x)},\qquad \theta = 1,2,\dots,T-1. \tag{7.53}$$

Estimating $w_N(x,x)$ and $w_N(x,y)$ by $W_{XX}/(NT)$ and $W_{XY}/(NT)$ and estimating $e_{N,\Delta\theta}(x,x)$ and $e_{N,\Delta\theta}(x,y)$ by $E_{XX,\Delta\theta}/(NT)$ and $E_{XY,\Delta\theta}/(NT)$, we obtain the N-consistent estimator[3]

$$\widehat{\beta}_{W\Delta\theta} = \frac{2W_{XY}-E_{XY,\Delta\theta}}{2W_{XX}-E_{XX\Delta\theta}} = \frac{2W_{XX}\widehat{\beta}_W - E_{XX,\Delta\theta}\widehat{\beta}_{\Delta\theta}}{2W_{XX}-E_{XX,\Delta\theta}}, \tag{7.54}$$

[3] If $\theta=T-1$, $\widehat{\beta}_{W\Delta\theta}$ becomes a '0/0-expression'. Therefore $\widehat{\beta}_{W\Delta\theta}$ is defined for $\theta = 1,\dots,T-2$, and can be interpreted as combining the inconsistent within-individual and first difference estimators. A similar result, obtained by combining plims of two inconsistent estimators, is given in Griliches and Hausman (1986, p. 95).

which combines the inconsistent estimators $\widehat{\beta}_W$ and $\widehat{\beta}_{\Delta\theta}$. This illustrates an important attraction of panel data. They enable us at the same time to come to grips with the endogeneity problem [$\lambda \neq 0$ in (7.38)] and the measurement error problem [$\sigma_\eta^2 > 0$ in (7.39)], without appealing to extraneous information. Such procedures would have been infeasible if we only had cross-section data ($T=1$).

7.4 **Extension II: Heterogeneity in the error**

7.4.1 MODEL

We return to the equation with full homogeneity in its 'structural part', (7.1):

$$
\begin{aligned}
&y_{it} = k + x_{it}^{*}\beta + u_{it}, \quad (u_{it}|X^{*}) \sim \mathsf{IID}(0,\sigma^2), \\
&i=1,\dots,N;\ t=1,\dots,T,
\end{aligned}
\tag{7.55}
$$

but extend the measurement error process (7.2) to a two-way, *three-component error*, one component relating to individual, one relating to period, and a remainder, so that the observed value of the regressor is given by

$$
\begin{aligned}
&x_{it} = x_{it}^{*} + \phi_i + \psi_t + \eta_{it}, \\
&(\phi_i|X^{*}) \sim \mathsf{IID}(0,\sigma_\phi^2),\ (\psi_t|X^{*}) \sim \mathsf{IID}(0,\sigma_\psi^2),\ (\eta_{it}|X^{*}) \sim \mathsf{IID}(0,\sigma_\eta^2), \\
&u_{it} \perp \phi_i \perp \psi_t \perp \eta_{it}, \\
&i = 1,\dots,N;\ t = 1,\dots,T.
\end{aligned}
\tag{7.56}
$$

The individual-specific measurement error component ϕ_i can represent individual, time-invariant 'habits' in error reporting, the period specific measurement error component ψ_t can represent errors relating to the period—correct measurement being more challenging to the data collector and the analyst in some periods than in others—while η_{it} is the genuine two-dimensional noise.

7.4.2 ESTIMATION

From (7.55)–(7.56), after elimination of x_{it}^{*}, we obtain

$$
y_{it} = k + x_{it}\beta + u_{it} - (\phi_i + \psi_t + \eta_{it})\beta, \quad i = 1,\dots,N;\ t = 1,\dots,T, \tag{7.57}
$$

while (7.6)–(7.7) are generalized to

$$\begin{aligned} w_{ij}(x,y) &= w_{ij}(x^*,x^*)\beta, \\ w_{ij}(x,x) &= w_{ij}(x^*,x^*) + \sigma_\psi^2 + \delta_{ij}\sigma_\eta^2, \end{aligned} \qquad i,j = 1,\dots,N, \tag{7.58}$$

$$\begin{aligned} v_{ts}(x,y) &= v_{ts}(x^*,x^*)\beta, \\ v_{ts}(x,x) &= v_{ts}(x^*,x^*) + \sigma_\phi^2 + \delta_{ts}\sigma_\eta^2, \end{aligned} \qquad t,s = 1,\dots,T. \tag{7.59}$$

Then (7.12) and (7.13) are generalized to

$$\operatorname*{plim}_{T\to\infty}(\widehat{\beta}_{Wij}) = \beta - \frac{(\sigma_\psi^2 + \delta_{ij}\sigma_\eta^2)\beta}{w_{ij}(x^*,x^*) + \sigma_\psi^2 + \delta_{ij}\sigma_\eta^2}, \quad i,j = 1,\dots,N, \tag{7.60}$$

$$\operatorname*{plim}_{N\to\infty}(\widehat{\beta}_{Vts}) = \beta - \frac{(\sigma_\phi^2 + \delta_{ts}\sigma_\eta^2)\,\beta}{v_{ts}(x^*,x^*) + \sigma_\phi^2 + \delta_{ts}\sigma_\eta^2}, \quad t,s = 1,\dots,T. \tag{7.61}$$

In this case, $\widehat{\beta}_{Wij}$ and $\widehat{\beta}_{Vts}$, unlike in the case with no error heterogeneity, are inconsistent for all (i,j) and all (t,s). Measurement errors bias not only the OLS estimators $\widehat{\beta}_{Wii}$ and $\widehat{\beta}_{Vtt}$, the error heterogeneity also destroys the consistency of $\widehat{\beta}_{Wij}$ $(i \neq j)$ and $\widehat{\beta}_{Vts}$ $(t \neq s)$. Strictly, however, the latter are no longer IV estimators, as they violate the instrument-error orthogonality for the following reason. Let $\tau_{it} = u_{it} - (\phi_i + \psi_t + \eta_{it})\beta$ denote the composite error/disturbance in (7.57). Then, $x_{it} - \bar{x}_{i\cdot}$ will not, for $i \neq j$, be a valid IV for $x_{jt} - \bar{x}_{j\cdot}$, since they both and $\tau_{jt} - \bar{\tau}_{j\cdot}$ contain $\psi_t - \bar{\psi}$, while $x_{it} - \bar{x}_{\cdot t}$ will not, for $t \neq s$, be a valid IV for $x_{is} - \bar{x}_{\cdot s}$, since they both and $\tau_{is} - \bar{\tau}_{\cdot s}$ contain $\phi_i - \bar{\phi}$.

Combining (7.58) and (7.59) with equations (7A.1)–(7A.6) in Appendix 7A, we obtain the results in Table 7.2. Comparing it with Table 7.1, we see the effect of allowing for the measurement error heterogeneity.

Table 7.2 Probability limits of aggregate estimators in Model (7.55)–(7.56)

Estimator	$\operatorname*{plim}_{N\to\infty}$	$\operatorname*{plim}_{T\to\infty}$	$\operatorname*{plim}_{N,T\to\infty}$
$\widehat{\beta}_W$	$\beta - \frac{[\sigma_\psi^2 + \sigma_\eta^2(1-\frac{1}{T})]\beta}{w_N^* + \sigma_\psi^2 + \sigma_\eta^2(1-\frac{1}{T})}$	$\beta - \frac{[\sigma_\psi^2 + \sigma_\eta^2]\beta}{w_T^* + \sigma_\psi^2 + \sigma_\eta^2}$	$\beta - \frac{[\sigma_\psi^2 + \sigma_\eta^2]\beta}{w_{NT}^* + \sigma_\psi^2 + \sigma_\eta^2}$
$\widehat{\beta}_B$	$\beta - \frac{[\sigma_\phi^2 + \sigma_\eta^2\frac{1}{T}]\beta}{b_N^* + \sigma_\phi^2 + \sigma_\eta^2\frac{1}{T}}$	$\beta - \frac{\sigma_\phi^2\beta}{b_T^* + \sigma_\phi^2}$	$\beta - \frac{\sigma_\phi^2\beta}{b_{NT}^* + \sigma_\phi^2}$
$\widehat{\beta}_V$	$\beta - \frac{[\sigma_\phi^2 + \sigma_\eta^2]\beta}{v_N^* + \sigma_\phi^2 + \sigma_\eta^2}$	$\beta - \frac{[\sigma_\phi^2 + \sigma_\eta^2(1-\frac{1}{N})]\beta}{v_T^* + \sigma_\phi^2 + \sigma_\eta^2(1-\frac{1}{N})}$	$\beta - \frac{[\sigma_\phi^2 + \sigma_\eta^2]\beta}{v_{NT}^* + \sigma_\phi^2 + \sigma_\eta^2}$
$\widehat{\beta}_C$	$\beta - \frac{\sigma_\psi^2\beta}{c_N^* + \sigma_\psi^2}$	$\beta - \frac{[\sigma_\psi^2 + \sigma_\eta^2\frac{1}{N}]\beta}{c_T^* + \sigma_\psi^2 + \sigma_\eta^2\frac{1}{N}}$	$\beta - \frac{\sigma_\psi^2\beta}{c_{NT}^* + \sigma_\psi^2}$
$\widehat{\beta}_R$	$\beta - \frac{\sigma_\eta^2(1-\frac{1}{T})\beta}{r_N^* + \sigma_\eta^2(1-\frac{1}{T})}$	$\beta - \frac{\sigma_\eta^2(1-\frac{1}{N})\beta}{r_T^* + \sigma_\eta^2(1-\frac{1}{N})}$	$\beta - \frac{\sigma_\eta^2\beta}{r_{NT}^* + \sigma_\eta^2}$

Using the same shorthand notation for plims of estimators ($\bar{\beta}_{RN}, \bar{\beta}_{RT}, \ldots$) as in Section 7.2.3, we obtain (for $\beta > 0$):

$$\bar{\beta}_{RN} < \bar{\beta}_{WN} < \bar{\beta}_{CN} < \beta \Longleftrightarrow 0 < T\frac{\sigma_\psi^2}{\sigma_\eta^2} r_N^* < (T-1)c_N^*,$$

$$\bar{\beta}_{CN} < \bar{\beta}_{WN} < \bar{\beta}_{RN} < \beta \Longleftrightarrow T\frac{\sigma_\psi^2}{\sigma_\eta^2} r_N^* > (T-1)c_N^*,$$

$$\bar{\beta}_{RN} < \bar{\beta}_{VN} < \bar{\beta}_{BN} < \beta \Longleftrightarrow (T\frac{\sigma_\phi^2}{\sigma_\eta^2} + 1) r_N^* < (T-1)b_N^*,$$

$$\bar{\beta}_{BN} < \bar{\beta}_{VN} < \bar{\beta}_{RN} < \beta \Longleftrightarrow (T\frac{\sigma_\phi^2}{\sigma_\eta^2} + 1) r_N^* > (T-1)b_N^*,$$

$$\bar{\beta}_{RT} < \bar{\beta}_{VT} < \bar{\beta}_{BT} < \beta \Longleftrightarrow 0 < N\frac{\sigma_\phi^2}{\sigma_\eta^2} r_T^* < (N-1)b_T^*,$$

$$\bar{\beta}_{BT} < \bar{\beta}_{VT} < \bar{\beta}_{RT} < \beta \Longleftrightarrow N\frac{\sigma_\phi^2}{\sigma_\eta^2} r_T^* > (N-1)b_T^*,$$

$$\bar{\beta}_{RT} < \bar{\beta}_{WT} < \bar{\beta}_{CT} < \beta \Longleftrightarrow (N\frac{\sigma_\psi^2}{\sigma_\eta^2} + 1) r_T^* < (N-1)c_T^*,$$

$$\bar{\beta}_{CT} < \bar{\beta}_{WT} < \bar{\beta}_{RT} < \beta \Longleftrightarrow (N\frac{\sigma_\psi^2}{\sigma_\eta^2} + 1) r_T^* > (N-1)c_T^*.$$

This demonstrates that a two-way, three-component design for the measurement errors may (1) for sufficiently large spread of the individual-specific measurement error, represented by $\sigma_\phi^2/\sigma_\eta^2$, give $\widehat{\beta}_B$ a stronger negative bias than $\widehat{\beta}_R$, and (2) for sufficiently large spread of the time-specific measurement error, represented by $\sigma_\psi^2/\sigma_\eta^2$, give $\widehat{\beta}_C$ a stronger negative bias than $\widehat{\beta}_R$.

Example: Assume that not only the measurement error, but also the latent regressor have a two-way, three-component design and specify:

$$x_{it}^* = \chi_i + \xi_t + \kappa_{it}, \quad \chi_i \sim \mathsf{IID}(\chi, \sigma_\chi^2), \quad \xi_t \sim \mathsf{IID}(0, \sigma_\xi^2), \quad \kappa_{it} \sim \mathsf{IID}(0, \sigma_\kappa^2).$$

Letting $\bar{\beta}_{ZNT} = \text{plim}_{N,T\to\infty}(\widehat{\beta}_Z)$ $(Z = W, B, V, C, R)$, the respective plims (corresponding to the last column of Table 7.2) can be expressed by the ratios between the noise and signal variance components $(\sigma_\phi^2, \sigma_\psi^2, \sigma_\eta^2)$ and $(\sigma_\chi^2, \sigma_\xi^2, \sigma_\kappa^2)$ as

$$\bar{\beta}_{WNT} = \frac{(\sigma_\xi^2 + \sigma_\kappa^2)\beta}{\sigma_\xi^2 + \sigma_\kappa^2 + \sigma_\psi^2 + \sigma_\eta^2},$$

$$\bar{\beta}_{BNT} = \frac{\sigma_\chi^2 \beta}{\sigma_\chi^2 + \sigma_\phi^2},$$

$$\bar{\beta}_{VNT} = \frac{(\sigma_\chi^2 + \sigma_\kappa^2)\beta}{\sigma_\chi^2 + \sigma_\kappa^2 + \sigma_\phi^2 + \sigma_\eta^2},$$

$$\bar{\beta}_{CNT} = \frac{\sigma_\xi^2 \beta}{\sigma_\xi^2 + \sigma_\psi^2},$$

$$\bar{\beta}_{RNT} = \frac{\sigma_\kappa^2 \beta}{\sigma_\kappa^2 + \sigma_\eta^2}.$$

7.4.3 COMBINING INCONSISTENT ESTIMATORS

Again, it is possible to estimate β consistently by combining inconsistent estimators. From (7.58) and (7.59) we derive

$$\begin{aligned} w_{ij}(x,x) &= w_{ij}(x,y)/\beta + \sigma_\psi^2 + \delta_{ij}\sigma_\eta^2, \qquad & i,j = 1,\dots,N, \\ v_{ts}(x,x) &= v_{ts}(x,y)/\beta + \sigma_\phi^2 + \delta_{ts}\sigma_\eta^2, \qquad & t,s = 1,\dots,T, \end{aligned}$$

and hence, letting a_{ij} $(i,j = 1,\dots,N)$ and b_{ts} $(t,s = 1,\dots,T)$ be constants,

$$\begin{aligned} \textstyle\sum_i \sum_j a_{ij} w_{ij}(x,x) &= \textstyle(1/\beta)\sum_i \sum_j a_{ij} w_{ij}(x,y) + \sigma_\psi^2 \sum_i \sum_j a_{ij} + \sigma_\eta^2 \sum_i a_{ii}, \\ \textstyle\sum_t \sum_s b_{ts} v_{ts}(x,x) &= \textstyle(1/\beta)\sum_t \sum_s b_{ts} v_{ts}(x,y) + \sigma_\phi^2 \sum_t \sum_s b_{ts} + \sigma_\eta^2 \sum_t b_{tt}. \end{aligned}$$

Choosing the a_{ij}s and b_{ts}s so that $\sum_i a_{ii} = \sum_t b_{tt} = 0$ and $\sum_i \sum_{j:j\neq i} a_{ij} = \sum_t \sum_{s:s\neq t} b_{ts} = 0$, it follows that β can be expressed as

$$\beta = \frac{\sum_i \sum_j a_{ij} w_{ij}(x,y)}{\sum_i \sum_j a_{ij} w_{ij}(x,x)} = \frac{\sum_t \sum_s b_{ts} v_{ts}(x,y)}{\sum_t \sum_s b_{ts} v_{ts}(x,x)}. \qquad (7.62)$$

Replacing $(w_{ij}(x,y), w_{ij}(x,x))$ by $(W_{XYij}/T, W_{XXij}/T)$ and $(v_{ts}(x,y), v_{ts}(x,x))$ by $(V_{XYts}/N, V_{XXts}/N)$, this can serve as an *estimator-generating equation.*

7.5 **Extension III: Memory in the error**

Consider a third generalization of the baseline model, (7.1)–(7.2):

$$\begin{aligned} &y_{it} = k + x_{it}^*\beta + u_{it}, \quad (u_{it}|X^*) \sim \mathsf{IID}(0,\sigma^2), \\ &i = 1,\dots,N;\ t = 1,\dots,T, \end{aligned} \qquad (7.63)$$

now assuming that the measurement error has a memory. This extension has relevance if, e.g., x_{it} is a stock obtained by cumulating flows, so that errors tend to vary cyclically. We discuss both the case where the measurement error has one component with memory, and a two-way, three-components design where both the time-specific and the two-dimensional components have memory.

7.5.1 ONE-COMPONENT ERROR WITH MEMORY

Let now (7.2) be generalized to

$$\begin{aligned} &x_{it}=x^*_{it}+\eta_{it}, \\ &\mathsf{E}(\eta_{it}|X^*)=0, \quad \mathsf{E}(\eta_{it}\eta_{js}|X^*)=\delta_{ij}r_{|t-s|}\sigma^2_\eta \ (r_0=1), \quad u_{it}\perp\eta_{it}, \end{aligned} \tag{7.64}$$

where $\{r_\theta\}_{\theta=1}^{\theta=T-1}$ is the correlogram of η_{it}. Since then $v_{ts}(\eta,\eta)=r_{|t-s|}\sigma^2_\eta$, we find that (7.7) and (7.13) are generalized to, respectively,

$$\begin{aligned} &v_{ts}(x,y)=v_{ts}(x^*,x^*)\beta, \\ &v_{ts}(x,x)=v_{ts}(x^*,x^*)+r_{|t-s|}\sigma^2_\eta \\ &\Longrightarrow v_{ts}(x,x)=v_{ts}(x,y)/\beta-r_{|t-s|}\sigma^2_\eta, \end{aligned} \tag{7.65}$$

$$\operatorname*{plim}_{N\to\infty}(\widehat{\beta}_{Vts})=\frac{v_{ts}(x,y)}{v_{ts}(x,x)}=\beta-\frac{r_{|t-s|}\sigma^2_\eta\beta}{v_{ts}(x^*,x^*)+r_{|t-s|}\sigma^2_\eta}. \tag{7.66}$$

Hence, $\widehat{\beta}_{Vts}$ is consistent only if $r_{|t-s|}=0$, i.e., if the measurement errors at a $|t-s|$ period distance are uncorrelated.

Let

$$G(r,T)=\tfrac{1}{T^2}\textstyle\sum_{q=1}^{T}\sum_{p=1}^{T}r_{|p-q|}\equiv\tfrac{1}{T^2}[T+2\sum_{s=1}^{T-1}(T-s)r_s].$$

Combining (7.65) and (7.14)–(7.17) and using similar algebra as in equations (7A.1)–(7A.6) in Appendix 7A, it follows that[4]

$$\begin{aligned} &v_N(x,x)-v_N(x,y)/\beta=v_N(\eta,\eta)=\sigma^2_\eta, \\ &b_N(x,x)-b_N(x,y)/\beta=b_N(\eta,\eta)=G(r,T)\,\sigma^2_\eta, \\ &c_N(x,x)-c_N(x,y)/\beta=c_N(\eta,\eta)=0, \\ &w_N(x,x)-w_N(x,y)/\beta=w_N(\eta,\eta)=[1-G(r,T)]\sigma^2_\eta, \\ &r_N(x,x)-r_N(x,y)/\beta=r_N(\eta,\eta)=[1-G(r,T)]\sigma^2_\eta. \end{aligned} \tag{7.67}$$

[4] The case with time-invariant, strongly persistent, measurement error, $x_{it}=x^*_{it}+\eta_i$, corresponds to $r_s=1, s=1,\dots,T-1\Longrightarrow G(r,T)=1$. Then it follows from (7.67) that $w_N(\eta,\eta)=r_N(\eta,\eta)=0$, so that $\widehat{\beta}_W$ and $\widehat{\beta}_R$ are consistent, because $x_{it}-\bar{x}_{i\cdot}$ is error-free.

Table 7.3 Probability limits in models without and with error memory

Estimator	$\text{plim}_{N\to\infty}$, no error memory	$\text{plim}_{N\to\infty}$, with error memory
$\widehat{\beta}_W$	$\beta - \dfrac{(1-\frac{1}{T})\sigma_\eta^2\beta}{w_N^*+(1-\frac{1}{T})\sigma_\eta^2}$	$\beta - \dfrac{[1-G(r,T)]\sigma_\eta^2\beta}{w_N^*+[1-G(r,T)]\sigma_\eta^2}$
$\widehat{\beta}_B$	$\beta - \dfrac{\frac{1}{T}\sigma_\eta^2\beta}{b_N^*+\frac{1}{T}\sigma_\eta^2}$	$\beta - \dfrac{G(r,T)\sigma_\eta^2\beta}{b_N^*+G(r,T)\sigma_\eta^2}$
$\widehat{\beta}_V$	$\beta - \dfrac{\sigma_\eta^2\beta}{v_N^*+\sigma_\eta^2}$	$\beta - \dfrac{\sigma_\eta^2\beta}{v_N^*+\sigma_\eta^2}$
$\widehat{\beta}_C$	β	β
$\widehat{\beta}_R$	$\beta - \dfrac{(1-\frac{1}{T})\sigma_\eta^2\beta}{r_N^*+(1-\frac{1}{T})\sigma_\eta^2}$	$\beta - \dfrac{[1-G(r,T)]\sigma_\eta^2\beta}{r_N^*+[1-G(r,T)]\sigma_\eta^2}$

The resulting plims of the aggregate estimators are given in Table 7.3, column 2, column 1 showing comparable plims for the no-memory case, which is characterized by $G(r,T)=\frac{1}{T}$. Still, the between-period estimator $\widehat{\beta}_C$ is N-consistent; the other estimators are negatively biased if $G(r,T)\in(0,1)$. While the plim of the within-period estimator $\widehat{\beta}_V$ does not depend on r, and T, $\widehat{\beta}_W$ $\widehat{\beta}_B$, and $\widehat{\beta}_R$ have plims depending, via $G(r,T)$, on the measurement error correlogram, we find

$$\begin{aligned}
&\bar{\beta}_{RN} < \bar{\beta}_{WN} < \bar{\beta}_{CN} = \beta,\\
&\bar{\beta}_{RN} < \bar{\beta}_{VN} < \bar{\beta}_{BN} < \beta \iff G(r,T)r_N^* < [1-G(r,T)]b_N^*,\\
&\bar{\beta}_{BN} < \bar{\beta}_{VN} < \bar{\beta}_{RN} < \beta \iff G(r,T)r_N^* > [1-G(r,T)]b_N^*.
\end{aligned}$$

Since (7.9) is generalized to

$$\begin{aligned}
&e_{ts}(x,y) = e_{ts}(x^*,x^*)\beta,\\
&e_{ts}(x,x) = e_{ts}(x^*,x^*) + 2(1-r_{|t-s|})\sigma_\eta^2\\
&\implies e_{ts}(x,x) = e_{ts}(x,y)/\beta + 2(1-r_{|t-s|})\sigma_\eta^2,
\end{aligned} \tag{7.68}$$

it follows, for the *difference estimators* defined in Section 7.2.5, that (7.31) is generalized to

$$\underset{N\to\infty}{\text{plim}}\,(\widehat{\beta}_{Ets}) = \frac{e_{ts}(x,y)}{e_{ts}(x,x)} = \beta - \frac{2(1-r_{|t-s|})\sigma_\eta^2\beta}{e_{ts}(x^*,x^*)+2(1-r_{|t-s|})\sigma_\eta^2}. \tag{7.69}$$

Obviously, $\widehat{\beta}_{Ets}$ is consistent if $r_{|t-s|}=1$. The intuition is that if the measurement errors at a $t-s$ period distance are perfectly correlated, differencing removes the error. Otherwise, the estimator is attenuated.

How can *N-consistent estimation* be ensured with this kind of estimator? Let $t=T$, $s=T-\theta$ and assume that $r_\theta=0$ for $\theta>M$. From (7.68) we obtain

$$e_{T,T-\theta}(x,x) = e_{T,T-\theta}(x,y)/\beta + 2(1-r_\theta)\sigma_\eta^2, \qquad \theta = 1,\dots,T-1,$$

which can be solved for $(\beta,\sigma_\eta^2,r_1,\dots,r_M)$ after having replaced $e_{T,T}, e_{T,T-1},\dots,e_{T,1}$ by their sample counterparts, provided that $M\leq T-3$.

7.5.2 THREE-COMPONENT SPECIFICATION

We extend (7.56) and (7.64) into a two-way, three-component version where both the time-specific and the two-dimensional component of the signal have memory and correlograms, respectively, $\{p_\theta\}_{\theta=1}^{\theta=T-1}$ and $\{r_\theta\}_{\theta=1}^{\theta=T-1}$:

$$\begin{aligned}
&x_{it} = x_{it}^* + \phi_i + \psi_t + \eta_{it},\\
&(\phi_i|X^*) \sim \mathsf{IID}(0,\sigma_\phi^2),\\
&\mathsf{E}(\psi_t|X^*) = 0,\ \mathsf{E}(\psi_t\psi_s|X^*) = p_{|t-s|}\sigma_\psi^2\ (p_0=1),\\
&\mathsf{E}(\eta_{it}|X^*) = 0,\ \mathsf{E}(\eta_{it}\,\eta_{js}|X^*) = \delta_{ij}r_{|t-s|}\sigma_\eta^2\ (r_0=1),\\
&\phi_i \perp \psi_t \perp \eta_{it} \perp u_{it},\\
&i,j = 1,\dots,N;\ t,s = 1,\dots,T.
\end{aligned} \tag{7.70}$$

Then (7.65)–(7.66) are extended to

$$\begin{aligned}
&v_{ts}(x,y) = v_{ts}(x^*,x^*)\beta,\\
&v_{ts}(x,x) = v_{ts}(x^*,x^*) + \sigma_\phi^2 + r_{|t-s|}\sigma_\eta^2,\\
&\Longrightarrow\ v_{ts}(x,x) = v_{ts}(x,y)/\beta + \sigma_\phi^2 + r_{|t-s|}\sigma_\eta^2,
\end{aligned} \tag{7.71}$$

$$\underset{N\to\infty}{\text{plim}}\,(\widehat{\beta}_{Vts}) = \frac{v_{ts}(x,y)}{v_{ts}(x,x)} = \beta - \frac{(\sigma_\phi^2 + r_{|t-s|}\sigma_\eta^2)\beta}{v_{ts}(x^*,x^*) + \sigma_\phi^2 + r_{|t-s|}\sigma_\eta^2}. \tag{7.72}$$

Hence, $\widehat{\beta}_{Vts}$ is inconsistent unless (by chance) $r_{|t-s|}=-\sigma_\phi^2/\sigma_\eta^2$.

Assume that not only the measurement error, but also the latent regressor x_{it}^* has a three-components structure and specify

$$\begin{aligned}
&x_{it}^* = \chi_i + \xi_t + \kappa_{it},\\
&\chi_i \sim \mathsf{IID}(\chi,\sigma_\chi^2),\\
&\mathsf{E}(\xi_t) = 0,\quad \mathsf{E}(\xi_t\xi_s) = \pi_{|t-s|}\,\sigma_\xi^2 \qquad (\pi_0=1),\\
&\mathsf{E}(\kappa_{it}) = 0,\quad \mathsf{E}(\kappa_{it}\,\kappa_{js}) = \delta_{ij}\,\rho_{|t-s|}\,\sigma_\kappa^2\ (\rho_0=1),\\
&\chi_i \perp \xi_t \perp \kappa_{it},\\
&i,j = 1,\dots,N;\ t,s = 1,\dots,T,
\end{aligned}$$

where both the time-specific and the two-dimensional component have memory and correlograms, respectively, $\{\pi_\theta\}_{\theta=1}^{\theta=T-1}$ and $\{\rho_\theta\}_{\theta=1}^{\theta=T-1}$, and let

$$G(\rho, T) = \tfrac{1}{T^2} \textstyle\sum_{q=1}^{T} \sum_{p=1}^{T} \rho_{|p-q|} = \tfrac{1}{T^2}[T + 2\sum_{s=1}^{T-1}(T-s)\rho_s].$$

We then have

$$\begin{aligned}
v_N(x^*, x^*) &= \sigma_\chi^2 + \sigma_\kappa^2, \\
b_N(x^*, x^*) &= \sigma_\chi^2 + G(\rho, T)\sigma_\kappa^2, \\
c_N(x^*, x^*) &= c_N(\xi+\kappa, \xi+\kappa) \approx \sigma_\xi^2, \\
w_N(x^*, x^*) &= w_N(\xi+\kappa, \xi+\kappa) \approx w_N(\xi, \xi) + w_N(\kappa, \kappa) \approx \sigma_\xi^2 + [1-G(\rho, T)]\sigma_\kappa^2, \\
r_N(x^*, x^*) &= [1-G(\rho, T)]\sigma_\kappa^2,
\end{aligned}$$

which implies that the entries in the first column of Table 7.2, for the *aggregate estimators* when $N \to \infty$ and T is finite, change to

$$\begin{aligned}
\bar{\beta}_{WN} &\approx \frac{(\sigma_\xi^2 + [1-G(\rho, T)]\sigma_\kappa^2)\beta}{\sigma_\xi^2 + [1-G(\rho, T)]\sigma_\kappa^2 + \sigma_\psi^2 + [1-G(r, T)]\sigma_\eta^2}, \\
\bar{\beta}_{BN} &= \frac{(\sigma_\chi^2 + G(\rho, T)\,\sigma_\kappa^2)\beta}{\sigma_\chi^2 + G(\rho, T)\,\sigma_\kappa^2 + \sigma_\phi^2 + G(r, T)\,\sigma_\eta^2}, \\
\bar{\beta}_{VN} &= \frac{(\sigma_\chi^2 + \sigma_\kappa^2)\,\beta}{\sigma_\chi^2 + \sigma_\kappa^2 + \sigma_\phi^2 + \sigma_\eta^2}, \\
\bar{\beta}_{CN} &\approx \frac{\sigma_\xi^2\,\beta}{\sigma_\xi^2 + \sigma_\psi^2}, \\
\bar{\beta}_{RN} &= \frac{[1-G(\rho, T)]\sigma_\kappa^2\beta}{[1-G(\rho, T)]\sigma_\kappa^2 + [1-G(r, T)]\sigma_\eta^2}.
\end{aligned}$$

These expressions give some interesting conclusions about how changes in the correlograms of, respectively, the two-dimensional component of the measurement error (noise) and the corresponding component of the latent regressor (signal) affect the estimator bias:

1. The biases of $\widehat{\beta}_C$ and $\widehat{\beta}_V$ do not depend on $\{r_\theta\}_{\theta=1}^{\theta=T-1}$ and $\{\rho_\theta\}_{\theta=1}^{\theta=T-1}$.
2. An increase in any element of the correlogram of the *two-dimensional noise* η_{it} *reduces* the bias of $\widehat{\beta}_R$ and $\widehat{\beta}_W$ and *increases* the bias of $\widehat{\beta}_B$. If, at the extreme, $r_1 = \cdots = r_{T-1} = 1 \Longrightarrow G(r, T) = 1$, $\widehat{\beta}_R$ is unbiased (as the residual transformation

eliminates the signal), while the plim of $\widehat{\beta}_W$ is positive (but less than β) as long as $\sigma_\psi^2 > 0$.

3. An increase in any element of the correlogram of the *two-dimensional signal* κ_{it} *increases* the bias of $\widehat{\beta}_R$ and $\widehat{\beta}_W$ and *reduces* the bias of $\widehat{\beta}_B$. If, at the extreme, $\rho_1 = \cdots = \rho_{T-1} = 1 \Longrightarrow G(\rho, T) = 1$, $\widehat{\beta}_R$ converges to zero (as the residual transformation eliminates the noise), while the plim of $\widehat{\beta}_W$ is positive (but less than β) when $\sigma_\xi^2 > 0$.

Turning once again to the *difference estimators*, it follows that (7.68) is generalized to

$$e_{ts}(x,y) = e_{ts}(x^* + \psi, x^*)\beta,$$
$$e_{ts}(x,x) = e_{ts}(x^* + \psi, x^* + \psi) + 2(1 - r_{|t-s|})\,\sigma_\eta^2, \quad t \neq s.$$

If $T - \theta$ is not too small, we have the approximations

$$\begin{aligned}\tfrac{1}{T-\theta}\textstyle\sum_{t=\theta+1}^T e_{t,t-\theta}(x^* + \psi, x^* + \psi) &\approx \tfrac{1}{T-\theta}\textstyle\sum_{t=\theta+1}^T e_{t,t-\theta}(x^*, x^*) + 2(1-p_\theta)\sigma_\psi^2 \\ &\approx 2(1-\pi_\theta)\sigma_\xi^2 + 2(1-\rho_\theta)\sigma_\kappa^2 + 2(1-p_\theta)\sigma_\psi^2, \\ \tfrac{1}{T-\theta}\textstyle\sum_{t=\theta+1}^T e_{t,t-\theta}(x^* + \psi, x^*) &\approx \tfrac{1}{T-\theta}\textstyle\sum_{t=\theta+1}^T e_{t,t-\theta}(x^*, x^*) \\ &\approx 2(1-\pi_\theta)\sigma_\xi^2 + 2(1-\rho_\theta)\sigma_\kappa^2,\end{aligned}$$

from which it follows, after some algebra, that (7.52) is modified to

$$\operatorname*{plim}_{N\to\infty}(\widehat{\beta}_{\Delta\theta}) \approx \beta - \frac{[(1-p_\theta)\sigma_\psi^2 + (1-r_\theta)\sigma_\eta^2]\beta}{(1-\pi_\theta)\sigma_\xi^2 + (1-\rho_\theta)\sigma_\kappa^2 + (1-p_\theta)\sigma_\psi^2 + (1-r_\theta)\sigma_\eta^2},$$
$$\theta = 1, 2, \dots, T-1.$$

Therefore:

1. An increased autocorrelation coefficient of the ψ_t component of the measurement error, p_θ, or in the autocorrelation coefficient of its η_{it} component, r_θ, will *reduce* the bias of the θ-period difference estimator. In the boundary case $r_\theta = p_\theta = 1$, the bias disappears, as differencing eliminates the noise.
2. An increased autocorrelation coefficient of the ξ_t component of the latent regressor, π_θ, or in the autocorrelation coefficient of its κ_{it} component, ρ_θ, will *increase* the bias of the θ-period difference estimator. In the boundary case $\rho_\theta = \pi_\theta = 1$, this estimator converges to zero, as the differencing eliminates the signal.

Briefly and intuitively, we can then conclude: the stronger the positive correlation of the measurement errors at a θ-period distance is, the 'more of the noise' will be eliminated when transforming the equation to a θ-period difference. The stronger the positive correlation of the latent exogenous variables at a θ-period distance is, the 'more of the signal' is eliminated when taking the θ-period differences.

7.6 **Generalized Method of Moments estimators**

We return to the model in Section 7.3, Model (7.39), which originates from (7.37), still with individual-specific heterogeneity specified as in (7.38). However, we will no longer stick strictly to the rather strong assumptions $(u_{it}|X^*) \sim \mathsf{IID}(0, \sigma^2)$ and $(\eta_{it}|X^*) \sim \mathsf{IID}(0, \sigma_\eta^2)$. They may be weakened in that the disturbance and the measurement error may be allowed to have memory. For such a modified Model (7.39) we consider estimation procedures which are more complex than those described in Sections 7.2.4, 7.3.2, and 7.3.3.

We specifically consider estimation by the GMM. This represents a large step forwards relative to the simple application of IVs in the basic estimators considered in Section 7.2.2. Another modification is that from now on the specific form of the heterogeneity will be immaterial since we, anyway, eliminate α_i or $\bar{x}_{i\cdot}^*\beta+w_i$ by taking the equation to differences.

7.6.1 GENERALITIES ON THE GMM

Before elaborating the GMM procedures for our panel data situation, we describe some generalities of this estimation principle, for later reference.[5] Assume, in general, that we want to estimate the $(K \times 1)$ coefficient *vector* $\boldsymbol{\beta}$ in the equation

$$y = \boldsymbol{x}\boldsymbol{\beta} + \epsilon, \tag{7.73}$$

where y and ϵ are scalars and $\boldsymbol{x}$ is a $(1 \times K)$ regressor *vector*.[6] We assume that an IV *vector* z, of dimension $(1 \times G)$, for $\boldsymbol{x}$ $(G \geq K)$, exists, satisfying the *orthogonality conditions*

$$\mathsf{E}(z'\epsilon) = \mathsf{E}[z'(y - \boldsymbol{x}\boldsymbol{\beta})] = 0_{G,1} \iff \mathsf{E}(z'y) = \mathsf{E}(z'\boldsymbol{x})\boldsymbol{\beta} \tag{7.74}$$

and the *rank condition*

$$\text{rank}[\mathsf{E}(z'\boldsymbol{x})] = K. \tag{7.75}$$

[5] Davidson and MacKinnon (1993, Chapter 17), Harris and Mátyás (1999), and Hall (2005) give more extensive and more technical expositions.

[6] Modifications required for panel data when x and z are extended to matrices and y and ϵ are extended to vectors will be explained below.

These conditions are assumed to be derived from the theory and the statistical hypotheses underlying our model.

We have n observations on $(y, \boldsymbol{x}, \boldsymbol{z})$, denoted as $(y_j, \boldsymbol{x}_j, \boldsymbol{z}_j), j = 1, \dots, n$, and define the vector valued $(G \times 1)$ function of corresponding means taken over all observations,

$$\boldsymbol{g}_n(y, \boldsymbol{x}, \boldsymbol{z}; \boldsymbol{\beta}) = \tfrac{1}{n} \textstyle\sum_{j=1}^{n} \boldsymbol{z}_j'(y_j - \boldsymbol{x}_j\boldsymbol{\beta}).$$

It may be regarded as the empirical counterpart to $\mathsf{E}[\boldsymbol{z}'(y - \boldsymbol{x}\boldsymbol{\beta})]$.

The *essence of the GMM* is to choose as estimator for $\boldsymbol{\beta}$ the value which brings the value of $\boldsymbol{g}_n(y, \boldsymbol{x}, \boldsymbol{z}; \boldsymbol{\beta})$ as close to its theoretical counterpart, the zero vector $\mathbf{0}_{G,1}$, as possible. If $G = K$, an exact solution to the equation $\boldsymbol{g}_n(y, \boldsymbol{x}, \boldsymbol{z}; \boldsymbol{\beta}) = \mathbf{0}_{G,1}$ exists and is the simple IV estimator

$$\boldsymbol{\beta}^* = [\textstyle\sum_j \boldsymbol{z}_j'\boldsymbol{x}_j]^{-1}[\textstyle\sum_j \boldsymbol{z}_j'y_j]. \tag{7.76}$$

If $G > K$, which is a more common situation, GMM solves the estimation problem by *minimizing a distance measure represented by a quadratic form in* $g_n(y, \boldsymbol{x}, \boldsymbol{z}; \boldsymbol{\beta})$ *for a suitably chosen positive definite* $(G \times G)$ *weighting matrix* $\boldsymbol{V}_n$, i.e.,

$$\boldsymbol{\beta}^*_{GMM} = \text{argmin}_{\boldsymbol{\beta}}[\boldsymbol{g}_n(y, \boldsymbol{x}, \boldsymbol{z}; \boldsymbol{\beta})'\boldsymbol{V}_n\boldsymbol{g}_n(y, \boldsymbol{x}, \boldsymbol{z}; \boldsymbol{\beta})]. \tag{7.77}$$

All estimators thus obtained are consistent. The choice of $\boldsymbol{V}_n$ determines the efficiency of the method. A choice which leads to an asymptotically efficient estimator of $\boldsymbol{\beta}$ is to set this weighting matrix equal (or proportional) to the inverse of (an estimate of) the (asymptotic) covariance matrix of $\frac{1}{n}\sum_{j=1}^{n} \boldsymbol{z}_j'\epsilon_j$; see, e.g., Davidson and MacKinnon (1993, Theorem 17.3) and Harris and Mátyás (1999, Section 1.3.3).

If ϵ is serially uncorrelated and homoskedastic, with variance σ_ϵ^2, the inverse of (the asymptotic) covariance matrix of $\frac{1}{n}\sum_{j=1}^{n} \boldsymbol{z}_j'\epsilon_j$ is simply $\boldsymbol{V}_n = [n^{-2}\sigma_\epsilon^2 \sum_{j=1}^{n} \boldsymbol{z}_j'\boldsymbol{z}_j]^{-1}$. The estimator following from (7.77) then becomes

$$\begin{aligned}\widehat{\boldsymbol{\beta}}_{GMM} &= [(\textstyle\sum_j \boldsymbol{x}_j'\boldsymbol{z}_j)(\textstyle\sum_j \boldsymbol{z}_j'\boldsymbol{z}_j)^{-1}(\textstyle\sum_j \boldsymbol{z}_j'\boldsymbol{x}_j)]^{-1} \\ &\quad \times [(\textstyle\sum_j \boldsymbol{x}_j'\boldsymbol{z}_j)(\textstyle\sum_j \boldsymbol{z}_j'\boldsymbol{z}_j)^{-1}(\textstyle\sum_j \boldsymbol{z}_j'y_j)],\end{aligned} \tag{7.78}$$

since σ_ϵ^2 cancels. It may be called the *step-one GMM estimator* and coincides with the 2SLS estimator and generalizes (7.76).

The GMM-procedure can, however, also be applied if ϵ_j has a *heteroskedasticity of unspecified form*. The procedure then consists in first constructing consistent residuals $\widehat{\epsilon}_j$, usually from (7.78), next estimating $\boldsymbol{V}_n$ by $\widehat{\boldsymbol{V}}_n = [n^{-2}\sum_j \boldsymbol{z}_j'\widehat{\epsilon}_j^2\boldsymbol{z}_j]^{-2}$ (see White (1984, Sections IV.3 and VI.2) and (1986, Section 3)), and finally inserting this expression in

(7.77) to obtain the *step-two GMM estimator*

$$\widetilde{\boldsymbol{\beta}}_{GMM} = [(\sum_j \boldsymbol{x}_j'\boldsymbol{z}_j)(\sum_j \boldsymbol{z}_j'\widehat{\epsilon}_j^2\boldsymbol{z}_j)^{-1}(\sum_j \boldsymbol{z}_j'\boldsymbol{x}_j)]^{-1} \\ \times\ [(\sum_j \boldsymbol{x}_j'\boldsymbol{z}_j)(\sum_j \boldsymbol{z}_j'\widehat{\epsilon}_j^2\boldsymbol{z}_j)^{-1}(\sum_j \boldsymbol{z}_j'y_j)]. \quad (7.79)$$

Under heteroskedasticity $\widetilde{\boldsymbol{\beta}}_{GMM}$ is (asymptotically) more efficient than $\widehat{\boldsymbol{\beta}}_{GMM}$. It may then be labelled as a 'heteroskedasticity robust' GMM-estimator.

The validity of the orthogonality conditions can be tested by the *Sargan–Hansen $\mathcal{J}$-statistic*, see Sargan (1958, 1959), Hansen (1982), and Newey (1985),

$$\mathcal{J} = [\sum_j \boldsymbol{x}_j'\boldsymbol{z}_j][\sum_j \boldsymbol{z}_j'\widehat{\epsilon}_j^2\boldsymbol{z}_j]^{-1}[\sum_j \boldsymbol{z}_j'\boldsymbol{x}_j]. \quad (7.80)$$

Under the null, i.e., all orthogonality conditions being satisfied, it is asymptotically distributed as χ^2 with a number of degrees of freedom equal to the number of overidentifying restrictions (the number of orthogonality conditions less the number of coefficients estimated under the null).

Equations (7.78)–(7.80) can be easily modified when $\boldsymbol{x}_j$ and $\boldsymbol{z}_j$ are extended to matrices and y_j and ϵ_j are extended to vectors, say $\boldsymbol{y}_j$ and $\boldsymbol{\epsilon}_j$, *inter alia*, for applications to panel data. The only essential changes needed are to replace y_j and $\widehat{\epsilon}_j^2$ by, respectively, $\boldsymbol{y}_j$ and $\widehat{\boldsymbol{\epsilon}}_j\widehat{\boldsymbol{\epsilon}}_j'$.

This finishes discussion of the generalities of GMM applied to a single linear equation. We proceed by demonstrating how the stepwise GMM estimators (7.78) and (7.79) and the $\mathcal{J}$-statistic (7.80) can be operationalized for the specific panel data model and variable transformations under consideration.[7]

7.6.2 GMM-ESTIMATION OF THE EQUATION IN DIFFERENCES

Equation (7.42), after differencing between periods t and s, takes the form

$$y_{it} - y_{is} = (x_{it} - x_{is})\beta + \epsilon_{it} - \epsilon_{is}, \quad (7.81)$$

where $\epsilon_{it} = u_{it} - \eta_{it}\beta$. We use as IV for $(x_{it} - x_{is})$ generally a so far unspecified variable z_i, which can be a scalar or a $(G \times 1)$-vector, when we utilize the orthogonality conditions, corresponding to (7.74),

$$\mathsf{E}[z_i'(\epsilon_{it} - \epsilon_{is})] = \mathsf{E}[z_i'[y_{it} - y_{is} - (x_{it} - x_{is})\beta]] = \mathbf{0}_{G,1}. \quad (7.82)$$

[7] Related operationalizations for autoregressive panel data models will be considered in Sections 8.2.4, 8.2.6, 8.3.2, and 8.3.3.

We construct estimators for β by replacing the expectation operation with the mean taken over i and minimizing the distance of these means from the zero vector.

For panel data there are usually several ways of formulating such minimization problems. The idea pursued is, generally, to *let z_i be equal to one or more of the level observations of x_{it} which are not involved in the differences.* We therefore set $z_i = x_{ip}$ for one or more $p \neq t, s$. We can operationalize this in three ways: use (7.82) with $z_i = x_{ip}$ for (a) all i, one (t, s) and one p; (b) all i, one (t, s) and several p; or (c) for all i, several (t, s) and several p simultaneously.

In case (a), where $G=1$, the sample counterpart of (7.82) can be satisfied exactly, see (7.76), and hence no optimization is required. In cases (b) and (c), more IVs than necessary exist, and we therefore optimize by involving quadratic forms in defining the empirical distances; see (7.77) and (7.78). Let

$$\Delta y_{its} = y_{it} - y_{is}, \qquad \Delta x_{its} = x_{it} - x_{is}, \qquad \Delta\epsilon_{its} = \epsilon_{it} - \epsilon_{is},$$

$$\Delta \boldsymbol{y}_{ts} = \begin{bmatrix} \Delta y_{1ts} \\ \vdots \\ \Delta y_{Nts} \end{bmatrix}, \quad \Delta \boldsymbol{x}_{ts} = \begin{bmatrix} \Delta x_{1ts} \\ \vdots \\ \Delta x_{Nts} \end{bmatrix}, \quad \Delta \boldsymbol{\epsilon}_{ts} = \begin{bmatrix} \Delta \epsilon_{1ts} \\ \vdots \\ \Delta \epsilon_{Nts} \end{bmatrix},$$

$$\boldsymbol{y}_{i\cdot} = \begin{bmatrix} y_{i1} \\ \vdots \\ y_{iT} \end{bmatrix}, \quad \boldsymbol{x}_{i\cdot} = \begin{bmatrix} x_{i1} \\ \vdots \\ x_{iT} \end{bmatrix}, \quad \boldsymbol{\epsilon}_{i\cdot} = \begin{bmatrix} \epsilon_{i1} \\ \vdots \\ \epsilon_{iT} \end{bmatrix}.$$

We first consider case (a). The sample counterpart to the orthogonality condition (7.82) for one (t, s, p)-combination gives

$$\widehat{\beta}_{\Delta(ts),p} = [\textstyle\sum_{i=1}^{N} x_{ip}(\Delta x_{its})]^{-1}[\sum_{i=1}^{N} x_{ip}(\Delta y_{its})]. \tag{7.83}$$

This is identical to the simple IV estimator (7.36). It is consistent, but usually has a low score in terms of efficiency, because of the usually weak empirical correlation (across i) between x_{ip} and Δx_{its}.

Next, consider case (b), i.e., estimation of β in (7.81) for one pair of periods (t, s), using as IV for Δx_{its} *all admissible x_{ip}s*. The inclusion of more x_{ip}-values normally makes the estimator more efficient than (7.83), but again, the strength of the correlation is of importance. To formalize this idea we define the selection matrices

$$\boldsymbol{P}_{ts} = \begin{bmatrix} ((T-2) \times T)\text{-matrix} \\ \text{obtained by deleting} \\ \text{from } \boldsymbol{I}_T \text{ rows } t \text{ and } s \end{bmatrix}, \qquad t, s = 1, \dots, T,$$

and use these to form

$$x'_{i(ts)} = P_{ts} x_{i\cdot},$$

etc. Here $x'_{i(ts)}$ denotes the $[(T-2) \times 1]$-vector of level values for the xs obtained by *excluding* rows t and p from the $(T \times 1)$-vector $x_{i\cdot}$. In general, we also let subscript (ts) on a vector denote *exclusion of* (ts)-differences. Placing the $[1 \times (T-2)]$-vectors $x_{i(ts)}$ for all individuals below each other, we get

$$X_{(ts)} = \begin{bmatrix} x_{1(ts)} \\ \vdots \\ x_{N(ts)} \end{bmatrix}.$$

Using $X_{(ts)}$ as IV matrix for Δx_{ts}, we obtain the following estimator for β, *specific for period* (t,s)*-differences and using as IVs all admissible* x*-level values*,

$$\begin{aligned}
\widehat{\beta}_{(ts)} &= [(\Delta x_{ts})' X_{(ts)} (X'_{(ts)} X_{(ts)})^{-1} X'_{(ts)} (\Delta x_{ts})]^{-1} \\
&\quad \times [(\Delta x_{ts})' X_{(ts)} (X'_{(ts)} X_{(ts)})^{-1} X'_{(ts)} (\Delta y_{ts})] \\
&= \{[\textstyle\sum_i (\Delta x_{its})' x_{i(ts)}][\sum_i x'_{i(ts)} x_{i(ts)}]^{-1} [\sum_i x'_{i(ts)} (\Delta x_{its})]\}^{-1} \\
&\quad \times \{[\textstyle\sum_i (\Delta x_{its})' x_{i(ts)}][\sum_i x'_{i(ts)} x_{i(ts)}]^{-1} [\sum_i x'_{i(ts)} (\Delta y_{its})]\}.
\end{aligned} \tag{7.84}$$

This estimator, exemplifying (7.78), exists if $X'_{(ts)} X_{(ts)} \equiv \sum_i x'_{i(ts)} x_{i(ts)}$ has rank $(T-2)$, which requires $N \geq T-2$. It utilizes the orthogonality condition $\mathsf{E}[x_{i(ts)}(\Delta \epsilon_{its})] = \mathbf{0}_{T-2,1}$, exemplifying (7.74), and minimizes the quadratic form

$$(\tfrac{1}{N} X'_{(ts)} \Delta \epsilon_{ts})' (\tfrac{1}{N^2} X'_{(ts)} X_{(ts)})^{-1} (\tfrac{1}{N} X'_{(ts)} \Delta \epsilon_{ts}).$$

The weight matrix $(N^{-2} X'_{(ts)} X_{(ts)})^{-1}$ is proportional to the inverse of (the asymptotic) covariance matrix of $N^{-1} X'_{(ts)} \Delta \epsilon_{ts}$ provided that the $\Delta \epsilon_{its}$s are IID over i, while the variance can depend on (t,s).

We finally consider case (c), i.e., GMM-estimation when *combining all orthogonality conditions obtained from one-period differences*. Consider (7.81) for all $s = t-1$. These $T-1$ equations for individual i are

$$\begin{bmatrix} \Delta y_{i21} \\ \Delta y_{i32} \\ \vdots \\ \Delta y_{i,T,T-1} \end{bmatrix} = \begin{bmatrix} \Delta x_{i21} \\ \Delta x_{i32} \\ \vdots \\ \Delta x_{i,T,T-1} \end{bmatrix} \beta + \begin{bmatrix} \Delta \epsilon_{i21} \\ \Delta \epsilon_{i32} \\ \vdots \\ \Delta \epsilon_{i,T,T-1} \end{bmatrix}, \tag{7.85}$$

or, in compact notation,

$$\Delta y_i = (\Delta x_i)\beta + \Delta \epsilon_i.$$

Note that these pooled equations, unlike (7.73), have a common scalar coefficient. The IV matrix of the $[(T-1) \times 1]$-vector Δx_i is the $[(T-1) \times (T-1)(T-2)]$-matrix

$$Z_i = \begin{bmatrix} x'_{i(21)} & 0 & \cdots & 0 \\ 0 & x'_{i(32)} & \cdots & 0 \\ \vdots & \vdots & \ddots & \vdots \\ 0 & 0 & \cdots & x'_{i(T,T-1)} \end{bmatrix}. \tag{7.86}$$

Let now

$$\Delta y = [(\Delta y_1)', \dots, (\Delta y_N)']', \; \Delta \epsilon = [(\Delta \epsilon_1)', \dots, (\Delta \epsilon_N)']',$$
$$\Delta x = [(\Delta x_1)', \dots, (\Delta x_N)']', \; Z = [Z'_1, \dots, Z'_N]'.$$

The GMM-estimator corresponding to the composite orthogonality condition $\mathsf{E}[Z'_i(\Delta \epsilon_i)] = 0_{(T-1)(T-2),1}$, which minimizes the quadratic form

$$\left(\tfrac{1}{N}(\Delta \epsilon)'Z\right)\left(\tfrac{1}{N^2}Z'Z\right)^{-1}\left(\tfrac{1}{N}Z'\Delta \epsilon\right),$$

can be written as

$$\begin{aligned} \widehat{\beta} &= [(\Delta x)'Z(Z'Z)^{-1}Z'(\Delta x)]^{-1}[(\Delta x)'Z(Z'Z)^{-1}Z'(\Delta y)] \\ &\equiv \{[\textstyle\sum_i(\Delta x_i)'Z_i][\sum_i Z'_iZ_i]^{-1}[\sum_i Z'_i(\Delta x_i)]\}^{-1} \\ &\quad \times \{[\textstyle\sum_i(\Delta x_i)'Z_i][\sum_i Z'_iZ_i]^{-1}[\sum_i Z'_i(\Delta y_i)]\}. \end{aligned} \tag{7.87}$$

This system *step-one GMM* estimator is an application of (7.78) for (balanced) panel data.

If $\Delta \epsilon$ has a non-scalar covariance matrix, we obtain an (asymptotically) more efficient GMM-estimator by proceeding as follows: form residuals from (7.87), $\widehat{\Delta \epsilon}_i = \Delta y_i - \Delta x_i \widehat{\beta}$, and replace $\sum_i Z'_iZ_i$ with $\sum_i Z'_i(\widehat{\Delta \epsilon}_i)(\widehat{\Delta \epsilon}_i)'Z_i$. This gives the asymptotically optimal GMM-estimator

$$\begin{aligned} \widetilde{\beta} &= \{[\textstyle\sum_i(\Delta x_i)'Z_i][\sum_i Z'_i\widehat{\Delta \epsilon}_i\widehat{\Delta \epsilon}'_iZ_i]^{-1}[\sum_i Z'_i(\Delta x_i)]\}^{-1} \\ &\quad \times \{[\textstyle\sum_i(\Delta x_i)'Z_i][\sum_i Z'_i\widehat{\Delta \epsilon}_i\widehat{\Delta \epsilon}'_iZ_i]^{-1}[\sum_i Z'_i(\Delta y_i)]\}. \end{aligned} \tag{7.88}$$

This (system) *step-two GMM* estimator is an application of (7.79).

The Sargan–Hansen statistic for testing the orthogonality conditions is

$$\mathcal{J} = [\sum_i (\Delta x_i)' Z_i][\sum_i Z_i' \widehat{\Delta\epsilon}_i \widehat{\Delta\epsilon}_i' Z_i]^{-1}[\sum_i Z_i'(\Delta x_i)]. \tag{7.89}$$

Example: This illustration, from Biørn (2003), utilizes firm data from Norwegian manufacturing of textiles and chemicals. Four cases and four estimators are considered; see Table 7.4. The four cases (rows) relate to (1) models where x measures log-output ($\ln Q$) and y measures log-input, for materials ($\ln M$) and capital in machinery ($\ln K$), respectively (rows 1, 3, 5, and 7), with β interpreted as an *input–output* elasticity, and to (2) models with reversed interpretation of x and y (rows 2, 4, 6, and 8), with β interpreted as an *output-input* elasticity. The four estimators (columns 1–4) are, respectively, step-one estimates using, respectively, x-IVs and y-IVs (columns 1 and 2) and corresponding step-two estimates (columns 3 and 4).

The estimated input–output elasticities (column 1, rows 1 and 3) are always lower than the inverse of the estimated output-input elasticities (column 2, rows 2 and 4).

Table 7.4 Input–output elasticities and their inverses: *one-step and two-step GMM on equation in differences, Q = output, M = materials, K = capital*

y, x	$\widehat{\beta}_{Dx}$	$\widehat{\beta}_{Dy}$	$\widetilde{\beta}_{Dx}$	$\widetilde{\beta}_{Dy}$	$\chi^2(\widetilde{\beta}_{Dx})$	$\chi^2(\widetilde{\beta}_{Dy})$
			Textiles: $N = 215, T = 8$			
$\ln(M), \ln(Q)$	1.0821	1.1275	1.0546	1.0825	51.71	70.39
	(0.0331)	(0.0346)	(0.0173)	(0.0169)	(0.2950)	(0.0152)
$\ln(Q), \ln(M)$	0.8404	0.8931	0.8917	0.9244	86.55	59.08
	(0.0283)	(0.0283)	(0.0143)	(0.0148)	(0.0004)	(0.1112)
$\ln(K), \ln(Q)$	0.5095	0.6425	0.5239	0.6092	115.68	121.29
	(0.0735)	(0.0700)	(0.0407)	(0.0314)	(0.0000)	(0.0000)
$\ln(Q), \ln(K)$	0.4170	0.6391	0.4499	0.6495	130.50	133.94
	(0.0409)	(0.0561)	(0.0248)	(0.0330)	(0.0000)	(0.0000)
			Chemicals: $N = 229, T = 8$			
$\ln(M), \ln(Q)$	1.0166	1.0540	1.0009	1.0394	54.29	81.64
	(0.0245)	(0.0241)	(0.0135)	(0.0138)	(0.2166)	(0.0013)
$\ln(Q), \ln(M)$	0.9205	0.9609	0.9323	0.9815	87.10	57.90
	(0.0230)	(0.0239)	(0.0122)	(0.0130)	(0.0003)	(0.1324)
$\ln(K), \ln(Q)$	0.9706	1.2497	1.0051	1.2672	90.42	85.36
	(0.0583)	(0.0633)	(0.0336)	(0.0489)	(0.0001)	(0.0005)
$\ln(Q), \ln(K)$	0.5550	0.7459	0.5700	0.7762	96.70	89.57
	(0.0317)	(0.0374)	(0.0236)	(0.0273)	(0.0000)	(0.0002)

Source: Based on Biørn (2003, Table 24.2).
$\widehat{\beta}_{Dx}, \widehat{\beta}_{Dy}$ = Step-one difference estimators using, respectively, level x-IVs and level y-IVs.
$\widetilde{\beta}_{Dx}, \widetilde{\beta}_{Dy}$ = Step-two difference estimators using level x-IVs and level y IVs, respectively.
$\chi^2(\widetilde{\beta}_{Dx}), \chi^2(\widetilde{\beta}_{Dy})$ = Sargan–Hansen $\mathcal{J}$-test-statistics for orthogonality conditions.
In parentheses, cols. 1–4: Std. errors, computed as described in Biørn and Krishnakumar (2008, Section 10.2.5).
In parentheses, cols. 5–6: p-values.

With both interpretations of (x, y), the estimates utilizing the y-IVs (column 2) tend to exceed those using the x-IVs (column 1). The corresponding step-two estimates (columns 3 and 4) have, unsurprisingly, smaller standard errors. All results for the *materials* input (rows 1, 2, 5, and 6) indicate an input elasticity greater than one. For the *capital* input, the results are less clear. For this input, it is only for the chemicals sector, when $y = $ log-input and $x = $ log-output, that input elasticity estimates around or larger than one are obtained (rows 7 and 8).

Sargan–Hansen statistics for testing the underlying orthogonality conditions (OC) are reported in columns 5 and 6. For *materials*, they indicate non-rejection of the full set of OCs when using the xs as IVs for the original interpretation of (x, y) (row 1) and the ys as IVs for the reversed interpretation (row 2) (i.e., the output variable in both cases), with p values exceeding 5%. The OCs when using the ys as IVs for the original interpretation of (x, y) and the xs as IVs for the reversed interpretation (i.e., the input variable in both cases) are, however, rejected. For the *capital* input, the p-values of the tests are very low in all cases, indicating rejection of the OCs. Explanations may be non-modelled lagged response, memory in the measurement errors or disturbances, or neglected trend effects.

7.6.3 EXTENSIONS AND MODIFICATIONS

When constructing GMM estimators, the roles of the levels and differences may be reversed, i.e., keeping the equation in levels and using the IVs in differences. We do not discuss this modification in the measurement error context further here, since Chapter 8 gives a more complete treatment of both versions for a situation which in several respects is similar. Empirical applications, and simulation experiments, e.g., Biørn (2003, 2015), indicate that, overall, GMM estimates based on equations kept in levels with IVs in differences are more precise and less biased than GMM estimates based on equations in differences with IVs in levels.

IV procedures valid for situations with memory-free errors can be modified to handle finite memory, e.g., formalized as moving average (MA) processes, by reducing the IV set. The essence of this reduction is to ensure that all remaining IVs get clear of the memory of the error process so that the IVs are uncorrelated with the errors/disturbances (the orthogonality condition), while being correlated with the variables for which they serve (the rank condition). This double claim restricts the admissible signal and noise memories for which GMM is feasible.

If the model has more than one regressor, the number of potential IVs, and hence the dimensions of the matrix elements in (7.87)–(7.89), grow correspondingly. Whether it is recommendable then to use all valid orthogonality conditions depends on the sample size and the processes generating the regressors. These issues are not dealt with here, but are discussed in several contexts in the panel data literature, *inter alia*, under the catchwords 'overfitting' and 'weak instruments', see, e.g., Nelson and Startz (1990), Davidson and MacKinnon (1993, Chapters 7 and 17), Bound, Jaeger, and Baker (1995), Staiger and Stock (1997), and Stock, Wright, and Yogo (2002). As noted by Bound *et al.* (1995, p. 443), (i) if a potential IV is only weakly correlated with the variable for which it serves, even a weak correlation between the IV and error term ('weak violation' of the orthogonality condition) tends to give large inconsistency in IV estimates, and (ii) the finite sample bias of 2SLS estimators (representing an optimal use of available IVs) has the same sign as have corresponding OLS estimators.

7.7 Concluding remarks

In this chapter we have exemplified utilization of IVs, and extensions of simple IV procedures to GMM procedures in estimating equations with correlation between composite disturbances and explanatory variables induced by measurement errors. We finally point out, and summarize, some extensions and unsolved problems.

First, in certain cases it is possible to apply y-values as IVs instead of, or as supplements to, x-values; see, e.g., Wansbeek (2001). Second, in some cases it is possible to estimate the equation consistently in its original level form, while using x-values (or y-values) in differences as IVs for the level xs, i.e., reversing the roles of the variables in levels and in differences. Third, we may estimate the equation while augmenting the orthogonality conditions in one-period differences with conditions in two-period differences or *longer differences*. Biørn and Klette (1998) discuss the potential of this extension and the distinction between essential and redundant orthogonality conditions in this context. Combining, e.g., two-period and one-period differences, redundancy may easily create singularity problems, as $\boldsymbol{x}_{it}-\boldsymbol{x}_{i,t-2} \equiv \Delta\boldsymbol{x}_{it}+\Delta\boldsymbol{x}_{i,t-1}$, etc., which should be addressed.

Fourth, the methods may be modified to account for memory in the measurement errors, or disturbances, e.g., specified as low-order moving averages. Then the IV set must be reduced to have all instruments 'getting clear of' the memory of the measurement error process to preserve orthogonality of the IVs and the measurement errors (disturbances), still ensuring correlation between the IV set and the observed explanatory variables (the rank condition). This double claim restricts the admissible signal and noise memories for GMM; see, e.g., Biørn (2003, Sections 24.5.1 and 24.5.2) and Biørn (2015, Sections 2 and 3) for elaboration. Fifth, using levels as IVs for differences, or vice versa, may raise problems related to 'overfitting' and 'weak instruments'. Finding operational ways of identifying 'essential' IVs and orthogonality conditions to reduce the potential damage of admissible, but 'inessential' IVs in terms of inefficiency, raises still unsolved problems.

Bun and Windmeijer (2010) propose a way of measuring IV strength for a panel data equation with one endogenous explanatory variable, based on a concentration parameter, which may be of some help.

Appendix 7A. **Asymptotics for aggregate estimators**

This appendix proves the results in Table 7.1. Using the notation exemplified by

$$\begin{aligned} w_N(z,q) &= \operatorname*{plim}_{N\to\infty}[\tfrac{1}{NT}W_{ZQ}],\\ w_T(z,q) &= \operatorname*{plim}_{T\to\infty}[\tfrac{1}{NT}W_{ZQ}],\\ w_{NT}(z,q) &= \operatorname*{plim}_{N,T\to\infty}[\tfrac{1}{NT}W_{ZQ}], \end{aligned}$$

in combination with (7.4) and (7.15)–(7.17), it follows that

$$w_T(z,q) = \tfrac{1}{N}\textstyle\sum_{i=1}^{N} w_{ii}(z,q), \tag{7A.1}$$

$$v_N(z,q) = \tfrac{1}{T}\textstyle\sum_{t=1}^{T} v_{tt}(z,q), \tag{7A.2}$$

$$b_N(z,q) = \tfrac{1}{T^2}\textstyle\sum_{t=1}^{T}\sum_{s=1}^{T} v_{ts}(z,q), \tag{7A.3}$$

$$c_T(z,q) = \tfrac{1}{N^2}\textstyle\sum_{i=1}^{N}\sum_{j=1}^{N} w_{ij}(z,q), \tag{7A.4}$$

$$r_T(z,q) = \tfrac{1}{N}\textstyle\sum_{i=1}^{N}[w_{ii}(z,q) - \tfrac{1}{N}\sum_{j=1}^{N} w_{ij}(z,q)], \tag{7A.5}$$

$$r_N(z,q) = \tfrac{1}{T}\textstyle\sum_{t=1}^{T}[v_{tt}(z,q) - \tfrac{1}{T}\sum_{s=1}^{T} v_{ts}(z,q)]. \tag{7A.6}$$

Since (7.1)–(7.2) imply

$$\begin{aligned} &v_N(\eta,\eta) = \sigma_\eta^2,\\ &c_N(\eta,\eta) = 0,\\ &w_N(\eta,\eta) = \sigma_\eta^2(1-\tfrac{1}{T}),\\ &b_N(\eta,\eta) = \sigma_\eta^2\tfrac{1}{T},\\ &r_N(\eta,\eta) = \sigma_\eta^2(1-\tfrac{1}{T}),\\ &w_T(\eta,\eta) = \sigma_\eta^2,\\ &b_T(\eta,\eta) = 0,\\ &v_T(\eta,\eta) = \sigma_\eta^2(1-\tfrac{1}{N}),\\ &c_T(\eta,\eta) = \sigma_\eta^2\tfrac{1}{N},\\ &r_T(\eta,\eta) = \sigma_\eta^2(1-\tfrac{1}{N}), \end{aligned}$$

the following respective relationships between plims hold:

$$\begin{aligned} w_N(x,y) &= w_N(x^*,x^*)\beta, \\ w_N(x,x) &= w_N(x^*,x^*) + \sigma_\eta^2(1-\tfrac{1}{T}), \end{aligned} \tag{7A.7}$$

$$\begin{aligned} v_N(x,y) &= v_N(x^*,x^*)\beta, \\ v_N(x,x) &= v_N(x^*,x^*) + \sigma_\eta^2, \end{aligned} \tag{7A.8}$$

$$\begin{aligned} b_N(x,y) &= b_N(x^*,x^*)\beta, \\ b_N(x,x) &= b_N(x^*,x^*) + \sigma_\eta^2\tfrac{1}{T}, \end{aligned} \tag{7A.9}$$

$$\begin{aligned} c_N(x,y) &= c_N(x^*,x^*)\beta, \\ c_N(x,x) &= c_N(x^*,x^*), \end{aligned} \tag{7A.10}$$

$$\begin{aligned} r_N(x,y) &= r_N(x^*,x^*)\beta, \\ r_N(x,x) &= r_N(x^*,x^*) + \sigma_\eta^2(1-\tfrac{1}{T}), \end{aligned} \tag{7A.11}$$

$$\begin{aligned} w_T(x,y) &= w_T(x^*,x^*)\beta, \\ w_T(x,x) &= w_T(x^*,x^*) + \sigma_\eta^2, \end{aligned} \tag{7A.12}$$

$$\begin{aligned} v_T(x,y) &= v_T(x^*,x^*)\beta, \\ v_T(x,x) &= v_T(x^*,x^*) + \sigma_\eta^2(1-\tfrac{1}{N}), \end{aligned} \tag{7A.13}$$

$$\begin{aligned} b_T(x,y) &= b_T(x^*,x^*)\beta, \\ b_T(x,x) &= b_T(x^*,x^*), \end{aligned} \tag{7A.14}$$

$$\begin{aligned} c_T(x,y) &= c_T(x^*,x^*)\beta, \\ c_T(x,x) &= c_T(x^*,x^*) + \sigma_\eta^2\tfrac{1}{N}, \end{aligned} \tag{7A.15}$$

$$\begin{aligned} r_T(x,y) &= r_T(x^*,x^*)\beta, \\ r_T(x,x) &= r_T(x^*,x^*) + \sigma_\eta^2(1-\tfrac{1}{N}). \end{aligned} \tag{7A.16}$$

Using $w_Z^*, v_Z^*, \dots$ as shorthand notation for $w_Z(x^*,x^*), v_Z(x^*,x^*), \dots$ $(Z = N, T, NT)$, it follows for the estimators (7.18)–(7.22) when N, respectively T, goes to infinity, that

$$\operatorname*{plim}_{N\to\infty}(\widehat{\beta}_W) = \frac{w_N(x,y)}{w_N(x,x)} = \beta - \frac{\sigma_\eta^2(1-\frac{1}{T})\beta}{w_N^* + \sigma_\eta^2(1-\frac{1}{T})}, \tag{7A.17}$$

$$\operatorname*{plim}_{N\to\infty}(\widehat{\beta}_B) = \frac{b_N(x,y)}{b_N(x,x)} = \beta - \frac{(\sigma_\eta^2\frac{1}{T})\beta}{b_N^* + \sigma_\eta^2\frac{1}{T}}, \tag{7A.18}$$

$$\operatorname*{plim}_{N\to\infty}(\widehat{\beta}_V) = \frac{v_N(x,y)}{v_N(x,x)} = \beta - \frac{\sigma_\eta^2\,\beta}{v_N^* + \sigma_\eta^2}, \tag{7A.19}$$

$$\operatorname*{plim}_{N\to\infty}(\widehat{\beta}_C) = \frac{c_N(x,y)}{c_N(x,x)} = \beta, \tag{7A.20}$$

$$\underset{N\to\infty}{\text{plim}}\,(\widehat{\beta}_R) = \frac{r_N(x,y)}{r_N(x,x)} = \beta - \frac{\sigma_\eta^2(1-\frac{1}{T})\beta}{r_N^* + \sigma_\eta^2(1-\frac{1}{T})}, \tag{7A.21}$$

$$\underset{T\to\infty}{\text{plim}}\,(\widehat{\beta}_W) = \frac{w_T(x,y)}{w_T(x,x)} = \beta - \frac{\sigma_\eta^2\beta}{w_T^* + \sigma_\eta^2}, \tag{7A.22}$$

$$\underset{T\to\infty}{\text{plim}}\,(\widehat{\beta}_B) = \frac{b_T(x,y)}{b_T(x,x)} = \beta, \tag{7A.23}$$

$$\underset{T\to\infty}{\text{plim}}\,(\widehat{\beta}_V) = \frac{v_T(x,y)}{v_T(x,x)} = \beta - \frac{\sigma_\eta^2(1-\frac{1}{N})\beta}{v_T^* + \sigma_\eta^2(1-\frac{1}{N})}, \tag{7A.24}$$

$$\underset{T\to\infty}{\text{plim}}\,(\widehat{\beta}_C) = \frac{c_T(x,y)}{c_T(x,x)} = \beta - \frac{(\sigma_\eta^2\frac{1}{N})\beta}{c_T^* + \sigma_\eta^2\frac{1}{N}}, \tag{7A.25}$$

$$\underset{T\to\infty}{\text{plim}}\,(\widehat{\beta}_R) = \frac{r_T(x,y)}{r_T(x,x)} = \beta - \frac{\sigma_\eta^2(1-\frac{1}{N})\beta}{r_T^* + \sigma_\eta^2(1-\frac{1}{N})}. \tag{7A.26}$$

When both N and T go to infinity, the corresponding expressions read

$$\underset{N,T\to\infty}{\text{plim}}\,(\widehat{\beta}_W) = \frac{w_{NT}(x,y)}{w_{NT}(x,x)} = \beta - \frac{\sigma_\eta^2\beta}{w_{NT}^* + \sigma_\eta^2}, \tag{7A.27}$$

$$\underset{N,T\to\infty}{\text{plim}}\,(\widehat{\beta}_B) = \frac{b_{NT}(x,y)}{b_{NT}(x,x)} = \beta, \tag{7A.28}$$

$$\underset{N,T\to\infty}{\text{plim}}\,(\widehat{\beta}_V) = \frac{v_{NT}(x,y)}{v_{NT}(x,x)} = \beta - \frac{\sigma_\eta^2\beta}{v_{NT}^* + \sigma_\eta^2}, \tag{7A.29}$$

$$\underset{N,T\to\infty}{\text{plim}}\,(\widehat{\beta}_C) = \frac{c_{NT}(x,y)}{c_{NT}(x,x)} = \beta, \tag{7A.30}$$

$$\underset{N,T\to\infty}{\text{plim}}\,(\widehat{\beta}_R) = \frac{r_{NT}(x,y)}{r_{NT}(x,x)} = \beta - \frac{\sigma_\eta^2\beta}{r_{NT}^* + \sigma_\eta^2}. \tag{7A.31}$$

8 Dynamic models

CHAPTER SUMMARY

First-order autoregressive models with individual-specific intercepts are considered. The within estimator, unlike its static fixed effects counterpart, has notable deficiencies when the time-series are short. OLS estimation of an equation in first-differences has similar deficiencies. Estimators utilizing IVs in levels for the equation in differences, or the opposite, may be more relevant. Also procedures using orthogonal forward deviations and procedures mixing levels and differences in other ways are considered. Versions of the GMM are discussed, and their extension to cases where the disturbance has memory is explained. For models with random effects, ML- and step-wise procedures are considered in models having both two-dimensional and individual-specific exogenous variables. Empirical examples are given.

8.1 Introduction

This chapter deals with specification and coefficient estimation in linear dynamic models for panel data, i.e., panel data models containing variables dated in different periods. Primary objectives of dynamic econometrics is the exploration of lags between stimulus and response and of 'short-run' versus 'long-run' effects, and dynamic panel data models have, during the last decades, received a steadily growing attention, methodologically, as well as with respect to applications. This is not surprising, as such models are well suited to confrontation with panel data. As remarked in the introductory chapter, the opportunity to handle models with lagged responses is a major advantage of panel data over pure cross-section data and time-series of cross-sections.

If exploration of lagged responses is a researcher's only concern, attention may be restricted to time-series models and data. However, panel data have several advantages when it comes to examining lags, since pure time-series data and models suited to such mechanisms cannot handle *individual* heterogeneity, the neglect of which—in particular when the time-series are linear aggregates across individuals—can bias inference on the dynamic pattern. With panel data it is possible to handle lags between time-indexed variables jointly with the 'nuisance' created by individual heterogeneity. So also in this respect, panel data are richer than pure cross-sections, time-series of non-overlapping cross-sections, and pure time-series data. In the panel data literature, substantial attention has been paid to *autoregressive (AR) models*, notably single equation first-order models, where the endogenous variable lagged one period, AR(1), is a predetermined regressor, usually together with (strictly) exogenous variables. An early contribution is Balestra and Nerlove (1966), followed by Nerlove (1967, 1971a) and Maddala (1971).

A selection of models and methods for dynamic equations will be considered, in particular stationary AR(1)-equations, with individual intercept heterogeneity. In equations for pure time series data, lagged endogenous regressors, being *predetermined*, have important properties in common with strictly exogenous variables when there is no memory in the disturbances; see Davidson and Mackinnon (2004, Sections 3.2 and 4.5) and Greene (2008, Section 13.2.2). The latter, however, does not, without modification, carry over to panel data models when time-invariant heterogeneity occurs, for two reasons. First, transformations of the equation to eliminate *fixed* intercept heterogeneity, notably within-individual or difference transformations, may introduce memory in the transformed disturbance and the transformed lagged variables. Second, intercept heterogeneity, modelled as *random* effects, uncorrelated with both the genuine disturbances and the strictly exogenous regressors, cannot be uncorrelated with the lagged endogenous regressors. On the contrary, its occurrence can raise problems resembling those created by classical measurement errors in static models, discussed in Chapter 7.

Therefore, models and procedures for autoregressive equations for time series data with measurement errors—see, e.g., Grether and Maddala (1973), Pagano (1974), and Maravall and Aigner (1977)—may be relevant when dealing with AR-models for panel data. Insights may also be obtained from studying the 'simultaneity problem' in classical econometrics and its similarity with the problems that arise when lagged endogenous variables occur jointly with a disturbance with memory.

We build up the argument step-wise, pointing out similarities between the problems raised by the coexistence of autocorrelation and individual heterogeneity and by the coexistence of measurement errors and heterogeneity. There are, however, important differences when it comes to ways of using IVs to handle such problems. We will mostly be concerned with *stationary* AR(1) models with intercept heterogeneity. We will, however, also briefly address problems related to unit roots and co-integration, a topic that, during the last two decades, has received increased attention not only for pure time series, but also in the panel data literature.

The chapter proceeds as follows. In Section 8.2 we discuss an AR(1) model with *fixed individual-specific intercept shifts*. It is the simplest specification imaginable, but lacking exogenous variables it has minor practical interest, except as a benchmark case. Several estimators are considered. We will show that the within estimator, unlike its counterpart for a static fixed effects model, has notable deficiencies when the times series are short, often denoted as *short panels*. OLS estimation of a differenced version of the equation has similar deficiencies. More relevant therefore are estimators that utilize IVs. The IV principle can be operationalized by transforming the equation to differences and using valid instruments in levels, or doing the opposite. Combining the two ways of mixing levels and differences is a third alternative. At least one differencing should be involved to handle the individual effects. Introducing exogenous covariates, which is straightforward, will be discussed in Section 8.3. The presence of strictly exogenous variables extends the set of potential instruments while increasing the coefficient set. Versions of the GMM approach here become useful. In Section 8.4, AR(1) models with heterogeneity treated as random are discussed, with attention given to the distinction between two-dimensional and individual-specific exogenous variables.

8.2 **Fixed effects AR-models**

8.2.1 A SIMPLE MODEL

Consider a simple AR(1) model with *fixed intercept heterogeneity* α_i^*:

$$\begin{aligned} &y_{it} = \alpha_i^* + y_{i,t-1}\gamma + u_{it},\ |\gamma| < 1,\ (u_{it}|y_i^{(t-1)}) \sim \mathsf{IID}(0,\sigma^2), \\ &i = 1,\dots,N;\ t = 1,\dots,T, \end{aligned} \tag{8.1}$$

where $y_i^{(t-1)} = (y_{i,t-1},\dots,y_{i1},y_{i0})'$, i.e., the vector containing all lagged y-observations, and u_{it} is a disturbance. In some cases, the conditioning of u_{it} on $y_i^{(t-1)}$ may be replaced by (the weaker) conditioning on $y_{i,t-1}$ only. We assume that the process has been effective back to $t \to -\infty$, but that y_{i0} is the first observation. If α_i^* were i-invariant, y_{it} would be a stationary variable with i-invariant expectation,[1] while if α_i^* is i-dependent, implying that $\mathsf{E}(y_{it})$ is i-dependent, different stationary processes are effective for each individual. It is important that u_{it} has no memory, otherwise the IID assumption may be relaxed. Since $\alpha_i^* \equiv \alpha_i^*/(1-\gamma) - \alpha_i^*\gamma/(1-\gamma)$, (8.1) can be rewritten as

$$\widetilde{y}_{it} = \widetilde{y}_{i,t-1}\gamma + u_{it}, \text{ where } \widetilde{y}_{it} = y_{it} - \alpha_i^*/(1-\gamma),$$

and $\widetilde{y}_{1t},\dots,\widetilde{y}_{Nt}$ are stationary, with zero expectation and common autoregressive coefficient and disturbance variance.

This model may be said to represent persistence, (strong) 'dependence on the past', in two ways: through the time-invariant parameter α_i^* and through the lagged endogenous variable. Intuition suggests that this double representation of sluggishness in the mechanism determining y_{it} may create problems in estimating γ, which a closer examination, to follow later, will confirm.

[1] If T is finite and the stationarity assumption is abandoned, $|\gamma| \geq 1$ is feasible. Equation (8.2), for example, holds whenever $|\gamma| \neq 1$.

Formally, (8.1) is, for any i, a first-order, linear stochastic difference equation. Its solution, when expressed by means of the first observation, y_{i0}, is

$$\begin{aligned} y_{it} &= \gamma^t y_{i0} + \textstyle\sum_{s=0}^{t-1} \gamma^s (\alpha_i^* + u_{i,t-s}) \\ &= \gamma^t y_{i0} + [(1-\gamma^t)/(1-\gamma)]\alpha_i^* + \textstyle\sum_{s=0}^{t-1} \gamma^s u_{i,t-s} \implies \\ \widetilde{y}_{it} &= \gamma^t \widetilde{y}_{i0} + \textstyle\sum_{s=0}^{t-1} \gamma^s u_{i,t-s}. \end{aligned} \tag{8.2}$$

Hence, $y_{i,t-1}$, while uncorrelated with u_{it}, is correlated with $u_{i,t-1}, u_{i,t-2}, \dots$ and $\bar{u}_{i\cdot}$. The case $\gamma = 1$, with a 'unit root' in the lag polynomial of y_{it}, gives

$$\begin{aligned} \Delta y_{it} &= \alpha_i^* + u_{it} \implies y_{it}^{\dagger} = y_{i,t-1}^{\dagger} + u_{it}, \text{ where } y_{it}^{\dagger} = y_{it} - t\alpha_i^* \implies \\ y_{it} &= y_{i0} + t\alpha_i^* + \textstyle\sum_{s=0}^{t-1} u_{i,t-s} \implies y_{it}^{\dagger} = y_{i0}^{\dagger} + \textstyle\sum_{s=0}^{t-1} u_{i,t-s}. \end{aligned}$$

The full solution to (8.2) when $|\gamma| < 1$ can be written as

$$y_{it} = \textstyle\sum_{s=0}^{\infty} \gamma^s (\alpha_i^* + u_{i,t-s}) = \alpha_i^*/(1-\gamma) + \textstyle\sum_{s=0}^{\infty} \gamma^s u_{i,t-s}. \tag{8.3}$$

Five types of estimators for γ will be discussed: first, the within estimator (Section 8.2.2); next simple IV estimators of the equation transformed to differences with IVs in levels (Section 8.2.3); then procedures constructed in the 'opposite' way, simple IV estimators of the equation in levels with IVs in differences (Section 8.2.4); and finally, extensions of the simple IV procedures, involving multiple IVs (Sections 8.2.5 and 8.2.6). The latter can be interpreted as *system GMM-estimators*. We here exploit the discussion of GMM for the static fixed effects panel data model with measurement errors in Chapter 7, Section 7.6.1, being a common reference; see also Section 8.3.4. In all cases, the within and the difference transformations serve to eliminate the fixed intercept heterogeneity.

8.2.2 WITHIN ESTIMATION: OTHER DIFFERENCE TRANSFORMATIONS

The regressor $y_{i,t-1}$ is a predetermined, not a (strictly) exogenous, variable, as (8.3) shows that $\text{cov}(y_{i,t-1}, u_{i,t-s}) \neq 0$ for $s = 1, 2, \dots$. Had strict exogeneity prevailed, OLS estimation of $\gamma, \alpha_1^*, \dots, \alpha_N^*$, which, for γ, coincides with the within estimator (see Section 2.1), would have given MVLUE. Consider first the properties of OLS in the present AR(1) case. It can be implemented by applying OLS on

$$(y_{it} - \bar{y}_{i\cdot}) = (y_{i,t-1} - \bar{y}_{i,-1})\gamma + (u_{it} - \bar{u}_{i\cdot}), \qquad i = 1, \dots, N;\ t = 1, \dots, T, \tag{8.4}$$

where $\bar{y}_{i,-1} = \frac{1}{T}\sum_{t=1}^{T} y_{i,t-1}$, giving[2]

$$\widehat{\gamma}_W = \frac{\sum_{i=1}^{N}\sum_{t=1}^{T}(y_{i,t-1}-\bar{y}_{i,-1})(y_{it}-\bar{y}_{i\cdot})}{\sum_{i=1}^{N}\sum_{t=1}^{T}(y_{i,t-1}-\bar{y}_{i,-1})^2}, \tag{8.5}$$

$$\widehat{\alpha}^*_{iW} = \bar{y}_{i\cdot}-\bar{y}_{i,-1}\widehat{\gamma}_W, \qquad i=1,\dots,N. \tag{8.6}$$

To see the 'anatomy' of the problem when $y_{i,t-1}$ is predetermined, we insert for y_{it} and $\bar{y}_{i\cdot}$ from (8.1), to obtain

$$\widehat{\gamma}_W-\gamma = \frac{\sum_{i=1}^{N}\sum_{t=1}^{T}(y_{i,t-1}-\bar{y}_{i,-1})u_{it}}{\sum_{i=1}^{N}\sum_{t=1}^{T}(y_{i,t-1}-\bar{y}_{i,-1})y_{i,t-1}} = \frac{C}{D}, \tag{8.7}$$

$$\widehat{\alpha}^*_{iW}-\alpha^*_i = -\bar{y}_{i,-1}(\widehat{\gamma}_W-\gamma)+\bar{u}_{i\cdot} = -\bar{y}_{i,-1}\frac{C}{D}+\bar{u}_{i\cdot}, \tag{8.8}$$

where

$$C = \frac{1}{NT}\sum_{i=1}^{N}\sum_{t=1}^{T}y_{i,t-1}u_{it}-\frac{1}{N}\sum_{i=1}^{N}\bar{y}_{i,-1}\bar{u}_{i\cdot},$$
$$D = \frac{1}{NT}\sum_{i=1}^{N}\sum_{t=1}^{T}y_{i,t-1}^2-\frac{1}{N}\sum_{i=1}^{N}\bar{y}_{i,-1}^2.$$

Usually, $\widehat{\gamma}_W$ and $\widehat{\alpha}^*_{iW}$ are biased for finite N and T. Since, as shown in Appendix 8A, (8A.12)–(8A.13)[3]

$$\operatorname*{plim}_{N\to\infty}(C) = -\frac{\sigma^2}{T^2(1-\gamma)}\left[T-\frac{1-\gamma^T}{1-\gamma}\right],$$

$$\operatorname*{plim}_{N\to\infty}(D) = \frac{\sigma^2}{1-\gamma^2}\left[1-\frac{1}{T}-\frac{2\gamma}{T^2(1-\gamma)}\left(T-\frac{1-\gamma^T}{1-\gamma}\right)\right],$$

the asymptotic bias of $\widehat{\gamma}_W$ depends on T (being of order $\frac{1}{T}$)

$$\operatorname*{plim}_{N\to\infty}(\widehat{\gamma}_W-\gamma) = \frac{\operatorname*{plim}_{N\to\infty}(C)}{\operatorname*{plim}_{N\to\infty}(D)} = -\frac{\dfrac{1+\gamma}{T-1}\left(1-\dfrac{1-\gamma^T}{T(1-\gamma)}\right)}{1-\dfrac{2\gamma}{(1-\gamma)(T-1)}\left(1-\dfrac{1-\gamma^T}{T(1-\gamma)}\right)}. \tag{8.9}$$

[2] If normality of disturbances is added, *ML estimation* of $\gamma,\alpha_1^*,\dots,\alpha_N^*$ is equivalent to minimization of $\sum_{i=1}^{N}\sum_{t=1}^{T}u_{it}^2$ when we either consider the y_{i0}s as non-stochastic and assume either that the individual-specific processes had started from these values, as in (8.2), or condition on y_{i0}, ignoring the mechanism which might have determined it. Correct specification of the generating process of the initial observation is critical for the properties of the ML estimators.

[3] See Nickell (1981), who first proved this result, and, for further discussion, Sevestre and Trognon (1985, Section 2), Hsiao (2003, p. 72), and Alvarez and Arellano (2003).

In particular,

$$\text{plim}_{N\to\infty}(\widehat{\gamma}_W - \gamma) = -\tfrac{1}{2}(1+\gamma) \text{ when } T=2,$$
$$\text{plim}_{N\to\infty}(\widehat{\gamma}_W - \gamma) = -\tfrac{1}{T} \qquad \text{when } \gamma = 0.$$

Hence, if $\gamma > 0$ and $T=2$, $\widehat{\gamma}_W$ has a negative asymptotic bias exceeding $\frac{1}{2}$, while if $\gamma=0$, $\widehat{\gamma}_W$ converges towards minus the inverse of the time-series length, which for any T less than, say, 10, also seems prohibitively large. *Therefore the common small T, large N case is problematic for application of the within estimator.*

Now, $\text{plim}_{N\to\infty}(C) < 0$ when $T < \infty$ because $(1-\gamma^T)/(1-\gamma) \equiv \sum_{k=0}^{T-1}\gamma^k < T$, while $\text{plim}_{N\to\infty}(D) > 0$ and $\text{plim}_{N\to\infty}(\bar{u}_{i\cdot}) \neq 0$. Therefore, (8.7)–(8.9) imply

$$\operatorname*{plim}_{N\to\infty}(\widehat{\gamma}_W - \gamma) < 0, \quad \operatorname*{plim}_{N\to\infty}(\widehat{\alpha}^*_{iW} - \alpha^*_i) \neq 0 \text{ for } 2 \leq T < \infty.$$

Since $\text{plim}_{T\to\infty}(\bar{u}_{i\cdot}) = 0$ and $\text{plim}_{N,T\to\infty}(C) = 0$, consistency is ensured if also $T \to \infty$:

$$\operatorname*{plim}_{N,T\to\infty}(\widehat{\gamma}_W - \gamma) = 0, \quad \operatorname*{plim}_{T\to\infty}(\widehat{\alpha}^*_{iW} - \alpha^*_i) = 0, \quad \text{when } |\gamma| < 1.$$

Consistency of $\widehat{\gamma}_W$ does not require $N \to \infty$, however. To see this we consider the more general model

$$y_{it} = \alpha^*_i + y_{i,t-1}\gamma_i + u_{it}; \ |\gamma_i| < 1, \ u_{it} \sim \mathsf{IID}(0,\sigma^2), \ \begin{matrix} i = 1,\dots,N; \\ t = 1,\dots,T, \end{matrix} \tag{8.10}$$

for which OLS gives

$$\widehat{\gamma}_i = \frac{\sum_{t=1}^{T}(y_{i,t-1} - \bar{y}_{i,-1})(y_{it} - \bar{y}_{i\cdot})}{\sum_{t=1}^{T}(y_{i,t-1} - \bar{y}_{i,-1})^2}, \quad \widehat{\alpha}^*_i = \bar{y}_{i\cdot} - \bar{y}_{i,-1}\widehat{\gamma}_i, \ i = 1,\dots,N.$$

Since these estimators are T-consistent for (γ_i, α^*_i) in Model (8.10), according to a familiar result for OLS regression on AR(1) models, see Greene (2008, Section 19.4), they are T-consistent for (γ, α^*_i) in Model (8.1) as well:

$$\operatorname*{plim}_{T\to\infty}(\widehat{\gamma}_i - \gamma) = \operatorname*{plim}_{T\to\infty}(\widehat{\alpha}^*_i - \alpha^*_i) = 0, \qquad i = 1,\dots,N.$$

This is because $\widehat{\gamma}_W$ is a weighted mean of the $\widehat{\gamma}_i$s, and hence

$$\operatorname*{plim}_{T\to\infty}(\widehat{\gamma}_W - \gamma) = 0, \quad \operatorname*{plim}_{T\to\infty}(\widehat{\alpha}^*_{iW} - \alpha^*_i) = 0 \quad \text{when } 2 \leq N < \infty; \ |\gamma| < 1.$$

We therefore conclude: *in Model (8.1), the within estimators of γ and α_i^* are (i) inconsistent if $N\to\infty$, T finite, and (ii) T-consistent for any N.*

The within transformation is definitely not the only way of eliminating fixed time-invariant effects. Let $d_{t1},\dots,d_{tT}$ be constants and form

$$\sum_{s=1}^{T} d_{ts}y_{is} = (\sum_{s=1}^{T} d_{ts})\alpha_i^* + (\sum_{s=1}^{T} d_{ts}y_{i,s-1})\gamma + \sum_{s=1}^{T} d_{ts}u_{is}, \tag{8.11}$$

or, letting $d_{t\cdot}=\sum_{s=1}^{T} d_{ts}$, $y_{it}^*=\sum_{s=1}^{T} d_{ts}y_{is}$, $u_{it}^*=\sum_{s=1}^{T} d_{ts}u_{is}$,

$$y_{it}^* = d_{t\cdot}\alpha_i^* + y_{it(-1)}^*\gamma + u_{it}^*. \tag{8.12}$$

If $d_{t\cdot}=0$ is satisfied, α_i^* is eliminated. Core examples are

$$d_{ts} = \begin{cases} 1-\frac{1}{T} & \text{for } s=t, \\ -\frac{1}{T} & \text{for } s\neq t, \end{cases}$$

$$d_{ts} = \begin{cases} 1 & \text{for } s=t, \\ -1 & \text{for } s=t-\theta, \\ 0 & \text{for } s\neq t, t-\theta, \end{cases}$$

which perform, respectively, the within transformation and the θ-period-difference transformation. When $|\gamma|<1$ and $d_{t\cdot}=0$, (8.12) has solution

$$y_{it}^* = \sum_{s=0}^{\infty} \gamma^s u_{i,t-s}^*. \tag{8.13}$$

In the differencing over θ periods example, (8.12) becomes

$$\begin{aligned}&(y_{it}-y_{i,t-\theta}) = (y_{i,t-1}-y_{i,t-\theta-1})\gamma + (u_{it}-u_{i,t-\theta}),\\ &\theta = 1,\dots,T-1;\ t=\theta+1,\dots,T,\end{aligned} \tag{8.14}$$

for which OLS, letting $\Delta_\theta z_{it}=z_{it}-z_{i,t-\theta}$, gives the following estimator of γ

$$\widehat{\gamma}_{\Delta,OLS}(\theta) = \frac{\sum_{i=1}^{N}\sum_{t=\theta+1}^{T}(\Delta_\theta y_{i,t-1})(\Delta_\theta y_{it})}{\sum_{i=1}^{N}\sum_{t=\theta+1}^{T}(\Delta_\theta y_{i,t-1})^2},\quad \theta=1,\dots,T-1. \tag{8.15}$$

This 'OLS on differences' estimator, like the within estimator (8.5), is inconsistent, since, *in general*, $\text{cov}(y_{it(-1)}^*, u_{it}^*)\neq 0$. For example, in

$$\widehat{\gamma}_{\Delta,OLS}(\theta) - \gamma = \frac{\frac{1}{N(T-\theta)}\sum_{i=1}^{N}\sum_{t=\theta+1}^{T}(\Delta_\theta y_{i,t-1})(\Delta_\theta u_{it})}{\frac{1}{N(T-\theta)}\sum_{i=1}^{N}\sum_{t=\theta+1}^{T}(\Delta_\theta y_{i,t-1})^2},$$

the numerator has non-zero plim since $\text{cov}(\Delta_\theta y_{i,t-1}, \Delta_\theta u_{it})\neq 0$ for any $\theta\geq 1$.

A good message is, however, that there exists a *particular* difference transformation, *orthogonal forward difference* (exemplifying the more general *Helmert transformation*), which retains the effective time-series length T and for which OLS is consistent. This transformation, considered by, e.g., Arellano and Bover (1995, pp. 41–3), can, for any z_{it}, be expressed as

$$z^*_{it} = \sqrt{\frac{T-t}{T-t+1}}\left(z_{it} - \frac{z_{i,t+1}+\cdots+z_{i,T}}{T-t}\right) \equiv \frac{\sum_{s=t+1}^{T}(z_{it}-z_{is})}{[(T-t)(T-t+1)]^{\frac{1}{2}}}, \tag{8.16}$$

obtained for

$$d_{ts} = \begin{cases} 0, & s < t, \\ \left(\dfrac{T-t}{T-t+1}\right)^{\frac{1}{2}}, & s = t, \\ -\dfrac{1}{[(T-t)(T-t+1)]^{\frac{1}{2}}}, & s > t. \end{cases}$$

The transformation constructs a weighted mean of forward differences. Applying it to u_{it}, we find, remarkably, that u^*_{it} *has the same properties as* u_{it}: $u_{it} \sim \mathsf{IID}(0,\sigma^2) \Longrightarrow u^*_{it} \sim \mathsf{IID}(0,\sigma^2)$. The proof is: assume, with no loss of generality, $0<t<\tau<T$ and let $\bar{u}_{i(tT)} = \frac{1}{T-t}\sum_{s=t+1}^{T} u_{is}$. Then

$$u_{it} \sim \mathsf{IID}(0,\sigma^2) \Longrightarrow \begin{cases} \mathsf{E}(u_{it}u_{i\tau}) = \mathsf{E}(u_{it}\bar{u}_{i(\tau T)}) = 0, \\ \mathsf{E}(u_{i\tau}\bar{u}_{i(tT)}) = \mathsf{E}(\bar{u}_{i(\tau T)}\bar{u}_{i(tT)}) = \frac{1}{T-t}\sigma^2, \\ \mathsf{E}(u_{it} - \bar{u}_{i(tT)})^2 = \frac{T-t+1}{T-t}\sigma^2. \end{cases}$$

From this it follows that $\mathsf{E}(u^{*2}_{it}) = \sigma^2$, $\mathsf{E}(u^*_{it}u^*_{i\tau}) = 0$, $t = 1,\dots,T$; $\tau = t+1,\dots,T$.

Since u^*_{it} has no memory while, in view of (8.13), $y^*_{i,t-1}$ depends on $u^*_{i,t-s}$ $(s \geq 1)$, OLS regression of y^*_{it} on $y^*_{i,t-1}$ is consistent for γ. The virtue of this transformation applied on Model (8.1) is therefore that it both removes the fixed heterogeneity and makes the lagged endogenous regressor and the disturbance uncorrelated: $\text{cov}(y^*_{i,t-1}, u^*_{i,t}) = 0$.[4]

8.2.3 EQUATION IN DIFFERENCES: SIMPLE ESTIMATION BY LEVEL IVs

Turning to IV estimation, we show how, by selecting a suitable IV-set, differenced equations of the form (8.14) can be consistently estimated. Consider the case $\theta = 1$, i.e.,

[4] The Stata module *tstransform* (see *http://www.kripfganz.de/stata*; last accessed March 2016) can be used to perform these (and several other) time-series transformations.

$$\Delta y_{it} = \Delta y_{i,t-1}\gamma + \Delta u_{it}, \qquad i = 1,\dots,N;\ t = 2,\dots,T. \tag{8.17}$$

Since (8.3) implies $\Delta y_{it} = \sum_{s=0}^{\infty}\gamma^s \Delta u_{i,t-s}$ and (8.1) implies that Δu_{it} is a MA(1) process, we have

$$\left\{\begin{matrix} y_{i,t-\tau}\ \&\ \Delta y_{i,t-\tau} \text{ for} \\ \tau = 2,3,\dots, \end{matrix}\right\} \text{ are } \left\{\begin{matrix} \text{correlated with } \Delta y_{i,t-1}, \\ \text{uncorrelated with } \Delta u_{it} \end{matrix}\right\}.$$

The *orthogonality conditions* for $y_{i,t-\tau}$ and $\Delta y_{i,t-\tau}$ therefore read:

$$\mathsf{E}(y_{i,t-\tau}\Delta u_{it}) = 0, \tag{8.18}$$

$$\mathsf{E}(\Delta y_{i,t-\tau}\Delta u_{it}) = 0, \qquad \text{for all } t \text{ and } \tau \geq 2, \tag{8.19}$$

which makes these variables valid IVs for $\Delta y_{i,t-1}$. If only one IV is used, following Anderson and Hsiao (1981, Section 8), we obtain, respectively,

$$\widehat{\gamma}_{\Delta IV}(\tau) = \frac{\sum_{i=1}^{N}\sum_{t=\tau}^{T} y_{i,t-\tau}\Delta y_{it}}{\sum_{i=1}^{N}\sum_{t=\tau}^{T} y_{i,t-\tau}\Delta y_{i,t-1}}, \qquad \tau = 2,\dots,T, \tag{8.20}$$

$$\widehat{\gamma}_{\Delta IV}(\Delta\tau) = \frac{\sum_{i=1}^{N}\sum_{t=\tau+1}^{T} \Delta y_{i,t-\tau}\Delta y_{it}}{\sum_{i=1}^{N}\sum_{t=\tau+1}^{T} \Delta y_{i,t-\tau}\Delta y_{i,t-1}}, \qquad \tau = 2,\dots,T-1, \tag{8.21}$$

where subscripts (τ) and $(\Delta\tau)$ indicate that the IV is lagged τ periods. In (8.20) a lagged y is used for $\Delta y_{i,t-1}$; in (8.21) a lagged Δy serves this purpose. Consistency follows because, in view of (8.18)–(8.19), the numerators of

$$\widehat{\gamma}_{\Delta IV}(\tau) - \gamma = \frac{\frac{1}{N(T-\tau+1)}\sum_{i=1}^{N}\sum_{t=\tau}^{T} y_{i,t-\tau}\Delta u_{it}}{\frac{1}{N(T-\tau+1)}\sum_{i=1}^{N}\sum_{t=\tau}^{T} y_{i,t-\tau}\Delta y_{i,t-1}},$$

$$\widehat{\gamma}_{\Delta,IV}(\Delta\tau) - \gamma = \frac{\frac{1}{N(T-\tau)}\sum_{i=1}^{N}\sum_{t=\tau+1}^{T} \Delta y_{i,t-\tau}\Delta u_{it}}{\frac{1}{N(T-\tau)}\sum_{i=1}^{N}\sum_{t=\tau+1}^{T} \Delta y_{i,t-\tau}\Delta y_{i,t-1}},$$

have zero plims as the lags in the IVs 'get clear of' the memory of Δu_{it}.[5]

Several modifications of these simple IV procedures are available. First, we could in (8.14) let $\theta = 2,3,\dots,T-1$, reformulate (8.18) accordingly, and use admissible IVs for the chosen difference span in a multi-IV procedure. Second, the equation could be kept

[5] Arellano (1989), examining more closely these Anderson–Hsiao estimators, finds that estimators using lagged Δys as IVs for $\Delta y_{i,t-1}$, as in (8.21), suffers from problems of existence and lack of efficiency and concludes that estimators using level ys as IVs, see (8.20), are definitely to be preferred.

in levels, *using differences of the form* $\Delta y_{i,t-\tau}$ *as IVs for* $y_{i,t-1}$, i.e., the 'roles' of differences and levels reversed. Third, we could use as IVs for $\Delta y_{i,t-1}$ *linear combinations of* $y_{i,t-\tau}$ *for several* $\tau \geq 2$ in a multi-IV procedure. The larger θ is set, however, the smaller is both the number of effective observations and $\text{corr}(\Delta_{i,t-1}, y_{i,t-\theta})$; see Appendix 8B. These ideas will be followed up in Sections 8.2.4–8.2.6.

8.2.4 EQUATION IN DIFFERENCES: SYSTEM GMM WITH LEVEL IVs

The previous section exemplified IV estimation of an AR(1)-equation in differences, using one IV. We extend it to a multi-IV procedure, considering (8.17) for $t=3,\dots,T$ as a *system of* $T-2$ *equations with* γ *as common coefficient:*

$$\begin{aligned} \Delta y_{i3} &= \Delta y_{i2}\gamma + \Delta u_{i3}, \\ \Delta y_{i4} &= \Delta y_{i3}\gamma + \Delta u_{i4}, \\ &\vdots \\ \Delta y_{iT} &= \Delta y_{i,T-1}\gamma + \Delta u_{iT}, \end{aligned} \tag{8.22}$$

or in compact notation,

$$\Delta \boldsymbol{y}_i = \Delta \boldsymbol{y}_{i,-1}\gamma + \Delta \boldsymbol{u}_i, \qquad i = 1,\dots,N. \tag{8.23}$$

Motivated by (8.18), we compile an IV matrix for (8.22) by using

$z_{i2} = y_{i0}$ for Δy_{i2} in the first equation,
$z_{i3} = (y_{i0}, y_{i1})$ for Δy_{i3} in the second equation,
$\vdots$
$z_{i,T-1} = (y_{i0}, y_{i1}, \dots, y_{i,T-3})$ for $\Delta y_{i,T-1}$ in the $(T-2)$'th equation.

Hence, different sets of lagged ys serve as IVs for Δys in different equations.[6]

A property of this approach, which may turn into a problem, is that, since the equation-specific IVs satisfy the recursion $z_{it} = (z_{i,t-1}, y_{i,t-2})$, *the IV-sets cumulate*, exemplifying a problem called *IV-proliferation*; see Roodman (2009). Unless T is very small, the number of candidates at the end may become excessive. There may be 'too many IVs' of 'poor quality'.[7] This method is therefore often labelled a *system IV estimator* appropriate for

[6] This is a more flexible way of IV selection than the standard approach for simultaneous equation systems, according to which the same IV-set is used for all equations. Schmidt (1990) and Wooldridge (1996) discuss the 'different IVs in different equations' idea in a general context, *inter alia*, in relation to the extension from two-stage to three-stage least squares.

[7] Appendix 8B gives some results on covariances and correlograms of levels and first-differences in strict $AR(1)$ models.

'*short panels*'. To condense the IV-set, by including at most two y-IVs in each equation, we may choose

$z_{i2} = y_{i0}$ for Δy_{i2} in the first equation,
$z_{i3} = (y_{i0}, y_{i1})$ for Δy_{i3} in the second equation,
$\vdots$
$z_{i,T-1} = (y_{i,T-4}, y_{i,T-3})$ for $\Delta y_{i,T-1}$ in the $(T-2)$'th equation.

Anyway, we stack the z_{it}s into an IV matrix for $\Delta y_{i,-1}$:

$$Z_i = \begin{bmatrix} z_{i2} & \mathbf{0} & \cdots & \mathbf{0} \\ \mathbf{0} & z_{i3} & \cdots & \mathbf{0} \\ \vdots & \vdots & \ddots & \vdots \\ \mathbf{0} & \mathbf{0} & \cdots & z_{i,T-1} \end{bmatrix}, \qquad i = 1, \dots, N, \tag{8.24}$$

and stack (8.23) across i to obtain

$$\Delta y = \Delta y_{-1}\gamma + \Delta u, \tag{8.25}$$

where Z acts as IV matrix for Δy_{-1}, letting

$$\Delta y = \begin{bmatrix} \Delta y_1 \\ \vdots \\ \Delta y_N \end{bmatrix}, \quad \Delta y_{-1} = \begin{bmatrix} \Delta y_{1,-1} \\ \vdots \\ \Delta y_{N,-1} \end{bmatrix}, \quad \Delta u = \begin{bmatrix} \Delta u_1 \\ \vdots \\ \Delta u_N \end{bmatrix}, \quad Z = \begin{bmatrix} Z_1 \\ \vdots \\ Z_N \end{bmatrix}.$$

This GMM problem has the same format as the one in Section 7.6.2, Δy_{-1} replacing Δx, which motivates the following *step-one GMM* estimator of γ:[8]

$$\begin{aligned} \widehat{\gamma}^D_{GMM} &= [\Delta y'_{-1}Z(Z'Z)^{-1}Z'\Delta y_{-1}]^{-1}[\Delta y'_{-1}Z(Z'Z)^{-1}Z'\Delta y] \\ &\equiv [(\textstyle\sum_{i=1}^N \Delta y'_{i,-1}Z_i)(\sum_{i=1}^N Z'_iZ_i)^{-1}(\sum_{i=1}^N Z'_i\Delta y_{i,-1})]^{-1} \\ &\quad \times [(\textstyle\sum_{i=1}^N \Delta y'_{i,-1}Z_i)(\sum_{i=1}^N Z'_iZ_i)^{-1}(\sum_{i=1}^N Z'_i\Delta y_i)] \end{aligned} \tag{8.26}$$

and the corresponding (heteroskedasticity-robust) *step-two-GMM* estimator

$$\begin{aligned} \widetilde{\gamma}^D_{GMM} &= [(\textstyle\sum_{i=1}^N \Delta y'_{i,-1}Z_i)(\sum_{i=1}^N Z'_i\widehat{\Delta u}_i\widehat{\Delta u}'_iZ_i)^{-1}(\sum_{i=1}^N Z'_i\Delta y_{i,-1})]^{-1} \\ &\quad \times [(\textstyle\sum_{i=1}^N \Delta y'_{i,-1}Z_i)(\sum_{i=1}^N Z'_i\widehat{\Delta u}_i\widehat{\Delta u}'_iZ_i)^{-1}(\sum_{i=1}^N Z'_i\Delta y_i)], \end{aligned} \tag{8.27}$$

[8] A formally similar GMM estimator for a measurement error model is (7.87).

where the $\widehat{\Delta u}_i$s are residual vectors obtained from the step-one estimates and superscript D signalizes that GMM is applied to an equation system in differences.

The Sargan–Hansen statistic for testing the validity of the orthogonality conditions, resembling (7.89), is

$$\mathcal{J}^D = (\textstyle\sum_{i=1}^N \Delta y'_{i,-1} Z_i)(\sum_{i=1}^N Z'_i \widehat{\Delta u}_i \widehat{\Delta u}'_i Z_i)^{-1}(\sum_{i=1}^N Z'_i \Delta y_{i,-1}). \tag{8.28}$$

8.2.5 EQUATION IN LEVELS: SIMPLE ESTIMATION BY DIFFERENCE IVs

We return to the level version of the equation, (8.1), and consider as IV for $y_{i,t-1}$ a lagged difference. Since

$$\textstyle\sum_i \sum_t (\Delta y_{i,t-\tau}) y_{it} = [\sum_i \sum_t (\Delta y_{i,t-\tau}) y_{i,t-1}]\gamma + \sum_i (\sum_t \Delta y_{i,t-\tau})(\alpha_i^* + u_{it}),$$

the following IV estimator for γ, symmetric with (8.20), is motivated:

$$\widetilde{\gamma}_{IV}(\Delta\tau) = \frac{\sum_{i=1}^N \sum_{t=\tau+1}^T (\Delta y_{i,t-\tau}) y_{it}}{\sum_{i=1}^N \sum_{t=\tau+1}^T (\Delta y_{i,t-\tau}) y_{i,t-1}}, \qquad \tau = 2, \dots, T. \tag{8.29}$$

Inserting for y_{it} from (8.1) gives

$$\widetilde{\gamma}_{IV(\Delta\tau)} - \gamma = \frac{\frac{1}{N}\sum_i (\frac{1}{T-\tau+1}\sum_t \Delta y_{i,t-\tau})\alpha_i^* + \frac{1}{N(T-\tau+1)}\sum_i \sum_t (\Delta y_{i,t-\tau}) u_{it}}{\frac{1}{N(T-\tau+1)}\sum_i \sum_t (\Delta y_{i,t-\tau}) y_{i,t-1}}.$$

When $N \to \infty$ the first term vanishes, regardless of T and τ, and the orthogonality condition, symmetric with (8.18),

$$\mathsf{E}[(\Delta y_{i,t-\tau}) u_{it}] = 0, \qquad \tau = 2, \dots, T, \tag{8.30}$$

ensures zero plim of the second term.

8.2.6 EQUATION IN LEVELS: SYSTEM GMM WITH DIFFERENCE IVs

The previous section exemplified a simple IV-procedure for an AR(1)-equation in levels. We extend it to a multi-IV procedure, considering (8.1) for $t = 3, \dots, T$ as a *system of* $T-2$ *equations with* γ *as common coefficient*:

$$
\begin{aligned}
y_{i3} &= \alpha_i^* + y_{i,2}\gamma + u_{i3},\\
y_{i4} &= \alpha_i^* + y_{i,3}\gamma + u_{i4},\\
&\vdots\\
y_{iT} &= \alpha_i^* + y_{i,T-1}\gamma + u_{iT},
\end{aligned}
\tag{8.31}
$$

or in compact notation, with $\boldsymbol{\alpha}_i^* = \boldsymbol{e}_{T-2}\alpha_i^*$,

$$
\boldsymbol{y}_i = \boldsymbol{\alpha}_i^* + \boldsymbol{y}_{i,-1}\gamma + \boldsymbol{u}_i, \qquad i = 1, \dots, N. \tag{8.32}
$$

Motivated by (8.30), we compile an IV matrix for (8.31) by using

$\Delta z_{i2} = \Delta y_{i1}$ for y_{i2} in the first equation,
$\Delta z_{i3} = (\Delta y_{i1}, \Delta y_{i2})$ for y_{i3} in the second equation,
$\vdots$
$\Delta z_{i,T-1} = (\Delta y_{i1}, \dots, \Delta y_{i,T-3})$ for $y_{i,T-1}$ in the $(T-2)$'th equation,

using *different sets of lagged Δys as IVs for ys in different equations.*

Since $\Delta z_{it} = (\Delta z_{i,t-1}, \Delta y_{i,t-2})$, the IV-sets cumulate and unless T is very small, the number of candidates at the end may become excessive.[9] To condense, by including at most two Δy-IVs in each equation, we may choose

$\Delta z_{i2} = \Delta y_{i1}$ for y_{i2} in the first equation,
$\Delta z_{i3} = (\Delta y_{i1}, \Delta y_{i2})$ for y_{i3} in the second equation,
$\vdots$
$\Delta z_{i,T-1} = (\Delta y_{i,T-3}, \Delta y_{i,T-2})$ for $y_{i,T-1}$ in the $(T-2)$'th equation.

Anyway, we stack these Δz_{it}s into an IV matrix for $\boldsymbol{y}_{i,-1}$:

$$
\Delta Z_i = \begin{bmatrix} \Delta z_{i2} & 0 & \cdots & 0 \\ 0 & \Delta z_{i3} & \cdots & 0 \\ \vdots & \vdots & \ddots & \vdots \\ 0 & 0 & \cdots & \Delta z_{i,T-1} \end{bmatrix}, \qquad i = 1, \dots, N, \tag{8.33}
$$

and stack (8.32) across i, letting

$$
\boldsymbol{y} = \begin{bmatrix} \boldsymbol{y}_1 \\ \vdots \\ \boldsymbol{y}_N \end{bmatrix}, \; \boldsymbol{y}_{-1} = \begin{bmatrix} \boldsymbol{y}_{1,-1} \\ \vdots \\ \boldsymbol{y}_{N,-1} \end{bmatrix}, \; \boldsymbol{u} = \begin{bmatrix} \boldsymbol{u}_1 \\ \vdots \\ \boldsymbol{u}_N \end{bmatrix}, \; \boldsymbol{\alpha}^* = \begin{bmatrix} \boldsymbol{\alpha}_1^* \\ \vdots \\ \boldsymbol{\alpha}_N^* \end{bmatrix}, \; \Delta Z = \begin{bmatrix} \Delta Z_1 \\ \vdots \\ \Delta Z_N \end{bmatrix},
$$

[9] Again, see Appendix 8B for results on covariances and correlograms of levels and first-differences in $AR(1)$ models.

to obtain

$$y = \alpha^* + y_{-1}\gamma + u, \tag{8.34}$$

where ΔZ acts as IV matrix for y_{-1}. This motivates the following *step-one GMM* estimator of γ:

$$\begin{aligned}\widehat{\gamma}^L_{GMM} &= [y'_{-1}\Delta Z(\Delta Z'\Delta Z)^{-1}\Delta Z' y_{-1}]^{-1}[y'_{-1}\Delta Z(\Delta Z'\Delta Z)^{-1}\Delta Z' y] \\ &\equiv [(\textstyle\sum_{i=1}^N y'_{i,-1}\Delta Z_i)(\sum_{i=1}^N \Delta Z'_i\Delta Z_i)^{-1}(\sum_{i=1}^N \Delta Z'_i y_{i,-1})]^{-1} \\ &\quad\times [(\textstyle\sum_{i=1}^N y'_{i,-1}\Delta Z_i)(\sum_{i=1}^N \Delta Z'_i\Delta Z_i)^{-1}(\sum_{i=1}^N \Delta Z'_i y_i)]\end{aligned} \tag{8.35}$$

and the corresponding *step-two GMM* estimator

$$\begin{aligned}\widetilde{\gamma}^L_{GMM} &= [(\textstyle\sum_{i=1}^N y'_{i,-1}\Delta Z_i)(\sum_{i=1}^N \Delta Z'_i\widehat{u}_i\widehat{u}'_i\Delta Z_i)^{-1}(\sum_{i=1}^N \Delta Z'_i y_{i,-1})]^{-1} \\ &\quad\times [(\textstyle\sum_{i=1}^N y'_{i,-1}\Delta Z_i)(\sum_{i=1}^N \Delta Z'_i\widehat{u}_i\widehat{u}'_i\Delta Z_i)^{-1}(\sum_{i=1}^N \Delta Z'_i y_i)],\end{aligned} \tag{8.36}$$

where the $\widehat{u}_i$s are residual vectors obtained from the step-one estimates and superscript L signalizes that GMM is applied to an equation system in levels.

The Sargan–Hansen statistic for testing the validity of the orthogonality conditions, underlying GMM estimation of the equation in levels, is

$$\mathcal{J}^L = (\textstyle\sum_{i=1}^N y'_{i,-1}\Delta Z_i)(\sum_{i=1}^N \Delta Z'_i\widehat{u}_i\widehat{u}'_i\Delta Z_i)^{-1}(\sum_{i=1}^N \Delta Z'_i y_{i,-1}). \tag{8.37}$$

The symmetry between (8.35)–(8.37) and (8.26)–(8.28) is obvious.

8.2.7 PANEL UNIT ROOTS AND PANEL CO-INTEGRATION

Above the AR-coefficient γ has (with a few exceptions) been assumed to be strictly less than one (in absolute value), an assumption necessary for stationarity of y_{it}. During the last decades, increasing attention has been given to models with unitary value of this coefficient and to the related models with co-integrated variables. This is partly motivated by related literature on models for non-stationary time-series and co-integration, of relevance for many economic variables and models. We comment briefly on the essence of such extensions, supplemented by references.

Consider first a model with both intercept and slope coefficient individual-specific. We write (8.10), with $\phi_i = \gamma_i - 1$, assuming $\gamma_i > 0$, as

$$\Delta y_{it} = \alpha_i^* + y_{i,t-1}\phi_i + u_{it}. \tag{8.38}$$

Stationarity of the AR-process for individual i requires $\phi_i < 0$ $(0 < \gamma_i < 1)$. Non-stationarity, in the form of a unit root entering the lag-polynomial of y_{it}, is characterized by $\phi_i = 0$ $(\gamma_i = 1)$, $i = 1, \dots, N$. The latter, as a null hypothesis H_0, can be tested against *either of* the alternative hypotheses, which imply stationarity:

$$H_{1a} : \phi_1 = \cdots = \phi_N = \phi < 0, \qquad \text{(common AR-coefficient)},$$
$$H_{1b} : \phi_1 < 0, \dots, \phi_M < 0, \qquad \text{(i-specific AR-coefficient)},$$

where, under H_{1b}, M is assumed to be less than N. A large number of such tests have been proposed, *inter alia*, based on the (augmented) Dickey–Fuller test, which is a specially designed t-test. A survey and synthesis is given in Breitung and Pesaran (2008, Sections 9.2 and 9.3); see also Levin, Lin, and Chu (2002), Im, Pesaran, and Shin (2003), and Westerlund (2005). A Lagrange Multiplier (LM) test based on residuals is proposed in Hadri (2000).[10]

A modified version of this model with $\gamma_i = \gamma$ $(\phi_i = \phi = \gamma - 1)$, containing also a (strictly) exogenous vector $\boldsymbol{x}_{it}$ and its one-period lag, is

$$y_{it} = \alpha_i^* + y_{i,t-1}\gamma + \boldsymbol{x}_{it}\boldsymbol{\beta}_0 + \boldsymbol{x}_{i,t-1}\boldsymbol{\beta}_1 + u_{it}. \tag{8.39}$$

This also is an extension of (8.1). If $\gamma = 1$, it can be rewritten as

$$\Delta y_{it} = \alpha_i^* + \Delta\boldsymbol{x}_{it}\boldsymbol{\beta}_0 + \boldsymbol{x}_{i,t-1}(\boldsymbol{\beta}_0 + \boldsymbol{\beta}_1) + u_{it}, \tag{8.40}$$

while if $\gamma < 1$ it can be reparameterized into

$$\Delta y_{it} = \Delta\boldsymbol{x}_{it}\boldsymbol{\beta}_0 - (1-\gamma)[y_{i,t-1} - \bar{\alpha}_i - \bar{\boldsymbol{\beta}}\boldsymbol{x}_{i,t-1}] + u_{it}, \tag{8.41}$$

where $\bar{\alpha}_i = \alpha_i^*/(1-\gamma)$ and $\bar{\boldsymbol{\beta}} = (\boldsymbol{\beta}_0 + \boldsymbol{\beta}_1)/(1-\gamma)$. If both y_{it} and $\boldsymbol{x}_{it}$ have unit roots, Δy_{it} and $\Delta\boldsymbol{x}_{it}$ are stationary. Then for u_{it} to be stationary, $y_{i,t-1} - \bar{\alpha}_i - \bar{\boldsymbol{\beta}}\boldsymbol{x}_{i,t-1}$ must be stationary. In such a case, y_{it} and $\boldsymbol{x}_{it}$ are said to co-integrated of first order, with co-integrating vector $\bar{\alpha}_i, \bar{\boldsymbol{\beta}}$.

The main focus of the panel co-integration literature dealing with testing has been on *residual-based approaches*, and tests are developed for different dynamic models and alternative hypotheses, e.g., based on OLS residuals from co-integration equations. See Breitung and Pesaran (2008, Sections 9.6, 9.7, and 9.9) for a survey, and Moon and

[10] A Stata module, `xtunitroot`, with several options, is available for performing such tests.

Perron (2004), Bai and Ng (2004), Pedroni (2004), and Westerlund (2005, 2007) for discussion of specific situations.

8.2.8 BIAS CORRECTION

The N-consistent estimators discussed in Sections 8.2.1–8.2.6 may have non-negligible *finite-sample bias*. It is far from certain that for small or moderate T, an N-consistent estimator, e.g., $\widehat{\gamma}^L_{GMM}$ or $\widetilde{\gamma}^L_{GMM}$, given by (8.35)–(8.36), has smaller bias than an N-inconsistent estimator, e.g., $\widehat{\gamma}_W$ given by (8.5). The former may well have a larger *finite-sample* bias for certain values of N, T, and γ. Such issues have been given substantial attention and can be examined by Monte Carlo simulations or by mathematical expansions of the bias formulae. Biased estimators may be 'corrected' by bias-factors or bias-corrections estimated from N-consistent estimates; see Kiviet (1995) and Bun and Carree (2005), and, for a more general discussion not specifically related to panel data, MacKinnon and Smith (1998). An example is that (8.9) may be estimated consistently from a consistent estimator of γ, e.g., from an IV-procedure. Although seemingly attractive, such bias correction procedures have drawbacks; see Harris, Mátyás, and Sevestre (2008, p. 254).

8.3 Fixed effects AR-models with exogenous variables

We have, in Sections 8.2.1–8.2.6, discussed in some detail estimation of a stylized, and for practical purposes not very appealing, model with only the lagged regressand as regressor. Including, as in the last part of Section 8.2.7, (strictly) exogenous variables increases the model's usefulness, but raises a few problems. There are more coefficients to be estimated, while the exogenous variables extend the IV-set. After specifying the model, we discuss *system GMM estimators* which generalize those in Sections 8.2.5 and 8.2.6, and give some empirical illustrations.

8.3.1 MODEL

Let $\boldsymbol{x}_{it}$ be a $(1 \times K)$-vector of (strictly) exogenous variables and $\boldsymbol{\beta}$ a $(K \times 1)$-vector of coefficients and extend Model (8.1) to[11]

[11] A limitation of this model, not to be discussed further, is that it only contains two-dimensional exogenous variables. Inclusion of time-invariant variables would have created problems with separating their effects from the impact of the fixed effects, related to those for static models discussed in Section 5.3.

$$
\begin{aligned}
&y_{it} = \alpha_i^* + y_{i,t-1}\gamma + \boldsymbol{x}_{it}\boldsymbol{\beta} + u_{it}, \quad |\gamma| < 1; \quad & i = 1,\dots,N; \\
&(u_{it}|X, y_i^{(t-1)}) \sim \mathsf{IID}(0, \sigma^2), & t = 1,\dots,T,
\end{aligned} \tag{8.42}
$$

where X denotes all values of $\boldsymbol{x}_{it}$ and $y_i^{(t-1)} = (y_{i,t-1},\dots,y_{i1},y_{i0})'$. Again it is important that u_{it} has no memory, making $y_{i,t-1}$ a predetermined variable uncorrelated with u_{it}; otherwise IID may be relaxed. The implied difference equation has solution

$$
\begin{aligned}
y_{it} &= \gamma^t y_{i0} + \textstyle\sum_{s=0}^{t-1} \gamma^s(\alpha_i^* + \boldsymbol{x}_{i,t-s}\boldsymbol{\beta} + u_{i,t-s}) \\
&= \gamma^t y_{i0} + \alpha_i^*(1-\gamma^t)/(1-\gamma) + \textstyle\sum_{s=0}^{t-1} \gamma^s(\boldsymbol{x}_{i,t-s}\boldsymbol{\beta} + u_{i,t-s}).
\end{aligned} \tag{8.43}
$$

This equation exists if $\gamma \neq 1$; it does not require $|\gamma| < 1$. The boundary case $\gamma = 1$, where the lag polynomial of y_{it} has a 'unit root' corresponding to the model in the last part of Section 8.2.7, gives

$$
\Delta y_{it} = \alpha_i^* + \boldsymbol{x}_{it}\boldsymbol{\beta} + u_{it} \implies y_{it}^\dagger = y_{i,t-1}^\dagger + \boldsymbol{x}_{it}\boldsymbol{\beta} + u_{it},
$$

where $y_{it}^\dagger = y_{it} - t\alpha_i^*$, which implies

$$
\begin{aligned}
y_{it} &= y_{i0} + t\alpha_i^* + \textstyle\sum_{s=0}^{t-1}(\boldsymbol{x}_{i,t-s}\boldsymbol{\beta} + u_{i,t-s}) \implies \\
y_{it}^\dagger &= y_{i0}^\dagger + \textstyle\sum_{s=0}^{t-1}(\boldsymbol{x}_{i,t-s}\boldsymbol{\beta} + u_{i,t-s}).
\end{aligned}
$$

The 'unit root' hypothesis can be tested by (augmented) Dickey–Fuller tests.

If the process had started infinitely long back in time, we get

$$
\begin{aligned}
y_{it} &= \textstyle\sum_{s=0}^{\infty} \gamma^s(\alpha_i^* + \boldsymbol{x}_{i,t-s}\boldsymbol{\beta} + u_{i,t-s}) \\
&= \alpha_i^*/(1-\gamma) + \textstyle\sum_{s=0}^{\infty} \gamma^s(\boldsymbol{x}_{i,t-s}\boldsymbol{\beta} + u_{i,t-s}).
\end{aligned} \tag{8.44}
$$

Transforming (8.42) into

$$
(y_{it} - \bar{y}_{i\cdot}) = (y_{i,t-1} - \bar{y}_{i,-1})\gamma + (\boldsymbol{x}_{it} - \bar{\boldsymbol{x}}_{i\cdot})\boldsymbol{\beta} + (u_{it} - \bar{u}_{i\cdot}), \tag{8.45}
$$

and applying OLS gives the *within estimator*, which are asymptotically biased *for both* γ *and* $\boldsymbol{\beta}$ when T is finite, because $(y_{i,t-1} - \bar{y}_{i,-1})$ is correlated with $(u_{it} - \bar{u}_{i\cdot})$, and $(y_{i,t-1} - \bar{y}_{i,-1})$, and $(\boldsymbol{x}_{it} - \bar{\boldsymbol{x}}_{i\cdot})$ are correlated. The problem is essentially the same as the problem discussed for (8.5). The within estimator is only T-consistent.

For (8.42) transformed to differences, since (8.44) implies

$$
\Delta y_{it} = \textstyle\sum_{s=0}^{\infty} \gamma^s(\Delta\boldsymbol{x}_{i,t-s}\boldsymbol{\beta} + \Delta u_{i,t-s}),
$$

the orthogonality properties $\mathsf{E}(y_{i,t-\tau}\Delta u_{it}) = \mathsf{E}(\Delta y_{i,t-\tau}\Delta u_{it}) = 0$, $\tau \geq 2$, motivates $y_{i,t-\tau}, \Delta y_{i,t-\tau}$ $(\tau \geq 2)$ and $\boldsymbol{x}_{i,t-\tau}, \Delta \boldsymbol{x}_{i,t-\tau}$ $(\tau \geq 1)$ as IV candidates for $\Delta y_{i,t-1}$ in

$$\Delta y_{it} = \Delta y_{i,t-1}\, \gamma + \Delta \boldsymbol{x}_{it}\boldsymbol{\beta} + \Delta u_{it}, \quad i = 1, \ldots, N;\ t = 2, \ldots, T. \tag{8.46}$$

These methods can be modified by exploiting difference transformations as in (8.11)–(8.12). Then we use

$$y^*_{it} = d_{t\cdot}\alpha^*_i + y^*_{it(-1)}\gamma + \boldsymbol{x}^*_{it}\boldsymbol{\beta} + u^*_{it}, \qquad i = 1, \ldots, N, \tag{8.47}$$

construct transformations of $y_{i0}, \ldots, y_{iT}$ and $\boldsymbol{x}_{i0}, \ldots, \boldsymbol{x}_{iT}$ to serve as IVs, and otherwise proceed as described in Section 8.2.2. We can, for example, exploit the orthogonal forward difference transformation (8.16) on $y_{it}, y_{i,t-1}$ and $\boldsymbol{x}_{it}$.

8.3.2 EQUATION IN DIFFERENCES: SYSTEM GMM WITH LEVEL IVs

We consider system GMM using level IVs. For $t = 3, \ldots, T$, (8.46) defines $T-2$ equations in differences:

$$\begin{aligned} \Delta y_{i3} &= \Delta y_{i2}\gamma + \Delta \boldsymbol{x}_{i3}\boldsymbol{\beta} + \Delta u_{i3} = \Delta \boldsymbol{q}_{i3}\boldsymbol{\delta} + \Delta u_{i3}, \\ \Delta y_{i4} &= \Delta y_{i3}\gamma + \Delta \boldsymbol{x}_{i4}\boldsymbol{\beta} + \Delta u_{i4} = \Delta \boldsymbol{q}_{i4}\boldsymbol{\delta} + \Delta u_{i4}, \\ &\vdots \\ \Delta y_{iT} &= \Delta y_{i,T-1}\gamma + \Delta \boldsymbol{x}_{iT}\boldsymbol{\beta} + \Delta u_{iT} = \Delta \boldsymbol{q}_{iT}\boldsymbol{\delta} + \Delta u_{iT}, \end{aligned} \tag{8.48}$$

or in compact notation

$$\Delta \boldsymbol{y}_i = \Delta \boldsymbol{Q}_i\boldsymbol{\delta} + \Delta \boldsymbol{u}_i, \qquad i = 1, \ldots, N, \tag{8.49}$$

where $\Delta \boldsymbol{q}_{it} = (\Delta y_{i,t-1}, \Delta \boldsymbol{x}_{it})$, $\Delta \boldsymbol{Q}'_i = [\Delta \boldsymbol{q}'_{i3}, \ldots, \Delta \boldsymbol{q}'_{iT}]$, $\boldsymbol{\delta} = (\gamma, \boldsymbol{\beta}')'$, etc. We compile an IV matrix by using as IVs

$\boldsymbol{z}_{i2} = (y_{i0}, \Delta \boldsymbol{x}_{i3})$ for $(\Delta y_{i2}, \Delta \boldsymbol{x}_{i3})$ in the first equation,
$\boldsymbol{z}_{i3} = (y_{i0}, y_{i1}, \Delta \boldsymbol{x}_{i4})$ for $(\Delta y_{i3}, \Delta \boldsymbol{x}_{i4})$ in the second equation,
$\vdots$
$\boldsymbol{z}_{i,T-1} = (y_{i0}, \ldots, y_{i,T-3}, \Delta \boldsymbol{x}_{iT})$ for $(\Delta y_{i,T-1}, \Delta \boldsymbol{x}_{iT})$ in the $(T-2)$'th equation,

or a parsimonious set which does not cumulate, with a maximum of two y-IVs,

$$
\begin{aligned}
&z_{i2} = (y_{i0}, \Delta x_{i3}) \text{ for } (\Delta y_{i2}, \Delta x_{i3}) \text{ in the first equation,}\\
&z_{i3} = (y_{i0}, y_{i1}, \Delta x_{i4}) \text{ for } (\Delta y_{i3}, \Delta x_{i4}) \text{ in the second equation,}\\
&\quad\vdots\\
&z_{i,T-1} = (y_{i,T-4}, y_{i,T-3}, \Delta x_{iT}) \text{ for } (\Delta y_{i,T-1}, \Delta x_{iT}) \text{ in the } (T-2)\text{'th equation.}
\end{aligned}
$$

The idea is to *use different IV-sets consisting of lagged ys together with the Δx in each equation in (8.48).*

We combine the level IVs into an IV matrix Z_i for ΔQ_i, of the form (8.24), with the reinterpreted z_{it}s, and stack (8.49) into

$$\Delta y = \Delta Q\delta + \Delta u, \tag{8.50}$$

letting

$$\Delta y = \begin{bmatrix} \Delta y_1 \\ \vdots \\ \Delta y_N \end{bmatrix}, \quad \Delta Q = \begin{bmatrix} \Delta Q_1 \\ \vdots \\ \Delta Q_N \end{bmatrix}, \quad \Delta u = \begin{bmatrix} \Delta u_1 \\ \vdots \\ \Delta u_N \end{bmatrix}, \quad Z = \begin{bmatrix} Z_1 \\ \vdots \\ Z_N \end{bmatrix}.$$

This motivates the following *step-one and step-two GMM* estimators of δ:

$$
\begin{aligned}
\widehat{\delta}^D_{GMM} &= [(\Delta Q')Z(Z'Z)^{-1}Z'(\Delta Q)]^{-1}[(\Delta Q')Z(Z'Z)^{-1}Z'(\Delta y)]\\
&\equiv [(\textstyle\sum_{i=1}^N (\Delta Q_i')Z_i)(\sum_{i=1}^N Z_i'Z_i)^{-1}(\sum_{i=1}^N Z_i'(\Delta Q_i))]^{-1}\\
&\quad \times [(\textstyle\sum_{i=1}^N (\Delta Q_i')Z_i)(\sum_{i=1}^N Z_i'Z_i)^{-1}(\sum_{i=1}^N Z_i'(\Delta y_i))], \qquad (8.51)\\
\widetilde{\delta}^D_{GMM} &= [(\textstyle\sum_{i=1}^N (\Delta Q_i')Z_i)(\sum_{i=1}^N Z_i'\widetilde{\Delta u}_i\widetilde{\Delta u}_i'Z_i)^{-1}(\sum_{i=1}^N Z_i'(\Delta Q_i))]^{-1}\\
&\quad \times [(\textstyle\sum_{i=1}^N (\Delta Q_i')Z_i)(\sum_{i=1}^N Z_i'\widetilde{\Delta u}_i\widetilde{\Delta u}_i'Z_i)^{-1}(\sum_{i=1}^N Z_i'(\Delta y_i))], \qquad (8.52)
\end{aligned}
$$

where the $\widetilde{\Delta u}_i$s are the residual vectors obtained from the step-one estimates. Arellano and Bond (1991) proposed this version of GMM, which generalizes (8.26) and (8.27) and has become quite popular in empirical applications.

The Sargan–Hansen statistic for testing the validity of the orthogonality conditions is

$$\mathcal{J}^D = (\textstyle\sum_{i=1}^N (\Delta Q_i')Z_i)(\sum_{i=1}^N Z_i'\widetilde{\Delta u}_i\widetilde{\Delta u}_i'Z_i)^{-1}(\sum_{i=1}^N Z_i'(\Delta Q_i)). \tag{8.53}$$

This estimation procedure, although N-consistent, may not perform well if γ is large or the latent individual-specific variation is large relative to the disturbance variation. Blundell and Bond (1998), building on Arellano and Bover (1995), propose a system estimator that exploits additional moment conditions, notably the additional orthogonality condition $\mathsf{E}(\Delta y_{i,t-1}u_{it}) = 0$; see also Harris, Mátyás, and Sevestre (2008, pp. 266–9). This motivates inclusion of lagged ys in the IV-set. This in a sense builds a bridge between what we call system GMM for equations in levels (see Section 8.3.3) and system GMM for equations in differences. Additional moment conditions to improve efficiency can also be obtained by exploiting that $\mathsf{E}[u_{it}(u_{i,t-s}-u_{i,t-s-1})] = 0,\ s \geq 1$, will often hold under mild conditions, as discussed in Ahn and Schmidt (1995).[12]

This modified system estimator is primarily designed for 'short panel' cases with many units. It assumes that there is no autocorrelation in the regular disturbances and *requires as an initial condition that the panel-level effects be uncorrelated with the first difference of the first observation of the dependent variable.* Such system GMM estimators can, when the autoregressive coefficient is close to one, give a dramatic improvement relative to the GMM estimator based only on the equation in differences. See Baltagi (2008, Section 8.5).

8.3.3 EQUATION IN LEVELS: SYSTEM GMM WITH DIFFERENCE IVs

Interchange again the variables in levels and in differences in GMM-estimation and consider (8.42), for $t = 3, \dots, T$, as a system of $T-2$ equations:

$$\begin{aligned} y_{i3} &= \alpha_i^* + y_{i2}\gamma + \boldsymbol{x}_{i3}\boldsymbol{\beta} + u_{i3} = \alpha_i^* + \boldsymbol{q}_{i3}\boldsymbol{\delta} + u_{i3}, \\ y_{i4} &= \alpha_i^* + y_{i3}\gamma + \boldsymbol{x}_{i4}\boldsymbol{\beta} + u_{i4} = \alpha_i^* + \boldsymbol{q}_{i4}\boldsymbol{\delta} + u_{i4}, \\ &\ \vdots \\ y_{iT} &= \alpha_i^* + y_{i,T-1}\gamma + \boldsymbol{x}_{iT}\boldsymbol{\beta} + u_{iT} = \alpha_i^* + \boldsymbol{q}_{iT}\boldsymbol{\delta} + u_{iT}, \end{aligned} \tag{8.54}$$

or in compact notation,

$$\boldsymbol{y}_i = \boldsymbol{\alpha}_i^* + \boldsymbol{Q}_i\boldsymbol{\delta} + \boldsymbol{u}_i, \qquad i = 1, \dots, N, \tag{8.55}$$

where $\boldsymbol{q}_{it} = (y_{i,t-1}, \boldsymbol{x}_{it})$, $\boldsymbol{Q}_i' = [\boldsymbol{q}_{i3}', \dots, \boldsymbol{q}_{iT}']$, $\boldsymbol{\delta}' = (\gamma, \boldsymbol{\beta}')$, etc. We compile an IV matrix by using as IVs

$\Delta \boldsymbol{z}_{i2} = (\Delta y_{i1}, \boldsymbol{x}_{i3})$ for $(y_{i2}, \boldsymbol{x}_{i3})$ in the first equation,
$\Delta \boldsymbol{z}_{i3} = (\Delta y_{i1}, \Delta y_{i2}, \boldsymbol{x}_{i4})$ for $(y_{i3}, \boldsymbol{x}_{i4})$ in the second equation,
$\vdots$
$\Delta \boldsymbol{z}_{i,T-1} = (\Delta y_{i1}, \dots, \Delta y_{i,T-2}, \boldsymbol{x}_{iT})$ for $(y_{i,T-1}, \boldsymbol{x}_{iT})$ in the $(T-2)$'th equation,

or a parsimonious, non-cumulative set, with a maximum of two Δy-IVs,

$\Delta \boldsymbol{z}_{i2} = (\Delta y_{i1}, \boldsymbol{x}_{i3})$ for $(y_{i2}, \boldsymbol{x}_{i3})$ in the first equation,
$\Delta \boldsymbol{z}_{i3} = (\Delta y_{i1}, \Delta y_{i2}, \boldsymbol{x}_{i4})$ for $(y_{i3}, \boldsymbol{x}_{i4})$ in the second equation,
$\vdots$
$\Delta \boldsymbol{z}_{i,T-1} = (\Delta y_{i,T-3}, \Delta y_{i,T-2}, \boldsymbol{x}_{iT})$ for $(y_{i,T-1}, \boldsymbol{x}_{iT})$ in the $(T-2)$'th equation.

12 Such moment conditions are, for example, implied by a random effect specification as $u_{it} = \alpha_i + \epsilon_{it}$ where ϵ_{it} is serially uncorrelated and homoskedastic and $\mathsf{E}(\alpha_i \epsilon_{it})$ is t-invariant.

Hence, we *use different IV-sets of lagged Δys together with the current $\boldsymbol{x}$ in each equation in (8.54)*. The Blundell–Bond approach considered in Section 8.3.2 has some resemblance to this approach.

We combine the difference IVs into an IV matrix, $\Delta \boldsymbol{Z}_i$ for $\boldsymbol{Q}_i$, of the form (8.33), with the reinterpreted Δz_{it}s, and stack (8.55) into

$$y = \boldsymbol{\alpha}^* + \boldsymbol{Q}\boldsymbol{\delta} + \boldsymbol{u}, \tag{8.56}$$

letting

$$y = \begin{bmatrix} y_1 \\ \vdots \\ y_N \end{bmatrix}, \ \boldsymbol{Q} = \begin{bmatrix} \boldsymbol{Q}_1 \\ \vdots \\ \boldsymbol{Q}_N \end{bmatrix}, \ \boldsymbol{u} = \begin{bmatrix} \boldsymbol{u}_1 \\ \vdots \\ \boldsymbol{u}_N \end{bmatrix}, \ \boldsymbol{\alpha}^* = \begin{bmatrix} \boldsymbol{\alpha}_1^* \\ \vdots \\ \boldsymbol{\alpha}_N^* \end{bmatrix}, \ \Delta \boldsymbol{Z} = \begin{bmatrix} \Delta \boldsymbol{Z}_1 \\ \vdots \\ \Delta \boldsymbol{Z}_N \end{bmatrix}.$$

This leads to the following *step-one and step-two GMM* estimators for $\boldsymbol{\delta}$:

$$\begin{aligned} \widehat{\boldsymbol{\delta}}^L_{GMM} &= [\boldsymbol{Q}'\Delta \boldsymbol{Z}(\Delta \boldsymbol{Z}'\Delta \boldsymbol{Z})^{-1}\Delta \boldsymbol{Z}'\boldsymbol{Q}]^{-1}[\boldsymbol{Q}'\Delta \boldsymbol{Z}(\Delta \boldsymbol{Z}'\Delta \boldsymbol{Z})^{-1}\Delta \boldsymbol{Z}'\boldsymbol{y})] \\ &= [(\textstyle\sum_{i=1}^N \boldsymbol{Q}_i'\Delta \boldsymbol{Z}_i)(\textstyle\sum_{i=1}^N \Delta \boldsymbol{Z}_i'\Delta \boldsymbol{Z}_i)^{-1}(\textstyle\sum_{i=1}^N \Delta \boldsymbol{Z}_i'\boldsymbol{Q}_i)]^{-1} \\ &\quad \times [(\textstyle\sum_{i=1}^N \boldsymbol{Q}_i'\Delta \boldsymbol{Z}_i)(\textstyle\sum_{i=1}^N \Delta \boldsymbol{Z}_i'\Delta \boldsymbol{Z}_i)^{-1}(\textstyle\sum_{i=1}^N \Delta \boldsymbol{Z}_i'\boldsymbol{y}_i)], \end{aligned} \tag{8.57}$$

$$\begin{aligned} \widetilde{\boldsymbol{\delta}}^L_{GMM} &= [(\textstyle\sum_{i=1}^N \boldsymbol{Q}_i'\Delta \boldsymbol{Z}_i)(\textstyle\sum_{i=1}^N \Delta \boldsymbol{Z}_i'\widetilde{\boldsymbol{u}}_i\widetilde{\boldsymbol{u}}_i'\Delta \boldsymbol{Z}_i)^{-1}(\textstyle\sum_{i=1}^N \Delta \boldsymbol{Z}_i'\boldsymbol{Q}_i)]^{-1} \\ &\quad \times [(\textstyle\sum_{i=1}^N \boldsymbol{Q}_i'\Delta \boldsymbol{Z}_i)(\textstyle\sum_{i=1}^N \Delta \boldsymbol{Z}_i'\widetilde{\boldsymbol{u}}_i\widetilde{\boldsymbol{u}}_i'\Delta \boldsymbol{Z}_i)^{-1}(\textstyle\sum_{i=1}^N \Delta \boldsymbol{Z}_i'\boldsymbol{y}_i)], \end{aligned} \tag{8.58}$$

where the $\widetilde{\boldsymbol{u}}_i$s are the residual vectors obtained from the step-one estimates.

The Sargan–Hansen statistic for testing the validity of the orthogonality conditions is

$$\mathcal{J}^L = (\textstyle\sum_{i=1}^N \boldsymbol{Q}_i'\Delta \boldsymbol{Z}_i)(\textstyle\sum_{i=1}^N \Delta \boldsymbol{Z}_i'\widetilde{\boldsymbol{u}}_i\widetilde{\boldsymbol{u}}_i'\Delta \boldsymbol{Z}_i)^{-1}(\textstyle\sum_{i=1}^N \Delta \boldsymbol{Z}_i'\boldsymbol{Q}_i). \tag{8.59}$$

The symmetry between (8.57)–(8.59) and (8.51)–(8.53) is obvious.

Example: Consider an autoregressive *labour demand equation* explaining a firm's employment by its lagged value, the real wage rate, the capital stock, and the output, all in logarithms. From the data set of Arellano and Bond (1991) a balanced subpanel for $N = 138$ firms in $T = 4$ years is extracted (source: http://www.stata-press.com/data; last accessed March 2016). Routines in the Stata software are used. Table 8.1 gives OLS estimates for three cases using, respectively, the level version neglecting heterogeneity altogether (column 1), fixed firm-specific heterogeneity included, i.e., within-firm estimation (column 2), and estimation based on one-year differences (column 3). All estimates have their expected signs, positive for the capital input and negative for the real wage rate. The coefficient estimate of the lagged regressor when the equation is in levels, is substantially larger than when using the differenced version or the within transformation, while for the wage rate and the capital stock the estimates are substantially smaller (in absolute value).

The results in Table 8.2, from step-one and step-two GMM estimation corresponding to (8.51)–(8.52), using the Arellano–Bond approach (columns 1 and 2), depart notably from the estimates based on OLS on differences (Table 8.1, column 3). The step-one and step-two results also differ notably. The GMM estimates of the autoregressive coefficient lie between the (inconsistent) estimates based on OLS on the within and the difference transformations (Table 8.1, columns 2 and 3), closer to the latter than to the former. The standard errors of the step-one GMM estimates from the 'robust' (and usually most reliable) procedures are much larger than those from 'non-robust' procedures. The estimates of the AR coefficient from the Blundell–Bond (1998) system-GMM approach, mixing equations and IVs in levels and in differences (Table 8.2, columns 3 and 4) are markedly higher than those from the Arellano–Bond approach (Table 8.2, columns 1 and 2). Overall, the former gives the smaller standard errors. The IV-quality depends on its correlation with the variable for which it serves, and the higher this correlation and the larger the spread of the instrumented variable are, the smaller the standard errors, *cet. par.* Appendix 8B contains some results for a stylized case which support this finding.

If more than one exogenous regressor is included, the dimension of the matrix elements in (8.57)–(8.59) grows with the dimension of Z. Using levels as instruments for differences or vice versa as a general estimation strategy within a GMM framework, may, as for static measurement error models (see Chapter 7), raise problems related to 'overfitting' and 'weak' or 'inessential' IVs; see, e.g., Nelson and Startz (1990), Bound, Jaeger, and

Table 8.1 Labour demand equation: OLS estimates. LHS-var: y = ln(employment). $N=138$, $T=4$

Variable	Eq. in levels, no heterog.	Eq. in levels, fixed effects	Eq. in diff.
y_{-1}	0.9230 (0.0091)	0.5074 (0.0406)	0.2191 (0.0372)
ln(real wage rate)	−0.0869 (0.0208)	−0.4574 (0.0665)	−0.4585 (0.0560)
ln(capital stock)	0.0717 (0.0081)	0.3568 (0.0347)	0.3460 (0.0288)
ln(output)	0.4457 (0.0628)	0.3670 (0.0678)	0.5849 (0.0710)
intercept	−1.7296 (0.3051)	0.3830 (0.4176)	

Standard errors in parentheses

Table 8.2 Labour demand equation: Arellano–Bond and Blundell–Bond GMM estimates. LHS-var: y = ln(employment). $N = 138$, $T = 4$

Variable	Eq. in diff., GMM: Arellano–Bond		System GMM: Blundell–Bond	
	Step-one	Step-two	Step-one	Step-two
y_{-1}	0.2670	0.3370	0.5724	0.5110
	(0.0800)	[0.1066]	(0.0541)	(0.0663)
	[0.1313]			
ln(real wage rate)	−0.4853	−0.5586	−0.4854	−0.5154
	(0.0592)	[0.1351]	(0.0626)	(0.1070)
	[0.1320]			
ln(capital stock)	0.3267	0.2958	0.2795	0.2760
	(0.0335)	[0.0643]	(0.0275)	(0.0523)
	[0.0641]			
ln(output)	0.6163	0.5300	0.5318	0.4725
	(0.0559)	[0.0931]	(0.0529)	(0.0699)
	[0.1020]			
intercept			−0.3943	0.0494
			(0.3721)	(0.5285)

Notes: Stata command: Cols. 1 and 2: `xtabond`. Cols. 3 and 4: `xtdpdsys`.
Standard errors in parentheses. Robust standard errors in brackets

Baker (1995), Staiger and Stock (1997), and Ziliak (1997). The remarks on the efficiency-bias trade-off at the end of Section 7.6.3 are equally appropriate here. Finding operational ways of identifying the 'essential' IVs and orthogonality conditions still remains as a challenge.

8.3.4 GMM ESTIMATION: AR-MODEL VERSUS EIV-MODEL

There are interesting similarities and discrepancies in the way GMM is used for fixed effects AR panel data models, as described in Sections 8.3.2 and 8.4.3, and the way it is used for *static* panel data models with errors in the regressors, as described in Sections 7.6 and 7.7. Before leaving the fixed effects AR-model, we briefly contrast the two model types from this viewpoint. In Biørn (2015), a synthesis of the two models, with applications of GMM, is considered.

The *common features* are: *first*, GMM exploits *orthogonality conditions* and *rank conditions* which jointly delimit a class of potential IVs. *Second*, the equation or its potential IV is transformed to differences to eliminate heterogeneity. Differencing usually increases memory, e.g., changes a white noise process to an MA(1)-process. GMM can be performed either on the equation in differences with IVs in levels, or on the reverse configuration. To handle the nuisance created by the fixed effects, either the equation or the IV-set must be in differences. *Third*, in choosing level IVs for an equation in differences, variables for periods *other than those defining the differences* are selected, while in choosing IVs in differences for an equation in levels, the period dating the level should be avoided as they violate the orthogonality conditions. *Fourth*, GMM can proceed in *one or two steps*, where the second step serves to improve efficiency by accounting for unspecified disturbance/error heteroskedasticity.

The *discrepancies* are: *first*, for the *AR-model*, *only lagged* endogenous and exogenous variables are admissible IVs. Their number may be excessive unless T is not very small, and parsimony is recommendable. This motivates inclusion of very few lagged values to prevent using many potentially weak IVs and reducing the effective number of observations. For the static *measurement error* model, *lagged and leaded* values of endogenous and exogenous variables can serve as IVs. Again, inclusion of only a few lags or leads is recommendable. *Second*, the memory pattern of the *AR-model* rationalizes both the orthogonality condition and the rank condition for the IV-set, both being parts of the theory. The static *measurement error* model has no implicit memory pattern for its observed variables. Therefore the validity of the IV rank condition must be postulated as a supplement to the theory behind the equation, and some mild restrictions must be imposed on the temporal properties of the latent exogenous variables.

8.3.5 EXTENSIONS AND MODIFICATIONS

So far we have considered fixed effects AR models whose disturbances have no memory, and all explanatory variables except the lagged endogenous variable have been strictly exogenous. When allowing for disturbance memory, the borderline between endogenous, predetermined and exogenous variables is changed, and the set of valid orthogonality conditions and potential IVs has to be modified. Briefly and intuitively, an error or disturbance memory, if finite, e.g., a moving average (MA) process, should not violate orthogonality conditions like (8.18) and (8.30). The situation somewhat resembles that in static regression models with measurement errors having memory; see Section 7.6.3. Keane and Runkle (1992, Section 2) consider memory of disturbances in connection with the distinction between exogeneity and predeterminedness, and propose procedures combining GMM and GLS; see also Arellano (2003, Chapter 8).

8.4 **Random effects AR(1) models**

8.4.1 A SIMPLE AR(1) MODEL

When considering static models up to this point, we have repeatedly remarked that random effects give far more restrictive and parsimonious parameterizations than fixed effects approaches, but have notable limitations. How should we balance the arguments when a strictly exogenous regressor is replaced by a predetermined, not strictly exogenous variable?

Consider first a strict AR(1) model, i.e., a baseline specification with one single predetermined, lagged endogenous variable and random effects. This is a counterpart to Model (8.1), $k+\alpha_i$ corresponding to α_i^*:

$$\begin{aligned} &y_{it} = k + y_{i,t-1}\gamma + \alpha_i + u_{it}, \quad |\gamma| < 1, \\ &(u_{it}|X, y_i^{(t-1)}) \sim \mathsf{IID}(0,\sigma^2), \ \ (\alpha_i|X) \sim \mathsf{IID}(0,\sigma_\alpha^2), \ \ u_{it} \perp \alpha_i, \\ &i=1,\dots,N;\ t=1,\dots,T, \end{aligned} \tag{8.60}$$

where still X denotes all values of x_{it} and $y_i^{(t-1)} = (y_{i,t-1},\dots,y_{i1},y_{i0})'$. An implication is that α_i *is correlated with all (current, lagged, and leaded) values of* y_{it}. This is seen by solving (8.60) as a difference equation, giving

$$y_{it} = \gamma^t y_{i0} + (k+\alpha_i)(1-\gamma^t)/(1-\gamma) + \textstyle\sum_{s=0}^{t-1}\gamma^s u_{i,t-s}, \tag{8.61}$$

and, provided that $|\gamma|<1$, in analogy with (8.3),

$$y_{it} = (k+\alpha_i)/(1-\gamma) + \textstyle\sum_{s=0}^{\infty}\gamma^s u_{i,t-s}. \tag{8.62}$$

It follows that $\text{cov}(y_{it},\alpha_i)=\sigma_\alpha^2/(1-\gamma)$. As in the fixed effects model, this reflects, loosely speaking, that the model represents *persistence* through both α_i and $y_{i,t-1}$. This relates to the more general problems of distinguishing between *state dependence* and heterogeneity in dynamic processes; see, e.g., Heckman (1991).

Writing in (8.60) α_i as $\alpha_i/(1-\gamma)-\alpha_i\gamma/(1-\gamma)$, we obtain

$$[y_{it}-\tfrac{\alpha_i}{1-\gamma}] = k + [y_{i,t-1}-\tfrac{\alpha_i}{1-\gamma}]\gamma + u_{it}, \text{ or } \widetilde{y}_{it} = k + \widetilde{y}_{i,t-1}\gamma + u_{it},$$

where $\widetilde{y}_{it} = y_{it}-\frac{\alpha_i}{1-\gamma}$, and can therefore interpret $\frac{\alpha_i}{1-\gamma}$ as an *individual-specific measurement error* in any y_{it}, and $\widetilde{y}_{it}$ as its systematic, latent counterpart, uncorrelated with the measurement error. Rewriting (8.61)–(8.62) as

$$\begin{aligned} \widetilde{y}_{it} &= \gamma^t\widetilde{y}_{i0} + k(1-\gamma^t)/(1-\gamma) + \textstyle\sum_{s=0}^{t-1}\gamma^s u_{i,t-s}, \\ \widetilde{y}_{it} &= k/(1-\gamma) + \textstyle\sum_{s=0}^{\infty}\gamma^s u_{i,t-s}, \end{aligned}$$

where $\text{cov}(\widetilde{y}_{i,t-1},u_{it})=\text{cov}(\widetilde{y}_{i,t-1},\alpha_i)=0$, we know that if (hypothetically) $\widetilde{y}_{it}$ were observable, k and γ could be estimated by regressing $\widetilde{y}_{it}$ on $\widetilde{y}_{i,t-1}$.

ML estimation of $k, \gamma, \sigma^2, \sigma_\alpha^2$, assuming normality of u_{it} and α_i, is feasible and ensures consistency in several, but far from all relevant cases; see Anderson and Hsiao (1981,1982), Bhargava and Sargan (1983), Sevestre and Trognon (1985, 1996), Hsiao (2003, sections 4.3.2 and 4.3.3), and Arellano (2003, Section 7.4). Consistent estimators could also be obtained by eliminating α_i and k through differencing and using level IVs, or by using IVs in differences on the equation in levels. This, however, would involve an efficiency loss, as elimination of α_i neglects its distributional assumptions in (8.60). A more attractive approach may be to combine several methods in a multi-step procedure. In Section 8.4.2, we describe one such procedure for a slightly more general model.

8.4.2 INCLUDING EXOGENOUS VARIABLES

We augment the simple AR(1) random effects model (8.60) by including two-dimensional and individual-specific regressors. Let $\boldsymbol{x}_{it}$ be the $(1 \times K_2)$-vector of two-dimensional exogenous variables, $\boldsymbol{z}_i$ be the $(1 \times K_1)$-vector of individual-specific exogenous variables, $\boldsymbol{\beta}$ and $\boldsymbol{\delta}$ their coefficient vectors, and consider

$$\begin{aligned} &y_{it} = k + y_{i,t-1}\gamma + \boldsymbol{x}_{it}\boldsymbol{\beta} + \boldsymbol{z}_i\boldsymbol{\delta} + \alpha_i + u_{it}, \; |\gamma| < 1, \; u_{it} \perp \alpha_i, \\ &(u_{it}|X, Z, y_i^{(t-1)}) \sim \mathsf{IID}(0, \sigma^2), \; (\alpha_i|X, Z) \sim \mathsf{IID}(0, \sigma_\alpha^2), \\ &i = 1, \ldots, N; \; t = 1, \ldots, T. \end{aligned} \tag{8.63}$$

ML estimation of $k, \gamma, \boldsymbol{\beta}, \boldsymbol{\delta}, \sigma^2, \sigma_\alpha^2$, assuming normality of u_{it} and α_i, is discussed in Anderson and Hsiao (1982) and Hsiao (2003, Section 4.3.3). They show that whether T- or N-consistency can be achieved depends on (i) the nature of the initial situation: whether y_{i0} or $\widetilde{y}_{i0} = y_{i0} - \alpha_i/(1-\gamma)$ are taken as starting values and (ii) whether these starting values are treated as fixed (pseudo-)parameters or as random variables with certain properties. A survey of results is given in Table 8.3. It is clear that consistency is more likely to be ensured for $\boldsymbol{\beta}$ than for $\boldsymbol{\delta}$. The ML-estimator of $\boldsymbol{\beta}$ is T- and N-consistent both when y_{i0} is fixed and when it is random. For $\boldsymbol{\delta}$, N-consistency is obtained both when y_{i0} is fixed and when it is random, while in no case T-consistency can be ensured when N is finite. The same holds for the ML-estimators of $\boldsymbol{\delta}$ when the initial situation is characterized by $\widetilde{y}_{i0}$ fixed, except that in neither case N-consistency is ensured for finite T. For a further discussion of the importance of the specification of the generating process of the initial observation for the properties of ML, see Sevestre and Trognon (1996, Section 7.2.4) and Harris, Mátyás, and Sevestre (2008, Section 8.5).

Also in this random effects case, *stepwise procedures* for consistent, although not fully efficient, estimation are available. As an example, we consider a mixture of GMM estimation of the equation in differences, between-individual estimation on levels, and FGLS.

Table 8.3 Asymptotics for ML estimators of $\boldsymbol{\beta}$ and $\boldsymbol{\delta}$ in Model (8.63)

		MLE of $\boldsymbol{\beta}$	MLE of $\boldsymbol{\delta}$
y_{i0} fixed	N finite, $T \to \infty$	Consistent	Inconsistent
y_{i0} fixed	T finite, $N \to \infty$	Consistent	Consistent
y_{i0} random	N finite, $T \to \infty$	Consistent	Inconsistent
y_{i0} random	T finite, $N \to \infty$	Consistent	Consistent
$\widetilde{y}_{i0}$ fixed	N finite, $T \to \infty$	Consistent	Inconsistent
$\widetilde{y}_{i0}$ fixed	T finite, $N \to \infty$	Inconsistent	Inconsistent
$\widetilde{y}_{i0}$ random	N finite, $T \to \infty$	Consistent	Inconsistent
$\widetilde{y}_{i0}$ random	T finite, $N \to \infty$	Consistent	Consistent

Source: based on Anderson and Hsiao (1982), Table 1.

This procedure may be seen as a way of handling some of the problems with ML-estimation noted above.

1. Transform (8.63) to differences, which eliminates z_i and gives

$$\Delta y_{it} = \Delta y_{i,t-1}\gamma + \Delta \boldsymbol{x}_{it}\boldsymbol{\beta} + \Delta u_{it}.$$

   Estimate γ and $\boldsymbol{\beta}$ by system GMM, as described for the corresponding fixed effects equation in Section 8.3.2; see (8.48)–(8.49). The resulting step-one estimator has the form (8.51). This gives $\widehat{\gamma}$ and $\widehat{\boldsymbol{\beta}}$.
2. Construct an *equation in individual means in levels*, replacing $(\gamma, \boldsymbol{\beta})$ with $(\widehat{\gamma}, \widehat{\boldsymbol{\beta}})$,

$$\bar{y}_{i\cdot} - \bar{y}_{i,-1}\widehat{\gamma} - \bar{\boldsymbol{x}}_{i\cdot}\widehat{\boldsymbol{\beta}} = k + \boldsymbol{z}_i\boldsymbol{\delta} + \alpha_i + \bar{u}_{i\cdot}\,.$$

   Its left-hand side variable, known from step 1, and its disturbance, $\alpha_i + \bar{u}_{i\cdot}$, has approximately (as estimated coefficients replace true ones) IID properties, since only the variation across i is effective. OLS estimation of this equation in individual means gives between estimates $\widehat{k}, \widehat{\boldsymbol{\delta}}$.
3. Construct from $\widehat{\gamma}, \widehat{\boldsymbol{\beta}}, \widehat{k}, \widehat{\boldsymbol{\delta}}$ corresponding $\epsilon_{it} = \alpha_i + u_{it}$ residuals,

$$\widehat{\epsilon}_{it} = y_{it} - \widehat{k} - y_{i,t-1}\widehat{\gamma} - \boldsymbol{x}_{it}\widehat{\boldsymbol{\beta}} - \boldsymbol{z}_i\widehat{\boldsymbol{\delta}},$$

   and estimate σ^2 and σ^2_α as for static equations (see Section 3.3). From the latter estimates we can again estimate the standard errors of the k, γ, $\boldsymbol{\beta}$, and $\boldsymbol{\delta}$ estimates, as explained in Section 3.4.3.

4. The procedure could be extended, using FGLS: construct

$$y_{it} - y_{i,t-1}\widehat{\gamma} = k + \boldsymbol{x}_{it}\boldsymbol{\beta} + \boldsymbol{z}_i\boldsymbol{\delta} + \epsilon_{it},$$

reestimate $\boldsymbol{\beta}$ and $\boldsymbol{\delta}$ by using FGLS with the estimated $(\sigma^2, \sigma_\alpha^2)$, update $\widehat{\epsilon}_{it}$ and continue repeating steps 2–4 until convergence (if possible). In this way, we update the $\boldsymbol{\beta}$ and $\boldsymbol{\delta}$ estimates, but retain the initial γ estimate, which may be considered a limitation of the method.

8.5 Conclusion

The linear AR(1) model with strictly exogenous regressors and latent individual (fixed or random) heterogeneity considered above defines one among several frameworks available for dynamic analysis of panel data. We end the chapter by indicating three directions for extensions.

First, the first-order setup could be extended to *higher-order*, linear autoregressive models with lags also in the exogenous variables. Holtz-Eakin, Newey, and Rosen (1988) consider generalizations in that direction, and extend to multi-equation models of the vector autoregressive (VAR) type, with exogenous explanatory variables, using combinations of 2SLS and GLS for estimation.

Second, lag distributions, in particular the combination *'long' distributions–'short' panels* is put in focus by Pakes and Griliches (1984). They specify a setup with N large and T small and, to preserve parsimony in parameterization, make specific assumptions about: (i) the contribution of the values of the unobserved presample exogenous variables to the current values of the endogenous variable; (ii) the relationship between the presample and in sample values of the exogenous variables; and (iii) functional form constraints on the lag coefficients.

Third, over the years, dynamic panel data models, both without and with strictly exogenous variables, have been the subject to substantial research regarding finite-sample efficiency, finite-sample bias, and bias correction. The rather strong disturbance assumption $(u_{it}|X, y_i^{(t-1)}) \sim \mathsf{IID}(0, \sigma^2)$ may be relaxed, e.g., heteroskedasticity allowed for, and the utilization of moment conditions modified. Suggestions have also been made to replace GMM with a version of the Limited Information Maximum Likelihood (LIML) procedure. The latter, unlike the former, relies on normality of the disturbance process and gives estimators that are invariant to the normalization of the equation; see, e.g., Arellano and Honoré (2001, Sections 3.2–3.3).

Appendix 8A. **Within estimation of the AR coefficient: Asymptotics**

In this appendix, we explore the asymptotics of $(\widehat{\gamma}_W-\gamma)$, as given by (8.7), for finite T, by, *inter alia*, deriving expressions for $\text{plim}_{N\to\infty}(C)$ and $\text{plim}_{N\to\infty}(D)$ needed for the plim of $(\widehat{\gamma}_W-\gamma)$. This variable has numerator and denominator, respectively,

$$C = \tfrac{1}{N}\sum_{i=1}^{N}[\tfrac{1}{T}\sum_{t=1}^{T} y_{i,t-1}u_{it} - \bar{y}_{i,-1}\bar{u}_{i\cdot}], \tag{8A.1}$$

$$D = \tfrac{1}{N}\sum_{i=1}^{N}[\tfrac{1}{T}\sum_{t=1}^{T} y_{i,t-1}^2 - \bar{y}_{i,-1}^2], \tag{8A.2}$$

where

$$y_{i,t-1} = \alpha_i^*/(1-\gamma) + \sum_{s=0}^{\infty}\gamma^s u_{i,t-s-1},$$

$$\bar{y}_{i,-1} = \alpha_i^*/(1-\gamma) + T^{-1}\sum_{t=1}^{T}\sum_{s=0}^{\infty}\gamma^s u_{i,t-s-1},$$

$$\bar{u}_{i\cdot} = T^{-1}\sum_{t=1}^{T} u_{it}.$$

Hence, since $u_{it} \sim \mathsf{IID}(0,\sigma^2)$,

$$\mathsf{E}(\sum_{t=1}^{T} y_{i,t-1}u_{it}) = 0, \tag{8A.3}$$

$$\mathsf{E}(\sum_{t=1}^{T} y_{i,t-1}^2) = T\alpha_i^{*2}/(1-\gamma)^2 + \mathsf{E}(\sum_{t=1}^{T}\sum_{s=0}^{\infty}\gamma^{2s}u_{i,t-s-1}^2), \tag{8A.4}$$

$$\mathsf{E}(\bar{y}_{i,-1}^2) = \alpha_i^{*2}/(1-\gamma)^2 + T^{-2}\mathsf{E}(\sum_{s=0}^{\infty}\gamma^s u_{i,t-s-1})^2, \tag{8A.5}$$

$$\mathsf{E}(\bar{y}_{i,-1}\bar{u}_{i\cdot}) = T^{-2}\mathsf{E}[\sum_{t=1}^{T} u_{it}][\sum_{\theta=1}^{T}\sum_{s=0}^{\infty}\gamma^s u_{i,\theta-s-1}]. \tag{8A.6}$$

To express (8A.4)–(8A.6) as functions of T and γ we need, using repeatedly the summation formula for a geometric succession,

$$a(T,\gamma) \equiv \sum_{t=1}^{T}(1-\gamma^{T-t}) \equiv T - \frac{1-\gamma^T}{1-\gamma}, \tag{8A.7}$$

$$\begin{aligned} b(T,\gamma) &\equiv \sum_{t=1}^{T}\sum_{\theta=1}^{T}\gamma^{|T-t|} \equiv \sum_{t=1}^{T}[\sum_{\theta=1}^{t}\gamma^{t-\theta} + \sum_{\theta=t+1}^{T}\gamma^{\theta-t}] \\ &\equiv (1-\gamma)^{-1}\sum_{t=1}^{T}[1-\gamma^t+\gamma(1-\gamma^{T-t})] \\ &\equiv \frac{1}{1-\gamma}\left[T(1+\gamma) - 2\gamma\frac{1-\gamma^T}{1-\gamma}\right] \equiv T + \frac{2\gamma}{1-\gamma}\left[T - \frac{1-\gamma^T}{1-\gamma}\right]. \end{aligned} \tag{8A.8}$$

Since

$$\mathsf{E}(\sum_{t=1}^{T}\sum_{s=0}^{\infty}\gamma^{2s}u_{i,t-s-1}^{2}) = \sigma^2/(1-\gamma^2),$$

we have, using (8A.4),

$$\mathsf{E}(y_{i,t-1}^2) = \frac{\alpha_i^{*2}}{(1-\gamma)^2} + \frac{\sigma^2}{1-\gamma^2}. \tag{8A.9}$$

Further, since

$$\begin{aligned}
&\mathsf{E}[\sum_{t=1}^{T} u_{it}][\sum_{\theta=1}^{T}\sum_{s=0}^{\infty}\gamma^{s}u_{i,\theta-s-1}] \\
&= \mathsf{E}[\sum_{t=1}^{T} u_{it}^{2}\sum_{s=0}^{T-t-1}\gamma^{s}] = \sigma^2\sum_{t=1}^{T}\sum_{s=0}^{T-t-1}\gamma^{s} \\
&= \frac{\sigma^2\sum_{t=1}^{T}(1-\gamma^{T-t})}{1-\gamma} = \frac{\sigma^2}{1-\gamma}\left[T - \frac{1-\gamma^{T}}{1-\gamma}\right],
\end{aligned}$$

we have, using (8A.6) and (8A.7),

$$\mathsf{E}(\bar{y}_{i,-1}\bar{u}_{i,\cdot}) = \frac{\sigma^2}{T^2(1-\gamma)}a(T,\gamma). \tag{8A.10}$$

For (8A.5) we need, substituting $\tau = t - \theta$,

$$\begin{aligned}
c(t,\theta,\gamma) \equiv c(\theta,t,\gamma) &\equiv \mathsf{E}[\sum_{z=0}^{\infty}\gamma^{z}u_{i,t-z-1}][\sum_{s=0}^{\infty}\gamma^{s}u_{i,\theta-s-1}] \\
&\equiv \mathsf{E}[\sum_{z=0}^{\tau-1}\gamma^{z}u_{i,\theta-(z-\tau)-1} + \sum_{z=\tau}^{\infty}\gamma^{z}u_{i,\theta-(z-\tau)-1}][\sum_{s=0}^{\infty}\gamma^{s}u_{i,\theta-s-1}] \\
&= \gamma^{\tau}(\sum_{z=\tau}^{\infty}\gamma^{z-\tau}u_{i,\theta-(z-\tau)-1})[\sum_{s=0}^{\infty}\gamma^{s}u_{i,\theta-s-1}],
\end{aligned}$$

which can be rewritten as

$$\begin{aligned}
c(t,\theta,\gamma) \equiv c(\theta,t,\gamma) &= \gamma^{|t-\theta|}\mathsf{E}[\sum_{s=0}^{\infty}\gamma^{s}u_{i,\theta-s-1}]^2 \\
&= \gamma^{|t-\theta|}\sigma^2\sum_{s=0}^{\infty}\gamma^{2s} = \frac{\sigma^2\gamma^{|t-\theta|}}{1-\gamma^2}.
\end{aligned}$$

It therefore follows, using (8A.5) and (8A.8), that

$$\mathsf{E}(\bar{y}_{i,-1}^2) = \frac{\alpha_i^{*2}}{(1-\gamma)^2} + \frac{\sigma^2\sum_{t=1}^{T}\sum_{\theta=1}^{T}c(t,\theta,\gamma)}{T^2}$$

$$= \frac{\alpha_i^{*2}}{(1-\gamma)^2} + \frac{\sigma^2 \sum_{t=1}^{T} \sum_{\theta=1}^{T} \gamma^{|t-\theta|}}{T^2(1-\gamma^2)}$$

$$= \frac{\alpha_i^{*2}}{(1-\gamma)^2} + \frac{\sigma^2 b(T,\gamma)}{T^2(1-\gamma^2)}. \tag{8A.11}$$

Inserting (8A.3) and (8A.9)–(8A.11) in (8A.1) and (8A.2) we get

$$\mathsf{E}(C) = -\frac{\sigma^2 a(T,\gamma)}{T^2(1-\gamma)},$$

$$\mathsf{E}(D) = \frac{\sigma^2}{1-\gamma^2} - \frac{\sigma^2 b(T,\gamma)}{T^2(1-\gamma^2)}.$$

The expressions after the equality signs are constant for any T. Therefore, when $N \to \infty$, the respective plims are equal to $\mathsf{E}(C)$ and $\mathsf{E}(D)$, so that we can finally conclude that

$$\operatorname*{plim}_{N\to\infty}(C) = \mathsf{E}(C) = -\frac{\sigma^2}{T^2(1-\gamma)}\left[T - \frac{1-\gamma^T}{1-\gamma}\right], \tag{8A.12}$$

$$\operatorname*{plim}_{N\to\infty}(D) = \mathsf{E}(D) = \frac{\sigma^2}{1-\gamma^2}\left[1 - \frac{1}{T} - \frac{2\gamma}{T^2(1-\gamma)}\left(T - \frac{1-\gamma^T}{1-\gamma}\right)\right]. \tag{8A.13}$$

Appendix 8B. **Autocovariances and correlograms of y_{it} and Δy_{it}**

In this appendix we derive the expressions for autocovariances and autocorrelations of y_{it} and Δy_{it} and related concepts in the simplest *fixed effects* panel data AR(1) model, (8.1). These are of interest, *inter alia*, for interpreting the use of lagged y_{it} as IVs for Δy_{it} and lagged Δy_{it} as IVs for y_{it}, which frequently occur in this chapter.

From the solution to the difference equation, (8.3), it first follows that when $|\gamma| < 1$,

$$\operatorname{var}(y_{it}) = \sigma_y^2 = \frac{1}{1-\gamma^2}\sigma^2, \tag{8B.1}$$

$$\operatorname{cov}(y_{it}, y_{i,t-s}) = \rho^s \sigma_y^2 = \frac{\gamma^s}{1-\gamma^2}\sigma^2, \qquad s = 1,2,\dots . \tag{8B.2}$$

Hence, because of the stationarity of $y_{it} - \alpha_i^*$, it follows from (8.1), using the notation $\Delta_s y_{it} = y_{it} - y_{i,t-s}$, that for $s = 1, 2, \dots$,

$$\text{var}(\Delta_s y_{it}) = 2(1-\gamma^s)\sigma_y^2 = \frac{2}{1+\gamma}\frac{1-\gamma^s}{1-\gamma}\sigma^2 = \frac{2(1+\gamma+\gamma^2+\cdots+\gamma^{s-1})}{1+\gamma}\sigma^2, \quad (8B.3)$$

which is increasing in s (for $0 < \gamma < 1$), with, for example,

$$\begin{aligned}
\text{var}(\Delta y_{it}) &= \frac{2}{1+\gamma}\sigma^2,\\
\text{var}(\Delta_2 y_{it}) &= 2\sigma^2,\\
\text{var}(\Delta_3 y_{it}) &= 2\left(1+\frac{\gamma^2}{1+\gamma}\right)\sigma^2,\\
\text{var}(\Delta_4 y_{it}) &= 2(1+\gamma^2)\sigma^2,
\end{aligned}$$

and that $\text{var}(\Delta_s y_{it})$ satisfies the recursion

$$\text{var}(\Delta_{s+1} y_{it}) = \text{var}(\Delta_s y_{it}) + \frac{2\gamma^s}{1+\gamma}\sigma^2 = \text{var}(\Delta_s y_{it}) + \gamma^s \text{var}(\Delta y_{it}), \quad s = 1,2,\ldots .$$

We have from (8B.1) and (8B.2)

$$\frac{\text{var}(\Delta_s y_{it})}{\text{var}(y_{it})} = 2(1-\gamma^s) \underset{<}{\overset{>}{=}} 1 \Longleftrightarrow \gamma^s \underset{>}{\overset{<}{=}} \frac{1}{2}. \quad (8B.4)$$

Covariances and correlations between ys and Δys: second, (8B.2) implies, for $s = 1,2,\ldots$,

$$\begin{aligned}
\text{cov}(y_{it}, \Delta y_{i,t-s}) &= \text{cov}(y_{it}, y_{i,t-s}) - \text{cov}(y_{it}, y_{i,t-s-1})\\
&= (\gamma^s - \gamma^{s+1})\sigma_y^2 = \frac{\gamma^s - \gamma^{s+1}}{1-\gamma^2}\sigma^2 = \frac{\gamma^s}{1+\gamma}\sigma^2,\\
\text{cov}(\Delta y_{it}, y_{i,t-s}) &= \text{cov}(y_{it}, y_{i,t-s}) - \text{cov}(y_{i,t-1}, y_{i,t-s})\\
&= (\gamma^s - \gamma^{s-1})\sigma_y^2 = \frac{\gamma^s - \gamma^{s-1}}{1-\gamma^2}\sigma^2 = -\frac{\gamma^{s-1}}{1+\gamma}\sigma^2 \quad \Longrightarrow\\
\text{cov}(\Delta y_{it}, \Delta y_{i,t-s}) &= \text{cov}(y_{it}, \Delta y_{i,t-s}) - \text{cov}(y_{i,t-1}, \Delta y_{i,t-s})\\
&= [(\gamma^s - \gamma^{s+1}) - (\gamma^{s-1} - \gamma^s)]\sigma_y^2 = -\gamma^{s-1}(1-\gamma)^2\sigma_y^2 = -\gamma^{s-1}\frac{1-\gamma}{1+\gamma}\sigma^2.
\end{aligned}$$

Autocorrelation coefficients: the corresponding autocorrelation coefficients (L and D symbolizing level and difference) are, for $s = 1,2,\ldots,$

$$\rho_{LLy}(s) \equiv \text{corr}(y_{it}, y_{i,t-s}) = \frac{\text{cov}(y_{it}, y_{i,t-s})}{\text{var}(y_{it})} = \gamma^s, \tag{8B.5}$$

$$\rho_{LDy}(s) \equiv \text{corr}(y_{it}, \Delta y_{i,t-s}) = \frac{\text{cov}(y_{it}, \Delta y_{i,t-s})}{[\text{var}(y_{it})\text{var}(\Delta y_{it})]^{1/2}} \tag{8B.6}$$

$$= \frac{\gamma^s - \gamma^{s+1}}{\sqrt{2(1-\gamma)}} = \gamma^s[\tfrac{1}{2}(1-\gamma)]^{1/2},$$

$$\rho_{DLy}(s) \equiv \text{corr}(\Delta y_{it}, y_{i,t-s}) = \frac{\text{cov}(\Delta y_{it}, y_{i,t-s})}{[\text{var}(\Delta y_{it})\text{var}(y_{it})]^{1/2}} \tag{8B.7}$$

$$= -\frac{\gamma^{s-1} - \gamma^s}{\sqrt{2(1-\gamma)}} = -\gamma^{s-1}[\tfrac{1}{2}(1-\gamma)]^{1/2},$$

$$\rho_{DDy}(s) \equiv \text{corr}(\Delta y_{it}, \Delta y_{i,t-s}) = \frac{\text{cov}(\Delta y_{it}, \Delta y_{i,t-s})}{\text{var}(\Delta y_{it})} \tag{8B.8}$$

$$= -\tfrac{1}{2}\gamma^{s-1}(1-\gamma),$$

all of which are decreasing in s, starting from different initial values. These equations also imply

$$\left[\frac{\rho_{LDy}(s)}{\rho_{LLy}(s)}\right]^2 = \frac{1-\gamma}{2} < 1,$$

$$\left[\frac{\rho_{DLy}(s)}{\rho_{DDy}(s)}\right]^2 = \frac{2}{1-\gamma} > 1,$$

$$\left[\frac{\rho_{LDy}(s)}{\rho_{DLy}(s)}\right]^2 = \gamma^2 < 1,$$

$$\left[\frac{\rho_{LDy}(s)}{\rho_{DDy}(s)}\right]^2 = \frac{2\gamma^2}{1-\gamma} \begin{smallmatrix} > \\ = \\ < \end{smallmatrix} 1 \iff \gamma \begin{smallmatrix} > \\ = \\ < \end{smallmatrix} \frac{1}{2}, \quad s = 1, 2, \dots .$$

The first two expressions imply that for both an AR-equation in levels and one in differences, a level y-IV shows, for any γ, higher correlation with an instrumented y-variable than a corresponding difference y-IV shows. However, as indicated by the last two expressions together with (8B.4), no general statement about the superiority of y-instruments in levels over corresponding y-instruments in differences can be given. Further investigations, including simulations, are required.

Because $\gamma^p(1-\gamma)$ attains its maximum for $\gamma = p/(p+1)$, it may also be of interest in considering 'instrument quality' to note that we have

$$\rho^2_{LDy}(s) = \text{max for } \gamma = \frac{2s}{2s+1}.$$

$$\rho^2_{DLy}(s) = \text{max for } \gamma = \frac{2(s-1)}{2s-1}.$$

$$\rho^2_{DDy}(s) = \text{max for } \gamma = \frac{s-1}{s}.$$

9 Analysis of discrete response

CHAPTER SUMMARY

Modelling qualitative responses, represented by binary variables is considered. Continuous latent variables, which may sometimes be given utility interpretations, underlying the responses, are also considered. Identification problems are discussed. Focus is on logit-models for binary responses with unobserved individual heterogeneity (fixed or random) and ML estimation. A conditional ML procedure for the binomial fixed effects logit model that ensures consistent coefficient estimation in short panels is explained by examples. Also briefly discussed are probit models and logit generalizations with more than two possible responses. Empirical examples are given.

9.1 Introduction

For several applications of panel data regression analysis, the assumption that the equations' dependent (response) variables are continuous with, in principle, unrestricted range is not satisfied. In this chapter we assume that the response to be explained is qualitative and represented by realizations of binary variables. These may take different values for different individuals and vary over time for any individual, i.e., are two-dimensional. A model for a binomial (dichotomic) choice (choice between two alternatives) may, e.g., indicate whether, in a specific period, a person smokes tobacco or not, owns a car or not, is employed or not. A model for multinomial choice (choice between more than two alternatives) may indicate which among several available transportation modes, regions of residence, types of housing, political parties, etc., is chosen. Explanatory variables for such discrete outcomes can be continuous or discrete. Underlying the discrete response may be continuous latent variables, to be explained later.

In such situations, we are motivated to represent the relationship between a binary endogenous variable and its explanatory variables by a *non-linear* function. It expresses the conditional expectation of the binary variable. This expectation is equal to the *probability* that the relevant outcome is observed, denoted as the *response probability*, which is a basic property of binary response models. A primary reason why modelling expected binary response variables (i.e., response probabilities) as linear functions of the covariates is problematic is, briefly, that unattractive claims will have to be made about the disturbance in the implied linear equation connecting the endogenous and the exogenous variables; see, e.g., Lewbel, Dong, and Yang (2012, p. 813).[1] Instead we choose non-linear functions with range from zero to one. A *linear probability model*, i.e., one that expresses conditional expectations (response probabilities) as linear functions of covariates, does not satisfy the latter claim, while a cumulative distribution function (cdf) derived from parametric probability distributions does. Core examples are the *probit model*, based on the standardized normal (Gaussian) distribution, and the *logit-model*, based on the standard logistic distribution. Models for discrete choice are prominent examples of *models with limited dependent variables*. Other examples will be considered in Chapter 11, where dependent variables which are, for some reason, observed partly as continuous, partly as discrete, are dealt with. The model types with discrete response and those with mixed discrete–continuous response variables are related, which will also be discussed in Chapter 11.

In this chapter, primary attention will be given to the logit-model with unobserved individual heterogeneity and parameter estimation by ML. Emphasis will be on models with two possible outcomes, so-called *binomial response*. The chapter proceeds, stepwise, as follows. In Section 9.2 we consider binomial, single-equation models, dealing with cases with no heterogeneity (Section 9.2.1), full heterogeneity with all coefficients treated as fixed individual-specific (Section 9.2.2), and a specification with fixed intercept heterogeneity and common coefficients (Section 9.2.3). They are all somewhat related to the linear models with continuous response variables considered in Chapter 2. The models in Sections 9.2.1 and 9.2.2 are special cases of model classes often denoted as, respectively, the *Generalized Linear Model (GLM)* and the *Generalized Linear Mixed Model (GLMM)*; see, e.g., Demidenko (2004, Chapter 7). Some attention will be given to *conditional* ML estimation, a variant of the ML-procedure for the logit model with fixed effects that has the attraction of admitting N-consistent estimation of coefficients even when the time-series are short (Section 9.2.4). Section 9.3 is concerned with a related model with random intercept heterogeneity and its ML estimation of the coeffcient vector. In Section 9.4, we briefly present extensions to multinomial (multi-equation) models, allowing for more than two possible responses.

9.2 **Binomial models: Fixed heterogeneity**

Three binomial panel data models, with different ways of treating fixed heterogeneity, will be discussed. In the way they represent heterogeneity they resemble the linear regression models considered in Chapter 2.

[1] The same is the case for a modified linear model including kinks in the response function to force its values to be in the (0,1) interval, making its first-derivative discontinuous at the kinks. Yet, there are authors who find linear probability models attractive for certain purposes and argue forcefully that they should be used, e.g., Angrist and Pischke (2009, Sections 3.1.3 and 3.4.2) and Wooldridge (2010, Section 15.2).

9.2.1 SIMPLE BINOMIAL MODEL: LOGIT AND PROBIT PARAMETERIZATIONS

It is convenient to introduce a continuous variable, y_{it}^*, imagined to underlie the discrete responses observed. In the baseline model it is determined by

$$\begin{aligned} & y_{it}^* = \boldsymbol{x}_{it}\boldsymbol{\beta} - u_{it}, \quad (u_{it}|X) \sim \mathsf{IID}(0, \sigma_u^2) \text{ with cdf } F(u_{it}), \\ & i = 1, \dots, N;\ t = 1, \dots, T, \end{aligned} \tag{9.1}$$

where $\boldsymbol{x}_{it} = (x_{1it}, \dots, x_{Kit})$ is a vector of explanatory variables (including one element attached to the intercept), $\boldsymbol{\beta} = (\beta_1, \dots, \beta_K)'$ is a coefficient vector (including the intercept), and u_{it} is a disturbance symmetrically distributed around its zero expectation.[2] The *endogenous* variable y_{it}^* is unobserved (latent); the *exogenous* vector $\boldsymbol{x}_{it}$ is observable. Throughout we again, in conditioning statements, use X as shorthand notation for 'all $\boldsymbol{x}_{it}$', even if a less restrictive conditioning would sometimes suffice. What we observe about y_{it}^* is only whether it is positive or negative, denoted as *positive, respectively negative response*.[3] We attach a binary variable, y_{it} to this, which makes y_{it} a step function of y_{it}^*:

$$y_{it} = \begin{cases} 1 \text{ if } y_{it}^* > 0, \\ 0 \text{ if } y_{it}^* \leq 0. \end{cases} \tag{9.2}$$

Let p_{it}, the *response probability*, be the probability that individual i in period t responds positively, $1-p_{it}$ being the *non-response probability*. It follows that

$$\begin{aligned} p_{it} = P(y_{it}=1|X) = P(y_{it}^*>0|X) = P(u_{it}<X_{it}\boldsymbol{\beta}|X) = F(\boldsymbol{x}_{it}\boldsymbol{\beta}), \\ \mathsf{E}(y_{it}|X) = P(y_{it}=1|X)\cdot 1 + P(y_{it}=0|X)\cdot 0 = F(\boldsymbol{x}_{it}\boldsymbol{\beta}). \end{aligned}$$

We here have an *identification problem* for $\boldsymbol{\beta}$ and σ_u, because y_{it}^* is latent and observed discretely through y_{it}. Since, for any positive c, $(\boldsymbol{\beta}, \sigma_u)$, and $(c\boldsymbol{\beta}, c\sigma_u)$ give the same observable outcome $(y_{it}, \boldsymbol{x}_{it})$ and the same response probability, we might, letting $c = 1/\sigma_u$, replace (9.1) with

$$y_{it}^{**} = \boldsymbol{x}_{it}(\boldsymbol{\beta}/\sigma_u) - \varepsilon_{it}, \quad (\varepsilon_{it}|X) \sim \mathsf{IID}(0, 1) \text{ with cdf } F_\varepsilon(\varepsilon_{it}) \equiv F(\sigma_u\varepsilon_{it}),$$

where $y_{it}^{**} = y_{it}^*/\sigma_u$ and $\varepsilon_{it} = u_{it}/\sigma_u$.[4]

[2] For convenience, we specify the disturbance with a minus-sign, which is inessential when its distribution is symmetric.

[3] The threshold value might well have been a non-zero constant, in which case we would be back in (9.2) by adjusting the intercept in (9.1) correspondingly.

[4] Essential to the argument is that σ_u is part of $F(\cdot)$, but not part of $F_\varepsilon(\cdot)$.

It follows that the expectations of y^*_{it} and y_{it} are given by, respectively,

$$\mathsf{E}(y^*_{it}|X) = \boldsymbol{x}_{it}\boldsymbol{\beta} \iff \mathsf{E}(y^{**}_{it}|X) = \boldsymbol{x}_{it}(\boldsymbol{\beta}/\sigma_u), \tag{9.3}$$

$$\mathsf{E}(y_{it}|X) = p_{it} = F(\boldsymbol{x}_{it}\boldsymbol{\beta}) = F_{\varepsilon}[\boldsymbol{x}_{it}(\boldsymbol{\beta}/\sigma_u)]. \tag{9.4}$$

Likewise,

$$\text{var}(y^*_{it}|X) = \sigma_u^2 \iff \text{var}(y^{**}_{it}|X) = 1, \tag{9.5}$$

$$\begin{aligned}\text{var}(y_{it}|X) &= p_{it}(1-p_{it})^2 + (1-p_{it})(-p_{it})^2 = p_{it}(1-p_{it})\\ &= F(\boldsymbol{x}_{it}\boldsymbol{\beta})[1-F(\boldsymbol{x}_{it}\boldsymbol{\beta})]\\ &= F_{\varepsilon}[\boldsymbol{x}_{it}(\boldsymbol{\beta}/\sigma_u)][1-F_{\varepsilon}[\boldsymbol{x}_{it}(\boldsymbol{\beta}/\sigma_u)]].\end{aligned} \tag{9.6}$$

For each (i, t) we have a *binomial situation*, where the response probability is not constant (as in the simple binomial distribution), but depends on $\boldsymbol{x}_{it}$.

Examples: [a] Let y^*_{it} be the expenditure of purchasing a (durable) good, say determined by a Linear Expenditure System through the maximization of a Stone–Geary utility function for exogenous total expenditure and prices. This outlay, although potentially observable, is not recorded in the data set. The only information is whether the outlay is positive or zero, i.e., whether there is a purchase or not, coded as $y_{it}=1$ and 0, and the associated $\boldsymbol{x}_{it}$. [b] Let y^*_{it} be the degree of satisfaction, genuinely unobservable, of being in a situation described by $\boldsymbol{x}_{it}$. Here 0 is the threshold above/below which the respondent feels sufficiently/insufficiently well to take/not take a certain action, e.g., supply labour, purchase an automobile, coded as $y_{it}=1$ and 0.

Since $p_{it}^{y_{it}}(1-p_{it})^{1-y_{it}} = p_{it}$ and $= 1-p_{it}$ for $y_{it}=1$ and $= 0$, respectively, we can write the likelihood-function for all y_{it}s as

$$\mathcal{L} = \textstyle\prod_{i=1}^{N}\prod_{t=1}^{T} p_{it}^{y_{it}}(1-p_{it})^{1-y_{it}}. \tag{9.7}$$

In Appendix 9A, (9A.7)–(9A.9), it is shown, letting $f(\boldsymbol{x}_{it}\boldsymbol{\beta}) = F'(\boldsymbol{x}_{it}\boldsymbol{\beta})$, that

$$\frac{\partial \ln(\mathcal{L})}{\partial \beta_k} = \sum_{i=1}^{N}\sum_{t=1}^{T}\left[\frac{y_{it}-F(\boldsymbol{x}_{it}\boldsymbol{\beta})}{1-F(\boldsymbol{x}_{it}\boldsymbol{\beta})}\right]\left[\frac{f(\boldsymbol{x}_{it}\boldsymbol{\beta})}{F(\boldsymbol{x}_{it}\boldsymbol{\beta})}\right]x_{kit}, \tag{9.8}$$

$$\begin{aligned}\frac{\partial^2 \ln(\mathcal{L})}{\partial \beta_k \partial \beta_r} = \sum_{i=1}^{N}\sum_{t=1}^{T}\Bigg[&\left(-\frac{y_{it}}{[F(\boldsymbol{x}_{it}\boldsymbol{\beta})]^2} + \frac{1-y_{it}}{[1-F(\boldsymbol{x}_{it}\boldsymbol{\beta})]^2}\right)[f(\boldsymbol{x}_{it}\boldsymbol{\beta})]^2\\ &+\left(\frac{y_{it}}{F(\boldsymbol{x}_{it}\boldsymbol{\beta})} - \frac{1-y_{it}}{1-F(\boldsymbol{x}_{it}\boldsymbol{\beta})}\right)f'(\boldsymbol{x}_{it}\boldsymbol{\beta})\Bigg]x_{kit}x_{rit},\end{aligned} \tag{9.9}$$

and that

$$-\mathsf{E}\left[\frac{\partial^2 \ln(\mathcal{L})}{\partial\beta_k\partial\beta_r}\bigg|X\right] = \sum_{i=1}^{N}\sum_{t=1}^{T}\left[\frac{[f(\boldsymbol{x}_{it}\boldsymbol{\beta})]^2}{F(\boldsymbol{x}_{it}\boldsymbol{\beta})[1-F(\boldsymbol{x}_{it}\boldsymbol{\beta})]}\right]x_{kit}x_{rit}. \tag{9.10}$$

We want to estimate $\boldsymbol{\beta}$ by *the ML* method and to test hypotheses about this coefficient vector. Can we really have the ambition to estimate $\boldsymbol{\beta}$, the response coefficient vector in (9.1), *measured in y^*-units* when only y-observations are available? Some reflection suggests that we should take care. The identification problem—that any $(\boldsymbol{\beta}, \sigma_u)$ rescaled by a common factor gives the same observable outcome, making only the relative coefficients in (9.1) identifiable—persists. This is usually 'solved' by reinterpreting $\boldsymbol{\beta}$ as being 'rescaled to u-standard-deviation units', which gives a ratio that can be identified.[5]

A general cdf for u_{it}, $F(\cdot)$, has so far been considered. A common assumption is that this disturbance follows a standard *logistic distribution*, in which the cdf and density are, respectively,[6]

$$F(u_{it}) = \Lambda(u_{it}) = \frac{e^{u_{it}}}{1+e^{u_{it}}}, \quad f(u_{it}) = \lambda(u_{it}) = \frac{e^{u_{it}}}{(1+e^{u_{it}})^2}. \tag{9.11}$$

This distribution is symmetric: $\Lambda(u_{it})+\Lambda(-u_{it})=1 \Longrightarrow \lambda(u_{it})=\lambda(-u_{it})$. A mathematically convenient property is that the two functions are related by

$$\lambda(u_{it}) \equiv \Lambda'(u_{it}) = \Lambda(u_{it})[1-\Lambda(u_{it})]. \tag{9.12}$$

The result is a *baseline binomial logit-model.* It satisfies: $\mathsf{E}(u_{it})=0$, $\text{var}(u_{it})=\sigma_u^2=\pi^2/3\approx 3.25$.

A *utility-based interpretation of the logit-model* can be given (the same holds for the probit model) in which individual i in period t is imagined to choose positive or negative responses depending on what gives the largest utility—letting y_{it}^* be the *difference* between the utilities of responding positively and negatively. If the utilities attached to the two choices are considered as stochastic and, conditional on the explanatory variables, follow

[5] As noted by Manski (1995, p. 93), 'A random utility model has no identifying power in the absence of information restricting the distribution of the unobserved (disturbance).' For a discussion of identification problems in (threshold-crossing) binary response models, *inter alia*, with focus on the distinction between structural and reduced form analysis, see Manski (1988). Hsiao (1991) discusses identification and ML estimation in binary choice models with measurement errors.

[6] The general logistic distribution, of which the 'standard' one is a member, is considered in, e.g., Evans, Hastings, and Peacock (1993, Chapter 24).

the same simple *extreme value distribution*, the response probabilities can be described by logit-probabilities; see, e.g., Cameron and Trivedi (2005, Sections 14.4.2 and 14.8).[7]

A competing parameterization lets ε_{it} follow a *standardized normal (Gaussian) distribution*, $\mathcal{N}(0,1)$, with cdf and density function, respectively,

$$F_\varepsilon(\varepsilon_{it}) = \Phi(\varepsilon_{it}) = \int_{-\infty}^{\varepsilon_{it}} \frac{1}{\sqrt{2\pi}} e^{-\frac{1}{2}z^2} dz, \quad f_\varepsilon(\varepsilon_{it}) = \phi(\varepsilon_{it}) = \frac{1}{\sqrt{2\pi}} e^{-\frac{1}{2}\varepsilon_{it}^2}, \tag{9.13}$$

which implies $F(u_{it}) = \Phi(u_{it}/\sigma_u)$ and $f(u_{it}) = \sigma_u^{-1}\phi(u_{it}/\sigma_u)$. It is also symmetric: $\Phi(\varepsilon_{it}) + \Phi(-\varepsilon_{it}) = 1 \Longrightarrow \phi(\varepsilon_{it}) = \phi(-\varepsilon_{it})$. Mathematical operations on this model can be facilitated by utilizing the relationship

$$\Phi''(\varepsilon_{it}) \equiv \phi'(\varepsilon_{it}) = -\varepsilon_{it}\phi(\varepsilon_{it}) \Longrightarrow \int_a^b \varepsilon_{it}\phi(\varepsilon_{it})d\varepsilon_{it} = \phi(a) - \phi(b). \tag{9.14}$$

This gives a *baseline binomial probit-model*. Amemiya (1985, Section 9.2.3) shows that the *log-likelihood* function of both the logit and the probit model is *globally concave*, so that multiple solutions to the ML problem can be disregarded.

Using (9.4) and (9.11) or (9.13) the respective response probabilities—the *logit* and the *probit probabilities*, for short—follow as

$$p_{it} = \Lambda(\boldsymbol{x}_{it}\boldsymbol{\beta}) = \frac{e^{\boldsymbol{x}_{it}\boldsymbol{\beta}}}{1 + e^{\boldsymbol{x}_{it}\boldsymbol{\beta}}}, \tag{9.15}$$

$$p_{it} = \Phi(\boldsymbol{x}_{it}\boldsymbol{\beta}/\sigma_u) = \int_{-\infty}^{\boldsymbol{x}_{it}\boldsymbol{\beta}/\sigma_u} \frac{1}{\sqrt{2\pi}} e^{-\frac{1}{2}z^2} dz. \tag{9.16}$$

The *log-odds ratio* for positive versus negative response is in the logit case simply

$$\ln\left(\frac{p_{it}}{1-p_{it}}\right) = \ln\left(\frac{\Lambda(\boldsymbol{x}_{it}\boldsymbol{\beta})}{1-\Lambda(\boldsymbol{x}_{it}\boldsymbol{\beta})}\right) = \boldsymbol{x}_{it}\boldsymbol{\beta},$$

while that of the probit is messy.

The difference in the 'metrics' of the logit and the probit is illustrated by the implied expressions for the 'marginal effects' (common shorthand term for the marginal impacts of the covariates on the response probabilities):

$$\text{Logit}: \qquad \text{ME}_k^L = \frac{\partial p_{it}}{\partial x_{kit}} = \lambda(\boldsymbol{x}_{it}\boldsymbol{\beta})\beta_k = \Lambda(\boldsymbol{x}_{it}\boldsymbol{\beta})[1-\Lambda(\boldsymbol{x}_{it}\boldsymbol{\beta})]\beta_k,$$

[7] This interpretation can be extended to situations with more than two alternatives involved (multinomial response), considered briefly in Section 9.4. However, acceptance of the utility-based interpretation is not required to meaningfully use the logit-model.

$$\text{Probit}: \qquad \mathrm{ME}_k^P = \frac{\partial p_{it}}{\partial x_{kit}} = \phi(\boldsymbol{x}_{it}\boldsymbol{\beta}/\sigma_u)(\beta_k/\sigma_u).$$

For $\boldsymbol{x}_{it}=\mathbf{0}$ we have, for example, since $\lambda(0)=\frac{1}{4}$ and $\phi(0)=1/\sqrt{2\pi}=0.399$, that $ME_k^L=0.25\beta_k$ and $ME_k^P=0.399\beta_k/\sigma_u$.

We will primarily consider the logit parameterization. In practice, this choice may not be crucial, at least not in modelling binomial responses, but may be of some importance in cases where $\boldsymbol{x}_{it}\boldsymbol{\beta}$ is very large or very small for some values of the explanatory variables. This is because the logistic distribution has heavier tails (larger kurtosis) than the normal distribution, see Greene (2008, p. 774).

The first-order conditions for ML implied by (9.8) and (9.12),

$$\begin{aligned}&\textstyle\sum_{i=1}^{N}\sum_{t=1}^{T}[y_{it}-\Lambda(\boldsymbol{x}_{it}\boldsymbol{\beta})]x_{kit}\\ &=\textstyle\sum_{i=1}^{N}\sum_{t=1}^{T}\Big(y_{it}-\frac{e^{\boldsymbol{x}_{it}\boldsymbol{\beta}}}{1+e^{\boldsymbol{x}_{it}\boldsymbol{\beta}}}\Big)x_{kit}=0, \qquad k=1,\dots,K,\end{aligned} \tag{9.17}$$

give a non-linear equation system in the K elements of $\boldsymbol{\beta}$. Its numerical solution is not complicated, but cannot be expressed in closed form. The asymptotic covariance matrix of the estimator can be estimated from the information matrix at maximum. In general, the *information matrix* is defined by

$$\boldsymbol{I}(\boldsymbol{\beta}) = -\mathsf{E}\left[\frac{\partial^2 \ln(\mathcal{L})}{\partial\boldsymbol{\beta}\partial\boldsymbol{\beta}'}\right],$$

where $\mathsf{E}(\partial^2 \ln(\mathcal{L}))/(\partial\boldsymbol{\beta}\partial\boldsymbol{\beta}')$ denotes the expectation, conditional on all $\boldsymbol{x}_{it}$s, of the matrix having $(\partial^2 \ln(\mathcal{L})/(\partial\beta_k\partial\beta_r)$ as element (k,r); confer (9.10). Then $\widehat{\boldsymbol{\beta}}$ has an asymptotic covariance matrix which can be estimated by $\boldsymbol{I}(\widehat{\boldsymbol{\beta}})^{-1}$, where $\widehat{\boldsymbol{\beta}}$ is the ML estimator of $\boldsymbol{\beta}$; see Greene (2008, Section 23.4). It follows from (9.10) and (9.12) that in the logit case, element (k,r) is[8]

$$-\mathsf{E}\left[\frac{\partial^2 \ln(\mathcal{L})}{\partial\beta_k\partial\beta_r}\middle| X\right] = \textstyle\sum_{i=1}^{N}\sum_{t=1}^{T}\Lambda(\boldsymbol{x}_{it}\boldsymbol{\beta})[1-\Lambda(\boldsymbol{x}_{it}\boldsymbol{\beta})]x_{kit}x_{rit}.$$

Gourieroux and Monfort (1981) demonstrate (strong) consistency of the ML estimator for the binary logit model and provide sufficient conditions for asymptotically normality of this estimator.

[8] To obtain the asymptotic covariance matrix for the corresponding probit model, the general expressions (9.8) and (9.10) must be used. This requires numerical integration.

Using the *Likelihood Ratio (LR) test principle*, we can, for the data set at hand, examine whether $\boldsymbol{\beta}$ satisfies P linear restrictions as follows. Having estimated the vector by ML under both H_0 (the restrictions apply) and H_1 (the restrictions do not apply), with likelihood values $\mathcal{L}_{H0}$ and $\mathcal{L}_{H1}$, respectively, we can use the statistic $LR = -2[\ln \mathcal{L}_{H0} - \ln \mathcal{L}_{H1}]$, which has *asymptotically* a $\chi^2(P)$-distribution under H_0.

Example: The data set for this example is extracted from a comprehensive cardiovascular screening program conducted by the former National Health Screening Service (presently the Norwegian Institute of Public Health), involving three screenings ($T = 3$) over the 1974–88 period, conducted approximately every fifth year (the t subscript referring to observation number, not to calendar year; see Chapter 10). The results, based on data for Finnmark county (used because it has a larger coverage than the other counties), are from a set of tentative explorations (unpublished) of binary responses for the use of alcohol and tobacco, obtained using the Stata software.

Table 9.1 gives estimates of $\boldsymbol{\beta}$ with standard errors for *both drugs (alcohol and cigarettes together)* (columns 1–3) and *cigarettes only* (column 4). For the former, results for males and females separately are also given, `mal` being the male dummy. The year of birth (`yrb`) has a clearer effect on the responses for females than for males. The effect of having children (`chi`) comes out as negative when using the pooled data set (columns 1 and 4). However, the gender-specific results for the combined drug category differ markedly: a positive children effect for males and a negative effect for females (columns 2 and 3). Increased length of schooling reduces the inclination to drug use and more so the higher is the education (represented by the dummies `ed1`, `ed2`, of which the latter indicates more than twelve years of schooling, including a university degree).

Table 9.1 Binomial logit analysis of drug use: no heterogeneity. $n = NT = 29454$, 14406 from males, 15048 from females

	Both drugs			*Cigarettes*
	All	Males	Females	All
`mal`	0.9874			0.5272
	(0.0248)			(0.0238)
`yrb`	0.0179	0.0048	0.0278	0.0204
	(0.0017)	(0.0026)	(0.0023)	(0.0017)
`chi`	−0.0906	0.1234	−0.2680	−0.0316
	(0.0518)	(0.0828)	(0.0701)	(0.0505)
`ed1`	−0.1012	−0.0912	−0.1225	−0.2628
	(0.0265)	(0.0396)	(0.0359)	(0.0255)
`ed2`	−0.4319	−0.3579	−0.5130	−0.8934
	(0.0486)	(0.0672)	(0.0711)	(0.0494)
`intercept`	−0.6125	0.8107	−0.9382	−0.8121
	(0.0614)	(0.0917)	(0.0792)	(0.0594)

Standard errors in parentheses

9.2.2 BINOMIAL MODEL WITH FULL FIXED HETEROGENEITY

An obvious extension to widen the applicability of the model is to allow for intercept and coefficient heterogeneity. This leads to

$$\begin{aligned}&y_{it}^{*}=\boldsymbol{x}_{it}\boldsymbol{\beta}_{i}+\alpha_i-u_{it}, \qquad (u_{it}|X)\sim \mathsf{IID}(0,\sigma_u^2),\\ &i=1,\dots,N;\; t=1,\dots,T,\end{aligned} \tag{9.18}$$

where $\boldsymbol{\beta}_i=(\beta_{1i},\dots,\beta_{Ki})'$ and α_i are *fixed* parameters, which—if we adhere to the utility-based interpretation—may represent individual heterogeneity in the utility evaluation not accounted for by $\boldsymbol{x}_{it}$.[9] We still observe $\boldsymbol{x}_{it}$ and y_{it} determined by (9.2). It follows that (9.4) and (9.6) are generalized to

$$\begin{aligned}\mathsf{E}(y_{it}|X)&=F(\boldsymbol{x}_{it}\boldsymbol{\beta}_i+\alpha_i),\\ \text{var}(y_{it}|X)&=F(\boldsymbol{x}_{it}\boldsymbol{\beta}_i+\alpha_i)[1-F(\boldsymbol{x}_{it}\boldsymbol{\beta}_i+\alpha_i)].\end{aligned}$$

The likelihood function still has the form (9.7), now with[10]

$$\frac{\partial \ln(\mathcal{L})}{\partial(\boldsymbol{x}_{it}\boldsymbol{\beta}_i+\alpha_i)}=y_{it}(1-p_{it})-(1-y_{it})p_{it}=y_{it}-p_{it}.$$

Again, our focus is on the logit version. A logistic distribution for u_{it} implies response probability and log-odds-ratio given by

$$\begin{aligned}p_{it}&=p_{it}(\alpha_i)=\Lambda(\boldsymbol{x}_{it}\boldsymbol{\beta}_i+\alpha_i)=\frac{e^{\boldsymbol{x}_{it}\boldsymbol{\beta}_i+\alpha_i}}{1+e^{\boldsymbol{x}_{it}\boldsymbol{\beta}_i+\alpha_i}},\\ \ln\left(\frac{p_{it}}{1-p_{it}}\right)&=\boldsymbol{x}_{it}\boldsymbol{\beta}_i+\alpha_i,\end{aligned} \tag{9.19}$$

and again, $\sigma_u^2=\pi^2/3$. Here α_i acts as a time-invariant shift in the log-odds ratio, or equivalently, in the critical value at which individual i responds positively.

Differentiating $\ln(\mathcal{L})$ with respect to $\boldsymbol{\beta}_i$ and α_i gives N sets of $K+1$ first-order conditions, each defining T-consistent estimators. If $N\to\infty$ the number of ML problems and the number of parameters to be estimated go to infinity, and an *incidental parameter-problem*, see Neyman and Scott (1948) and Lancaster (2000), arises. The ML estimators are then inconsistent for finite T.

[9] In the utility-related interpretation, α_i can be interpreted as individual idiosyncrasies in the utility evaluation not accounted for by $F(\cdot)$ and $\boldsymbol{x}_{it}$.

[10] The *identification problem* now concerns $\boldsymbol{\beta}_i$, α_i, and σ_u, as $(\boldsymbol{\beta}_i,\alpha_i,\sigma_u)$ and $(k\boldsymbol{\beta},k\alpha_i,k\sigma_u)$ give for any k the same value of y_{it} and the same response probability. We might therefore have replaced (9.18) with $y_{it}^{**}=\boldsymbol{x}_{it}(\boldsymbol{\beta}_i/\sigma_u)+(\alpha_i/\sigma_u)-\varepsilon_{it}$, $(\varepsilon_{it}|X)\sim\mathsf{IID}(0,1)$, where $y_{it}^{**}=y_{it}^{*}/\sigma_u$ and $\varepsilon_{it}=u_{it}/\sigma_u$.

9.2.3 BINOMIAL MODEL WITH FIXED INTERCEPT HETEROGENEITY

The third model imposes on (9.18) $\boldsymbol{\beta}_i = \boldsymbol{\beta}$ $(i = 1, \dots, N)$, giving

$$y_{it}^* = \boldsymbol{x}_{it}\boldsymbol{\beta} + \alpha_i - u_{it}, \qquad (u_{it}|\boldsymbol{X}) \sim \mathsf{IID}(0, \sigma_u^2), \tag{9.20}$$

$$p_{it} = p_{it}(\alpha_i) = \Lambda(\boldsymbol{x}_{it}\boldsymbol{\beta} + \alpha_i) = \frac{e^{\boldsymbol{x}_{it}\boldsymbol{\beta}+\alpha_i}}{1+e^{\boldsymbol{x}_{it}\boldsymbol{\beta}+\alpha_i}}, \tag{9.21}$$

$$\ln\left(\frac{p_{it}}{1-p_{it}}\right) = \boldsymbol{x}_{it}\boldsymbol{\beta} + \alpha_i,$$

$$i = 1, \dots, N;\ t = 1, \dots, T.$$

The likelihood function again has the form (9.7), and it follows that

$$\frac{\partial \ln(\mathcal{L})}{\partial(\boldsymbol{x}_{it}\boldsymbol{\beta} + \alpha_i)} = y_{it}(1-p_{it}) - (1-y_{it})p_{it} = y_{it} - p_{it}.$$

Hence, $\partial \ln(\mathcal{L})/\partial\beta_k = (y_{it} - p_{it})x_{kit}$ and $\partial \ln(\mathcal{L})/\partial\alpha_i = y_{it} - p_{it}$. The first-order conditions give $K+N$ non-linear equations in $\boldsymbol{\beta}$ and $\alpha_1, \dots, \alpha_N$. The solution leads to T-consistent estimators of these parameters. If $N \to \infty$ while T is finite, the number of unknown parameters increases, and we have an incidental parameter problem for the α_is. However, the ML estimators are *inconsistent not only for the α_is, but also for $\boldsymbol{\beta}$*. This is because the parameters enter non-linearly; a consequence is that the inconsistency in estimating α_i for finite T 'infects' the estimation of $\boldsymbol{\beta}$. The model differs in this respect from the *linear* regression model with *continuous* regressand; see Section 2.1.2. For the finite T case in the latter type of model, the incidental parameter-problem for the intercepts did not prevent consistent estimation of the coefficient vector. This is because in a linear model, the estimator of $\boldsymbol{\beta}$ is uncorrelated with the estimator of α_i, a property which does not carry over to the present, non-linear model.[11]

9.2.4 FIXED INTERCEPT HETEROGENEITY, SMALL *T* AND CONDITIONAL ML

A way of coming to grips with the incidental parameter problem in analysis of fixed intercept logit models when T is finite, specifically appealing for this model type, is to use a *conditional ML procedure* considered by Chamberlain (1984, Section 3.2); see also

[11] For illustrations of the nature of the problem, see Chamberlain (1980, Section 2), Hsiao (2003, Section 7.3.1.a), and Demidenko (2004, Section 7.2.2), the latter considering the corresponding unbalanced case.

Andersen (1970). Its essence is first, to perform a transformation which eliminates the individual effects, and next to *perform (sequences of) ML estimations conditional on the number of times each individual responds positively.*[12] This number may be $0, 1, \dots, T$. To explain its essence we initially notice that relative logit odds-ratios for individual i across different periods do not involve α_i, as (9.21) implies, for example,

$$\left(\frac{p_{it}}{1-p_{it}}\right) / \left(\frac{p_{is}}{1-p_{is}}\right) = e^{(\boldsymbol{x}_{it}-\boldsymbol{x}_{is})\boldsymbol{\beta}}, \qquad t,s = 1,\dots,T;\ t \neq s.$$

We will explain the idea in some detail for $T=2$ and $T=3$.[13]

The case $T=2$. Since $y_{i1}+y_{i2}=0 \Leftrightarrow y_{i1}=y_{i2}=0$, $y_{i1}+y_{i2}=2 \Leftrightarrow y_{i1}=y_{i2}=1$,

$$P(y_{i1} = y_{i2} = 0|X, y_{i1}+y_{i2} = 0) = P(y_{i1} = y_{i2} = 1|X, y_{i1}+y_{i2} = 2) = 1.$$

Therefore, conditioning on negative or positive responses twice gives no contribution to the conditional log-likelihood. The only observations of interest for making inference on $\boldsymbol{\beta}$ come from individuals who change their response. The probability that individual i responds positively once is

$$P(y_{i1}+y_{i2}=1|X) = p_{i1}(1-p_{i2}) + (1-p_{i1})p_{i2},$$

as $(y_{i1}, y_{i2}) = (1,0)$ and $(0,1)$ make this happen. Let $B_{1.2} = \{i : y_{i1}+y_{i2}=1\}$ be the index set for the individuals who respond positively once when $T=2$. From (9.21) we find, after rearrangement, the conditional probabilities

$$\begin{aligned} P[(y_{i1}, y_{i2}) &= (1,0)|X, y_{i1} + y_{i2} = 1] \\ &= \frac{p_{i1}(1-p_{i2})}{p_{i1}(1-p_{i2}) + (1-p_{i1})p_{i2}} = \frac{e^{(x_{i1}-x_{i2})\beta}}{1+e^{(x_{i1}-x_{i2})\beta}}, \\ P[(y_{i1}, y_{i2}) &= (0,1)|X, y_{i1} + y_{i2} = 1] \\ &= \frac{(1-p_{i1})p_{i2}}{p_{i1}(1-p_{i2}) + (1-p_{i1})p_{i2}} = \frac{1}{1+e^{(x_{i1}-x_{i2})\beta}}, \end{aligned} \tag{9.22}$$

from which α_i is eliminated, as the common factor e^{α_i} cancels. All individual-specific explanatory variables also vanish, which makes their coefficients unidentified. Introducing binary variables

[12] This transformation and the procedure it motivates utilize that $\sum_t y_{it}$ is a *sufficient statistic* for α_i, see Chamberlain (1980, pp. 228–9). For further discussion, see Magnac (2004) and, for elaboration of the sufficiency concept in relation to econometrics, Gourieroux and Monfort (1995, Section 3.1).

[13] See, e.g., Demidenko (2004, Section 7.2.3) for a more compact description.

$$\begin{aligned} z_{i10} &= 1\{(y_{i1}, y_{i2}) = (1,0) | y_{i1} + y_{i2} = 1\}, \\ z_{i01} &= 1\{(y_{i1}, y_{i2}) = (0,1) | y_{i1} + y_{i2} = 1\}, \end{aligned} \quad i \in B_{1.2},$$

where $1\{\mathcal{S}\} = 1$ if $\mathcal{S}$ is true and $= 0$ if $\mathcal{S}$ is false, (9.22) reads

$$\begin{aligned} \pi_{i10} &= P(z_{i10} = 1 | X) = \frac{e^{(x_{i1} - x_{i2})\beta}}{1 + e^{(x_{i1} - x_{i2})\beta}}, \\ \pi_{i01} &= P(z_{i01} = 1 | X) = \frac{1}{1 + e^{(x_{i1} - x_{i2})\beta}}, \end{aligned} \quad i \in B_{1.2}. \tag{9.23}$$

These expressions are analogous to p_{it} and $1 - p_{it}$ given by (9.15), except that the covariates are differences between the covariates from the first and the second observation. No level information on $\boldsymbol{x}_{it}$ enters the expressions for the conditional response probabilities. This algebra may be seen as a counterpart to eliminating fixed effects in linear regression models by linear transformations, like taking differences or deducting individuals means. In analogy with (9.7), the likelihood for all z_i, conditional on $y_{i1} + y_{i2} = 1$ and $\boldsymbol{x}_{i1} - \boldsymbol{x}_{i2}$, is

$$\mathcal{L}_{B_{1.2}} = \prod_{i \in B_{1.2}} \pi_{i10}^{z_{i10}} \pi_{i01}^{z_{i01}}, \tag{9.24}$$

with first-order conditions for conditional ML

$$\sum_{i \in B_{1.2}} [z_{i10} - \pi_{i10}](x_{ki1} - x_{ki2}) = \sum_{i \in B_{1.2}} \left[z_{i10} - \frac{e^{(x_{i1} - x_{i2})\beta}}{1 + e^{(x_{i1} - x_{i2})\beta}} \right] (x_{ki1} - x_{ki2}) = 0,$$
$$k = 1, \ldots, K.$$

The solution for $\boldsymbol{\beta}$ defines *the conditional ML estimator*. It is consistent when the number of individuals in $B_{1.2}$ goes to infinity. A far from innocent problem is that the effect of individual-specific covariates, which are eliminated from the likelihood function together with α_i, cannot be identified.

The case $T = 3$. Since $y_{i1} + y_{i2} + y_{i3} = 0 \Leftrightarrow y_{i1} = y_{i2} = y_{i3} = 0$, $y_{i1} + y_{i2} + y_{i3} = 3 \Leftrightarrow y_{i1} = y_{i2} = y_{i3} = 1$,

$$\begin{aligned} & P(y_{i1} = y_{i2} = y_{i3} = 0 | X, \textstyle\sum_{k=1}^{3} y_{ik} = 0) \\ & \quad = P(y_{i1} = y_{i2} = y_{i3} = 1 | X, \textstyle\sum_{k=1}^{3} = 3) = 1. \end{aligned}$$

Therefore, conditioning on positive responses zero or three times does not contribute to the conditional log-likelihood. The only observations of interest are those from individuals who respond positively once or twice, i.e., change their response at least once. The latter events have probabilities, respectively,

$$P(\sum_{k=1}^{3} y_{ik}=1|X)$$
$$= p_{i1}(1-p_{i2})(1-p_{i3})+(1-p_{i1})p_{i2}(1-p_{i3})+(1-p_{i1})(1-p_{i2})p_{i3},$$
$$P(\sum_{k=1}^{3} y_{ik}=2|X)$$
$$= p_{i1}p_{i2}(1-p_{i3})+p_{i1}(1-p_{i2})p_{i3}+(1-p_{i1})p_{i2}p_{i3},$$

as $(y_{i1}, y_{i2}, y_{i3}) = (1,0,0), (0,1,0), (0,0,1)$ and $(1,1,0), (1,0,1), (0,1,1)$ make respectively the former and the latter happen. Introducing the binary variables

$$\begin{aligned}
z_{i100} &= 1\{(y_{i1}, y_{i2}, y_{i3}) = (1,0,0)|\textstyle\sum_{k=1}^{3} y_{ik}=1\},\\
z_{i010} &= 1\{(y_{i1}, y_{i2}, y_{i3}) = (0,1,0)|\textstyle\sum_{k=1}^{3} y_{ik}=1\},\\
z_{i001} &= 1\{(y_{i1}, y_{i2}, y_{i3}) = (0,0,1)|\textstyle\sum_{k=1}^{3} y_{ik}=1\},\\
z_{i110} &= 1\{(y_{i1}, y_{i2}, y_{i3}) = (1,1,0)|\textstyle\sum_{k=1}^{3} y_{ik}=2\},\\
z_{i101} &= 1\{(y_{i1}, y_{i2}, y_{i3}) = (1,0,1)|\textstyle\sum_{k=1}^{3} y_{ik}=2\},\\
z_{i011} &= 1\{(y_{i1}, y_{i2}, y_{i3}) = (0,1,1)|\textstyle\sum_{k=1}^{3} y_{ik}=2\},
\end{aligned}$$

the relevant conditional probabilities, from which the factor e^{α_i} cancels, are[14]

$$\begin{aligned}
\pi_{i100} = P(z_{i100}=1|X) &= \frac{p_{i1}(1-p_{i2})(1-p_{i3})}{P(\sum_{k=1}^{3} y_{ik}=1|X)} = \frac{e^{(x_{i1}-x_{i3})\beta}}{1+e^{(x_{i1}-x_{i3})\beta}+e^{(x_{i2}-x_{i3})\beta}},\\
\pi_{i010} = P(z_{i010}=1|X) &= \frac{(1-p_{i1})p_{i2}(1-p_{i3})}{P(\sum_{k=1}^{3} y_{ik}=1|X)} = \frac{e^{(x_{i2}-x_{i3})\beta}}{1+e^{(x_{i1}-x_{i3})\beta}+e^{(x_{i2}-x_{i3})\beta}},\\
\pi_{i001} = P(z_{i001}=1|X) &= \frac{(1-p_{i1})(1-p_{i2})p_{i3}}{P(\sum_{k=1}^{3} y_{ik}=1|X)} = \frac{1}{1+e^{(x_{i1}-x_{i3})\beta}+e^{(x_{i2}-x_{i3})\beta}},\\
&\qquad i \in B_{1.3},
\end{aligned} \tag{9.25}$$

$$\begin{aligned}
\pi_{i110} = P(z_{i110}=1|X) &= \frac{p_{i1}p_{i2}(1-p_{i3})}{P(\sum_{k=1}^{3} y_{ik}=2|X)} = \frac{e^{(x_{i1}-x_{i3})\beta}}{1+e^{(x_{i1}-x_{i3})\beta}+e^{(x_{i1}-x_{i2})\beta}},\\
\pi_{i101} = P(z_{i101}=1|X) &= \frac{p_{i1}(1-p_{i2})p_{i3}}{P(\sum_{k=1}^{3} y_{ik}=2|X)} = \frac{e^{(x_{i1}-x_{i2})\beta}}{1+e^{(x_{i1}-x_{i3})\beta}+e^{(x_{i1}-x_{i2})\beta}},\\
\pi_{i011} = P(z_{i011}=1|X) &= \frac{(1-p_{i1})p_{i2}p_{i3}}{P(\sum_{k=1}^{3} y_{ik}=2|X)} = \frac{1}{1+e^{(x_{i1}-x_{i3})\beta}+e^{(x_{i1}-x_{i2})\beta}},\\
&\qquad i \in B_{2.3},
\end{aligned} \tag{9.26}$$

$B_{s.T}$ in general denoting the index set of the individuals who respond positively s times among T. Since $(z_{i100}, z_{i010}, z_{i001})$ and $(z_{i110}, z_{i101}, z_{i011})$ are *trinomially* distributed, with probabilities, respectively, $(\pi_{i100}, \pi_{i010}, \pi_{i001})$ and $(\pi_{i110}, \pi_{i101}, \pi_{i011})$, the likelihoods of all $(z_{i100}, z_{i010}, z_{i001})$ and $(z_{i110}, z_{i101}, z_{i011})$, conditional on $\sum_{k=1}^{3} y_{ik}=1$ and $\sum_{k=1}^{3} y_{ik}=2$, respectively, are

[14] We here manipulate expressions of the form $p_{i1}p_{i2}p_{i3} = \prod_{k=1}^{3}[e^{x_{ik}\beta}/(1+e^{x_{ik}\beta})]$.

$$\mathcal{L}_{B_{1.3}} = \prod_{i \in B_{1.3}} \pi_{i100}^{z_{i100}} \pi_{i010}^{z_{i010}} \pi_{i001}^{z_{i001}}, \tag{9.27}$$

$$\mathcal{L}_{B_{2.3}} = \prod_{i \in B_{2.3}} \pi_{i110}^{z_{i110}} \pi_{i101}^{z_{i101}} \pi_{i011}^{z_{i011}}. \tag{9.28}$$

Since for any $V_1, V_2, \dots, \delta_{jr}$ being Kronecker-deltas, we have

$$g_j = \frac{e^{V_j}}{1+\sum_r e^{V_r}} \; (j=1,2,\dots) \implies \frac{\partial \ln(g_j)}{\partial V_r} = \delta_{jr} - g_r, \tag{9.29}$$

$$\frac{\partial}{\partial[(\boldsymbol{x}_{i1}-\boldsymbol{x}_{i3})\boldsymbol{\beta}]} \begin{bmatrix} \ln(\pi_{i100}) \\ \ln(\pi_{i010}) \\ \ln(\pi_{i001}) \end{bmatrix} = \begin{bmatrix} 1-\pi_{i100} \\ -\pi_{i100} \\ -\pi_{i100} \end{bmatrix},$$

$$\frac{\partial}{\partial[(\boldsymbol{x}_{i2}-\boldsymbol{x}_{i3})\boldsymbol{\beta}]} \begin{bmatrix} \ln(\pi_{i100}) \\ \ln(\pi_{i010}) \\ \ln(\pi_{i001}) \end{bmatrix} = \begin{bmatrix} -\pi_{i010} \\ 1-\pi_{i010} \\ -\pi_{i010} \end{bmatrix},$$

$$\frac{\partial}{\partial[(\boldsymbol{x}_{i1}-\boldsymbol{x}_{i3})\boldsymbol{\beta}]} \begin{bmatrix} \ln(\pi_{i110}) \\ \ln(\pi_{i101}) \\ \ln(\pi_{i011}) \end{bmatrix} = \begin{bmatrix} 1-\pi_{i110} \\ -\pi_{i110} \\ -\pi_{i110} \end{bmatrix},$$

$$\frac{\partial}{\partial[(\boldsymbol{x}_{i1}-\boldsymbol{x}_{i2})\boldsymbol{\beta}]} \begin{bmatrix} \ln(\pi_{i110}) \\ \ln(\pi_{i101}) \\ \ln(\pi_{i011}) \end{bmatrix} = \begin{bmatrix} -\pi_{i101} \\ 1-\pi_{i101} \\ -\pi_{i101} \end{bmatrix},$$

and hence

$$\begin{aligned}
\frac{\partial \ln(\mathcal{L}_{B_{1.3}})}{\partial[(\boldsymbol{x}_{i1}-\boldsymbol{x}_{i3})\boldsymbol{\beta}]} &= \sum[z_{i100}(1-\pi_{i100}) - z_{i010}\pi_{i100} - z_{i001}\pi_{i100}] \\
&\equiv \sum(z_{i100}-\pi_{i100}), \\
\frac{\partial \ln(\mathcal{L}_{B_{1.3}})}{\partial[(\boldsymbol{x}_{i2}-\boldsymbol{x}_{i3})\boldsymbol{\beta}]} &= \sum[-z_{i100}\pi_{i010} + z_{i010}(1-\pi_{i010}) - z_{i001}\pi_{i010}] \\
&\equiv \sum(z_{i010}-\pi_{i010}), \\
\frac{\partial \ln(\mathcal{L}_{B_{2.3}})}{\partial[(\boldsymbol{x}_{i1}-\boldsymbol{x}_{i3})\boldsymbol{\beta}]} &= \sum[z_{i110}(1-\pi_{i110}) - z_{i101}\pi_{i110} - z_{i011}\pi_{i110}] \\
&\equiv \sum(z_{i110}-\pi_{i110}), \\
\frac{\partial \ln(\mathcal{L}_{B_{2.3}})}{\partial[(\boldsymbol{x}_{i1}-\boldsymbol{x}_{i2})\boldsymbol{\beta}]} &= \sum[-z_{i110}\pi_{i101} + z_{i101}(1-\pi_{i101}) - z_{i011}\pi_{i101}] \\
&\equiv \sum(z_{i101}-\pi_{i101}).
\end{aligned}$$

Therefore, the first-order conditions for ML estimation of $\boldsymbol{\beta}$ based on observations from the individuals in $B_{1.3}$ and $B_{2.3}$ become, respectively,

$$\sum_{i\in B_{1.3}}[(z_{i100}-\pi_{i100})(x_{ki1}-x_{ki3})+(z_{i010}-\pi_{i010})(x_{ki2}-x_{ki3})]=0,$$
$$\sum_{i\in B_{2.3}}[(z_{i110}-\pi_{i110})(x_{ki1}-x_{ki3})+(z_{i101}-\pi_{i101})(x_{ki1}-x_{ki2})]=0,$$
$$k=1,\dots,K.$$

The solutions for $\boldsymbol{\beta}$ define, when the number of individuals in, respectively, $B_{1.3}$ and $B_{2.3}$, goes to infinity, consistent conditional ML estimators.

Maximization of $\mathcal{L}_{B_{1.3}}$ and of $\mathcal{L}_{B_{2.3}}$ usually give different results, and efficiency is improved by combining the two problems. Since the observations from the individuals in $B_{1.3}$ and $B_{2.3}$ are independent, the log-likelihood function to be maximized with respect to $\boldsymbol{\beta}$, after inserting (9.25)–(9.28), becomes

$$\begin{aligned}\ln(\mathcal{L}_{B_{1.3\&2.3}}) &= \ln(\mathcal{L}_{B_{1.3}})+\ln(\mathcal{L}_{B_{2.3}})\\ &= \sum_{i\in B_{1.3}}[z_{i100}\ln(\pi_{i100})+z_{i010}\ln(\pi_{i010})+z_{i001}\ln(\pi_{i001})]\\ &\quad+\sum_{i\in B_{2.3}}[z_{i110}\ln(\pi_{i110})+z_{i101}\ln(\pi_{i101})+z_{i011}\ln(\pi_{i011})].\end{aligned} \tag{9.30}$$

The general case. The procedures described in detail for $T=2$ and 3 can be generalized. If $T=4$, there are four ways of observing positive response once, six ways of observing this outcome twice, and four ways of observing it three times, corresponding to multinomial situations with, respectively, four, six, and four alternatives. More generally, for an arbitrary T there are $\binom{T}{s}$ ways of observing an outcome with s positive responses, which correspond to multinomial situations with $\binom{T}{s}$ alternatives ($s=1,\dots,T-1$). Since the binomial formula implies $\sum_{s=0}^{T}\binom{T}{s}=2^T \Longrightarrow \sum_{s=1}^{T-1}\binom{T}{s}=2^T-2$, as $\binom{T}{0}=\binom{T}{T}=1$, the number of alternative responses, and hence the combined log-likelihood function generalizing (9.30) can, even for moderate T, be prohibitively large. For $T=10$ the number is, for example, 1022. This method will therefore be practicable only when T is small.

9.3 **Binomial model: Random heterogeneity**

9.3.1 MODEL

We consider a model similar to that in Section 9.2.3, except that α_i, is treated as random, generated by a specified distribution. Then (9.20) is replaced by

$$\begin{aligned} &y_{it}^* = \boldsymbol{x}_{it}\boldsymbol{\beta}+\alpha_i - u_{it}, \\ &(u_{it}|X) \sim \text{IID Logit}, \quad (\alpha_i|X) \text{ has density } g(\alpha_i;\boldsymbol{\lambda}), \\ &i = 1,\dots,N;\ t=1,\dots,T, \end{aligned} \tag{9.31}$$

where α_i, if we adhere to the utility-based interpretation, represents a stochastic intercept shift in individual i's utility evaluation, g is a known functional form, and $\boldsymbol{\lambda}$ is a parameter vector. Relative to the fixed effect formulation, this is strongly parameter-saving, as in linear regression models. However, the implication that α_i and X are stochastically independent (provided that γ does not characterize the distribution of X) may be unrealistic.[15] The observations still are the $\boldsymbol{x}_{it}$s and the y_{it}s generated by (9.2).[16]

The expressions for the response probability, *conditional on* α_i, has the same form as (9.21), and hence the conditional version of this function and the log-odds ratio are, respectively,

$$\begin{aligned} p_{it}(\alpha_i) &= P(y_{it}=1|X,\alpha_i) = \Lambda(\boldsymbol{x}_{it}\boldsymbol{\beta}+\alpha_i) = \frac{e^{\boldsymbol{x}_{it}\boldsymbol{\beta}+\alpha_i}}{1+e^{\boldsymbol{x}_{it}\boldsymbol{\beta}+\alpha_i}}, \\ \ln\left(\frac{p_{it}(\alpha_i)}{1-p_{it}(\alpha_i)}\right) &= \boldsymbol{x}_{it}\boldsymbol{\beta}+\alpha_i. \end{aligned} \tag{9.32}$$

Letting

$$\mathcal{L}_{it}(\alpha_i) = p_{it}(\alpha_i)^{y_{it}}(1-p_{it}(\alpha_i))^{1-y_{it}}, \tag{9.33}$$

$$\mathcal{L}_i(\alpha_i) = \prod_{t=1}^{T} \mathcal{L}_{it}(\alpha_i), \tag{9.34}$$

where $\mathcal{L}_i(\alpha_i)$ is individual i's part of the likelihood function conditional on α_i, and assuming $y_{i1},\dots,y_{iT}$ independent (conditional on α_i and X), we can express the corresponding part of the marginal likelihood function, after multiplication by the density $g(\alpha_i;\boldsymbol{\lambda})$ and integration over α_i, as

$$\begin{aligned} \mathcal{L}_i &= \int_{-\infty}^{\infty} \prod_{t=1}^{T} \mathcal{L}_i(\alpha_i) g(\alpha_i;\boldsymbol{\lambda})d\alpha_i \\ &= \int_{-\infty}^{\infty} \prod_{t=1}^{T} p_{it}(\alpha_i)^{y_{it}}(1-p_{it}(\alpha_i))^{1-y_{it}} g(\alpha_i;\boldsymbol{\lambda})d\alpha_i. \end{aligned} \tag{9.35}$$

15 MaCurdy (1981, p. 1065), for example, argues along these lines when considering the (individual-specific) Lagrange Multiplier of the intertemporal budget constraint of a life-cycle model as part of a fixed, not a random, effect.

16 Discrete response modelling for panel data with stochastic parameters has some resemblance to Bayesian approaches. See, e.g., Koop, Poirier, and Tobias (2007) on hierarchical models (Chapter 12) and latent variable models (Chapter 14), as well as the remarks on mixed logit approaches to be given in Section 9.4.1.

The joint likelihood function of all y_{it}s then becomes the product of these elements, as the individuals are independently observed, and we get

$$\mathcal{L} = \prod_{i=1}^{N} \int_{-\infty}^{\infty} \left\{ \prod_{t=1}^{T} p_{it}(\alpha_i)^{y_{it}} (1 - p_{it}(\alpha_i))^{1-y_{it}} g(\alpha_i; \boldsymbol{\lambda}) \right\} d\alpha_i. \tag{9.36}$$

9.3.2 ML ESTIMATION

Maximizing $\mathcal{L}$, or simpler, $\ln(\mathcal{L})$, with respect to $(\boldsymbol{\beta}, \boldsymbol{\lambda})$, provided that the function has properties which ensure a unique solution, we get their ML estimators. In practice this problem is solved numerically.[17] Since only single integration is needed, the solution is usually not time-consuming. For further discussion, including numerical aspects and approximations, see, Hsiao (1996a, Section 16.3), Demidenko (2004, Sections 7.3.1–7.3.4.), and Lechner, Lollivier, and Magnac (2008, Sections 7.2.3–7.2.4). The latter also survey simulation methods.

We might well have assumed u_{it} normally, instead of logistically, distributed. This would have given a *probit model* with random heterogeneity. We then replace the conditional probability (9.32) by $p_{it}(\alpha_i) = \Phi(\boldsymbol{x}_{it}\boldsymbol{\beta} + \alpha_i)$ and may, for example, also let α_i be normally distributed, replacing $g(\alpha_i; \boldsymbol{\lambda})$ with the normal density. Because $\Phi(\cdot)$ is defined by an integral, the solution procedure would involve numerical integration twice.

Modelling heterogeneity as random, with a parametric distribution, has the advantage that N-consistent estimation of $\boldsymbol{\beta}$ and $\boldsymbol{\gamma}$ can be ensured (if a solution exists and is unique), even for T finite (and small), and, unlike conditional logit, it utilizes all NT observations and allows identification of the coefficients of individual-specific explanatory variables. This is another example of a gain obtainable by choosing a parsimonious parameterization of the response probabilities, contrasting with conditional ML estimation of the logit model, which eliminates the individual effects and all individual-specific regressors, and neglects all observations from individuals who do not change responses. Drawbacks are that this procedure may be numerically cumbersome and that its (asymptotic) properties are not robust to violation of the implied independence of the latent effect and the covariates.

Another way of facilitating numerical integration, is to choose a distribution for α_i simpler than the normal, for example the uniform distribution.

Example *(continued):* Table 9.2 contains results corresponding to those in Table 9.1, except that latent heterogeneity, modelled by *normally distributed* random effects, are

[17] It is possible to proceed as in Sections 9.2.3 and 9.2.4: condition on the values of the α_is realized and neglecting their distributional properties, or perform conditional ML estimation. Both, however, involve a loss of information and a loss of efficiency.

Table 9.2 Binomial logit analysis of drug use: *heterogeneity, as random effects, accounted for.* $N=9818$ (4802 males, 5016 females). $T=3$

	Both drugs			*Cigarettes*
	All	Males	Females	All
mal	4.7342 (0.1089)			1.9245 (0.1207)
yrb	0.0336 (0.0051)	0.0254 (0.0185)	0.0689 (0.0154)	0.0755 (0.0081)
chi	0.4769 (0.1360)	1.3868 (0.2905)	0.2983 (0.2917)	0.4853 (0.1294)
ed1	−0.0811 (0.0789)	−0.2326 (0.2942)	−0.3275 (0.2639)	−0.9437 (0.1271)
ed2	−0.5050 (0.1273)	−1.4377 (0.4936)	−3.0352 (0.3132)	−3.1716 (0.2251)
intercept	−0.2310 (0.2088)	7.2543 (0.6798)	−2.3308 (0.5390)	−3.1068 (0.2919)
ρ	0.8938	0.9736	0.8957	0.8813

Standard errors in parentheses

allowed. Heterogeneity is strong, with an estimated $\rho = \text{var}(\alpha_i)/[\text{var}(\alpha_i)+\text{var}(u_{it})]$ around 0.9. The coefficient estimates are substantially changed, and on the whole increased. The sign of the children effect is reversed, except for males, where it, for the two drugs combined, is still positive. For females it comes out as (insignificantly) positive. Again, the birth-year effect is stronger for females than for males. The ed1 dummy (schooling for fewer than twelve years) now has a negative, but insignificant effect on the two drugs combined ('t-values' around -1, columns 1–3), while the coefficient of ed2 is significantly negative. For cigarettes only, however, both education dummies come out with significantly negative coefficients, and the effect is stronger the higher is the education.

It can be shown, see Demidenko (2004, Section 7.2.1), that a consequence of ignoring random intercept heterogeneity in logit analysis is that the coefficients are reduced ('attenuated') by a factor $1/(1+\sigma_\alpha^2)^{\frac{1}{2}}$, where $\sigma_\alpha^2 = \text{var}(\alpha_i^2)$. Considering the large estimate of ρ, it therefore comes as no surprise that, overall, the size of the coefficient estimates in Table 9.1 are substantially smaller than in Table 9.2 (although the reduction is far from proportional, and, as noted, some estimates also differ in sign).

9.4 **Multinomial model: Other extensions**

An obvious limitation of bivariate logit models is that, for each (i, t), only two responses are allowed. We in this section outline extensions to handle cases with J alternative responses (in the binomial model, $J=2$), with individual-specific heterogeneity represented by latent individual effects.

9.4.1 MODEL

We let the multinomial model contain two kinds of explanatory variables (regressors). Like the binomial model it includes K two-dimensional regressors, $\boldsymbol{x}_{it}=(x_{1it},\dots,x_{Kit})$ for individual, period (i,t), *common to all alternatives*, and L alternative- and individual-specific regressors, for alternative j, individual i, $\boldsymbol{z}_{ji}=(z_{j1i},\dots,z_{jLi})$. For each individual a latent effect is attached to each alternative, collected in the random vector $\boldsymbol{\alpha}_i=(\alpha_{1i},\dots,\alpha_{Ji})$. While $\boldsymbol{x}_{it}$ has alternative-specific coefficient vectors, $\boldsymbol{\beta}_j=(\beta_{j1},\dots,\beta_{jK})'$, $\boldsymbol{z}_{ji}$ has alternative-invariant coefficients, the vector $\boldsymbol{\gamma}=(\gamma_1,\dots,\gamma_L)'$. We assume that $\boldsymbol{\alpha}_i$, conditional on all $\boldsymbol{x}_{it}$ and all $\boldsymbol{z}_{ji}$, has density $g(\boldsymbol{\alpha}_i,\boldsymbol{\lambda})$, which is the $(J-1)$-dimensional multivariate generalization of $g(\alpha_i,\boldsymbol{\lambda})$. For convenience, we introduce

$$V_{jit}(\boldsymbol{\alpha}_i)=\boldsymbol{z}_{ji}\boldsymbol{\gamma}+\boldsymbol{x}_{it}\boldsymbol{\beta}_j+\alpha_{ji},\ j=1,\dots,J;\, i=1,\dots,N;\, t=1,\dots,T, \tag{9.37}$$

interpreted as a function of the full vector $\boldsymbol{\alpha}_i$ (see below).[18]

This description is modified slightly, by taking $j=1$ as the *base alternative*, and measuring alternative-specific variables and coefficients from those in the base alternative. This reflects that for any (i,t), one alternative among the J is realized,[19] and formalized by

$$z_{1i}=0_{L,1},\ \beta_{1k}=0,\ \alpha_{1i}=0 \implies V_{1it}(\boldsymbol{\alpha}_i)=0,\ k=1,\dots,K;\ i=1,\dots,N,$$

which imply

$$V_{jit}(\boldsymbol{\alpha}_i)-V_{rit}(\boldsymbol{\alpha}_i)=(\boldsymbol{z}_{ji}-\boldsymbol{z}_{ri})\boldsymbol{\gamma}+\boldsymbol{x}_{it}(\boldsymbol{\beta}_j-\boldsymbol{\beta}_r)+\alpha_{ji}-\alpha_{ri},\ j,r=2,\dots,J.$$

Letting

$$p_{jit}=P(\text{alternative } j \text{ is realized in observation } (i,t)),$$

the multinomial response probabilities conditional on $\boldsymbol{\alpha}_i$ can be written as

$$p_{jit}=p_{jit}(\boldsymbol{\alpha}_i)=\frac{e^{V_{jit}}}{1+\sum_{k=2}^{J}e^{V_{kit}(\boldsymbol{\alpha}_i)}}=\frac{e^{\boldsymbol{z}_{ji}\boldsymbol{\gamma}+\boldsymbol{x}_{it}\boldsymbol{\beta}_j+\alpha_{ji}}}{1+\sum_{k=2}^{J}e^{\boldsymbol{z}_{ki}\boldsymbol{\gamma}+\boldsymbol{x}_{it}\boldsymbol{\beta}_k+\alpha_{ki}}},$$
$$i=1,\dots,N;\ t=1,\dots,T;\ j=1,\dots,J. \tag{9.38}$$

[18] Its counterpart in the binomial model, (9.20) or (9.31), is $V_{it}(\alpha_i)=\boldsymbol{x}_{it}\boldsymbol{\beta}+\alpha_i$.
[19] The binomial model has non-response as base alternative.

In the binomial case ($J=2$), p_{it} and $1-p_{it}$ correspond to p_{2it} and p_{1it}. This generalization of (9.32) implies that the probability that, in observation (i,t), j is realized given that either j or r is realized (conditional on $\boldsymbol{\alpha}_i$), is

$$\frac{p_{jit}(\boldsymbol{\alpha}_i)}{p_{jit}(\boldsymbol{\alpha}_i)+p_{rit}(\boldsymbol{\alpha}_i)} = \frac{1}{1+e^{V_{jit}(\boldsymbol{\alpha}_i)-V_{rit}(\boldsymbol{\alpha}_i)}},$$

and that the *log-odds ratio (conditional on $\boldsymbol{\alpha}_i$) between alternatives* (j,r) is

$$\ln\left[\frac{p_{jit}(\boldsymbol{\alpha}_i)}{p_{rit}(\boldsymbol{\alpha}_i)}\right] = V_{jit}(\boldsymbol{\alpha}_i)-V_{rit}(\boldsymbol{\alpha}_i) = (z_{ji}-z_{ri})\boldsymbol{\gamma} + \boldsymbol{x}_{it}(\boldsymbol{\beta}_j-\boldsymbol{\beta}_r)+\alpha_{ji}-\alpha_{ri}.$$

Neither of these expressions involve V_{kit} for $k \neq j,r$.

Important properties of this system of conditional probabilities and log-odds ratios are therefore: (a) variables belonging to the γ-coefficient vector are z-differences between alternatives j and r; (b) coefficients belonging to $\boldsymbol{x}$-variables are $\boldsymbol{\beta}$-differences between alternatives j and r; and (c) attributes of alternatives other than (j,r) are irrelevant for the choice between these two alternatives; confer the last two expressions. Property (c), labelled *Independence of Irrelevant Alternatives (IIA)*, is in several contexts unrealistic and is often considered a severe limitation of the logit-parameterization.

The multinomial logit model and generalizations of it are often used to represent *individual probabilistic choice* in a utility-related setting. Relying on this interpretation is not necessary, however, as the 'responses' may be, e.g., diseases, outcomes of medical treatment, or outcomes of traffic accidents. When sticking to a *utility-based interpretation*, response probabilities of multinomial logit form follow when three assumptions are satisfied. (1) Individual i is in period t imagined to choose the alternative among the J available which gives the largest utility. (2) The random utility is for alternative j, observation (i,t) represented by, see (9.37),

$$V_{jit}(\boldsymbol{\alpha}_i)+u_{jit}=z_{ji}\boldsymbol{\gamma}+\boldsymbol{x}_{it}\boldsymbol{\beta}_j+\alpha_{ji}+u_{jit},$$
$$j=1,\dots,J;\ i=1,\dots,N;\ t=1,\dots,T,$$

where u_{jit} is a random component in the utility, with zero expectation, and $V_{jit}(\boldsymbol{\alpha}_i)$ is the *expected utility* obtained by choosing alternative j, conditional on z_{ji}, $\boldsymbol{x}_{it}$, and α_{ji}. (3) All u_{jit} are independent and follow *the same* simple *extreme value distribution*.[20]

[20] The detailed proof is omitted. It can be found at several places, e.g., in Cameron and Trivedi (2005, Sections 15.5.1 and 15.5.2).

The normalizations which lead to $V_{1it}(\boldsymbol{\alpha}_i)=0$ reflect that for all (i,t), the expected utility in the base alternative ($j=1$) is taken as benchmark for the utility level when compared with the other alternatives.

Multinomial probit does not have the limitation denoted as IIA. This may be considered an attraction and follows because the model is based on stochastic utilities modelled by the multivariate *normal* distribution, which does not, in general, assume a diagonal covariance matrix of the stochastic elements. It therefore has more parameters. However, implementing the above assumptions (1) and (2) in the likelihood function for ML-estimation may raise numerical problems, *inter alia*, related to numerical evaluation of multiple integrals, and may be time-consuming. In many applications, *inter alia*, in transportation research, it is, however, used, and practical techniques for implementing and estimating the model have been proposed, see, e.g., Bolduc (1999).

Mixed logit, a model class more general than the standard logit, gives another way of dispensing with the IIA implication, without requiring so heavy computer work as multinomial probit. Its idea is, loosely expressed, that the logit parameter vectors $\boldsymbol{\beta}$ and $\boldsymbol{\gamma}$ are replaced by *stochastic individual-specific parameters*, $\boldsymbol{\beta}_i$ and $\boldsymbol{\gamma}_i$, generated by (parametric or non-parametric) distributions, and *estimation performed by simulation*; see, e.g., Train (2009, Chapter 6). Simulation is, on the whole, a very useful device to save computer time in estimation for models with limited dependent variables. Other solutions are given by GLLAMMs (Generalized Linear Latent and Mixed Models) model class, by means of which we can handle, *inter alia*, nested multilevel models and several generalizations for both panel data and cross-section data; see Skrondal and Rabe-Hesketh (2004), Rabe-Hesketh, Skrondal, and Pickles (2005), and Rabe-Hesketh and Skrondal (2006). Needless to say, the (numerical) multidimensional integration involved may require substantial computer time.

9.4.2 LIKELIHOOD FUNCTION AND ML ESTIMATION

The set of binary variables involved in the likelihood function of the multinomial logit is defined by

$$y_{jit}=1\{\text{alternative } j \text{ is realized in observation } (i,t)\}. \tag{9.39}$$

There is one such variable for each alternative, individual and period, in total JNT variables. The assumption that there is one possible response for each (i,t) implies $\prod_{j=1}^{J}y_{jit}=0$ and $\sum_{j=1}^{J}y_{jit}=1\ \forall i\,\&\,t$. The element of the *conditional* likelihood function which belongs to observation (i,t), respectively, to individual i, conditional on $\boldsymbol{\alpha}_i$, generalizing (9.33)–(9.34), can be written as

$$\mathcal{L}_{it}(\boldsymbol{\alpha}_i) = p_{1it}(\boldsymbol{\alpha}_i)^{y_{1it}} p_{2it}(\boldsymbol{\alpha}_i)^{y_{2it}} \cdots p_{Jit}(\boldsymbol{\alpha}_i)^{y_{Jit}}, \tag{9.40}$$

$$\mathcal{L}_i(\boldsymbol{\alpha}_i) = \prod_{t=1}^{T} \mathcal{L}_{it}(\boldsymbol{\alpha}_i). \tag{9.41}$$

The part of the *marginal* likelihood function that belongs to individual i is obtained by multiplying $\mathcal{L}_i(\boldsymbol{\alpha}_i)$ by the joint density $g(\boldsymbol{\alpha}_i, \boldsymbol{\lambda})$ and integrating over $\boldsymbol{\alpha}_i$, which gives ($\int_{\boldsymbol{\alpha}_i}$ symbolizing this $(J-1)$-dimensional integration)

$$\begin{aligned}\mathcal{L}_i &= \int_{\boldsymbol{\alpha}_i} \mathcal{L}_i(\boldsymbol{\alpha}_i) g(\boldsymbol{\alpha}_i, \boldsymbol{\lambda}) d\boldsymbol{\alpha}_i \\ &= \int_{\boldsymbol{\alpha}_i} \prod_{t=1}^{T} p_{1it}(\boldsymbol{\alpha}_i)^{y_{1it}} \cdots p_{Jit}(\boldsymbol{\alpha}_i)^{y_{Jit}} g(\boldsymbol{\alpha}_i, \boldsymbol{\lambda}) d\boldsymbol{\alpha}_i. \end{aligned} \tag{9.42}$$

Then the full (marginal) likelihood function emerges as their product, since the individuals are independently observed:

$$\mathcal{L} \equiv \prod_{i=1}^{N} \mathcal{L}_i = \prod_{i=1}^{N} \int_{\boldsymbol{\alpha}_i} \prod_{t=1}^{T} p_{1it}(\boldsymbol{\alpha}_i)^{y_{1it}} \cdots p_{Jit}(\boldsymbol{\alpha}_i)^{y_{Jit}} g(\boldsymbol{\alpha}_i, \boldsymbol{\lambda}) d\boldsymbol{\alpha}_i. \tag{9.43}$$

This is the multinomial counterpart to (9.36) and leads to the full ML problem: maximize $\mathcal{L}$, or $\ln(\mathcal{L})$, with respect to $\boldsymbol{\beta}_1, \ldots, \boldsymbol{\beta}_J, \boldsymbol{\gamma}, \boldsymbol{\lambda}$. If the solution exists and is unique, it defines the (marginal) ML estimators of these parameters.

9.4.3 ML ESTIMATION CONDITIONAL ON THE INDIVIDUAL EFFECTS

We end with a brief description of the ML problem conditional on the individual effects $\boldsymbol{\alpha}_i$ and the problems such a fixed effects approach would create. The conditional ML-problem is now to maximize, with respect to $\boldsymbol{\beta}_1, \ldots, \boldsymbol{\beta}_J, \boldsymbol{\gamma}, \boldsymbol{\alpha}$, $\ln[\mathcal{L}(\boldsymbol{\alpha})] = \sum_{i=1}^{N} \ln[\mathcal{L}_i(\boldsymbol{\alpha}_i)]$. In Appendix 9B it is shown that

$$\frac{\partial \ln[\mathcal{L}_i(\boldsymbol{\alpha}_i)]}{\partial \boldsymbol{\beta}_k} = \sum_{t=1}^{T} \left(y_{kit} - \frac{e^{z_{ki}\gamma} + {}^{x_{it}\beta_k} + {}^{\alpha_{ki}}}{1 + \sum_{j=2}^{J} e^{z_{ki}\gamma + x_{it}\beta_j + \alpha_{ji}}} \right) \boldsymbol{x}_{it},$$

$$\frac{\partial \ln[\mathcal{L}_i(\boldsymbol{\alpha}_i)]}{\partial \boldsymbol{\gamma}} = \sum_{t=1}^{T} \sum_{k=1}^{J} \left(y_{kit} - \frac{e^{z_{ki}\gamma} + {}^{x_{it}\beta_k} + {}^{\alpha_{ki}}}{1 + \sum_{j=2}^{J} e^{z_{ki}\gamma + x_{it}\beta_j + \alpha_{ji}}} \right) z_{ki},$$

$$\frac{\partial \ln[\mathcal{L}_i(\boldsymbol{\alpha}_i)]}{\partial \boldsymbol{\alpha}_i} = \sum_{t=1}^{T}\sum_{k=1}^{J}\left(y_{kit} - \frac{e^{z_{ki}\gamma + x_{it}\beta_k + \alpha_{ki}}}{1+\sum_{j=2}^{J} e^{z_{ki}\gamma + x_{it}\beta_j + \alpha_{ji}}}\right),$$

from which it follows that the first-order conditions are, see Appendix 9B, (9B.6)–(9B.8),

$$\sum_{i=1}^{N}\sum_{t=1}^{T}\left[y_{kit} - \frac{e^{z_{ki}\gamma + x_{it}\beta_k + \alpha_{ki}}}{1+\sum_{j=2}^{J} e^{z_{ki}\gamma + x_{it}\beta_j + \alpha_{ji}}}\right]\boldsymbol{x}_{it} = \boldsymbol{0},\ k=2,\dots,J, \tag{9.44}$$

$$\sum_{i=1}^{N}\sum_{t=1}^{T}\sum_{k=1}^{J}\left[y_{kit} - \frac{e^{z_{ki}\gamma + x_{it}\beta_k + \alpha_{ki}}}{1+\sum_{j=2}^{J} e^{z_{ki}\gamma + x_{it}\beta_j + \alpha_{ji}}}\right]\boldsymbol{z}_{ki} = \boldsymbol{0}, \tag{9.45}$$

$$\sum_{t=1}^{T}\sum_{k=1}^{J}\left[y_{kit} - \frac{e^{z_{ki}\gamma + x_{it}\beta_k + \alpha_{ki}}}{1+\sum_{j=2}^{J} e^{z_{ki}\gamma + x_{it}\beta_j + \alpha_{ji}}}\right] = 0,\ i=1,\dots,N. \tag{9.46}$$

However, these equations are *not independent* when $J > 2$, because satisfaction of (9.46) implies satisfaction of (9.45) for any z_{ki}. Therefore, specifying a full set of alternative-individual-specific α_{ji}s will not work in ML estimation conditional on the α_{ji}s. The situation resembles that in single-equation (and multi-equation) linear regression analysis when fixed individual-specific effects are combined with individual-specific regressors; see Section 5.3. To obtain a solution, the (fixed) latent heterogeneity will have to be restricted in some way, e.g., by setting some of the α_{ji}s equal or equal to zero, by removing the time-invariant explanatory variables, or by imposing more general linear restrictions. This will break the dependence of (9.45) on (9.46).[21] Moreover, since the number of α_{ji}s increases with N, an incidental parameter problem is likely to arise when T is finite; see the discussion of the similar limitation of the binomial model in Section 9.2.2.

Appendix 9A. **The general binomial model: ML estimation**

In this Appendix, related to Section 9.2.1, the algebra for ML estimation of a binomial discrete choice model with unspecified distribution of the disturbances, is elaborated.

[21] Such restrictions may also simplify the unconditional ML problem in Section 9.4.2 and speed up the computation, as the dimension of the numerical integration required will be reduced.

From (9.4) and (9.7), since $\partial(\boldsymbol{x}_{it}\boldsymbol{\beta})/\partial\beta_k = x_{kit}$, it follows that

$$\frac{\partial \ln(\mathcal{L})}{\partial\beta_k} = \sum_{i=1}^{N}\sum_{t=1}^{T}\left[y_{it}\frac{\partial \ln[F(\boldsymbol{x}_{it}\boldsymbol{\beta})]}{\partial(\boldsymbol{x}_{it}\boldsymbol{\beta})} + (1-y_{it})\frac{\partial \ln[1-F(\boldsymbol{x}_{it}\boldsymbol{\beta})]}{\partial(\boldsymbol{x}_{it}\boldsymbol{\beta})}\right]x_{kit}, \tag{9A.1}$$

$$\frac{\partial^2 \ln(\mathcal{L})}{\partial\beta_k\partial\beta_r} = \sum_{i=1}^{N}\sum_{t=1}^{T}\left[y_{it}\frac{\partial^2 \ln[F(\boldsymbol{x}_{it}\boldsymbol{\beta})]}{\partial(\boldsymbol{x}_{it}\boldsymbol{\beta})^2} + (1-y_{it})\frac{\partial^2 \ln[1-F(\boldsymbol{x}_{it}\boldsymbol{\beta})]}{\partial(\boldsymbol{x}_{it}\boldsymbol{\beta})^2}\right]x_{kit}x_{rit}, \tag{9A.2}$$

Since $F'(\boldsymbol{x}_{it}\boldsymbol{\beta}) = f(\boldsymbol{x}_{it}\boldsymbol{\beta})$, we have

$$\frac{\partial \ln[F(\boldsymbol{x}_{it}\boldsymbol{\beta})]}{\partial(\boldsymbol{x}_{it}\boldsymbol{\beta})} = \frac{f(\boldsymbol{x}_{it}\boldsymbol{\beta})}{F(\boldsymbol{x}_{it}\boldsymbol{\beta})}, \tag{9A.3}$$

$$\frac{\partial \ln[1-F(\boldsymbol{x}_{it}\boldsymbol{\beta})]}{\partial(\boldsymbol{x}_{it}\boldsymbol{\beta})} = -\frac{f(\boldsymbol{x}_{it}\boldsymbol{\beta})}{1-F(\boldsymbol{x}_{it}\boldsymbol{\beta})}, \tag{9A.4}$$

$$\frac{\partial^2 \ln[F(\boldsymbol{x}_{it}\boldsymbol{\beta})]}{\partial(\boldsymbol{x}_{it}\boldsymbol{\beta})^2} = \frac{F(\boldsymbol{x}_{it}\boldsymbol{\beta})f'(\boldsymbol{x}_{it}\boldsymbol{\beta}) - [f(\boldsymbol{x}_{it}\boldsymbol{\beta})]^2}{[F(\boldsymbol{x}_{it}\boldsymbol{\beta})]^2}, \tag{9A.5}$$

$$\frac{\partial^2 \ln[1-F(\boldsymbol{x}_{it}\boldsymbol{\beta})]}{\partial(\boldsymbol{x}_{it}\boldsymbol{\beta})^2} = -\frac{[1-F(\boldsymbol{x}_{it}\boldsymbol{\beta})]f'(\boldsymbol{x}_{it}\boldsymbol{\beta}) + [f(\boldsymbol{x}_{it}\boldsymbol{\beta})]^2}{[1-F(\boldsymbol{x}_{it}\boldsymbol{\beta})]^2}, \tag{9A.6}$$

which when inserted in (9A.1)–(9A.2) leads to

$$\begin{aligned}\frac{\partial \ln(\mathcal{L})}{\partial\beta_k} &= \sum_{i=1}^{N}\sum_{t=1}^{T}\left[\frac{y_{it}}{F(\boldsymbol{x}_{it}\boldsymbol{\beta})} - \frac{1-y_{it}}{1-F(\boldsymbol{x}_{it}\boldsymbol{\beta})}\right]f(\boldsymbol{x}_{it}\boldsymbol{\beta})x_{kit}\\ &= \sum_{i=1}^{N}\sum_{t=1}^{T}\left[\frac{y_{it}-F(\boldsymbol{x}_{it}\boldsymbol{\beta})}{1-F(\boldsymbol{x}_{it}\boldsymbol{\beta})}\right]\left[\frac{f(\boldsymbol{x}_{it}\boldsymbol{\beta})}{F(\boldsymbol{x}_{it}\boldsymbol{\beta})}\right]x_{kit},\end{aligned} \tag{9A.7}$$

$$\begin{aligned}\frac{\partial^2 \ln(\mathcal{L})}{\partial\beta_k\partial\beta_r} &= \sum_{i=1}^{N}\sum_{t=1}^{T}\Bigg[y_{it}\frac{F(\boldsymbol{x}_{it}\boldsymbol{\beta})f'(\boldsymbol{x}_{it}\boldsymbol{\beta}) - [f(\boldsymbol{x}_{it}\boldsymbol{\beta})]^2}{[F(\boldsymbol{x}_{it}\boldsymbol{\beta})]^2}\\ &\quad - (1-y_{it})\frac{[1-F(\boldsymbol{x}_{it}\boldsymbol{\beta})]f'(\boldsymbol{x}_{it}\boldsymbol{\beta}) + [f(\boldsymbol{x}_{it}\boldsymbol{\beta})]^2}{[1-F(\boldsymbol{x}_{it}\boldsymbol{\beta})]^2}\Bigg]x_{kit}x_{rit}\\ &= \sum_{i=1}^{N}\sum_{t=1}^{T}\Bigg[\left(-\frac{y_{it}}{[F(\boldsymbol{x}_{it}\boldsymbol{\beta})]^2} + \frac{1-y_{it}}{[1-F(\boldsymbol{x}_{it}\boldsymbol{\beta})]^2}\right)[f(\boldsymbol{x}_{it}\boldsymbol{\beta})]^2\\ &\quad + \left(\frac{y_{it}}{F(\boldsymbol{x}_{it}\boldsymbol{\beta})} - \frac{1-y_{it}}{1-F(\boldsymbol{x}_{it}\boldsymbol{\beta})}\right)f'(\boldsymbol{x}_{it}\boldsymbol{\beta})\Bigg]x_{kit}x_{rit}.\end{aligned} \tag{9A.8}$$

It follows from (9A.8), since (9.4) implies $\mathsf{E}(y_{it}|X) = F(\boldsymbol{x}_{it}\boldsymbol{\beta})$, that

$$-\mathsf{E}\left[\frac{\partial^2 \ln(\mathcal{L})}{\partial\beta_k\partial\beta_r}\bigg|X\right] = \sum_{i=1}^{N}\sum_{t=1}^{T}\left[\frac{[f(\boldsymbol{x}_{it}\boldsymbol{\beta})]^2}{F(\boldsymbol{x}_{it}\boldsymbol{\beta})[1-F(\boldsymbol{x}_{it}\boldsymbol{\beta})]}\right]x_{kit}x_{rit}. \tag{9A.9}$$

Appendix 9B. **The multinomial logit model: Conditional ML estimation**

This appendix gives details for the first-order conditions for the ML problem for the multinomial logit model when conditioning on the individual- and alternative-specific effects, resembling a fixed effects version of the model. It follows from (9.38) and (9.41) that

$$\frac{\partial \ln[\mathcal{L}_i(\boldsymbol{\alpha}_i)]}{\partial V_{kit}(\boldsymbol{\alpha}_i)} = \sum_{t=1}^{T}\sum_{j=1}^{J} y_{jit}\frac{\partial \ln(p_{jit})}{\partial V_{kit}(\boldsymbol{\alpha}_i)}. \tag{9B.1}$$

From (9.38), δ_{jk} still denoting Kronecker-deltas, we have

$$\frac{\partial \ln[p_{jit}(\boldsymbol{\alpha}_i)]}{\partial V_{kit}(\boldsymbol{\alpha}_i)} = \delta_{kj} - p_{kit}(\boldsymbol{\alpha}_i).$$

Therefore, because $\sum_{j=1}^{J} y_{jit} = 1 \Longrightarrow \sum_{j=1}^{J} y_{jit}[\delta_{kj} - p_{kit}(\boldsymbol{\alpha}_i)] \equiv y_{kit} - p_{kit}(\boldsymbol{\alpha}_i)$,

$$\sum_{i=1}^{N}\frac{\partial \ln[\mathcal{L}_i(\boldsymbol{\alpha}_i)]}{\partial V_{kit}(\boldsymbol{\alpha}_i)} = \sum_{i=1}^{N}\sum_{t=1}^{T}[y_{kit} - p_{kit}(\boldsymbol{\alpha}_i)]. \tag{9B.2}$$

Since, from (9.37),

$$\partial V_{jit}(\boldsymbol{\alpha}_i)/\partial \boldsymbol{\beta}_k = \boldsymbol{x}_{it}, \quad \partial V_{jit}(\boldsymbol{\alpha}_i)/\partial \boldsymbol{\gamma} = \boldsymbol{z}_{ji}, \quad \partial V_{jit}(\boldsymbol{\alpha}_i)/\partial \alpha_{ji} = 1,$$

we obtain, using (9B.1) and (9B.2) and the chain rule, that

$$\begin{aligned}\frac{\partial \ln[\mathcal{L}_i(\boldsymbol{\alpha}_i)]}{\partial \boldsymbol{\beta}_k} &= \frac{\partial \ln[\mathcal{L}_i(\boldsymbol{\alpha})]}{\partial V_{kit}(\boldsymbol{\alpha}_i)}\frac{\partial V_{kit}(\boldsymbol{\alpha}_i)}{\partial \boldsymbol{\beta}_k}\\ &= \sum_{i=1}^{N}\sum_{t=1}^{T}[y_{kit} - p_{kit}(\boldsymbol{\alpha}_i)]\boldsymbol{x}_{it},\end{aligned} \tag{9B.3}$$

$$\frac{\partial \ln[\mathcal{L}_i(\boldsymbol{\alpha}_i)]}{\partial \boldsymbol{\gamma}} = \sum_{k=1}^{J} \frac{\partial \ln[\mathcal{L}_i(\boldsymbol{\alpha}_i)]}{\partial V_{kit}(\boldsymbol{\alpha}_i)} \frac{\partial V_{kit}(\boldsymbol{\alpha}_i)}{\partial \boldsymbol{\gamma}}$$

$$= \sum_{i=1}^{N}\sum_{t=1}^{T}\sum_{k=1}^{J}[y_{kit} - p_{kit}(\boldsymbol{\alpha}_i)]z_{ki}, \tag{9B.4}$$

$$\frac{\partial \ln[\mathcal{L}_i(\boldsymbol{\alpha}_i)]}{\partial \boldsymbol{\alpha}_i} = \sum_{k=1}^{J} \frac{\partial \ln[\mathcal{L}(\boldsymbol{\alpha})]}{\partial V_{kit}(\boldsymbol{\alpha}_i)}$$

$$= \sum_{t=1}^{T}\sum_{k=1}^{J}[y_{kit} - p_{kit}(\boldsymbol{\alpha}_i)]. \tag{9B.5}$$

Hence, the first-order conditions for ML estimation conditional on $\boldsymbol{\alpha}$,

$$\sum_{i=1}^{N} \frac{\partial \ln[\mathcal{L}_i(\boldsymbol{\alpha}_i)]}{\partial \boldsymbol{\beta}_k} = 0, \qquad k = 2, \dots, J,$$

$$\sum_{i=1}^{N} \frac{\partial \ln[\mathcal{L}_i(\boldsymbol{\alpha}_i)]}{\partial \boldsymbol{\gamma}} = 0,$$

$$\frac{\partial \ln[\mathcal{L}_i(\boldsymbol{\alpha}_i)]}{\partial \boldsymbol{\alpha}_i} = 0, \qquad i = 1, \dots, N,$$

lead to

$$\sum_{i=1}^{N}\sum_{t=1}^{T}\left(y_{kit} - \frac{e^{z_{ki}\gamma} + {}^{x_{it}\beta_k} + \alpha_{ki}}{1+\sum_{j=2}^{J} e^{z_{ki}\gamma + x_{it}\beta_j + \alpha_{ji}}}\right) x_{it} = 0, \;\; k = 2, \dots, J, \tag{9B.6}$$

$$\sum_{i=1}^{N}\sum_{t=1}^{T}\sum_{k=1}^{J}\left(y_{kit} - \frac{e^{z_{ki}\gamma} + {}^{x_{it}\beta_k} + \alpha_{ki}}{1+\sum_{j=2}^{J} e^{z_{ki}\gamma + x_{it}\beta_j + \alpha_{ji}}}\right) z_{ki} = 0, \tag{9B.7}$$

$$\sum_{t=1}^{T}\sum_{k=1}^{J}\left(y_{kit} - \frac{e^{z_{ki}\gamma} + {}^{x_{it}\beta_k} + \alpha_{ki}}{1+\sum_{j=2}^{J} e^{z_{ki}\gamma + x_{it}\beta_j + \alpha_{ji}}}\right) = 0, \;\; i = 1, \dots, N. \tag{9B.8}$$

10 Unbalanced panel data

CHAPTER SUMMARY

This chapter extends models and procedures discussed in Chapters 2 and 3 to handle unbalanced panel data. Typologies of data and types of unbalance and models are discussed. Since the nature of the unbalance may affect the preferred procedures, attention is given to the required modifications of the within, between, GLS, and OLS estimators and to the relationships between them. Two kinds of between estimators and three kinds of weighted global means are involved. Procedures for estimation of the disturbance variance components and joint ML estimation of coefficients and variance components are discussed. Empirical illustrations are given.

10.1 Introduction

Quite often panel data researchers do not have time-series of equal length for all individuals. Such a data set is said to be *unbalanced*, or *incomplete*, the data types considered earlier being denoted as balanced or complete. We would have been badly situated if panel data econometrics were confined to balanced (complete) data sets and existing software could handle such data only. Fortunately, this is not the case.

How could a data set arise where *not the same individuals, or units, are observed in all periods considered*? One answer may be that unbalanced panel data occur *unintentionally*. The data-collector may want to obtain a balanced data set, but is unable to do so because observations are unavailable for some or all variables for some individuals in certain periods. There may be exits from and entries to a survey, firms may disappear due to bankruptcies, households may be dissolved, etc. We could consider sets of unbalanced panel data as a (hypothetically) balanced data set with *missing observations*.[1]

An important category of unbalanced panel data is *rotating panel data*. It is panel data obtained from *sample surveys*, where the sample of units changes over time in a systematic way which is part of the sample design. Here the non-balance is *intended*. The data-collector chooses to replace, for example, a fixed share, say 20 per cent, of the respondents in one wave (vintage) with a fresh sample of units next year, so that no unit is observed in more than a given number of periods (in the cited example five) and some in fewer years.

[1] Methods for statistical analysis with missing observations, although not specifically in panel data contexts, are discussed in Little and Rubin (1987). Unbalanced panel data, primarily in analysis of variance (ANOVA) situations, is a main topic in Searle (1987).

Such a sample is said to *rotate*. There may be pragmatic reasons why a data collector may prefer rotating designs to balanced ones. One reason may be the desire to avoid imposing large burdens on the respondents in the hope of reducing non-response in cases with voluntary participation.[2]

Unbalanced panel data may also follow from *endogenous selection*. This means that the selection of observation units in different periods is entirely or partly determined by variables we want to explain. This may give rise to inconsistent coefficient estimates and biased test procedures if they are not given due attention. Selection problems of this kind may also occur in cross-section data.[3] In case of endogenous selection, both the sampling process and the values of the endogenous variables can be said to be determined from a common set of exogenous factors. One example can be investigations of individuals' employment histories. If we want to use panel data to quantify factors which determine individuals' choice of employment and only observations from individuals who are employed in the actual years, a typical case with endogenous selection occurs. Another example is exploring the determinants of purchases of alcoholic beverages from household budget survey data. If the rate of non-response is higher for individuals and in periods with relatively large consumption of alcohol than for individuals and in periods with less such consumption or nothing at all, endogenous selection occurs. A substantial literature on this exists, related to cross-section data and to panel data. This problem is not addressed in the present chapter. Some aspects, partly related to modeling and partly related to estimation to avoid biased interference, will be discussed in Chapter 11. See also Verbeek and Nijman (1996).

What can be done if a data set is unbalanced and this is not due to endogenous selection? First, we can *delete individuals (or periods)* to make the panel balanced. We then, however, run the risk of discarding a lot of observations, loose important data information, and reduce the estimation precision obtainable. Second, we can treat unbalanced data sets as a case with *missing observations* and attempt to reconstruct (impute) the observations missing from those available in some way, to obtain full-length time-series for all individuals; see Little and Rubin (1987, Section 4.5). Third, we can *modify methods constructed for balanced panel data* to make them applicable to unbalanced data, for example, revise the within, between, GLS, and ML estimators. We in this chapter, which to some extent generalizes Chapters 2 and 3, pursue the third strategy. For simplicity, we consider only static regression equations without measurement errors and with strictly exogenous regressors only. Period-specific unobserved heterogeneity will not be treated explicitly. Throughout, the latent (individual-specific) heterogeneity is assumed to be uncorrelated with the regressors.[4]

[2] Questions related to *optimal rotation designs* in such contexts are discussed in Biørn (1985) and Nijman, Verbeek, and van Soest (1991).

[3] On the distinction between 'ignorable' and 'non-ignorable' selection, see, e.g., Little and Rubin (1987, Sections 1.3–1.6) and Chapter 11.

[4] Deleting incomplete observation records in order to make a panel data set with gaps balanced will often involve an efficiency loss in coefficient estimation because of the reduced number of degrees of freedom.

The rest of the chapter proceeds as follows. In Section 10.2 we present the main single-equation model for unbalanced panel data and the notation needed. Section 10.3 considers a model version where heterogeneity as fixed individual-specific effects occurs. Within-individual and between-individual estimation are reconsidered. Section 10.4 considers the related model with heterogeneity as random effects. As in the balanced case, GLS is a primary estimation method, and its relationship to the within- and between-individual estimators are reconsidered. We also discuss estimation of the variance components, and finally, in Section 10.5, the basic aspects of ML estimation.

10.2 **Basic model and notation**

We consider a regression equation with K regressors,

$$y_{it} = \alpha_i^* + \boldsymbol{x}_{it}\boldsymbol{\beta} + u_{it}, \qquad (u_{it}|X) \sim \mathsf{IID}(0, \sigma^2), \tag{10.1}$$

where α_i^* is an individual-specific (non-stochastic or stochastic) effect; $\boldsymbol{\beta}$ and $\boldsymbol{x}_{it}$ are, respectively, $(K \times 1)$ and $(1 \times K)$ vectors; and $\boldsymbol{X}$, as before, denotes all values of $\boldsymbol{x}_{it}$ (see Section 10.3.1 for a precise definition). So far the ranges of i and t are unspecified. They will define which type of unbalanced panel data exists.

10.2.1 FORMALIZATION OF THE NON-BALANCE

To simplify the model description we let the individuals and periods from which observations are available be represented by index sets, in that

$$\begin{aligned} I_t &= \text{Index set of individuals observed in period } t, & t &= 1, \ldots, T, \\ P_i &= \text{Index set of periods where individual } i \text{ is observed}, & i &= 1, \ldots, N, \end{aligned}$$

where T is the number of periods with *at least one* individual observed and N is the number of individuals observed in *at least one* period. Then the (i, t)-combinations in the data set can be characterized by either the index sets $I_1, \ldots, I_T$ or the index sets $P_1, \ldots, P_N$. This general description may cover any type of panel data. A balanced panel data set follows when

$$I_t = [1, \ldots, N], \quad t = 1, \ldots, T \iff P_i = [1, \ldots, T], \quad i = 1, \ldots, N.$$

However, this is not necessarily the case if some parameters, say variance components in a random effects model, are estimated with non-negligible finite sample bias. FGLS estimators based on the full unbalanced data set may be inferior to the corresponding estimators based on the 'curtailed' balanced data set, a problem discussed and illustrated through Monte Carlo simulations by Mátyás and Lovrics (1991).

Then, for any panel data set we have

$$\begin{aligned} I_1 \cup I_2 \cup \cdots \cup I_T &= [1,\ldots,N], \\ P_1 \cup P_2 \cup \cdots \cup P_N &= [1,\ldots,T], \end{aligned}$$

$$\begin{aligned} I_t \cap I_s &\neq \emptyset \text{ for at least one } t \neq s, \\ P_i \cap P_j &\neq \emptyset \text{ for at least one } i \neq j, \end{aligned}$$

while $I_1 \cap I_2 \cap \cdots \cap I_T$ and $P_1 \cap P_2 \cap \cdots \cap P_N$ may be empty sets, which means that no individual is observed in all periods, as in the example below. Data sets with non-overlapping cross-sections from different periods, useful for constructing pseudo-panel data (see Section 1.4), are characterized by

$$I_t \cap I_s \neq \emptyset \text{ for all } t \neq s.$$

Let $\boldsymbol{D}$ be the $(N \times T)$-matrix whose element (i,t) is the binary variable

$$d_{it} = \begin{cases} 1 \text{ if individual } i \text{ is observed in period } t, & i = 1,\ldots,N, \\ 0 \text{ if individual } i \text{ is not observed in period } t, & t = 1,\ldots,T. \end{cases} \tag{10.2}$$

This implies

$$N_t = \textstyle\sum_{i=1}^{N} d_{it} = \text{No. of individuals observed in period } t, \tag{10.3}$$

$$T_i = \textstyle\sum_{t=1}^{T} d_{it} = \text{No. of periods where individual } i \text{ is observed.} \tag{10.4}$$

Example: Let $N=6$, $T=4$ and assume

$$I_1 = \{1,2,4,6\},\ I_2 = \{2,3,6\},\ I_3 = \{1,3,5\},\ I_4 = \{1,2,3,5\},$$

equivalently,

$$P_1 = \{1,3,4\},\ P_2 = \{1,2,4\},\ P_3 = \{2,3,4\},\ P_4 = \{1\},\ P_5 = \{3,4\},\ P_6 = \{1,2\}.$$

Then,

$$\begin{aligned} (N_1,N_2,N_3,N_4) &= (4,3,3,4), \\ (T_1,T_2,T_3,T_4,T_5,T_6) &= (3,3,3,1,2,2), \end{aligned}$$

$$\begin{aligned} I_1 \cup I_2 \cup I_3 \cup I_4 &= \{1,2,3,4,5,6\}, & I_1 \cap I_2 \cap I_3 \cap I_4 &= \emptyset, \\ P_1 \cup P_2 \cup P_3 \cup P_4 \cup P_5 \cup P_6 &= \{1,2,3,4\}, & P_1 \cap P_2 \cap P_3 \cap P_4 \cap P_5 \cap P_6 &= \emptyset, \end{aligned}$$

and the (6×4) matrix of observation dummies is

$$D = \begin{bmatrix} 1 & 0 & 1 & 1 \\ 1 & 1 & 0 & 1 \\ 0 & 1 & 1 & 1 \\ 1 & 0 & 0 & 0 \\ 0 & 0 & 1 & 1 \\ 1 & 1 & 0 & 0 \end{bmatrix}.$$

10.2.2 INDIVIDUAL-SPECIFIC, PERIOD-SPECIFIC, AND GLOBAL MEANS

For unbalanced data, several types of means can be distinguished, the individual-specific and period-specific means being still the most important. We exemplify their definitions for y. The *individual-specific mean* of the observed y-values for individual i is

$$\bar{y}_{i\cdot} = \frac{\sum_{t=1}^{T} d_{it}y_{it}}{\sum_{t=1}^{T} d_{it}} \equiv \frac{\sum_{t=1}^{T} d_{it}y_{it}}{T_i} \equiv \frac{\sum_{t\in P_i} y_{it}}{T_i}, \qquad i = 1,\dots,N,$$

where the values of y_{it} for $t \notin P_i$ can be chosen freely, as they are multiplied by zero. Symmetrically, the *period-specific mean* for period t is

$$\bar{y}_{\cdot t} = \frac{\sum_{i=1}^{N} d_{it}y_{it}}{\sum_{i=1}^{N} d_{it}} \equiv \frac{\sum_{i=1}^{N} d_{it}y_{it}}{N_t} \equiv \frac{\sum_{i\in I_t} y_{it}}{N_t}, \qquad t = 1,\dots,T,$$

where the values of y_{it} for $i \notin I_t$ can be chosen freely. The *global mean* can be expressed alternatively as:

$$\bar{y} = \frac{\sum_{i=1}^{N}\sum_{t=1}^{T} d_{it}y_{it}}{\sum_{i=1}^{N}\sum_{t=1}^{T} d_{it}} \equiv \frac{\sum_{i=1}^{N} T_i\bar{y}_{i\cdot}}{\sum_{i=1}^{N} T_i} \equiv \frac{\sum_{t=1}^{T} N_t\bar{y}_{\cdot t}}{\sum_{t=1}^{T} N_t}. \tag{10.5}$$

Hence, it emerges as a *weighted mean* of the individual-specific, respectively, the period-specific means, with weights proportional to the number of times the individuals, respectively the periods, are included. In balanced situations ($T_i = T$ for all i, $N_t = N$ for all t) the corresponding means are non-weighted: $\bar{y} = \frac{1}{N}\sum_{i=1}^{N}\bar{y}_{i\cdot} = \frac{1}{T}\sum_{t=1}^{T}\bar{y}_{\cdot t}$, etc.

Referring to the distinction between endogenous (non-ignorable) and exogenous (ignorable) sample selection, see Section 11.1, the former may be viewed as corresponding to $\text{cov}(d_{it}, y_{it}) \neq 0$ and the latter to $\text{cov}(d_{it}, y_{it}) = 0$.

10.3 The fixed effects case

In this section, we treat $\alpha_1^*,\dots,\alpha_N^*$ in (10.1) as N unknown constants. We first discuss the one-regressor case (Sections 10.3.1–10.3.2) and next the general case (Sections 10.3.3–10.3.4).

10.3.1 THE ONE-REGRESSOR CASE

We assume $K=1$ and let x_{it} and β denote the regressor and its coefficient. The OLS problem is

$$\min_{\alpha_1^*,\dots,\alpha_N^*,\beta} \sum_{i=1}^N \sum_{t\in P_i}(y_{it}-\alpha_i^*-x_{it}\beta)^2,$$

where the sum of squares goes across all available observations. Letting in general

$$W_{ZQ}=\sum_{i=1}^N \sum_{t\in P_i}(z_{it}-\bar{z}_{i\cdot})(q_{it}-\bar{q}_{i\cdot}),$$

the first-order conditions lead to

$$\widehat{\beta}_W=\frac{W_{XY}}{W_{XX}}=\frac{\sum_{i=1}^N \sum_{t\in P_i}(x_{it}-\bar{x}_{i\cdot})(y_{it}-\bar{y}_{i\cdot})}{\sum_{i=1}^N \sum_{t\in P_i}(x_{it}-\bar{x}_{i\cdot})^2}, \tag{10.6}$$

$$\widehat{\alpha}_{iW}^*=\bar{y}_{i\cdot}-\bar{x}_{i\cdot}\widehat{\beta}_W, \qquad i=1,\dots,N. \tag{10.7}$$

Still $\widehat{\beta}_W$ is MVLUE and is denoted as the *within-individual estimator*.

Since inserting for y_{it} from (10.1) in (10.6) and (10.7) gives

$$\widehat{\beta}_W-\beta=\frac{W_{XU}}{W_{XX}}, \quad \widehat{\alpha}_{iW}^*-\alpha_i^*=\bar{u}_{i\cdot}-\bar{x}_{i\cdot}(\widehat{\beta}_W-\beta), \quad i=1,\dots,N,$$

and since $\mathrm{var}(W_{XU}|X)=\sigma^2 W_{XX}$, $\widehat{\beta}_W$ and $\widehat{\alpha}_{iW}^*$ are unbiased, with

$$\mathrm{var}(\widehat{\beta}_W|X)=\mathrm{var}\left(\frac{W_{XU}}{W_{XX}}|X\right)=\frac{\sigma^2}{W_{XX}}=\frac{\sigma^2}{\sum_{i=1}^N \sum_{t\in P_i}(x_{it}-\bar{x}_{i\cdot})^2}, \tag{10.8}$$

where, as before, X denotes all observations on x_{it}, i.e., in the present context,

$$X=\{x_{it}: i\in I_t, t=1,\dots,T\}\equiv\{x_{it}: t\in P_i, i=1,\dots,N\}.$$

The estimator $\widehat{\beta}_W$ only exploits the variation in x and y within individuals. The variation between individuals, represented by the variation in the individual-specific means, is spent in estimating the intercepts, as in the balanced case (Section 2.1.3). As always in classical OLS regression, an unbiased estimator of σ^2 is the sum of squares of residuals divided by the number of degrees of freedom:

$$\widehat{\sigma}^2 = \frac{1}{n-N-1} \sum_{i=1}^{N} \sum_{t \in P_i} (y_{it} - \widehat{\alpha}_i^* - x_{it}\widehat{\beta}_W)^2, \tag{10.9}$$

where $n = \sum_{i=1}^{N} T_i = \sum_{t=1}^{T} N_t$.

When applying an unbalanced panel data set, *the interpretation of the period index* is worth reflection. Three situations can be distinguished:

(a) All individuals belong to the panel from period 1 and are observed over a varying number of *contiguous* periods, i.e., the time-series contain *no gaps*. Individual i drops out after T_i periods, so that $P_i = [1, 2, \dots, T_i]$.

(b) Not all individuals are included in the data set from the start. Individual i is observed in T_i *successive* periods, for example $P_i = [\tau_i+1, \dots, \tau_i+T_i]$, where τ_i is the last period before the starting period for individual i.

(c) The T_i observations from at least one individual, i, are non-contiguous, but are dispersed over the T periods covered by the panel data set, i.e., the time-series, and hence the elements in P_i, have one or more gaps.

In (a), t represents both the calendar period and the observation number, while in (b) and (c), t is still the calendar period, but it differs from the observation number for some individuals. In (a) and (b), we have contiguous time-series for all individuals. *Rotating panel data are usually contiguous and belong to type (b).* In (c) gaps may occur in the individual-specific time-series.

If the model is static and contains no period-specific variables, there is no problem in reinterpreting (y_{it}, x_{it}) from being the values of (y, x) in period t for individual i to being the values *in the period where individual i gives observation no. t, regardless of whether the data set is of type (a), (b), or (c).* We then can write the observation index sets as

$$P_i = [1, 2, \dots, T_i], \qquad i = 1, \dots, N. \tag{10.10}$$

If, however, x_{it}, with t interpreted as the calendar period, represents *lagged values* of y_{it} or of some other variable[5] and we are in situations (b) or (c), complications arise. A notable complication also occurs if x_{it} represents a period-specific variable, because such a variable has a meaning different from an observation-number-specific variable if the individual time-series start in different periods. For example, a price index for the year

[5] In Chapter 8, balanced data sets were assumed throughout.

1990 may represent observation no. 10 for firm no. 2 and observation no. 5 for firm no. 9. *Period-specific variables may therefore appear as two-dimensional variables in the model* when t is given the interpretation as observation number and the situation is not as in case (a).

Assume that (10.10) holds, and let $\boldsymbol{y}_i, \boldsymbol{x}_i, \boldsymbol{u}_i$ be the $(T_i \times 1)$ vectors which contain the T_i successively numbered values of y_{it}, x_{it}, u_{it} for individual i:

$$\boldsymbol{y}_i = \begin{bmatrix} y_{i1} \\ \vdots \\ y_{i,T_i} \end{bmatrix}, \quad \boldsymbol{x}_i = \begin{bmatrix} x_{i1} \\ \vdots \\ x_{i,T_i} \end{bmatrix}, \quad \boldsymbol{u}_i = \begin{bmatrix} u_{i1} \\ \vdots \\ u_{i,T_i} \end{bmatrix}, \quad i = 1, \dots, N. \tag{10.11}$$

Since, in general, $\bar{q}_{i\cdot} = \frac{1}{T_i}\boldsymbol{e}'_{T_i}\boldsymbol{q}_i$, $\bar{z}_{i\cdot} = \frac{1}{T_i}\boldsymbol{e}'_{T_i}\boldsymbol{z}_i$, and $W_{ZQ} = \sum_{i=1}^{N} \boldsymbol{z}'_i \boldsymbol{B}_{T_i} \boldsymbol{q}_i$, (10.6)–(10.7) can be written as

$$\widehat{\beta}_W = \frac{\sum_{i=1}^{N} \boldsymbol{x}'_i \boldsymbol{B}_{T_i} \boldsymbol{y}_i}{\sum_{i=1}^{N} \boldsymbol{x}'_i \boldsymbol{B}_{T_i} \boldsymbol{x}_i}, \tag{10.12}$$

$$\widehat{\alpha}^*_{iW} = \tfrac{1}{T_i}\boldsymbol{e}'_{T_i}(\boldsymbol{y}_i - \boldsymbol{x}_i \widehat{\boldsymbol{\beta}}_W), \qquad i = 1, \dots, N. \tag{10.13}$$

10.3.2 BETWEEN- AND OLS-ESTIMATION IN THE ONE-REGRESSOR CASE

There are several ways of forming equations in individual-specific means. First, summing (10.1) over $t \in P_i$ and dividing by T_i, we get

$$\bar{y}_{i\cdot} = \alpha^*_i + \bar{x}_{i\cdot}\beta + \bar{u}_{i\cdot}, \quad \mathsf{E}(\bar{u}_{i\cdot}|X) = 0, \ \ \mathrm{var}(\bar{u}_{i\cdot}|X) = \tfrac{1}{T_i}\sigma^2, \tag{10.14}$$

where $\bar{u}_{i\cdot}$ is heteroskedastic, with a variance which is inversely proportional with T_i, because a different number of observations underlies the individual-specific means. This could be compensated through multiplication by $\sqrt{T_i}$, giving[6]

$$\sqrt{T_i}\bar{y}_{i\cdot} = \sqrt{T_i}\alpha^*_i + \sqrt{T_i}\bar{x}_{i\cdot}\beta + \sqrt{T_i}\bar{u}_{i\cdot}, \qquad \sqrt{T_i}\bar{u}_{i\cdot} \sim \mathsf{IID}(0, \sigma^2). \tag{10.15}$$

In the absence of individual-specific heterogeneity ($\alpha^*_i = \alpha$ for all i), we have

$$\bar{y}_{i\cdot} = \alpha + \bar{x}_{i\cdot}\beta + \bar{u}_{i\cdot}, \tag{10.16}$$

$$\sqrt{T_i}\bar{y}_{i\cdot} = \sqrt{T_i}\alpha + \sqrt{T_i}\bar{x}_{i\cdot}\beta + \sqrt{T_i}\bar{u}_{i\cdot}, \qquad i = 1, \dots, N. \tag{10.17}$$

[6] This corresponds to the transformation often recommended for regression analysis based on data for group means only, and exemplifying weighted regression.

Application of OLS on (10.16) and (10.17) defines *alternative between-individual estimators* for β and α, denoted as $(\widehat{\beta}_{B1}, \widehat{\alpha}_{B1})$ and $(\widehat{\beta}_{B2}, \widehat{\alpha}_{B2})$. The former application gives

$$\widehat{\beta}_{B1} = \frac{\sum_{i=1}^{N}(\bar{x}_{i\cdot} - \bar{\bar{x}})(\bar{y}_{i\cdot} - \bar{\bar{y}})}{\sum_{i=1}^{N}(\bar{x}_{i\cdot} - \bar{\bar{x}})^2}, \qquad \widehat{\alpha}_{B1} = \bar{\bar{y}} - \bar{\bar{x}}\widehat{\beta}_{B1}, \tag{10.18}$$

where $\bar{\bar{y}}$ and $\bar{\bar{x}}$ are global means formed as *non-weighted* means of the individual-specific means, i.e.,

$$\begin{aligned} \bar{\bar{y}} &= \tfrac{1}{N}\textstyle\sum_{i=1}^{N}\bar{y}_{i\cdot} = \tfrac{1}{n}\sum_{i=1}^{N}(\bar{T}/T_i)\sum_{t=1}^{T_i} y_{it}, \\ \bar{\bar{x}} &= \tfrac{1}{N}\textstyle\sum_{i=1}^{N}\bar{x}_{i\cdot} = \tfrac{1}{n}\sum_{i=1}^{N}(\bar{T}/T_i)\sum_{t=1}^{T_i} x_{it}, \end{aligned} \tag{10.19}$$

where $\bar{T} = \frac{1}{N}\sum_{i=1}^{N} T_i = n/N$ is the average number of observations per individual. Unlike in $\bar{y}$, defined by (10.5), the $n = \sum_i T_i$ observations have unequal weight in $\bar{\bar{y}}$, the weight of individual i being proportional to $\bar{T}/T_i$. The latter application gives, see Appendix 10A for details,

$$\widehat{\beta}_{B2} = \frac{\sum_i T_i\bar{x}_{i\cdot}\bar{y}_{i\cdot} - n\bar{x}\bar{y}}{\sum_i T_i\bar{x}_{i\cdot}^2 - n\bar{x}^2}, \quad \widehat{\alpha}_{B2} = \frac{(\sum_i T_i\bar{x}_{i\cdot}^2)\bar{y} - (\sum_i T_i\bar{x}_{i\cdot}\bar{y}_{i\cdot})\bar{x}}{\sum_i T_i\bar{x}_{i\cdot}^2 - n\bar{x}^2} \iff$$

$$\widehat{\beta}_{B2} = \frac{\sum_{i=1}^{N} T_i(\bar{x}_{i\cdot} - \bar{x})(\bar{y}_{i\cdot} - \bar{y})}{\sum_{i=1}^{N} T_i(\bar{x}_{i\cdot} - \bar{x})^2}, \qquad \widehat{\alpha}_{B2} = \bar{y} - \bar{x}\widehat{\beta}_{B2}. \tag{10.20}$$

The estimators (10.18) and (10.20) are equal for balanced data and differ for unbalanced panel data. Using the averaging matrix $\boldsymbol{A}_{T_i}$, $\widehat{\beta}_{B2}$ can be written as

$$\widehat{\beta}_{B2} = \frac{\sum_{i=1}^{N} \boldsymbol{x}_i'\boldsymbol{A}_{T_i}\boldsymbol{y}_i - n\bar{x}\bar{y}}{\sum_{i=1}^{N} \boldsymbol{x}_i'\boldsymbol{A}_{T_i}\boldsymbol{x}_i - n\bar{x}^2}. \tag{10.21}$$

More generally, we may attach weights $\boldsymbol{v} = (v_1, \dots, v_N)$ to the individual-specific means, giving a *generalized weighted global mean* of the form

$$\widetilde{q} = \widetilde{q}(\boldsymbol{v}) = \frac{\sum_{i=1}^{N} v_i\bar{q}_{i\cdot}}{\sum_{i=1}^{N} v_i}. \tag{10.22}$$

From (10.16) and (10.22) we obtain

$$\sqrt{v_i}(\bar{y}_{i\cdot} - \widetilde{y}) = \sqrt{v_i}(\bar{x}_{i\cdot} - \widetilde{x})\beta + \sqrt{v_i}(\bar{u}_{i\cdot} - \widetilde{u}), \quad i = 1, \dots, N. \tag{10.23}$$

Applying OLS on (10.23) gives

$$\widehat{\beta}_B(v) = \frac{\sum_{i=1}^N v_i(\bar{x}_{i\cdot} - \widetilde{x})(\bar{y}_{i\cdot} - \widetilde{y})}{\sum_{i=1}^N v_i(\bar{x}_{i\cdot} - \widetilde{x})^2}, \qquad \widehat{\alpha}_B(v) = \widetilde{y} - \widetilde{x}\widehat{\beta}_B(v), \tag{10.24}$$

and hence

$$\begin{aligned} \widehat{\beta}_{B1} &= \widehat{\beta}_B(1,\dots,1), & \widehat{\alpha}_{B1} &= \widehat{\alpha}_B(1,\dots,1), \\ \widehat{\beta}_{B2} &= \widehat{\beta}_B(T_1,\dots,T_N), & \widehat{\alpha}_{B2} &= \widehat{\alpha}_B(T_1,\dots,T_N). \end{aligned}$$

Is there some relationship between the OLS, the within-individual, and the between-individual estimators for the slope coefficient similar to that in the balanced case? The answer is yes if the latter is defined as $\widehat{\beta}_{B2}$. We can, still assuming (10.10), decompose the global (co)variation of any z and q as

$$\begin{aligned} G_{ZQ} &= \sum_{i=1}^N \sum_{t=1}^{T_i} (z_{it} - \bar{z})(q_{it} - \bar{q}) \equiv W_{ZQ} + B_{ZQ}, \\ W_{ZQ} &= \sum_{i=1}^N \sum_{t=1}^{T_i} (z_{it} - \bar{z}_{i\cdot})(q_{it} - \bar{q}_{i\cdot}) \equiv \sum_{i=1}^N z_i' B_{T_i} q_i, \\ B_{ZQ} &= \sum_{i=1}^N T_i(\bar{z}_{i\cdot} - \bar{z})(\bar{q}_{i\cdot} - \bar{q}) \equiv \sum_{i=1}^N z_i' A_{T_i} q_i - n\bar{z}\bar{q}. \end{aligned}$$

Then we can, using (10.12) and (10.20)–(10.21), express the OLS estimator of β as a weighted mean of $\widehat{\beta}_W$ and $\widehat{\beta}_{B2}$, with the within-individual and the between-individual variation in the xs as weights:

$$\begin{aligned} \widehat{\beta}_{OLS} &= \frac{G_{XY}}{G_{XX}} = \frac{\sum_{i=1}^N \sum_{t=1}^{T_i} (x_{it} - \bar{x})(y_{it} - \bar{y})}{\sum_{i=1}^N \sum_{t=1}^{T_i} (x_{it} - \bar{x})^2} = \frac{\sum_{i=1}^N \boldsymbol{x}_i' \boldsymbol{y}_i - n\bar{x}\bar{y}}{\sum_{i=1}^N \boldsymbol{x}_i' \boldsymbol{x}_i - n\bar{x}^2} \\ &\equiv \frac{\sum_{i=1}^N \boldsymbol{x}_i'(\boldsymbol{B}_{T_i} + \boldsymbol{A}_{T_i})\boldsymbol{y}_i - n\bar{x}\bar{y}}{\sum_{i=1}^N \boldsymbol{x}_i'(\boldsymbol{B}_{T_i} + \boldsymbol{A}_{T_i})\boldsymbol{x}_i - n\bar{x}^2} = \frac{W_{XX}\widehat{\beta}_W + B_{XX}\widehat{\beta}_{B2}}{W_{XX} + B_{XX}}, \end{aligned} \tag{10.25}$$

which generalizes the result for the balanced situation in Section 2.1.4.

10.3.3 THE MULTI-REGRESSOR CASE

Next, we let in (10.1) K be arbitrary and consider the OLS problem:

$$\min_{\alpha_1^*,\dots,\alpha_N^*,\boldsymbol{\beta}} \sum_{i=1}^N \sum_{t \in P_i} (y_{it} - \alpha_i^* - \boldsymbol{x}_{it}\boldsymbol{\beta})^2,$$

the first-order conditions of which lead to

$$\widehat{\boldsymbol{\beta}}_W = \boldsymbol{W}_{XX}^{-1}\boldsymbol{W}_{XY} = [\sum_{i=1}^{N} \boldsymbol{X}_i'\boldsymbol{B}_{T_i}\boldsymbol{X}_i]^{-1}[\sum_{i=1}^{N} \boldsymbol{X}_i'\boldsymbol{B}_{T_i}\boldsymbol{y}_i], \tag{10.26}$$

$$\widehat{\alpha}_{iW}^* = \bar{y}_{i\cdot} - \bar{\boldsymbol{x}}_{i\cdot}\widehat{\boldsymbol{\beta}}_W = \tfrac{1}{T_i}\boldsymbol{e}_{T_i}'(\boldsymbol{y}_i - \boldsymbol{X}_i\widehat{\boldsymbol{\beta}}_W), \qquad i = 1,\dots,N. \tag{10.27}$$

Since (10.1) and (10.6)–(10.7) imply $\widehat{\boldsymbol{\beta}}_W - \boldsymbol{\beta} = \boldsymbol{W}_{XX}^{-1}\boldsymbol{W}_{XU}$, $\widehat{\alpha}_{iW}^* - \alpha_i^* = \bar{u}_{i\cdot} - \bar{\boldsymbol{x}}_{i\cdot}(\widehat{\boldsymbol{\beta}}_W - \boldsymbol{\beta})$, and $\mathsf{V}(\boldsymbol{W}_{XU}|\boldsymbol{X}) = \sigma^2\boldsymbol{W}_{XX}$, it follows that $\widehat{\beta}_W$ and $\widehat{\alpha}_{iW}^*$ are unbiased, with

$$\mathsf{V}(\widehat{\boldsymbol{\beta}}_W|\boldsymbol{X}) = \sigma^2\boldsymbol{W}_{XX}^{-1}. \tag{10.28}$$

The unbiased estimator for σ^2, generalizing (10.9), now is

$$\widehat{\sigma}^2 = \tfrac{1}{n-N-K}\sum_{i=1}^{N}\sum_{t\in P_i}(y_{it} - \widehat{\alpha}_i^* - \boldsymbol{x}_{it}\widehat{\boldsymbol{\beta}}_W)^2. \tag{10.29}$$

Still assuming (10.10), we here let $\boldsymbol{y}_i$, $\boldsymbol{X}_i$, and $\boldsymbol{u}_i$ be, respectively, the $(T_i \times 1)$ vector, the $(T_i \times K)$ matrix, and the $(T_i \times 1)$ vector which contain the T_i contiguous values of y_{it}, $\boldsymbol{x}_{it}$, and u_{it} for individual i, i.e.,

$$\boldsymbol{y}_i = \begin{bmatrix} y_{i1} \\ \vdots \\ y_{i,T_i} \end{bmatrix}, \; \boldsymbol{X}_i = \begin{bmatrix} \boldsymbol{x}_{i1} \\ \vdots \\ \boldsymbol{x}_{i,T_i} \end{bmatrix}, \; \boldsymbol{u}_i = \begin{bmatrix} u_{i1} \\ \vdots \\ u_{i,T_i} \end{bmatrix}, \; i = 1,\dots,N. \tag{10.30}$$

10.3.4 BETWEEN- AND OLS-ESTIMATION IN THE GENERAL CASE

In the absence of heterogeneity, (10.16) and (10.23) are generalized to, respectively,

$$\bar{y}_{i\cdot} = \alpha + \bar{\boldsymbol{x}}_{i\cdot}\boldsymbol{\beta} + \bar{u}_{i\cdot}, \tag{10.31}$$

$$\sqrt{v_i}(\bar{y}_{i\cdot} - \widetilde{y}) = \sqrt{v_i}(\bar{\boldsymbol{x}}_{i\cdot} - \widetilde{\boldsymbol{x}})\boldsymbol{\beta} + \sqrt{v_i}(\bar{u}_{i\cdot} - \widetilde{u}), \quad i = 1,\dots,N. \tag{10.32}$$

Applying OLS on (10.32) gives the following generalization of (10.24):

$$\begin{aligned} \widehat{\boldsymbol{\beta}}_B(v) &= [\sum_{i=1}^{N} v_i(\bar{\boldsymbol{x}}_{i\cdot} - \widetilde{\boldsymbol{x}})'(\bar{\boldsymbol{x}}_{i\cdot} - \widetilde{\boldsymbol{x}})]^{-1}[\sum_{i=1}^{N} v_i(\bar{\boldsymbol{x}}_{i\cdot} - \widetilde{\boldsymbol{x}})'(\bar{y}_{i\cdot} - \widetilde{y})], \\ \widehat{\alpha}_B(v) &= \widetilde{y} - \widetilde{\boldsymbol{x}}\widehat{\boldsymbol{\beta}}_B(v), \end{aligned} \tag{10.33}$$

and $v_i = T_i$ gives

$$\begin{aligned} \widehat{\boldsymbol{\beta}}_{B2} &= [\sum_{i=1}^{N} \boldsymbol{X}_i'\boldsymbol{A}_{T_i}\boldsymbol{X}_i - n\bar{\boldsymbol{x}}'\bar{\boldsymbol{x}}]^{-1}[\sum_{i=1}^{N} \boldsymbol{X}_i'\boldsymbol{A}_{T_i}\boldsymbol{y}_i - n\bar{\boldsymbol{x}}'\bar{y}], \\ \widehat{\alpha}_{B2} &= \bar{y} - \bar{\boldsymbol{x}}\widehat{\boldsymbol{\beta}}_{B2}. \end{aligned} \tag{10.34}$$

which generalizes (10.21).

The OLS estimator of $\boldsymbol{\beta}$ can be expressed as a matrix-weighted mean of the within- and the between-individual estimators, provided that the latter is defined as $\widehat{\boldsymbol{\beta}}_{B2}$. The decomposition of the global (co)variation now reads

$$\begin{aligned}
G_{ZQ} &= \textstyle\sum_{i=1}^{N}\sum_{t=1}^{T_i}(z_{it}-\bar{z})'(q_{it}-\bar{q}) \equiv W_{ZQ}+B_{ZQ},\\
W_{ZQ} &= \textstyle\sum_{i=1}^{N}\sum_{t=1}^{T_i}(z_{it}-\bar{z}_{i\cdot})'(q_{it}-\bar{q}_{i\cdot}) \equiv \sum_{i=1}^{N} Z_i'B_{T_i}Q_i,\\
B_{ZQ} &= \textstyle\sum_{i=1}^{N} T_i(\bar{z}_{i\cdot}-\bar{z})'(\bar{q}_{i\cdot}-\bar{q}) \equiv \sum_{i=1}^{N} Q_i'A_{T_i}Q_i-n\bar{z}'\bar{q},
\end{aligned}$$

and, using (10.26) and (10.34), we find that (10.25) is generalized to

$$\begin{aligned}
\widehat{\boldsymbol{\beta}}_{OLS} &= G_{XX}^{-1}G_{XY}\\
&= [\textstyle\sum_{i=1}^{N}\sum_{t=1}^{T_i}(x_{it}-\bar{x})'(x_{it}-\bar{x})]^{-1}[\sum_{i=1}^{N}\sum_{t=1}^{T_i}(x_{it}-\bar{x})'(y_{it}-\bar{y})]\\
&= [\textstyle\sum_{i=1}^{N}X_i'X_i-n\bar{x}'\bar{x}]^{-1}[\sum_{i=1}^{N}X_i'y_i-n\bar{x}'\bar{y}]\\
&\equiv [\textstyle\sum_{i=1}^{N}X_i'(B_{T_i}+A_{T_i})X_i-n\bar{x}'\bar{x}]^{-1}\\
&\quad\times [\textstyle\sum_{i=1}^{N}X_i'(B_{T_i}+A_{T_i})y_i-n\bar{x}'\bar{y}]\\
&= [W_{XX}+B_{XX}]^{-1}[W_{XX}\widehat{\boldsymbol{\beta}}_W+B_{XX}\widehat{\boldsymbol{\beta}}_{B2}].
\end{aligned} \tag{10.35}$$

This generalizes the expression for the balanced case in Section 2.2.4 as well.

10.4 The random effects case

The regression equation still has the form (10.1), except that we interpret the α_i^*s as realizations of stochastic, IID variables, with expectation k and variance σ_α^2. We write the model, letting $\alpha_i=\alpha_i^*-k$, as

$$\begin{aligned}
&y_{it} = k + x_{it}\boldsymbol{\beta} + \alpha_i + u_{it},\\
&(u_{it}|X) \sim \mathsf{IID}(0,\sigma^2), \quad (\alpha_i|X) \sim \mathsf{IID}(0,\sigma_\alpha^2), \quad \alpha_i \perp u_{it},\\
&i = 1,\dots,N;\ t = 1,\dots,T_i,
\end{aligned} \tag{10.36}$$

again assuming that (10.10) holds.[7]

[7] This specification is related to regression models for unbalanced panel data as discussed by Biørn (1981), Baltagi (1985), Wansbeek and Kapteyn (1989), and Kumbhakar (1992).

10.4.1 THE ONE-REGRESSOR CASE

We first let $K=1$ and write the model, with $x_i = (x_{i1}, \dots, x_{i,T_i})'$, etc., x_{it} and β being scalars, as

$$\begin{aligned} &y_i = e_{T_i}k + x_i\beta + \epsilon_i, \;\; \epsilon_i = e_{T_i}\alpha_i + u_i, \;\; \mathsf{E}(\epsilon_i|X) = 0_{T_i,1}, \\ &\mathsf{V}(\epsilon_i|X) = \Omega_{T_i} = \sigma_\alpha^2(e_{T_i}e'_{T_i}) + \sigma^2 I_{T_i}, \;\; \epsilon_i \perp \epsilon_j \; (i \neq j), \\ &i,j = 1,\dots,N, \end{aligned} \tag{10.37}$$

and hence

$$\Omega_{T_i} = \sigma^2 B_{T_i} + (\sigma^2 + T_i\sigma_\alpha^2)A_{T_i}. \tag{10.38}$$

Stacking the equation by individuals, we get

$$\begin{bmatrix} y_1 \\ \vdots \\ y_N \end{bmatrix} = \begin{bmatrix} e_{T_1} \\ \vdots \\ e_{T_N} \end{bmatrix} k + \begin{bmatrix} x_1 \\ \vdots \\ x_N \end{bmatrix} \beta + \begin{bmatrix} \epsilon_1 \\ \vdots \\ \epsilon_N \end{bmatrix},$$

or compactly, with $x=[x'_1,\dots,x'_N]'$, $u=[u'_1,\dots,u'_N]'$, $\alpha=[e'_{T_1}\alpha_1,\dots,e'_{T_N}\alpha_N]'$, etc.,

$$y = e_n k + x\beta + \epsilon, \quad \epsilon = \alpha + u, \tag{10.39}$$

where

$$\mathsf{V}(\epsilon|X) = \Omega = \begin{bmatrix} \Omega_{T_1} & \cdots & 0 \\ \vdots & \ddots & \vdots \\ 0 & \cdots & \Omega_{T_N} \end{bmatrix} = \text{diag}[\Omega_{T_1},\dots,\Omega_{T_N}]. \tag{10.40}$$

A consequence of the unbalance is that α and Ω cannot be written as Kronecker-products.

GLS estimation of (10.39), provided that Ω is known, proceeds as follows. From (10.38), using Appendix 3A, Theorem 3A.1, we have

$$\Omega_{T_i}^r = (\sigma^2)^r B_{T_i} + (\sigma^2 + T_i\sigma_\alpha^2)^r A_{T_i} \equiv (\sigma^2)^r[B_{T_i} + \theta_{Bi}^{-r} A_{T_i}], \tag{10.41}$$

where

$$\theta_{Bi} = \frac{\sigma^2}{\sigma^2 + T_i\sigma_\alpha^2} = \frac{1-\rho}{1+(T_i-1)\rho}, \tag{10.42}$$

and $\rho = \sigma_\alpha^2/(\sigma^2+\sigma_\alpha^2)$. Hence, computation of the r'th power of $\boldsymbol{\Omega}_{T_i}$ only requires that σ^2 and $(\sigma^2+T_i\sigma_\alpha^2)$ are raised to the r'th power.[8]

As in the balanced case, the GLS problem can be transformed into an OLS problem. The form of the transformation depends on the disturbance covariances and the unbalance. Since (10.40) and (10.41) imply

$$\boldsymbol{\Omega}^r = \begin{bmatrix} \boldsymbol{\Omega}_{T_1}^r & \cdots & \mathbf{0} \\ \vdots & \ddots & \vdots \\ \mathbf{0} & \cdots & \boldsymbol{\Omega}_{T_N}^r \end{bmatrix},$$

$$\boldsymbol{S}_{T_i} = \boldsymbol{\Omega}_{T_i}^{-\frac{1}{2}} \equiv \sigma^{-1}(\boldsymbol{B}_{T_i}+\sqrt{\theta_{Bi}}\boldsymbol{A}_{T_i}) \equiv \sigma^{-1}[\boldsymbol{I}_{T_i}-(1-\sqrt{\theta_{Bi}})\boldsymbol{A}_{T_i}], \qquad (10.43)$$

the minimand can be written as

$$\begin{aligned} Q &= (\boldsymbol{y}-\boldsymbol{e}_n k-\boldsymbol{x}\boldsymbol{\beta})'\boldsymbol{\Omega}^{-1}(\boldsymbol{y}-\boldsymbol{e}_n k-\boldsymbol{x}\boldsymbol{\beta}) \\ &= \textstyle\sum_{i=1}^N (\boldsymbol{y}_i-\boldsymbol{e}_{T_i}k-\boldsymbol{x}_i\boldsymbol{\beta})'\boldsymbol{\Omega}_{T_i}^{-1}(\boldsymbol{y}_i-\boldsymbol{e}_{T_i}k-\boldsymbol{x}_i\boldsymbol{\beta}) \\ &= \sigma^{-2}\textstyle\sum_{i=1}^N (\boldsymbol{y}_i-\boldsymbol{e}_{T_i}k-\boldsymbol{x}_i\boldsymbol{\beta})'(\sigma\boldsymbol{S}_{T_i})'(\sigma\boldsymbol{S}_{T_i})(\boldsymbol{y}_i-\boldsymbol{e}_{T_i}k-\boldsymbol{x}_i\boldsymbol{\beta}) \\ &= \sigma^{-2}\textstyle\sum_{i=1}^N (\sigma\boldsymbol{S}_{T_i}\boldsymbol{\epsilon}_i)'(\sigma\boldsymbol{S}_{T_i}\boldsymbol{\epsilon}_i). \end{aligned} \qquad (10.44)$$

Therefore

$$Q^* = \sigma^2 Q = \textstyle\sum_{i=1}^N \boldsymbol{\epsilon}_i^{*\prime}\boldsymbol{\epsilon}_i^*, \qquad (10.45)$$

where

$$\boldsymbol{\epsilon}_i^* = \sigma\boldsymbol{S}_{T_i}\boldsymbol{\epsilon}_i = [\boldsymbol{I}_{T_i}-(1-\sqrt{\theta_{Bi}})\boldsymbol{A}_{T_i}]\boldsymbol{\epsilon}_i = \boldsymbol{y}_i^*-\boldsymbol{e}_{T_i}\sqrt{\theta_{Bi}}k-\boldsymbol{x}_i^*\boldsymbol{\beta}, \qquad (10.46)$$

with $\boldsymbol{y}_i^* = \sigma\boldsymbol{S}_{T_i}\boldsymbol{y}_i$, $\boldsymbol{x}_i^* = \sigma\boldsymbol{S}_{T_i}\boldsymbol{x}_i$, (10.43) giving $\mathsf{V}(\boldsymbol{\epsilon}_i^*|\boldsymbol{X}) = \sigma^2(\boldsymbol{S}_{T_i}\boldsymbol{\Omega}_{T_i}\boldsymbol{S}_{T_i}') = \boldsymbol{I}_{T_i}$. Hence, a prescription for minimizing Q^* is:

Subtract from $\boldsymbol{y}_i$ and $\boldsymbol{x}_i$ a share $(1-\sqrt{\theta_{Bi}})$ of the corresponding means, and apply OLS on the resulting equation, $\boldsymbol{y}_i^* = \boldsymbol{e}_{T_i}\sqrt{\theta_{Bi}}k + \boldsymbol{x}_i^*\boldsymbol{\beta} + \boldsymbol{\epsilon}_i^*$.

Since θ_{Bi} is decreasing in T_i and in ρ, a larger share of the means should be deducted from the original observations (i) the longer the time series for individual i, and (ii) the stronger the heterogeneity, measured by σ_α^2.

[8] Its rationale is that (10.38) is the *spectral decomposition* of $\boldsymbol{\Omega}_{T_i}$ and that σ^2 and $(\sigma^2+T_i\sigma_\alpha^2)$ are its eigenvalues, with multiplicity, respectively, T_i-1 and 1; confer Sections 3.2.1 and 3.8.3.

For the balanced random effects case, we examined in Section 3.2.3 the relationship between the GLS and the within- and between-estimators. Does a similar relationship hold in the unbalanced case? The answer is a conditional yes. In Appendix 10B, Section 10B.1, it is shown that Q^*, written as

$$Q^* = \sum_{i=1}^{N}(y_i - e_{T_i}k - x_i\beta)' C_{T_i}(y_i - e_{T_i}k - x_i\beta), \tag{10.47}$$

where

$$C_{T_i} = \sigma^2 S_{T_i}^2 = \sigma^2 \boldsymbol{\Omega}_{T_i}^{-1} = \boldsymbol{B}_{T_i} + \theta_{Bi}\boldsymbol{A}_{T_i}, \qquad i = 1,\ldots,N, \tag{10.48}$$

is minimized for

$$\widehat{\beta}_{GLS} = \frac{[W_{XY}+\sum_i \theta_{Bi}T_i\bar{x}_{i\cdot}\bar{y}_{i\cdot}][\sum_i \theta_{Bi}T_i]-[\sum_i \theta_{Bi}T_i\bar{x}_{i\cdot}][\sum_i \theta_{Bi}T_i\bar{y}_{i\cdot}]}{[W_{XX}+\sum_i \theta_{Bi}T_i\bar{x}_{i\cdot}^2][\sum_i \theta_{Bi}T_i]-[\sum_i \theta_{Bi}T_i\bar{x}_{i\cdot}]^2}, \tag{10.49}$$

$$\widehat{k}_{GLS} = \frac{\sum_i \theta_{Bi}T_i\bar{y}_{i\cdot}}{\sum_i \theta_{Bi}T_i} - \frac{\sum_i \theta_{Bi}T_i\bar{x}_{i\cdot}}{\sum_i \theta_{Bi}T_i}\widehat{\beta}_{GLS}. \tag{10.50}$$

These expressions can be rewritten in a form comparable with that in the balanced case. Defining from (10.22) weighted global means, using $v_i = \theta_{Bi}T_i$,

$$\begin{aligned} \widetilde{\bar{y}} &= \frac{\sum_{i=1}^{N}\theta_{Bi}T_i\bar{y}_{i\cdot}}{\sum_{i=1}^{N}\theta_{Bi}T_i}, \\ \widetilde{\bar{x}} &= \frac{\sum_{i=1}^{N}\theta_{Bi}T_i\bar{x}_{i\cdot}}{\sum_{i=1}^{N}\theta_{Bi}T_i}, \end{aligned} \tag{10.51}$$

we obtain

$$\widehat{\beta}_{GLS} = \frac{W_{XY} + \sum_i \theta_{Bi}T_i(\bar{x}_{i\cdot} - \widetilde{\bar{x}})(\bar{y}_{i\cdot} - \widetilde{\bar{y}})}{W_{XX} + \sum_i \theta_{Bi}T_i(\bar{x}_{i\cdot} - \widetilde{\bar{x}})^2}, \tag{10.52}$$

$$\widehat{k}_{GLS} = \widetilde{\bar{y}} - \widetilde{\bar{x}}\widehat{\beta}_{GLS}. \tag{10.53}$$

An alternative way of writing $\widehat{\beta}_{GLS}$ is

$$\widehat{\beta}_{GLS} = \frac{\sum_{i=1}^{N} x_i' \boldsymbol{B}_{T_i} y_i + \sum_{i=1}^{N}\theta_{Bi}x_i'\boldsymbol{A}_{T_i}y_i - (\sum_{i=1}^{N}\theta_{Bi}T_i)\widetilde{\bar{x}}\widetilde{\bar{y}}}{\sum_{i=1}^{N} x_i' \boldsymbol{B}_{T_i} x_i + \sum_{i=1}^{N}\theta_{Bi}x_i'\boldsymbol{A}_{T_i}x_i - (\sum_{i=1}^{N}\theta_{Bi}T_i)\widetilde{\bar{x}}^2}. \tag{10.54}$$

A comparison of this expression with (10.12) and (10.25) shows that the within-individual and the OLS estimators correspond to, respectively, $\theta_{Bi} = 0$ and $\theta_{Bi} = 1$. However, since, for $\sigma_\alpha^2 > 0$, $\theta_{Bi} < 1$, and varies with i, we cannot, as in the balanced case, interpret the GLS estimator of $\boldsymbol{\beta}$ as a weighted mean of the within estimator and *one common* between estimator. This is the answer to the above question.

10.4.2 THE MULTI-REGRESSOR CASE

We next let K be arbitrary and extend (10.37) to

$$\begin{aligned} &y_i = e_{T_i}k + X_i\boldsymbol{\beta} + \boldsymbol{\epsilon}_i, \ \ \mathsf{E}(\boldsymbol{\epsilon}_i|X) = \mathbf{0}_{T_i,1}, \\ &\mathsf{V}(\boldsymbol{\epsilon}_i|X) = \boldsymbol{\Omega}_{T_i} = \sigma_\alpha^2(e_{T_i}e'_{T_i}) + \sigma^2 \boldsymbol{I}_{T_i}, \ \ \boldsymbol{\epsilon}_i \perp \boldsymbol{\epsilon}_j \ (i \neq j), \\ &i,j = 1,\dots,N. \end{aligned} \tag{10.55}$$

Stacking by individuals yields

$$\begin{bmatrix} y_1 \\ \vdots \\ y_N \end{bmatrix} = \begin{bmatrix} e_{T_1} \\ \vdots \\ e_{T_N} \end{bmatrix} k + \begin{bmatrix} X_1 \\ \vdots \\ X_N \end{bmatrix} \boldsymbol{\beta} + \begin{bmatrix} \boldsymbol{\epsilon}_1 \\ \vdots \\ \boldsymbol{\epsilon}_N \end{bmatrix},$$

or compactly,

$$y = e_n k + X\boldsymbol{\beta} + \boldsymbol{\epsilon}. \tag{10.56}$$

The GLS minimand is

$$\begin{aligned} Q &= (y - e_n k - X\boldsymbol{\beta})'\boldsymbol{\Omega}^{-1}(y - e_n k - X\boldsymbol{\beta}) \\ &= \textstyle\sum_{i=1}^N (y_i - e_{T_i}k - X_i\boldsymbol{\beta})'\boldsymbol{\Omega}_{T_i}^{-1}(y_i - e_{T_i}k - X_i\boldsymbol{\beta}) \\ &= \sigma^{-2}\textstyle\sum_{i=1}^N (y_i - e_{T_i}k - X_i\boldsymbol{\beta})'(\sigma S_{T_i})'(\sigma S_{T_i})(y_i - e_{T_i}k - X_i\boldsymbol{\beta}) \\ &= \sigma^{-2}\textstyle\sum_{i=1}^N (\sigma S_{T_i}\boldsymbol{\epsilon}_i)'(\sigma S_{T_i}\boldsymbol{\epsilon}_i), \end{aligned} \tag{10.57}$$

still making $Q^* = \sigma^2 Q$ a sum of squares in transformed disturbances:

$$\boldsymbol{\epsilon}_i^* = \sigma S_{T_i}\boldsymbol{\epsilon}_i = y_i^* - e_{T_i}\sqrt{\theta_{Bi}}k - X_i^*\boldsymbol{\beta}, \tag{10.58}$$

with $y_i^* = \sigma S_{T_i} y_i$ and $X_i^* = \sigma S_{T_i} X_i$. Hence, the GLS-prescription is:

> *Subtract from y_i and X_i a share $(1-\sqrt{\theta_{Bi}})$ of the corresponding means, and apply OLS on the resulting equation, $y_i^* = e_{T_i}\sqrt{\theta_{Bi}}k + X_i^*\boldsymbol{\beta} + \boldsymbol{\epsilon}_i^*$.*

The corresponding generalizations of (10.47) and (10.49)–(10.50) are, see Appendix 10B, Section 10B.2,

$$Q^* = \sum_{i=1}^{N}(y_i - e_{T_i}k - X_i\beta)' C_{T_i}(y_i - e_{T_i}k - X_i\beta), \tag{10.59}$$

$$\begin{aligned}\widehat{\beta}_{GLS} &= \big([W_{XX} + \textstyle\sum_i \theta_{Bi} T_i \bar{x}'_{i\cdot}\bar{x}_{i\cdot}][\sum_i \theta_{Bi} T_i] - [\sum_i \theta_{Bi} T_i \bar{x}'_{i\cdot}][\sum_i \theta_{Bi} T_i \bar{x}_{i\cdot}]\big)^{-1} \\ &\quad \times \big([W_{XY} + \textstyle\sum_i \theta_{Bi} T_i \bar{x}'_{i\cdot}\bar{y}_{i\cdot}][\sum_i \theta_{Bi} T_i] - [\sum_i \theta_{Bi} T_i \bar{x}'_{i\cdot}][\sum_i \theta_{Bi} T_i \bar{y}_{i\cdot}]\big),\end{aligned} \tag{10.60}$$

$$\widehat{k}_{GLS} = \frac{\sum_i \theta_{Bi} T_i \bar{y}_{i\cdot}}{\sum_i \theta_{Bi} T_i} - \frac{\sum_i \theta_{Bi} T_i \bar{x}_{i\cdot}}{\sum_i \theta_{Bi} T_i}\widehat{\beta}_{GLS}. \tag{10.61}$$

Defining $\widetilde{\bar{y}}$ and $\widetilde{\bar{x}}$ as in the one-regressor case, we obtain

$$\begin{aligned}\widehat{\beta}_{GLS} &= \big[W_{XX} + \textstyle\sum_i \theta_{Bi} T_i (\bar{x}_{i\cdot} - \widetilde{\bar{x}})'(\bar{x}_{i\cdot} - \widetilde{\bar{x}})\big]^{-1} \\ &\quad \times \big[W_{XY} + \textstyle\sum_i \theta_{Bi} T_i (\bar{x}_{i\cdot} - \widetilde{\bar{x}})'(\bar{y}_{i\cdot} - \widetilde{\bar{y}})\big],\end{aligned} \tag{10.62}$$

$$\widehat{k}_{GLS} = \widetilde{\bar{y}} - \widetilde{\bar{x}}\widehat{\beta}_{GLS}. \tag{10.63}$$

An alternative way of writing $\widehat{\beta}_{GLS}$ is

$$\begin{aligned}\widehat{\beta}_{GLS} &= [\textstyle\sum_{i=1}^{N} X_i' B_{T_i} X_i + \sum_{i=1}^{N} \theta_{Bi} X_i' A_{T_i} X_i - (\sum_{i=1}^{N} \theta_{Bi} T_i)\widetilde{\bar{x}}'\widetilde{\bar{x}}]^{-1} \\ &\quad \times [\textstyle\sum_{i=1}^{N} X_i' B_{T_i} y_i + \sum_{i=1}^{N} \theta_{Bi} X_i' A_{T_i} y_i - (\sum_{i=1}^{N} \theta_{Bi} T_i)\widetilde{\bar{x}}'\widetilde{\bar{y}}].\end{aligned} \tag{10.64}$$

The three last equations generalize (10.52)–(10.54).

The above discussion of unbalanced panel data has involved three kinds of global means defined from individual-specific means as special cases of (10.22) for an arbitrary variable q: the unweighted mean $\bar{\bar{q}}$; the T_i-weighted mean $\bar{q}$; and the $\theta_{Bi}T_i$-weighted mean $\widetilde{\bar{q}}$; see (10.19), (10.5), and (10.51). If $\sigma_\alpha^2 > 0$, they are equal only in the balanced case $(T_i = T, \theta_{Bi} = \theta_B)$.

10.4.3 ESTIMATING THE VARIANCE COMPONENTS: FGLS

We finally show how the procedure for estimation of σ^2 and σ_α^2 from a balanced panel data set, described in Section 3.3.3, is modified when there is an unbalance.

In (3.42)–(3.43) we showed that when $T_i = T$, $n = \sum_i T_i = NT$, then

$$\mathsf{E}(W_{\epsilon\epsilon}|X) = \sigma^2 N(T-1),$$
$$\mathsf{E}(B_{\epsilon\epsilon}|X) = (T\sigma_\alpha^2 + \sigma^2)(N-1).$$

In Appendix 10C, (10C.6)–(10C.7), we derive the generalizations

$$\mathsf{E}(W_{\epsilon\epsilon}|X) = (n-N)\sigma^2, \tag{10.65}$$
$$\mathsf{E}(B_{\epsilon\epsilon}|X) = (n-\sum T_i^2/n)\sigma_\alpha^2 + (N-1)\sigma^2. \tag{10.66}$$

If $\boldsymbol{\beta}$ and k were known, making ϵ_{it} observable, the following unbiased 'estimators' based on disturbances are therefore motivated:[9]

$$\widehat{\sigma}^2 = \frac{W_{\epsilon\epsilon}}{n-N}, \tag{10.67}$$
$$\widehat{\sigma}_\alpha^2 = \frac{B_{\epsilon\epsilon} - \dfrac{N-1}{n-N} W_{\epsilon\epsilon}}{n - \dfrac{\sum T_i^2}{n}}. \tag{10.68}$$

Their counterparts in the balanced case, see (3.38) and (3.40), are

$$\widehat{\sigma}^2 = \frac{W_{\epsilon\epsilon}}{N(T-1)},$$
$$\widehat{\sigma}_\alpha^2 = \frac{1}{T}\left[\frac{B_{\epsilon\epsilon}}{N-1} - \frac{W_{\epsilon\epsilon}}{N(T-1)}\right].$$

In practice, (consistent) residuals are used in estimating σ^2 and σ_α^2. Overall, this motivates the following stepwise procedure for FGLS estimation:

1. Estimate $\boldsymbol{\beta}$ and k by OLS on (10.56) and extract the residuals $\widehat{\epsilon}_{it}$.
2. Compute $\widehat{\sigma}^2$, $\widehat{\sigma}_\alpha^2$, and $\widehat{\theta}_{Bi}$ from (10.67), (10.68), and (10.42), with ϵ_{it} replaced by $\widehat{\epsilon}_{it}$.
3. Reestimate $\boldsymbol{\beta}$ and k from (10.62)–(10.63), with θ_{Bi} replaced by $\widehat{\theta}_{Bi}$.

This procedure can be iterated by recomputing the residuals and repeating steps 2 and 3 until convergence according to some criterion.

A comparative study of properties of alternative estimators for this kind of model is given in Baltagi and Chang (1994).

Example: We want to compare results based on unbalanced and on balanced panel data, using a data set extracted from the *Journal of Applied Econometrics Archive*, used in Riphahn, Wambach, and Million (2003) (from the German Socioeconomic Panel) from the years 1984–88, 1991, and 1994 (T=7). The balanced data set is obtained by omitting all individuals not having full-length time series. The full data set contains $n = 28326$ observations from $N = 7293$ individuals observed between 1 and 7 times (mean=3.7). The number of observations per individual, a very useful variable, is denoted as `numobs`.

[9] See also Searle, Casella, and McCulloch (1992, p. 71).

Table 10.1 Unbalanced panel data: health satisfaction example. Regressand=`hsat`. Regression results for full panel and sub-panels

Regressor	*Random effects model*			*Fixed effects model*		
	Unbal.1–7	Unbal.4–7	Bal.7	Unbal.1–7	Unbal.4–7	Bal.7
`cohort`	−0.0293	−0.0315	−0.0167			
	(0.0034)	(0.0043)	(0.0082)			
`age`	−0.0710	−0.0701	−0.0559	−0.0727	−0.0725	−0.0580
	(0.0035)	(0.0038)	(0.0060)	(0.0037)	(0.0038)	(0.0060)
`working`	0.1570	0.1420	0.2791	−0.0058	−0.0145	0.0982
	(0.0313)	(0.0365)	(0.0690)	(0.0405)	(0.0442)	(0.0792)
`docvis`	−0.0945	−0.0932	−0.0953	−0.0690	−0.0706	−0.0790
	(0.0021)	(0.0024)	(0.0044)	(0.0024)	(0.0026)	(0.0046)
`intercept`	67.1237	71.2667	41.7426	10.1742	10.2147	9.4431
	(6.8350)	(8.4824)	(16.1976)	(0.1610)	(0.1725)	(0.2724)
n	28326	21168	6209	28326	21168	6209
N	7293	3864	887	7293	3864	887
n/N	3.7	5.5	7	3.7	5.5	7

Standard errors in parentheses

Table 10.1 gives fixed effects (columns 1–3) and random effects estimates (columns 4–6). Two versions of unbalanced data sets—one containing the full set, one containing $n = 21,168$ observations from 3,864 individuals observed at least 4 times (columns 1, 2, 4, and 5)—are considered, the comparable results based on the curtailed balanced panel data set (columns 3 and 6) are based on observations from $N=887$ individuals. The regressand is `hsat` (self-reported health satisfaction), coded ordinally, from 0 (low) to 10 (high). The regressors are `cohort` (year of birth), `age` (age in years), `working` (dummy for being employed), and `docvis` (number of doctor visits during the last three months). The effect of `cohort` (individual specific) is in the fixed effects regressions captured by the individual dummies and therefore excluded. For `cohort`, `age`, and `working`, the coefficient estimates vary notably with choice of data set, especially between the full unbalanced and the balanced data sets, both when using the random and the fixed effects approach. There are also notable differences between the random and the fixed effects estimates, also with respect to sign. For example, the random effects results give an estimated impact of the working dummy of 0.28 when using the balanced panel and 0.16 for the full unbalanced one (both significant at standard levels). On the other hand, none of the fixed effects estimates for this variable come out as significant.

Some 'background' for the sensitivity of the results is given in Table 10.2, containing correlation coefficients between the regressand and the regressors for the full unbalanced and the balanced data set (columns 1 and 2), and for cross section data for the first and last year in the data period (1984: 3874 observations; 1994: 3377

Table 10.2 Correlation, regressor vs. regressand `hsat`

Regressor	Unbal.1–7	Bal.7	CS, 1984	CS, 1994
`cohort`	0.2208	0.1889	0.2844	0.2195
`age`	−0.2409	−0.2108	−0.2844	−0.2195
`year`	−0.0331	−0.0964	–	–
`working`	0.1386	0.1747	0.1745	0.1590
`docvis`	−0.3702	−0.3837	−0.3931	−0.4012
n	28326	6209	3874	3377
N	7293	887	3874	3377
n/N	3.7	7	1	1

observations) (columns 3 and 4). For example, `working` is more strongly correlated with `hsat` in the balanced sub-panel than in the full data set. Signs of 'lack of representativity' of the data set is also seen from the following descriptive regression, showing, for the full data set, how `numobs` is 'empirically' related to `hsat` and `working` (standard errors in parentheses):

$$\texttt{numobs} = -0.0275\,(0.0048)^*\texttt{hsat} + 0.3472\,(0.0233)^*\texttt{working} + 4.8493\,(0.0356).$$

No specific 'diagnosis' can, of course, be given from this single finding, except that a larger number of individual observations seems to be included in the panel the lower is the respondent's reported health satisfaction and the stronger the inclination to be working. It *may* indicate that the selection is non-ignorable, which is an issue to be addressed in a more general context in Chapter 11.

10.5 Maximum Likelihood estimation

We finally describe a procedure for joint estimation of the coefficient vector $\boldsymbol{\beta}$, the intercept k, and the variance components σ^2 and σ_α^2 related to the application of ML to balanced panel data for a one-way random effects model in Section 3.4.

10.5.1 A CONVENIENT NOTATION AND REORDERING

It is convenient to *rearrange the N individuals in groups according to the number of observations*, and to introduce corresponding notation:

$$D_{ip} = 1\{\text{Individual } i \text{ is observed } p \text{ times}\}, \quad p = 1, \ldots, P,$$

as before letting $1\{\mathcal{S}\}=1$ if $\mathcal{S}$ is true and $=0$ if $\mathcal{S}$ is untrue. Let M_p be the number of individuals which are observed p times, to be denoted as *group* p, assuming $p \leq P \leq T$, i.e.,

$$M_p = \sum_{i=1}^{N} D_{ip}, \quad p = 1, \dots, P. \tag{10.69}$$

The binary variables D_{ip} and d_{it}, the latter defined by (10.2), are related by

$$D_{ip} = 1\{\sum_{t=1}^{T} d_{it} = p\}, \quad i = 1, \dots, N;\ p = 1, \dots, P. \tag{10.70}$$

The total number of individuals and the total number of observations can then be expressed as, respectively,

$$N = \sum_{p=1}^{P} M_p = \sum_{p=1}^{P} \sum_{i=1}^{N} D_{ip}, \tag{10.71}$$

$$n = \sum_{p=1}^{P} M_p p. \tag{10.72}$$

While for a balanced data set with T replications, $P=T$, $D_{iT}=1$, $M_T=N$, and $D_{ip}=M_p=0$ for $p \neq T$, an unbalanced panel data set may have any M_p positive; see Section 10.2.1.

Corresponding to the reordering of individuals, we *change indexation*, letting an individual be represented by an index pair (j, p), p representing the group, j indexing the *individual* in the group. The *observation* number index for each individual is k, so that $\alpha_{(j,p)}$ is the individual-specific effect for individual (j, p), and $(y_{(j,p),k}, \boldsymbol{x}_{(j,p),k}, u_{(j,p),k}, \epsilon_{(j,p),k})$ are the values of $(y, \boldsymbol{x}, u, \epsilon)$ for observation k from this individual, $k = 1, \dots, p$; $j = 1, \dots, M_p$; $p = 1, \dots, P$.

10.5.2 REFORMULATING THE MODEL

In this revised notation, Model (10.55) takes the form

$$\begin{aligned} &\boldsymbol{y}_{(jp)} = \boldsymbol{e}_p k + \boldsymbol{X}_{(jp)}\boldsymbol{\beta} + \boldsymbol{\epsilon}_{(jp)}, \quad \boldsymbol{\epsilon}_{(jp)} = \boldsymbol{e}_p \alpha_{(jp)} + \boldsymbol{u}_{(jp)}, \\ &\mathsf{E}(\boldsymbol{\epsilon}_{(jp)}|\boldsymbol{X}) = \boldsymbol{0}_{p,1}, \quad \mathsf{V}(\boldsymbol{\epsilon}_{(jp)}|\boldsymbol{X}) = \boldsymbol{\Omega}_p = \sigma_\alpha^2(\boldsymbol{e}_p\boldsymbol{e}_p') + \sigma^2 \boldsymbol{I}_p, \\ &j = 1, \dots, M_p;\ p = 1, \dots, P, \end{aligned} \tag{10.73}$$

where

$$\boldsymbol{y}_{(jp)} = \begin{bmatrix} y_{(jp)1} \\ \vdots \\ y_{(jp)p} \end{bmatrix}, \quad \boldsymbol{X}_{(jp)} = \begin{bmatrix} \boldsymbol{x}_{(jp)1} \\ \vdots \\ \boldsymbol{x}_{(jp)p} \end{bmatrix}, \quad \boldsymbol{u}_{(jp)} = \begin{bmatrix} u_{(jp)1} \\ \vdots \\ u_{(jp)p} \end{bmatrix}.$$

In analogy with (10.38) we let

$$\boldsymbol{\Omega}_p = \sigma^2 \boldsymbol{B}_p + (\sigma^2 + p\sigma_\alpha^2)\boldsymbol{A}_p, \qquad p = 1, \dots, P. \tag{10.74}$$

10.5.3 'ESTIMATING' THE VARIANCE COMPONENTS FROM DISTURBANCES

First, we consider 'estimation' of the group-specific variance components for $\epsilon_{(jp)k}$ known. We then proceed as if *the data set contains P balanced data sets, set p containing the observations from the individuals in group p*. Accordingly, we let

$$\begin{aligned}
\boldsymbol{W}_{XX(p)} &= \textstyle\sum_{j=1}^{M_p} \sum_{k=1}^{p} (\boldsymbol{x}_{(jp)k} - \bar{\boldsymbol{x}}_{(jp)})'(\boldsymbol{x}_{(jp)k} - \bar{\boldsymbol{x}}_{(jp)}), \\
\boldsymbol{B}_{XX(p)} &= \textstyle\sum_{j=1}^{M_p} p(\bar{\boldsymbol{x}}_{(jp)} - \bar{\boldsymbol{x}}_{(p)})'(\bar{\boldsymbol{x}}_{(jp)} - \bar{\boldsymbol{x}}_{(p)}), \\
\boldsymbol{W}_{XY(p)} &= \textstyle\sum_{j=1}^{M_p} \sum_{k=1}^{p} (\boldsymbol{x}_{(jp)k} - \bar{\boldsymbol{x}}_{(jp)})'(y_{(jp)k} - \bar{y}_{(jp)}), \\
\boldsymbol{B}_{XY(p)} &= \textstyle\sum_{j=1}^{M_p} p(\bar{\boldsymbol{x}}_{(jp)} - \bar{\boldsymbol{x}}_{(p)})'(\bar{y}_{(jp)} - \bar{y}_{(p)}),
\end{aligned}$$

etc., where $\bar{\boldsymbol{x}}_{(jp)} = \frac{1}{p}\sum_{k=1}^{p} \boldsymbol{x}_{(jp)k}$, $\bar{\boldsymbol{x}}_{(p)} = (M_p p)^{-1}\sum_{j=1}^{M_p}\sum_{k=1}^{p} \boldsymbol{x}_{(jp)k}$, etc. Then variance components can be estimated for group p by proceeding as in the balanced case, (M_p, p) corresponding to (N, T). For $M_p \geq 2$, in analogy with (3.38)–(3.39), this gives group-p-specific 'estimators' of σ^2 and $\sigma_\alpha^2 + \frac{1}{p}\sigma^2$:

$$\widehat{\sigma}^2_{(p)} = \frac{W_{\epsilon\epsilon(p)}}{M_p(p-1)}, \tag{10.75}$$

$$\left(\widehat{\sigma_\alpha^2 + \frac{\sigma^2}{p}}\right)_{(p)} = \frac{B_{\epsilon\epsilon(p)}}{(M_p - 1)p}, \qquad p = 2, \dots, P, \tag{10.76}$$

and hence

$$\widehat{\sigma}^2_{\alpha(p)} = \frac{B_{\epsilon\epsilon(p)}}{(M_p - 1)p} - \frac{W_{\epsilon\epsilon(p)}}{M_p p(p-1)}, \quad p = 2, \dots, P. \tag{10.77}$$

For group $p = 1$, the 'estimators' collapse to

$$\widehat{\sigma^2_{\alpha\,(1)} + \sigma^2_{(1)}} = \frac{B_{\epsilon\epsilon\,(1)}}{M_1 - 1} = \frac{\sum_{j=1}^{M_1}(\bar{\epsilon}_{(j1)1} - \bar{\epsilon}_{(1)})^2}{M_1 - 1}. \tag{10.78}$$

Groupwise estimation of σ^2 and σ_α^2 gives a partial solution only, since obtaining $P-1$ different estimators of σ^2 and P different estimators of σ_α^2 is clearly inefficient. Compromises may be constructed, in a somewhat *ad hoc* way, by weighting the estimators for $p = 2, \dots, P$, by, for example, $M_p(p-1)$. This gives

$$\widehat{\sigma}^2 = \frac{\sum_{p=2}^{P} M_p(p-1)\widehat{\sigma}^2_{(p)}}{\sum_{p=2}^{P} M_p(p-1)} = \frac{\sum_{p=2}^{P} W_{\epsilon\epsilon(p)}}{\sum_{p=2}^{P} M_p(p-1)}, \tag{10.79}$$

$$\widehat{\sigma}_\alpha^2 = \frac{\sum_{p=2}^{P} M_p(p-1)\widehat{\sigma}^2_{\alpha\,(p)}}{\sum_{p=2}^{P} M_p(p-1)}$$

$$= \frac{\sum_{p=2}^{P}[M_p(p-1)]/[(M_p-1)p]B_{\epsilon\epsilon(p)}}{\sum_{p=2}^{P} M_p(p-1)} - \frac{\sum_{p=2}^{P} W_{\epsilon\epsilon(p)}/p}{\sum_{p=2}^{P} M_p(p-1)}. \tag{10.80}$$

Having obtained consistent residuals, we could, following (10.62)–(10.63), insert the implied $\widehat{\theta}_{Bi}$ in a stepwise FGLS-procedure, which could be iterated.

10.5.4 THE LOG-LIKELIHOOD FUNCTION

The log-likelihood function of $(y_{1p}, \dots, y_{M_p p}|X_{1p}, \dots, X_{M_p p})$, i.e., for group p, is, in analogy with the balanced panel data case, see (3.46),

$$\ln(\mathcal{L}_p) = -\tfrac{1}{2}M_p[p\ln(2\pi) + \ln(|\boldsymbol{\Omega}_{(p)}|)]$$

$$-\tfrac{1}{2}\sum_{j=1}^{M_p}[y_{(jp)} - e_p k - X_{(jp)}\boldsymbol{\beta}]'\boldsymbol{\Omega}_{(p)}^{-1}[y_{(jp)} - e_p k - X_{(jp)}\boldsymbol{\beta}]$$

$$= -\tfrac{1}{2}M_p p\ln(2\pi) - \tfrac{1}{2}g_p, \qquad p = 1, \dots, P, \tag{10.81}$$

where

$$g_p = M_p\ln(|\boldsymbol{\Omega}_{(p)}|) + \sum_{j=1}^{M_p}\boldsymbol{\epsilon}'_{(jp)}\boldsymbol{\Omega}_{(p)}^{-1}\boldsymbol{\epsilon}_{(jp)}. \tag{10.82}$$

Since, from Theorem 3A.1 in Appendix 3A, $\boldsymbol{\Omega}_{(p)}^{-1} = \sigma^{-2}\boldsymbol{B}_p + (\sigma^2 + p\sigma_\alpha^2)^{-1}\boldsymbol{A}_p$ and since $|\boldsymbol{\Omega}_{(p)}| = \sigma^{2(p-1)}(\sigma^2 + p\sigma_\alpha^2)$, (10.82) can be written as

$$g_p = M_p[(p-1)\ln(\sigma^2)+\ln(\sigma^2+p\sigma_\alpha^2))]$$
$$+\frac{\sum_{j=1}^{M_p}\boldsymbol{\epsilon}'_{(jp)}\boldsymbol{B}_p\boldsymbol{\epsilon}_{(jp)}}{\sigma^2}+\frac{\sum_{j=1}^{M_p}\boldsymbol{\epsilon}'_{(jp)}\boldsymbol{A}_p\boldsymbol{\epsilon}_{(jp)}}{\sigma^2+p\sigma_\alpha^2}$$
$$= M_p[(p-1)\ln(\sigma^2)+\ln(\sigma^2+p\sigma_\alpha^2))]+\frac{W_{\epsilon\epsilon(p)}}{\sigma^2}+\frac{B_{\epsilon\epsilon(p)}}{\sigma^2+p\sigma_\alpha^2}. \tag{10.83}$$

Because the observations from the different individuals are independent, the overall *log-likelihood function*, obtained by summing (10.81) across p, is

$$\ln(\mathcal{L}) = \sum_{p=1}^{P}\ln(\mathcal{L}_p) = -\tfrac{1}{2}n\ln(2\pi) - \tfrac{1}{2}g, \tag{10.84}$$

where

$$g = \sum_{p=1}^{P} M_p\ln(|\boldsymbol{\Omega}_{(p)}|) + Q, \tag{10.85}$$
$$Q = \sum_{p=1}^{P}\sum_{j=1}^{M_p}\boldsymbol{\epsilon}'_{(jp)}\boldsymbol{\Omega}_{(p)}^{-1}\boldsymbol{\epsilon}_{(jp)}. \tag{10.86}$$

Obviously, $\ln(\mathcal{L})$ is maximized when g is minimized, and for given σ^2 and σ_α^2,

$$\max_{k,\boldsymbol{\beta}}[\ln(\mathcal{L})] \iff \min_{k,\boldsymbol{\beta}}[Q],$$

The latter problem is identical to the GLS problem for known variance components, discussed in Section 10.4.2, except that the ordering of observations differs. As in our earlier applications of ML, we split the problem into:

Sub-problem A: maximization of $\ln(\mathcal{L})$ *with respect to* $(\boldsymbol{\beta}, k)$, *given* $(\sigma^2, \sigma_\alpha^2)$.

Sub-problem B: maximization of $\ln(\mathcal{L})$ *with respect to* $(\sigma^2, \sigma_\alpha^2)$, *given* $(\boldsymbol{\beta}, k)$.

Sub-problem A coincides with the GLS problem. Using the changed notation, the (conditional) estimators (10.62)–(10.63) can be written as

$$\widetilde{\boldsymbol{\beta}} = \widetilde{\boldsymbol{\beta}}(\sigma^2,\sigma_\alpha^2)$$
$$= [\sum_{p=1}^{P} W_{XX(p)} + \sum_{p=1}^{P}\sum_{j=1}^{M_p}\theta_{Bp}p(\bar{\boldsymbol{x}}_{(jp)}-\bar{\bar{\boldsymbol{x}}})'(\bar{\boldsymbol{x}}_{(jp)}-\bar{\bar{\boldsymbol{x}}})]^{-1}$$
$$\times [\sum_{p=1}^{P} W_{XY(p)} + \sum_{p=1}^{P}\sum_{j=1}^{M_p}\theta_{Bp}p(\bar{\boldsymbol{x}}_{(jp)}-\bar{\bar{\boldsymbol{x}}})'(\bar{y}_{(jp)}-\bar{\bar{y}})], \tag{10.87}$$
$$\widetilde{k} = \widetilde{k}(\sigma^2,\sigma_\alpha^2) = \bar{\bar{y}} - \bar{\bar{\boldsymbol{x}}}\widetilde{\boldsymbol{\beta}}, \tag{10.88}$$

where $\widetilde{\bar{y}}$ and $\widetilde{\bar{x}}$, formerly given by (10.51), now are expressed as

$$\begin{aligned}\widetilde{\bar{y}} &= \frac{\sum_{p=1}^{P}\sum_{j=1}^{M_p}\theta_{Bp}p\,\bar{y}_{(jp)}}{\sum_{p=1}^{P}\sum_{j=1}^{M_p}\theta_{Bp}p},\\ \widetilde{\bar{\boldsymbol{x}}} &= \frac{\sum_{p=1}^{P}\sum_{j=1}^{M_p}\theta_{Bp}p\,\bar{\boldsymbol{x}}_{(jp)}}{\sum_{p=1}^{P}\sum_{j=1}^{M_p}\theta_{Bp}p}.\end{aligned} \tag{10.89}$$

Sub-problem B has first-order conditions:

$$\sum_{p=1}^{P}\frac{\partial g_p}{\partial\sigma^2} = \sum_{p=1}^{P}\frac{\partial g_p}{\partial\sigma_\alpha^2} = 0. \tag{10.90}$$

Since it follows from (10.83) that

$$\begin{aligned}\frac{\partial g_p}{\partial\sigma^2} &= M_p\left[\frac{p-1}{\sigma^2}+\frac{1}{\sigma^2+p\sigma_\alpha^2}\right]-\left[\frac{W_{\epsilon\epsilon(p)}}{(\sigma^2)^2}+\frac{B_{\epsilon\epsilon(p)}}{(\sigma^2+p\sigma_\alpha^2)^2}\right],\\ \frac{\partial g_p}{\partial\sigma_\alpha^2} &= \frac{M_p p}{\sigma^2+p\sigma_\alpha^2}-\frac{pB_{\epsilon\epsilon(p)}}{(\sigma^2+p\sigma_\alpha^2)^2},\end{aligned}$$

we obtain a non-linear equation system in σ^2 and σ_α^2:

$$\sum_{p=1}^{P}\left[\frac{M_p p}{\widetilde{\sigma}^2+p\widetilde{\sigma}_\alpha^2}\right] = \sum_{p=1}^{P}\left[\frac{pB_{\epsilon\epsilon(p)}}{(\widetilde{\sigma}^2+p\widetilde{\sigma}_\alpha^2)^2}\right], \tag{10.91}$$

$$\sum_{p=1}^{P}M_p\left[\frac{p-1}{\widetilde{\sigma}^2}+\frac{1}{\widetilde{\sigma}^2+p\widetilde{\sigma}_\alpha^2}\right] = \sum_{p=1}^{P}\left[\frac{W_{\epsilon\epsilon(p)}}{(\widetilde{\sigma}^2)^2}+\frac{B_{\epsilon\epsilon(p)}}{(\widetilde{\sigma}^2+p\widetilde{\sigma}_\alpha^2)^2}\right]. \tag{10.92}$$

Its solution, denoted by tildes, cannot be written in closed form, but $\widetilde{\sigma}^2$ and $\widetilde{\sigma}_\alpha^2$ can be computed iteratively by choosing suitable starting values, for example, those obtained from (10.79)–(10.80).

How can this be condensed in a prescription for ML estimation? Again, maximization can proceed iteratively, for example as follows:

1. Set $\widetilde{\sigma}_\alpha^2 = 0$, and compute $\widetilde{\boldsymbol{\beta}}$ by OLS, which is consistent.
2. Compute the residuals $\widetilde{\epsilon}_{(jp)k}$, their within- and between-individual sums of squares $W_{\epsilon\epsilon(p)}$ and $B_{\epsilon\epsilon(p)}$, and $\widetilde{\sigma}^2 = \widetilde{\sigma}^2(\widetilde{\boldsymbol{\beta}}, \widetilde{k})$ and $\widetilde{\sigma}_\alpha^2 = \widetilde{\sigma}_\alpha^2(\widetilde{\boldsymbol{\beta}}, \widetilde{k})$ by solving (10.91)–(10.92) iteratively.

3. Compute $\widetilde{\boldsymbol{\beta}}=\widetilde{\boldsymbol{\beta}}(\widetilde{\sigma}^2,\widetilde{\sigma}_\alpha^2)$ and $\widetilde{k}=\widetilde{k}(\widetilde{\sigma}^2,\widetilde{\sigma}_\alpha^2)$, from (10.87)–(10.88).
4. Compute $\ln(\mathcal{L})$ from (10.84)–(10.86). If convergence is confirmed, finish and proceed to step 5. Otherwise, repeat steps 2–4.
5. Finally, compute $\widetilde{\sigma}^2 = \widetilde{\sigma}^2(\widetilde{\boldsymbol{\beta}},\widetilde{k})$ and $\widetilde{\sigma}_\alpha^2 = \widetilde{\sigma}_\alpha^2(\widetilde{\boldsymbol{\beta}},\widetilde{k})$.

A generalization of this ML-related procedure for single-equation models, for a *system* of regression equations, which also generalizes the procedures for the regression systems considered in Section 12.2 for the balanced case, is considered in Biørn (2004).

Appendix 10A. **Between estimation: Proofs**

In this appendix we show that OLS applied on the $\sqrt{T_i}$-weighted regression equation in individual-specific means, (10.17), leads to (10.20). Taking *origo* regression of $\sqrt{T_i}\bar{y}_{i\cdot}$ on $\sqrt{T_i}$ and $\sqrt{T_i}\bar{x}_{i\cdot}$, gives

$$\widehat{\beta}_{B2} = \frac{\big[\sum_i(\sqrt{T_i}\bar{y}_{i\cdot})(\sqrt{T_i}\bar{x}_{i\cdot})\big]\big[\sum_i(\sqrt{T_i})^2\big]-\big[\sum_i(\sqrt{T_i}\bar{y}_{i\cdot})(\sqrt{T_i})\big]\big[\sum_i(\sqrt{T_i})(\sqrt{T_i}\bar{x}_{i\cdot})\big]}{\big[\sum_i(\sqrt{T_i})^2\big]\big[\sum_i(\sqrt{T_i}\bar{x}_{i\cdot})^2\big]-\big[\sum_i(\sqrt{T_i})(\sqrt{T_i}\bar{x}_{i\cdot})\big]^2},$$

$$\widehat{\alpha}_{B2} = \frac{\big[\sum_i(\sqrt{T_i}\bar{y}_{i\cdot})(\sqrt{T_i})\big]\big[\sum_i(\sqrt{T_i}\bar{x}_{i\cdot})^2\big]-\big[\sum_i(\sqrt{T_i}\bar{y}_{i\cdot})(\sqrt{T_i}\bar{x}_{i\cdot})\big]\big[\sum_i(\sqrt{T_i})(\sqrt{T_i}\bar{x}_{i\cdot})\big]}{\big[\sum_i(\sqrt{T_i})^2\big]\big[\sum_i(\sqrt{T_i}\bar{x}_{i\cdot})^2\big]-\big[\sum_i(\sqrt{T_i})(\sqrt{T_i}\bar{x}_{i\cdot})\big]^2},$$

which can be rearranged to

$$\widehat{\beta}_{B2} = \frac{[\sum_i T_i\bar{x}_{i\cdot}\bar{y}_{i\cdot}][\sum_i T_i]-[\sum_i T_i\bar{x}_{i\cdot}][\sum_i T_i\bar{y}_{i\cdot}]}{[\sum_i T_i][\sum_i T_i\bar{x}_{i\cdot}^2]-[\sum_i T_i\bar{x}_{i\cdot}]^2}, \tag{10A.1}$$

$$\widehat{\alpha}_{B2} = \frac{[\sum_i T_i\bar{y}_{i\cdot}][\sum_i T_i\bar{x}_{i\cdot}^2]-[\sum_i T_i\bar{x}_{i\cdot}\bar{y}_{i\cdot}][\sum_i T_i\bar{x}_{i\cdot}]}{[\sum_i T_i][\sum_i T_i\bar{x}_{i\cdot}^2]-[\sum_i T_i\bar{x}_{i\cdot}]^2}. \tag{10A.2}$$

Since $\sum_i T_i = n$, these expressions can be further rewritten as

$$\widehat{\beta}_{B2} = \frac{(\sum_i T_i\bar{x}_{i\cdot}\bar{y}_{i\cdot})n-(n\bar{x})(n\bar{y})}{n(\sum_i T_i\bar{x}_{i\cdot}^2)-(n\bar{x})^2} \equiv \frac{\sum_i T_i\bar{x}_{i\cdot}\bar{y}_{i\cdot}-n\bar{x}\bar{y}}{\sum_i T_i\bar{x}_{i\cdot}^2-n\bar{x}^2}, \tag{10A.3}$$

$$\widehat{\alpha}_{B2} = \frac{n\bar{y}(\sum_i T_i\bar{x}_{i\cdot}^2)-(\sum_i T_i\bar{x}_{i\cdot}\bar{y}_{i\cdot})n\bar{x}}{n(\sum_i T_i\bar{x}_{i\cdot}^2)-(n\bar{x})^2} \equiv \frac{(\sum_i T_i\bar{x}_{i\cdot}^2)\bar{y}-(\sum_i T_i\bar{x}_{i\cdot}\bar{y}_{i\cdot})\bar{x}}{\sum_i T_i\bar{x}_{i\cdot}^2-n\bar{x}^2}, \tag{10A.4}$$

which can be rearranged to (10.20).

Appendix 10B. **GLS estimation: Proofs**

In this appendix, we give proofs, first of (10.49)–(10.50) ($K=1$), next of (10.60)–(10.61) (K arbitrary).

10B.1 The one-regressor case: since from (10.47) we have

$$Q^* = \sigma^2 Q = \textstyle\sum_{i=1}^{N} (y_i - e_{T_i} k - x_i \beta)' C_{T_i} (y_i - e_{T_i} k - x_i \beta), \tag{10B.1}$$

Q^* can be rewritten as

$$\begin{aligned} Q^* = &\textstyle\sum_i y_i' C_{T_i} y_i + k^2 \sum_i e_{T_i}' C_{T_i} e_{T_i} + \beta^2 \sum_i x_i' C_{T_i} x_i \\ &- 2k \textstyle\sum_i e_{T_i}' C_{T_i} y_i - 2\beta \sum_i x_i' C_{T_i} y_i + 2k\beta \sum_i e_{T_i}' C_{T_i} x_i. \end{aligned}$$

The first-order conditions for minimization of Q^* then become

$$\begin{aligned} \frac{\partial Q^*}{\partial k} &= 2k(\textstyle\sum_i e_{T_i}' C_{T_i} e_{T_i}) - 2(\sum_i e_{T_i}' C_{T_i} y_i) + 2\beta(\sum_i e_{T_i}' C_{T_i} x_i) = 0, \\ \frac{\partial Q^*}{\partial \beta} &= 2\beta(\textstyle\sum_i x_i' C_{T_i} x_i) - 2(\sum_i x_i' C_{T_i} y_i) + 2k(\sum_i e_{T_i}' C_{T_i} x_i) = 0, \end{aligned}$$

giving as solution values

$$\widehat{\beta}_{GLS} = \frac{(\sum_i x_i' C_{T_i} y_i)(\sum_i e_{T_i}' C_{T_i} e_{T_i}) - (\sum_i e_{T_i}' C_{T_i} y_i)(\sum_i e_{T_i}' C_{T_i} x_i)}{(\sum_i x_i' C_{T_i} x_i)(\sum_i e_{T_i}' C_{T_i} e_{T_i}) - (\sum_i e_{T_i}' C_{T_i} x_i)^2}, \tag{10B.2}$$

$$\widehat{k}_{GLS} = \frac{\sum_i e_{T_i}' C_{T_i} y_i}{\sum_i e_{T_i}' C_{T_i} e_{T_i}} - \frac{\sum_i e_{T_i}' C_{T_i} x_i}{\sum_i e_{T_i}' C_{T_i} e_{T_i}} \widehat{\beta}_{GLS}. \tag{10B.3}$$

Using (10.48), since $A_{T_i} e_{T_i} = e_{T_i}$, $B_{T_i} e_{T_i} = 0_{T_i,1}$, $e_{T_i}' e_{T_i} = T_i$, it follows that

$$\begin{aligned} &\textstyle\sum_i e_{T_i}' C_{T_i} e_{T_i} = \sum_i \theta_{Bi} e_{T_i}' e_{T_i} = \sum_i \theta_{Bi} T_i, \\ &\textstyle\sum_i e_{T_i}' C_{T_i} x_i = \sum_i \theta_{Bi} e_{T_i}' x_i = \sum_i \theta_{Bi} T_i \bar{x}_{i\cdot}, \\ &\textstyle\sum_i e_{T_i}' C_{T_i} y_i = \sum_i \theta_{Bi} e_{T_i}' y_i = \sum_i \theta_{Bi} T_i \bar{y}_{i\cdot}, \\ &\textstyle\sum_i x_i' C_{T_i} x_i = \sum_i x_i' B_{T_i} x_i + \sum_i \theta_{Bi} x_i' A_{T_i} x_i = W_{XX} + \sum_i \theta_{Bi} T_i \bar{x}_{i\cdot}^2, \\ &\textstyle\sum_i x_i' C_{T_i} y_i = \sum_i x_i' B_{T_i} y_i + \sum_i \theta_{Bi} x_i' A_{T_i} y_i = W_{XY} + \sum_i \theta_{Bi} T_i \bar{x}_{i\cdot} \bar{y}_{i\cdot}. \end{aligned}$$

The GLS estimators can therefore be rewritten as

$$\widehat{\beta}_{GLS} = \frac{[W_{XY} + \sum_i \theta_{Bi} T_i \bar{x}_{i\cdot} \bar{y}_{i\cdot}][\sum_i \theta_{Bi} T_i] - [\sum_i \theta_{Bi} T_i \bar{x}_{i\cdot}][\sum_i \theta_{Bi} T_i \bar{y}_{i\cdot}]}{[W_{XX} + \sum_i \theta_{Bi} T_i \bar{x}_{i\cdot}^2][\sum_i \theta_{Bi} T_i] - [\sum_i \theta_{Bi} T_i \bar{x}_{i\cdot}]^2}, \tag{10B.4}$$

$$\widehat{k}_{GLS} = \frac{\sum_i \theta_{Bi} T_i \bar{y}_{i\cdot}}{\sum_i \theta_{Bi} T_i} - \frac{\sum_i \theta_{Bi} T_i \bar{x}_{i\cdot}}{\sum_i \theta_{Bi} T_i} \widehat{\beta}_{GLS}. \tag{10B.5}$$

10B.2 The K-regressor case: since from (10.59) we have

$$Q^* = \sigma^2 Q = \sum_{i=1}^{N} (y_i - e_{T_i} k - X_i \boldsymbol{\beta})' C_{T_i} (y_i - e_{T_i} k - X_i \boldsymbol{\beta}), \tag{10B.6}$$

Q^* can be written as

$$\begin{aligned} Q^* &= \textstyle\sum_i y_i' C_{T_i} y_i + k^2 \sum_i e_{T_i}' C_{T_i} e_{T_i} + \boldsymbol{\beta}' (\sum_i X_i' C_{T_i} X_i) \boldsymbol{\beta} \\ &\quad - 2k \textstyle\sum_i e_{T_i}' C_{T_i} y_i - 2\boldsymbol{\beta}' \sum_i X_i' C_{T_i} y_i + 2k \boldsymbol{\beta}' (\sum_i X_i' C_{T_i} e_{T_i}). \end{aligned}$$

Since, in general, $(\partial \boldsymbol{a}' \boldsymbol{M} \boldsymbol{a})/(\partial \boldsymbol{a}) = 2\boldsymbol{M}\boldsymbol{a}$ and $(\partial \boldsymbol{a}' \boldsymbol{B})/(\partial \boldsymbol{a}) = \boldsymbol{B}$, see, e.g., Greene (2008, Appendix A.8.1), the first-order conditions for minimization of Q^* become

$$\begin{aligned} \frac{\partial Q^*}{\partial k} &= 2k(\textstyle\sum_i e_{T_i}' C_{T_i} e_{T_i}) - 2(\sum_i e_{T_i}' C_{T_i} y_i) + 2\boldsymbol{\beta}' (\sum_i X_i' C_{T_i} e_{T_i}) = 0, \\ \frac{\partial Q^*}{\partial \boldsymbol{\beta}} &= 2(\textstyle\sum_i X_i' C_{T_i} X_i) \boldsymbol{\beta} - 2(\sum_i X_i' C_{T_i} y_i) + 2k(\sum_i X_i' C_{T_i} e_{T_i}) = \boldsymbol{0}. \end{aligned}$$

The GLS estimators can therefore be rewritten as

$$\begin{aligned} \widehat{\boldsymbol{\beta}}_{GLS} &= [(\textstyle\sum_i X_i' C_{T_i} X_i)(\sum_i e_{T_i}' C_{T_i} e_{T_i}) - (\sum_i e_{T_i}' C_{T_i} X_i)(\sum_i X_i' C_{T_i} e_{T_i})]^{-1} \\ &\quad \times [(\textstyle\sum_i X_i' C_{T_i} y_i)(\sum_i e_{T_i}' C_{T_i} e_{T_i}) - (\sum_i e_{T_i}' C_{T_i} y_i)(\sum_i X_i' C_{T_i} e_{T_i})], \end{aligned} \tag{10B.7}$$

$$\widehat{k}_{GLS} = \frac{\sum_i e_{T_i}' C_{T_i} y_i}{\sum_i e_{T_i}' C_{T_i} e_{T_i}} - \frac{\sum_i e_{T_i}' C_{T_i} X_i}{\sum_i e_{T_i}' C_{T_i} e_{T_i}} \widehat{\boldsymbol{\beta}}_{GLS}. \tag{10B.8}$$

Using algebra similar to that for $K = 1$, we find that (10B.4)–(10B.5) are generalized to

$$\begin{aligned} \widehat{\boldsymbol{\beta}}_{GLS} &= \left([W_{XX} + \textstyle\sum_i \theta_{Bi} T_i \bar{x}_{i\cdot}' \bar{x}_{i\cdot}][\sum_i \theta_{Bi} T_i] - [\sum_i \theta_{Bi} T_i \bar{x}_{i\cdot}'][\sum_i \theta_{Bi} T_i \bar{x}_{i\cdot}]\right)^{-1} \\ &\quad \times \left([W_{XY} + \textstyle\sum_i \theta_{Bi} T_i \bar{x}_{i\cdot}' \bar{y}_{i\cdot}][\sum_i \theta_{Bi} T_i] - [\sum_i \theta_{Bi} T_i \bar{x}_{i\cdot}'][\sum_i \theta_{Bi} T_i \bar{y}_{i\cdot}]\right), \end{aligned} \tag{10B.9}$$

$$\widehat{k}_{GLS} = \frac{\sum_i \theta_{Bi} T_i \bar{y}_{i\cdot}}{\sum_i \theta_{Bi} T_i} - \frac{\sum_i \theta_{Bi} T_i \bar{x}_{i\cdot}}{\sum_i \theta_{Bi} T_i} \widehat{\boldsymbol{\beta}}_{GLS}. \tag{10B.10}$$

Appendix 10C. **Estimation of variance components: Details**

In this appendix we prove (10.65)–(10.66). Since the α_is and u_{it}s are independent, we have

$$\mathsf{E}(W_{\epsilon\epsilon}|X) = \mathsf{E}(W_{uu}|X), \quad (10C.1)$$

$$\mathsf{E}(B_{\epsilon\epsilon}|X) = \mathsf{E}(B_{\alpha\alpha}|X) + \mathsf{E}(B_{uu}|X), \quad (10C.2)$$

where

$$\begin{aligned}
W_{\epsilon\epsilon} &= \textstyle\sum_{i=1}^{N}\sum_{t=1}^{T_i}(\epsilon_{it} - \bar{\epsilon}_{i\cdot})^2 = \sum_{i=1}^{N}\sum_{t=1}^{T_i}\epsilon_{it}^2 - \sum_{i=1}^{N} T_i\bar{\epsilon}_{i\cdot}^2, \\
B_{\epsilon\epsilon} &= \textstyle\sum_{i=1}^{N} T_i(\bar{\epsilon}_{i\cdot} - \bar{\epsilon})^2 = \sum_{i=1}^{N}\sum_{t=1}^{T_i}\epsilon_{it}^2 - \sum_{i=1}^{N} T_i\bar{\epsilon}_{i\cdot}^2, \\
W_{uu} &= \textstyle\sum_{i=1}^{N}\sum_{t=1}^{T_i}(u_{it} - \bar{u}_{i\cdot})^2 = \sum_{i=1}^{N}\sum_{t=1}^{T_i} u_{it}^2 - \sum_{i=1}^{N} T_i\bar{u}_{i\cdot}^2, \\
B_{uu} &= \textstyle\sum_{i=1}^{N} T_i(\bar{u}_{i\cdot} - \bar{u})^2 = \sum_{i=1}^{N} T_i\bar{u}_{i\cdot}^2 - (\sum_{i=1}^{N} T_i)\bar{u}^2, \\
B_{\alpha\alpha} &= \textstyle\sum_{i=1}^{N} T_i(\alpha_i - \bar{\alpha})^2 = \sum_{i=1}^{N} T_i\alpha_i^2 - (\sum_{i=1}^{N} T_i)\bar{\alpha}^2, \\
\bar{\epsilon}_{i\cdot} &= \textstyle\sum_{t=1}^{T_i}\epsilon_{it}/T_i, \\
\bar{u}_{i\cdot} &= \textstyle\sum_{t=1}^{T_i} u_{it}/T_i, \\
\bar{\epsilon} &= \textstyle(\sum_{i=1}^{N} T_i\bar{\epsilon}_{i\cdot})/(\sum_{i=1}^{N} T_i), \\
\bar{u} &= \textstyle(\sum_{i=1}^{N} T_i\bar{u}_{i\cdot})/(\sum_{i=1}^{N} T_i), \\
\bar{\alpha} &= \textstyle(\sum_{i=1}^{N} T_i\alpha_i)/(\sum_{i=1}^{N} T_i).
\end{aligned}$$

Note that $\bar{\alpha}$ is a *weighted* mean of the α_is. From (10.36) it follows that

$$\begin{aligned}
\mathsf{E}(\bar{u}_{i\cdot}^2|X) &= \frac{\sigma^2}{T_i}, \\
\mathsf{E}(\bar{u}^2|X) &= \frac{\sigma^2}{\sum_i T_i}, \\
\mathsf{E}(\bar{\alpha}^2|X) &= \frac{(\sum T_i^2)\sigma_\alpha^2}{(\sum T_i)^2}.
\end{aligned}$$

Hence,

$$\mathsf{E}(W_{uu}|X) = (\textstyle\sum T_i - N)\sigma^2 = (n - N)\sigma^2, \quad (10C.3)$$

$$\mathsf{E}(B_{uu}|X) = (N - 1)\sigma^2, \quad (10C.4)$$

$$\mathsf{E}(B_{\alpha\alpha}|X) = \left(\sum T_i - \frac{\sum T_i^2}{\sum T_i}\right)\sigma_\alpha^2 = \left(n - \frac{\sum T_i^2}{n}\right)\sigma_\alpha^2. \tag{10C.5}$$

Combining (10C.1)–(10C.5) it finally follows that

$$\mathsf{E}(W_{\epsilon\epsilon}|X) = (n-N)\sigma^2, \tag{10C.6}$$

$$\mathsf{E}(B_{\epsilon\epsilon}|X) = \left(n - \frac{\sum T_i^2}{n}\right)\sigma_\alpha^2 + (N-1)\sigma^2. \tag{10C.7}$$

11 Panel data with systematic unbalance

CHAPTER SUMMARY

The chapter relates to, and extends parts of, Chapters 9 and 10. It focuses on observation (selection) rules and systematically unbalanced panel data. The unbalance may follow from the sampling process, which often mirrors properties of the endogenous variables and violates 'classical' assumptions in regression analysis. The observations may be distorted by the data generating process. Key concepts are censoring and truncation, and the truncated normal and binormal distributions (properties of which are given in an appendix) play important roles. Questions addressed are, *inter alia*, which kind of biases arise when the observation rules are neglected and how proceed by ML estimation when paying regard to these rules). Empirical examples are given.

11.1 Introduction: Observation rules

When a set of panel data is unbalanced, there is every reason for its user to ask why this is so. The answer may motivate the kind of model and method to be used. The situation discussed in Chapter 10 related to cases where the data set is generated from a mechanism denoted, somewhat vaguely, as one where observations are missing in a non-systematic, or 'ignorable' way. What is meant by this, and how should we proceed if there is reason to believe that the panel data set contains observations that are missing in a *systematic, non-ignorable* way? In this chapter we seek to provide *some* answers to these questions and, as parts of the answers, introduce other concepts, such as censoring, truncation, and selection.

Systematic selection arguably occurs in virtually any panel (and cross-section) data set. We cannot fully avoid it. For example, people having decided (in all periods covered by a panel or in some of them) to live in certain regions, having decided not to taste alcohol, not to smoke, or not to have a driving licence may be idiosyncratic in some (other) sense. It is impossible to obtain (by statistically funded procedures) a sample that is completely representative 'in any direction' or 'completely random'. The question is always: random with respect to what? A profound, unsettled question is whether it is possible to obtain randomness with respect to (genuinely) latent variables affecting the observed variable of interest. Anyway, when judging whether a method is 'sound' relative to a specific model, it is, as always, essential to ask how the model and results are to be applied.

Motivating examples will be given as a start. Let y^*_{it} denote the value for individual i in period t of a *potentially unobserved* variable y^*, determined by

$$y^*_{it} = \boldsymbol{x}_{it}\boldsymbol{\beta} + \alpha_i - u_{it}, \tag{11.1}$$

where $\boldsymbol{x}_{it}$ is a vector of observed explanatory variables, α_i is a latent individual-specific effect, and u_{it} is a disturbance. This equation has the same form as the equation for the latent y^*_{it} in the discrete response model in Sections 9.2.3 and 9.3.1, there assumed to determine an observed variable, y_{it}, through a step function, representing a very simple observation mechanism. We now have

$$\mathsf{E}(y^*_{it}|X) = \boldsymbol{x}_{it}\boldsymbol{\beta} + \mathsf{E}(\alpha_i|X) - \mathsf{E}(u_{it}|X), \tag{11.2}$$

$$\mathsf{E}(y^*_{it}|X,\alpha_i) = \boldsymbol{x}_{it}\boldsymbol{\beta} + \alpha_i - \mathsf{E}(u_{it}|X,\alpha_i), \tag{11.3}$$

X still denoting all realizations of $\boldsymbol{x}_{it}$. Let y_{it} denote the observation on the endogenous variable, if it exists, and let R_{it} symbolize a mechanism for (potential) realization (i,t) such that: if R_{it} is true, $y_{it} = y^*_{it}$, while if R_{it} is untrue, denoted as R^*_{it}, we may have either (A) no observation of y_{it} at all or (B) a distorted observation given by $y_{it} = H(y^*_{it})$, where $H(y^*_{it})$ may well be a constant. We call R_{it} an *observation (selection) rule*. It may be technically or institutionally based or rooted in individual behaviour. In the latter case, a decision of the respondent determines which kind of observation, if any, we shall have. The sample emerges as a set of unbalanced panel data, *and the non-balance pattern is endogenous*, described by the model. If the decision determines whether we shall have an observation, as in case (A), the mechanism may be called *self-selection*. We will classify a panel data set as being *systematically unbalanced* when it contains a mixture of distorted and non-distorted observations, as in case (B), even if the observations cover the same period for all individuals.

Consider the expectation of y_{it} when an observation rule is effective. In case (A) (no observation under R^*_{it}), we have

$$f_R(\boldsymbol{x}_{it}) \equiv \mathsf{E}(y_{it}|X,R_{it}) = \boldsymbol{x}_{it}\boldsymbol{\beta} + \mathsf{E}(\alpha_i|X,R_{it}) - \mathsf{E}(u_{it}|X,R_{it}), \tag{11.4}$$

$$f_{R\alpha}(\boldsymbol{x}_{it}) \equiv \mathsf{E}(y_{it}|X,\alpha_i,R_{it}) = \boldsymbol{x}_{it}\boldsymbol{\beta} + \alpha_i - \mathsf{E}(u_{it}|X,\alpha_i,R_{it}). \tag{11.5}$$

In case (B) (distorted observation under R^*_{it}), $P(R_{it}|X)$ denoting the probability that the observation rule is satisfied, the rule of iterated expectation implies

$$g_R(\boldsymbol{x}_{it}) \equiv \mathsf{E}(y_{it}|X) = \mathsf{E}(y_{it}|X,R_{it})P(R_{it}|X) + \mathsf{E}(H(y^*_{it})|X,R^*_{it})[1-P(R_{it}|X)], \tag{11.6}$$

$$g_{R\alpha}(\boldsymbol{x}_{it}) \equiv \mathsf{E}(y_{it}|X,\alpha_i) = \mathsf{E}(y_{it}|X,\alpha_i,R_{it})P(R_{it}|X,\alpha_i) + \mathsf{E}(H(y^*_{it})|X,\alpha_i,R^*_{it})[1-P(R_{it}|X,\alpha_i)]. \tag{11.7}$$

Our aim is to uncover $\boldsymbol{\beta}$ from functions like (11.4)–(11.7) by confronting them with observations on $(y_{it}, \boldsymbol{x}_{it})$.

We illustrate this somewhat abstract framework by three examples leading to specific $f_R(\boldsymbol{x}_{it})$ and $f_{R\alpha}(\boldsymbol{x}_{it})$ functions:[1] $(y_{it}, \boldsymbol{x}_{it})$ exist if, respectively, (1) y_{it} belongs to an interval, (2) $\boldsymbol{x}_{it}$ is in some region, $\mathcal{A}$, and (3) α_i is in some region, $\mathcal{B}$:

(1). $y_{it} \in (a, b) \implies$

$$\begin{aligned}
\mathsf{E}[y_{it}|X, y_{it} \in (a,b)] &= \boldsymbol{x}_{it}\boldsymbol{\beta} + \mathsf{E}[\alpha_i|X, \boldsymbol{x}_{it}\boldsymbol{\beta}+\alpha_i-b < u_{it} < \boldsymbol{x}_{it}\boldsymbol{\beta}+\alpha_i-a] \\
&\quad - \mathsf{E}[u_{it}|X, \boldsymbol{x}_{it}\boldsymbol{\beta}+\alpha_i-b < u_{it} < \boldsymbol{x}_{it}\boldsymbol{\beta}+\alpha_i-a], \\
\mathsf{E}[y_{it}|X, \alpha_i, y_{it} \in (a,b)] &= \boldsymbol{x}_{it}\boldsymbol{\beta}+\alpha_i-\mathsf{E}(u_{it}|X, \boldsymbol{x}_{it}\boldsymbol{\beta}+\alpha_i-b < u_{it} < \boldsymbol{x}_{it}\boldsymbol{\beta}+\alpha_i-a).
\end{aligned}$$

(2). $\boldsymbol{x}_{it} \in \mathcal{A} \implies$

$$\begin{aligned}
\mathsf{E}(y_{it}|X, \boldsymbol{x}_{it} \in \mathcal{A}) &= \boldsymbol{x}_{it}\boldsymbol{\beta} + \mathsf{E}[\alpha_i|X, \boldsymbol{x}_{it} \in \mathcal{A}] - \mathsf{E}[u_{it}|X, \boldsymbol{x}_{it} \in \mathcal{A}], \\
\mathsf{E}(y_{it}|X, \alpha_i, \boldsymbol{x}_{it} \in \mathcal{A}) &= \boldsymbol{x}_{it}\boldsymbol{\beta}+\alpha_i-\mathsf{E}[u_{it}|X, \alpha_i, \boldsymbol{x}_{it} \in \mathcal{A}].
\end{aligned}$$

(3). $\alpha_i \in \mathcal{B} \implies$

$$\mathsf{E}(y_{it}|X, \alpha_i \in \mathcal{B}) = \boldsymbol{x}_{it}\boldsymbol{\beta}+\mathsf{E}(\alpha_i|X, \alpha_i \in \mathcal{B})-\mathsf{E}[u_{it}|X, \alpha_i \in \mathcal{B}).$$

In all examples, $f_R(\boldsymbol{x}_{it})$ and $f_{R\alpha}(\boldsymbol{x}_{it})$ depend on the distribution of $(\boldsymbol{x}_{it}, \alpha_i, u_{it})$. In (1), they also depend on (a, b), while in (2) and (3) they also depend on, respectively, $\mathcal{A}$ and $\mathcal{B}$. In (1), the observation rule involves y_{it} and therefore u_{it} and $\boldsymbol{x}_{it}$ (as exogeneity of the latter implies no feedback from y_{it} to $\boldsymbol{x}_{it}$). In (2), the observation rule involves $\boldsymbol{x}_{it}$, and hence involves α_i only if α_i depends on $\boldsymbol{x}_{it}$, while in (3), the observation rule involves α_i and hence involves u_{it} only if α_i depends on u_{it}.

If we in addition assume that $\boldsymbol{x}_{it}$ and u_{it} as well as α_i and u_{it} are independent, then

$$\begin{aligned}
\mathsf{E}[y_{it}|X, \alpha_i, y_{it} \in (a,b)] &= \boldsymbol{x}_{it}\boldsymbol{\beta}+\alpha_i-\mathsf{E}(u_{it}|\boldsymbol{x}_{it}\boldsymbol{\beta}+\alpha_i-b < u_{it} < \boldsymbol{x}_{it}\boldsymbol{\beta}+\alpha_i-a), \\
\mathsf{E}(y_{it}|X, \boldsymbol{x}_{it} \in \mathcal{A}) &= \boldsymbol{x}_{it}\boldsymbol{\beta}+\mathsf{E}(\alpha_i|X, \boldsymbol{x}_{it} \in \mathcal{A}), \\
\mathsf{E}(y_{it}|X, \alpha_i \in \mathcal{B}) &= \boldsymbol{x}_{it}\boldsymbol{\beta}+\mathsf{E}(\alpha_i|X, \alpha_i \in \mathcal{B}).
\end{aligned}$$

If, still stronger, $\boldsymbol{x}_{it}$, u_{it}, *and* α_i are all independent, we have $\mathsf{E}(y_{it}|X, \boldsymbol{x}_{it} \in \mathcal{A}) = \mathsf{E}(y_{it}|X) = \boldsymbol{x}_{it}\boldsymbol{\beta}$ irrespective of $\mathcal{A}$. The latter is a case where the observation rule is ignorable. On the other hand, $\mathsf{E}[y_{it}|X, \alpha_i, y_{it} \in (a,b)]$ and $\mathsf{E}(y_{it}|X, \alpha_i \in \mathcal{B})$ still represent $\boldsymbol{x}_{it}\boldsymbol{\beta}$ in a distorted way, making their observation rules non-ignorable.

[1] If also $H(y^*_{it})$, $P(R_{it}|X)$, and $P(R_{it}|X, \alpha_i)$ are specified, the corresponding $g_R(\boldsymbol{x}_{it})$ and $g_{R\alpha}(\boldsymbol{x}_{it})$ can be obtained, see (11.6) and (11.7).

A situation as in example (2) may occur if the functional form in (11.1) is *mis-specified*, e.g., a linear form used instead of a quadratic or cubic. The range restriction on $\boldsymbol{x}_{it}$ may then give $\mathsf{E}(u_{it}|X, \boldsymbol{x}_{it} \in \mathcal{A}) \neq 0$ even if $\mathsf{E}(u_{it}|X) = 0$.

A concrete interpretation of example (3) may be: a panel data set collected at some place where drivers of own cars are more likely to be observed than are persons usually going by (usually slower) public transport. Then we may over-represent impatient persons with a 'fast lifestyle' who consider time a precious good. Assume further that neither of y_{it} and $\boldsymbol{x}_{it}$ involves transportation activities. Then the relationship between $\mathsf{E}(y_{it}|X)$ and $\boldsymbol{x}_{it}$, and hence our inference on $\boldsymbol{\beta}$, may be distorted if impatience and 'fast lifestyle', being 'part of' α_i, affects $\boldsymbol{x}_{it}$ and this mechanism is not modelled.

Our aim is to estimate $\boldsymbol{\beta}$ from observations on $(y_{it}, \boldsymbol{x}_{it})$. Examples (1)–(3) indicate that only exceptionally this coefficient vector can be uncovered by linearizing functions like (11.4)–(11.7) and attempting to estimate their first-derivatives. An interesting related question, to be addressed, is which properties classical linear regression has when the observation rules are neglected.

We leave examples (2) and (3) here. In the rest of the chapter, dealing with situations related to example (1), focus will be on the distinction between (A) (no observation if R_{it} untrue) and (B) (distorted observation if R_{it} untrue). In Section 11.2 we consider models for truncated and censored data, disregarding latent heterogeneity, and how their parameters can be estimated by ML and multi-step procedures. Section 11.3 extends by introducing individual-specific effects, and modifies the methods accordingly. In Section 11.4 we consider multi-equation models where the truncation or censoring of the variable explained in one equation may involve endogenous variables determined in other equations.

11.2 Truncation and censoring: Baseline models

With Section 11.1 as background, we consider a baseline model without heterogeneity and explain how it can represent observation rules denoted as truncation and censoring (Section 11.2.1). We discuss biases arising (Sections 11.2.2 and 11.2.3) and procedures for consistent estimation (Sections 11.2.4 and 11.2.5).

11.2.1 BASIC CONCEPTS AND POINT OF DEPARTURE

Consider an equation of the form (11.1), with α_i omitted:

$$\begin{aligned} y_{it}^* &= \boldsymbol{x}_{it}\boldsymbol{\beta} - u_{it}, \qquad (u_{it}|X) \sim \mathsf{IID}(0, \sigma^2), \\ i &= 1, \ldots, N;\ t = 1, \ldots, T. \end{aligned} \tag{11.8}$$

A key question is which values i and t take in the data set. Its answer describes the type of data we have and whether the observations mechanism is ignorable or should be accounted for to avoid biased inference. Although (11.8) is assumed to hold for $i = 1,\dots,N$; $t = 1,\dots,T$, not all realizations of $(y^*_{it}, \boldsymbol{x}_{it})$ are recorded. As in Section 10.2.1, we could let I_t denote the index set of individuals observed in period t ($t = 1,\dots,T$), and let P_i denote the index set of periods where individual i is observed ($i = 1,\dots,N$), letting T be the number of periods in which *at least one* individual is observed, and N be the number of individuals observed at least once. Our concern now is that I_t and P_i are determined in a systematic way, relative to the model: *they are endogenous.*

Two situations can be distinguished. (A) We observe $(y_{it}, \boldsymbol{x}_{it}) = (y^*_{it}, \boldsymbol{x}_{it})$ in certain regions (entry in panel), depending on y^*_{it}. Elsewhere we observe neither y^*_{it} nor $\boldsymbol{x}_{it}$ (exit from panel). (B) We observe $y_{it} = y^*_{it}$ in certain regions, depending on y^*_{it}. Elsewhere we observe a y_{it} different from y^*_{it}, for example a constant. We have panel data where the individuals switch systematically between having their responses correctly and incorrectly recorded, in both cases observing $\boldsymbol{x}_{it}$. (A) will be denoted as *truncation* (a truncated data set); (B) will be denoted as *censoring* (a censored data set). We classify both (A) and (B) as giving systematically unbalanced panel data sets. We will assume that $u_{it} \sim \mathcal{N}(0, \sigma^2)$ and write (11.8) with $\varepsilon_{it} = u_{it}/\sigma$ as

$$\begin{aligned} &y^*_{it} = \boldsymbol{x}_{it}\boldsymbol{\beta} - \sigma\varepsilon_{it}, \quad (\varepsilon_{it}|X) \sim \mathsf{IIN}(0,1), \\ &i = 1,\dots,N;\ t = 1,\dots,T. \end{aligned} \tag{11.9}$$

11.2.2 TRUNCATION AND TRUNCATION BIAS

Truncation at zero from below (from the left), which means that y^*_{it} and $\boldsymbol{x}_{it}$ are unobserved when y^*_{it} is zero or negative, is described by the observation rule

$$\begin{aligned} &(y_{it}, \boldsymbol{x}_{it}) = (y^*_{it}, \boldsymbol{x}_{it}) = (\boldsymbol{x}_{it}\boldsymbol{\beta} - \sigma\varepsilon_{it}, \boldsymbol{x}_{it}) && \text{if } \varepsilon_{it} < \boldsymbol{x}_{it}\tfrac{\boldsymbol{\beta}}{\sigma}, \\ &(y_{it}, \boldsymbol{x}_{it}) \text{ are unobserved} && \text{if } \varepsilon_{it} \geq \boldsymbol{x}_{it}\tfrac{\boldsymbol{\beta}}{\sigma}. \end{aligned} \tag{11.10}$$

Examples: [a] y^*_{it} denotes supply of labour hours and the data set includes observations of the hours worked and its determinants—including, e.g., the wage rate and the working conditions—in the periods where the individual works, and no observation otherwise.[2] [b] Observations of the purchase expenditure for a commodity, y^*_{it}, and its determinants exist for individuals if a purchase takes place, otherwise no record of neither the zero expenditure, nor its determinants exist. This exemplifies *self-selection.*

[2] A negative y^*_{it} might (somewhat artificially) be interpreted as a latent demand for hours.

Symmetrically, *truncation at zero from above (from the right)*, which means that y^*_{it} and $\boldsymbol{x}_{it}$ are unobserved if y^*_{it} is zero or positive, while both are observed if y^*_{it} is negative, occurs if

$$\begin{aligned}(y_{it},\boldsymbol{x}_{it}) &= (y^*_{it},\boldsymbol{x}_{it}) = (\boldsymbol{x}_{it}\boldsymbol{\beta}-\sigma\varepsilon_{it},\boldsymbol{x}_{it}) && \text{if} \quad \varepsilon_{it} > \boldsymbol{x}_{it}\tfrac{\boldsymbol{\beta}}{\sigma},\\ (y_{it},\boldsymbol{x}_{it}) &\text{ are unobserved} && \text{if} \quad \varepsilon_{it} \le \boldsymbol{x}_{it}\tfrac{\boldsymbol{\beta}}{\sigma}.\end{aligned} \tag{11.11}$$

In both cases $\boldsymbol{\beta}$ can be identified, because the observed y_{it} gives an 'anchor' for the $\boldsymbol{\beta}$-'metric'. This differs from discrete response (e.g., logit and probit) cases where the link between y^*_{it} and y_{it} is a simple step function; confer the identification problem noted in Section 9.2.1.

It follows that

$$\begin{aligned}\mathsf{E}(y_{it}|X,y_{it}>0) &= \mathsf{E}(y^*_{it}|X,y^*_{it}>0) = \boldsymbol{x}_{it}\boldsymbol{\beta}-\sigma\,\mathsf{E}(\varepsilon_{it}|X,\varepsilon_{it}<\boldsymbol{x}_{it}\tfrac{\boldsymbol{\beta}}{\sigma}),\\ \mathsf{E}(y_{it}|X,y_{it}<0) &= \mathsf{E}(y^*_{it}|X,y^*_{it}<0) = \boldsymbol{x}_{it}\boldsymbol{\beta}-\sigma\,\mathsf{E}(\varepsilon_{it}|X,\varepsilon_{it}>\boldsymbol{x}_{it}\tfrac{\boldsymbol{\beta}}{\sigma}),\end{aligned} \tag{11.12}$$

$$\begin{aligned}\text{var}(y_{it}|X,y_{it}>0) &= \text{var}(y^*_{it}|X,y^*_{it}>0) = \sigma^2\text{var}(\varepsilon_{it}|X,\varepsilon_{it}<\boldsymbol{x}_{it}\tfrac{\boldsymbol{\beta}}{\sigma}),\\ \text{var}(y_{it}|X,y_{it}<0) &= \text{var}(y^*_{it}|X,y^*_{it}<0) = \sigma^2\text{var}(\varepsilon_{it}|X,\varepsilon_{it}>\boldsymbol{x}_{it}\tfrac{\boldsymbol{\beta}}{\sigma}).\end{aligned} \tag{11.13}$$

To make these relationships operational, properties of the truncated normal distribution will have to be involved. In Appendix 11A, (11A.9)–(11A.12), it is shown that

$$\varepsilon_{it} \sim \mathcal{N}(0,1) \Longrightarrow \begin{cases}\mathsf{E}(\varepsilon_{it}|\varepsilon_{it}>a) = \lambda_A(a),\\ \text{var}(\varepsilon_{it}|\varepsilon_{it}>a) = 1+a\lambda_A(a)-[\lambda_A(a)]^2,\\ \mathsf{E}(\varepsilon_{it}|\varepsilon_{it}<b) = -\lambda_B(b),\\ \text{var}(\varepsilon_{it}|\varepsilon_{it}<b) = 1-b\lambda_B(b)-[\lambda_B(b)]^2,\end{cases} \tag{11.14}$$

where

$$\lambda_A(a) = \frac{\phi(a)}{1-\Phi(a)} = \lambda_B(-a), \tag{11.15}$$

$$\lambda_B(b) = \frac{\phi(b)}{\Phi(b)} = \lambda_A(-b), \tag{11.16}$$

$\phi(\cdot)$ and $\Phi(\cdot)$ denoting the density and the cdf of $\mathcal{N}(0,1)$. The symmetry of the normal distribution implies $\phi(-a)=\phi(a)$, $\Phi(-a)+\Phi(a)=1 \Longrightarrow \lambda_A(-b)=\lambda_B(b)$, $\lambda_B(-a)=\lambda_A(a)$. Subscripts A and B indicate that the actual variable (ε_{it}) is restricted to be *above (at the right of)*, respectively *below (at the left of)* the argument value (the minus sign is not part of $\lambda_B(b)$). Using the notation

$$\Phi_{it} \equiv \Phi\left(x_{it}\frac{\beta}{\sigma}\right), \quad \phi_{it} \equiv \phi\left(x_{it}\frac{\beta}{\sigma}\right), \tag{11.17}$$

$$\lambda_{Ait} \equiv \lambda_A\left(x_{it}\frac{\beta}{\sigma}\right) = \frac{\phi_{it}}{1-\Phi_{it}}, \quad \lambda_{Bit} \equiv \lambda_B\left(x_{it}\frac{\beta}{\sigma}\right) = \frac{\phi_{it}}{\Phi_{it}}, \tag{11.18}$$

we obtain from (11.12)–(11.14)

$$\mathsf{E}(y_{it}|X, y_{it}>0) = x_{it}\boldsymbol{\beta} + \sigma\lambda_{Bit}, \quad \mathsf{E}(y_{it}|X, y_{it}<0) = x_{it}\boldsymbol{\beta} - \sigma\lambda_{Ait}, \tag{11.19}$$

$$\mathrm{var}(y_{it}|X, y_{it}>0) = \sigma^2[1-x_{it}\tfrac{\beta}{\sigma}\lambda_{Bit}-\lambda_{Bit}^2], \quad \mathrm{var}(y_{it}|X, y_{it}<0) = \sigma^2[1+x_{it}\tfrac{\beta}{\sigma}\lambda_{Ait}-\lambda_{Ait}^2]. \tag{11.20}$$

Let $\eta_{Ait} = y_{it} - \mathsf{E}(y_{it}|X, y_{it}>0)$, $\eta_{Bit} = y_{it} - \mathsf{E}(y_{it}|X, y_{it}<0)$, which are disturbances satisfying $\mathsf{E}(\eta_{Ait}|X, y_{it}>0)=0$ and $\mathsf{E}(\eta_{Bit}|X, y_{it}<0)=0$ in the respective regression equations:

$$y_{it} = x_{it}\boldsymbol{\beta} + \sigma\lambda_{Bit} + \eta_{Ait} \quad \text{(truncation from the left)}, \tag{11.21}$$

$$y_{it} = x_{it}\boldsymbol{\beta} - \sigma\lambda_{Ait} + \eta_{Bit} \quad \text{(truncation from the right)}. \tag{11.22}$$

If we, by OLS regression of y_{it} on x_{it}, attempt to estimate $\boldsymbol{\beta}$ from a truncated panel data set, two complications arise: [1] λ_{Bit} or λ_{Ait} are omitted, and [2] the disturbances η_{Ait} or η_{Bit} have variances depending on $x_{it}\boldsymbol{\beta}/\sigma$.

What is known about the *partial (marginal) effects*, i.e., the first-derivatives of the theoretical regressions, obtained when regressing y_{it} linearly on x_{it}, mimicking coefficients obtained from linearized versions of the theoretical regressions? Let x_{kit} and β_k be element k of, respectively, x_{it} and $\boldsymbol{\beta}$. In Appendix 11B, (11B.5) and (11B.6), it is shown that the answer is that the truncation has the following impact on the marginal effects:

$$\frac{\partial\mathsf{E}(y_{it}|x_{it}, y_{it}>0)}{\partial x_{kit}} = \beta_k[1-\lambda_{Bit}(\lambda_{Bit}+x_{it}\tfrac{\beta}{\sigma})], \tag{11.23}$$

$$\frac{\partial\mathsf{E}(y_{it}|x_{it}, y_{it}<0)}{\partial x_{kit}} = \beta_k[1-\lambda_{Ait}(\lambda_{Ait}-x_{it}\tfrac{\beta}{\sigma})]. \tag{11.24}$$

The factors in the square brackets, the *bias factors*, are the same for all k: *proportional attenuation* prevails; see Heckman (1976), Goldberger (1981), and Amemiya (1985, p. 367).[3]

[3] Note that expressions for partial (marginal) effects obtained by taking conditional expectations prior to differentiation, for non-linear equations, differ from the expressions obtained by taking the two operations in opposite succession; see, e.g., Wooldridge (2010, Section 2.2).

11.2.3 CENSORING AND CENSORING BIAS

We next consider *censoring from below (from the left)*. Then we observe more than under a similar truncation, as the data set includes the observations of $\boldsymbol{x}_{it}$ together with the zero observations of y_{it}. Therefore the observation rule is:

$$y_{it} = \max[y^*_{it}, 0] = \max[\boldsymbol{x}_{it}\boldsymbol{\beta} - \sigma\varepsilon_{it}, 0], \tag{11.25}$$

with related probabilities

$$\begin{aligned} P(y_{it} = y^*_{it}|X) &= P(y^*_{it} > 0|X) = P(\varepsilon_{it} < \boldsymbol{x}_{it}\tfrac{\boldsymbol{\beta}}{\sigma}|X) = \Phi_{it}, \\ P(y_{it} = 0|X) &= P(y^*_{it} \leq 0|X) = P(\varepsilon_{it} \geq \boldsymbol{x}_{it}\tfrac{\boldsymbol{\beta}}{\sigma}|X) = 1 - \Phi_{it}. \end{aligned}$$

We may interpret this censored data set as obtained by augmenting the truncated data set, described by the observation rule (11.10), by adding the zero y_{it} values and the related $\boldsymbol{x}_{it}$ values. Again, the observed y_{it} gives an 'anchor' for the $\boldsymbol{\beta}$-'metric'. The rule of iterated expectation and (11.12) imply

$$\begin{aligned} \mathsf{E}(y_{it}|X, y_{it} \geq 0) &= \mathsf{E}(y^*_{it}|X, y^*_{it} \geq 0) \\ &= \mathsf{E}(y^*_{it}|X, y^*_{it} > 0)P(y^*_{it} > 0|X) + 0P(y^*_{it} \leq 0|X) \\ &= [\boldsymbol{x}_{it}\boldsymbol{\beta} - \sigma\mathsf{E}(\varepsilon_{it}|x_{it}, \varepsilon_{it} < \boldsymbol{x}_{it}\tfrac{\boldsymbol{\beta}}{\sigma})]P(\varepsilon_{it} < \boldsymbol{x}_{it}\tfrac{\boldsymbol{\beta}}{\sigma}|X), \end{aligned}$$

and hence, when utilizing (11.17)–(11.18),

$$\mathsf{E}(y_{it}|X, y_{it} \geq 0) = (\boldsymbol{x}_{it}\boldsymbol{\beta} + \sigma\lambda_{Bit})\Phi_{it} \equiv \boldsymbol{x}_{it}\boldsymbol{\beta}\Phi_{it} + \sigma\phi_{it}. \tag{11.26}$$

Examples: [a] y^*_{it} is an individual's supply of labour hours, and the data set records observations, y_{it}, of the hours worked if, in the actual period, the individual is working, and zero otherwise. In both cases, the determinants of the response are recorded, including, for example, the wage rate motivating the labour supply of respondents who do not work. [b] Observations of the purchase expenditure for a commodity and its determinants exist for all actual individuals both in periods when there is a purchase and in periods with no purchase.

Symmetrically, if the *censoring is from above (from the right)*, the data set includes the zero observations of y_{it} and the related $\boldsymbol{x}_{it}$:

$$y_{it} = \min[y^*_{it}, 0] = \min[\boldsymbol{x}_{it}\boldsymbol{\beta} - \sigma\varepsilon_{it}, 0]. \tag{11.27}$$

The related probabilities are

$$P(y_{it}=y^*_{it}|X) = P(y^*_{it} < 0|X) = P(\varepsilon_{it} > \boldsymbol{x}_{it}\tfrac{\boldsymbol{\beta}}{\sigma}|X) = 1-\Phi_{it},$$
$$P(y_{it}=0|X) = P(y^*_{it} \geq 0|X) = P(\varepsilon_{it} \leq \boldsymbol{x}_{it}\tfrac{\boldsymbol{\beta}}{\sigma}|X) = \Phi_{it}.$$

We may interpret such a censored data set as obtained by *augmenting the truncated data set (11.11) with the zero y_{it} values and the related $\boldsymbol{x}_{it}$-values*. The rule of iterated expectation and (11.12) imply

$$\begin{aligned}\mathsf{E}(y_{it}|X, y_{it} \leq 0) &= \mathsf{E}(y^*_{it}|X, y^*_{it} \leq 0)\\ &= \mathsf{E}(y^*_{it}|X, y^*_{it} < 0)P(y^*_{it} < 0|X) + 0P(y^*_{it} \geq 0|X)\\ &= [\boldsymbol{x}_{it}\boldsymbol{\beta} - \sigma\,\mathsf{E}(\varepsilon_{it}|X, \varepsilon_{it} > \boldsymbol{x}_{it}\tfrac{\boldsymbol{\beta}}{\sigma})]P(\varepsilon_{it} > \boldsymbol{x}_{it}\tfrac{\boldsymbol{\beta}}{\sigma}|X),\end{aligned}$$

and hence, utilizing (11.17)–(11.18),

$$\mathsf{E}(y_{it}|X, y_{it} \leq 0) = (\boldsymbol{x}_{it}\boldsymbol{\beta} + \sigma\lambda_{Ait})[1-\Phi_{it}] \equiv \boldsymbol{x}_{it}\boldsymbol{\beta}[1-\Phi_{it}] - \sigma\phi_{it}. \tag{11.28}$$

Let $\mu_{Ait} = y_{it} - \mathsf{E}(y_{it}|X, y_{it} \geq 0)$, $\mu_{Bit} = y_{it} - \mathsf{E}(y_{it}|X, y_{it} \leq 0)$, which are disturbances satisfying $\mathsf{E}(\mu_{Ait}|X, y_{it} \geq 0) = 0$ and $\mathsf{E}(\mu_{Bit}|X, y_{it} \leq 0) = 0$ in the respective regression equations:

$$y_{it} = \boldsymbol{x}_{it}\Phi_{it}\boldsymbol{\beta} + \sigma\phi_{it} + \mu_{Ait} \qquad \text{(censoring from the left)}, \tag{11.29}$$
$$y_{it} = \boldsymbol{x}_{it}[1-\Phi_{it}]\boldsymbol{\beta} - \sigma\phi_{it} + \mu_{Bit} \qquad \text{(censoring from the right)}. \tag{11.30}$$

If we, by OLS regression of y_{it} on $\boldsymbol{x}_{it}$, attempt to estimate $\boldsymbol{\beta}$ from a censored data set, three complications arise. [1] The (first) regressor is systematically mis-measured: instead of $\boldsymbol{x}_{it}$ it should have been $\boldsymbol{x}_{it}\Phi_{it}$, respectively, $\boldsymbol{x}_{it}[1-\Phi_{it}]$. [2] ϕ_{it}, respectively $-\phi_{it}$, are omitted variables. [3] The disturbances μ_{Ait} and μ_{Bit} have variances depending on $\boldsymbol{x}_{it}\boldsymbol{\beta}/\sigma$.

What is known about the *partial (marginal) effects*, i.e., the first-derivatives of the theoretical regression, obtained when regressing y_{it} linearly on $\boldsymbol{x}_{it}$, mimicking coefficients obtained from linearized versions of the theoretical regressions? Let x_{kit} and β_k be element k of, respectively, $\boldsymbol{x}_{it}$ and $\boldsymbol{\beta}$. In Appendix 11B, (11B.3) and (11B.4), it is shown from (11.26) and (11.28) that censoring has the following impact on the marginal effects:

$$\frac{\partial\,\mathsf{E}(y_{it}|X, y_{it} \geq 0)}{\partial x_{kit}} = \beta_k\Phi_{it}, \tag{11.31}$$
$$\frac{\partial\,\mathsf{E}(y_{it}|X, y_{it} \leq 0)}{\partial x_{kit}} = \beta_k[1-\Phi_{it}]. \tag{11.32}$$

These expressions differ from β_k as well as from the corresponding expressions under truncation, (11.23)–(11.24). Again, there is proportional attenuation: all explanatory variables have the same *bias factors*, Φ_{it} and $1-\Phi_{it}$.[4]

The contrast between censoring and truncation is reflected in the following ratios, which show how inclusion/exclusion of the zero y_{it}-observations impacts the conditional expectation of the y_{it}s:

$$\frac{\mathsf{E}(y_{it}|X, y_{it}\geq 0)}{\mathsf{E}(y_{it}|X, y_{it}>0)} = P(y^*_{it}>0|X) = \Phi_{it} < 1 \qquad \text{(from the left)},$$

$$\frac{\mathsf{E}(y_{it}|X, y_{it}\leq 0)}{\mathsf{E}(y_{it}|X, y_{it}<0)} = P(y^*_{it}<0|X) = 1-\Phi_{it} < 1 \qquad \text{(from the right)}.$$

11.2.4 MAXIMUM LIKELIHOOD IN CASE OF TRUNCATION

The likelihood element belonging to individual i in period t, as generated by (11.10),[5] is the density of y_{it}, conditional on $y_{it}>0$. It follows from $(\varepsilon_{it}|X) \sim \mathcal{N}(0,1)$ that $(y_{it}|X)$ has density $(1/\sigma)\phi[(y_{it}-\boldsymbol{x}_{it}\boldsymbol{\beta})/\sigma]$ unconditionally and that $P(y_{it}>0|X)=\Phi(\boldsymbol{x}_{it}\boldsymbol{\beta}/\sigma)$,[6] and therefore this likelihood element can be expressed as

$$\mathcal{L}_{it} = \frac{\dfrac{1}{\sigma}\phi\left(\dfrac{y_{it}-\boldsymbol{x}_{it}\boldsymbol{\beta}}{\sigma}\right)}{\Phi\left(\dfrac{\boldsymbol{x}_{it}\boldsymbol{\beta}}{\sigma}\right)}.$$

Since $y_{i1},\dots,y_{iT}$ are independent (conditional on X), the likelihood element relating to individual i becomes

$$\mathcal{L}_i = \prod_{t:y_{it}>0} \mathcal{L}_{it},$$

where '$t: y_{it}>0$' denotes a product over all observations with y_{it} positive. The likelihood function is the product of the individual-specific elements, which gives

[4] Again, expressions for partial effects obtained by taking conditional expectations prior to differentiation differ from the expressions obtained by reversing the two operations.

[5] If $(y_{it}|X)$ is generated by (11.11), replace $\Phi(x_{it}\beta/\sigma)$ by $1-\Phi(x_{it}\beta/\sigma)$, and otherwise proceed as specified.

[6] $P(y_{it}>0|X)$ corresponds to $P(R_{it}|X)$ in the general setup in Section 11.1.

$$\mathcal{L} = \prod_{i=1}^{N} \mathcal{L}_i = \prod_{i=1}^{N} \prod_{t:y_{it}>0} \left[\frac{\frac{1}{\sigma}\phi\left(\frac{y_{it} - \mathbf{x}_{it}\boldsymbol{\beta}}{\sigma}\right)}{\Phi\left(\frac{\mathbf{x}_{it}\boldsymbol{\beta}}{\sigma}\right)} \right]. \tag{11.33}$$

Maximizing $\mathcal{L}$, or somewhat easier, maximizing $\ln(\mathcal{L})$, with respect to $(\boldsymbol{\beta}, \sigma)$, provided that the solution exists and is unique, gives their ML estimators.

11.2.5 MAXIMUM LIKELIHOOD IN CASE OF CENSORING

To obtain the likelihood function of $(y_{it}|X)$, which is given by (11.25),[7] we combine elements from the regions where $y_{it} = y^*_{it}$ and $y_{it} = 0$. When y_{it} is observed continuously, its cdf and density function equal those of y^*_{it}, giving the likelihood element

$$\mathcal{L}_{1it} \equiv \frac{1}{\sigma}\phi\left(\frac{y_{it} - \mathbf{x}_{it}\boldsymbol{\beta}}{\sigma}\right) = \frac{1}{\sigma}\phi\left(\frac{y^*_{it} - \mathbf{x}_{it}\boldsymbol{\beta}}{\sigma}\right).$$

When y_{it} is observed discretely as 0, the likelihood element is a point probability equal to the cdf of y^*_{it} at the censoring point:

$$\mathcal{L}_{0it} \equiv P(y_{it} = 0|X) = P(y^*_{it} \leq 0|X) = P[\varepsilon_{it} \geq \mathbf{x}_{it}\boldsymbol{\beta}/\sigma|X] = 1 - \Phi(\mathbf{x}_{it}\boldsymbol{\beta}/\sigma).$$

Combining the two elements gives, since $y_{i1}, \ldots, y_{iT}$ are independent (conditional on X), the likelihood element of individual i:

$$\mathcal{L}_i = \prod_{t:y_{it}>0} \mathcal{L}_{1it} \prod_{t:y_{it}=0} \mathcal{L}_{0it},$$

where '$t{:}y_{it} > 0$' and '$t{:}y_{it} = 0$' denote products over all observations with, respectively, $y_{it} > 0$ and $y_{it} = 0$. Again, the full likelihood function is the product of the individual-specific elements, which now reads:

$$\mathcal{L} = \prod_{i=1}^{N} \mathcal{L}_i = \prod_{i=1}^{N} \prod_{t:y_{it}>0} \left[\frac{1}{\sigma}\phi\left(\frac{y_{it} - \mathbf{x}_{it}\boldsymbol{\beta}}{\sigma}\right)\right] \prod_{t:y_{it}=0} \left[1 - \Phi\left(\frac{\mathbf{x}_{it}\boldsymbol{\beta}}{\sigma}\right)\right]. \tag{11.34}$$

Maximizing $\mathcal{L}$, or equivalently, maximizing $\ln(\mathcal{L})$, with respect to $(\boldsymbol{\beta}, \sigma)$, we obtain the ML estimators.

[7] If $(y_{it}|X)$ is generated by (11.27), replace $1 - \Phi(\mathbf{x}_{it}\boldsymbol{\beta}/\sigma)$ by $\Phi(\mathbf{x}_{it}\boldsymbol{\beta}/\sigma)$ and otherwise proceed as specified.

Amemiya (1973) gives a further discussion of ML estimators. It can be shown that the corresponding $\ln(\mathcal{L})$ is globally concave, see Olsen (1978) and Amemiya (1985, Section 10.4.5), which ensures uniqueness of the estimators. The consistency of the estimators is not robust to violation of the normality assumption, which makes testing for normality important; see Nelson (1981) and Amemiya (1985, Section 10.5.4) for further discussion.

A comparison of (11.34) with (11.33) clarifies the different 'roles' of the density and cdf of the $\mathcal{N}(0,1)$ distribution in the maximands in the cases with truncation and censoring. A truncated or censored data set enables us to identify $\boldsymbol{\beta}$ and σ, not only their ratio, as in discrete response cases, because we now *in a certain region* observe y^*_{it} as a continuous variable in its defined 'metric'. This gives an 'anchor' for measuring y_{it}. This is sufficient for identification.

This kind of procedure is often called '*Tobit analysis*', after Tobin (1958); see also Amemiya (1984, 1985). A model with likelihood given by (11.34) may be denoted as 'the standard Tobit model', an abbreviation of 'Tobin's probit model', see Amemiya (1985, Equation (10.2.5)).

To escape the complications often arising in numerical maximization of likelihood functions, we may, as a technical simplification, proceed stepwise, following a procedure proposed by Heckman (1976, 1979):[8]

1. Perform *probit analysis*, exploiting only the information of whether y_{it} is censored or not, i.e., whether $y^*_{it} > 0$ or $y^*_{it} \leq 0$, and the corresponding $\boldsymbol{x}_{it}$. This gives an estimate of $\boldsymbol{\beta}/\sigma$, $\widehat{\boldsymbol{\beta}/\sigma}$, as described in Section 9.2.1.
2. Compute from (11.17)–(11.18) $\lambda_{Bit} = \lambda_B(\boldsymbol{x}_{it}\boldsymbol{\beta}/\sigma)$ by replacing $\boldsymbol{x}_{it}\boldsymbol{\beta}/\sigma$ with $\boldsymbol{x}_{it}\widehat{(\boldsymbol{\beta}/\sigma)}$.
3. Regress, for the non-censored observations, i.e., with $y_{it} > 0$, y_{it} on $\boldsymbol{x}_{it}$ and $\widehat{\lambda}_{Bit}$ by using (11.21). This gives $\widehat{\boldsymbol{\beta}}$ and $\widehat{\sigma}$.

11.3 Truncation and censoring: Heterogeneity

To widen applicability of the framework described in Section 11.2.1 for microeconomic problems, allowing for individual-specific heterogeneity is clearly important. We specify, using (11.1),

$$\begin{aligned} &y^*_{it} = \boldsymbol{x}_{it}\boldsymbol{\beta} + \alpha_i - \sigma\varepsilon_{it}, \quad i = 1,\dots,N;\ t = 1,\dots,T, \\ &(\varepsilon_{it}|X) \sim \mathsf{IIN}(0,1), \quad (\alpha_i|X) \sim \mathsf{IID} \text{ with density } g(\alpha_i, \boldsymbol{\lambda}), \quad \varepsilon_{it} \perp \alpha_i, \end{aligned} \tag{11.35}$$

where α_i is a random latent effect and $\boldsymbol{\lambda}$ is a parameter vector.

[8] Amemiya (1985, Section 10.4.3) discusses the properties of this procedure.

11.3.1 TRUNCATION: MAXIMUM LIKELIHOOD ESTIMATION

The extended version of (11.10), valid for truncation at zero from below,[9] reads:

$$\begin{array}{ll}(y_{it},\boldsymbol{x}_{it})=(y^*_{it},\boldsymbol{x}_{it})=(\boldsymbol{x}_{it}\boldsymbol{\beta}+\alpha_i-\sigma\varepsilon_{it},\boldsymbol{x}_{it}) & \text{if } \varepsilon_{it}<(\boldsymbol{x}_{it}\boldsymbol{\beta}+\alpha_i)/\sigma,\\ (y_{it},\boldsymbol{x}_{it}) \text{ are unobserved} & \text{if } \varepsilon_{it}\geq(\boldsymbol{x}_{it}\boldsymbol{\beta}+\alpha_i)/\sigma.\end{array} \tag{11.36}$$

A related theoretical regression, extending (11.19), is

$$\mathsf{E}(y_{it}|X,\alpha_i,y_{it}>0)=\boldsymbol{x}_{it}\boldsymbol{\beta}+\alpha_i+\sigma\lambda_B((\boldsymbol{x}_{it}\boldsymbol{\beta}+\alpha_i)/\sigma).$$

The likelihood elements, conditional on α_i, for, respectively, observation (i,t) and individual i are

$$\mathcal{L}_{it}(\alpha_i)=\frac{\dfrac{1}{\sigma}\phi\left(\dfrac{y_{it}-\boldsymbol{x}_{it}\boldsymbol{\beta}-\alpha_i}{\sigma}\right)}{\Phi\left(\dfrac{\boldsymbol{x}_{it}\boldsymbol{\beta}+\alpha_i}{\sigma}\right)} \qquad (y_{it}>0),$$

$$\mathcal{L}_i(\alpha_i)=\prod_{t:y_{it}>0}\mathcal{L}_{it}(\alpha_i).$$

The unconditional counterpart to $\mathcal{L}_i(\alpha_i)$, obtained by multiplication with $g(\alpha_i,\boldsymbol{\lambda})$ and integration over α_i, becomes $\mathcal{L}^*_i=\int_{-\infty}^{\infty}\mathcal{L}_i(\alpha_i)g(\alpha_i,\boldsymbol{\lambda})d\alpha_i$, and finally, the full likelihood function follows as the product of these elements, since the individuals are independently observed:

$$\mathcal{L}^*=\prod_{i=1}^{N}\mathcal{L}^*_i=\prod_{i=1}^{N}\int_{-\infty}^{\infty}\prod_{t:y_{it}>0}\left[\frac{\dfrac{1}{\sigma}\phi\left(\dfrac{y_{it}-\boldsymbol{x}_{it}\boldsymbol{\beta}-\alpha_i}{\sigma}\right)}{\Phi\left(\dfrac{\boldsymbol{x}_{it}\boldsymbol{\beta}+\alpha_i}{\sigma}\right)}\right]g(\alpha_i,\boldsymbol{\lambda})d\alpha_i. \tag{11.37}$$

This is the counterpart to (11.33) when random heterogeneity is allowed for.

Maximizing $\mathcal{L}^*$, or $\ln(\mathcal{L}^*)$, with respect to $(\boldsymbol{\beta},\sigma,\boldsymbol{\lambda})$, again provided that the solution exists and is unique, we get their ML estimators. The solution requires (numerical) integration twice, as the (log)-likelihood function involves integration over α_i, and $\Phi(\cdot)$ is defined by an integral.

A *fixed effects version* of the ML procedure is defined as maximizing $\prod_{i=1}^{N}\mathcal{L}_i(\alpha_i)$ with respect to $(\boldsymbol{\beta},\alpha_1,\ldots,\alpha_N,\sigma)$. This, however, will create incidental parameter problems

[9] If the truncation is from above, and $(y_{it}|X)$ is generated by the extended version of (11.11), replace $\Phi((\boldsymbol{x}_{it}\boldsymbol{\beta}+\alpha_i)/\sigma)$ by $1-\Phi((\boldsymbol{x}_{it}\boldsymbol{\beta}+\alpha_i)/\sigma)$, and otherwise proceed as specified.

and ensuing inconsistency problems when $N \to \infty$ and T is finite. So the practical interest of this model version may be limited, in particular for short panels.

11.3.2 CENSORING: MAXIMUM LIKELIHOOD ESTIMATION

The extended version of (11.25)[10] reads:

$$y_{it} = \max[y_{it}^*, 0] = \max[\boldsymbol{x}_{it}\boldsymbol{\beta} + \alpha_i - \sigma\varepsilon_{it}, 0]. \tag{11.38}$$

A related theoretical regression, extending (11.26), is

$$\mathsf{E}(y_{it}|X, \alpha_i, y_{it} \geq 0) = [\boldsymbol{x}_{it}\boldsymbol{\beta} + \alpha_i]\Phi((\boldsymbol{x}_{it}\boldsymbol{\beta} + \alpha_i)/\sigma) + \sigma\phi((\boldsymbol{x}_{it}\boldsymbol{\beta} + \alpha_i)/\sigma).$$

In the region where y_{it} is observed continuously, its likelihood element, conditional on α_i, is

$$\mathcal{L}_{1it}(\alpha_i) \equiv \frac{1}{\sigma}\phi\left(\frac{y_{it} - \boldsymbol{x}_{it}\boldsymbol{\beta} - \alpha_i}{\sigma}\right) = \frac{1}{\sigma}\phi\left(\frac{y_{it}^* - \boldsymbol{x}_{it}\boldsymbol{\beta} - \alpha_i}{\sigma}\right),$$

while in the region where y_{it} is observed discretely, as 0, its likelihood element is

$$\begin{aligned}\mathcal{L}_{0it}(\alpha_i) &\equiv P(y_{it} = 0|X, \alpha_i) = P(y_{it}^* \leq 0|X, \alpha_i) \\ &= P[\varepsilon_{it} \geq (\boldsymbol{x}_{it}\boldsymbol{\beta} + \alpha_i)/\sigma\,|X, \alpha_i] = 1 - \Phi[(\boldsymbol{x}_{it}\boldsymbol{\beta} + \alpha_i)/\sigma].\end{aligned}$$

Combining the two elements, we obtain the likelihood element for individual i as

$$\mathcal{L}_i(\alpha_i) = \prod_{t:y_{it}>0} \mathcal{L}_{1it}(\alpha_i) \prod_{t:y_{it}=0} \mathcal{L}_{0it}(\alpha_i).$$

The unconditional counterpart to $\mathcal{L}_i(\alpha_i)$, obtained by multiplication with $g(\alpha_i; \boldsymbol{\lambda})$ and integration over α_i, becomes $\mathcal{L}_i^* \equiv \int_{-\infty}^{\infty} \mathcal{L}_i(\alpha_i) g(\alpha_i; \boldsymbol{\lambda}) d\alpha_i$, and finally, the full likelihood function is the product of these elements, since the individuals are independently observed:

[10] If the censoring is from above, and $y_{it} = \min[y_{it}^*, 0]$, replace $1 - \Phi((\boldsymbol{x}_{it}\boldsymbol{\beta} + \alpha_i)/\sigma)$ by $\Phi((\boldsymbol{x}_{it}\boldsymbol{\beta} + \alpha_i)/\sigma)$, and otherwise proceed as specified.

$$\mathcal{L}^* = \prod_{i=1}^{N} \mathcal{L}_i^* = \prod_{i=1}^{N} \int_{-\infty}^{\infty} \prod_{t:y_{it}>0} \left[\frac{1}{\sigma} \phi \left(\frac{y_{it} - \mathbf{x}_{it}\boldsymbol{\beta} - \alpha_i}{\sigma} \right) \right]$$

$$\times \prod_{t:y_{it}=0} \left[1 - \Phi \left(\frac{\mathbf{x}_{it}\boldsymbol{\beta} + \alpha_i}{\sigma} \right) \right] g(\alpha_i; \boldsymbol{\lambda}) d\alpha_i. \tag{11.39}$$

This is the counterpart to (11.34) under random heterogeneity.

Maximizing $\mathcal{L}^*$, or $\ln(\mathcal{L}^*)$, with respect to $(\boldsymbol{\beta}, \sigma, \boldsymbol{\lambda})$, if the solution exists and is unique, we get their ML estimators. Again, the solution involves integration twice. A comparison of (11.39) and (11.37) shows the different 'roles' of the density and the cdf of $\mathcal{N}(0, 1)$ in the likelihood functions under truncation and censoring.

Example: Consider a relationship between the (deflated) wage rate (in logs), y, and a dummy for trade union membership *(union)*, the age *(age)*, and the grade at exam *(grade)* of the respondent, using unbalanced US panel data from 4148 individuals observed from 1 to 12 years (mean 4.6 years) (source: National Longitudinal Survey: http://www.stata-press.com/data; last accessed March 2016). The threshold is, as an illustration, set to ln(wage)=y=2 for *right*-censoring and -truncation and to ln(wage)=y=1 for *left*-censoring and -truncation. The results, obtained by using Stata modules, are given in Table 11.1 for 7 cases. In case 1, the data set is neither truncated nor censored (but ignorably unbalanced). The contrast between right-censoring, right-truncation, and censored regression when censoring is accounted for in estimation, is exemplified by comparing cases 2, 3, and 4. Similarly, the contrast between left-censoring and left-truncation and censored regression, when censoring is accounted for in estimation, is exemplified by comparing cases 5, 6, and 7. The prevalence of unobserved heterogeneity, measured by $\rho = \text{var}(\alpha_i)/[\text{var}(\alpha_i)+\text{var}(u_{it})]$, and the number of observations used in estimation are given at the bottom of the table.

All illustrations use unbalanced panel data. To summarize: case 1, as mentioned, relates to *non-systematic* (ignorable) unbalance. Cases 2, 3, 5, and 6 exemplify systematic unbalance not accounted for by the chosen procedure. Cases 2 and 5 illustrate the censoring bias, as formalized in (11.31)–(11.32), while cases 3 and 6 illustrate the truncation bias, as formalized in (11.23)–(11.24). Cases 4 and 7 illustrate the use of censored regression (Tobit analysis) *to account for* the censoring bias problem that affects the estimates in cases 2 and 5, respectively.

A *fixed effects version* of this ML procedure is defined by maximizing $\prod_{i=1}^{N} \mathcal{L}_i(\alpha_i)$ with respect to $(\boldsymbol{\beta}, \alpha_1, \ldots, \alpha_N, \sigma)$. Again, an incidental parameter problem would occur for $N \to \infty$, T finite, but the finite-sample bias of the parameter estimates of interest may sometimes be small, as exemplified by Greene (2004).

A problem with ML procedures assuming normally distributed ε_{it}-disturbances for this kind of non-linear model is, in both the fixed and the random effects cases, that

Table 11.1 Censoring and truncation: equation for female log(wage rate)

	1	2	3	4	5	6	7
union	0.1280	0.1064	0.1041	0.1438	0.1182	0.1056	0.1215
	(0.0065)	(0.0050)	(0.0063)	(0.0068)	(0.0061)	(0.0060	(0.0063)
age	0.0137	0.0066	0.0038	0.0110	0.0131	0.0132	0.0134
	(0.0004)	(0.0003)	(0.0004)	(0.0004)	(0.0004)	(0.0004	(0.0004)
grade	0.0816	0.0573	0.0429	0.0841	0.0784	0.0757	0.0806
	(0.0022)	(0.0017)	(0.0019)	(0.0023)	(0.0020)	(0.0020	(0.0021)
ρ	0.6134	0.6019	0.5255	0.6220	0.5990	0.5976	0.6085
No. of obs.	19227	19227	13730	19227	19227	18591	19227
Of which censored	–	5497	–	5497	636	–	636

Notes: Standard errors in parentheses.
Model and procedures:
1: No censoring or truncation, random effects model: GLS.
2: Observations right-censored at $y = 2$. GLS, censoring not allowed for.
3: Observations right-truncated at $y = 2$. GLS, truncation not allowed for.
4: Observations censored with upper limit $y = 2$, allowed for in estimation (Tobit).
5: Observations left-censored at $y = 1$. GLS, censoring not allowed for.
6: Observations left-truncated at $y = 1$. GLS, truncation not allowed for.
7: Observations censored with lower limit $y = 1$, allowed for in estimation (Tobit).

the estimates may be sensitive to violation of this assumption; a mis-specified form of the distribution may make the estimates N-inconsistent. This lack of robustness has motivated the use of *semiparametric* approaches, as discussed in Kyriazidou (1997) and Honoré and Kyriazidou (2000). For surveys, see Arellano and Honoré (2001, Section 7) and Honoré, Vella, and Verbeek (2008, Sections 12.5.5, 12.6.5, and 12.6.6).

11.4 Truncation and censoring: Cross-effects

The models and methods considered in Sections 11.2 and 11.3 have one equation and one endogenous variable. Quite often, however, our situation is one where the censoring or truncation mechanism for one variable *involves other variables determined within the same model.* In this section we give examples of such models and consider estimation procedures, building on the results for the single equation models.[11]

[11] Related examples are discussed by Amemiya (1984, Chapter 10). He also suggests a typology that contains a limited number of relevant censoring models of the Tobit type. Arguably, the number of such models is infinitely large, especially when censoring, truncation, and missing observations occur simultaneously, which may well happen in practice; see, e.g., Biørn and Wangen (2012) for an attempt to describe the typology.

11.4.1 MOTIVATION AND COMMON MODEL ELEMENTS

Consider a pair of continuous latent variables, y^*_{1it} and y^*_{2it}, determined by a two-equation extension of Model (11.8), with vectors of explanatory variables, respectively, $\boldsymbol{x}_{1it}$ and $\boldsymbol{x}_{2it}$. First, we consider the case with no latent heterogeneity (Sections 11.4.1–11.4.3) and next allow for heterogeneity (Section 11.4.4). Still, the disturbances (u_{1it}, u_{2it}) are binormally distributed, as $\mathcal{N}_2(0,0,\sigma_1^2,\sigma_2^2,\sigma_{12})$. Again, it is convenient to work with standardized disturbances, $\varepsilon_{1it} = u_{1it}/\sigma_1, \varepsilon_{2it} = u_{2it}/\sigma_2$, and we let $\rho = \text{corr}(\varepsilon_{1it}, \varepsilon_{2it}) = \sigma_{12}/(\sigma_1\sigma_2)$. The model is

$$\begin{aligned}
&y^*_{1it} = \boldsymbol{x}_{1it}\boldsymbol{\beta}_1 - \sigma_1\varepsilon_{1it}, \\
&y^*_{2it} = \boldsymbol{x}_{2it}\boldsymbol{\beta}_2 - \sigma_2\varepsilon_{2it}, \\
&(\varepsilon_{1it}, \varepsilon_{2it}|\boldsymbol{X}) \sim \mathsf{IIN}_2(0,0,1,1,\rho), \\
&i = 1,\dots,N;\ t = 1,\dots,T.
\end{aligned} \tag{11.40}$$

We still condition on $\boldsymbol{X}$, which now denotes all $(\boldsymbol{x}_{1it}, \boldsymbol{x}_{2it})$-values. The two endogenous variables are observed either as truncated or as censored, *and the mechanism involves* y^*_{2it} for both.

Example: We want to estimate a *wage equation* for individuals, y_{1it} being the observed wage rate. Jointly with it an equation for the hours supplied (briefly, a *hours equation*) exists, y_{2it} being the observed number of hours worked. We have observations of both sets of explanatory variables, $\boldsymbol{x}_{1it}$ and $\boldsymbol{x}_{2it}$ (which may have common elements). However, y^*_{1it} is observed only for respondents who deliver a positive number of hours, $y^*_{2it} > 0$. Otherwise, y^*_{1it} and y^*_{2it} are both either unobserved (truncation) or are observed as zero together with their explanatory variables (censoring). This generalizes observation rules (11.10) and (11.25), respectively. In this panel data set, the truncation or censoring may be effective in different periods. Indeed, the most interesting observations may come from individuals who change 'status' during the observation period. For simplicity, only truncation or censoring, at zero, from below is considered.

The observation rule under *truncation* is

$$\begin{aligned}
&(y_{1it}, y_{2it}, \boldsymbol{x}_{1it}, \boldsymbol{x}_{2it}) = (y^*_{1it}, y^*_{2it}, \boldsymbol{x}_{1it}, \boldsymbol{x}_{1it}) &&\text{if} \quad \varepsilon_{2it} < \boldsymbol{x}_{2it}\tfrac{\boldsymbol{\beta}_2}{\sigma_2}, \\
&(y_{1it}, y_{2it}, \boldsymbol{x}_{1it}, \boldsymbol{x}_{2it}) \text{ are unobserved} &&\text{if} \quad \varepsilon_{2it} \geq \boldsymbol{x}_{2it}\tfrac{\boldsymbol{\beta}_2}{\sigma_2},
\end{aligned} \tag{11.41}$$

while under *censoring*, still letting $\mathbf{1}\{S\}=1$ if S is true and $=0$ if S is false,

$$\begin{aligned}
y_{1it} &= y^*_{1it}\mathbf{1}\{y^*_{2it} > 0\} = [\boldsymbol{x}_{1it}\boldsymbol{\beta}_1 - \sigma_1\varepsilon_{1it}]\mathbf{1}\{\varepsilon_{2it} < \boldsymbol{x}_{2it}\tfrac{\boldsymbol{\beta}_2}{\sigma_2}\}, \\
y_{2it} &= y^*_{2it}\mathbf{1}\{y^*_{2it} > 0\} = [\boldsymbol{x}_{2it}\boldsymbol{\beta}_2 - \sigma_2\varepsilon_{2it}]\mathbf{1}\{\varepsilon_{2it} < \boldsymbol{x}_{2it}\tfrac{\boldsymbol{\beta}_2}{\sigma_2}\},
\end{aligned} \tag{11.42}$$

and $\boldsymbol{x}_{1it}$ and $\boldsymbol{x}_{2it}$ are observed for all (i, t).

11.4.2 IMPLIED THEORETICAL REGRESSIONS FOR THE OBSERVABLE VARIABLES

To connect the observed endogenous and exogenous variables, properties of truncated binormal distributions will have to be exploited, while in the single-equation model we needed the univariate counterparts. In Appendix 11A, see (11A.9), (11A.10), (11A.15), and (11A.16), it is shown that:

$$(\varepsilon_{1it}, \varepsilon_{2it}) \sim \mathcal{N}_2(0,0,1,1,\rho) \Longrightarrow \begin{cases} \mathsf{E}(\varepsilon_{kit}|\varepsilon_{jit} > a) = \begin{cases} \lambda_A(a), & k=j, \\ \rho\lambda_A(a), & k \neq j, \end{cases} \\ \mathsf{E}(\varepsilon_{kit}|\varepsilon_{jit} < b) = \begin{cases} -\lambda_B(b), & k=j, \\ -\rho\lambda_B(b), & k \neq j, \end{cases} \end{cases}$$
$$k,j = 1,2. \tag{11.43}$$

This supplements (11.14).[12] Hence, using the notation, confer (11.15)–(11.18),

$$\begin{aligned} \Phi_{kit} &\equiv \Phi\left(\boldsymbol{x}_{kit}\frac{\boldsymbol{\beta}_k}{\sigma_k}\right), \\ \phi_{kit} &\equiv \phi\left(\boldsymbol{x}_{kit}\frac{\boldsymbol{\beta}_k}{\sigma_k}\right), \end{aligned} \tag{11.44}$$

$$\left. \begin{aligned} \lambda_{Akit} &\equiv \lambda_A(\boldsymbol{x}_{kit}\tfrac{\boldsymbol{\beta}_k}{\sigma_k}) = \frac{\phi_{kit}}{1-\Phi_{kit}}, \\ \lambda_{Bkit} &\equiv \lambda_B(\boldsymbol{x}_{kit}\tfrac{\boldsymbol{\beta}_k}{\sigma_k}) = \frac{\phi_{kit}}{\Phi_{kit}}, \end{aligned} \right. \quad k = 1,2, \tag{11.45}$$

we obtain

$$\begin{aligned} \mathsf{E}(\varepsilon_{kit}|\boldsymbol{X}, \varepsilon_{jit} > \boldsymbol{x}_{jit}\tfrac{\boldsymbol{\beta}_j}{\sigma_j}) &= \begin{cases} \lambda_{Akit}, & k=j, \\ \rho\lambda_{Ajit}, & k \neq j. \end{cases} \\ \mathsf{E}(\varepsilon_{kit}|\boldsymbol{X}, \varepsilon_{jit} < \boldsymbol{x}_{jit}\tfrac{\boldsymbol{\beta}_j}{\sigma_j}) &= \begin{cases} -\lambda_{Bkit}, & k=j, \\ -\rho\lambda_{Bjit}, & k \neq j. \end{cases} \end{aligned} \tag{11.46}$$

From (11.40) it follows that

$$\mathsf{E}(y^*_{kit}|\boldsymbol{X}, y^*_{jit} > 0) = \boldsymbol{x}_{kit}\boldsymbol{\beta}_k - \sigma_k \mathsf{E}(\varepsilon_{kit}|\boldsymbol{X}, \varepsilon_{jit} < \boldsymbol{x}_{jit}\tfrac{\boldsymbol{\beta}_j}{\sigma_j}). \tag{11.47}$$

[12] The variance and covariance formulae are suppressed; see Tallis (1961, 1965) and Rosenbaum (1961) for further results.

This quite general expression can be combined with (11.41) and (11.42) in several ways. To preserve generality before proceeding to the examples, we continue labelling the variables as (k,j) and find, using (11.46):

Observation rule truncation, based on y_{jit}, gives

$$\mathsf{E}(y_{kit}|X, y_{jit} > 0) = \begin{cases} x_{kit}\boldsymbol{\beta}_k + \sigma_k\lambda_{Bkit}, & k=j, \\ x_{kit}\boldsymbol{\beta}_k + \rho\sigma_k\lambda_{Bjit}, & k \neq j. \end{cases} \tag{11.48}$$

Observation rule censoring, based on y_{jit} (confer (11.26)), gives

$$\begin{aligned} \mathsf{E}(y_{kit}|X, y_{jit} \geq 0) &= \mathsf{E}(y_{kit}|X, y_{jit} > 0)P(y_{jit} > 0|X) \\ &= \begin{cases} x_{kit}\boldsymbol{\beta}_k\Phi_{kit} + \sigma_k\phi_{kit}, & k=j, \\ x_{kit}\boldsymbol{\beta}_k\Phi_{jit} + \rho\sigma_k\phi_{jit}, & k \neq j. \end{cases} \end{aligned} \tag{11.49}$$

Since σ_k, Φ_{jit}, ϕ_{jit}, and λ_{Bjit} are positive,

$$\mathsf{E}(y_{kit}|X, y_{jit} > 0) \gtreqless x_{kit}\boldsymbol{\beta}_k \iff \rho \gtreqless 0 \qquad \text{(truncation)} \qquad (k \neq j),$$

$$\mathsf{E}(y_{kit}|X, y_{jit} \geq 0) \gtreqless x_{kit}\boldsymbol{\beta}_k\Phi_{jit} \iff \rho \gtreqless 0 \qquad \text{(censoring)} \qquad (k \neq j).$$

Hence, if in (11.40) equations k and j have correlated disturbances ($\rho \neq 0$), the theoretical regression $\mathsf{E}(y_{kit}|X, y_{jit} > 0)$ depends not only on $\boldsymbol{x}_{kit}$ and $\boldsymbol{\beta}_k$, but also on $\boldsymbol{x}_{jit}$ and $\boldsymbol{\beta}_j$. If the disturbances are uncorrelated ($\rho = 0$), then $\mathsf{E}(y_{kit}|X, y_{jit} > 0) = x_{kit}\boldsymbol{\beta}_k$ regardless of $\boldsymbol{x}_{jit}$ and $\boldsymbol{\beta}_j$, and y_{jit} and $\boldsymbol{x}_{jit}$ do not need to be known. We then do not need observations of the explanatory variables for y_{jit} to ensure consistent estimation of $\boldsymbol{\beta}_k$.

11.4.3 STEPWISE ESTIMATION: EXAMPLES

Let $\kappa_{kjit} = y_{kit} - \mathsf{E}(y_{kit}|X, y_{jit} > 0)$ and $\xi_{kjit} = y_{kit} - \mathsf{E}(y_{kit}|X, y_{jit} \geq 0)$, which can be interpreted as disturbances in (11.48) and (11.49) satisfying, respectively, $\mathsf{E}(\kappa_{kjit}|X, y_{jit} > 0) = 0$ and $\mathsf{E}(\xi_{kjit}|X, y_{jit} \geq 0) = 0$, giving

$$y_{kit} = x_{kit}\boldsymbol{\beta}_k + \begin{cases} \sigma_k\lambda_{Bkit} + \kappa_{kkit}, & k=j, \\ \rho\sigma_k\lambda_{Bjit} + \kappa_{kjit}, & k\neq j, \end{cases} \qquad \text{(truncation)}$$

$$y_{kit} = \begin{cases} x_{kit}\boldsymbol{\beta}_k\Phi_{kit} + \sigma_k\phi_{kit} + \xi_{kkit}, & k=j, \\ x_{kit}\boldsymbol{\beta}_k\Phi_{jit} + \rho\sigma_k\phi_{jit} + \xi_{kjit}, & k\neq j. \end{cases} \qquad \text{(censoring)}$$

Both are *two-equation regression systems, non-linear in the exogenous variables.* However, the equations in the truncation case are *linear* in $(\boldsymbol{x}_{kit}, \lambda_{Bkit})$ $(k=j)$ and $(\boldsymbol{x}_{kit}, \lambda_{Bjit})$ $(k \neq j)$, respectively, while in the censoring case they are *linear* in $(\boldsymbol{x}_{kit}\Phi_{kit}, \phi_{kit})$ $(k=j)$ and $(\boldsymbol{x}_{kit}\Phi_{jit}, \phi_{jit})$ $(k \neq j)$, respectively.

We consider stepwise estimation in four examples, related to the method appropriate for a one-equation model discussed at the end of Section 11.2.5, the first two examples also considered by Heckman (1979).

Example 1 *Truncation of y_1 (wage rate) based on y_2 (hours).* We specify

$$\begin{aligned} y_{1it} &= \boldsymbol{x}_{1it}\boldsymbol{\beta}_1 + \rho\sigma_1\lambda_{B2it} + \kappa_{12it}, \\ y_{2it} &= \boldsymbol{x}_{2it}\boldsymbol{\beta}_2 + \sigma_2\lambda_{B2it} + \kappa_{22it}. \end{aligned} \tag{11.50}$$

1. *Probit-step:* estimate the rescaled coefficient vector $\frac{\boldsymbol{\beta}_2}{\sigma_2}$ from the complete *censored* data set by applying binomial probit on the hours equation (see Section 9.2.1), and compute from the estimates $\widehat{\lambda}_{B2it}$. This involves $\boldsymbol{x}_{2it}$ for all (i, t).
2. *Coefficient estimation step:* replace in (11.50) λ_{B2it} with $\widehat{\lambda}_{B2it}$, and estimate by OLS *from the sub-sample where $y_{2it} > 0$*, $\boldsymbol{\beta}_1$ and $\rho\sigma_1$ from the wage equation, $\boldsymbol{\beta}_2$ and σ_2 from the hours equation. A meaningful result requires that the last estimate is positive. We cannot identify ρ and σ_1 in this way, only their product. This involves $\boldsymbol{x}_{1it}$ and $\boldsymbol{x}_{2it}$ only for the non-truncated observations. We may use OLS, which is consistent (if the model setup is correct), but since the disturbances are obviously heteroskedastic, weighted regression conducted in a stepwise manner has the potential to improve efficiency.

Example 2 *Censoring of y_1 (wage rate) based on y_2 (hours).* We specify

$$\begin{aligned} y_{1it} &= \boldsymbol{x}_{1it}\boldsymbol{\beta}_1\Phi_{2it} + \rho\sigma_1\phi_{2it} + \xi_{12it}, \\ y_{2it} &= \boldsymbol{x}_{2it}\boldsymbol{\beta}_2\Phi_{2it} + \sigma_2\phi_{2it} + \xi_{22it}. \end{aligned} \tag{11.51}$$

1. *Probit step:* estimate $\frac{\boldsymbol{\beta}_2}{\sigma_2}$ by binomial probit analysis as in Example 1 and compute from the estimates $\widehat{\Phi}_{2it}$ and $\widehat{\phi}_{2it}$. This involves $\boldsymbol{x}_{2it}$ for all (i, t).
2. *Coefficient estimation step:* replace in (11.51) (Φ_{2it}, ϕ_{2it}) with $(\widehat{\Phi}_{B2i}, \widehat{\phi}_{B2i})$, and estimate by OLS *using the (full) sample with $y_{2it} \geq 0$*, $\boldsymbol{\beta}_1$ and $\rho\sigma_1$ from the wage equation, $\boldsymbol{\beta}_2$ and σ_2 from the hours equation. A meaningful result requires that the last estimate is positive. We cannot identify ρ and σ_1 in this way, only their product. This involves $\boldsymbol{x}_{1it}$ and $\boldsymbol{x}_{2it}$ for all non-censored and censored observations. Again, OLS may be used, but since the disturbances are obviously heteroskedastic, weighted regression (proceeding stepwise) has potential for improvement.

In neither of these examples observations on $\boldsymbol{x}_{1it}$ from censored individuals are used. A lesson from them is that even if our interest only is in the parameters of the first (wage) equation, specification and estimation of (properties of) its second (hours) equation is required, except when the wage and hours equations have uncorrelated disturbances.

The next two examples are variations on the two first. Concretely, they may be interpreted as related to another market, containing (reduced form) price and quantity equations for a housing market, y_1 and y_2 being, respectively, the residential user cost per unit of dwelling area and the area of the dwelling, being explained by, e.g., income, occupation, household size, dwelling standard, building costs, interest level, location. We want to estimate the equations valid regardless of whether the user is an owner or a renter, but the data set is incomplete in that observations of the rental cost, y_1, exist only for renters and observations on dwelling area, y_2, exist only for individuals who own their dwelling. The statistical interpretation is that $y_1(>0)$ is recorded only for (i,t)-values representing renters, and that $y_2(>0)$ is recorded only for (i,t)-values representing owners. Hence, there is a *self-selection* for individuals who (in all or in certain periods) choose to be a renter rather than an owner, or the opposite.[13] Our aim is to obtain unbiased estimation of individuals' response of dwelling area and rental price paid with respect to changes in exogenous variables. The inference should not be conditional on the respondent being a renter, but should be intended to have validity regardless of the owner status. Example 3 relates to truncation, Example 4 to censoring.

Example 3 *Truncation of y_1 based on y_2, and vice versa.* We then specify

$$\begin{aligned} y_{1it} &= \boldsymbol{x}_{1it}\boldsymbol{\beta}_1 + \rho\sigma_1\lambda_{B2it} + \kappa_{12it}, \\ y_{2it} &= \boldsymbol{x}_{2it}\boldsymbol{\beta}_2 + \rho\sigma_2\lambda_{B1it} + \kappa_{21it}. \end{aligned} \tag{11.52}$$

1. *Probit step:* estimate rescaled coefficients and compute from them $\widehat{\lambda}_{B1it}$ and $\widehat{\lambda}_{B2it}$, using binomial probit analysis on both equations. This requires $\boldsymbol{x}_{1it}$ and $\boldsymbol{x}_{2it}$ for all (i,t).
2. *Coefficient estimation step:* replace in (11.52) $(\lambda_{B1it}, \lambda_{B2it})$ with $(\widehat{\lambda}_{B1it}, \widehat{\lambda}_{B2it})$. Estimate by OLS (or weighted regression) $\boldsymbol{\beta}_1$ and $\rho\sigma_1$ from the rental price equation, using the sub-sample of renters. Estimate by OLS (or weighted regression) $\boldsymbol{\beta}_2$ and $\rho\sigma_2$ from the area equation, using the sub-sample of owners. We then are unable to identify ρ, σ_1, σ_2, only $\rho\sigma_1$ and $\rho\sigma_2$. This step requires $\boldsymbol{x}_{1it}$ and $\boldsymbol{x}_{2it}$ only for the truncated observations.

Example 4 *Censoring of y_1 based on y_2, and vice versa.* We then specify

$$\begin{aligned} y_{1it} &= \boldsymbol{x}_{1it}\boldsymbol{\beta}_1\Phi_{2it} + \rho\sigma_1\phi_{2it} + \xi_{12it}, \\ y_{2it} &= \boldsymbol{x}_{2it}\boldsymbol{\beta}_2\Phi_{1it} + \rho\sigma_2\phi_{1it} + \xi_{21it}. \end{aligned} \tag{11.53}$$

[13] These, admittedly stylized, assumptions are made for expositional simplicity and might well have been relaxed.

1. *Probit step:* this is identical to step 1 in Example 3, except that we compute from the estimated rescaled coefficients $\widehat{\Phi}_{1it}, \widehat{\phi}_{1it}$ and $\widehat{\Phi}_{2it}, \widehat{\phi}_{2it}$. This step requires $\boldsymbol{x}_{1it}$ and $\boldsymbol{x}_{2it}$ for all (i, t).
2. *Coefficient estimation step:* replace in (11.53) $(\Phi_{B1it}, \phi_{B1it}, \Phi_{B2it}, \phi_{B2it})$ with $(\widehat{\Phi}_{B1it}, \widehat{\phi}_{B1it}, \widehat{\Phi}_{B2it}, \widehat{\phi}_{B2it})$. Estimate by OLS (or weighted regression) $\boldsymbol{\beta}_1$ and $\rho\sigma_1$ from the rental price equation, using the sub-sample of renters. Estimate by OLS $\boldsymbol{\beta}_2$ and $\rho\sigma_2$ from the area equation, using the sub-sample of owners. Again, we are unable to identify ρ, σ_1, σ_2, only $\rho\sigma_1$ and $\rho\sigma_2$ are identifiable, and again, this requires $\boldsymbol{x}_{1it}$ and $\boldsymbol{x}_{2it}$ only for the observations which are truncated.

11.4.4 EXTENSIONS: ML ESTIMATION—HETEROGENEITY

Using stepwise estimation, as in Examples 1 through 4, some efficiency is usually lost. Another limitation of these examples is their neglect of latent heterogeneity. We end by sketching three modifications of Example 2; see (11.51).

Example 2 with ML estimation. The starting point is the binormal density $\psi(\varepsilon_{1it}, \varepsilon_{2it})$; see Appendix 11A. Since $(y^*_{1it}, y^*_{2it}|X)$ is formally a non-singular transformation of $(\varepsilon_{1it}, \varepsilon_{2it})$, their joint density can be constructed from this density. It gets the form $\psi_y(y^*_{1it}, y^*_{2it}; \boldsymbol{x}_{1it}, \boldsymbol{x}_{2it}, \boldsymbol{\beta}_1, \boldsymbol{\beta}_2, \boldsymbol{\sigma})$, where $\boldsymbol{\sigma} = (\sigma_1^2, \sigma_2^2, \sigma_{12})$, from which can be constructed (by integration over y^*_{2it}) the density of y^*_{1it} given that $y^*_{2it} > 0$, symbolized by

$$g_{y1|2}(y^*_{1it}; \boldsymbol{x}_{1it}, \boldsymbol{x}_{2it}, \boldsymbol{\beta}_1, \boldsymbol{\beta}_2, \boldsymbol{\sigma}).$$

This is the function appropriate for constructing the likelihood element of observation (i, t) when there is truncation of y_{1it} based on y_{2it}. In analogy with the truncation model in Section 11.2.4, we let

$$\mathcal{L}_{it} = g_{y1|2}(y_{1it}; \boldsymbol{x}_{1it}, \boldsymbol{x}_{2it}, \boldsymbol{\beta}_1, \boldsymbol{\beta}_2, \boldsymbol{\sigma}),$$

and since $y_{i1}, \dots, y_{iT}$ are independent (conditional on X), the likelihood element relating to individual i becomes $\mathcal{L}_i = \prod_{t:y_{2it}>0} \mathcal{L}_{it}$, where '$t : y_{2it} > 0$' denotes a product over all observations with y_{2it} positive. The likelihood function is the product of the individual-specific elements, which gives

$$\mathcal{L} = \prod_{i=1}^{N} \mathcal{L}_i = \prod_{i=1}^{N} \prod_{t:y_{2it}>0} g_{y1|2}(y_{1it}; \boldsymbol{x}_{1it}, \boldsymbol{x}_{2it}, \boldsymbol{\beta}_1, \boldsymbol{\beta}_2, \boldsymbol{\sigma}).$$

Maximizing $\mathcal{L}$, or somewhat easier, maximizing $\ln(\mathcal{L})$, with respect to $(\boldsymbol{\beta}_1, \boldsymbol{\beta}_2, \boldsymbol{\sigma})$, provided that the solution exists and is unique, we obtain the ML estimators.

Example 2 with random heterogeneity and ML estimation. This example modifies the previous one in that its starting point is the joint density of (y^*_{1it}, y^*_{2it}) conditional on the latent effects $\boldsymbol{\alpha}_i$.[14] The density of y^*_{1it} conditional on $y^*_{2it} > 0$ and $\boldsymbol{\alpha}_i = (\alpha_{1i}, \alpha_{2i})$ therefore has the form

$$g_{y1|2}(y^*_{1it}; \boldsymbol{x}_{1it}, \boldsymbol{x}_{2it}, \boldsymbol{\alpha}_i, \boldsymbol{\beta}_1, \boldsymbol{\beta}_2, \boldsymbol{\sigma}).$$

This is the function appropriate for constructing the likelihood element of observation (i, t) conditional on $\boldsymbol{\alpha}_i$:

$$\mathcal{L}_{it}(\boldsymbol{\alpha}_i) = g_{y1|2}(y_{1it}; \boldsymbol{x}_{1it}, \boldsymbol{x}_{2it}, \boldsymbol{\alpha}_i, \boldsymbol{\beta}_1, \boldsymbol{\beta}_2, \boldsymbol{\sigma}),$$

and since $y_{i1}, \dots, y_{iT}$ are independent (conditional on $\boldsymbol{X}$ and $\boldsymbol{\alpha}_i$), the conditional likelihood element of individual i becomes $\mathcal{L}_i(\boldsymbol{\alpha}_i) = \prod_{t:y_{2it}>0} \mathcal{L}_{it}(\boldsymbol{\alpha}_i)$. Its marginal counterpart follows by multiplication with the joint density $g(\boldsymbol{\alpha}_i; \boldsymbol{\lambda})$ and integration over $\boldsymbol{\alpha}_i$. This gives $\mathcal{L}^*_i \equiv \int_{\boldsymbol{\alpha}_i} \mathcal{L}_i(\boldsymbol{\alpha}_i) g(\boldsymbol{\alpha}_i; \boldsymbol{\lambda}) d\boldsymbol{\alpha}_i$, and hence the full likelihood function becomes

$$\mathcal{L}^* = \prod_{i=1}^{N} \mathcal{L}^*_i = \prod_{i=1}^{N} \int_{\boldsymbol{\alpha}_i} \prod_{t:y_{2it}>0} g_{y1|2}(y_{1it}; \boldsymbol{x}_{1it}, \boldsymbol{x}_{2it}, \boldsymbol{\alpha}_i, \boldsymbol{\beta}_1, \boldsymbol{\beta}_2, \boldsymbol{\sigma}) g(\boldsymbol{\alpha}_i; \boldsymbol{\lambda}) d\boldsymbol{\alpha}_i.$$

Maximizing $\mathcal{L}^*$ with respect to $\boldsymbol{\beta}_1, \boldsymbol{\beta}_2, \boldsymbol{\sigma}, \boldsymbol{\lambda}$—which may *not* be a straightforward numerical problem—gives their ML estimates.

Example 2 in case of fixed heterogeneity. For the fixed heterogeneity case, Kyriazidou (1997) has proposed a stepwise procedure which, relative to the initial setup in Section 11.4.1, briefly described, starts from the following interesting idea. Include in the equations in (11.40) individual-specific effects, α_{1i}, α_{2i}. The modified version of (11.42) can then be written as

$$\begin{aligned} y_{1it} &= [\boldsymbol{x}_{1it}\boldsymbol{\beta}_1 + \alpha_{1i} - \sigma_1\varepsilon_{1it}]\mathbf{1}\{y_{2it} > 0\}, \\ y_{2it} &= [\boldsymbol{x}_{2it}\boldsymbol{\beta}_2 + \alpha_{2i} - \sigma_2\varepsilon_{2it}]\mathbf{1}\{y_{2it} > 0\}. \end{aligned}$$

It then follows that the heterogeneity, conditional on $y_{2it} > 0$, can be eliminated by a simple differencing to obtain:

$$\begin{aligned} \Delta y_{1it} &= \Delta \boldsymbol{x}_{1it}\boldsymbol{\beta}_1 - \sigma_1 \Delta\varepsilon_{1it} \quad && \text{if } y_{2it} > 0, \\ \Delta y_{2it} &= \Delta \boldsymbol{x}_{2it}\boldsymbol{\beta}_2 - \sigma_2 \Delta\varepsilon_{2it} \quad && \text{if } y_{2it} > 0. \end{aligned}$$

[14] The following sketch only aims at describing the 'logic' of the problem.

Since the censoring effect is not eliminated in this way, a combination of the latter equations and a modified version of the Heckman procedure, see Examples 1 and 2, is proposed. Proceeding in this way, Kyriazidou designed a method for coming to grips with the 'nuisance' created by the fixed effects and the sample selection simultaneously. This method is less complicated numerically and potentially less robust than the ML procedure sketched above.

When practising ML estimation in limited dependent variables models, as exemplified by models for discrete response, truncation, and censoring, *simulation* may be a way of overcoming numerical problems arising in (multiple) integration. This is discussed in, e.g., Hajivassiliou and Ruud (1994) and Gourieroux and Monfort (1996).

Appendix 11A. **On truncated normal distributions**

This appendix collects some properties of truncated *uni- and bivariate* normal distributions, useful when considering regression models with truncated or censored variables. For extensive discussion of these distributions, see Kotz, Balakrishnan, and Johnson (2000, Chapter 46.9), as well as Tallis (1961, 1965), Rosenbaum (1961), and Muthén (1990).

11A.1. *Single conditioning*: consider first two *standardized binormally distributed variables*: $(v_1, v_2) \sim \mathcal{N}_2(0, 0, 1, 1, \rho)$, having marginal, simultaneous, and conditional densities, respectively,

$$\phi(v_i) = \frac{1}{\sqrt{2\pi}} \exp\left[-\tfrac{1}{2}v_i^2\right], \qquad i = 1, 2, \tag{11A.1}$$

$$\psi(v_1, v_2) = \frac{1}{2\pi}\frac{1}{(1-\rho^2)^{\frac{1}{2}}} \exp\left[-\frac{1}{2}\frac{v_1^2 - 2\rho\, v_1 v_2 + v_2^2}{1-\rho^2}\right], \tag{11A.2}$$

$$\psi_{i|j}(v_i|v_j) \equiv \frac{\psi(v_i, v_j)}{\phi(v_j)} = \frac{1}{[2\pi(1-\rho^2)]^{\frac{1}{2}}} \exp\left[-\frac{(v_i - \rho v_j)^2}{2(1-\rho^2)}\right],\ i,j = (1,2),(2,1). \tag{11A.3}$$

Hence, $(v_i|v_j) \sim \mathcal{N}(\rho v_j, 1-\rho^2)$, and v_i, truncated to be in the interval (a, b), has density

$$f_{ab}(v_i|a < v_i < b) = \frac{\phi(v_i)}{\Phi(b) - \Phi(a)}, \qquad i = 1, 2. \tag{11A.4}$$

Since (11A.1) implies, see also (9.14),

$$\phi'(v_i) = -v_i\phi(v_i), \tag{11A.5}$$

we have

$$\begin{aligned}\int_a^b v_i\phi(v_i)dv_i &= -\int_a^b \phi'(v_i)dv_i = \phi(a)-\phi(b),\\ \int_a^b v_i^2\phi(v_i)dv_i &= -\int_a^b v_i\phi'(v_i)dv_i = |_a^b[\phi(v_i) - v_i\phi(v_i)]\\ &= [\Phi(b)-\Phi(a)] - [b\phi(b)-a\phi(a)],\end{aligned}$$

since $d[v_i\phi(v_i)]/dv_i \equiv v_i\phi'(v_i)+\phi(v_i)$ implies $\int_a^b[v_i\phi'(v_i) + \phi(v_i)]dv_i \equiv b\phi(b) - a\phi(a)$. We then obtain, when truncation is from both the left and the right:

$$\begin{aligned}\mathsf{E}(v_i|a<v_i<b) &\equiv \int_a^b v_i f_{ab}(v_i|a<v_i<b)dv_i\\ &= \frac{\int_a^b v_i\phi(v_i)dv_i}{\int_a^b \phi(v_i)dv_i} = \frac{\phi(a)-\phi(b)}{\Phi(b)-\Phi(a)},\end{aligned} \tag{11A.6}$$

$$\begin{aligned}\mathsf{E}(v_i^2|a<v_i<b) &\equiv \int_a^b v_i^2 f_{ab}(v_i|a<v_i<b)dv_i\\ &= \frac{\int_a^b v_i^2\phi(v_i)dv_i}{\int_a^b \phi(v_i)dv_i} = 1-\frac{b\phi(b)-a\phi(a)}{\Phi(b)-\Phi(a)},\end{aligned} \tag{11A.7}$$

$$\begin{aligned}\mathrm{var}(v_i|a<v_i<b) &\equiv \mathsf{E}(v_i^2|a<v_i<b) - [\mathsf{E}(v_i|a<v_i<b)]^2\\ &= 1 - \frac{b\phi(b)-a\phi(a)}{\Phi(b)-\Phi(a)} - \left[\frac{\phi(b)-\phi(a)}{\Phi(b)-\Phi(a)}\right]^2.\end{aligned} \tag{11A.8}$$

Special cases, for single truncation, obtained for $b \to \infty$ (only left-truncation) and $a =\to -\infty$ (only right-truncation), confer (11.15)–(11.16), are

$$\mathsf{E}(v_i|v_i>a) = \frac{\phi(a)}{1-\Phi(a)} \equiv \lambda_A(a), \tag{11A.9}$$

$$\mathsf{E}(v_i|v_i<b) = -\frac{\phi(b)}{\Phi(b)} \equiv -\lambda_B(b), \tag{11A.10}$$

$$\begin{aligned}\mathrm{var}(v_i|v_i>a) &= 1+\frac{a\phi(a)}{1-\Phi(a)} - \left[\frac{\phi(a)}{1-\Phi(a)}\right]^2\\ &= 1 + \lambda_A(a)[a - \lambda_A(a)]],\end{aligned} \tag{11A.11}$$

$$\text{var}(v_i|v_i < b) = 1 - \frac{b\phi(b)}{\Phi(b)} - \left[\frac{\phi(b)}{\Phi(b)}\right]^2$$
$$= 1 - \lambda_B(b)[b + \lambda_B(b)]]. \tag{11A.12}$$

Using $\mathsf{E}(v_j|v_i) = \rho v_i$, $\text{var}(v_j|v_i) = (1-\rho^2)$ $(i \neq j)$, (11A.3), (11A.6), (11A.8), and the rule of iterated expectations, it follows that

$$\mathsf{E}(v_j|a < v_i < b) = \rho\mathsf{E}(v_i|a < v_i < b) = \rho\frac{\int_a^b v_i\phi(v_i)dv_i}{\int_a^b \phi(v_i)dv_i} = \rho\frac{\phi(a)-\phi(b)}{\Phi(b)-\Phi(a)}, \tag{11A.13}$$

$$\text{var}(v_j|a < v_i < b) = \mathsf{E}[\text{var}(v_j|a < v_i < b] + \text{var}[\mathsf{E}(v_j|a < v_i < b]$$
$$= \mathsf{E}(1-\rho^2) + \text{var}[\rho v_i|a < v_i < b]$$
$$= 1-\rho^2\left\{\frac{b\phi(b)-a\phi(a)}{\Phi(b)-\Phi(a)} + \left[\frac{\phi(b)-\phi(a)}{\Phi(b)-\Phi(a)}\right]^2\right\}. \tag{11A.14}$$

Special cases, for single truncation, are

$$\mathsf{E}(v_j|v_i > a) = \rho\frac{\phi(a)}{1-\Phi(a)} = \rho\lambda_A(a), \tag{11A.15}$$

$$\mathsf{E}(v_j|v_i < b) = -\rho\frac{\phi(b)}{\Phi(b)} = -\rho\lambda_B(b), \tag{11A.16}$$

$$\text{var}(v_j|v_i > a) = 1 + \rho^2\left[\frac{a\phi(a)}{1-\Phi(a)} - \frac{[\phi(a)]^2}{[1-\Phi(a)]^2}\right]$$
$$= 1 + \rho^2\lambda_A(a)[a - \lambda_A(a)], \tag{11A.17}$$

$$\text{var}(v_j|v_i < b) = 1 - \rho^2\left[\frac{b\phi(b)}{\Phi(b)} + \frac{[\phi(b)]^2}{[\Phi(b)]^2}\right]$$
$$= 1 - \rho^2\lambda_B(b)[b + \lambda_B(b)]. \tag{11A.18}$$

11A.2. Deriving implications of these results for *general binormal variables* is straightforward. Results for $(p, q) \sim \mathcal{N}_2(\mu_p, \mu_q; \sigma_p^2, \sigma_p^2, \sigma_{pq})$ can be easily derived by inserting $u = (p - \mu_p)/\sigma_p$, $v = (q - \mu_q)/\sigma_q \Longrightarrow p = \mu_p + \sigma_p u$, $q = \mu_q + \sigma_q v$. The counterparts to (11A.9)–(11A.10) and (11A.15)–(11A.16) become respectively

$$\mathsf{E}(q|q > A) = \mu_q + \sigma_q\mathsf{E}\left(v|v > \frac{A-\mu_q}{\sigma_q}\right) = \mu_q + \sigma_q\lambda_A\left(\frac{A-\mu_q}{\sigma_q}\right), \tag{11A.19}$$

$$\mathsf{E}(q|q < B) = \mu_q + \sigma_q\mathsf{E}\left(v|v < \frac{B-\mu_q}{\sigma_q}\right) = \mu_q - \sigma_q\lambda_B\left(\frac{B-\mu_q}{\sigma_q}\right), \tag{11A.20}$$

$$\mathsf{E}(q|p>A) = \mu_q + \sigma_q \mathsf{E}\left(v|u > \frac{A-\mu_p}{\sigma_p}\right) = \mu_q + \sigma_q \rho \lambda_A\left(\frac{A-\mu_p}{\sigma_p}\right), \tag{11A.21}$$

$$\mathsf{E}(q|p<B) = \mu_q + \sigma_q \mathsf{E}\left(v|u < \frac{B-\mu_p}{\sigma_p}\right) = \mu_q - \sigma_q \rho \lambda_B\left(\frac{B-\mu_p}{\sigma_p}\right). \tag{11A.22}$$

11A.3. Returning to the standardized distribution, we let $(u,v) \sim \mathcal{N}_2(0,0,1,1,\rho)$ and define

$$\begin{aligned}\delta \equiv \delta(a,b,c,d) &\equiv P(a<u<c,\ b<v<d) = \textstyle\int_a^c \int_b^d \psi(u,v)\,du\,dv \\ &= \Psi(c,d) - \Psi(c,b) - \Psi(a,d) + \Psi(a,b), \end{aligned} \tag{11A.23}$$

$$\gamma \equiv \gamma(a,b,c,d) \equiv \textstyle\int_a^c \int_b^d u\,\psi(u,v)\,du\,dv, \tag{11A.24}$$

where $\Psi(\cdot,\cdot)$ is the cdf corresponding to the density $\psi(v_1,v_2)$. We can then express the expectation of u when both u and v are doubly truncated, as

$$\mathsf{E}(u|a<u<c, b<v<d) = \frac{\gamma(a,b,c,d)}{\delta(a,b,c,d)} \equiv \mu(a,b,c,d). \tag{11A.25}$$

From (11A.2) and (11A.24) it follows that

$$\begin{aligned}\gamma &= \frac{1}{2\pi}\frac{1}{\sqrt{1-\rho^2}}\int_a^c\int_b^d u\exp\left(-\frac{v^2-2\rho v u+u^2}{2(1-\rho^2)}\right)dv\,du \\ &\equiv \frac{1}{2\pi}\frac{1}{\sqrt{1-\rho^2}}\int_a^c u\exp\left(-\frac{u^2}{2}\right)\left[\int_b^d \exp\left(-\frac{(v-\rho u)^2}{2(1-\rho^2)}\right)dv\right]du.\end{aligned}$$

Substituting $\tau = 1/\sqrt{1-\rho^2}$ and $z=\tau(v-\rho u)$, this can be written as

$$\gamma = \frac{1}{2\pi}\int_a^c ue^{-u^2/2}\left[\int_{\tau(b-\rho u)}^{\tau(d-\rho u)} e^{-z^2/2}dz\right]du.$$

Using integration by parts, defining

$$\begin{aligned}s'(u) &= ue^{-u^2/2} \equiv -\sqrt{2\pi}\,u\phi(u) \implies \\ s(u) &= -e^{-u^2/2} \equiv -\sqrt{2\pi}\phi(u), \\ t(u) &= \int_{\tau(b-\rho u)}^{\tau(d-\rho u)} e^{-z^2/2}dz \equiv \sqrt{2\pi}[\Phi(\tau(d-\rho u)) - \Phi(\tau(b-\rho u))] \implies \\ t'(u) &= -\sqrt{2\pi}\,\rho\tau[\phi(\tau(d-\rho u)) - \phi(\tau(b-\rho u))],\end{aligned}$$

γ can be written as

$$\gamma = \frac{1}{2\pi}\int_a^c s'(u)t(u)du \equiv \frac{1}{2\pi}\left[s(c)t(c)-s(a)t(a)-\int_a^c s(u)t'(u)du\right]. \qquad (11A.26)$$

Now, from the above definitions we have

$$s(u)t(u) = -(2\pi)\phi(u)[\Phi(\tau(d-\rho u)) - \Phi(\tau(b-\rho u))], \qquad (11A.27)$$

$$\begin{aligned} s(u)t'(u) &= (2\pi)\rho\tau\phi(u)[\phi(\tau(d-\rho u))-\phi(\tau(b-\rho u))] \\ &\equiv (2\pi)\rho\tau[\phi(d)\phi(\tau(u-\rho d))-\phi(b)\phi(\tau(u-\rho b))] \end{aligned} \qquad (11A.28)$$

where the last equality follows because $\phi(u)\phi(\tau(d-\rho u)) \equiv \phi(d)\phi(\tau(u-\rho d))$ and $\phi(u)\phi(\tau(b-\rho u)) \equiv \phi(b)\phi(\tau(u-\rho b))$. Therefore (11A.26), (11A.27), and (11A.28) imply

$$\begin{aligned} \int_a^c s(u)t'(u)du = (2\pi)\rho\{&\phi(d)[\Phi(\tau(c-\rho d))-\Phi(\tau(a-\rho d))] \\ &- \phi(b)[\Phi(\tau(c-\rho b))-\Phi(\tau(a-\rho b))]\}. \end{aligned}$$

Combining the three last results with (11A.24), we obtain

$$\begin{aligned} \gamma(a,b,c,d) = &\ \phi(a)[\Phi(\tau(d-\rho a))-\Phi(\tau(b-\rho a))] \\ &- \phi(c)[\Phi(\tau(d-\rho c))-\Phi(\tau(b-\rho c))] \\ &+ \rho\phi(b)[\Phi(\tau(c-\rho b))-\Phi(\tau(a-\rho b))] \\ &- \rho\phi(d)[\Phi(\tau(c-\rho d)) - \Phi(\tau(a-\rho d))]. \end{aligned} \qquad (11A.29)$$

Muthén (1990) has derived a related expression in a somewhat more general setting. The final expression for $\mu(a,b,c,d)$ follows by inserting (11A.23) and (11A.29) in (11A.25).

Finally, consider two special cases:

Single truncation from below: $(a,b) = (-\infty,-\infty) \Longrightarrow$

$$\begin{aligned} \mathsf{E}(u|u<c, v<d) &= \frac{\gamma(-\infty,-\infty,c,d)}{\delta(-\infty,-\infty,c,d)} \\ &= -\frac{\phi(c)\Phi(\tau(d-\rho c))+\rho\phi(d)\Phi(\tau(c-\rho d))}{\Psi(c,d)}. \end{aligned}$$

Double truncation, uncorrelated (independent) disturbances: $\rho = 0 \Longrightarrow \tau = 1 \Longrightarrow$

$$\gamma(a,b,c,d) = \int_a^c \int_b^d u\,\phi(u)\phi(v)\,du\,dv = [\int_a^c u\,\phi(u)du][\int_b^d \phi(v)dv]$$
$$= [\phi(a) - \phi(c)][\Phi(d) - \Phi(b)],$$
$$\delta(a,b,c,d) = \int_a^c \int_b^d \phi(u)\phi(v)\,du\,dv = [\int_a^c \phi(u)du][\int_b^d \phi(v)dv]$$
$$= [\Phi(c) - \Phi(a)][\Phi(d) - \Phi(b)].$$

In this case, conditioning on $v \in (b,d)$ is irrelevant, since

$$\mathsf{E}(u|a < u < c, b < v < d) = \frac{\gamma(a,b,c,d)}{\delta(a,b,c,d)} = \frac{\phi(a) - \phi(c)}{\Phi(c) - \Phi(a)} = \mathsf{E}(u|a < u < c).$$

Appendix 11B. **Partial effects in censoring models**

Can we indicate which partial (marginal) effects we in reality attempt to estimate instead of $\boldsymbol{\beta}$ when regressing y_{it} on $\boldsymbol{x}_{it}$, using a truncated or a censored sample? The following results can help in answering these questions.

Let x_{kit} and β_k denote element k of, respectively, $\boldsymbol{x}_{it}$ and $\boldsymbol{\beta}$. We find, using $\Phi'(c) = \phi(c)$ and $\phi'(c) = -c\phi(c)$, see (11A.5), by differentiating (11.15) and (11.16), that

$$\frac{\partial\lambda_A(a)}{\partial a} = \frac{[1-\Phi(a)]\phi'(a)+[\phi(a)]^2}{[1-\Phi(a)]^2} = \frac{[\phi(a)]^2 - a\,\phi(a)[1-\Phi(a)]}{[1-\Phi(a)]^2},$$
$$\frac{\partial\lambda_B(b)}{\partial b} = \frac{\Phi(b)\phi'(b) - [\phi(b)]^2}{[\Phi(b)]^2} = -\frac{b\phi(b)\Phi(b)+[\phi(b)]^2}{[\Phi(b)]^2},$$

and hence

$$\frac{\partial\lambda_A(a)}{\partial a} = \lambda_A(a)[\lambda_A(a) - a], \tag{11B.1}$$
$$\frac{\partial\lambda_B(b)}{\partial b} = -\lambda_B(b)[\lambda_B(b) + b]. \tag{11B.2}$$

Using these derivatives in combination with (11.12), (11.26), and (11.28) we obtain

$$\frac{\partial\mathsf{E}(y_{it}|\boldsymbol{X}, y_{it} \geq 0)}{\partial x_{kit}} = \beta_k\Phi_{it} + (\boldsymbol{x}_{it}\boldsymbol{\beta})\phi_{it}\tfrac{\beta_k}{\sigma} + \sigma(-\boldsymbol{x}_{it}\tfrac{\boldsymbol{\beta}}{\sigma})\phi_{it}\tfrac{\beta_k}{\sigma},$$

$$\frac{\partial \mathsf{E}(y_{it}|X, y_{it} \le 0)}{\partial x_{kit}} = \beta_k[1-\Phi_{it}] - (x_{it\beta})\phi_{it}\frac{\beta_k}{\sigma} - \sigma(-x_{it}\frac{\beta}{\sigma})\phi_{it}\frac{\beta_k}{\sigma},$$

$$\frac{\partial \mathsf{E}(y_{it}|X, y_{it} > 0)}{\partial x_{kit}} = \beta_k - \sigma[\lambda_{Bit}(\lambda_{Bit} + x_{it}\frac{\beta}{\sigma})]\frac{\beta_k}{\sigma},$$

$$\frac{\partial \mathsf{E}(y_{it}|X, y_{it} < 0)}{\partial x_{kit}} = \beta_k - \sigma[\lambda_{Ait}(\lambda_{Ait} - x_{it}\frac{\beta}{\sigma})]\frac{\beta_k}{\sigma},$$

and hence

$$\frac{\partial \mathsf{E}(y_{it}|X, y_{it} \ge 0)}{\partial x_{kit}} = \beta_k\Phi_{it}, \qquad (11B.3)$$

$$\frac{\partial \mathsf{E}(y_{it}|X, y_{it} \le 0)}{\partial x_{kit}} = \beta_k[1-\Phi_{it}], \qquad (11B.4)$$

$$\frac{\partial \mathsf{E}(y_{it}|X, y_{it} > 0)}{\partial x_{kit}} = \beta_k[1-\lambda_{Bit}(\lambda_{Bit}+x_{it}\frac{\beta}{\sigma})], \qquad (11B.5)$$

$$\frac{\partial \mathsf{E}(y_{it}|X, y_{it} < 0)}{\partial x_{kit}} = \beta_k[1-\lambda_{Ait}(\lambda_{Ait}-x_{it}\frac{\beta}{\sigma})]. \qquad (11B.6)$$

For extensions to, *inter alia*, cases where the normality assumption is relaxed, see Rosett and Nelson (1975) and McDonald and Moffitt (1980).

12 Multi-equation models

CHAPTER SUMMARY

Two kinds of multi-equation models are in focus: systems of regression equations and interdependent models. In the former, systems with only individual-specific random intercepts and systems with both individual-specific and period-specific random effects are considered. In the latter, estimation of single equations is considered first and next system estimation of all equations. We here draw on results from earlier chapters regarding within-, between-, GLS (including the Zellner SUR idea), and ML estimators, as well as elements from two-stage and three-stage least squares (2SLS, 3SLS). Two ways of ordering variables and coefficients in matrices, serving different purposes, are considered. Empirical examples are given.

12.1 Introduction

All preceding chapters have been concerned almost exclusively with single-equation models, each having one endogenous variable.[1] The tools and procedures for making inference from panel data are definitely not confined to situations with one (structural) equation. In this chapter we consider multi-equation models for balanced panel data and estimation methods for such models. A formal property of all multi-equation models for panel data is that the exogenous and endogenous variables have *three subscripts*, referring to the equation, the individual, and the period. Certain variables may be common to all equations, to all individuals, or to all periods, i.e., have fewer than three subscripts.

Multi-equation models may be divided into: *systems of regression equations*—whose main characteristic is that each equation has one endogenous variable—and

[1] This is not strictly true, depending on what is understood by 'one variable'. Sometimes it has been convenient to formally consider one econometric equation with observations from N individuals in T periods *either* as N equations with T observations (period being the observation unit), *or* as T equations with N observations (individual being the observations unit), both with identical coefficients. The multinomial choice models discussed in Chapter 9 are by their nature multi-equation models, although non-linear, to comply with the restrictions on the response probabilities. The same is true for the limited dependent variables models in Section 11.4.

interdependent models—in which at least one equation has more than one endogenous variable. Examples in the first category are systems of demand functions for consumption goods and factor inputs, in the second category are systems of structural macro-economic equations (say neo-keynesian) for several countries. For both categories, several problems discussed earlier might have been reconsidered, e.g., fixed vs. random intercepts and coefficients, dynamic mechanisms, unidimensional variables, unbalanced data, and measurement errors. We will confine attention to selected problems related to multi-equation panel data models, including systems of regression equations of the type often labelled 'SUR systems' (Sections 12.2 and 12.3) and interdependent models (Sections 12.4 and 12.5). Maintained assumptions will be: balanced panel, no measurement error, static, linear equations with endogenous variables continuous; all slope coefficients deterministic with no heterogeneity, censoring, and truncation of observations disregarded; and random individual-specific or period-specific intercept heterogeneity.

The chapter proceeds as follows. Section 12.2 deals with systems of regression equations with individual-specific random effects. Section 12.3 generalizes by adding period-specific random effects. In Section 12.4 we take a first step into models with several endogenous variables in at least some equations and consider estimation of *single equations* in such simultaneous systems. Section 12.5 is concerned with methods for *system estimation* of all equations. All sections draw on results from earlier chapters. Ingredients in the methods will be, on the one hand, within-, between-, and GLS estimators, previously discussed for single-equation regression models, and on the other hand, elements from two-stage and three-stage least squares (2SLS, 3SLS), two fairly standard estimation methods for simultaneous equation models.

12.2 **Regression system with one-way random effects**

The regression models to be considered have, in principle, *four dimensions*: variable, equation, individual, and period. In scalar notation, each will be represented by a specific subscript. Taking care when organizing panel data sets in matrix files for use in econometric software packages or modules for a specific problem can give profits when the econometric work is carried through. We first give a model description in (mostly) scalar notation (Section 12.2.1), next present two versions in matrix formulation, with different ordering of the elements (Section 12.2.2), and then consider estimation by GLS and FGLS (Section 12.2.3) and ML (Section 12.2.4).

12.2.1 MODEL DESCRIPTION

Consider a model with G equations, indexed by $g = 1, \ldots, G$, individuals indexed by $i = 1, \ldots, N$, and periods by $t = 1, \ldots, T$. Equation g has K_g regressors:

$$\begin{aligned}
&y_{git} = \boldsymbol{x}_{git}\boldsymbol{\beta}_g + \alpha_{gi} + u_{git} = \boldsymbol{x}_{git}\boldsymbol{\beta}_g + \epsilon_{git},\\
&\epsilon_{git} = \alpha_{gi} + u_{git}, \quad \alpha_{gi} \perp u_{git},\\
&\mathsf{E}(\alpha_{gi}|X) = 0, \qquad \mathsf{E}(\alpha_{gi}\alpha_{hj}|X) = \delta_{ij}\sigma^{\alpha}_{gh},\\
&\mathsf{E}(u_{git}|X) = 0, \qquad \mathsf{E}(u_{git}u_{hjs}|X) = \delta_{ij}\delta_{ts}\sigma^{u}_{gh},\\
&g,h=1,\ldots,G;\ i,j=1,\ldots,N;\ t,s=1,\ldots,T,
\end{aligned} \tag{12.1}$$

where, for equation g, y_{git} is the regressand, $\boldsymbol{x}_{git} = (x_{g1it}, \ldots, x_{gK_git})$ is the $(1 \times K_g)$-vector of regressors (including a one attached to the intercept), $\boldsymbol{\beta}_g = (\beta_{g1}, \ldots, \beta_{gK_g})'$ is the corresponding $(K_g \times 1)$-vector of coefficients (including intercept), α_{gi} is a stochastic individual-specific effect, u_{git} is a genuine disturbance, and X (in general) denotes all values of $\boldsymbol{x}_{git}$ (in any equation). This allows for correlated individual-specific effects across equations ($\sigma^{\alpha}_{gh} \neq 0,\ g \neq h$) and genuine disturbances correlated across equations ($\sigma^{u}_{gh} \neq 0,\ g \neq h$). Within each equation the disturbance components are homoskedastic and uncorrelated. Then

$$\mathsf{E}(\epsilon_{git}|X)=0,\ \mathsf{E}(\epsilon_{git}\epsilon_{hjs}|X) = \begin{cases} \sigma^{\alpha}_{gh}+\sigma^{u}_{gh}, & i=j,\ t=s,\\ \sigma^{\alpha}_{gh}, & i=j,\ t\neq s,\\ 0, & i\neq j. \end{cases} \tag{12.2}$$

Since in general $\frac{1}{2}GNT(GNT+1)$ second-order moments exist between the ϵ_{git}s, this is a drastic reduction of the parameter set, even for moderate G, N, and T, since by (12.2) they are structured by $\frac{1}{2}G(G+1)$ σ^{α}_{gh}s and $\frac{1}{2}G(G+1)$ σ^{u}_{gh}s.

12.2.2 MATRIX VERSION: TWO FORMULATIONS

Two ways of ordering variables and coefficients in (12.1) are of interest when bringing the model to matrix form, denoted as *ordering by equation* and *ordering by individual*. The first will be useful, *inter alia*, for GLS estimation when using the Zellner SUR approach; see Zellner (1962). The second will be convenient, *inter alia*, for explaining estimation of disturbance covariance matrices.

Ordering by equation: we arrange, for equation g, the NT elements in (12.1) in vectors and matrices by individual and period in the same way as for the single-equation models in Chapter 3, defining

$$y_g = \begin{bmatrix} y_{g11} \\ \vdots \\ y_{g1T} \\ \vdots \\ y_{gN1} \\ \vdots \\ y_{gNT} \end{bmatrix}, \quad u_g = \begin{bmatrix} u_{g11} \\ \vdots \\ u_{g1T} \\ \vdots \\ u_{gN1} \\ \vdots \\ u_{gNT} \end{bmatrix}, \quad \epsilon_g = \begin{bmatrix} \epsilon_{g11} \\ \vdots \\ \epsilon_{g1T} \\ \vdots \\ \epsilon_{gN1} \\ \vdots \\ \epsilon_{gNT} \end{bmatrix}, \quad X_g = \begin{bmatrix} x_{g11} \\ \vdots \\ x_{g1T} \\ \vdots \\ x_{gN1} \\ \vdots \\ x_{gNT} \end{bmatrix},$$

and $\boldsymbol{\alpha}_g = (\alpha_{g1}, \dots, \alpha_{gN})'$. Then (12.1)–(12.2) take the form

$$\begin{aligned} & y_g = X_g\boldsymbol{\beta}_g + (\boldsymbol{\alpha}_g \otimes e_T) + u_g = X_g\boldsymbol{\beta}_g + \boldsymbol{\epsilon}_g, \\ & \boldsymbol{\epsilon}_g = (\boldsymbol{\alpha}_g \otimes e_T) + u_g, \quad \boldsymbol{\alpha}_g \perp u_g, \\ & \mathsf{E}(\boldsymbol{\alpha}_g|X) = \mathbf{0}_{N,1}, \qquad \mathsf{E}(\boldsymbol{\alpha}_g\boldsymbol{\alpha}_h'|X) = \sigma_{gh}^{\alpha}\boldsymbol{I}_N, \\ & \mathsf{E}(\boldsymbol{u}_g|X) = \mathbf{0}_{NT,1}, \qquad \mathsf{E}(\boldsymbol{u}_g\boldsymbol{u}_h'|X) = \sigma_{gh}^{u}(\boldsymbol{I}_N \otimes \boldsymbol{I}_T), \end{aligned} \tag{12.3}$$

$$\begin{aligned} & \mathsf{E}(\boldsymbol{\epsilon}_g|X) = \mathbf{0}_{NT,1}, \\ & \mathsf{E}(\boldsymbol{\epsilon}_g\boldsymbol{\epsilon}_h'|X) = \boldsymbol{\Omega}_{gh} = \sigma_{gh}^{\alpha}\boldsymbol{I}_N \otimes (\boldsymbol{e}_T\boldsymbol{e}_T') + \sigma_{gh}^{u}(\boldsymbol{I}_N \otimes \boldsymbol{I}_T), \\ & \qquad g, h = 1, \dots, G. \end{aligned} \tag{12.4}$$

We define

$$y = \begin{bmatrix} y_1 \\ \vdots \\ y_G \end{bmatrix}, \quad u = \begin{bmatrix} u_1 \\ \vdots \\ u_G \end{bmatrix}, \quad \epsilon = \begin{bmatrix} \epsilon_1 \\ \vdots \\ \epsilon_G \end{bmatrix}, \quad X = \begin{bmatrix} X_1 & \cdots & 0 \\ \vdots & \ddots & \vdots \\ 0 & \cdots & X_G \end{bmatrix},$$

so that when moving along a vector, the equation subscript g 'runs slow', the individual subscript i 'runs faster', and the period subscript t 'runs fastest'. We further let $\boldsymbol{\alpha}$ be the $(GNT \times 1)$-vector which contains all N individual-specific effects, ordered by equation, each element repeated T times, and let $\boldsymbol{\beta}$ be the $(\sum_{g=1}^{G} K_g \times 1)$-vector which contains all regression coefficients (including the intercepts), ordered by equation, i.e.,

$$\boldsymbol{\alpha} = \begin{bmatrix} \boldsymbol{\alpha}_1 \otimes \boldsymbol{e}_T \\ \vdots \\ \boldsymbol{\alpha}_G \otimes \boldsymbol{e}_T \end{bmatrix}, \qquad \boldsymbol{\beta} = \begin{bmatrix} \boldsymbol{\beta}_1 \\ \vdots \\ \boldsymbol{\beta}_G \end{bmatrix}. \tag{12.5}$$

This allows us to write (12.3) compactly as

$$\begin{aligned}
&y = X\beta + \alpha + u = X\beta + \epsilon, \quad \epsilon = \alpha + u, \quad \alpha \perp u, \\
&\mathsf{E}(\alpha|X) = 0_{GNT,1}, \qquad \mathsf{E}(\alpha\alpha'|X) = \Sigma_\alpha \otimes I_N \otimes (e_T e_T'), \\
&\mathsf{E}(u|X) = 0_{GNT,1}, \qquad \mathsf{E}(uu'|X) = \Sigma_u \otimes I_N \otimes I_T,
\end{aligned} \tag{12.6}$$

where, when letting $\widetilde{\alpha}_i = (\alpha_{1i}, \dots, \alpha_{Gi})'$ and $\widetilde{u}_{it} = (u_{1it}, \dots, u_{Git})'$,

$$\Sigma_\alpha = \mathsf{E}[\widetilde{\alpha}_i \widetilde{\alpha}_i'|X] = \begin{bmatrix} \sigma_{11}^\alpha & \cdots & \sigma_{1G}^\alpha \\ \vdots & & \vdots \\ \sigma_{G1}^\alpha & \cdots & \sigma_{GG}^\alpha \end{bmatrix},$$

$$\Sigma_u = \mathsf{E}[\widetilde{u}_{it} \widetilde{u}_{it}'|X] = \begin{bmatrix} \sigma_{11}^u & \cdots & \sigma_{1G}^u \\ \vdots & & \vdots \\ \sigma_{G1}^u & \cdots & \sigma_{GG}^u \end{bmatrix}.$$

The covariance matrix of the $(GNT \times 1)$-vector ϵ can then be written either as

$$\Omega = \mathsf{E}(\epsilon\epsilon'|X) = \begin{bmatrix} \Omega_{11} & \cdots & \Omega_{1G} \\ \vdots & & \vdots \\ \Omega_{G1} & \cdots & \Omega_{GG} \end{bmatrix}, \tag{12.7}$$

or, by using (12.4), as

$$\begin{aligned}
\Omega &= \Sigma_\alpha \otimes I_N \otimes (e_T e_T') + \Sigma_u \otimes I_N \otimes I_T \\
&\equiv (\Sigma_u + T\Sigma_\alpha) \otimes I_N \otimes A_T + \Sigma_u \otimes I_N \otimes B_T.
\end{aligned} \tag{12.8}$$

From Theorem 1 in Appendix 3A, Section 3A.1, it follows that

$$\Omega^{-1} = (\Sigma_u + T\Sigma_\alpha)^{-1} \otimes I_N \otimes A_T + \Sigma_u^{-1} \otimes I_N \otimes B_T. \tag{12.9}$$

This is a very useful expression to economize on computer capacity in estimating β by GLS, as Ω^{-1} is obtained by inverting two $(G \times G)$-matrices and adding two Kronecker-products in these inverses. Direct inversion of the $(GNT \times GNT)$-matrix Ω would have been a formidable computer task even for moderate G, N, and T. Denoting block (g, h) of Ω^{-1} by Ω^{gh}, the inverse of Ω can alternatively be written, in analogy with (12.7), as:

$$\Omega^{-1} = \begin{bmatrix} \Omega^{11} & \cdots & \Omega^{1G} \\ \vdots & & \vdots \\ \Omega^{G1} & \cdots & \Omega^{GG} \end{bmatrix}. \tag{12.10}$$

Ordering by individual: we alternatively order, for individual and period (i,t), the G elements in (12.1), defining

$$\widetilde{y}_{it} = \begin{bmatrix} y_{1it} \\ \vdots \\ y_{Git} \end{bmatrix}, \quad \widetilde{u}_{it} = \begin{bmatrix} u_{1it} \\ \vdots \\ u_{Git} \end{bmatrix}, \quad \widetilde{\epsilon}_{it} = \begin{bmatrix} \epsilon_{1it} \\ \vdots \\ \epsilon_{Git} \end{bmatrix}, \quad \widetilde{X}_{it} = \begin{bmatrix} x_{1it} & \cdots & 0 \\ \vdots & \ddots & \vdots \\ 0 & \cdots & x_{Git} \end{bmatrix}.$$

Then (12.1) and (12.2) take the form

$$\begin{aligned} &\widetilde{y}_{it} = \widetilde{X}_{it}\boldsymbol{\beta} + \widetilde{\boldsymbol{\alpha}}_i + \widetilde{u}_{it} = \widetilde{X}_{it}\boldsymbol{\beta} + \widetilde{\epsilon}_{it}, \\ &\widetilde{\epsilon}_{it} = \widetilde{\boldsymbol{\alpha}}_i + \widetilde{u}_{it}, \quad \widetilde{\boldsymbol{\alpha}}_i \perp \widetilde{u}_{it}, \\ &\mathsf{E}(\widetilde{\boldsymbol{\alpha}}_i|X) = \mathbf{0}_{G,1}, \qquad \mathsf{E}(\widetilde{\boldsymbol{\alpha}}_i\widetilde{\boldsymbol{\alpha}}_j'|X) = \delta_{ij}\boldsymbol{\Sigma}_{\alpha}, \\ &\mathsf{E}(\widetilde{u}_{it}|X) = \mathbf{0}_{G,1}, \qquad \mathsf{E}(\widetilde{u}_{it}\widetilde{u}_{js}'|X) = \delta_{ij}\delta_{ts}\boldsymbol{\Sigma}_{u}, \end{aligned} \tag{12.11}$$

$$\mathsf{E}(\widetilde{\epsilon}_{it}|X) = \mathbf{0}_{G,1}, \quad \mathsf{E}(\widetilde{\epsilon}_{it}\widetilde{\epsilon}_{js}'|X) = \begin{cases} \boldsymbol{\Sigma}_{\alpha} + \boldsymbol{\Sigma}_{u}, & i=j,\ t=s, \\ \boldsymbol{\Sigma}_{\alpha}, & i=j,\ t\neq s, \\ \mathbf{0}_{G,G}, & i\neq j. \end{cases} \tag{12.12}$$

$$i,j = 1,\dots,N; \quad t,s = 1,\dots,T.$$

We stack the NT equations, defining

$$\widetilde{y}_i = \begin{bmatrix} \widetilde{y}_{i1} \\ \vdots \\ \widetilde{y}_{iT} \end{bmatrix}, \quad \widetilde{u}_i = \begin{bmatrix} \widetilde{u}_{i1} \\ \vdots \\ \widetilde{u}_{iT} \end{bmatrix}, \quad \widetilde{\epsilon}_i = \begin{bmatrix} \widetilde{\epsilon}_{i1} \\ \vdots \\ \widetilde{\epsilon}_{iT} \end{bmatrix}, \quad \widetilde{X}_i = \begin{bmatrix} \widetilde{X}_{i1} \\ \vdots \\ \widetilde{X}_{iT} \end{bmatrix},$$

$$\widetilde{y} = \begin{bmatrix} \widetilde{y}_{1} \\ \vdots \\ \widetilde{y}_{N} \end{bmatrix}, \quad \widetilde{u} = \begin{bmatrix} \widetilde{u}_{1} \\ \vdots \\ \widetilde{u}_{N} \end{bmatrix}, \quad \widetilde{\epsilon} = \begin{bmatrix} \widetilde{\epsilon}_{1} \\ \vdots \\ \widetilde{\epsilon}_{N} \end{bmatrix}, \quad \widetilde{X} = \begin{bmatrix} \widetilde{X}_{1} \\ \vdots \\ \widetilde{X}_{N} \end{bmatrix},$$

so that when moving along a tilded vector, the individual index i runs slow, the period index t runs faster, and the equation index g runs fastest. We further let $\widetilde{\boldsymbol{\alpha}}$ be the $\boldsymbol{\alpha}$ vector containing all the N individual-specific effects, ordered by individual, each vector element repeated T times, i.e.,

$$\widetilde{\boldsymbol{\alpha}} = \begin{bmatrix} e_T \otimes \widetilde{\boldsymbol{\alpha}}_1 \\ \vdots \\ e_T \otimes \widetilde{\boldsymbol{\alpha}}_N \end{bmatrix}. \tag{12.13}$$

The $\boldsymbol{\beta}$ vector does not change since the columns represent the regressors in both X_g and $\widetilde{X}_i$ and hence in both X and $\widetilde{X}$. Then we can write (12.11) as

$$\begin{aligned} &\widetilde{y} = \widetilde{X}\boldsymbol{\beta} + \widetilde{\alpha} + \widetilde{u} = \widetilde{X}\boldsymbol{\beta} + \widetilde{\epsilon}, \quad \widetilde{\epsilon} = \widetilde{\alpha} + \widetilde{u}, \quad \widetilde{\alpha} \perp \widetilde{u}, \\ &\mathsf{E}(\widetilde{\alpha}|X) = 0_{NTG,1}, \qquad \mathsf{E}(\widetilde{\alpha}\widetilde{\alpha}'|X) = I_N \otimes (e_T e_T') \otimes \boldsymbol{\Sigma}_\alpha, \\ &\mathsf{E}(\widetilde{u}|X) = 0_{NTG,1}, \qquad \mathsf{E}(\widetilde{u}\widetilde{u}'|X) = I_N \otimes I_T \otimes \boldsymbol{\Sigma}_u. \end{aligned} \tag{12.14}$$

The expression for the covariance matrix $\mathsf{E}(\widetilde{\epsilon}\widetilde{\epsilon}'|X)$, equivalent to (12.8), is

$$\begin{aligned} \widetilde{\boldsymbol{\Omega}} &= I_N \otimes (e_T e_T') \otimes \boldsymbol{\Sigma}_\alpha + I_N \otimes I_T \otimes \boldsymbol{\Sigma}_u \\ &\equiv I_N \otimes [A_T \otimes (\boldsymbol{\Sigma}_u + T\boldsymbol{\Sigma}_\alpha) + B_T \otimes \boldsymbol{\Sigma}_u]. \end{aligned} \tag{12.15}$$

It differs from (12.8) solely by the ordering of the factors: $\boldsymbol{\Sigma}_\alpha$ and $\boldsymbol{\Sigma}_u$ come first in $\boldsymbol{\Omega}$ and last in $\widetilde{\boldsymbol{\Omega}}$. The counterpart to (12.9) therefore is

$$\widetilde{\boldsymbol{\Omega}}^{-1} = I_N \otimes [A_T \otimes (\boldsymbol{\Sigma}_u + T\boldsymbol{\Sigma}_\alpha)^{-1} + B_T \otimes \boldsymbol{\Sigma}_u^{-1}]. \tag{12.16}$$

12.2.3 GLS ESTIMATION

We next describe the GLS problem when all σ^u_{gh}s and σ^α_{gh}s, i.e., $\boldsymbol{\Sigma}_u$ and $\boldsymbol{\Sigma}_\alpha$, are known.

When *ordering by equation*, using (12.6), the GLS estimator of $\boldsymbol{\beta}$ and its covariance matrix can be written as

$$\widehat{\boldsymbol{\beta}}_{GLS} = (X'\boldsymbol{\Omega}^{-1}X)^{-1}(X'\boldsymbol{\Omega}^{-1}y), \tag{12.17}$$

$$\mathsf{V}(\widehat{\boldsymbol{\beta}}_{GLS}|X) = (X'\boldsymbol{\Omega}^{-1}X)^{-1}, \tag{12.18}$$

and by using (12.9) as, respectively,

$$\begin{aligned} \widehat{\boldsymbol{\beta}}_{GLS} = &\{X'[(\boldsymbol{\Sigma}_u + T\boldsymbol{\Sigma}_\alpha)^{-1} \otimes I_N \otimes A_T + \boldsymbol{\Sigma}_u^{-1} \otimes I_N \otimes B_T]X\}^{-1} \\ &\times \{X'[(\boldsymbol{\Sigma}_u + T\boldsymbol{\Sigma}_\alpha)^{-1} \otimes I_N \otimes A_T + \boldsymbol{\Sigma}_u^{-1} \otimes I_N \otimes B_T]y\}, \end{aligned} \tag{12.19}$$

$$\mathsf{V}(\widehat{\boldsymbol{\beta}}_{GLS}|X) = \{X'[(\boldsymbol{\Sigma}_u + T\boldsymbol{\Sigma}_\alpha)^{-1} \otimes I_N \otimes A_T + \boldsymbol{\Sigma}_u^{-1} \otimes I_N \otimes B_T]X\}^{-1}. \tag{12.20}$$

Using (12.10), we can alternatively write (12.17)–(12.18) as

$$\widehat{\boldsymbol{\beta}}_{GLS} = \begin{bmatrix} X_1'\boldsymbol{\Omega}^{11}X_1 & \cdots & X_1'\boldsymbol{\Omega}^{1G}X_G \\ \vdots & & \vdots \\ X_G'\boldsymbol{\Omega}^{G1}X_1 & \cdots & X_G'\boldsymbol{\Omega}^{GG}X_G \end{bmatrix}^{-1} \begin{bmatrix} \sum_{g=1}^{G} X_1'\boldsymbol{\Omega}^{1g}y_g \\ \vdots \\ \sum_{g=1}^{G} X_G'\boldsymbol{\Omega}^{Gg}y_g \end{bmatrix}, \tag{12.21}$$

$$\mathsf{V}(\widehat{\boldsymbol{\beta}}_{GLS}) = \begin{bmatrix} X_1'\boldsymbol{\Omega}^{11}X_1 & \cdots & X_1'\boldsymbol{\Omega}^{1G}X_G \\ \vdots & & \vdots \\ X_G'\boldsymbol{\Omega}^{G1}X_1 & \cdots & X_G'\boldsymbol{\Omega}^{GG}X_G \end{bmatrix}^{-1}. \tag{12.22}$$

If the disturbances are uncorrelated across equations ($\boldsymbol{\Omega}_{gh}=\mathbf{0}$, $g \neq h$), making $\boldsymbol{\Omega}$ and $\boldsymbol{\Omega}^{-1}$ block-diagonal ($\boldsymbol{\Omega}^{gg}=\boldsymbol{\Omega}_{gg}^{-1}$), we have

$$\begin{aligned}
\boldsymbol{\Omega}_{gg} &= (I_N \otimes B_T)\sigma^u_{gg} + (I_N \otimes A_T)(\sigma^u_{gg} + T\sigma^\alpha_{gg}), \\
\boldsymbol{\Omega}^{gg} &= \frac{I_N \otimes B_T}{\sigma^u_{gg}} + \frac{I_N \otimes A_T}{\sigma^u_{gg} + T\sigma^\alpha_{gg}}, \\
\widehat{\boldsymbol{\beta}}_{GLS} &= \begin{bmatrix} X_1'\boldsymbol{\Omega}^{11}X_1 & \cdots & \mathbf{0} \\ \vdots & \ddots & \vdots \\ \mathbf{0} & \cdots & X_G'\boldsymbol{\Omega}^{GG}X_G \end{bmatrix}^{-1} \begin{bmatrix} X_1'\boldsymbol{\Omega}^{11}y_1 \\ \vdots \\ X_G'\boldsymbol{\Omega}^{GG}y_G \end{bmatrix}, \\
\mathsf{V}(\widehat{\boldsymbol{\beta}}_{GLS}) &= \begin{bmatrix} X_1'\boldsymbol{\Omega}^{11}X_1 & \cdots & \mathbf{0} \\ \vdots & \ddots & \vdots \\ \mathbf{0} & \cdots & X_G'\boldsymbol{\Omega}^{GG}X_G \end{bmatrix}^{-1}.
\end{aligned}$$

This means that GLS is applied to each equation separately:

$$\begin{aligned}
\widehat{\boldsymbol{\beta}}_{g,GLS} &= (X_g'\boldsymbol{\Omega}^{gg}X_g)^{-1}(X_g'\boldsymbol{\Omega}^{gg}y_g), \\
\mathsf{V}(\widehat{\boldsymbol{\beta}}_{g,GLS}) &= (X_g'\boldsymbol{\Omega}^{gg}X_g)^{-1}, \qquad\qquad g = 1,\ldots,G.
\end{aligned}$$

The model and estimator formats (12.6) and (12.21)–(12.22) rely on an idea of Zellner (1962), Seemingly Unrelated Regressions (SUR) handled by GLS, frequently used in general analysis of systems of regression equations. A familiar, remarkable implication of this *Zellner SUR-GLS idea* is:[2] *if the equations have identical regressors*, GLS estimation of a composite equation $\boldsymbol{y}=\boldsymbol{X\beta}+\boldsymbol{u}$, $\mathsf{E}(\boldsymbol{u}|X) = \mathbf{0}$ simplifies to application of *OLS* equation by equation. This holds even if the disturbances in different equations are correlated. However, as pointed out by Avery (1977), and further elaborated by Baltagi (1980), this does not invariably carry over to panel data situations, because the Zellner result presumes that $\boldsymbol{\Omega}$ is an unrestricted covariance matrix, while (12.7)–(12.8) *impose a particular structure on it.*

The latter is illustrated by the fact that the above expression for $\widehat{\boldsymbol{\beta}}_{g,GLS}$ in the absence of cross-equation disturbance correlation, always depends on $\boldsymbol{\Omega}^{gg}$. In particular, $X_g=\bar{X}$

[2] See Greene (2008, Section 10.2.2).

gives $\widehat{\boldsymbol{\beta}}_{g,GLS} = (\bar{X}'\boldsymbol{\Omega}^{gg}\bar{X})^{-1}(\bar{X}'\boldsymbol{\Omega}^{gg}y_g)$. However, if the equation system has not only identical regressors, but also no individual-specific effects ($\boldsymbol{\Sigma}_\alpha = \mathbf{0}_{G,G} \Longrightarrow \boldsymbol{\Omega} = \boldsymbol{\Sigma}_u \otimes \boldsymbol{I}_{NT}$), then (12.9)–(12.10) yield $\boldsymbol{\Omega}^{-1} = \boldsymbol{\Sigma}_u^{-1} \otimes \boldsymbol{I}_{NT}$, and the Zellner SUR-GLS idea simplifies to applying OLS equation by equation. This follows because inserting $\boldsymbol{\Omega}^{-1} = \boldsymbol{\Sigma}_u^{-1} \otimes \boldsymbol{I}_{NT}$ and $X = \boldsymbol{I}_G \otimes \bar{X}$ in (12.17) (using rules for Kronecker-products, see Sections 2.4.1 and 2.4.2) leads to

$$
\begin{aligned}
\widehat{\boldsymbol{\beta}}_{GLS} &= [(\boldsymbol{I}_G \otimes \bar{X}')(\boldsymbol{\Sigma}_u^{-1} \otimes \boldsymbol{I}_{NT})(\boldsymbol{I}_G \otimes \bar{X})]^{-1}[(\boldsymbol{I}_G \otimes \bar{X}')(\boldsymbol{\Sigma}_u^{-1} \otimes \boldsymbol{I}_{NT})y] \\
&= [\boldsymbol{\Sigma}_u^{-1} \otimes (\bar{X}'\bar{X})]^{-1}[\boldsymbol{\Sigma}_u^{-1} \otimes \bar{X}']y = [\boldsymbol{I}_G \otimes (\bar{X}'\bar{X})^{-1}\bar{X}']y \\
&\equiv \begin{bmatrix} (\bar{X}'\bar{X})^{-1}\bar{X}' & \cdots & 0 \\ \vdots & \ddots & \vdots \\ 0 & \cdots & (\bar{X}'\bar{X})^{-1}\bar{X}' \end{bmatrix} \begin{bmatrix} y_1 \\ \vdots \\ y_G \end{bmatrix} \Longrightarrow \\
\widehat{\boldsymbol{\beta}}_{g,GLS} &= (\bar{X}'\bar{X})^{-1}(\bar{X}'y_g), \qquad g = 1, \dots, G.
\end{aligned}
$$

When *ordering by individual* (i.e., not following the Zellner SUR-GLS idea) the GLS estimator and its covariance matrix, using (12.16), take the form

$$\widehat{\boldsymbol{\beta}}_{GLS} = (\widetilde{X}'\widetilde{\boldsymbol{\Omega}}^{-1}\widetilde{X})^{-1}(\widetilde{X}'\widetilde{\boldsymbol{\Omega}}^{-1}\widetilde{y}), \tag{12.23}$$

$$\mathsf{V}(\widehat{\boldsymbol{\beta}}_{GLS}|X) = (\widetilde{X}'\widetilde{\boldsymbol{\Omega}}^{-1}\widetilde{X})^{-1}, \tag{12.24}$$

which since $\widetilde{\boldsymbol{\Omega}}^{-1}$ is block-diagonal, with one block per individual, implies

$$
\begin{aligned}
\widehat{\boldsymbol{\beta}}_{GLS} = \{&\textstyle\sum_{i=1}^N \widetilde{X}_i'[A_T \otimes (\boldsymbol{\Sigma}_u + T\boldsymbol{\Sigma}_\alpha)^{-1} + B_T \otimes \boldsymbol{\Sigma}_u^{-1}]\widetilde{X}_i\}^{-1} \\
&\times \{\textstyle\sum_{i=1}^N \widetilde{X}_i'[A_T \otimes (\boldsymbol{\Sigma}_u + T\boldsymbol{\Sigma}_\alpha)^{-1} + B_T \otimes \boldsymbol{\Sigma}_u^{-1}]\widetilde{y}_i\},
\end{aligned} \tag{12.25}
$$

$$\mathsf{V}(\widehat{\boldsymbol{\beta}}_{GLS}|X) = \{\textstyle\sum_{i=1}^N \widetilde{X}_i'[A_T \otimes (\boldsymbol{\Sigma}_u + T\boldsymbol{\Sigma}_\alpha)^{-1} + B_T \otimes \boldsymbol{\Sigma}_u^{-1}]\widetilde{X}_i\}^{-1}. \tag{12.26}$$

We have in this section expressed the GLS estimators and their covariance matrices in three forms: (12.19)–(12.20), (12.21)–(12.22), and (12.25)–(12.26). The context dictates which is preferable. Estimation of $\boldsymbol{\Sigma}_u$ and $\boldsymbol{\Sigma}_\alpha$, to obtain FGLS estimators, is discussed in Appendix 12A, Section 12A.1.

12.2.4 MAXIMUM LIKELIHOOD ESTIMATION

We next consider the more ambitious problem of estimating $\boldsymbol{\beta}$, $\boldsymbol{\Sigma}_u$, and $\boldsymbol{\Sigma}_\alpha$ jointly. We then stick, for convenience, to the ordering by individual, (12.14), assuming in addition that $\widetilde{\boldsymbol{\alpha}}_i$ and $\widetilde{\boldsymbol{u}}_i$ are independent and *multinormal*. Since $\widetilde{\boldsymbol{\epsilon}}_i$ is a linear transformation of these vectors, it is also multinormal. Therefore,

$$\widetilde{\boldsymbol{y}} = \widetilde{\boldsymbol{X}}\boldsymbol{\beta}+\widetilde{\boldsymbol{\epsilon}}, \quad \widetilde{\boldsymbol{\epsilon}} = \widetilde{\boldsymbol{\alpha}}+\widetilde{\boldsymbol{u}} \sim \mathsf{N}(\boldsymbol{0}_{NTG,1}, \widetilde{\boldsymbol{\Omega}}) \iff \tag{12.27}$$

$$\widetilde{\boldsymbol{y}}_i = \widetilde{\boldsymbol{X}}_i\boldsymbol{\beta}+\widetilde{\boldsymbol{\epsilon}}_i, \; \widetilde{\boldsymbol{\epsilon}}_i=(\boldsymbol{e}_T \otimes \widetilde{\boldsymbol{\alpha}}_i)+\widetilde{\boldsymbol{u}}_i \sim \mathsf{IIN}(\boldsymbol{0}_{GT,1}, \boldsymbol{\Omega}_T), \; i=1,\dots,N, \tag{12.28}$$

where $\widetilde{\boldsymbol{\Omega}}=\boldsymbol{I}_N\otimes\boldsymbol{\Omega}_T$, with

$$\boldsymbol{\Omega}_T = \boldsymbol{A}_T\otimes(\boldsymbol{\Sigma}_u+T\boldsymbol{\Sigma}_\alpha) + \boldsymbol{B}_T\otimes\boldsymbol{\Sigma}_u, \tag{12.29}$$

see (12.15). This is a generalization of the model considered in Section 3.4, with a changed interpretation of $\boldsymbol{\Omega}_T$, the scalars σ^2 and σ_α^2 being extended to $\boldsymbol{\Sigma}_u$ and $\boldsymbol{\Sigma}_\alpha$; see (3.5). Then the log-density functions of $\widetilde{\boldsymbol{\epsilon}}_i$ and $\widetilde{\boldsymbol{\epsilon}}$ are, respectively,

$$\ln(\mathcal{L}_i) = -\tfrac{1}{2}[GT\ln(2\pi)+\ln|\boldsymbol{\Omega}_T|+\widetilde{\boldsymbol{\epsilon}}_i'\boldsymbol{\Omega}_T^{-1}\widetilde{\boldsymbol{\epsilon}}_i], \tag{12.30}$$

$$\ln(\mathcal{L}) = -\tfrac{1}{2}[NTG\ln(2\pi)+N\ln(|\boldsymbol{\Omega}_T|)+\textstyle\sum_{i=1}^N\widetilde{\boldsymbol{\epsilon}}_i'\boldsymbol{\Omega}_T^{-1}\widetilde{\boldsymbol{\epsilon}}_i]. \tag{12.31}$$

Inserting $\widetilde{\boldsymbol{\epsilon}}_i=\widetilde{\boldsymbol{y}}_i-\widetilde{\boldsymbol{X}}_i\boldsymbol{\beta}$ gives the following generalization of (3.48):

$$\ln(\mathcal{L})=-\tfrac{1}{2}[NTG\ln(2\pi)+N\ln(|\boldsymbol{\Omega}_T|)+Q(\boldsymbol{\beta},\boldsymbol{\Sigma}_u,\boldsymbol{\Sigma}_\alpha)], \tag{12.32}$$

where

$$\begin{aligned} Q(\boldsymbol{\beta}, \boldsymbol{\Sigma}_u, \boldsymbol{\Sigma}_\alpha) &= [\widetilde{\boldsymbol{y}}-\widetilde{\boldsymbol{X}}\boldsymbol{\beta}]'\boldsymbol{\Omega}^{-1}[\widetilde{\boldsymbol{y}}-\widetilde{\boldsymbol{X}}\boldsymbol{\beta}] \\ &\equiv \textstyle\sum_{i=1}^N[\widetilde{\boldsymbol{y}}_i-\widetilde{\boldsymbol{X}}_i\boldsymbol{\beta}]'\boldsymbol{\Omega}_T^{-1}[\widetilde{\boldsymbol{y}}_i-\widetilde{\boldsymbol{X}}_i\boldsymbol{\beta}]. \end{aligned} \tag{12.33}$$

Direct maximization of $\ln(\mathcal{L})$ is complicated. Its particular structure can, however, as in the single-equation model, be utilized to simplify the solution, *inter alia*, by exploiting the solution to the GLS problem and suitable matrix operations. To derive the first-order conditions we split the problem into:

Sub-problem A: maximization of $\ln(\mathcal{L})$ *with respect to* $\boldsymbol{\beta}$ *for given* $(\boldsymbol{\Sigma}_u, \boldsymbol{\Sigma}_\alpha)$.
Sub-problem B: maximization of $\ln(\mathcal{L})$ *with respect to* $(\boldsymbol{\Sigma}_u, \boldsymbol{\Sigma}_\alpha)$ *for given* $\boldsymbol{\beta}$.

Sub-problem A is identical to the GLS problem, as maximizing $\ln(\mathcal{L})$ with respect to $\boldsymbol{\beta}$ is equivalent to minimizing Q. Therefore, (12.25)–(12.26) give

$$\begin{aligned} \widehat{\boldsymbol{\beta}} &= \{\textstyle\sum_{i=1}^N\widetilde{\boldsymbol{X}}_i'[\boldsymbol{A}_T\otimes(\boldsymbol{\Sigma}_u+T\boldsymbol{\Sigma}_\alpha)^{-1}+\boldsymbol{B}_T\otimes\boldsymbol{\Sigma}_u^{-1}]\widetilde{\boldsymbol{X}}_i\}^{-1} \\ &\quad\times\{\textstyle\sum_{i=1}^N\widetilde{\boldsymbol{X}}_i'[\boldsymbol{A}_T\otimes(\boldsymbol{\Sigma}_u+T\boldsymbol{\Sigma}_\alpha)^{-1}+\boldsymbol{B}_T\otimes\boldsymbol{\Sigma}_u^{-1}]\widetilde{\boldsymbol{y}}_i\}, \end{aligned} \tag{12.34}$$

$$\mathsf{V}(\widehat{\boldsymbol{\beta}}|X) = \{\textstyle\sum_{i=1}^{N}\widetilde{X}_i'[A_T\otimes(\boldsymbol{\Sigma}_u+T\boldsymbol{\Sigma}_\alpha)^{-1}+B_T\otimes\boldsymbol{\Sigma}_u^{-1}]\widetilde{X}_i\}^{-1}. \tag{12.35}$$

Sub-problem B requires derivatives of Q and $\ln(|\boldsymbol{\Omega}_T|)$. The relevant expressions can be obtained by exploiting (12.29) and results in Appendix 12B. Let first

$$Q_i = \widetilde{\boldsymbol{\epsilon}}_i'\boldsymbol{\Omega}_T^{-1}\widetilde{\boldsymbol{\epsilon}}_i = \widetilde{\boldsymbol{\epsilon}}_i'[A_T\otimes(\boldsymbol{\Sigma}_u+T\boldsymbol{\Sigma}_\alpha)^{-1}+B_T\otimes\boldsymbol{\Sigma}_u^{-1}]\widetilde{\boldsymbol{\epsilon}}_i \tag{12.36}$$

and

$$\widetilde{E}_i = [\widetilde{\boldsymbol{\epsilon}}_{i1},\dots,\widetilde{\boldsymbol{\epsilon}}_{iT}] = \begin{bmatrix} \epsilon_{1i1} & \cdots & \epsilon_{1iT} \\ \vdots & & \vdots \\ \epsilon_{Gi1} & \cdots & \epsilon_{GiT} \end{bmatrix} \Longrightarrow \widetilde{\boldsymbol{\epsilon}}_i = \mathrm{vec}(\widetilde{E}_i).$$

Next, using (12B.2) and (12B.3) (see Sections 12B.1–12B.2) and after that (12B.4) and (12B.5) (see Sections 12B.3–12B.4), we get

$$\begin{aligned}
Q_i &= \mathrm{tr}(Q_i) = \mathrm{tr}[\widetilde{E}_i'(\boldsymbol{\Sigma}_u+T\boldsymbol{\Sigma}_\alpha)^{-1}\widetilde{E}_iA_T] + \mathrm{tr}[\widetilde{E}_i'\boldsymbol{\Sigma}_u^{-1}\widetilde{E}_iB_T] \\
&= \mathrm{tr}[\widetilde{E}_iA_T\widetilde{E}_i'(\boldsymbol{\Sigma}_u+T\boldsymbol{\Sigma}_\alpha)^{-1}] + \mathrm{tr}[\widetilde{E}_iB_T\widetilde{E}_i'\boldsymbol{\Sigma}_u^{-1}], \\
|\boldsymbol{\Omega}_T| &= |A_T\otimes(\boldsymbol{\Sigma}_u+T\boldsymbol{\Sigma}_\alpha) + B_T\otimes\boldsymbol{\Sigma}_u| = |\boldsymbol{\Sigma}_u+T\boldsymbol{\Sigma}_\alpha||\boldsymbol{\Sigma}_u|^{T-1}, \\
\frac{\partial Q_i}{\partial\boldsymbol{\Sigma}_u} &= -(\boldsymbol{\Sigma}_u+T\boldsymbol{\Sigma}_\alpha)^{-1}\widetilde{E}_iA_T\widetilde{E}_i'(\boldsymbol{\Sigma}_u+T\boldsymbol{\Sigma}_\alpha)^{-1} - \boldsymbol{\Sigma}_u^{-1}\widetilde{E}_iB_T\widetilde{E}_i'\boldsymbol{\Sigma}_u^{-1}, \\
\frac{\partial Q_i}{\partial\boldsymbol{\Sigma}_\alpha} &= -T(\boldsymbol{\Sigma}_u+T\boldsymbol{\Sigma}_\alpha)^{-1}\widetilde{E}_iA_T\widetilde{E}_i'(\boldsymbol{\Sigma}_u+T\boldsymbol{\Sigma}_\alpha)^{-1}, \\
\frac{\partial\ln|\boldsymbol{\Omega}_T|}{\partial\boldsymbol{\Sigma}_u} &= \frac{\partial\ln|\boldsymbol{\Sigma}_u+T\boldsymbol{\Sigma}_\alpha|}{\partial\boldsymbol{\Sigma}_u} + (T-1)\frac{\partial\ln|\boldsymbol{\Sigma}_u|}{\partial\boldsymbol{\Sigma}_u} \\
&= (\boldsymbol{\Sigma}_u+T\boldsymbol{\Sigma}_\alpha)^{-1}+(T-1)\boldsymbol{\Sigma}_u^{-1}, \\
\frac{\partial\ln|\boldsymbol{\Omega}_T|}{\partial\boldsymbol{\Sigma}_\alpha} &= \frac{\partial\ln|\boldsymbol{\Sigma}_u+T\boldsymbol{\Sigma}_\alpha|}{\partial\boldsymbol{\Sigma}_\alpha} = T(\boldsymbol{\Sigma}_u+T\boldsymbol{\Sigma}_\alpha)^{-1}.
\end{aligned}$$

Combining (12.30) with the four last expressions, we obtain

$$\begin{aligned}
\frac{\partial\ln(\mathcal{L}_i)}{\partial\boldsymbol{\Sigma}_u} &= -\tfrac{1}{2}[(\boldsymbol{\Sigma}_u+T\boldsymbol{\Sigma}_\alpha)^{-1} + (T-1)\boldsymbol{\Sigma}_u^{-1} \\
&\quad - (\boldsymbol{\Sigma}_u+T\boldsymbol{\Sigma}_\alpha)^{-1}\widetilde{E}_iA_T\widetilde{E}_i'(\boldsymbol{\Sigma}_u+T\boldsymbol{\Sigma}_\alpha)^{-1} - \boldsymbol{\Sigma}_u^{-1}\widetilde{E}_iB_T\widetilde{E}_i'\boldsymbol{\Sigma}_u^{-1}], \\
\frac{\partial\ln(\mathcal{L}_i)}{\partial\boldsymbol{\Sigma}_\alpha} &= -\tfrac{1}{2}[T(\boldsymbol{\Sigma}_u+T\boldsymbol{\Sigma}_\alpha)^{-1} - T(\boldsymbol{\Sigma}_u+T\boldsymbol{\Sigma}_\alpha)^{-1}\widetilde{E}_iA_T\widetilde{E}_i'(\boldsymbol{\Sigma}_u+T\boldsymbol{\Sigma}_\alpha)^{-1}].
\end{aligned}$$

Finally, $\partial \ln(\mathcal{L})/\partial \boldsymbol{\Sigma}_u = \partial \ln(\mathcal{L})/\partial \boldsymbol{\Sigma}_\alpha = \mathbf{0}$, with these expressions inserted give[3]

$$\widehat{\boldsymbol{\Sigma}}_u = \widehat{\boldsymbol{\Sigma}}_u(\boldsymbol{\beta}) = \tfrac{1}{N(T-1)} \textstyle\sum_{i=1}^N \widetilde{\boldsymbol{E}}_i \boldsymbol{B}_T \widetilde{\boldsymbol{E}}_i', \tag{12.37}$$

$$\widehat{\boldsymbol{\Sigma}_u + T\boldsymbol{\Sigma}_\alpha} = \widehat{\boldsymbol{\Sigma}}_u(\boldsymbol{\beta}) + T\widehat{\boldsymbol{\Sigma}}_\alpha(\boldsymbol{\beta}) = \tfrac{1}{N} \textstyle\sum_{i=1}^N \widetilde{\boldsymbol{E}}_i \boldsymbol{A}_T \widetilde{\boldsymbol{E}}_i', \tag{12.38}$$

and hence,

$$\widehat{\boldsymbol{\Sigma}}_\alpha = \widehat{\boldsymbol{\Sigma}}_\alpha(\boldsymbol{\beta}) = \tfrac{1}{NT}[\textstyle\sum_{i=1}^N \widetilde{\boldsymbol{E}}_i \boldsymbol{A}_T \widetilde{\boldsymbol{E}}_i' - \tfrac{1}{T-1} \textstyle\sum_{i=1}^N \widetilde{\boldsymbol{E}}_i \boldsymbol{B}_T \widetilde{\boldsymbol{E}}_i']. \tag{12.39}$$

The above conditions for solving sub-problems A and B can be condensed in a prescription for iterative estimation:

1. *Estimate $\boldsymbol{\beta}_1, \dots, \boldsymbol{\beta}_G$ by OLS on each equation, and extract the residuals.*
2. *Compute, using (12.37)–(12.38), $\widehat{\boldsymbol{\Sigma}}_u$ and $\widehat{\boldsymbol{\Sigma}_u + T\boldsymbol{\Sigma}_\alpha}$.*
3. *Compute, using (12.34)–(12.35), $\widehat{\boldsymbol{\beta}}$ and $\mathsf{V}(\widehat{\boldsymbol{\beta}}|X)$.*
4. *Compute $\ln(\mathcal{L})$ by (12.32)–(12.33) and check for convergence. If convergence is confirmed, proceed to step 5. Otherwise, repeat steps 2–4.*
5. *Finally, compute $\widehat{\boldsymbol{\Sigma}}_u(\widehat{\boldsymbol{\beta}})$ and $\widehat{\boldsymbol{\Sigma}}_\alpha(\widehat{\boldsymbol{\beta}})$ from (12.37) and (12.39).*

12.3 **Regression system with two-way random effects**

We extend the model in Section 12.2 by including two-way random effects, supplementing, for equation g, the individual-specific effect α_{gi} by period-specific effects γ_{gt} and corresponding terms in the disturbance covariance matrices. The model also extends the single-equation two-way model in Section 3.5.1.

12.3.1 MODEL DESCRIPTION

The resulting extension of (12.1) is

$$\begin{aligned}
&y_{git} = \boldsymbol{x}_{git}\boldsymbol{\beta}_g + \alpha_{gi} + \gamma_{gt} + u_{git} = \boldsymbol{x}_{git}\boldsymbol{\beta}_g + \epsilon_{git},\\
&\epsilon_{git} = \alpha_{gi} + \gamma_{gt} + u_{git}, \quad \alpha_{gi} \perp \gamma_{gt} \perp u_{git},\\
&\mathsf{E}(\alpha_{gi}|X) = 0, \qquad \mathsf{E}(\alpha_{gi}\alpha_{hj}|X) = \delta_{ij}\sigma^\alpha_{gh},\\
&\mathsf{E}(\gamma_{gt}|X) = 0, \qquad \mathsf{E}(\gamma_{gt}\gamma_{hs}|X) = \delta_{ts}\sigma^\gamma_{gh},\\
&\mathsf{E}(u_{git}|X) = 0, \qquad \mathsf{E}(u_{git}u_{hjs}|X) = \delta_{ij}\delta_{ts}\sigma^u_{gh},\\
&g,h = 1,\dots,G;\ i,j = 1,\dots,N;\ t,s = 1,\dots,T.
\end{aligned} \tag{12.40}$$

[3] These estimators, one small modification apart, coincide with Appendix 12A, (12A.3)–(12A.4).

It allows for individual-specific and period-specific effects correlated across equations ($\sigma^{\alpha}_{gh}\neq 0$, $\sigma^{\gamma}_{gh}\neq 0$, $g\neq h$) and genuine disturbances correlated across equations ($\sigma^{u}_{gh}\neq 0$, $g\neq h$). Within each equation the disturbance components are assumed homoskedastic and uncorrelated. Then (12.2) is extended to

$$\mathsf{E}(\epsilon_{git}|X)=0,\qquad \mathsf{E}(\epsilon_{git}\epsilon_{hjs}|X)=\begin{cases}\sigma^{\alpha}_{gh}+\sigma^{\gamma}_{gh}+\sigma^{u}_{gh}, & i=j,t=s,\\ \sigma^{\alpha}_{gh}, & i=j,t\neq s,\\ \sigma^{\gamma}_{gh}, & t=s,i\neq j,\\ 0, & i\neq j,t\neq s.\end{cases} \tag{12.41}$$

The $\frac{1}{2}GNT(GNT+1)$ second-order moments of the ϵ_{git}s are now structured by $\frac{1}{2}G(G+1)$ σ^{α}_{gh}s, $\frac{1}{2}G(G+1)$ σ^{γ}_{gh}s, and $\frac{1}{2}G(G+1)$ σ^{u}_{gh}s. This is a sizable reduction of the parameter set, but less drastic than (12.2).

12.3.2 MATRIX VERSION: TWO FORMULATIONS

Ordering by equation: we stack, for equation g, the NT elements in (12.40) in vectors and matrices and let $\boldsymbol{\gamma}_g=(\gamma_{g1},\dots,\gamma_{gT})'$. Then (12.40)–(12.41) take the form, which generalizes (12.3)–(12.4),

$$\begin{aligned}&\boldsymbol{y}_g=\boldsymbol{X}_g\boldsymbol{\beta}_g+(\boldsymbol{\alpha}_g\otimes\boldsymbol{e}_T)+(\boldsymbol{e}_N\otimes\boldsymbol{\gamma}_g)+\boldsymbol{u}_g=\boldsymbol{X}_g\boldsymbol{\beta}_g+\boldsymbol{\epsilon}_g,\\ &\boldsymbol{\epsilon}_g=(\boldsymbol{\alpha}_g\otimes\boldsymbol{e}_T)+(\boldsymbol{e}_N\otimes\boldsymbol{\gamma}_g)+\boldsymbol{u}_g,\quad \boldsymbol{\alpha}_g\perp\boldsymbol{\gamma}_g\perp\boldsymbol{u}_g,\\ &\mathsf{E}(\boldsymbol{\alpha}_g|\boldsymbol{X})=\boldsymbol{0}_{N,1},\qquad \mathsf{E}(\boldsymbol{\alpha}_g\boldsymbol{\alpha}'_h|\boldsymbol{X})=\sigma^{\alpha}_{gh}\boldsymbol{I}_N,\\ &\mathsf{E}(\boldsymbol{\gamma}_g|\boldsymbol{X})=\boldsymbol{0}_{T,1},\qquad \mathsf{E}(\boldsymbol{\gamma}_g\boldsymbol{\gamma}'_h|\boldsymbol{X})=\sigma^{\gamma}_{gh}\boldsymbol{I}_T,\\ &\mathsf{E}(\boldsymbol{u}_g|\boldsymbol{X})=\boldsymbol{0}_{NT,1},\qquad \mathsf{E}(\boldsymbol{u}_g\boldsymbol{u}'_h|\boldsymbol{X})=\sigma^{u}_{gh}(\boldsymbol{I}_N\otimes\boldsymbol{I}_T),\end{aligned} \tag{12.42}$$

$$\begin{aligned}&\mathsf{E}(\boldsymbol{\epsilon}_g|\boldsymbol{X})=\boldsymbol{0}_{NT,1},\\ &\mathsf{E}(\boldsymbol{\epsilon}_g\boldsymbol{\epsilon}'_h|\boldsymbol{X})=\boldsymbol{\Omega}_{gh}\\ &\quad=\sigma^{\alpha}_{gh}[\boldsymbol{I}_N\otimes(\boldsymbol{e}_T\boldsymbol{e}'_T)]+\sigma^{\gamma}_{gh}[(\boldsymbol{e}_N\boldsymbol{e}'_N)\otimes\boldsymbol{I}_T]+\sigma^{u}_{gh}[\boldsymbol{I}_N\otimes\boldsymbol{I}_T].\end{aligned} \tag{12.43}$$

Stacking the G equations, letting $\boldsymbol{\gamma}$ contain all period-specific effects ordered by equation, the elements repeated N times,

$$\boldsymbol{\gamma}=\begin{bmatrix}\boldsymbol{e}_N\otimes\boldsymbol{\gamma}_1\\ \vdots\\ \boldsymbol{e}_N\otimes\boldsymbol{\gamma}_G\end{bmatrix}, \tag{12.44}$$

we write (12.42) as the following generalization of (12.6):

$$\begin{aligned}
&\boldsymbol{y} = \boldsymbol{X\beta} + \boldsymbol{\alpha} + \boldsymbol{\gamma} + \boldsymbol{u} = \boldsymbol{X\beta} + \boldsymbol{\epsilon}, \ \boldsymbol{\epsilon} = \boldsymbol{\alpha} + \boldsymbol{\gamma} + \boldsymbol{u}, \ \boldsymbol{\alpha} \perp \boldsymbol{\gamma} \perp \boldsymbol{u}, \\
&\mathsf{E}(\boldsymbol{\alpha}|X) = \boldsymbol{0}_{GNT,1}, \qquad \mathsf{E}(\boldsymbol{\alpha\alpha}'|X) = \boldsymbol{\Sigma}_{\alpha} \otimes \boldsymbol{I}_N \otimes (\boldsymbol{e}_T \boldsymbol{e}_T'), \\
&\mathsf{E}(\boldsymbol{\gamma}|X) = \boldsymbol{0}_{GNT,1}, \qquad \mathsf{E}(\boldsymbol{\gamma\gamma}'|X) = \boldsymbol{\Sigma}_{\gamma} \otimes (\boldsymbol{e}_N \boldsymbol{e}_N') \otimes \boldsymbol{I}_T, \\
&\mathsf{E}(\boldsymbol{u}|X) = \boldsymbol{0}_{GNT,1}, \qquad \mathsf{E}(\boldsymbol{uu}'|X) = \boldsymbol{\Sigma}_{u} \otimes \boldsymbol{I}_N \otimes \boldsymbol{I}_T,
\end{aligned} \tag{12.45}$$

where

$$\boldsymbol{\Sigma}_{\gamma} = \mathsf{E}[\widetilde{\boldsymbol{\gamma}}_t \widetilde{\boldsymbol{\gamma}}_t'|X] = \begin{bmatrix} \sigma_{11}^{\gamma} & \cdots & \sigma_{1G}^{\gamma} \\ \vdots & & \vdots \\ \sigma_{G1}^{\gamma} & \cdots & \sigma_{GG}^{\gamma} \end{bmatrix}.$$

Then the covariance matrix $\mathsf{E}(\boldsymbol{\epsilon\epsilon}'|X)$ can be expressed alternatively as

$$\boldsymbol{\Omega} = \begin{bmatrix} \boldsymbol{\Omega}_{11} & \cdots & \boldsymbol{\Omega}_{1G} \\ \vdots & & \vdots \\ \boldsymbol{\Omega}_{G1} & \cdots & \boldsymbol{\Omega}_{GG} \end{bmatrix}, \tag{12.46}$$

$$\begin{aligned}
\boldsymbol{\Omega} &= \boldsymbol{\Sigma}_{\alpha} \otimes \boldsymbol{I}_N \otimes (\boldsymbol{e}_T \boldsymbol{e}_T') + \boldsymbol{\Sigma}_{\gamma} \otimes (\boldsymbol{e}_N \boldsymbol{e}_N') \otimes \boldsymbol{I}_T + \boldsymbol{\Sigma}_u \otimes \boldsymbol{I}_N \otimes \boldsymbol{I}_T \\
&\equiv (\boldsymbol{\Sigma}_u + T\boldsymbol{\Sigma}_{\alpha} + N\boldsymbol{\Sigma}_{\gamma}) \otimes \boldsymbol{A}_N \otimes \boldsymbol{A}_T \\
&\quad + (\boldsymbol{\Sigma}_u + T\boldsymbol{\Sigma}_{\alpha}) \otimes \boldsymbol{B}_N \otimes \boldsymbol{A}_T \\
&\quad + (\boldsymbol{\Sigma}_u + N\boldsymbol{\Sigma}_{\gamma}) \otimes \boldsymbol{A}_N \otimes \boldsymbol{B}_T \\
&\quad + \boldsymbol{\Sigma}_u \otimes \boldsymbol{B}_N \otimes \boldsymbol{B}_T,
\end{aligned} \tag{12.47}$$

the latter expression generalizing (12.8). The inverse of $\boldsymbol{\Omega}$ can still be written as (12.10), or, by using (12.47) and Theorem 1 in Appendix 3A, Section 3A.1, as the following generalization of (12.9):

$$\begin{aligned}
\boldsymbol{\Omega}^{-1} &= (\boldsymbol{\Sigma}_u + T\boldsymbol{\Sigma}_{\alpha} + N\boldsymbol{\Sigma}_{\gamma})^{-1} \otimes \boldsymbol{A}_N \otimes \boldsymbol{A}_T \\
&\quad + (\boldsymbol{\Sigma}_u + T\boldsymbol{\Sigma}_{\alpha})^{-1} \otimes \boldsymbol{B}_N \otimes \boldsymbol{A}_T \\
&\quad + (\boldsymbol{\Sigma}_u + N\boldsymbol{\Sigma}_{\gamma})^{-1} \otimes \boldsymbol{A}_N \otimes \boldsymbol{B}_T \\
&\quad + \boldsymbol{\Sigma}_u^{-1} \otimes \boldsymbol{B}_N \otimes \boldsymbol{B}_T.
\end{aligned} \tag{12.48}$$

This is also a generalization of $\boldsymbol{\Omega}^{-1}$, given by (3.59), with the scalars σ^2, σ_{α}^2, and σ_{γ}^2 extended to $\boldsymbol{\Sigma}_u$, $\boldsymbol{\Sigma}_{\alpha}$, and $\boldsymbol{\Sigma}_{\gamma}$.

Ordering by individual: stacking, for individual and period (i, t), the G elements in vectors and matrices, letting $\widetilde{\boldsymbol{\gamma}}_t = (\gamma_{1t}, \dots, \gamma_{Gt})'$, (12.40) and (12.41) take the form, which generalizes (12.11)–(12.12),

$$\begin{aligned}
&\widetilde{y}_{it} = \widetilde{X}_{it}\boldsymbol{\beta} + \widetilde{\boldsymbol{\alpha}}_i + \widetilde{\boldsymbol{\gamma}}_t + \widetilde{\boldsymbol{u}}_{it} = \widetilde{X}_{it}\boldsymbol{\beta} + \widetilde{\boldsymbol{\epsilon}}_{it},\\
&\widetilde{\boldsymbol{\epsilon}}_{it} = \widetilde{\boldsymbol{\alpha}}_i + \widetilde{\boldsymbol{\gamma}}_t + \widetilde{\boldsymbol{u}}_{it}, \quad \widetilde{\boldsymbol{\alpha}}_i \perp \widetilde{\boldsymbol{\gamma}}_t \perp \widetilde{\boldsymbol{u}}_{it},\\
&\mathsf{E}(\widetilde{\boldsymbol{\alpha}}_i|X) = \mathbf{0}_{G,1}, \qquad \mathsf{E}(\widetilde{\boldsymbol{\alpha}}_i\widetilde{\boldsymbol{\alpha}}_j'|X) = \delta_{ij}\boldsymbol{\Sigma}_{\alpha}, \quad i,j = 1,\dots,N,\\
&\mathsf{E}(\widetilde{\boldsymbol{\gamma}}_t|X) = \mathbf{0}_{G,1}, \qquad \mathsf{E}(\widetilde{\boldsymbol{\gamma}}_t\widetilde{\boldsymbol{\gamma}}_s'|X) = \delta_{ts}\boldsymbol{\Sigma}_{\gamma}, \quad t,s = 1,\dots,T,\\
&\mathsf{E}(\widetilde{\boldsymbol{u}}_{it}|X) = \mathbf{0}_{G,1}, \qquad \mathsf{E}(\widetilde{\boldsymbol{u}}_{it}\widetilde{\boldsymbol{u}}_{js}'|X) = \delta_{ij}\delta_{ts}\boldsymbol{\Sigma}_{u},
\end{aligned} \tag{12.49}$$

$$\mathsf{E}(\widetilde{\boldsymbol{\epsilon}}_{it}|X) = \mathbf{0}_{G,1}, \quad \mathsf{E}(\widetilde{\boldsymbol{\epsilon}}_{it}\widetilde{\boldsymbol{\epsilon}}_{js}'|X) = \begin{cases} \boldsymbol{\Sigma}_{\alpha}+\boldsymbol{\Sigma}_{\gamma}+\boldsymbol{\Sigma}_{u}, & i=j, s=t,\\ \boldsymbol{\Sigma}_{\alpha}, & i=j, t\neq s,\\ \boldsymbol{\Sigma}_{\gamma}, & t=s, i\neq j,\\ \mathbf{0}_{G,G}, & i\neq j, t\neq s. \end{cases} \tag{12.50}$$

Stacking the NT equations, letting

$$\widetilde{\boldsymbol{\gamma}} = \boldsymbol{e}_N \otimes \begin{bmatrix} \widetilde{\boldsymbol{\gamma}}_1 \\ \vdots \\ \widetilde{\boldsymbol{\gamma}}_T \end{bmatrix}, \tag{12.51}$$

we can write (12.49) as the following extension of (12.14):

$$\begin{aligned}
&\widetilde{y} = \widetilde{X}\boldsymbol{\beta} + \widetilde{\boldsymbol{\alpha}} + \widetilde{\boldsymbol{\gamma}} + \widetilde{\boldsymbol{u}} = \widetilde{X}\boldsymbol{\beta} + \widetilde{\boldsymbol{\epsilon}},\\
&\widetilde{\boldsymbol{\epsilon}} = \widetilde{\boldsymbol{\alpha}} + \widetilde{\boldsymbol{\gamma}} + \widetilde{\boldsymbol{u}}, \quad \widetilde{\boldsymbol{\alpha}} \perp \widetilde{\boldsymbol{\gamma}} \perp \widetilde{\boldsymbol{u}},\\
&\mathsf{E}(\widetilde{\boldsymbol{\alpha}}|X) = \mathbf{0}_{NTG,1}, \quad \mathsf{E}(\widetilde{\boldsymbol{\alpha}}\widetilde{\boldsymbol{\alpha}}'|X) = \boldsymbol{I}_N \otimes (\boldsymbol{e}_T\boldsymbol{e}_T') \otimes \boldsymbol{\Sigma}_{\alpha},\\
&\mathsf{E}(\widetilde{\boldsymbol{\gamma}}|X) = \mathbf{0}_{NTG,1}, \quad \mathsf{E}(\widetilde{\boldsymbol{\gamma}}\widetilde{\boldsymbol{\gamma}}'|X) = (\boldsymbol{e}_N\boldsymbol{e}_N') \otimes \boldsymbol{I}_T \otimes \boldsymbol{\Sigma}_{\gamma},\\
&\mathsf{E}(\widetilde{\boldsymbol{u}}|X) = \mathbf{0}_{NTG,1}, \quad \mathsf{E}(\widetilde{\boldsymbol{u}}\widetilde{\boldsymbol{u}}'|X) = \boldsymbol{I}_N \otimes \boldsymbol{I}_T \otimes \boldsymbol{\Sigma}_{u}.
\end{aligned} \tag{12.52}$$

Hence, (12.15) and (12.16) are generalized to

$$\begin{aligned}
\widetilde{\boldsymbol{\Omega}} &= \boldsymbol{I}_N \otimes (\boldsymbol{e}_T\boldsymbol{e}_T') \otimes \boldsymbol{\Sigma}_{\alpha} + (\boldsymbol{e}_N\boldsymbol{e}_N') \otimes \boldsymbol{I}_T \otimes \boldsymbol{\Sigma}_{\gamma} + \boldsymbol{I}_N \otimes \boldsymbol{I}_T \otimes \boldsymbol{\Sigma}_{u}\\
&\equiv \boldsymbol{A}_N \otimes \boldsymbol{A}_T \otimes (\boldsymbol{\Sigma}_u + T\boldsymbol{\Sigma}_{\alpha} + N\boldsymbol{\Sigma}_{\gamma})\\
&\quad + \boldsymbol{B}_N \otimes \boldsymbol{A}_T \otimes (\boldsymbol{\Sigma}_u + T\boldsymbol{\Sigma}_{\alpha})\\
&\quad + \boldsymbol{A}_N \otimes \boldsymbol{B}_T \otimes (\boldsymbol{\Sigma}_u + N\boldsymbol{\Sigma}_{\gamma})\\
&\quad + \boldsymbol{B}_N \otimes \boldsymbol{B}_T \otimes \boldsymbol{\Sigma}_u,
\end{aligned} \tag{12.53}$$

$$\begin{aligned}
\widetilde{\boldsymbol{\Omega}}^{-1} &= \boldsymbol{A}_N \otimes \boldsymbol{A}_T \otimes (\boldsymbol{\Sigma}_u + T\boldsymbol{\Sigma}_{\alpha} + N\boldsymbol{\Sigma}_{\gamma})^{-1}\\
&\quad + \boldsymbol{B}_N \otimes \boldsymbol{A}_T \otimes (\boldsymbol{\Sigma}_u + T\boldsymbol{\Sigma}_{\alpha})^{-1}\\
&\quad + \boldsymbol{A}_N \otimes \boldsymbol{B}_T \otimes (\boldsymbol{\Sigma}_u + N\boldsymbol{\Sigma}_{\gamma})^{-1}\\
&\quad + \boldsymbol{B}_N \otimes \boldsymbol{B}_T \otimes \boldsymbol{\Sigma}_u^{-1}.
\end{aligned} \tag{12.54}$$

12.3.3 GLS ESTIMATION

Using the results in Section 12.3.2, we can briefly describe the GLS procedure for $\boldsymbol{\beta}$ when $\boldsymbol{\Sigma}_u$, $\boldsymbol{\Sigma}_\alpha$, and $\boldsymbol{\Sigma}_\gamma$ are known.

When *ordering by equation* and $\boldsymbol{\Omega}$ is given by (12.46)–(12.47), the GLS estimator and its covariance matrix have the form (12.17)–(12.18). The estimator $\widehat{\boldsymbol{\beta}}_{GLS}$ and its covariance matrix can be written in partitioned form as (12.21)–(12.22), with the changed interpretation of the $\boldsymbol{\Omega}^{gh}$s. From (12.48) we get alternative expressions which generalize (12.19)–(12.20). Estimation of $\boldsymbol{\Sigma}_u$, $\boldsymbol{\Sigma}_\alpha$, and $\boldsymbol{\Sigma}_\gamma$ is considered in Appendix 12A, Section 12A.2.

If $\boldsymbol{\Omega}$, and hence $\boldsymbol{\Omega}^{-1}$, is block-diagonal ($\sigma^u_{gh}=\sigma^\alpha_{gh}=\sigma^\gamma_{gh}=0$, $\boldsymbol{\Omega}_{gh}=\mathbf{0}_{NT,NT}, g\neq h$), the procedure simplifies to using GLS equation by equation:

$$\begin{aligned}\widehat{\boldsymbol{\beta}}_{g,GLS} &= (\boldsymbol{X}_g'\boldsymbol{\Omega}^{gg}\boldsymbol{X}_g)^{-1}(\boldsymbol{X}_g'\boldsymbol{\Omega}^{gg}\boldsymbol{y}_g),\\ \mathsf{V}(\widehat{\boldsymbol{\beta}}_{g,GLS}) &= (\boldsymbol{X}_g'\boldsymbol{\Omega}^{gg}\boldsymbol{X}_g)^{-1},\end{aligned}$$

where

$$\begin{aligned}\boldsymbol{\Omega}_{gg} &= (\boldsymbol{A}_N\otimes\boldsymbol{A}_T)(\sigma^u_{gg}+T\sigma^\alpha_{gg}+N\sigma^\gamma_{gg}) + (\boldsymbol{B}_N\otimes\boldsymbol{A}_T)(\sigma^u_{gg}+T\sigma^\alpha_{gg})\\ &\quad + (\boldsymbol{A}_N\otimes\boldsymbol{B}_T)(\sigma^u_{gg}+N\sigma^\gamma_{gg}) + (\boldsymbol{B}_N\otimes\boldsymbol{B}_T)\sigma^u_{gg},\\ \boldsymbol{\Omega}^{gg} &= \frac{\boldsymbol{A}_N\otimes\boldsymbol{A}_T}{\sigma^u_{gg}+T\sigma^\alpha_{gg}+N\sigma^\gamma_{gg}} + \frac{\boldsymbol{B}_N\otimes\boldsymbol{A}_T}{\sigma^u_{gg}+T\sigma^\alpha_{gg}} + \frac{\boldsymbol{A}_N\otimes\boldsymbol{B}_T}{\sigma^u_{gg}+N\sigma^\gamma_{gg}} + \frac{\boldsymbol{B}_N\otimes\boldsymbol{B}_T}{\sigma^u_{gg}},\\ &\qquad g = 1,\dots,G.\end{aligned}$$

When *ordering by individual*, as in (12.52), the GLS estimator of $\boldsymbol{\beta}$ and its covariance matrix still take the form (12.23)–(12.24), now with $\widetilde{\boldsymbol{\Omega}}^{-1}$ given by (12.54). The expressions obtained generalize (12.25)–(12.26).

12.4 Interdependent model: One-equation estimation

We take a substantial step and consider multi-equation panel data models *with one-way random effects* which are not regression systems. This means that at least two endogenous variables enter some equations. In general econometrics, such models are often denoted as *interdependent models*, or models with jointly endogenous variables. Since the (genuine) disturbances and some of the explanatory variables in the equation are then usually correlated, consistent estimation requires methods more advanced than GLS or FGLS.

The procedures to be considered involve methods for handling the simultaneity problem, notably IVs, in interaction with the Zellner SUR-GLS idea for panel data. Because of the joint endogeneity, SUR-GLS procedures alone, which only address the problems related to the non-scalar disturbance covariance matrix, usually lead to inconsistent estimators.

Following, as in the first part of Section 12.2.2, *ordering by equation*, we assume that the model has G equations and write equation g as

$$\begin{aligned} y_g &= Z_g\gamma_g + (\alpha_g \otimes e_T) + u_g = Z_g\gamma_g + \epsilon_g, \\ \epsilon_g &= (\alpha_g \otimes e_T) + u_g, \qquad g = 1,\dots,G, \end{aligned} \tag{12.55}$$

α_g containing the N individual-specific, random effects and u_g is the vector of genuine disturbances; confer (12.3). Here y_g, ϵ_g, and u_g are $(NT \times 1)$-vectors, while the matrix of explanatory variables, Z_g, with coefficient (column) vector γ_g, has NT rows and a number of columns equal to the number of explanatory variables in equation g (including the unit entry attached to the intercept), the individual index running slow and the period index running fast. Since Z_g contains variables that are jointly endogenous within the full model system, but usually also exogenous variables, it is correlated with ϵ_g and a simultaneity problem arises.[4]

Let $\bar{X}$ be an IV matrix for Z_g. Implied in this is the requirement for valid IVs (including the full rank condition for $\bar{X}'Z_g$) funded on *theoretical* probability distributions and motivated by the theory behind the model to which equation g belongs. This IV matrix can, for example, be the matrix containing the values of the full set of exogenous variables (those included in Z_g as well as those entering at least one other equation). We specifically assume[5]

$$\begin{aligned} &\mathsf{E}(\alpha_g|\bar{X}) = 0_{N,1}, \qquad \mathsf{E}(\alpha_g\alpha_h'|\bar{X}) = \sigma^{\alpha}_{gh}I_N, \quad g,h=1,\dots,G, \\ &\mathsf{E}(u_g|\bar{X}) = 0_{NT,1}, \qquad \mathsf{E}(u_g u_h'|\bar{X}) = \sigma^{u}_{gh}(I_N \otimes I_T), \end{aligned} \tag{12.56}$$

the left column expressing the double exogeneity of $\bar{X}$, which implies

$$\begin{aligned} \mathsf{E}(\epsilon_g|\bar{X}) &= 0_{NT,1}, \\ \mathsf{E}(\epsilon_g\epsilon_h'|\bar{X}) &= \sigma^{\alpha}_{gh}[I_N \otimes (e_T e_T')] + \sigma^{u}_{gh}[I_N \otimes I_T] \\ &= (\sigma^{u}_{gh} + T\sigma^{\alpha}_{gh})(I_N \otimes A_T) + \sigma^{u}_{gh}(I_N \otimes B_T). \end{aligned} \tag{12.57}$$

[4] The basic idea behind the procedures exposed in the following relies on Baltagi (1981b). See also Balestra and Varadharajan-Krishnakumar (1987), Baltagi and Li (1992), and Biørn and Krishnakumar (2008, Section 10.4).

[5] Since no assumption for $g \neq h$ will be involved in the rest of this section, the corresponding parts of (12.56)–(12.57) are irrelevant. First in Section 12.5 the full set of assumptions come into play; see (12.83).

We here condition on the exogenous variables, while in the previous models the conditioning concerned the regressors, exogenous by assumption; see (12.3)–(12.4). An implication is that $\bar{X}$ is uncorrelated with both $\boldsymbol{\alpha}_g$ and $\boldsymbol{u}_g$, and it includes the exogenous part of $\boldsymbol{Z}_g$. In other words, the elements of $\bar{X}$ are *doubly exogenous* relative to (12.55). For the endogenous components of $\boldsymbol{Z}_g$, the distinction between double and single endogeneity is important. Aspects of the single endogeneity problem for single-equation models were discussed in Chapter 6 in relation to correlation between explanatory variables and latent heterogeneity, the maintained assumption there being that all explanatory variables were uncorrelated with the equation's genuine disturbance. Now violation of the latter assumption becomes a core issue.

Three single-equation estimators will be discussed, the first two utilizing, respectively, within-variation and between-variation (Section 12.4.1), the third combining the two (Section 12.4.2).

12.4.1 WITHIN AND BETWEEN TWO-STAGE LEAST SQUARES

Consider first IV estimation exploiting either the within- or the between-variation.

Following Section 2.4.3, we premultiply (12.55) with, respectively, the 'within-individual operator' $(\boldsymbol{I}_N \otimes \boldsymbol{B}_T)$ and the 'between-individual operator' $(\boldsymbol{B}_N \otimes \boldsymbol{A}_T)$, which give the *within-individual and between-individual transformations* of equation g[6]

$$(\boldsymbol{I}_N \otimes \boldsymbol{B}_T)\boldsymbol{y}_g = (\boldsymbol{I}_N \otimes \boldsymbol{B}_T)\boldsymbol{Z}_g\boldsymbol{\gamma}_g + (\boldsymbol{I}_N \otimes \boldsymbol{B}_T)\boldsymbol{\epsilon}_g, \qquad (12.58)$$

$$(\boldsymbol{B}_N \otimes \boldsymbol{A}_T)\boldsymbol{y}_g = (\boldsymbol{B}_N \otimes \boldsymbol{A}_T)\boldsymbol{Z}_g\boldsymbol{\gamma}_g + (\boldsymbol{B}_N \otimes \boldsymbol{A}_T)\boldsymbol{\epsilon}_g. \qquad (12.59)$$

Using for any $(NT \times 1)$-vector $\boldsymbol{q}$ or $(NT \times M)$-matrix $\boldsymbol{Q}$ the notation

$$\boldsymbol{q}_W = (\boldsymbol{I}_N \otimes \boldsymbol{B}_T)\boldsymbol{q}, \qquad \boldsymbol{Q}_W = (\boldsymbol{I}_N \otimes \boldsymbol{B}_T)\boldsymbol{Q},$$
$$\boldsymbol{q}_B = (\boldsymbol{B}_N \otimes \boldsymbol{A}_T)\boldsymbol{q}, \qquad \boldsymbol{Q}_B = (\boldsymbol{B}_N \otimes \boldsymbol{A}_T)\boldsymbol{Q},$$

which, because $\boldsymbol{A}_T\boldsymbol{B}_T = \boldsymbol{0}_{T,T}$, satisfy $\boldsymbol{q}'_W\boldsymbol{q}_B = 0$, $\boldsymbol{Q}'_W\boldsymbol{Q}_B = \boldsymbol{0}$, we can write these equations as

$$\boldsymbol{y}_{Wg} = \boldsymbol{Z}_{Wg}\boldsymbol{\gamma}_g + \boldsymbol{\epsilon}_{Wg}, \qquad (12.60)$$

$$\boldsymbol{y}_{Bg} = \boldsymbol{Z}_{Bg}\boldsymbol{\gamma}_g + \boldsymbol{\epsilon}_{Bg}. \qquad (12.61)$$

[6] In the following, all variables are assumed two-dimensional. If some elements in $\boldsymbol{Z}_g$ are individual-specific, the within estimators of their coefficients do not exist and the procedures must be modified accordingly. The procedures for variance components estimation, which combine within- and between-variation are feasible; see Cornwell, Schmidt, and Wyhowski (1992) as well as Sections 5.3 and 5.4.

From (12.57) and the within–between orthogonality it follows that $\boldsymbol{\epsilon}_{Wg}$ and $\boldsymbol{\epsilon}_{Bg}$ are uncorrelated, conditional on $\bar{X}$, and that

$$\mathsf{V}(\boldsymbol{\epsilon}_{Wg}|\bar{X}) = \mathsf{V}[(I_N \otimes B_T)\boldsymbol{\epsilon}_g|\bar{X}] = \sigma^u_{gg}(I_N \otimes B_T), \tag{12.62}$$

$$\mathsf{V}(\boldsymbol{\epsilon}_{Bg}|\bar{X}) = \mathsf{V}[(B_N \otimes A_T)\boldsymbol{\epsilon}_g|\bar{X}] = (\sigma^u_{gg} + T\sigma^\alpha_{gg})(B_N \otimes A_T). \tag{12.63}$$

Estimators labeled as the *within-individual two-stage least squares estimator (W2SLS)* and the *between-individual two-stage least squares estimator (B2SLS)* of $\boldsymbol{\gamma}_g$ now follow by using as IVs within- and between-transformed variables, respectively,

$\bar{X}_W = (I_N \otimes B_T)\bar{X}$ as IV matrix for $Z_{Wg} = (I_N \otimes B_T)Z_g$ in (12.60),
$\bar{X}_B = (B_N \otimes A_T)\bar{X}$ as IV matrix for $Z_{Bg} = (B_N \otimes A_T)Z_g$ in (12.61).

This gives[7]

$$\begin{aligned}\widehat{\boldsymbol{\gamma}}_{W2SLSg} &= [Z'_{Wg}\bar{X}_W(\bar{X}'_W\bar{X}_W)^{-1}\bar{X}'_W Z_{Wg}]^{-1} \\ &\quad \times [Z'_{Wg}\bar{X}_W(\bar{X}'_W\bar{X}_W)^{-1}\bar{X}'_W \boldsymbol{y}_{Wg}],\end{aligned} \tag{12.64}$$

$$\begin{aligned}\widehat{\boldsymbol{\gamma}}_{B2SLSg} &= [Z'_{Bg}\bar{X}_B(\bar{X}'_B\bar{X}_B)^{-1}\bar{X}'_B Z_{Bg}]^{-1} \\ &\quad \times [Z'_{Bg}\bar{X}_B(\bar{X}'_B\bar{X}_B)^{-1}\bar{X}'_B \boldsymbol{y}_{Bg}].\end{aligned} \tag{12.65}$$

If Z_g and $\bar{X}$ had the same dimension, and hence $\bar{X}'_W Z_{Wg}$ and $\bar{X}'_B Z_{Bg}$ were quadratic and non-singular, the two estimators would collapse to simple IV estimators:

$$\begin{aligned}\widehat{\boldsymbol{\gamma}}_{W2SLSg} &= [\bar{X}'_W Z_{Wg}]^{-1}[\bar{X}'_W \boldsymbol{y}_{Wg}], \\ \widehat{\boldsymbol{\gamma}}_{B2SLSg} &= [\bar{X}'_B Z_{Bg}]^{-1}[\bar{X}'_B \boldsymbol{y}_{Bg}],\end{aligned}$$

while the more general 2SLS estimators involve, respectively,

$$P_{WX} = \bar{X}_W(\bar{X}'_W\bar{X}_W)^{-1}\bar{X}'_W, \tag{12.66}$$

$$P_{BX} = \bar{X}_B(\bar{X}'_B\bar{X}_B)^{-1}\bar{X}'_B, \tag{12.67}$$

which satisfy $P_{WX}P_{BX} = \mathbf{0}$ because $\bar{X}'_W\bar{X}_B = \mathbf{0}$. Then the two estimators can in general be written as

[7] Since $A_T B_T = \mathbf{0}_{T,T}$, $\bar{X}'_W Q_W = \bar{X}'_W Q$, and $\bar{X}'_B Q_B = \bar{X}'_B Q$, while $\bar{X}'_W Q_B = \bar{X}'_B Q_W = \mathbf{0}$ for any Q. Therefore, *using $\bar{X}_W$ as IV matrix for Z_{Wg} in (12.60)* is equivalent to *using it as IV matrix for Z_g in (12.55)* and *using $\bar{X}_B$ as IV matrix for Z_{Bg} in (12.61)* is equivalent to *using $\bar{X}_B$ as IV matrix for Z_g in (12.55).*

$$\widehat{\boldsymbol{\gamma}}_{W2SLSg} = [\boldsymbol{Z}_g'\boldsymbol{P}_{WX}\boldsymbol{Z}_g]^{-1}[\boldsymbol{Z}_g'\boldsymbol{P}_{WX}\boldsymbol{y}_g], \tag{12.68}$$

$$\widehat{\boldsymbol{\gamma}}_{B2SLSg} = [\boldsymbol{Z}_g'\boldsymbol{P}_{BX}\boldsymbol{Z}_g]^{-1}[\boldsymbol{Z}_g'\boldsymbol{P}_{BX}\boldsymbol{y}_g]. \tag{12.69}$$

They can be given the following reinterpretation, useful when the procedures are extended, by invoking GLS, to increase efficiency: premultiply (12.55) with $\bar{\boldsymbol{X}}_W'$ and $\bar{\boldsymbol{X}}_B'$,

$$\bar{\boldsymbol{X}}_W'\boldsymbol{y}_g = \bar{\boldsymbol{X}}_W'\boldsymbol{Z}_g\boldsymbol{\gamma}_g + \bar{\boldsymbol{X}}_W'\boldsymbol{\epsilon}_g, \tag{12.70}$$

$$\bar{\boldsymbol{X}}_B'\boldsymbol{y}_g = \bar{\boldsymbol{X}}_B'\boldsymbol{Z}_g\boldsymbol{\gamma}_g + \bar{\boldsymbol{X}}_B'\boldsymbol{\epsilon}_g, \tag{12.71}$$

whose disturbance vectors, recalling (12.62)–(12.63), satisfy

$$\mathsf{V}(\bar{\boldsymbol{X}}_W'\boldsymbol{\epsilon}_g|\bar{\boldsymbol{X}}) = \sigma_{gg}^u\bar{\boldsymbol{X}}_W'\bar{\boldsymbol{X}}_W, \tag{12.72}$$

$$\mathsf{V}(\bar{\boldsymbol{X}}_B'\boldsymbol{\epsilon}_g|\bar{\boldsymbol{X}}) = (\sigma_{gg}^u + T\sigma_{gg}^\alpha)\bar{\boldsymbol{X}}_B'\bar{\boldsymbol{X}}_B, \tag{12.73}$$

and apply *GLS* on (12.70)–(12.71). This yields, respectively,

$$\begin{aligned}
\widehat{\boldsymbol{\gamma}}_{W2SLSg} &= [(\bar{\boldsymbol{X}}_W'\boldsymbol{Z}_g)'\mathsf{V}(\bar{\boldsymbol{X}}_W'\boldsymbol{\epsilon}_g|\bar{\boldsymbol{X}})^{-1}(\bar{\boldsymbol{X}}_W'\boldsymbol{Z}_g)]^{-1} \\
&\quad \times [(\bar{\boldsymbol{X}}_W'\boldsymbol{Z}_g)'\mathsf{V}(\bar{\boldsymbol{X}}_W'\boldsymbol{\epsilon}_g|\bar{\boldsymbol{X}})^{-1}(\bar{\boldsymbol{X}}_W'\boldsymbol{y}_g)], \\
\widehat{\boldsymbol{\gamma}}_{B2SLSg} &= [(\bar{\boldsymbol{X}}_B'\boldsymbol{Z}_g)'\mathsf{V}(\bar{\boldsymbol{X}}_B'\boldsymbol{\epsilon}_g|\bar{\boldsymbol{X}})^{-1}(\bar{\boldsymbol{X}}_B'\boldsymbol{Z}_g)]^{-1} \\
&\quad \times [(\bar{\boldsymbol{X}}_B'\boldsymbol{Z}_g)'\mathsf{V}(\bar{\boldsymbol{X}}_B'\boldsymbol{\epsilon}_g|\bar{\boldsymbol{X}})^{-1}(\bar{\boldsymbol{X}}_B'\boldsymbol{y}_g)],
\end{aligned}$$

which simplify to (12.68)–(12.69).

12.4.2 VARIANCE COMPONENTS TWO-STAGE LEAST SQUARES

We next stack the two transformed versions of equation g, (12.70)–(12.71), having $\boldsymbol{\gamma}_g$ as their common coefficient vector, and use GLS. This improves efficiency because the stacking into one equation exploits the within- and between-variation in the data jointly with disturbance covariance structure. We then construct

$$\begin{bmatrix} \bar{\boldsymbol{X}}_W'\boldsymbol{y}_g \\ \bar{\boldsymbol{X}}_B'\boldsymbol{y}_g \end{bmatrix} = \begin{bmatrix} \bar{\boldsymbol{X}}_W'\boldsymbol{Z}_g \\ \bar{\boldsymbol{X}}_B'\boldsymbol{Z}_g \end{bmatrix}\boldsymbol{\gamma}_g + \begin{bmatrix} \bar{\boldsymbol{X}}_W'\boldsymbol{\epsilon}_g \\ \bar{\boldsymbol{X}}_B'\boldsymbol{\epsilon}_g \end{bmatrix}, \tag{12.74}$$

which since $\bar{\boldsymbol{X}}_W'\bar{\boldsymbol{X}}_B = \boldsymbol{0}$ (implied by the within–between orthogonality) has a composite disturbance vector with block-diagonal covariance matrix:

$$\mathsf{V}\begin{bmatrix}\bar{X}_W'\epsilon_g|\bar{X}\\ \bar{X}_B'\epsilon_g|\bar{X}\end{bmatrix}=\begin{bmatrix}\sigma_{gg}^u\bar{X}_W'\bar{X}_W & 0\\ 0 & (\sigma_{gg}^u+T\sigma_{gg}^\alpha)\bar{X}_B'\bar{X}_B\end{bmatrix}, \tag{12.75}$$

and hence

$$\left\{\mathsf{V}\begin{bmatrix}\bar{X}_W'\epsilon_g|\bar{X}\\ \bar{X}_B'\epsilon_g|\bar{X}\end{bmatrix}\right\}^{-1}=\begin{bmatrix}\dfrac{[\bar{X}_W'\bar{X}_W]^{-1}}{\sigma_{gg}^u} & 0\\ 0 & \dfrac{[\bar{X}_B'\bar{X}_B]^{-1}}{\sigma_{gg}^u+T\sigma_{gg}^\alpha}\end{bmatrix}.$$

Application of *GLS* on the stacked equation (12.74) gives the following estimator of $\boldsymbol{\gamma}_g$, denoted as *the variance components two-stage least squares estimator (VC2SLS)*:

$$\begin{aligned}\widehat{\boldsymbol{\gamma}}_{VC2SLSg}=&\left[\begin{bmatrix}\bar{X}_W'Z_g\\ \bar{X}_B'Z_g\end{bmatrix}'\left\{\mathsf{V}\begin{bmatrix}\bar{X}_W'\epsilon_g|X\\ \bar{X}_B'\epsilon_g|X\end{bmatrix}\right\}^{-1}\begin{bmatrix}\bar{X}_W'Z_g\\ \bar{X}_B'Z_g\end{bmatrix}\right]^{-1}\\ &\times\left[\begin{bmatrix}\bar{X}_W'Z_g\\ \bar{X}_B'Z_g\end{bmatrix}'\left\{\mathsf{V}\begin{bmatrix}\bar{X}_W'\epsilon_g|X\\ \bar{X}_B'\epsilon_g|X\end{bmatrix}\right\}^{-1}\begin{bmatrix}\bar{X}_W'y_g\\ \bar{X}_B'y_g\end{bmatrix}\right],\end{aligned}$$

which, when again using (12.66)–(12.67), can be simplified to

$$\begin{aligned}\widehat{\boldsymbol{\gamma}}_{VC2SLSg}=&\left[\frac{Z_g'P_{WX}Z_g}{\sigma_{gg}^u}+\frac{Z_g'P_{BX}Z_g}{\sigma_{gg}^u+T\sigma_{gg}^\alpha}\right]^{-1}\\ &\times\left[\frac{Z_g'P_{WX}y_g}{\sigma_{gg}^u}+\frac{Z_g'P_{BX}y_g}{\sigma_{gg}^u+T\sigma_{gg}^\alpha}\right].\end{aligned} \tag{12.76}$$

Since $Z_g'P_{WX}y_g=Z_g'P_{WX}Z_g\widehat{\boldsymbol{\gamma}}_{W2SLSg}$ and $Z_g'P_{BX}y_g=Z_g'P_{BX}Z_g\widehat{\boldsymbol{\gamma}}_{B2SLSg}$, which follows from (12.68)–(12.69), we can express $\widehat{\boldsymbol{\gamma}}_{VC2SLSg}$ as a matrix-weighted average of $\widehat{\boldsymbol{\gamma}}_{W2SLSg}$ and $\widehat{\boldsymbol{\gamma}}_{B2SLSg}$:

$$\begin{aligned}\widehat{\boldsymbol{\gamma}}_{VC2SLSg}=&\left[\frac{Z_g'P_{WX}Z_g}{\sigma_{gg}^u}+\frac{Z_g'P_{BX}Z_g}{\sigma_{gg}^u+T\sigma_{gg}^\alpha}\right]^{-1}\\ &\times\left[\frac{Z_g'P_{WX}Z_g}{\sigma_{gg}^u}\widehat{\boldsymbol{\gamma}}_{W2SLSg}+\frac{Z_g'P_{BX}Z_g}{\sigma_{gg}^u+T\sigma_{gg}^\alpha}\widehat{\boldsymbol{\gamma}}_{B2SLSg}\right].\end{aligned}$$

This GLS estimator, however, is not feasible unless σ^u_{gg} and σ^α_{gg} are known. Estimating these parameters is therefore a problem to address.

Estimation of the variance components. The variance components σ^u_{gg} and σ^α_{gg} needed to compute (12.76) can be estimated consistently from the W2SLS- and B2SLS-residual vectors. We first note that[8]

$$\begin{aligned}
\mathsf{E}[\boldsymbol{\epsilon}'_g(\boldsymbol{I}_N \otimes \boldsymbol{B}_T)\boldsymbol{\epsilon}_g|\bar{\boldsymbol{X}}] &= \mathsf{E}[\mathrm{tr}(\boldsymbol{\epsilon}'_g(\boldsymbol{I}_N \otimes \boldsymbol{B}_T)\boldsymbol{\epsilon}_g)|\bar{\boldsymbol{X}}] \\
&= \mathsf{E}[\mathrm{tr}(\boldsymbol{\epsilon}_g\boldsymbol{\epsilon}'_g(\boldsymbol{I}_N \otimes \boldsymbol{B}_T))|\boldsymbol{X}] \\
&= \mathrm{tr}[\mathsf{E}(\boldsymbol{\epsilon}_g\boldsymbol{\epsilon}'_g)(\boldsymbol{I}_N \otimes \boldsymbol{B}_T)|\bar{\boldsymbol{X}}], \\
\mathsf{E}[\boldsymbol{\epsilon}'_g(\boldsymbol{B}_N \otimes \boldsymbol{A}_T)\boldsymbol{\epsilon}_g|\bar{\boldsymbol{X}}] &= \mathsf{E}[\mathrm{tr}(\boldsymbol{\epsilon}'_g(\boldsymbol{B}_N \otimes \boldsymbol{A}_T)\boldsymbol{\epsilon}_g)|\boldsymbol{X}] \\
&= \mathsf{E}[\mathrm{tr}(\boldsymbol{\epsilon}_g\boldsymbol{\epsilon}'_g(\boldsymbol{B}_N \otimes \boldsymbol{A}_T))|\bar{\boldsymbol{X}}] \\
&= \mathrm{tr}[\mathsf{E}(\boldsymbol{\epsilon}_g\boldsymbol{\epsilon}'_g)(\boldsymbol{B}_N \otimes \boldsymbol{A}_T)|\bar{\boldsymbol{X}}].
\end{aligned}$$

Since $\boldsymbol{\epsilon}_g = \boldsymbol{\alpha}_g \otimes \boldsymbol{e}_T + \boldsymbol{u}_g$ and $\boldsymbol{\alpha}_g \perp \boldsymbol{u}_g$, we next have

$$\begin{aligned}
\mathsf{E}(\boldsymbol{\epsilon}_g\boldsymbol{\epsilon}'_g|\bar{\boldsymbol{X}}) &= \mathsf{E}(\boldsymbol{\alpha}_g\boldsymbol{\alpha}'_g|\bar{\boldsymbol{X}}) \otimes (\boldsymbol{e}_T\boldsymbol{e}'_T) + \mathsf{E}(\boldsymbol{u}_g\boldsymbol{u}'_g|\bar{\boldsymbol{X}}) \\
&= T\sigma^\alpha_{gg}(\boldsymbol{I}_N \otimes \boldsymbol{A}_T) + \sigma^u_{gg}(\boldsymbol{I}_N \otimes \boldsymbol{I}_T),
\end{aligned}$$

and hence, since (2.86) implies $\mathrm{tr}(\boldsymbol{I}_N \otimes \boldsymbol{B}_T) = N(T-1)$, $\mathrm{tr}(\boldsymbol{B}_N \otimes \boldsymbol{A}_T) = N-1$,

$$\begin{aligned}
\mathrm{tr}[\mathsf{E}(\boldsymbol{\epsilon}_g\boldsymbol{\epsilon}'_g)(\boldsymbol{I}_N \otimes \boldsymbol{B}_T)|\bar{\boldsymbol{X}}] &= \sigma^u_{gg}\mathrm{tr}(\boldsymbol{I}_N \otimes \boldsymbol{B}_T) = \sigma^u_{gg}N(T-1), \\
\mathrm{tr}[\mathsf{E}(\boldsymbol{\epsilon}_g\boldsymbol{\epsilon}'_g)(\boldsymbol{B}_N \otimes \boldsymbol{A}_T)|\bar{\boldsymbol{X}}] &= (T\sigma^\alpha_{gg} + \sigma^u_{gg})\mathrm{tr}(\boldsymbol{B}_N \otimes \boldsymbol{A}_T) = (T\sigma^\alpha_{gg} + \sigma^u_{gg})(N-1).
\end{aligned}$$

Collecting the results, we find

$$\frac{\mathsf{E}[\boldsymbol{\epsilon}'_g(\boldsymbol{I}_N \otimes \boldsymbol{B}_T)\boldsymbol{\epsilon}_g|\bar{\boldsymbol{X}}]}{N(T-1)} = \sigma^u_{gg}, \tag{12.77}$$

$$\frac{\mathsf{E}[\boldsymbol{\epsilon}'_g(\boldsymbol{B}_N \otimes \boldsymbol{A}_T)\boldsymbol{\epsilon}_g|\bar{\boldsymbol{X}}]}{N-1} = T\sigma^\alpha_{gg} + \sigma^u_{gg}. \tag{12.78}$$

Constructing $\boldsymbol{\epsilon}_g$ residual vectors implied by the W2SLS- and B2SLS-estimates,

$$\begin{aligned}
\widehat{\boldsymbol{\epsilon}}_{W2SLSg} &= \boldsymbol{y}_g - \boldsymbol{Z}_g\widehat{\boldsymbol{\gamma}}_{W2SLSg}, \\
\widehat{\boldsymbol{\epsilon}}_{B2SLSg} &= \boldsymbol{y}_g - \boldsymbol{Z}_g\widehat{\boldsymbol{\gamma}}_{B2SLSg},
\end{aligned}$$

[8] Confer the algebra for $\boldsymbol{\epsilon}'(\boldsymbol{I}_N \otimes \boldsymbol{B}_T)\boldsymbol{\epsilon}$ and $\boldsymbol{\epsilon}'(\boldsymbol{B}_N \otimes \boldsymbol{A}_T)\boldsymbol{\epsilon}$ used in Section 3.3.2 and Appendix 12A.

we are therefore led to estimate the disturbance variances consistently by:

$$\widehat{\sigma}^{u}_{gg} = \frac{\widehat{\boldsymbol{\epsilon}}'_{W2SLSg}(\boldsymbol{I}_N \otimes \boldsymbol{B}_T)\widehat{\boldsymbol{\epsilon}}_{W2SLSg}}{N(T-1)}, \tag{12.79}$$

$$\widehat{T\sigma^{\alpha}_{gg}+\sigma^{u}_{gg}} = \frac{\widehat{\boldsymbol{\epsilon}}'_{B2SLSg}(\boldsymbol{B}_N \otimes \boldsymbol{A}_T)\widehat{\boldsymbol{\epsilon}}_{B2SLSg}}{N-1}, \quad g = 1,\dots,G. \tag{12.80}$$

Inserting these estimators in (12.76) makes the above application of the variance-components 2SLS-estimator feasible. For estimation of the covariance matrices of $\widehat{\boldsymbol{\gamma}}_{W2SLSg}$, $\widehat{\boldsymbol{\gamma}}_{B2SLSg}$, and $\widehat{\boldsymbol{\gamma}}_{VC2SLSg}$, see Appendix 12C, Section 12C.1.

Example: In this illustration we attempt to explore how the female wage rate, in logs (`ln(wage)`), is related to age, its square, and the number of years employed at the present place (`age, age2, tenure`) as well as dummies for being unionized, being black, and living in the south (`union, black, south`). Unbalanced data with 19,007 observations from 4,134 young women of age 14–28 years in 1968 from US National Longitudinal Survey (source: http://www.stata-press.com/data; last accessed March 2016) and routines in Stata are used. In Tables 12.1 and 12.2 are given results based on standard random effects models and FGLS (columns labelled a) and results based on error components 2SLS (columns labelled b or c), treating `tenure` as jointly endogenous with `ln(wage)`, while the assumed exogenous variables `age, age2, union, black, south` are IVs for `tenure`. The column c results are based on VC2SLS as described above, while the column b results rely on G2SLS, denoting a version of the method, proposed by Balestra and Varadharajan-Krishnakumar (1987), which treats the IVs somewhat differently when combining 2SLS and GLS; see Baltagi and Li (1992, Section 2.1).

We find that increased age and longer tenure tend to increase the female wage rate, and that the wage–age relation shows a slight concavity. The union dummy contributes positively as a regressor according to the results from in the standard random effects model, while the dummies `black, south` have negative impacts.

When `tenure` is treated as jointly endogenous with wage and instrumented, its wage effect comes out as stronger, while the `age` effect is weakened (both significant) (compare columns a with b and c in Table 12.2). The latent individual-specific heterogeneity accounts for a substantial part of the total disturbance variance (ρ), but the VC2SLS and G2SLS estimates of this parameter are notably lower than the FGLS estimates. The reduced form equation for *tenure*, estimated by FGLS, indicates a rather strong relationship between this variable and the five exogenous variables:

`age`	`age2`	`union`	`south`	`black`
0.1038	0.0031	0.7315	−0.2642	0.4043
(0.0328)	(0.0005)	(0.0640)	(0.0807)	(0.1038)

Table 12.1 Wage equation, simple: OLS and panel data GLS-2SLS estimates. *n* = *19007*, *N* = *4134*. Unbalanced panel, $\bar{T} = 4.6$ (max $T_i = 12$, min $T_i = 1$)

	a	a	b	c
`age`	0.0568 (0.0027)	0.0336 (0.0033)	0.0212 (0.0061)	0.0346 (0.0040)
`age2`	−0.0008 (0.0000)	−0.0004 (0.0001)	−0.0008 (0.0001)	−0.0006 (0.0001)
`tenure`	0.0260 (0.0007)	0.0227 (0.0008)	0.1591 (0.0105)	0.0639 (0.0026)
`union`		0.1198 (0.0066)		
`intercept`	0.6137 (0.0395)	0.9928 (0.0505)	1.3422 (0.0954)	1.0498 (0.0621)
ρ	0.5610	0.6577	0.2587	0.2587

Notes: Standard errors in parentheses.
ρ = variance of individual disturbance components/total disturbance variance.
a: Standard random effects, GLS.
b: Random effects, G2SLS, IVs for tenure: age, age2, union, south, black.
c: Random effects, VC2SLS, IVs for tenure: age, age2, union, south, black.

Table 12.2 Wage equation, extended: OLS and panel data GLS-2SLS estimates. *n* = *19007*, *N* = *4134*. Unbalanced panel, $\bar{T} = 4.6$. (max $T_i = 12$, min $T_i = 1$)

	a	a	b	c
`age`	0.0345 (0.0033)	0.0344 (0.0033)	0.0233 (0.0066)	0.0392 (0.0041)
`age2`	−0.0004 (0.0001)	−0.0004 (0.0001)	−0.0009 (0.0001)	−0.0007 (0.0001)
`tenure`	0.0230 (0.0008)	0.0229 (0.0007)	0.1742 (0.0116)	0.0627 (0.0025)
`union`	0.1237 (0.0066)	0.1177 (0.0066)		
`black`	−0.1510 (0.0133)	−0.1187 (0.0134)	−0.1744 (0.0153)	−0.1231 (0.0092)
`south`		−0.1103 (0.0093)	−0.1030 (0.0129)	−0.1427 (0.0079)
`intercept`	1.0215 (0.0505)	1.0586 (0.0506)	1.3967 (0.1029)	1.0671 (0.0621)
ρ	0.6473	0.6406	0.2088	0.2088

Notes: Standard errors in parentheses.
ρ = variance of individual disturbance components/total disturbance variance.
a: Standard random effects, GLS.
b: Random effects, G2SLS, IVs for tenure: age, age2, union, south, black.
c: Random effects, VC2SLS, IVs for tenure: age, age2, union, south, black.

12.5 Interdependent model: Joint estimation

Having considered three methods for single-equation estimation in an interdependent system with one-way random effects, we turn to the more challenging problem of multi-equation estimation, again relying on Baltagi (1981b). We set out to estimate the coefficients in the full G-equation system jointly, *assuming all equations identifiable* (and at least some of them overidentified), following the general idea which takes 2SLS to 3SLS; see Greene (2008, Section 13.6.1).

First, we stack all the G equations (12.55) into

$$\begin{bmatrix} y_1 \\ \vdots \\ y_G \end{bmatrix} = \begin{bmatrix} Z_1 & \cdots & 0 \\ \vdots & \ddots & \vdots \\ 0 & \cdots & Z_G \end{bmatrix} \begin{bmatrix} \gamma_1 \\ \vdots \\ \gamma_G \end{bmatrix} + \begin{bmatrix} \epsilon_1 \\ \vdots \\ \epsilon_G \end{bmatrix}, \tag{12.81}$$

or compactly,

$$y = Z\gamma + \epsilon. \tag{12.82}$$

From (12.57) it follows that

$$\begin{aligned} \mathsf{E}(\epsilon|\bar{X}) &= 0, \\ \mathsf{E}(\epsilon\epsilon'|\bar{X}) &= \boldsymbol{\Sigma}_\alpha \otimes \boldsymbol{I}_N \otimes (e_T e_T') + \boldsymbol{\Sigma}_u \otimes \boldsymbol{I}_N \otimes \boldsymbol{I}_T \\ &\equiv (\boldsymbol{\Sigma}_u + T\boldsymbol{\Sigma}_\alpha) \otimes \boldsymbol{I}_N \otimes \boldsymbol{A}_T + \boldsymbol{\Sigma}_u \otimes \boldsymbol{I}_N \otimes \boldsymbol{B}_T, \end{aligned} \tag{12.83}$$

where

$$\boldsymbol{\Sigma}_\alpha = \begin{bmatrix} \sigma^\alpha_{11} & \cdots & \sigma^\alpha_{1G} \\ \vdots & & \vdots \\ \sigma^\alpha_{G1} & \cdots & \sigma^\alpha_{GG} \end{bmatrix},$$

$$\boldsymbol{\Sigma}_u = \begin{bmatrix} \sigma^u_{11} & \cdots & \sigma^u_{1G} \\ \vdots & & \vdots \\ \sigma^u_{G1} & \cdots & \sigma^u_{GG} \end{bmatrix}.$$

It is worth noticing that this model, compactly described by (12.82)–(12.83), by including latent variables in a multi-equation structure, belong to the wide class of simultaneous equation structural models surveyed in, e.g., Aigner *et al.* (1984). What is particular with this member of the class, from a formal point of view, is that the latent effects, $(\boldsymbol{\alpha}_g \otimes e_T)$, $g = 1, \ldots, G$, being part of ϵ, are not integrated in the model structure as latent (and potentially exogenous or endogenous) variables with unknown coefficients. They are added to the rest of the equation system as normalized in (12.82) and have a full-specified coefficient matrix consisting of one- and zero-entries. This indicates an avenue for possible extensions.

12.5.1 WITHIN AND BETWEEN THREE-STAGE LEAST SQUARES

Again, we exploit IV-based procedures with GLS-ingredients and proceed stepwise. First, we consider estimators utilizing either the within- or the between-variation, taking alternatively $\bar{X}_W = (I_N \otimes B_T)\bar{X}$ and $\bar{X}_B = (B_N \otimes A_T)\bar{X}$ as IV matrices for each of $Z_1, \dots, Z_G$. We still assume that (12.56)–(12.57) hold and that $\bar{X}$ has at least as many columns as the largest Z_g.

A succession of matrix expressions and matrix operations will be needed to present the idea. We start by premultiplying (12.81) with, respectively, $(I_G \otimes I_N \otimes B_T)$ and $(I_G \otimes B_N \otimes A_T)$, and obtain

$$\begin{bmatrix} y_{W1} \\ \vdots \\ y_{WG} \end{bmatrix} = \begin{bmatrix} Z_{W1} & \cdots & 0 \\ \vdots & \ddots & \vdots \\ 0 & \cdots & Z_{WG} \end{bmatrix} \begin{bmatrix} \gamma_1 \\ \vdots \\ \gamma_G \end{bmatrix} + \begin{bmatrix} \epsilon_{W1} \\ \vdots \\ \epsilon_{WG} \end{bmatrix}, \tag{12.84}$$

$$\begin{bmatrix} y_{B1} \\ \vdots \\ y_{BG} \end{bmatrix} = \begin{bmatrix} Z_{B1} & \cdots & 0 \\ \vdots & \ddots & \vdots \\ 0 & \cdots & Z_{BG} \end{bmatrix} \begin{bmatrix} \gamma_1 \\ \vdots \\ \gamma_G \end{bmatrix} + \begin{bmatrix} \epsilon_{B1} \\ \vdots \\ \epsilon_{BG} \end{bmatrix}. \tag{12.85}$$

These are the systems which follow from stacking, respectively, (12.60) and (12.61) across g. In compact notation they read

$$y_W = Z_W \gamma + \epsilon_W, \tag{12.86}$$

$$y_B = Z_B \gamma + \epsilon_B, \tag{12.87}$$

where $Z_W = \text{diag}[Z_{W1}, \dots, Z_{WG}]$, $Z_B = \text{diag}[Z_{B1}, \dots, Z_{BG}]$, etc. We consider

$$(I_G \otimes \bar{X}'_W) \equiv (I_G \otimes \bar{X}')(I_G \otimes I_N \otimes B_T),$$
$$(I_G \otimes \bar{X}'_B) \equiv (I_G \otimes \bar{X}')(I_G \otimes B_N \otimes A_T),$$

as IV matrices for, respectively, Z_W in (12.86) and Z_B in (12.87), operationalized by premultiplying (12.81) with these respective matrices. This gives

$$\begin{bmatrix} \bar{X}'_W y_1 \\ \vdots \\ \bar{X}'_W y_G \end{bmatrix} = \begin{bmatrix} \bar{X}'_W Z_1 & \dots & 0 \\ \vdots & \ddots & \vdots \\ 0 & \dots & \bar{X}'_W Z_G \end{bmatrix} \begin{bmatrix} \gamma_1 \\ \vdots \\ \gamma_G \end{bmatrix} + \begin{bmatrix} \bar{X}'_W \epsilon_1 \\ \vdots \\ \bar{X}'_W \epsilon_G \end{bmatrix}, \tag{12.88}$$

$$\begin{bmatrix} \bar{X}'_B y_1 \\ \vdots \\ \bar{X}'_B y_G \end{bmatrix} = \begin{bmatrix} \bar{X}'_B Z_1 & \dots & 0 \\ \vdots & \ddots & \vdots \\ 0 & \dots & \bar{X}'_B Z_G \end{bmatrix} \begin{bmatrix} \gamma_1 \\ \vdots \\ \gamma_G \end{bmatrix} + \begin{bmatrix} \bar{X}'_B \epsilon_1 \\ \vdots \\ \bar{X}'_B \epsilon_G \end{bmatrix}, \tag{12.89}$$

or compactly,

$$(I_G \otimes \bar{X}'_W) y = (I_G \otimes \bar{X}'_W) Z \gamma + (I_G \otimes \bar{X}'_W) \epsilon, \tag{12.90}$$

$$(I_G \otimes \bar{X}'_B) y = (I_G \otimes \bar{X}'_B) Z \gamma + (I_G \otimes \bar{X}'_B) \epsilon, \tag{12.91}$$

where

$$(I_G \otimes \bar{X}'_W) Z = \text{diag}[\bar{X}'_W Z_1, \dots, \bar{X}'_W Z_G],$$
$$(I_G \otimes \bar{X}'_B) Z = \text{diag}[\bar{X}'_B Z_1, \dots, \bar{X}'_B Z_G].$$

It follows from (12.83) and the within–between orthogonality that the composite disturbance vectors $(I_G \otimes \bar{X}'_W)\epsilon$ and $(I_G \otimes \bar{X}'_B)\epsilon$ are uncorrelated (conditional on $\bar{X}$) and have covariance matrices, respectively,

$$\begin{aligned} \mathsf{V}[(I_G \otimes \bar{X}'_W)\epsilon | \bar{X}] &= \boldsymbol{\Sigma}_u \otimes (\bar{X}'_W \bar{X}_W) \\ &\equiv \boldsymbol{\Sigma}_u \otimes [\bar{X}'(I_N \otimes B_T)\bar{X}], \end{aligned} \tag{12.92}$$

$$\begin{aligned} \mathsf{V}[(I_G \otimes \bar{X}'_B)\epsilon | \bar{X}] &= (\boldsymbol{\Sigma}_u + T\boldsymbol{\Sigma}_\alpha) \otimes (\bar{X}'_B \bar{X}_B) \\ &\equiv (\boldsymbol{\Sigma}_u + T\boldsymbol{\Sigma}_\alpha) \otimes [\bar{X}'(B_N \otimes A_T)\bar{X}]. \end{aligned} \tag{12.93}$$

Application of GLS on (12.90) and (12.91) then gives, respectively,

$$\begin{aligned} \widehat{\gamma}_{W3SLS} = {} & [\{(I_G \otimes \bar{X}'_W)Z\}'[\boldsymbol{\Sigma}_u \otimes (\bar{X}'_W \bar{X}_W)]^{-1}\{(I_G \otimes \bar{X}'_W)Z\}]^{-1} \\ & \times [\{(I_G \otimes \bar{X}'_W)Z\}'[\boldsymbol{\Sigma}_u \otimes (\bar{X}'_W \bar{X}_W)]^{-1}\{(I_G \otimes \bar{X}'_W)y\}], \end{aligned}$$

$$\begin{aligned} \widehat{\gamma}_{B3SLS} = {} & [\{(I_G \otimes \bar{X}'_B)Z\}'[(\boldsymbol{\Sigma}_u + T\boldsymbol{\Sigma}_\alpha) \otimes (\bar{X}'_B \bar{X}_B)]^{-1}\{(I_G \otimes \bar{X}'_B)Z\}]^{-1} \\ & \times [\{(I_G \otimes \bar{X}'_B)Z\}'[(\boldsymbol{\Sigma}_u + T\boldsymbol{\Sigma}_\alpha) \otimes (\bar{X}'_B \bar{X}_B)]^{-1}\{(I_G \otimes \bar{X}'_B)y\}]. \end{aligned}$$

Using once again (12.66)–(12.67), these expressions can be simplified to

$$\widehat{\boldsymbol{\gamma}}_{W3SLS} = [\boldsymbol{Z}'(\boldsymbol{\Sigma}_u^{-1} \otimes \boldsymbol{P}_{WX})\boldsymbol{Z}]^{-1}[\boldsymbol{Z}'(\boldsymbol{\Sigma}_u^{-1} \otimes \boldsymbol{P}_{WX})\boldsymbol{y}], \tag{12.94}$$

$$\widehat{\boldsymbol{\gamma}}_{B3SLS} = \left[\boldsymbol{Z}'[(\boldsymbol{\Sigma}_u + T\boldsymbol{\Sigma}_\alpha)^{-1} \otimes \boldsymbol{P}_{BX}]\boldsymbol{Z}\right]^{-1} \times \left[\boldsymbol{Z}'[(\boldsymbol{\Sigma}_u + T\boldsymbol{\Sigma}_\alpha)^{-1} \otimes \boldsymbol{P}_{BX}]\boldsymbol{y}\right]. \tag{12.95}$$

These two estimators can be denoted as, respectively, the *within three-stage least squares estimator* and the *between three-stage least squares estimator* of $\boldsymbol{\gamma}$. They are multi-equation counterparts to (12.68)–(12.69).

12.5.2 VARIANCE COMPONENTS THREE-STAGE LEAST SQUARES

The final step consists in stacking the transformed versions of (12.81), given by (12.90) and (12.91), with $\boldsymbol{\gamma}$ as the common coefficient vector, and use GLS. This serves to improve efficiency. The intuitive reason for this is that the two types of data variation are exploited in combination with the variance components structure of the equation system. The multi-equation generalization of (12.74) thus obtained is:

$$\begin{bmatrix} (\boldsymbol{I}_G \otimes \bar{\boldsymbol{X}}'_W)\boldsymbol{y} \\ (\boldsymbol{I}_G \otimes \bar{\boldsymbol{X}}'_B)\boldsymbol{y} \end{bmatrix} = \begin{bmatrix} (\boldsymbol{I}_G \otimes \bar{\boldsymbol{X}}'_W)\boldsymbol{Z} \\ (\boldsymbol{I}_G \otimes \bar{\boldsymbol{X}}'_B)\boldsymbol{Z} \end{bmatrix}\boldsymbol{\gamma} + \begin{bmatrix} (\boldsymbol{I}_G \otimes \bar{\boldsymbol{X}}'_W)\boldsymbol{\epsilon} \\ (\boldsymbol{I}_G \otimes \bar{\boldsymbol{X}}'_B)\boldsymbol{\epsilon} \end{bmatrix}. \tag{12.96}$$

From (12.92)–(12.93) and $\bar{\boldsymbol{X}}'_W\bar{\boldsymbol{X}}_B = \boldsymbol{0}$ we find that the disturbance vector in (12.96) has block-diagonal covariance matrix

$$\mathsf{V}\begin{bmatrix} (\boldsymbol{I}_G \otimes \bar{\boldsymbol{X}}'_W)\boldsymbol{\epsilon}|\bar{\boldsymbol{X}} \\ (\boldsymbol{I}_G \otimes \bar{\boldsymbol{X}}'_B)\boldsymbol{\epsilon}|\bar{\boldsymbol{X}} \end{bmatrix} = \begin{bmatrix} \boldsymbol{\Sigma}_u \otimes (\bar{\boldsymbol{X}}'_W\bar{\boldsymbol{X}}_W) & \boldsymbol{0} \\ \boldsymbol{0} & (\boldsymbol{\Sigma}_u + T\boldsymbol{\Sigma}_\alpha) \otimes (\bar{\boldsymbol{X}}'_B\bar{\boldsymbol{X}}_B) \end{bmatrix}, \tag{12.97}$$

and hence

$$\left\{\mathsf{V}\begin{bmatrix} (\boldsymbol{I}_G \otimes \bar{\boldsymbol{X}}'_W)\boldsymbol{\epsilon}|\bar{\boldsymbol{X}} \\ (\boldsymbol{I}_G \otimes \bar{\boldsymbol{X}}'_B)\boldsymbol{\epsilon}|\bar{\boldsymbol{X}} \end{bmatrix}\right\}^{-1} = \begin{bmatrix} \boldsymbol{\Sigma}_u^{-1} \otimes (\bar{\boldsymbol{X}}'_W\bar{\boldsymbol{X}}_W)^{-1} & \boldsymbol{0} \\ \boldsymbol{0} & (\boldsymbol{\Sigma}_u + T\boldsymbol{\Sigma}_\alpha)^{-1} \otimes (\bar{\boldsymbol{X}}'_B\bar{\boldsymbol{X}}_B)^{-1} \end{bmatrix}.$$

Application of GLS on (12.96) gives the estimator

$$\widehat{\boldsymbol{\gamma}}_{VC3SLS} = \left[\begin{bmatrix} (\boldsymbol{I}_G \otimes \bar{\boldsymbol{X}}'_W)\boldsymbol{Z} \\ (\boldsymbol{I}_G \otimes \bar{\boldsymbol{X}}'_B)\boldsymbol{Z} \end{bmatrix}' \left\{\mathsf{V}\begin{bmatrix} (\boldsymbol{I}_G \otimes \bar{\boldsymbol{X}}'_W)\boldsymbol{\epsilon}|\boldsymbol{X} \\ (\boldsymbol{I}_G \otimes \bar{\boldsymbol{X}}'_B)\boldsymbol{\epsilon}|\boldsymbol{X} \end{bmatrix}\right\}^{-1} \begin{bmatrix} (\boldsymbol{I}_G \otimes \bar{\boldsymbol{X}}'_W)\boldsymbol{Z} \\ (\boldsymbol{I}_G \otimes \bar{\boldsymbol{X}}'_B)\boldsymbol{Z} \end{bmatrix}\right]^{-1}$$
$$\times \left[\begin{bmatrix} (\boldsymbol{I}_G \otimes \bar{\boldsymbol{X}}'_W)\boldsymbol{Z} \\ (\boldsymbol{I}_G \otimes \bar{\boldsymbol{X}}'_B)\boldsymbol{Z} \end{bmatrix}' \left\{\mathsf{V}\begin{bmatrix} (\boldsymbol{I}_G \otimes \bar{\boldsymbol{X}}'_W)\boldsymbol{\epsilon}|\boldsymbol{X} \\ (\boldsymbol{I}_G \otimes \bar{\boldsymbol{X}}'_B)\boldsymbol{\epsilon}|\boldsymbol{X} \end{bmatrix}\right\}^{-1} \begin{bmatrix} (\boldsymbol{I}_G \otimes \bar{\boldsymbol{X}}'_W)\boldsymbol{y} \\ (\boldsymbol{I}_G \otimes \bar{\boldsymbol{X}}'_B)\boldsymbol{y} \end{bmatrix}\right],$$

which, when again using (12.66)–(12.67), can be rearranged to

$$\widehat{\gamma}_{VC3SLS} = \{Z'[\Sigma_u^{-1}\otimes P_{WX}]Z+Z'[(\Sigma_u+T\Sigma_\alpha)^{-1}\otimes P_{BX}]Z\}^{-1} \times \{Z'[\Sigma_u^{-1} \otimes P_{WX}]y+Z'(\Sigma_u+T\Sigma_\alpha)^{-1}\otimes P_{BX}]y\}. \tag{12.98}$$

This is the *variance components three-stage least squares (VC3SLS) estimator.* Since (12.94)–(12.95) imply

$$Z'[\Sigma_u^{-1}\otimes P_{WX}]y = Z'[\Sigma_u^{-1}\otimes P_{WX}]Z\widehat{\gamma}_{W3SLS},$$
$$Z'[(\Sigma_u+T\Sigma_\alpha)^{-1}\otimes P_{BX}]y = Z'[(\Sigma_u+T\Sigma_\alpha)^{-1}\otimes P_{BX}]Z\widehat{\gamma}_{B3SLS},$$

it emerges as a matrix-weighted average of $\widehat{\gamma}_{W3SLS}$ and $\widehat{\gamma}_{B3SLS}$:

$$\widehat{\gamma}_{VC3SLS}=\{Z'[\Sigma_u^{-1}\otimes P_{WX}]Z+Z'[(\Sigma_u+T\Sigma_\alpha)^{-1}\otimes P_{BX}]Z\}^{-1} \times \{Z'[\Sigma_u^{-1}\otimes P_{WX}]Z\widehat{\gamma}_{W3SLS}+Z'(\Sigma_u+T\Sigma_\alpha)^{-1}\otimes P_{BX}]Z\widehat{\gamma}_{B3SLS}\}.$$

Estimation of variance components matrices: the matrices Σ_u and Σ_α needed for computation of (12.98) can be estimated *from the W2SLS- and B2SLS-residual vectors of all G equations.* Briefly, the procedure is: we extend (12.77)–(12.78) to

$$\frac{\mathsf{E}[\epsilon_g'(I_N\otimes B_T)\epsilon_h]}{N(T-1)} = \sigma_{gh}^u, \tag{12.99}$$

$$\frac{\mathsf{E}[\epsilon_g'(B_N\otimes A_T)\epsilon_h]}{N-1} = T\sigma_{gh}^\alpha+\sigma_{gh}^u, \tag{12.100}$$

which motivate the following estimators, as natural extensions of (12.79)–(12.80):

$$\widehat{\sigma}_{gh}^u = \frac{\widehat{\epsilon}'_{W2SLSg}(I_N\otimes B_T)\widehat{\epsilon}_{W2SLSh}}{N(T-1)}, \tag{12.101}$$

$$\widehat{T\sigma_{gh}^\alpha+\sigma_{gh}^u} = \frac{\widehat{\epsilon}'_{B2SLSg}(B_N\otimes A_T)\widehat{\epsilon}_{B2SLSh}}{N-1}, \quad g,h = 1,\dots,G. \tag{12.102}$$

From these estimators for the respective elements we can form $\widehat{\Sigma}_u$ and $\widehat{\Sigma_u+T\Sigma_\alpha}$. Inserting these estimators in (12.94), (12.95), and (12.98) makes the respective 3SLS-procedures feasible.

For estimation of the covariance matrices of the one-way variance components versions of the within-, between-, and 3SLS-estimators, see Appendix 12C, Section 12C.2.

Appendix 12A. **Estimation of error component covariance matrices**

In this appendix, procedures for estimating the covariance matrices of the error components in the regression systems with one-way and two-way heterogeneity in Sections 12.2 and 12.3 are considered.

12A.1 One-way model: to obtain from GLS estimators FGLS procedures for the one-way regression system, we need expressions for the estimators for $\boldsymbol{\Sigma}_u$ and $\boldsymbol{\Sigma}_\alpha$ that generalize those for single equation models in Section 3.3. We start from the following expressions, using rules for trace-operations:

$$\begin{aligned}
\mathsf{E}[\boldsymbol{\epsilon}_g'(\boldsymbol{I}_N \otimes \boldsymbol{B}_T)\boldsymbol{\epsilon}_h|\boldsymbol{X}] &= \mathsf{E}[\mathrm{tr}(\boldsymbol{\epsilon}_g'(\boldsymbol{I}_N \otimes \boldsymbol{B}_T)\boldsymbol{\epsilon}_h)|\boldsymbol{X}] \\
&= \mathsf{E}[\mathrm{tr}(\boldsymbol{\epsilon}_g\boldsymbol{\epsilon}_h'(\boldsymbol{I}_N \otimes \boldsymbol{B}_T))|\boldsymbol{X}] \\
&= \mathrm{tr}[\mathsf{E}(\boldsymbol{\epsilon}_g\boldsymbol{\epsilon}_h')(\boldsymbol{I}_N \otimes \boldsymbol{B}_T)|\boldsymbol{X}], \\
\mathsf{E}[\boldsymbol{\epsilon}_g'(\boldsymbol{B}_N \otimes \boldsymbol{A}_T)\boldsymbol{\epsilon}_h|\boldsymbol{X}] &= \mathsf{E}[\mathrm{tr}(\boldsymbol{\epsilon}_g'(\boldsymbol{B}_N \otimes \boldsymbol{A}_T)\boldsymbol{\epsilon}_h)|\boldsymbol{X}] \\
&= \mathsf{E}[\mathrm{tr}(\boldsymbol{\epsilon}_g\boldsymbol{\epsilon}_h'(\boldsymbol{B}_N \otimes \boldsymbol{A}_T))|\boldsymbol{X}] \\
&= \mathrm{tr}[\mathsf{E}(\boldsymbol{\epsilon}_g\boldsymbol{\epsilon}_h')(\boldsymbol{B}_N \otimes \boldsymbol{A}_T)|\boldsymbol{X}].
\end{aligned}$$

Since (12.4) implies

$$\mathsf{E}(\boldsymbol{\epsilon}_g\boldsymbol{\epsilon}_h'|\boldsymbol{X}) = T\sigma^\alpha_{gh}(\boldsymbol{I}_N \otimes \boldsymbol{A}_T) + \sigma^u_{gh}(\boldsymbol{I}_N \otimes \boldsymbol{I}_T),$$

and hence, since $\mathrm{tr}(\boldsymbol{A}_T)=1$ and $\mathrm{tr}(\boldsymbol{B}_T)=T-1$,

$$\begin{aligned}
\mathrm{tr}[\mathsf{E}(\boldsymbol{\epsilon}_g\boldsymbol{\epsilon}_h')(\boldsymbol{I}_N \otimes \boldsymbol{B}_T)|\boldsymbol{X}] &= \sigma^u_{gh}\mathrm{tr}(\boldsymbol{I}_N \otimes \boldsymbol{B}_T) = \sigma^u_{gh}N(T-1), \\
\mathrm{tr}[\mathsf{E}(\boldsymbol{\epsilon}_g\boldsymbol{\epsilon}_h')(\boldsymbol{B}_N \otimes \boldsymbol{A}_T)|\boldsymbol{X}] &= (T\sigma^\alpha_{gh}+\sigma^u_{gh})\mathrm{tr}(\boldsymbol{B}_N \otimes \boldsymbol{A}_T) = (T\sigma^\alpha_{gh}+\sigma^u_{gh})(N-1),
\end{aligned}$$

we obtain

$$\mathsf{E}[\boldsymbol{\epsilon}_g'(\boldsymbol{I}_N \otimes \boldsymbol{B}_T)\boldsymbol{\epsilon}_h|\boldsymbol{X}] = \sigma^u_{gh}N(T-1), \tag{12A.1}$$

$$\mathsf{E}[\boldsymbol{\epsilon}_g'(\boldsymbol{B}_N \otimes \boldsymbol{A}_T)\boldsymbol{\epsilon}_h|\boldsymbol{X}] = (T\sigma^\alpha_{gh}+\sigma^u_{gh})(N-1). \tag{12A.2}$$

Letting $\widehat{\boldsymbol{\epsilon}}_g$ denote residuals obtained by OLS on equation g, this motivates the estimators

$$\widehat{\sigma}^u_{gh} = \frac{\widehat{\boldsymbol{\epsilon}}_g'(\boldsymbol{I}_N \otimes \boldsymbol{B}_T)\widehat{\boldsymbol{\epsilon}}_h}{N(T-1)}, \tag{12A.3}$$

$$\widehat{T\sigma_{gh}^{\alpha}+\sigma_{gh}^{u}} = \frac{\widehat{\boldsymbol{\epsilon}}_g'(B_N \otimes A_T)\widehat{\boldsymbol{\epsilon}}_h}{N-1}, \tag{12A.4}$$

leading to

$$\widehat{\sigma}_{gh}^{\alpha} = \frac{\widehat{\boldsymbol{\epsilon}}_g'(I_N \otimes A_T)\widehat{\boldsymbol{\epsilon}}_h}{(N-1)T} - \frac{\widehat{\boldsymbol{\epsilon}}_g'(B_N \otimes B_T)\widehat{\boldsymbol{\epsilon}}_h}{NT(T-1)}.$$

From these estimators we form $\widehat{\boldsymbol{\Sigma}}_u$ and $\widehat{T\boldsymbol{\Sigma}_\alpha+\boldsymbol{\Sigma}_u}$, needed for computing the FGLS estimator of $\boldsymbol{\beta}$ and its estimated covariance matrix from (12.19) and (12.20).

12A.2 Two-way model: to obtain from GLS estimators FGLS procedures for the two-way model (12.42), we need expressions for the estimators of $\boldsymbol{\Sigma}_u$, $\boldsymbol{\Sigma}_\alpha$, and $\boldsymbol{\Sigma}_\gamma$ that generalize those for single-equation models in Section 3.5. We have

$$\begin{aligned}
\mathsf{E}[\boldsymbol{\epsilon}_g'(B_N \otimes B_T)\boldsymbol{\epsilon}_h|X] &= \mathsf{E}[\mathrm{tr}(\boldsymbol{\epsilon}_g'(B_N \otimes B_T)\boldsymbol{\epsilon}_h)|X] \\
&= \mathsf{E}[\mathrm{tr}(\boldsymbol{\epsilon}_g\boldsymbol{\epsilon}_h'(B_N \otimes B_T))|X] \\
&= \mathrm{tr}[\mathsf{E}(\boldsymbol{\epsilon}_g\boldsymbol{\epsilon}_h')(B_N \otimes B_T)|X], \\
\mathsf{E}[\boldsymbol{\epsilon}_g'(B_N \otimes A_T)\boldsymbol{\epsilon}_h|X] &= \mathsf{E}[\mathrm{tr}(\boldsymbol{\epsilon}_g'(B_N \otimes A_T)\boldsymbol{\epsilon}_h)|X] \\
&= \mathsf{E}[\mathrm{tr}(\boldsymbol{\epsilon}_g\boldsymbol{\epsilon}_h'(B_N \otimes A_T))|X] \\
&= \mathrm{tr}[\mathsf{E}(\boldsymbol{\epsilon}_g\boldsymbol{\epsilon}_h')(B_N \otimes A_T)|X], \\
\mathsf{E}[\boldsymbol{\epsilon}_g'(A_N \otimes B_T)\boldsymbol{\epsilon}_h|X] &= \mathsf{E}[\mathrm{tr}(\boldsymbol{\epsilon}_g'(A_N \otimes B_T)\boldsymbol{\epsilon}_h)|X] \\
&= \mathsf{E}[\mathrm{tr}(\boldsymbol{\epsilon}_g\boldsymbol{\epsilon}_h'(A_N \otimes B_T))|X] \\
&= \mathrm{tr}[\mathsf{E}(\boldsymbol{\epsilon}_g\boldsymbol{\epsilon}_h')(A_N \otimes B_T)|X].
\end{aligned}$$

Since (12.43) implies

$$\mathsf{E}(\boldsymbol{\epsilon}_g\boldsymbol{\epsilon}_h'|X) = T\sigma_{gh}^{\alpha}(I_N \otimes A_T) + N\sigma_{gh}^{\gamma}(A_N \otimes I_T) + \sigma_{gh}^{u}(I_N \otimes I_T),$$

and hence

$$\begin{aligned}
\mathrm{tr}[\mathsf{E}(\boldsymbol{\epsilon}_g\boldsymbol{\epsilon}_h')(B_N \otimes B_T)|X] &= \sigma_{gh}^{u}\mathrm{tr}(B_N \otimes B_T) = \sigma_{gh}^{u}(N-1)(T-1), \\
\mathrm{tr}[\mathsf{E}(\boldsymbol{\epsilon}_g\boldsymbol{\epsilon}_h')(B_N \otimes A_T)|X] &= (T\sigma_{gh}^{\alpha}+\sigma_{gh}^{u})\mathrm{tr}(B_N \otimes A_T) = (T\sigma_{gh}^{\alpha}+\sigma_{gh}^{u})(N-1), \\
\mathrm{tr}[\mathsf{E}(\boldsymbol{\epsilon}_g\boldsymbol{\epsilon}_h')(A_N \otimes B_T)|X] &= (N\sigma_{gh}^{\gamma}+\sigma_{gh}^{u})\mathrm{tr}(A_N \otimes B_T) = (N\sigma_{gh}^{\gamma}+\sigma_{gh}^{u})(T-1),
\end{aligned}$$

we obtain

$$\mathsf{E}[\epsilon_g'(B_N \otimes B_T)\epsilon_h|X] = \sigma^u_{gh}(N-1)(T-1), \tag{12A.5}$$
$$\mathsf{E}[\epsilon_g'(B_N \otimes A_T)\epsilon_h|X] = (T\sigma^\alpha_{gh}+\sigma^u_{gh})(N-1), \tag{12A.6}$$
$$\mathsf{E}[\epsilon_g'(A_N \otimes B_T)\epsilon_h|X] = (N\sigma^\gamma_{gh}+\sigma^u_{gh})(T-1). \tag{12A.7}$$

Letting $\widehat{\epsilon}_g$ denote residuals obtained by OLS on equation g, this motivates the estimators

$$\widehat{\sigma}^u_{gh} = \frac{\widehat{\epsilon}_g'(B_N \otimes B_T)\widehat{\epsilon}_h}{(N-1)(T-1)}, \tag{12A.8}$$
$$\widehat{T\sigma^\alpha_{gh}+\sigma^u_{gh}} = \frac{\widehat{\epsilon}_g'(B_N \otimes A_T)\widehat{\epsilon}_h}{N-1}, \tag{12A.9}$$
$$\widehat{N\sigma^\gamma_{gh}+\sigma^u_{gh}} = \frac{\widehat{\epsilon}_g'(A_N \otimes B_T)\widehat{\epsilon}_h}{T-1}, \tag{12A.10}$$

leading to

$$\widehat{\sigma}^\alpha_{gh} = \frac{1}{(N-1)T}\left[\widehat{\epsilon}_g'(B_N \otimes A_T)\widehat{\epsilon}_h - \frac{\widehat{\epsilon}_g'(B_N \otimes B_T)\widehat{\epsilon}_h}{T-1}\right],$$
$$\widehat{\sigma}^\gamma_{gh} = \frac{1}{N(T-1)}\left[\widehat{\epsilon}_g'(A_N \otimes B_T)\widehat{\epsilon}_h - \frac{\widehat{\epsilon}_g'(B_N \otimes B_T)\widehat{\epsilon}_h}{N-1}\right].$$

From these estimators we form $\widehat{\boldsymbol{\Sigma}}_u$, $\widehat{T\boldsymbol{\Sigma}_\alpha+\boldsymbol{\Sigma}_u}$, and $\widehat{N\boldsymbol{\Sigma}_\gamma+\boldsymbol{\Sigma}_u}$ needed for computing the FGLS estimator of $\boldsymbol{\beta}$ and its estimated covariance matrix.

Appendix 12B. **Matrix differentiation: Useful results**

In this appendix we collect, with suitable references (without referring proofs), some results for certain functions of quadratic matrices and their derivatives which are utilized in Section 12.2.4 to simplify the algebra in deriving the ML estimators for systems of regression equations for panel data.

12B.1 Let the matrices A and C have dimensions $(m \times n)$ and $(n \times m)$. Then the trace of their product can be written as, see Lütkepohl (1996, p. 41),

$$\mathrm{tr}(AC) = \mathrm{tr}(CA) = \mathrm{vec}(A')'\mathrm{vec}(C) = \mathrm{vec}(C')'\mathrm{vec}(A). \tag{12B.1}$$

A generalization of this result which involves a four-factor matrix product is: let A, B, C, and D be matrices such that $ABCD$ is defined. Then we have, see Lütkepohl (1996, p. 42),

$$\mathrm{tr}(ABCD) = \mathrm{tr}(CDAB) = \mathrm{vec}(A')'(D' \otimes B)\mathrm{vec}(C) = \mathrm{vec}(C')'(B' \otimes D)\mathrm{vec}(A). \tag{12B.2}$$

Equation (12B.1) follows as the special case where B and D are identity matrices.

12B.2 Let C and D be $(m \times m)$ matrices, and let $A_T = (e_T e'_T)/T$ (trace=1), $B_T = I_T - (e_T e'_T)/T$ (trace=$T-1$). Then the $(mT \times mT)$-matrix $[(A_T \otimes C) + (B_T \otimes D)]$ has determinant value equal to, see Magnus (1982, Lemma 2.1),

$$|(A_T \otimes C) + (B_T \otimes D)| = |C|\,|D|^{T-1}. \tag{12B.3}$$

12B.3 Let A be a quadratic, non-singular $(m \times m)$-matrix. The derivative of its determinant value with respect to the matrix of its elements is given by the $(m \times m)$-matrix; see Magnus and Neudecker (1988, p. 179) or Lütkepohl (1996, p. 181):

$$\frac{\partial |A|}{\partial A} = |A|\,(A')^{-1} = (A')^{\mathrm{adj}},$$

where $(A')^{\mathrm{adj}}$ is the adjoint of A'. From this, since $(\partial \ln |A|)/(\partial |A|) = 1/|A|$, it follows that

$$\frac{\partial \ln |A|}{\partial A} = (A')^{-1}. \tag{12B.4}$$

12B.4 Let B and C be quadratic, non-singular $(m \times m)$-matrices. Then the trace of CB^{-1} satisfies; see Magnus and Neudecker (1988, p. 178) or Lütkepohl (1996, p. 179):

$$\frac{\partial \mathrm{tr}(CB^{-1})}{\partial B} = -(B^{-1}CB^{-1})'. \tag{12B.5}$$

Appendix 12C. Estimator covariance matrices in interdependent models

In this appendix we describe core elements in the procedures for estimating covariance matrices of the coefficient estimator vectors of the interdependent models considered in Sections 12.4 (single-equation estimation) and 12.5 (joint estimation of all equations). The discussion is confined to situations with one-way heterogeneity only.

12C.1 *Single-equation estimation:* from (12.55) and (12.64)–(12.65), after rearrangement, it follows that

$$\sqrt{NT}(\widehat{\boldsymbol{\gamma}}_{W2SLSg}-\boldsymbol{\gamma}_g)$$

$$=\left[\frac{Z'_{Wg}\bar{X}_W}{NT}\left(\frac{\bar{X}'_W\bar{X}_W}{NT}\right)^{-1}\frac{\bar{X}'_W Z_{Wg}}{NT}\right]^{-1}\left[\frac{Z'_{Wg}\bar{X}_W}{NT}\left(\frac{\bar{X}'_W\bar{X}_W}{NT}\right)^{-1}\frac{\bar{X}'_W\boldsymbol{\epsilon}_{Wg}}{\sqrt{NT}}\right], \tag{12C.1}$$

$$\sqrt{NT}(\widehat{\boldsymbol{\gamma}}_{B2SLSg}-\boldsymbol{\gamma}_g)$$

$$=\left[\frac{Z'_{Bg}\bar{X}_B}{NT}\left(\frac{\bar{X}'_B\bar{X}_B}{NT}\right)^{-1}\frac{\bar{X}'_B Z_{Bg}}{NT}\right]^{-1}\left[\frac{Z'_{Bg}\bar{X}_B}{NT}\left(\frac{\bar{X}'_B\bar{X}_B}{NT}\right)^{-1}\frac{\bar{X}'_B\boldsymbol{\epsilon}_{Bg}}{\sqrt{NT}}\right]. \tag{12C.2}$$

Let

$$\boldsymbol{\Sigma}_{WXZg} = \operatorname*{plim}_{N,T\to\infty}\left(\frac{\bar{X}'_W Z_{Wg}}{NT}\right),$$

$$\boldsymbol{\Sigma}_{BXZg} = \operatorname*{plim}_{N,T\to\infty}\left(\frac{\bar{X}'_B Z_{Bg}}{NT}\right),$$

$$\boldsymbol{\Sigma}_{WXX} = \operatorname*{plim}_{N,T\to\infty}\left(\frac{\bar{X}'_W\bar{X}_W}{NT}\right),$$

$$\boldsymbol{\Sigma}_{BXX} = \operatorname*{plim}_{N,T\to\infty}\left(\frac{\bar{X}'_B\bar{X}_B}{NT}\right).$$

Under suitable regularity conditions, using (12.56)–(12.57), we also have

$$\operatorname*{plim}_{N,T\to\infty}\left(\frac{\bar{X}'_W\boldsymbol{\epsilon}_{Wg}}{\sqrt{NT}}\frac{\boldsymbol{\epsilon}'_{Wg}\bar{X}_W}{\sqrt{NT}}\right)=\sigma^u_{gg}\operatorname*{plim}_{N,T\to\infty}\left(\frac{\bar{X}'_W\bar{X}_W}{NT}\right)=\sigma^u_{gg}\boldsymbol{\Sigma}_{WXX},$$

$$\operatorname*{plim}_{N,T\to\infty}\left(\frac{\bar{X}'_B\boldsymbol{\epsilon}_{Bg}}{\sqrt{NT}}\frac{\boldsymbol{\epsilon}'_{Bg}\bar{X}_B}{\sqrt{NT}}\right)=(\sigma^u_{gg}+T\sigma^{\alpha}_{gg})\operatorname*{plim}_{N,T\to\infty}\left(\frac{\bar{X}'_B\bar{X}_B}{NT}\right)=(\sigma^u_{gg}+T\sigma^{\alpha}_{gg})\boldsymbol{\Sigma}_{BXX}.$$

Then it can be shown that $\sqrt{NT}(\widehat{\boldsymbol{\gamma}}_{W2SLSg}-\boldsymbol{\gamma}_g)$ and $\sqrt{NT}(\widehat{\boldsymbol{\gamma}}_{B2SLSg}-\boldsymbol{\gamma}_g)$ have limiting distributions which are normal with zero mean vectors and (asymptotic) covariance matrices, respectively,

$$aV[\sqrt{NT}(\widehat{\boldsymbol{\gamma}}_{W2SLSg}-\boldsymbol{\gamma}_g)] = \sigma^u_{gg}[\boldsymbol{\Sigma}'_{WXZg}\boldsymbol{\Sigma}^{-1}_{WXX}\boldsymbol{\Sigma}_{WXZg}]^{-1}, \quad (12C.3)$$

$$aV[\sqrt{NT}(\widehat{\boldsymbol{\gamma}}_{B2SLSg}-\boldsymbol{\gamma}_g)] = (\sigma^u_{gg}+T\sigma^{\alpha}_{gg})[\boldsymbol{\Sigma}'_{BXZg}\boldsymbol{\Sigma}^{-1}_{BXX}\boldsymbol{\Sigma}_{BXZg}]^{-1}. \quad (12C.4)$$

By similar algebra it can be shown from (12.76) that $\sqrt{NT}(\widehat{\boldsymbol{\gamma}}_{VC2SLSg}-\boldsymbol{\gamma}_g)$ has a limiting distribution which is normal with zero mean vector and (asymptotic) covariance matrix

$$aV[\sqrt{NT}(\widehat{\boldsymbol{\gamma}}_{VC2SLSg}-\boldsymbol{\gamma}_g)] = \left[\frac{\boldsymbol{\Sigma}'_{WXZg}\boldsymbol{\Sigma}^{-1}_{WXX}\boldsymbol{\Sigma}_{WXZg}}{\sigma^u_{gg}}+\frac{\boldsymbol{\Sigma}'_{BXZg}\boldsymbol{\Sigma}^{-1}_{BXX}\boldsymbol{\Sigma}_{BXZg}}{\sigma^u_{gg}+T\sigma^{\alpha}_{gg}}\right]^{-1}. \quad (12C.5)$$

12C.2 *Simultaneous equation estimation:* rearranging (12.94) and (12.95), using (12.66)–(12.67), it follows that

$$\sqrt{NT}(\widehat{\boldsymbol{\gamma}}_{W3SLS}-\gamma) = \left[\frac{Z'}{\sqrt{NT}}\left(\boldsymbol{\Sigma}^{-1}_u\otimes\frac{\bar{X}_W}{\sqrt{NT}}\left(\frac{\bar{X}'_W\bar{X}_W}{NT}\right)^{-1}\frac{\bar{X}'_W}{\sqrt{NT}}\right)\frac{Z}{\sqrt{NT}}\right]^{-1}$$
$$\times\left[\frac{Z'}{\sqrt{NT}}\left(\boldsymbol{\Sigma}^{-1}_u\otimes\frac{\bar{X}_W}{\sqrt{NT}}\left(\frac{\bar{X}'_W\bar{X}_W}{NT}\right)^{-1}\frac{\bar{X}'_W}{\sqrt{NT}}\right)\boldsymbol{\epsilon}\right],$$

$$\sqrt{NT}(\widehat{\boldsymbol{\gamma}}_{B3SLS}-\gamma) = \left[\frac{Z'}{\sqrt{NT}}\left((\boldsymbol{\Sigma}_u+T\boldsymbol{\Sigma}_\alpha)^{-1}\otimes\frac{\bar{X}_B}{\sqrt{NT}}\left(\frac{\bar{X}'_B\bar{X}_B}{NT}\right)^{-1}\frac{\bar{X}'_B}{\sqrt{NT}}\right)\frac{Z}{\sqrt{NT}}\right]^{-1}$$
$$\times\left[\frac{Z'}{\sqrt{NT}}\left((\boldsymbol{\Sigma}_u+T\boldsymbol{\Sigma}_\alpha)^{-1}\otimes\frac{\bar{X}_B}{\sqrt{NT}}\left(\frac{\bar{X}'_B\bar{X}_B}{NT}\right)^{-1}\frac{\bar{X}'_B}{\sqrt{NT}}\right)\boldsymbol{\epsilon}\right].$$

Letting

$$Q_W = \boldsymbol{\Sigma}_u^{-\frac{1}{2}}\otimes\left[\bar{X}_W\left(\frac{\bar{X}'_W\bar{X}_W}{\sqrt{NT}}\right)^{-\frac{1}{2}}\right],$$

$$Q_B = (\boldsymbol{\Sigma}_u+T\boldsymbol{\Sigma}_\alpha)^{-\frac{1}{2}}\otimes\left[\bar{X}_B\left(\frac{\bar{X}'_B\bar{X}_B}{\sqrt{NT}}\right)^{-\frac{1}{2}}\right],$$

these expressions can be simplified to

$$\sqrt{NT}(\widehat{\boldsymbol{\gamma}}_{W3SLS}-\gamma) = \left[\frac{Z'}{\sqrt{NT}}\frac{Q_W}{\sqrt{NT}}\frac{Q'_W}{\sqrt{NT}}\frac{Z}{\sqrt{NT}}\right]^{-1}\left[\frac{Z'}{\sqrt{NT}}\frac{Q_W}{\sqrt{NT}}\frac{Q'_W}{\sqrt{NT}}\boldsymbol{\epsilon}\right], \quad (12C.6)$$

$$\sqrt{NT}(\widehat{\boldsymbol{\gamma}}_{B3SLS}-\gamma) = \left[\frac{Z'}{\sqrt{NT}}\frac{Q_B}{\sqrt{NT}}\frac{Q_B'}{\sqrt{NT}}\frac{Z}{\sqrt{NT}}\right]^{-1}\left[\frac{Z'}{\sqrt{NT}}\frac{Q_B}{\sqrt{NT}}\frac{Q_B'}{\sqrt{NT}}\boldsymbol{\epsilon}\right]. \quad (12C.7)$$

It can then be shown from (12.83), letting

$$\boldsymbol{\Sigma}_{WQZ} = \operatorname*{plim}_{N,T\to\infty}\left(\frac{Q_W'Z}{NT}\right),$$

$$\boldsymbol{\Sigma}_{BQZ} = \operatorname*{plim}_{N,T\to\infty}\left(\frac{Q_B'Z}{NT}\right),$$

that, under suitable regularity conditions, $\sqrt{NT}(\widehat{\boldsymbol{\gamma}}_{W3SLS}-\boldsymbol{\gamma})$ and $\sqrt{NT}(\widehat{\boldsymbol{\gamma}}_{B3SLS}-\boldsymbol{\gamma})$ have limiting distributions which are normal with zero mean vectors and (asymptotic) covariance matrices, respectively,

$$a\mathsf{V}[\sqrt{NT}(\widehat{\boldsymbol{\gamma}}_{W3SLS}-\boldsymbol{\gamma})] = [\boldsymbol{\Sigma}_{WQZ}'\boldsymbol{\Sigma}_{WQZ}]^{-1}, \quad (12C.8)$$

$$a\mathsf{V}[\sqrt{NT}(\widehat{\boldsymbol{\gamma}}_{B3SLS}-\boldsymbol{\gamma})] = [\boldsymbol{\Sigma}_{BQZ}'\boldsymbol{\Sigma}_{BQZ}]^{-1}. \quad (12C.9)$$

By similar algebra it can be shown from (12.98) that $\sqrt{NT}(\widehat{\boldsymbol{\gamma}}_{VC3SLS}-\boldsymbol{\gamma})$ has a limiting distribution which is normal with zero mean vector and (asymptotic) covariance matrix

$$a\mathsf{V}[\sqrt{NT}(\widehat{\boldsymbol{\gamma}}_{VC3SLS}-\boldsymbol{\gamma})] = [\boldsymbol{\Sigma}_{WQZ}'\boldsymbol{\Sigma}_{WQZ} + \boldsymbol{\Sigma}_{BQZ}'\boldsymbol{\Sigma}_{BQZ}]^{-1}. \quad (12C.10)$$

REFERENCES

Ahn, S.C. and Schmidt, P. (1995) Efficient Estimation of Models for Dynamic Panel Data. *Journal of Econometrics* **68**, 5–27.

Aigner, D.J., Hsiao, C., Kapteyn, A., and Wansbeek, T. (1984) Latent Variable Models in Econometrics. Chapter 23 in: Griliches, Z. and Intriligator, M.D. (eds.): *Handbook of Econometrics, Volume 2*. Amsterdam: North-Holland.

Alvarez, J. and Arellano, M. (2003) The Time Series and Cross-Section Asymptotics of Dynamic Panel Data Estimators. *Econometrica* **71**, 1121–59.

Amemiya, T. (1971) The Estimation of the Variances in a Variance-Components Model. *International Economic Review* **12**, 1–13.

Amemiya, T. (1973) Regression Analysis When the Dependent Variable Is Truncated Normal. *Econometrica* **41**, 997–1016.

Amemiya, T. (1984) Tobit Models: A Survey. *Journal of Econometrics* **24**, 3–61.

Amemiya, T. (1985) *Advanced Econometrics*. Cambridge, MA: Harvard University Press.

Amemiya, T. and MaCurdy, T.E. (1986) Instrumental-Variable Estimation of an Error-Components Model. *Econometrica* **54**, 869–80.

Andersen, E.B. (1970) Asymptotic Properties of Conditional Maximum-Likelihood Estimators. *Journal of the Royal Statistical Society. Series B* **32**, 283–301.

Anderson, T.W. and Hsiao, C. (1981) Estimation of Dynamic Models with Error Components. *Journal of the American Statistical Association* **76**, 598–606.

Anderson, T.W. and Hsiao, C. (1982) Formulation and Estimation of Dynamic Models Using Panel Data. *Journal of Econometrics* **18**, 47–82.

Angrist, J. and Pischke, J.-S. (2009) *Mostly Harmless Econometrics: An Empiricist's Companion*. Princeton: Princeton University Press.

Arellano, M. (1989) A Note on the Anderson–Hsiao Estimator for Panel Data. *Economics Letters* **31**, 337–41.

Arellano, M. (2003) *Panel Data Econometrics*. Oxford. Oxford University Press.

Arellano, M. and Bond, S. (1991) Some Tests of Specification for Panel Data: Monte Carlo Evidence and an Application to Employment Equations. *Review of Economic Studies* **58**, 277–97.

Arellano, M. and Bover, O. (1995) Another Look at the Instrumental Variable Estimation of Error-Components Models. *Journal of Econometrics* **68**, 29–51.

Arellano, M. and Honoré, B. (2001) Panel Data Models: Some Recent Developments. Chapter 53 in: Heckman, J.J. and Leamer, E. (eds.): *Handbook of Econometrics, Volume 5*. Amsterdam: North-Holland.

Avery, R.B. (1977) Error Components and Seemingly Unrelated Regressions. *Econometrica* **45**, 199–209.

Bai, J. and Ng, S. (2004) A PANIC Attack on Unit Roots and Cointegration. *Econometrica* **72**, 1172–77.

Balestra, P. and Nerlove, M. (1966) Pooling Cross Section and Time Series Data in the Estimation of a Dynamic Model: The Demand for Natural Gas. *Econometrica* **34**, 585–612.

Balestra, P. and Varadharajan-Krishnakumar, J. (1987) Full Information Estimations of a System of Simultaneous Equations with Error Component Structure. *Econometric Theory* **3**, 223–46.

Baltagi, B.H. (1980) On Seemingly Unrelated Regressions with Error Components. *Econometrica* **48**, 1547–51.

Baltagi, B.H. (1981a) Pooling: An Experimental Study of Alternative Testing and Estimation Procedures in a Two-Way Error Component Model. *Journal of Econometrics* 17, 21–49.

Baltagi, B.H. (1981b) Simultaneous Equations with Error Components. *Journal of Econometrics* 17, 189–200.

Baltagi, B.H. (1985) Pooling Cross-Sections with Unequal Time-Series Lengths. *Economics Letters* **18**, 133–6.

Baltagi, B.H. (2005) *Econometric Analysis of Panel Data*, Third edition. Chichester: Wiley.

Baltagi, B.H. (2008) *Econometric Analysis of Panel Data*, Fourth edition. Chichester: Wiley.

Baltagi, B.H., Bresson, G., and Pirotte, A. (2005) Adaptive Estimation of Heteroskedastic Error Component Models. *Econometric Reviews* **24**, 39–58.

Baltagi, B.H., Bresson, G., and Pirotte, A. (2006) Joint LM Test for Heteroskedasticity in a One-Way Error Component Model. *Journal of Econometrics* **134**, 401–17.

Baltagi, B.H. and Chang, Y.-J. (1994) Incomplete Panels: A Comparative Study of Alternative Estimators for the Unbalanced One-Way Error Component Regression Model. *Journal of Econometrics* **62**, 67–89.

Baltagi, B.H. and Griffin, J.M. (1983) Gasoline Demand in the OECD: An Application of Pooling and Testing Procedures. *European Economic Review* **22**, 117–37.

Baltagi, B.H. and Griffin, J.M. (1988) A Generalized Error Component Model with Heteroscedastic Disturbances. *International Economic Review* **29**, 745–53.

Baltagi, B.H., Jung, B.C., and Song, S.H. (2010) Testing for Heteroskedasticity and Serial Correlation in a Random Effects Panel Data Model. *Journal of Econometrics* **154**, 122–4.

Baltagi, B.H. and Li, Q. (1991) A Transformation that Will Circumvent the Problem of Autocorrelation in an Error Component Model. *Journal of Econometrics* **48**, 385–93.

Baltagi, B.H. and Li, Q. (1992) A Note on the Estimation of Simultaneous Equations with Error Components. *Econometric Theory* **8**, 113–19.

Baltagi, B.H. and Li, Q. (1995) Testing AR(1) against MA(1) Disturbances in an Error Component Model. *Journal of Econometrics* **68**, 133–51.

Berzeg, K. (1979) The Error Components Model: Conditions for the Existence of the Maximum Likelihood Estimates. *Journal of Econometrics* **10**, 99–102.

Bhargava, A., Franzini, L., and Narendranathan, W. (1982) Serial Correlation and the Fixed Effects Model. *Review of Economic Studies* **49**, 533–49.

Bhargava, A. and Sargan, J.D. (1983) Estimating Dynamic Random Effects Models from Panel Data Covering Short Time Periods. *Econometrica* **51**, 1635–59.

Biørn, E. (1981) Estimating Economic Relations from Incomplete Cross-Section/Time-Series Data. *Journal of Econometrics* **16**, 221–36.

Biørn, E. (1985) On the Prediction of Population Totals from Sample Surveys Based on Rotating Panels. Statistics Norway, Discussion Paper No. 3.

Biørn, E. (1992) The Bias of Some Estimators for Panel Data Models with Measurement Errors. *Empirical Economics* 17, 51–66.

Biørn, E. (1994) Moment Estimators and the Estimation of Marginal Budget Shares from Household Panel Data. *Structural Change and Economic Dynamics* **5**, 133–54.

Biørn, E. (1996) Panel Data with Measurement Errors. Chapter 10 in: Mátyás, L. and Sevestre, P. (eds.): *The Econometrics of Panel Data. A Handbook of the Theory with Applications*, Second edition. Dordrecht: Kluwer.

Biørn, E. (2000) Panel Data with Measurement Errors: Instrumental Variables and GMM Procedures Combining Levels and Differences. *Econometric Reviews* **19**, 391–424.

Biørn, E. (2001) The Efficiency of Panel Data Estimators: GLS Versus Estimators Which Do Not Depend on Variance Components. Department of Economics, University of Oslo. Memorandum No. 28/2001.

Biørn, E. (2003) Handling the Measurement Error Problem by Means of Panel Data: Moment Methods Applied on Firm Data. Chapter 24 in: Stigum, B.P. (ed.): *Econometrics and the Philosophy of Economics*. Princeton: Princeton University Press.

Biørn, E. (2004) Regression Systems for Unbalanced Panel Data: A Stepwise Maximum Likelihood Procedure. *Journal of Econometrics* **122**, 281–91.

Biørn, E. (2005) Constructing Panel Data Estimators by Aggregation: A General Moment Estimator and a Suggested Synthesis. Statistics Norway, Discussion Paper No. 420.

Biørn, E. (2014) Estimating SUR Systems with Random Coefficients: The Unbalanced Panel Data Case. *Empirical Economics* **47**, 451–68.

Biørn, E. (2015) Panel Data Dynamics with Mis-measured Variables: Modeling and GMM Estimation. *Empirical Economics* **48**, 517–35.

Biørn, E., Hagen, T.P., Iversen, T., and Magnussen, J. (2010) How Different Are Hospitals' Responses to a Financial Reform? The Impact on Efficiency of Activity-Based Financing. *Health Care Management Science* **13**, 1–16.

Biørn, E. and Klette, T.J. (1998) Panel Data with Errors-in-Variables: Essential and Redundant Orthogonality Conditions in GMM-Estimation. *Economics Letters* **59**, 275–82.

Biørn, E. and Krishnakumar, J. (2008) Measurement Errors and Simultaneity. Chapter 10 in: Mátyás, L. and Sevestre, P. (eds.): *The Econometrics of Panel Data. Fundamentals and Recent Developments in Theory and Practice, Third edition*. Berlin–Heidelberg: Springer.

Biørn, E. and Wangen, K.R. (2012) New Taxonomies for Limited Dependent Variables Models. Munich Personal RePEc Archive, MPRA Paper No. 41461.

Blundell, R. and Bond, S. (1998) Initial Conditions and Moment Restrictions in Dynamic Panel Data Models. *Journal of Econometrics* **87**, 115–43.

Blundell, R. and Stoker, T.M. (2005) Heterogeneity and Aggregation. *Journal of Economic Literature* **53**, 347–91.

Bolduc, D. (1999) A Practical Technique to Estimate Multinomial Probit Models in Transportation. *Transportation Research Part B: Methodological* **33**, 63–79.

Boumahdi, R. and Thomas, A. (2008) Endogenous Regressors and Correlated Effects. Chapter 4 in: Mátyás, L. and Sevestre, P. (eds.): *The Econometrics of Panel Data. Fundamentals and Recent Developments in Theory and Practice, Third edition*. Berlin–Heidelberg: Springer.

Bound, J., Jaeger, D.A., and Baker, R.M. (1995) Problems with Instrumental Variables Estimation When the Correlation between the Instruments and the Endogeneous Explanatory Variable is Weak. *Journal of the American Statistical Association* **90**, 443–50.

Breitung, J. and Pesaran, M.H. (2008) Unit Roots and Cointegration in Panels. Chapter 9 in: Mátyás, L. and Sevestre, P. (eds.): *The Econometrics of Panel Data. Fundamentals and Recent Developments in Theory and Practice, Third edition*. Berlin–Heidelberg: Springer.

Breusch, T.S. (1987) Maximum Likelihood Estimation of Random Effects Models. *Journal of Econometrics* **36**, 383–9.

Breusch, T.S., Mizon, G.E., and Schmidt, P. (1989) Efficient Estimation Using Panel Data. *Econometrica* **57**, 695–700.

Breusch, T.S. and Pagan, A.R. (1979) A Simple Test for Heteroskedasticity and Random Coefficient Variation. *Econometrica* **47**, 1287–94.

Bun, M.J.G. and Carree, M.A. (2005) Bias-Corrected Estimation in Dynamic Panel Data Models. *Journal of Business & Economic Statistics* **23**, 200–10.

Bun, M.J.G. and Windmeijer, F. (2010) The Weak Instrument Problem of the System GMM Estimator in Dynamic Panel Data Models. *Econometrics Journal* **13**, 95–126.

Burke, S.P., Godfrey, L.G., and Tremayne, A.R. (1990) Testing AR(1) Against MA(1) Disturbances in the Linear Regression Model: An Alternative Procedure. *Review of Economic Studies* **57**, 135–45.

Cameron, A.C. and Trivedi, P.K. (2005) *Microeconometrics. Methods and Applications.* Cambridge: Cambridge University Press.

Chamberlain, G. (1980) Analysis of Covariance with Qualitative Data. *Review of Economic Studies* **47**, 225–38.

Chamberlain, G. (1984) Panel Data. Chapter 22 in: Griliches, Z. and Intriligator, M.D. (eds.): *Handbook of Econometrics, Volume 2.* Amsterdam: North-Holland.

Cornwell, C. and Rupert, P. (1988) Efficient Estimation With Panel Data: An Empirical Comparison of Instrumental Variables Estimators. *Journal of Applied Econometrics* **3**, 149–55.

Cornwell, C., Schmidt, P., and Wyhowski, D. (1992) Simultaneous Equations and Panel Data. *Journal of Econometrics* **51**, 151–81.

Davidson, R. and MacKinnon, J.G. (1993) *Estimation and Inference in Econometrics*. Oxford: Oxford University Press.

Davidson, R. and MacKinnon, J.G. (2004) *Econometric Theory and Methods*. Oxford: Oxford University Press.

Deaton, A. (1985) Panel Data from Time Series of Cross Sections. *Journal of Econometrics* **30**, 109–26.

Demidenko, E. (2004) *Mixed Models: Theory and Applications*. Hoboken, NJ: Wiley.

Drukker, D.M. (2003) Testing for Serial Correlation in Linear Panel-Data Models. *Stata Journal* **3**, 168–77.

Durbin, J. and Watson, G.S. (1950) Testing for Serial Correlation in Least Squares Regression, I. *Biometrika* **37**, 409–28.

Durbin, J. and Watson, G.S. (1951) Testing for Serial Correlation in Least Squares Regression, II. *Biometrika* **38**, 159–79.

Evans, M., Hastings, N., and Peacock, B. (1993) *Statistical Distributions*, Second edition. New York: Wiley.

Frisch, R. and Waugh, F.V. (1933) Partial Time Regressions as Compared with Individual Trends. *Econometrica* **1**, 387–401.

Fuller, W.A. (1987) *Measurement Error Models*. New York: Wiley.

Fuller, W.A. and Battese, G.E. (1973) Transformations for Estimation of Linear Models with Nested Error Structure. *Journal of the American Statistical Association* **68**, 626–32.

Fuller, W.A. and Battese, G.E. (1974) Estimation of Linear Models with Crossed-Error Structure. *Journal of Econometrics* **2**, 67–78.

Goldberger, A.S. (1962) Best Linear Unbiased Prediction in the Generalized Linear Regression Model. *Journal of the American Statistical Association* **57**, 369–75.

Goldberger, A.S. (1981) Linear Regression After Selection. *Journal of Econometrics* **15**, 357–66.

Gourieroux, C. and Monfort, A. (1981) Asymptotic Properties of the Maximum Likelihood Estimator in Dichotomous Logit Models. *Journal of Econometrics* **17**, 83–97.

Gourieroux, C. and Monfort, A. (1995) *Statistics and Econometric Models, Volumes 1-2.* Cambridge: Cambridge University Press.

Gourieroux, C. and Monfort, A. (1996) *Simulation-Based Econometric Models.* Oxford: Oxford University Press.

Greene, W.H. (2004) Fixed Effects and Bias Due to the Incidental Parameters Problem in the Tobit Model. *Econometric Reviews* **23**, 125–47.

Greene, W.H. (2008) *Econometric Analysis*, Sixth edition. New Jersey: Prentice Hall.

Grether, D.M. and Maddala, G.S. (1973) Errors in Variables and Serially Correlated Disturbances in Distributed Lag Models. *Econometrica* **41**, 255–62.

Griliches, Z. (1977) Estimating the Returns to Schooling: Some Econometric Problems. *Econometrica* **45**, 1–22.

Griliches, Z. (1986) Economic Data Issues. Chapter 25 in: Griliches, Z. and Intriligator, M.D. (eds.): *Handbook of Econometrics, Volume 3.* Amsterdam: North-Holland.

Griliches, Z. and Hausman, J.A. (1986) Errors in Variables in Panel Data. *Journal of Econometrics* **31**, 93–118.

Haavelmo, T. (1944) The Probability Approach in Econometrics. *Econometrica* **12**, Supplement, 1–115.

Hadri, K. (2000) Testing for Stationarity in Heterogeneous Panel Data. *Econometrics Journal* **3**, 148–61.

Hajivassiliou, V.A. and Ruud, P.A. (1994) Classical Estimation Methods for LDV Models Using Simulation. Chapter 40 in: Engle, R.E. and McFadden, D.L. (eds.): *Handbook of Econometrics, Volume 4.* Amsterdam: North-Holland.

Hall, A.R. (2005) *Generalized Method of Moments.* Oxford: Oxford University Press.

Hansen, L.P. (1982) Large Sample Properties of Generalized Method of Moments Estimators. *Econometrica* **50**, 1029–54.

Harris, D. and Mátyás, L. (1999) Introduction to the Generalized Method of Moments Estimation. Chapter 1 in: Mátyás, L. (ed.): *Generalized Method of Moments Estimation.* Cambridge: Cambridge University Press.

Harris, M.N., Mátyás, L., and Sevestre, P. (2008) Dynamic Models for Short Panels. Chapter 8 in: Mátyás, L. and Sevestre, P. (eds.): *The Econometrics of Panel Data. Fundamentals and Recent Developments in Theory and Practice, Third edition.* Berlin–Heidelberg: Springer.

Hatfield, G. (2006) Kant on the Perception of Space (and Time). Chapter 2 in: Guyer, P. (ed.): *The Cambridge Companion to Kant and Modern Philosophy.* Cambridge: Cambridge University Press.

Hausman, J.A. (1978) Specification Tests in Econometrics. *Econometrica* **46**, 1251–71.

Hausman, J.A. and Taylor, W.E. (1981) Panel Data and Unobservable Individual Effects. *Econometrica* **49**, 1377–98.

Heckman, J.J. (1976) The Common Structure of Statistical Models of Truncation, Sample Selection and Limited Dependent Variables and a Simple Estimator for Such Models. *Annals of Ecconomic and Social Measurement* **5**, 475–92.

Heckman, J.J. (1979) Sample Selection Bias as a Specification Error. *Econometrica* **47**, 153–161.

Heckman, J.J. (1991) Identifying the Hand of the Past: Distinguishing State Dependence from Heterogeneity. *American Economic Review, Papers and Proceedings* **81**, 75–9.

Holly, A. and Gardiol, L. (2000) A Score Test for Individual Heteroscedasticity in a One-way Error Components Model. Chapter 10 in: Krishnakumar, J. and Ronchetti, E. (eds.), *Panel Data Econometrics: Future Directions.* Amsterdam: North-Holland.

Holtz-Eakin, D., Newey, W., and Rosen, H.S. (1988) Estimating Vector Autoregressions with Panel Data. *Econometrica* **56**, 1371–95.

Honda, Y. (1985) Testing the Error Components Model with Non-normal Disturbances. *Review of Economic Studies* **52**, 681–90.

Honoré, B.E. and Kyriazidou, E. (2000) Estimation of Tobit-type Models with Individual Specific Effects. *Econometric Reviews* **19**, 341–66.

Honoré, B.E., Vella, F., and Verbeek, M. (2008) Attrition, Selection Bias and Censored Regressions. Chapter 12 in: Mátyás, L. and Sevestre, P. (eds.): *The Econometrics of Panel Data. Fundamentals and Recent Developments in Theory and Practice, Third edition*. Berlin–Heidelberg: Springer.

Hsiao, C. (1974) Statistical Inference for a Model with Both Random Cross-Sectional and Time Effects. *International Economic Review* **15**, 12–30.

Hsiao, C. (1975) Some Estimation Methods for a Random Coefficient Model. *Econometrica* **43**, 305–25.

Hsiao, C. (1991) Identification and Estimation of Dichotomous Latent Variables Models Using Panel Data, *Review of Economic Studies* **58**, 717–31.

Hsiao, C. (1996a) Logit and Probit Models. Chapter 16 in: Mátyás, L. and Sevestre, P. (eds.): *The Econometrics of Panel Data. A Handbook of the Theory with Applications*, Second edition. Dordrecht: Kluwer.

Hsiao, C. (1996b) Random Coefficient Models. Chapter 5 in: Mátyás, L. and Sevestre, P. (eds.): *The Econometrics of Panel Data. A Handbook of the Theory with Applications*, Second edition. Dordrecht: Kluwer.

Hsiao, C. (2003) *Analysis of Panel Data*, Second edition. Cambridge: Cambridge University Press.

Hsiao, C. and Pesaran, M.H. (2008) Random Coefficients Models. Chapter 6 in: Mátyás, L. and Sevestre, P. (eds.): *The Econometrics of Panel Data. Fundamentals and Recent Developments in Theory and Practice, Third edition*. Berlin-Heidelberg: Springer.

Im, K.S., Pesaran, M.H., and Shin, Y. (2003) Testing for Unit Roots in Heterogeneous Panels. *Journal of Econometrics* **115**, 53–74.

Jones, R.H. (1993) *Longitudinal Data with Serial Correlation: A State-space Approach*. London: Chapman & Hall.

Keane, M.P. and Runkle, D.E. (1992) On the Estimation of Panel-Data Models with Serial Correlation When Instruments Are Not Strictly Exogenous. *Journal of Business & Economic Statistics* **10**, 1–9.

Kirman, A.P. (1992) Whom or What Docs the Representative Individual Represent? *Journal of Economic Perspectives* **6**, 117–36.

Kiviet, J.F. (1995) On Bias, Inconsistency, and Efficiency of Various Estimators in Dynamic Panel Data Models. *Journal of Econometrics* **68**, 53–78.

Koop, G., Poirier, D.J., and Tobias, J.L. (2007) *Bayesian Econometric Methods*. Cambridge: Cambridge University Press.

Kotz, S., Balakrishnan, N., and Johnson, N.L. (2000) *Continuous Multivariate Distributions, Volume 1, Models and Applications, Second edition*. New York: Wiley.

Kuh, E. (1959) The Validity of Cross-Sectionally Estimated Behavior Equations in Time Series Applications. *Econometrica* **27**, 197–214.

Kumbhakar, S.C. (1992) Efficiency Estimation Using Rotating Panel Data Models. *Economics Letters* **41**, 11–16.

Kyriazidou, E. (1997) Estimation of a Panel Data Sample Selection Model. *Econometrica* **65**, 1335–64.

Lancaster, T. (2000) The Incidental Parameter Problem Since 1948. *Journal of Econometrics* **95**, 391–413.

Lancaster, T. (2006) *An Introduction to Modern Bayesian Econometrics*. Malden, MA: Blackwell.

Lechner, M., Lollivier, S., and Magnac, T. (2008) Parametric Binary Choice Models: Random Coefficients Models. Chapter 7 in: Mátyás, L. and Sevestre, P. (eds.): *The Econometrics of Panel Data. Fundamentals and Recent Developments in Theory and Practice, Third edition*. Berlin–Heidelberg: Springer.

Levin, A., Lin, C.-F., and Chu, C.-S.J. (2002) Unit Root Tests in Panel Data: Asymptotic and Finite-Sample Properties. *Journal of Econometrics* **108**, 1–24.

Lewbel, A., Dong, Y., and Yang, T.T. (2012) Comparing Features of Convenient Estimators for Binary Choice Models with Endogenous Regressors. *Canadian Journal of Economics* **45**, 809–29.

Li, Q. and Stengos, T. (1994) Adaptive Estimation in the Panel Data Error Component Model with Heteroskedasticity of Unknown Form. *International Economic Review* **35**, 981–1000.

Little, R.J.A. and Rubin, D.B. (1987) *Statistical Analysis with Missing Data*. New York: Wiley.

Lütkepohl, H. (1996) *Handbook of Matrices*. Chichester: Wiley.

MaCurdy, T.E. (1981) An Empirical Model of Labor Supply in a Life-Cycle Setting. *Journal of Political Economy* **89**, 1059–85.

McDonald, J.F. and Moffitt, R. (1980) The Uses of Tobit Analysis. *Review of Economics and Statistics* **62**, 318–21.

McFadden, D. (1974) Conditional Logit Analysis in Qualitative Choice Behavior. Chapter 4 in: Zarembka, P. (ed.): *Frontiers in Econometrics*. New York: Academic Press.

MacKinnon, J.G. and Smith, A.A. (1998) Approximate Bias Correction in Econometrics. *Journal of Econometrics* **85**, 205–30.

Maddala, G.S. (1971) The Use of Variance Components Models in Pooling Cross Section and Time Series Data. *Econometrica* **39**, 341–58.

Maddala, G.S. (1987) Limited Dependent Variable Models Using Panel Data. *Journal of Human Resources* **22**, 307–38.

Magnac, T. (2004) Panel Binary Variables and Sufficiency: Generalizing Conditionial Logit. *Econometrica* **72**, 1859–76.

Magnus, J.R. (1982) Multivariate Error Components Analysis of Linear and Nonlinear Regression Models by Maximum Likelihood. *Journal of Econometrics* **19**, 239–85.

Magnus, J.R. and Neudecker, H. (1988) *Matrix Differential Calculus with Applications in Statistics and Econometrics*. Chichester: Wiley.

Malinvaud, E. (1978) *Méthodes Statistiques de l'économétrie*, Third edition. Paris: Dunod.

Manski, C.F. (1988) Identification of Binary Response Models. *Journal of the American Statistical Association* **83**, 729–38.

Manski, C.F. (1995) *Identification Problems in the Social Sciences*. London: Harvard University Press.

Maravall, A. and Aigner, D.J. (1977) Identification of the Dynamic Shock-Error Model: The Case of Dynamic Regression. Chapter 18 in: Aigner, D.J. and Goldberger, A.S. (eds.): *Latent Variables in Socio-Economic Models*. Amsterdam: North-Holland.

Marschak, J. (1953) Economic Measurements for Policy and Prediction. Chapter 1 in: Hood, W.C and Koopmans, T.C. (eds.): *Studies in Econometric Methods*. New York: Wiley.

Mátyás, L. and Lovrics, L. (1991) Missing Observations and Panel Data: A Monte-Carlo Analysis. *Economics Letters* **37**, 39–44.

Moffitt, R. (1993) Identification and Estimation of Dynamic Models with a Time Series of Repeated Cross-sections. *Journal of Econometrics* **59**, 99–123.

Moon, H.R. and Perron, B. (2004) Testing for a Unit Root in Panels with Dynamic Factors. *Journal of Econometrics* **122**, 81–126.

Mundlak, Y. (1978) On the Pooling of Time Series and Cross Section Data. *Econometrica* **46**, 69–85.

Muthén, B. (1990) Moments of the Censored and Truncated Bivariate Normal Distribution. *British Journal of Mathematical and Statistical Psychology* **43**, 131–43.

Nelson, C.R. and Startz, R. (1990) Some Further Results on the Exact Small Sample Properties of the Instrumental Variable Estimator. *Econometrica* **58**, 967–76.

Nelson, F.D. (1981) A Test for Misspecification in the Censored Normal Model. *Econometrica* **49**, 1317–29.

Nerlove, M. (1967) Experimental Evidence on the Estimation of Dynamic Economic Relations from a Time Series of Cross-Sections. *Economic Studies Quarterly* **18**, 42–74.

Nerlove, M. (1971a) Further Evidence on the Estimation of Dynamic Relations from a Time Series of Cross Sections. *Econometrica* **39**, 359–82.

Nerlove, M. (1971b) A Note on Error Components Models. *Econometrica* **39**, 383–96.

Nerlove, M. (2002) *Essays in Panel Data Econometrics.* Cambridge: Cambridge University Press.

Nerlove, M. (2014) Individual Heterogeneity and State Dependence: From George Biddell Airy to James Joseph Heckman. *Oeconomia* **4**, 281–320.

Nerlove, N., Sevestre, P., and Balestra, P. (2008) Introduction. Chapter 1 in: Mátyás, L. and Sevestre, P. (eds.): *The Econometrics of Panel Data. Fundamentals and Recent Developments in Theory and Practice, Third edition.* Berlin–Heidelberg: Springer.

Newey, W.K. (1985) Generalized Method of Moments Specification Testing. *Journal of Econometrics* **29**, 229–56.

Neyman, J. and Scott, E.L. (1948) Consistent Estimates Based on Partially Consistent Observations. *Econometrica* **16**, 1–32.

Nickell, S. (1981) Biases in Dynamic Models with Fixed Effects. *Econometrica* **49**, 1417–26.

Nijman, T.E., Verbeek, M., and Soest, A. van (1991) The Efficiency of Rotating-Panel Designs in an Analysis-of-Variance Model. *Journal of Econometrics* **49**, 373–99.

Oberhofer, W. and Kmenta, J. (1974) A General Procedure for Obtaining Maximum Likelihood Estimates in Generalized Regression Models. *Econometrica* **42**, 579–90.

Olsen, R.J. (1978) Note on the Uniqueness of the Maximum Likelihood Estimator for the Tobit Model. *Econometrica* **46**, 1211–15.

Pagano, M. (1974) Estimation of Models of Autoregressive Signal Plus White Noise. *Annals of Statistics* **2**, 99–108.

Pakes, A. and Griliches, Z. (1984) Estimating Distributed Lags in Short Panels with an Application to the Specification of Depreciation Patterns and Capital Stock Constructs. *Review of Economic Studies* **51**, 243–62.

Pedroni, P. (2004) Panel Cointegration: Asymptotic and Finite Sample Properties of Pooled Time Series Tests with an Application to the PPP Hypothesis. *Econometric Theory* **20**, 597–625.

Rabe-Hesketh, S. and Skrondal, A. (2006) Multilevel Modelling of Complex Survey Data. *Journal of the Royal Statistical Society. Series A* **169**, 805–27.

Rabe-Hesketh, S., Skrondal, A., and Pickles, A. (2005) Maximum Likelihood Estimation of Limited and Discrete Dependent Variable Models with Nested Random Effects. *Journal of Econometrics* **128**, 301–23.

Randolph, W.C. (1988) A Transformation for Heteroscedastic Error Components Regression Models. *Economics Letters* **27**, 349–54.

Rao, P.S.R.S. (1997) *Variance Components Estimation. Mixed Models, Methodologies and Applications.* London: Chapman & Hall.

Rendon, S.E. (2013) Fixed and Random Effects in Classical and Bayesian Regression. *Oxford Bulletin of Economics and Statistics* **75**, 460–76.

Riphahn, R.T., Wambach, A., and Million, A. (2003) Incentive Effects in the Demand for Health Care: A Bivariate Panel Count Data Estimation. *Journal of Applied Econometrics* **18**, 387–405.

Robinson, G.K. (1991) That BLUP is a Good Thing: The Estimation of Random Effects. *Statistical Science* **6**, 15–32.

Roodman, D. (2009) A Note on the Theme of Too Many Instruments. *Oxford Bulletin of Economics and Statistics* **71** 135–58.

Rosenbaum, B. (1961) Moments of a Truncated Bivariate Normal Distribution. *Journal of the Royal Statistical Society. Series B* **23**, 405–8.

Rosett, R.N. and Nelson, F.D. (1975) Estimation of the Two-Limit Probit Regression Model. *Econometrica* **43**, 141–6.

Sarafidis, V. and Wansbeek, T. (2012) Cross-Sectional Dependence in Panel Data Analysis. *Econometric Reviews* **31**, 483–531.

Sargan, J.D. (1958) The Estimation of Economic Relationships using Instrumental Variables. *Econometrica* **26**, 393–415.

Sargan, J.D. (1959) The Estimation of Relationships with Autocorrelated Residuals by the Use of Instrumental Variables. *Journal of the Royal Statistical Society. Series B* **21**, 91–105.

Searle, S.R. (1987) *Linear Models for Unbalanced Data*. New York: Wiley.

Schmidt, P. (1990) Three-Stage Least Squares with Different Instruments for Different Equations. *Journal of Econometrics* **43**, 389–94.

Searle, S.R., Casella, G., and McCulloch, C.E. (1992) *Variance Components*. New York: Wiley.

Sevestre, P. and Trognon, A. (1985) A Note on Autoregressive Error Components Models. *Journal of Econometrics* **28**, 231–45.

Sevestre, P. and Trognon, A. (1996) Dynamic Linear Models. Chapter 7 in: Mátyás, L. and Sevestre, P. (eds.): *The Econometrics of Panel Data. A Handbook of the Theory with Applications, Second edition*. Dordrecht: Kluwer.

Skrondal, A. and Rabe-Hesketh, S. (2004) *Generalized Latent Variable Modeling: Multilevel, Longitudinal and Structural Equation Models*. Boca Raton: Chapman & Hall/CRC Press.

Staiger, D. and Stock, J.H. (1997) Instrumental Variables Regression with Weak Instruments. *Econometrica* **65**, 557–86.

Stock, J.H., Wright, J.H., and Yogo, M. (2002) A Survey of Weak Instruments and Weak Identification in Generalized Method of Moments. *Journal of Business & Economic Statistics* **20**, 518–29.

Stoker, T.M. (1993) Empirical Approaches to the Problem of Aggregation Over Individuals. *Journal of Economic Literature* **31**, 1827–74.

Swamy, P.A.V.B. (1970) Efficient Estimation in a Random Coefficient Regression Model. *Econometrica* **38**, 311–23.

Swamy, P.A.V.B. (1971) *Statistical Inference in Random Coefficient Regression Models*. New York: Springer.

Swamy, P.A.V.B. (1974) Linear Models with Random Coefficients. Chapter 5 in: Zarembka, P. (ed.): *Frontiers in Econometrics*. New York: Academic Press.

Swamy, P.A.V.B. and Arora, S.S. (1972) The Exact Finite Sample Properties of the Estimators of Coefficients in the Error Components Regression Models. *Econometrica* **40**, 261–75.

Tallis, G.M. (1961) The Moment Generating Function of the Truncated Multi-normal Distribution. *Journal of the Royal Statistical Society. Series B* **23**, 223–9.

Tallis, G.M. (1965) Plane Truncation in Normal Populations. *Journal of the Royal Statistical Society. Series B* **27**, 301–7.

Taylor, W.E. (1980) Small Sample Considerations in Estimation from Panel Data. *Journal of Econometrics* **13**, 203–23.

Tobin, J. (1958) Estimation of Relationships for Limited Dependent Variables. *Econometrica* **26**, 24–36.

Train, K. (2009) *Discrete Choice Methods with Simulation, Second edition.* Cambridge: Cambridge University Press.

Verbeek, M. and Nijman, T.E. (1996) Incomplete Panels and Selection Bias. Chapter 18 in: Mátyás, L. and Sevestre, P. (eds.): *The Econometrics of Panel Data. A Handbook of the Theory with Applications, Second edition.* Dordrecht: Kluwer.

Wallace, T.D. and Hussain, A. (1969) The Use of Error Components Models in Combining Cross Section with Time Series Data. *Econometrica* **37**, 55–72.

Wansbeek, T. (2001) GMM Estimation in Panel Data Models with Measurement Error. *Journal of Econometrics* **104**, 259–68.

Wansbeek, T. and Kapteyn, A. (1981) Estimators of the Covariance Structure of a Model for Longitudinal Data. Chapter 15 in: Charatsis, E.G. (ed.): *Proceedings of the Econometric Society European Meeting 1979.* Amsterdam: North-Holland.

Wansbeek, T. and Kapteyn, A. (1982) A Class of Decompositions of the Variance-Covariance Matrix of a Generalized Error Components Model. *Econometrica* **50**, 713–24.

Wansbeek, T. and Kapteyn, A. (1983) A Note on Spectral Decomposition and Maximum Likelihood Estimation in ANOVA Models with Balanced Data. *Statistics & Probability Letters* **1**, 213–15.

Wansbeek, T. and Kapteyn, A. (1989) Estimation of the Error Components Model with Incomplete Panels. *Journal of Econometrics* **41**, 341–61.

Wansbeek, T. and Koning, R.H. (1991) Measurement Error and Panel Data. *Statistica Neerlandica* **45**, 85–92.

Wansbeek, T. and Meijer, E. (2000) *Measurement Error and Latent Variables in Econometrics.* Amsterdam: North-Holland.

Westerlund, J. (2005) New Simple Tests for Panel Cointegration. *Econometric Reviews* **24**, 297–316.

Westerlund, J. (2007) Testing for Error Correction in Panel Data. *Oxford Bulletin of Economics and Statistics* **69**, 709–48.

White, H. (1984) *Asymptotic Theory for Econometricians.* Orlando: Academic Press.

White, H. (1986) Instrumental Variables Analogs of Generalized Least Squares Estimators. In: Mariano, R.S. (ed.): *Advances in Statistical Analysis and Statistical Computing. Theory and Applications, Volume 1*, pp. 173–227. New York: JAI Press.

Wooldridge, J.M. (1996) Estimating Systems of Equations with Different Instruments for Different Equations. *Journal of Econometrics* **74**, 387–405.

Wooldridge, J.M. (2010) *Econometric Analysis of Cross Section and Panel Data*, Second edition. Cambridge, MA: MIT Press.

Wu, D.-M. (1973) Alternative Tests of Independence between Stochastic Regressors and Disturbances. *Econometrica* **41**, 733–50.

Wyhowski, D.J. (1994) Estimation of a Panel Data Model in the Presence of Correlation Between Regressors and a Two-Way Error Component. *Econometric Theory* **10**, 130–9.

Zellner, A. (1962) An Efficient Method of Estimating Seemingly Unrelated Regressions and Tests for Aggregation Bias. *Journal of the American Statistical Association* **57**, 348–68.

Ziliak, J.P. (1997) Efficient Estimation with Panel Data When Instruments Are Predetermined: An Empirical Comparison of Moment-Condition Estimators. *Journal of Business & Economic Statistics* **15**, 419–31.

INDEX